SUBJECT AND STRUCTURE

An Anthology for Writers

SEVENTH EDITION

SUBJECT AND STRUCTURE

An Anthology for Writers

JOHN M. WASSON
Washington State University

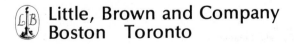
Little, Brown and Company
Boston   Toronto

Library of Congress Catalog Card No. 80-82946

ISBN 0-316-924237

9 8 7 6 5 4 3 2 1

MU

Published simultaneously in Canada
by Little, Brown & Company (Canada) Limited

Printed in the United States of America

PREFACE

This seventh edition retains the dual focus of earlier editions of *Subject and Structure:* in each section, every selection is on the same general subject and illustrates the same rhetorical technique. Students are thus provided with a number of examples of the way different writers approach the same task. This arrangement should stimulate comparison of structure and technique — as well as content — during class discussion.

This edition features a larger number of short essays approximating the length of student themes and clearly illustrating the rhetorical technique under consideration, thus providing more direct models for student composition than did earlier editions. In general, the selections within each section are arranged in increasing order of difficulty, with short stories and poems placed last.

The introductions to the sections discuss the philosophy, importance, and utility of each rhetorical technique. They also offer general principles to guide students in their theme writing and to warn them against pitfalls common to each writing problem.

The questions for discussion following each essay have been divided into two categories: "Subject" and "Structure." Students are thus encouraged to see that organization, sentence construction, and perhaps even word choice depend upon both the subject and the author's choice of rhetorical technique. Most structure questions are aimed at solutions to specific writing problems and often refer back to the general principles outlined in the introduction to the section. These structure questions should consume at least as much class discussion time as those dealing with subject matter.

The questions for discussion are followed in every case by "Suggestions for Writing." These are intended not to be exhaustive but to stimulate thinking about the kind of essay students might write employing the particular rhetorical technique being studied. They should prove useful because they are aimed at showing the students that writing is less a matter of "inspiration" than of identifying a writing "problem" and finding a means to solve it.

The author and the publisher are eager to receive from both students and teachers suggestions and evaluations of this book's effectiveness. Only through such communication can we hope to arrive at a truly satisfactory text. To this end we have included at the back of the book an evaluation form, which users are urged to complete and return to Little, Brown.

The editor would like to acknowledge the helpful suggestions and comments of instructors who have used earlier editions of *Subject and Structure*, including Charlene J. Allen, Norma Bains, Sarah R. Barnhill, Sue Blumer, Bruce Brandt, L. A. Cheever, Judith Danielson, Eileen B. Evans, Kris Ferguson, Frederick J. Fosher, Philippe Gacon, G. Dale Gleason, Charles H. Harper, Philip Headings, Marilyn Helgerson, Dennis Hoilman, O. P. Jones, Bernita Krumm, Reginald Martin, Joan Mullah, George O'Brien, Jon Olson, Brenda Paulsen, Robert C. Petersen, Suzanne Poirier, Harry Preble, Alan Reinhardt, David G. Riede, V. C. Rudolph, John G. Rudy, Nancy Schick, George G. Slutsky, Mary Smith, Rose M. Sweeney, Robert Wess, and Michael Yetman, as well as the many students who took the time to fill out and mail the questionnaire at the back of the book. As always the editorial staff at Little, Brown were particularly encouraging and helpful. Special thanks go to Charles Christensen, Joan Feinberg, and Jane Muse.

CONTENTS

3

PLAYSCHOOLS AND COLLEGES 91

Comparison and Contrast

5

THE FAMILY UNDER STRESS   207

Cause and Effect

7

FREEDOM AND RESPONSIBILITY 315

Argument

9

LOOKING AHEAD   447

Evaluation

SUBJECT AND STRUCTURE
An Anthology for Writers

1

TURNING POINTS

Example

Among the first lessons a writer must learn is that personal opinions and generalizations usually need illustrations drawn from firsthand observation if the reader is to understand them clearly and be convinced of their validity. Although one example cannot prove an opinion's worth, it will at least make clear what the writer means and will indicate that supporting evidence is available. Because of its versatility, the personal example is one of the writer's basic tools: it may be, and usually is, employed as secondary support for every other method of developing ideas described in this book.

Almost certainly the earliest attempts at written communication were in the form of pictures, at first single pictures and then a related series of pictures which told a story, perhaps of a warrior's success in battle or of a narrow escape from some wild animal. From such crude beginnings, written languages were developed, based at first on stylized abbreviations of the earlier picture writing. But as early as the Sumerian culture of 3000 B.C., people had discovered that they needed phonetic characters to express concepts which could not be "pictured." The subsequent history of written languages shows a clear trend toward developing simpler, more flexible alphabets capable of expressing relationships between ideas in words which refer to no "pictures" at all — "God is love," "Truth is Beauty," and so on.

Until comparatively recently, however, people were so accustomed to thinking in pictures that they instinctively avoided such totally abstract statements whenever possible. They preferred to ex-

1

press the abstract though in "pictorial" language. When the author of Ecclesiastes wrote "all is vanity," he added "and chasing after wind." When Shakespeare wanted his character Macbeth to complain that life is meaningless, he avoided the unimpressive abstract statement in favor of the now famous lines:

> Life's but a walking shadow, a poor player
> That struts and frets his hour upon the stage,
> And then is heard no more: it is a tale
> Told by an idiot, full of sound and fury,
> Signifying nothing.   5

The ability to express generalizations in abstract language is certainly an important advance: scientific laws, for instance, can be expressed in pictorial language only with difficulty and at great length. But we must recognize that there are certain weaknesses in abstract language and that we are not justified in dismissing the pictorial techniques of the older writers without good reason.

At its best, a generalization in abstract language forces readers to supply concrete illustration from their own experience. The writer thus loses an important means of control, for the readers' illustration may vary widely from what the author has in mind. To avoid this, the writer of a physics textbook, for instance, who states Boyle's law of gases in general terms, is careful either to give specific illustrations of the law's application or to give instructions for a controlled experiment whereby readers can see for themselves the operation of Boyle's law.

At its worst, highly abstract language may leave readers with only the vaguest notion of its meaning and without a ready example to clarify it. Suppose you were to read, instead of Shakespeare's clear statement "Life's but a walking shadow . . . ," something as atrocious as this:

> In the opinion of the author of the present
> investigation, it is a not unjustifiable assumption
> that the normal experiences of human existence
> seem to indicate that it may be without a demonstrable
> teleological basis.   5

There are two related methods of avoiding this sort of vagueness: (1) the use of specific, concrete language, including figures of speech where appropriate (a figure of speech should always be used to *clarify*, not to *decorate* the writing); and (2) the use of examples. You should not, of course, try to fill your writing with imagery of the florid, "limpid pools in the moonlight" variety. And you need not pile

Example   3

up superfluous examples. But you should remember to support and clarify your generalizations with illustrative evidence.

When asked to write opinion papers, college students often feel handicapped by a lack of adequate knowledge. They may even disregard as unimportant their best source of material, personal experience and observation. The best writers in every age have used their personal experiences as examples of general principles, partly because they can relate these experiences vividly and partly because firsthand reports are usually more reliable than borrowed ones. Many fiction writers — nearly all of the best novelists, in fact — have kept notebooks in which they jotted down for future use firsthand observations of places, events, and people. A wealth of such material is available to anyone who will use eyes and memory, even to an "inexperienced" college student. If you think back carefully, you may find that your experience includes acquaintance with such apparently remote subjects as communism (a room and toys "communally" owned by you and a brother or sister) and totalitarianism (a father or mother, perhaps, whose "word was law" in the home).

Even though your personal experiences may not seem to be of tremendous significance, there are several good reasons why you should draw on them for illustrative evidence. (1) Accurate personal observation makes writing more *vivid*. When you give a vague hypothetical example or none at all, readers get no mental picture from the writing; and what they can "see" clearly they understand better. If you are writing about the need for minimum speed laws on freeways, describe in graphic detail the time you nearly smashed into the back end of a slow-moving vehicle in the midst of sixty-mile-per-hour traffic.

(2) Such writing is not only clearer, but it is more *interesting*. You must know from experience how dull a textbook can be when the writer fails to give concrete examples. You may "read" several pages and suddenly realize you haven't any notion of what you have read. And you probably remember as a child that you avoided checking out library books which contained no pictures. While adults can usually maintain interest without pictures, they want at least "word-pictures."

(3) Personal examples make writing more *convincing*. A hypothetical example beginning, "Someone might be driving along the highway sometime when . . ." would hardly carry the authoritative force of "I had pushed my '69 Ford up to seventy on the long straight stretch of Highway 101 just south of San Jose when . . . ." Readers might, at worst, argue that your example isn't typical, but they would still be convinced that it did actually happen. And if the

example does not seem too unlikely, readers will probably be reminded of supporting evidence from their own experience.

(4) Finally, writing containing accounts of firsthand experiences is necessarily more *personal:* that is, it establishes a bond of intimacy between you and your readers. Readers, feeling that you are taking them into your confidence and that you sincerely want to communicate with them, will be much more willing to give you a fair chance to make your point. Nothing will alienate readers more quickly than the suspicion that you do not really care whether or not they understand and agree with you. An impersonal approach is a great producer of that suspicion.

In relating personal examples, be sure to include enough concrete facts to create a clear picture for your reader. Use actual names of people, places, and things when possible, and select verbs that convey a sense of action. "The coffee burned my tongue" is much more vivid than "The coffee was hot" and is just as easy to write if you employ verbs which carry part of the meaning of the sentence instead of being mere *links.* Try to re-create your experience in such a way that the reader can relive it vicariously. As you read the selections in this section, notice how the writers have accomplished this sense of vicarious experience through the use of concrete detail and active verbs. Note, for instance, how Brother Malcolm, in "The First Major Turning Point," gives names of actual people, quotes his teacher as nearly as he can remember, and even recalls such apparently unimportant details as the particular jobs his classmates were interested in — details which, precisely because there would be no sense reporting them unless they were true, give the account its impact of immediacy.

One word of caution: be sure to avoid trite expressions in relating a personal experience. In striving for vividness, you may be tempted to use such "tried and true" phrases as those in this passage from a student theme.

I was so excited I could hardly wait for the trip to start. But the day finally came. We arose bright-eyed and bushy-tailed, ate a hurried breakfast, and were on our way.

Such worn-out phrases destroy the very bond of intimacy you are trying to establish between you and your readers. The readers feel that you are not interested enough in what you are saying to think up your own expressions. Furthermore, they lose interest because they feel that they have "read all this before." Trite language, in short, destroys the sense of uniqueness your writing should convey. Readers are not concerned just with the nature of your experience; they

Example 5

are interested in your personal view of it and your reaction to it. For it is precisely your point of view that makes your experience unique and therefore worth reading: remember that no two people experience events in precisely the same way. Even two people in the same automobile accident will "see" it differently because of differences in past experience, intelligence, and emotional nature. Do not sell yourself short; your experience does count, and it will be worth reading if you write it so that it will be "seen" in the way that you saw it.

The First Major Turning Point

Malcolm X

Malcolm X, born Malcolm Little in Omaha, Nebraska, in 1925, was assassinated in Harlem on February 21, 1965. The ultimate influence in this powerful civil rights leader's turbulent career is still difficult to assess, partly because his own views changed from black militancy to black nationalism to a deep sense of the brotherhood of man. It can be said with assurance that more than any other leader he gave the black man a sense of his manhood, and that, as Wyatt Tee Walker says, "Malcolm had the 'book' on white America and he read it loud and clear for all to hear." The Autobiography of Malcolm X (1964), whatever one thinks of its author, is probably the most sensitive book yet written by an Afro-American. The following extract is about his experience in junior high school at Mason, Michigan, early in 1941.

I kept close to the top of the class, though. The topmost scholastic standing, I remember, kept shifting between me, a girl named Audrey Slaugh, and a boy named Jimmy Cotton. 1

It went on that way, as I became increasingly restless and disturbed through the first semester. And then one day, just about when those of us who had passed were about to move up to 8-A, from which we would enter high school the next year, something happened which was to become the first major turning point of my life. 2

Somehow, I happened to be alone in the classroom with Mr. Ostrowski, my English teacher. He was a tall, rather reddish white man and he had a thick mustache. I had gotten some of my best marks under him, and he had always made me feel that he liked me. He was, as I have mentioned, a natural-born "advisor," about what you ought to read, to do, or think — about any and everything. We used to make unkind jokes about him: why was he teaching in Mason instead of somewhere else, getting for himself some of the "success in life" that he kept telling us how to get? 3

I know that he probably meant well in what he happened to advise me that day. I doubt that he meant any harm. It was just in his nature as an American white man. I was one of his top students, one of the school's top 4 students — but all he could see for me was the kind of future "in your place" that all white people see for black people.

He told me, "Malcolm, you ought to be thinking about a career. Have you been giving it thought?"

The truth is, I hadn't. I never have figured out why I told him, "Well, yes sir, I've been thinking I'd like to be a lawyer." Lansing certainly had no Negro lawyers — or doctors either — in those days, to hold up an image I might have aspired to. All I really knew for certain was that a lawyer didn't wash dishes, as I was doing.

Mr. Ostrowski looked surprised, I remember, and leaned back in his chair and clasped his hands behind his head. He kind of half-smiled and said, "Malcolm, one of life's first needs is for us to be realistic. Don't misunderstand me, now. We all here like you, you know that. But you've got to be realistic about being a nigger. A lawyer — that's no realistic goal for a nigger. You need to think about something you *can* be. You're good with your hands — making things. Everybody admires your carpentry shop work. Why don't you plan on carpentry? People like you as a person — you'd get all kinds of work."

The more I thought afterwards about what he said, the more uneasy it made me. It just kept treading around in my mind.

What made it really begin to disturb me was Mr. Ostrowski's advice to others in my class — all of them white. Most of them had told him they were planning to become farmers, like their parents — to one day take over their family farms. But those who wanted to strike out on their own, to try something new, he had encouraged. Some, mostly girls, wanted to be teachers. A few wanted other professions, such as one boy who wanted to become a county agent; another, a veterinarian; and one girl wanted to be a nurse. They all reported that Mr. Ostrowski had encouraged whatever they had wanted. Yet nearly none of them had earned marks equal to mine.

It was a surprising thing that I had never thought of it that way before, but I realized that whatever I wasn't, I *was* smarter than nearly all of those white kids. But apparently I was still not intelligent enough, in their eyes, to become whatever I wanted to be.

It was then that I began to change — inside.

SUBJECT QUESTIONS

1. Do you think Mr. Ostrowski's advice to Malcolm arises from (perhaps unrecognized) prejudice, or from an honest desire to be "realistic"? What does Malcolm think?

2. Malcolm relates this incident with calm objectivity. Since it is to be a "major turning point," should he have jazzed it up a bit?

3. What is Malcolm's attitude toward Mr. Ostrowski after twenty-four

years? Does this attitude seem characteristic of a man who had become an impassioned denouncer of white racism? What clues do you have that the attitude is genuine?

4. Does the account make clear why Malcolm should have been so disturbed by Mr. Ostrowski's advice — considering that Malcolm had no intention of being a lawyer, anyway? (Note that Malcolm was more upset by the advice than by being called "nigger." Clearly he was already aware of his "difference" from the other students in the class.)

STRUCTURE QUESTIONS

1. Since Mr. Ostrowski is referred to a number of times, it is clearly more convenient to call him by his name than to keep repeating "my English teacher." But the same reasoning does not explain Malcolm's inclusion of the names Audrey Slaugh and Jimmy Cotton, who are not referred to again. What effect does Malcolm achieve by naming them, an effect which would be lost if he simply wrote "two other students"?

2. Point out some of the descriptive details which have nothing to do with the aim of the story but which help reconstruct the scene in the reader's mind. (Note that Malcolm does not clutter the account with such details — just enough for verisimilitude.)

3. Malcolm might have achieved more marked contrast between the advice he received and that of the whites had he included some with less realistic ambitions than nurse, schoolteacher, or extension agent. Why do you suppose he doesn't? (Even if he had invented a couple of ambitions — brain surgeon, ambassador, president — no reader would be greatly surprised by such responses from eighth graders.)

4. This account describes, of course, a purely personal experience; does Malcolm give any indication that he thinks of it as an example of a much more widespread problem? Using this essay as an example, consider the problem of making a personal experience seem both unique and something which "speaks" to the readers.

SUGGESTION FOR WRITING

Describe a childhood confrontation with a teacher or other adult. Try to show both how you felt and how the adult must have felt about you. (Do this through carefully selected details rather than direct interpretation: "She clenched her teeth and sucked in her breath" instead of "She was trying desperately to control herself.")

Salvation

Langston Hughes

*Langston Hughes (1902–1967) was a poet, jazz expert, and columnist for
The New York Post. At the age of twenty, he quit college for several
years and worked as a common seaman, whence the title of his autobiography,* The Big Sea *(1940), from which the following episode is taken.*

I was saved from sin when I was going on thirteen. But not really saved. It
happened like this. There was a big revival at my Auntie Reed's church.
Every night for weeks there had been much preaching, singing, praying, and
shouting, and some very hardened sinners had been brought to Christ, and
the membership of the church had grown by leaps and bounds. Then just
before the revival ended, they held a special meeting for children, "to bring
the young lambs to the fold." My aunt spoke of it for days ahead. That night
I was escorted to the front row and placed on the mourners' bench with all
the other young sinners, who had not yet been brought to Jesus.

My aunt told me that when you were saved you saw a light, and something happened to you inside! And Jesus came into your life! And God was
with you from then on! She said you could see and hear and feel Jesus in
your soul. I believed her. I had heard a great many old people say the same
thing and it seemed to me they ought to know. So I sat there calmly in the
hot, crowded church, waiting for Jesus to come to me.

The preacher preached a wonderful rhythmical sermon, all moans and
shouts and lonely cries and dire pictures of hell, and then he sang a song
about the ninety and nine safe in the fold, but one little lamb was left out in
the cold. Then he said: "Won't you come? Won't you come to Jesus? Young
lambs, won't you come?" And he held out his arms to all us young sinners
there on the mourners' bench. And the little girls cried. And some of them
jumped up and went to Jesus right away. But most of us just sat there.

A great many old people came and knelt around us and prayed, old
women with jet-black faces and braided hair, old men with work-gnarled
hands. And the church sang a song about the lower lights are burning, some
poor sinners to be saved. And the whole building rocked with prayer and
song.

Still I kept waiting to *see* Jesus.

Finally all the young people had gone to the altar and were saved, but   6
one boy and me. He was a rounder's son named Westley. Westley and I
were surrounded by sisters and deacons praying. It was very hot in the
church, and getting late now. Finally Westley said to me in a whisper: "God
damn! I'm tired o' sitting here. Let's get up and be saved." So he got up and
was saved.

Then I was left all alone on the mourners' bench. My aunt came and   7
knelt at my knees and cried, while prayers and songs swirled all around me
in the little church. The whole congregation prayed for me alone, in a
mighty wail of moans and voices. And I kept waiting serenely for Jesus, waiting, waiting — but he didn't come. I wanted to see him, but nothing happened to me. Nothing! I wanted something to happen to me, but nothing
happened.

I heard the songs and the minister saying: "Why don't you come? My   8
dear child, why don't you come to Jesus? Jesus is waiting for you. He wants
you. Why don't you come? Sister Reed, what is this child's name?"

"Langston," my aunt sobbed.   9

"Langston, why don't you come? Why don't you come and be saved?   10
Oh, Lamb of God! Why don't you come?"

Now it was really getting late. I began to be ashamed of myself, hold-   11
ing everything up so long. I began to wonder what God thought about Westley, who certainly hadn't seen Jesus either, but who was now sitting proudly
on the platform, swinging his knickerbockered legs and grinning down at
me, surrounded by deacons and old women on their knees praying. God had
not struck Westley dead for taking his name in vain or for lying in the
temple. So I decided that maybe to save further trouble, I'd better lie, too,
and say that Jesus had come, and get up and be saved.

So I got up.   12

Suddenly the whole room broke into a sea of shouting, as they saw me   13
rise. Waves of rejoicing swept the place. Women leaped in the air. My aunt
threw her arms around me. The minister took me by the hand and led me to
the platform.

When things quieted down, in a hushed silence, punctuated by a few   14
ecstatic "Amens," all the new young lambs were blessed in the name of God.
Then joyous singing filled the room.

That night, for the last time in my life but one — for I was a big boy   15
twelve years old — I cried. I cried, in bed alone, and couldn't stop. I buried
my head under the quilts, but my aunt heard me. She woke up and told my
uncle I was crying because the Holy Ghost had come into my life, and
because I had seen Jesus. But I was really crying because I couldn't bear to
tell her that I had lied, that I had deceived everybody in the church, and I
hadn't seen Jesus, and that now I didn't believe there was a Jesus any more,
since he didn't come to help me.

SUBJECT QUESTIONS

1. Do you think that Hughes is concentrating more on giving an honest self-analysis or on entertaining the reader with the humorous account itself? What saves the story from being funny but pointless?
2. Does Langston's pretense at salvation seem to be a typical trick for a boy that age? Is it at least believable? How would you have reacted at age twelve to pressures like those exerted on Hughes?
3. Hughes implies in his last paragraph that this apparently harmless event had an important and lasting effect on him. Does this seem psychologically valid? Can you recall any small events from your childhood which have had lasting effects?
4. Do you think that, in addition to the analysis of himself, Hughes intends some social criticism? Of religion? Of "saving" children at too early an age?

STRUCTURE QUESTIONS

1. Examine Hughes's employment of concrete detail. Point out details which are especially effective in making the essay vivid, authentic, and interesting.
2. What special devices does Hughes employ to achieve realism? Were you able to picture yourself in his place?
3. How does Hughes convey the impression that the story is told from the point of view of a young boy? Analyze the sentence structure in the second and third paragraphs, for instance.

SUGGESTIONS FOR WRITING

1. Think about the earliest experience in your childhood that you can recall vividly. Try to decide why you remember it. (Many such memories at first seem silly or unimportant.) Then relate that event in such a way that the reader can experience it vicariously. Do not *tell* readers how to feel (nobody told you how to react when you had the experience), but try to bring it alive for them with vivid detail.
2. Probably at some time in the past you have acted in a way that made you feel embarrassed or ashamed afterwards — kicked a kindergarten teacher in the shins, perhaps, or tried to steal a toy from the dime store. Try to re-create the situation verbally in such a way that the reader can understand how you felt when you did it. Don't attempt an abstract self-analysis or character explanation; instead, paint a picture vivid enough for the reader to experience.

A Whole Society of Loners and Dreamers

William Allen

William Allen (b. 1940) attended North Texas State and California State, Long Beach before doing his graduate work in creative writing at the University of Iowa. He now teaches at Ohio State University. Allen has published many short stories, articles, and books, including Starkweather *(1976). His first novel was* To Tojo from Billy-Bob Jones *(1977), and he is editor of the literary magazine* Ohio Journal. *The essay (1972) which follows may read like fiction, but it is based on Allen's own experiences; he has wanted to be a writer since he was twelve. Students may feel some comfort that a successful writer's career began thus unpromisingly.*

On Sunday afternoons here, if you're tired of taking walks in the country 1
and fighting off the green-bellied hogflies, your next best choice is thumbing magazines at the downtown drugstore. One Sunday not long ago, when I ran out of anything else to thumb, I started looking through one of those magazines geared toward helping new writers achieve success. I used to pore over them a lot when I was a teenager, and the first thing I noticed now was that the ads haven't changed much over the past fifteen years:

"IMAGINE MAKING $5,000 A YEAR WRITING IN YOUR SPARE 2
TIME! Fantastic? Not at all. . . . Hundreds of People Make That Much or More Every Year — and Have Fun Doing It!"

"TO PEOPLE WHO WANT TO WRITE FOR PROFIT BUT CAN'T 3
GET STARTED. Have You Natural Writing Ability? Now a Chance to Test Yourself — FREE!"

"I FIRE WRITERS . . . with enthusiasm for developing God-given 4
talent. You'll 'get fired' too with my 48-lesson home study course. Over-the-shoulder coaching . . . personalized critiques! Amazing sales opportunity the first week. Write for my FREE STARTER KIT."

The ad that struck me the most showed a picture of a handsome and 5
darkly serious young man sitting on a hill, picking his teeth with a weed, and gazing out over the countryside. The caption read: DO YOU HAVE THE "FAULTS" THAT COULD MEAN YOU WERE MEANT TO BE A

WRITER? The ad went on to list the outstanding characteristics of writers. They are dreamers, loners, bookworms. They are too impractical, too intense, too idealistic.

When I was fourteen and had just started trying to write, I saw an ad much like this and was overwhelmed by it. That fellow on the hill was just like me, I thought. It was a tremendous feeling to discover that I might not be alone — that there was a whole society of loners and dreamers, that they were called writers, and that by sending off for a free writing IQ test I could find out by return mail if I qualified to climb the hill and chew straw with them.

I took that test and blew the top off it. The writing school said I demonstrated a rare creative potential unlike anything they had seen in years. They did wonder, though, if I had what it took to stick with them through long months of arduous training to develop my raw talent. If I really did have that kind of fortitude, the next step would be to send in some actual samples of my writing.

Spurred, I sent off everything I had ever written — two stories of about 200 words each. One was about some unidentified creatures who lived in dread of an unidentified monster who came around every week or so to slaughter as many of them as he could. Some of the persecuted creatures had the option of running, hopping, scurrying, or crawling to safety, but the others, for some unexplained reason, couldn't move and had just to stand there and take it. There was a description of the monster's roaring approach. Then the last line hit the reader like a left hook: "The lawn mower ran swiftly over. . . ."

The other story I have preserved these many years:

The Race

Two gleaming hot rods stand side by side, poised and tensed — eager to scream down the hot asphalt track, each secretly confident that he will be the supreme victor. The time is drawing close now; in just a few minutes the race will be on.

There is a last minute check of both cars . . . everything is ready. A yell rings out for everyone to clear the track. The flagman raises the starting flag above his head, pauses for a second, and with a downward thrust of the flag, he sends the cars leaping forward with frightening speed.

They fly down the track, side by side, neither able to take the lead. They are gaining speed with every second. Faster and faster they go, approaching the half-way mark with incredible momentum. . . .

Wait! Something is wrong — one of the cars is going out of control and skidding toward the other car! The rending sound of ripping metal and sliding tires cuts through the air as the two autos collide and spin crazily off the track.

For a moment the tragic panorama is hidden by a self-made curtain of dust, but it isn't a second before the curtain is pulled away by the wind, revealing the horrible sight. There are the two hot rods, one turned over, both broken and smashed. All is quiet. . . .

Two small children, a boy and a girl, get up from the curb where they have been sitting. They eye each other accusingly as they walk slowly across the street where the two broken toy cars lay silent. . . . "Woman driver," grumbles the little boy.

The End

The correspondence school's copy desk quickly replied that the writ-   10
ing samples confirmed my aptitude test results and that they looked forward to working with me to the point of publication and beyond. I couldn't
imagine what could be beyond publication but finally figured out they
meant to handle my work later as agent-representative. They praised my
choice of subject matter, sense of drama, and powerful surprise
endings — all of which they said indicated I could sell to the sci-fi market.
This made sense, because science fiction was all I had ever read voluntarily except for *Comic Classics* and, as a child, *Uncle Wiggily*. The school was
particularly impressed by my style, which they said was practically poetry,
in places. They made reference to my use of alliteration ("rending sound of
ripping metal") and of metaphor ("self-made curtain of dust . . . pulled
away by the wind").

They were quick to make clear, however, that what I had here were   11
only germs of stories. They needed to be expanded to publishable lengths
and had to have better character development — particularly the one
about the bugs and grass being slaughtered by the lawn mower. They said
a good writer could give even an insect an interesting personality.

The next step was to send them $10 for each of the two stories — the   12
standard fee for detailed, over-the-shoulder copy-desk criticism. Then after
these stories had been redone and rushed off for publication, I should enroll in their thirty-six-lesson course, in which I would be taught the ins and
outs of plotting, characterization, point of view, theme, tone, and setting.
The fee was $10 a lesson, and after my successful completion of the course
they would then handle my literary properties, protect my legal rights,
etc., for the regular 10 per cent.

At this point I began to wonder if I might be going in over my head. I   13
was getting only a dollar a week from my folks and didn't understand half of
what the writing school was talking about. In English class I had heard of
such terms as "alliteration," "tone," and "point of view" but had no clear
idea what they meant. Also I felt like an imposter. I had given my age as
twenty-one. Of course, I was strutting because at fourteen I was doing
better than anybody they had worked with in years, but I wondered if I
could keep it up. "Rending sound of ripping metal" was genius, but could I
crank out lines like that on a daily basis? I decided to try.

First I wrote them that I was a little short of cash this month and asked if just to get started, it would be all right to work on one story for $10 instead of two for $20. They replied that that would be fine — just send in the ten bucks so they could get rolling.

Meanwhile I hadn't been able to get even that much money together. I approached my family and was turned down flat because my father thought there was something unhealthy about people who wanted to write. He was bothered by the school's remark that my writing was like poetry. "If you were a girl, it might be different," he said, and showed me a copy of *Men's Adventure.* "Look here, why don't you get one of these two ninety-eight worm ranches? Or one of these small-game boomerangs?"

After a few days of trying to drum up work around the neighborhood, I realized I wasn't going to be able to pull it off and decided just not to write back. But in a week I got a curt note saying they wanted to help me, were trying to be patient, but I was going to have to be more responsible. They said that writing was 1 per cent inspiration and 99 per cent perspiration and wondered if in my case the figures might be reversed.

This both goaded and scared me. I wrote back that on account of unexpected medical expenses I could afford to give them only $5 at first. Could they possibly let me have a cut rate? They replied that it was strictly against their policy, but in view of my undeniably vast potential the copydesk team had voted to go along with me just this once — send the $5.

By mowing lawns and selling bottles, I had by this time scraped together $3, but there my earning potential dropped sharply. Another week went by, and I made only 48 cents more. Then a letter arrived stamped in red, front and back: URGENT! IMPORTANT! DO NOT DISCARD! It said I had violated an agreement based on mutual trust and had exactly twenty-four hours to send in the $5. Without exactly spelling it out, they gave the impression that legal action might be taken. The letter ended: "Frankly, Mr. Allen, we're about at our wits' end with you."

I was hurt as well as shaken. I felt that I just didn't have what it takes. If there ever had been a chance of my climbing that hill and sitting with that elite group of loners and dreamers, it was gone now. I had my mother write them that I had suddenly been struck down with polio and was unable even to write my name, much less take their course. I hung onto the litte money I had in case I had to give it to them to avoid a lawsuit, but I didn't hear from them after that. In a few weeks I relaxed and mailed off for the $2.98 worm ranch.

SUBJECT QUESTIONS

1. The title is supposed to refer to adolescents who are potential professional writers; does the phrase "loners and dreamers" include

more people than that? Would the advertisements be aimed at a broad, or very limited, group of teenagers?

2. Have you ever answered, or been tempted to answer, an advertisement offering a free talent test — for art, stenography, computer programming, and so on? How objective would you expect the advertiser to be in assessing your potential?

3. Compare the mail-order advertisements in two very different sorts of magazines — *Playboy* and a child's comic book, for instance, or *Cosmopolitan* and *Sunset*. For what reasons would the advertisements in one magazine be inappropriate for the other?

4. Have you ever got yourself into an awkward financial obligation by answering an "irresistible" advertisement — "free postage stamp offer," "choose any six records for only one dollar," "the first volume absolutely free"? Does Allen seem to assume that his readers will have had experiences similar to his own?

5. Examine Allen's reactions to the six letters he received from the writing school; do they seem typical of a fourteen-year-old? Is he displaying a basic dishonesty or simple panic?

6. Consider the praises which the writing school gave Allen's two stories; which of the virtues do you think Allen consciously put into his writing? Has an English teacher ever praised you for something you didn't know you'd done?

STRUCTURE QUESTIONS

1. What would have been lost — or gained — had Allen written this essay from the point of view of the teen-aged boy instead of the adult looking back on his boyhood?

2. The final sentence, about the worm ranch, is not necessary to the conclusion of the story. What purposes does it serve?

3. What stylistic differences can you detect between the article itself and the story, "The Race," included in it? The story includes some rather ambitious vocabulary; what marks it as immature?

4. Allen's "adult" style is a very correct informal style; yet it contains some expressions more appropriate to a "colloquial" style: "blew the top off," "hit like a left hook," "ten bucks," and so on. What do such expressions contribute to the "tone" of the essay? Does Allen's purpose justify their inclusion?

5. Identify some of the specific nouns which, while not necessary to the meaning, help to make the essay seem authentic. Test the effect of substituting general nouns for these specific ones.

SUGGESTIONS FOR WRITING

1. Re-create a childhood experience in which your good intentions resulted in an embarrassing situation. Be sure to provide concrete and specific details.
2. If you have had an awkward experience with a mail-order company — joined a book club, requested free postage stamps, ordered an ant farm, and so on — recount the experience using as much accurate detail as you can recall.
3. Write an essay about handing in a paper and receiving praise or advice from an English teacher which you didn't fully understand. Illustrate the kind of writing which prompted the teacher's comments. (If you have "learned," there should be a contrast between this paper and the earlier one.)

My Sixth Christmas

Floyd Dell

*Floyd Dell (1887–1969) was born in Barry, Illinois. Although he was a pro-
lific writer, his radical politics and pacifism fifty years before such beliefs
were fashionable have caused him to be virtually obliterated from bio-
graphies and histories of politics and literature. During World War I, he
was editor of a radical journal,* The Masses *(1914–17). When the paper,
with Dell as defendant, was accused of violating the Espionage Act, Dell
promptly started another radical journal,* The Liberator *(1918–24). During
the twenties and early thirties, Dell published ten novels, six books of
nonfiction, numerous plays, and his autobiography,* Homecoming
(1933) — from which the following passage is taken.

That fall, before it was discovered that the soles of both my shoes were worn   1
clear through, I still went to Sunday school. And one time the Sunday-school
superintendent made a speech to all the classes. He said that these were
hard times, and that many poor children weren't getting enough to eat. It
was the first that I had heard about it. He asked everybody to bring some
food for the poor children next Sunday. I felt very sorry for the poor children.

Also, little envelopes were distributed to all the classes. Each little boy   2
and girl was to bring money for the poor, next Sunday. The pretty Sunday-
school teacher explained that we were to write our names, or have our
parents write them, up in the left-hand corner of the little envelopes. . . . I
told my mother all about it when I came home. And my mother gave me,
the next Sunday, a small bag of potatoes to carry to Sunday school. I supposed the poor children's mothers would make potato soup out of them.
. . . Potato soup was good. My father, who was quite a joker, would always
say, as if he were surprised, "Ah! I see we have some nourishing potato soup
today!" It was so good that we had it every day. My father was at home all
day long and every day, now; and I liked that, even if he was grumpy as he
sat reading Grant's "Memoirs." I had my parents all to myself, too; the
others were away. My oldest brother was in Quincy, and memory does not
reveal where the others were: perhaps with relatives in the country.

Taking my small bag of potatoes to Sunday school, I looked around for   3 the poor children; I was disappointed not to see them. I had heard about poor children in stories. But I was told just to put my contribution with the others on the big table in the side room.

I had brought with me the little yellow envelope, with some money in   4
it for the poor children. My mother had put the money in it and sealed it up. She wouldn't tell me how much money she had put in it, but it felt like several dimes. Only she wouldn't let me write my name on the envelope. I had learned to write my name, and I was proud of being able to do it. But my mother said firmly, no, I must not write my name on the envelope; she didn't tell my why. On the way to Sunday school I had pressed the envelope against the coins until I could tell what they were; they weren't dimes but pennies.

When I handed in my envelope, my Sunday-school teacher noticed   5
that my name wasn't on it, and she gave me a pencil; I could write my own name, she said. So I did. But I was confused because my mother had said not to; and when I came home, I confessed what I had done. She looked distressed. "I told you not to!" she said. But she didn't explain why. . . .

I didn't go back to school that fall. My mother said it was because I was   6
sick. I did have a cold the week that school opened; I had been playing in the gutters and had got my feet wet, because there were holes in my shoes. My father cut insoles out of cardboard, and I wore those in my shoes. As long as I had to stay in the house anyway, they were all right.

I stayed cooped up in the house, without any companionship. We   7
didn't take a Sunday paper any more, but the Barry *Adage* came every week in the mails; and though I did not read small print, I could see the Santa Clauses and holly wreaths in the advertisements.

There was a calendar in the kitchen. The red days were Sundays and   8
holidays; and that red 25 was Christmas. (It was on a Monday, and the two red figures would come right together in 1893; but this represents research in the World Almanac, not memory.) I knew when Sunday was, because I could look out of the window and see the neighbor's children, all dressed up, going to Sunday school. I knew just when Christmas was going to be.

But there was something queer! My father and mother didn't say a   9
word about Christmas. And once, when I spoke of it, there was a strange, embarrassed silence; so I didn't say anything more about it. But I wondered, and was troubled. Why didn't they say anything about it? Was what I had said I wanted (memory refuses to supply that detail) too expensive?

I wasn't arrogant and talkative now. I was silent and frightened. What   10
was the matter? Why didn't my father and mother say anything about Christmas? As the day approached, my chest grew tighter with anxiety.

Now it was the day before Christmas. I couldn't be mistaken. But not a   11
word about it from my father and mother. I waited in painful bewilderment all day. I had supper with them, and was allowed to sit up for an hour. I was

waiting for them to say something. "It's time for you to go to bed," my mother said gently. I had to say something.

"This is Christmas Eve, isn't it?" I asked, as if I didn't know.   12

My father and mother looked at one another. Then my mother looked   13
away. Her face was pale and stony. My father cleared his throat, and his face took on a joking look. He pretended he hadn't known it was Christmas Eve, because he hadn't been reading the papers. He said he would go downtown and find out.

My mother got up and walked out of the room. I didn't want my father   14
to have to keep on being funny about it, so I got up and went to bed. I went by myself without having a light. I undressed in the dark and crawled into bed.

I was numb. As if I had been hit by something. It was hard to breathe.   15
I ached all through. I was stunned — with finding out the truth.

My body knew before my mind quite did. In a minute, when I could   16
think, my mind would know. And as the pain in my body ebbed, the pain in my mind began. I knew. I couldn't put it into words yet. But I knew why I had taken only a little bag of potatoes to Sunday school that fall. I knew why there had been only pennies in my little yellow envelope. I knew why I hadn't gone to school that fall — why I hadn't any new shoes — why we had been living on potato soup all winter. All these things, and others, many others, fitted themselves together in my mind, and meant something.

Then the words came into my mind and I whispered them into the   17
darkness:

"We're poor!"   18

That was it. I was one of those poor children I had been sorry for,   19
when I heard about them in Sunday school. My mother hadn't told me. My father was out of work, and we hadn't any money. That was why there wasn't going to be any Christmas at our house.

Then I remembered something that made me squirm with shame — a   20
boast. (Memory will not yield this up. Had I said to some Nice little boy, "I'm going to be President of the United States"? Or to a Nice little girl: "I'll marry you when I grow up"? It was some boast as horribly shameful to remember.)

"We're poor." There in bed in the dark, I whispered it over and over   21
to myself. I was making myself get used to it. (Or — just torturing myself, as one presses the tongue against a sore tooth? No, memory says not like that — but to keep myself from ever being such a fool again: suffering now, to keep this awful thing from ever happening again. Memory is clear on that; it was more like pulling the tooth, to get it over with — never mind the pain, this will be the end!)

It wasn't so bad, now that I knew. I just hadn't known! I had thought   22
all sorts of foolish things: that I was going to Ann Arbor — going to be a

lawyer — going to make speeches in the Square, going to be President. Now I knew better.

I had wanted (something) for Christmas. I didn't want it, now. I didn't want anything. 23

I lay there in the dark, feeling the cold emotion of renunciation. (The tendrils of desire unfold their clasp on the outer world of objects, withdraw, shrivel up. Wishes shrivel up, turn black, die. It is like that.) 24

It hurt. But nothing would ever hurt again. I would never let myself want anything again. 25

I lay there stretched out straight and stiff in the dark, my fists clenched hard upon Nothing. . . . 26

In the morning it had been like a nightmare that is not clearly remembered — that one wishes to forget. Though I hadn't hung up any stocking, there was one hanging at the foot of my bed. A bag of popcorn, and a lead pencil, for me. They had done the best they could, now they realized that I knew about Christmas. But they needn't have thought they had to. I didn't want anything. 27

SUBJECT QUESTIONS

1. At what point in the story does the reader become aware that the Dell family is poor? Why does it take the child so much longer to make this discovery?
2. Given Floyd's new attitude at the end, how might he have felt had his family received some of the Sunday school's gifts for poor children? How does his mother feel about letting people know the family is poor? Why?
3. In some ways Christmas Eve was the worst possible time for Floyd to make his discovery; in what respects might it be the right time?
4. The worst part of the discovery for the boy is the shame over his boast; shouldn't the prospect of hunger and hardship be more of a worry? Which is normally more important to a person, the preservation of his life or of his self-respect?

STRUCTURE QUESTIONS

1. Which details in this passage mark it as uniquely Dell's experience? Which details make it a typical example of the experiences of almost all poor children in America?
2. How does Dell separate the immediate experience of the child from his mature comments on that experience? The device is somewhat mechanical; does it work all right? Would there have been a better

way to achieve the same separation? What do the "grown-ups's" comments add to the story?

3. Contrast the way feelings are communicated in paragraphs 4 and 10; which way is more effective? How could Dell have improved the weaker paragraph?

4. Since the reader finds out almost at once the point of Floyd's much later discovery, how does the author maintain interest (or suspense) until he can come to the boy's crucial reaction to this discovery?

SUGGESTION FOR WRITING

Describe an experience that forced you to reexamine yourself in the light of facts that could not be ignored — a determination to attend a certain college, which your parents could not afford, perhaps; or even a childhood insistence on a pony for Christmas, when you lived in a city apartment complex. Try to provide descriptive details that you would have noticed when you were at the age at which the experience took place.

On Self-Respect

Joan Didion

Joan Didion (b. 1934) is a native of California and graduated from the University of California. She has had a busy writing career since her first job as associate feature editor of Vogue; *she has been a columnist for the* Saturday Evening Post *and* Esquire *and a contributing editor for* National Review. *Her novels include* Run River *(1963),* Play It as It Lays *(1971), and* A Book of Common Prayer *(1977). A collection of her essays,* The White Album, *was published in 1979. She has also been coauthor of several screenplays, including* A Star Is Born *(1976). The following essay was written early in her career, when she was only a few years out of college.*

Once, in a dry season, I wrote in large letters across two pages of a notebook that innocence ends when one is stripped of the delusion that one likes oneself. Although now, some years later, I marvel that a mind on the outs with itself should have nonetheless made painstaking record of its every tremor, I recall with embarrassing clarity the flavor of those particular ashes. It was a matter of misplaced self-respect. 1

I had not been elected to Phi Beta Kappa. This failure could scarcely have been more predictable or less ambiguous (I simply did not have the grades), but I was unnerved by it; I had somehow thought myself a kind of academic Raskolnikov, curiously exempt from the cause-effect relationships which hampered others. Although even the humorless nineteen-year-old that I was must have recognized that the situation lacked real tragic stature, the day that I did not make Phi Beta Kappa nonetheless marked the end of something, and innocence may well be the word for it. I lost the conviction that lights would always turn green for me, the pleasant certainty that those rather passive virtues which had won me approval as a child automatically guaranteed me not only Phi Beta Kappa keys but happiness, honor, and the love of a good man; lost a certain touching faith in the totem power of good manners, clean hair, and proven competence on the Stanford-Binet scale. To such doubtful amulets had my self-respect been pinned, and I faced myself that day with the nonplused apprehension of someone who has come across a vampire and has no crucifix at hand. 2

Although to be driven back upon oneself is an uneasy affair at best, 3

Reprinted by permission of Farrar, Straus & Giroux, Inc. "On Self-Respect" from *Slouching Towards Bethlehem* by Joan Didion. Copyright © 1961 by Joan Didion.

23

rather like trying to cross a border with borrowed credentials, it seems to me now the one condition necessary to the beginnings of real self-respect. Most of our platitudes notwithstanding, self-deception remains the most difficult deception. The tricks that work on others count for nothing in that very well-lit back alley where one keeps assignations with oneself: no winning smiles will do here, no prettily drawn lists of good intentions. One shuffles flashily but in vain through one's marked cards — the kindness done for the wrong reason, the apparent triumph which involved no real effort, the seemingly heroic act into which one had been shamed. The dismal fact is that self-respect has nothing to do with the approval of others — who are, after all, deceived easily enough; has nothing to do with reputation, which, as Rhett Butler told Scarlett O'Hara, is something people with courage can do without.

To do without self-respect, on the other hand, is to be an unwilling audience of one to an interminable documentary that details one's failings, both real and imagined, with fresh footage spliced in for every screening. *There's the glass you broke in anger, there's the hurt on X's face; watch now, this next scene, the night Y came back from Houston, see how you muff this one.* To live without self-respect is to lie awake some night, beyond the reach of warm milk, phenobarbital, and the sleeping hand on the coverlet, counting up the sins of commission and omission, the trusts betrayed, the promises subtly broken, the gifts irrevocably wasted through sloth or cowardice or carelessness. However long we postpone it, we eventually lie down alone in that notoriously uncomfortable bed, the one we make ourselves. Whether or not we sleep in it depends, of course, on whether or not we respect ourselves. 4

To protest that some fairly improbable people, some people who *could not possibly respect themselves,* seem to sleep easily enough is to miss the point entirely, as surely as those people miss it who think that self-respect has necessarily to do with not having safety pins in one's underwear. There is a common superstition that "self-respect" is a kind of charm against snakes, something that keeps those who have it locked in some unblighted Eden, out of strange beds, ambivalent conversations, and trouble in general. It does not at all. It has nothing to do with the face of things, but concerns instead a separate peace, a private reconciliation. Although the careless, suicidal Julian English in *Appointment in Samarra* and the careless, incurably dishonest Jordan Baker in *The Great Gatsby* seem equally improbable candidates for self-respect, Jordan Baker had it, Julian English did not. With that genius for accommodation more often seen in women than in men, Jordan took her own measure, made her own peace, avoided threats to that peace: "I hate careless people," she told Nick Carraway. "It takes two to make an accident." 5

Like Jordan Baker, people with self-respect have the courage of their 6 mistakes. They know the price of things. If they choose to commit adultery, they do not then go running, in an access of bad conscience, to receive absolution from the wronged parties; nor do they complain unduly of the unfairness, the undeserved embarrassment, of being named co-respondent. In brief, people with self-respect exhibit a certain toughness, a kind of moral nerve; they display what was once called *character*, a quality which, although approved in the abstract, sometimes loses ground to other, more instantly negotiable virtues. The measure of its slipping prestige is that one tends to think of it only in connection with homely children and United States senators who have been defeated, preferably in the primary, for reelection. Nonetheless, character — the willingness to accept responsibility for one's own life — is the source from which self-respect springs.

Self-respect is something that our grandparents, whether or not they had   7
it, knew all about. They had instilled in them, young, a certain discipline, the sense that one lives by doing things one does not particularly want to do, by putting fears and doubts to one side, by weighing immediate comforts against the possibility of larger, even intangible, comforts. It seemed to the nineteenth century admirable, but not remarkable, that Chinese Gordon put on a clean white suit and held Khartoum against the Mahdi; it did not seem unjust that the way to free land in California involved death and difficulty and dirt. In a diary kept during the winter of 1846, an emigrating twelve-year-old named Narcissa Cornwall noted coolly: "Father was busy reading and did not notice that the house was being filled with strange Indians until Mother spoke about it." Even lacking any clue as to what Mother said, one can scarcely fail to be impressed by the entire incident: the father reading, the Indians filing in, the mother choosing the words that would not alarm, the child duly recording the event and noting further that those particular Indians were not, "fortunately for us," hostile. Indians were simply part of the *donnée*.

In one guise or another, Indians always are. Again, it is a question of   8
recognizing that anything worth having has its price. People who respect themselves are willing to accept the risk that the Indians will be hostile, that the venture will go bankrupt, that the liaison may not turn out to be one in which *every day is a holiday because you're married to me*. They are willing to invest something of themselves; they may not play at all, but when they do play, they know the odds.

That kind of self-respect is a discipline, a habit of mind that can never be   9
faked but can be developed, trained, coaxed forth. It was once suggested to me that, as an antidote to crying, I put my head in a paper bag. As it

happens, there is a sound physiological reason, something to do with oxygen, for doing exactly that, but the psychological effect alone is incalculable: it is difficult in the extreme to continue fancying oneself Cathy in *Wuthering Heights* with one's head in a Food Fair bag. There is a similar case for all the small disciplines, unimportant in themselves; imagine maintaining any kind of swoon, commiserative or carnal, in a cold shower.

But those small disciplines are valuable only insofar as they represent   10
larger ones. To say that Waterloo was won on the playing fields of Eton is not to say that Napoleon might have been saved by a crash program in cricket; to give formal dinners in the rain forest would be pointless did not the candlelight flickering on the liana call forth deeper, stronger disciplines, values instilled long before. It is a kind of ritual, helping us to remember who and what we are. In order to remember it, one must have known it.

To have that sense of one's intrinsic worth which constitutes self-   11
respect is potentially to have everything: the ability to discriminate, to love and to remain indifferent. To lack it is to be locked within oneself, paradoxically incapable of either love or indifference. If we do not respect ourselves, we are on the one hand forced to despise those who have so few resources as to consort with us, so little perception as to remain blind to our fatal weaknesses. On the other, we are peculiarly in thrall to everyone we see, curiously determined to live out — since our self-image is untenable — their false notions of us. We flatter ourselves by thinking this compulsion to please others an attractive trait: a gist for imaginative empathy, evidence of our willingness to give. *Of course* I will play Francesca to your Paolo, Helen Keller to anyone's Annie Sullivan: no expectation is too misplaced, no role too ludicrous. At the mercy of those we cannot but hold in contempt, we play roles doomed to failure before they are begun, each defeat generating fresh despair at the urgency of divining and meeting the next demand made upon us.

It is the phenomenon sometimes called "alienation from self." In its   12
advanced stages, we no longer answer the telephone, because someone might want something; that we could say *no* without drowning in self-reproach is an idea alien to this game. Every encounter demands too much, tears the nerves, drains the will, and the specter of something as small as an unanswered letter arouses such disproportionate guilt that answering it becomes out of the question. To assign unanswered letters their proper weight, to free us from the expectations of others, to give us back to ourselves — there lies the great, the singular power of self-respect. Without it, one eventually discovers the final turn of the screw: one runs away to find oneself, and finds no one at home.

SUBJECT QUESTIONS

1. Like Didion, many students who earned high grades without much effort in high school find themselves nearer the middle of the heap in college. Is this phenomenon usually a blow to one's sense of self-respect? How does one cope with it?
2. Didion suggests that she was typical in being a "humorless nineteen-year-old." Obviously, teenagers have a sense of humor; in what area might they lack the perspective necessary to see humor in a situation?
3. According to this essay, if one lacks self-respect, the two most likely courses are a) excessive concern for self and b) desperate attempts to please others and live out "their false notions of us." Are these two courses generally observable among college students? Which seems more prevalent? Suggest some ways in which the attempt manifests itself.
4. Does Didion give any helpful suggestions on how to achieve self-respect? Does she make clear what it is? Why doesn't she simply define it?
5. As a college student, the author achieved part of her sense of "self" by identifying with characters from films and novels. Is this typical practice? How does one gain a sense of self before one has achieved very much on one's own?

STRUCTURE QUESTIONS

1. Didion begins the essay by using herself as a personal example, but after the second paragraph she generalizes from "I" to "we." Would she have made her point more clearly had she kept herself as the focus? Does she ever return to herself as personal example?
2. How does the author keep her generalizations from being vague? (Consider both the language and examples other than personal ones.)
3. Didion can hardly expect any one reader to be familiar with all of the novels and historical events to which she makes reference. Can the reader understand her point without knowing the references intimately? Can you formulate any rule about how to use supporting evidence from history and fiction?
4. The author is less concerned with defining "self-respect" than with pointing out its importance to a mature and responsible human being. Yet she must make clear what she means by the term, and distinguish it from other concepts — particularly from "reputation" and "the approval of others." How does she accomplish those tasks?
5. This is what is called a "reflective essay": readers are encouraged to read slowly, pausing to think about the points being made, to relate them to their own lives, rather than to read quickly through for "the

facts." Can you see any differences in style or language between this essay and the earlier essays in this section which make this one more "reflective"?

SUGGESTIONS FOR WRITING

1. Using yourself and acquaintances as examples, write an essay in which you discuss one of the problems of transmuting from "a big frog in the little pond" of high school to "a little frog in the big pond" of college. Choose any area particularly noticeable to you — athletics, academic work, social life, some extracurricular activity.
2. Write an essay, using yourself as chief example, on the difficulty of finding a balance between pleasing yourself and pleasing others. (You may want to concentrate on some limited area, such as writing essays, or deciding what to do on Friday night.)
3. If you have had an experience which, like Didion's, caused your own self-image to crumble, recount it in such a way that the reader can see both the weakness in your prior self-image and why the experience exposed that weakness.

Death in the Woods

Sherwood Anderson

Sherwood Anderson (1876–1941) began his literary career as a journalist and newspaper editor, but he is known today as one of America's finest short story writers. His best-known work is Winesburg, Ohio *(1920), a collection of Freudian stories about the inhabitants of a small town. "Death in the Woods," typical of Anderson's abiding interest in everyday, unimportant people, was written in 1926.*

She was an old woman and lived on a farm near the town in which I lived. All country and small-town people have seen such old women, but no one knows much about them. Such an old woman comes into town driving an old worn-out horse or she comes afoot carrying a basket. She may own a few hens and have eggs to sell. She brings them in a basket and takes them to a grocer. There she trades them in. She gets some salt pork and some beans. Then she gets a pound or two of sugar and some flour.

Afterwards she goes to the butcher's and asks for some dog-meat. She may spend ten or fifteen cents, but when she does she asks for something. Formerly the butchers gave liver to any one who wanted to carry it away. In our family we were always having it. Once one of my brothers got a whole cow's liver at the slaughter-house near the fairgrounds in our town. We had it until we were sick of it. It never cost a cent. I have hated the thought of it ever since.

The old farm woman got some liver and a soup-bone. She never visited with any one, and as soon as she got what she wanted she lit out for home. It made quite a load for such an old body. No one gave her a lift. People drive right down a road and never notice an old woman like that.

There was such an old woman who used to come into town past our house one Summer and Fall when I was a young boy and was sick with what was called inflammatory rheumatism. She went home later carrying a heavy pack on her back. Two or three large gaunt-looking dogs followed at her heels.

The old woman was nothing special. She was one of the nameless ones that hardly any one knows, but she got into my thoughts. I have just suddenly now, after all these years, remembered her and what happened. It is a

29

story. Her name was Grimes, and she lived with her husband and son in a small unpainted house on the bank of a small creek four miles from town.

The husband and son were a tough lot. Although the son was but   6
twenty-one, he had already served a term in jail. It was whispered about that the woman's husband stole horses and ran them off to some other county. Now and then, when a horse turned up missing, the man had also disappeared. No one ever caught him. Once, when I was loafing at Tom Whitehead's livery-barn, the man came there and sat on the bench in front. Two or three other men were there, but no one spoke to him. He sat for a few minutes and then got up and went away. When he was leaving he turned around and stared at the men. There was a look of defiance in his eyes. "Well, I have tried to be friendly. You don't want to talk to me. It has been so wherever I have gone in this town. If, some day, one of your fine horses turns up missing, well, then what?" He did not say anything actually: "I'd like to bust one of you on the jaw," was about what his eyes said. I remember how the look in his eyes made me shiver.

The old man belonged to a family that had had money once. His name   7
was Jake Grimes. It all comes back clearly now. His father, John Grimes, had owned a sawmill when the country was new, and had made money. Then he got to drinking and running after women. When he died there wasn't much left.

Jake blew in the rest. Pretty soon there wasn't any more lumber to cut   8
and his land was nearly all gone.

He got his wife off a German farmer, for whom he went to work one   9
June day in the wheat harvest. She was a young thing then and scared to death. You see, the farmer was up to something with the girl — she was, I think, a bound girl and his wife had her suspicions. She took it out on the girl when the man wasn't around. Then, when the wife had to go off to town for supplies, the farmer got after her. She told young Jake that nothing really ever happened, but he didn't know whether to believe it or not.

He got her pretty easy himself, the first time he was out with her. He   10
wouldn't have married her if the German farmer hadn't tried to tell him where to get off. He got her to go riding with him in his buggy one night when he was threshing on the place, and then he came for her the next Sunday night.

She managed to get out of the house without her employer's seeing,   11
but when she was getting into the buggy he showed up. It was almost dark, and he just popped up suddenly at the horse's head. He grabbed the horse by the bridle and Jake got out his buggy-whip.

They had it out all right! The German was a tough one. Maybe he   12
didn't care whether his wife knew or not. Jake hit him over the face and shoulders with the buggy-whip, but the horse got to acting up and he had to get out.

Then the two men went for it. The girl didn't see it. The horse started   13
to run away and went nearly a mile down the road before the girl got him
stopped. Then she managed to tie him to a tree beside the road. (I wonder
how I know all this. It must have stuck in my mind from small-town tales
when I was a boy.) Jake found her there after he got through with the German. She was huddled up in the buggy seat, crying, scared to death. She
told Jake a lot of stuff, how the German had tried to get her, how he chased
her once into the barn, how another time, when they happened to be alone
in the house together, he tore her dress open clear down the front. The German, she said, might have got her that time if he hadn't heard his old woman
drive in at the gate. She had been off to town for supplies. Well, she would
be putting the horse in the barn. The German managed to sneak off to the
fields without his wife seeing. He told the girl he would kill her if she told.
What could she do? She told a lie about ripping her dress in the barn when
she was feeding the stock. I remember now that she was a bound girl and
did not know where her father and mother were. Maybe she did not have
any father. You know what I mean.

Such bound children were often enough cruelly treated. They were   14
children who had no parents, slaves really. There were very few orphan
homes then. They were legally bound into some home. It was a matter of
pure luck how it came out.

II

She married Jake and had a son and daughter, but the daughter died.   15

Then she settled down to feed stock. That was her job. At the Ger-   16
man's place she had cooked the food for the German and his wife. The wife
was a strong woman with big hips and worked most of the time in the fields
with her husband. She fed them and fed the cows in the barn, fed the pigs,
the horses and the chickens. Every moment of every day, as a young girl,
was spent feeding something.

Then she married Jake Grimes and he had to be fed. She was a slight   17
thing, and when she had been married for three or four years, and after the
two children were born, her slender shoulders became stooped.

Jake always had a lot of big dogs around the house, that stood near the   18
unused sawmill near the creek. He was always trading horses when he
wasn't stealing something and had a lot of poor bony ones about. Also he
kept three or four pigs and a cow. They were all pastured in the few acres
left of the Grimes place and Jake did little enough work.

He went into debt for a threshing outfit and ran it for several years, but   19
it did not pay. People did not trust him. They were afraid he would steal the
grain at night. He had to go a long way off to get work and it cost too much
to get there. In the Winter he hunted and cut a little firewood, to be sold in

some nearby town. When the son grew up he was just like the father. They got drunk together. If there wasn't anything to eat in the house when they came home the old man gave his old woman a cut over the head. She had a few chickens of her own and had to kill one of them in a hurry. When they were all killed she wouldn't have any eggs to sell when she went to town, and then what would she do?

She had to scheme all her life about getting things fed, getting the pigs   20
fed so they would grow fat and could be butchered in the Fall. When they were butchered her husband took most of the meat off to town and sold it. If he did not do it first the boy did. They fought sometimes and when they fought the old woman stood aside trembling.

She had got the habit of silence anyway — that was fixed. Sometimes,   21
when she began to look old — she wasn't forty yet — and when the husband and son were both off, trading horses or drinking or hunting or stealing, she went around the house and the barnyard muttering to herself.

How was she going to get everything fed — that was her problem. The   22
dogs had to be fed. There wasn't enough hay in the barn for the horses and the cow. If she didn't feed the chickens how could they lay eggs? Without eggs to sell how could she get things in town, things she had to have to keep the life of the farm going? Thank heaven, she did not have to feed her husband — in a certain way. That hadn't lasted long after their marriage and after the babies came. Where he went on his long trips she did not know. Sometimes he was gone from home for weeks, and after the boy grew up they went off together.

They left everything at home for her to manage and she had no money.   23
She knew no one. No one ever talked to her in town. When it was Winter she had to gather sticks of wood for her fire, had to try to keep the stock fed with very little grain.

The stock in the barn cried to her hungrily, the dogs followed her   24
about. In the Winter the hens laid few enough eggs. They huddled in the corners of the barn and she kept watching them. If a hen lays an egg in the barn in the Winter and you do not find it, it freezes and breaks.

One day in Winter the old woman went off to town with a few eggs and   25
the dogs followed her. She did not get started until nearly three o'clock and the snow was heavy. She hadn't been feeling very well for several days and so she went muttering along, scantily clad, her shoulders stooped. She had an old grain bag in which she carried her eggs, tucked away down in the bottom. There weren't many of them, but in Winter the price of eggs is up. She would get a little meat in exchange for the eggs, some salt pork, a little sugar, and some coffee perhaps. It might be the butcher would give her a piece of liver.

When she had got to town and was trading in her eggs the dogs lay by   26
the door outside. She did pretty well, got the things she needed, more than

she had hoped. Then she went to the butcher and he gave her some liver and some dog-meat.

It was the first time any one had spoken to her in a friendly way for a long time. The butcher was alone in his shop when she came in and was annoyed by the thought of such a sick-looking old woman out on such a day. It was bitter cold and the snow, that had let up during the afternoon, was falling again. The butcher said something about her husband and her son, swore at them, and the old woman stared at him, a look of mild surprise in her eyes as he talked. He said that if either the husband or the son were going to get any of the liver or the heavy bones with scraps of meat hanging to them that he had put into the grain bag, he'd see him starve first. 27

Starve, eh? Well, things had to be fed. Men had to be fed, and the horses that weren't any good but maybe could be traded off, and the poor thin cow that hadn't given any milk for three months. 28

Horses, cows, pigs, dogs, men. 29

III

The old woman had to get back before darkness came if she could. The dogs followed at her heels, sniffing at the heavy grain bag she had fastened on her back. When she got to the edge of town she stopped by a fence and tied the bag on her back with a piece of rope she had carried in her dress-pocket for just that purpose. That was an easier way to carry it. Her arms ached. It was hard when she had to crawl over fences and once she fell over and landed in the snow. The dogs went frisking about. She had to struggle to get to her feet again, but she made it. The point of climbing over the fences was that there was a short cut over a hill and through a woods. She might have gone around by the road, but it was a mile farther that way. She was afraid she couldn't make it. And then, besides, the stock had to be fed. There was a little hay left and a little corn. Perhaps her husband and son would bring some home when they came. The had driven off in the only buggy the Grimes family had, a rickety thing, a rickety horse hitched to the buggy, two other rickety horses led by halters. They were going to trade horses, get a little money if they could. They might come home drunk. It would be well to have something in the house when they came back. 30

The son had an affair on with a woman at the county seat, fifteen miles away. She was a rough enough woman, a tough one. Once, in the Summer, the son had brought her to the house. Both she and the son had been drinking. Jake Grimes was away and the son and his woman ordered the old woman about like a servant. She didn't mind much; she was used to it. Whatever happened she never said anything. That was her way of getting along. She had managed that way when she was a young girl at the German's and ever since she had married Jake. That time her son brought his woman 31 to the house they stayed all night, sleeping together just as though they were married. It hadn't shocked the old woman, not much. She had got past being shocked early in life.

With the pack on her back she went painfully along across an open field, wading in the deep snow, and got into the woods. 32

There was a path, but it was hard to follow. Just beyond the top of the hill, where the woods was thickest, there was a small clearing. Had some one once thought of building a house there? The clearing was as large as a building lot in town, large enough for a house and a garden. The path ran along the side of the clearing, and when she got there the old woman sat down to rest at the foot of a tree. 33

It was a foolish thing to do. When she got herself placed, the pack against the tree's trunk, it was nice, but what about getting up again? She worried about that for a moment and then quietly closed her eyes. 34

She must have slept for a time. When you are about so cold you can't get any colder. The afternoon grew a little warmer and the snow came thicker than ever. Then after a time the weather cleared. The moon even came out. 35

There were four Grimes dogs that had followed Mrs. Grimes into town, all tall gaunt fellows. Such men as Jake Grimes and his son always keep just such dogs. They kick and abuse them, but they stay. The Grimes dogs, in order to keep from starving, had to do a lot of foraging for themselves, and they had been at it while the old woman slept with her back to the tree at the side of the clearing. They had been chasing rabbits in the woods and in adjoining fields and in their ranging had picked up three other farm dogs. 36

After a time all the dogs came back to the clearing. They were excited about something. Such nights, cold and clear and with a moon, do things to dogs. It may be that some old instinct, come down from the time when they were wolves and ranged the woods in packs on Winter nights, comes back into them. 37

The dogs in the clearing, before the old woman, had caught two or three rabbits and their immediate hunger had been satisfied. They began to play, running in circles in the clearing. Round and round they ran, each dog's nose at the tail of the next dog. In the clearing, under the snow-laden trees and under the wintry moon they made a strange picture, running thus silently, in a circle their running had beaten in the soft snow. The dogs made no sound. They ran around and around in the circle. 38

It may have been that the old woman saw them doing that before she died. She may have awakened once or twice and looked at the strange sight with dim old eyes. 39

She wouldn't be very cold now, just drowsy. Life hangs on a long time. Perhaps the old woman was out of her head. She may have dreamed of her 40 girlhood, at the German's, and before that, when she was a child and before her mother lit out and left her.

Her dreams couldn't have been very pleasant. Not many pleasant things had happened to her. Now and then one of the Grimes dogs left the running circle and came to stand before her. The dog thrust his face close to her face. His red tongue was hanging out. 41

The running of the dogs may have been a kind of death ceremony. It may have been that the primitive instinct of the wolf, having been aroused in the dogs by the night and the running, made them somehow afraid. 42

"Now we are no longer wolves. We are dogs, the servants of men. Keep alive, man! When man dies we become wolves again." 43

When one of the dogs came to where the old woman sat with her back against the tree and thrust his nose close to her face he seemed satisfied and went back to run with the pack. All the Grimes dogs did it at some time during the evening, before she died. I knew all about it afterward, when I grew to be a man, because once in a woods in Illinois, on another Winter night, I saw a pack of dogs act just like that. The dogs were waiting for me to die as they had waited for the old woman that night when I was a child, but when it happened to me I was a young man and had no intention whatever of dying. 44

The old woman died softly and quietly. When she was dead and when one of the Grimes dogs had come to her and had found her dead all the dogs stopped running. 45

They gathered about her. 46

Well, she was dead now. She had fed the Grimes dogs when she was alive, what about now? 47

There was the pack on her back, the grain bag containing the piece of salt pork, the liver the butcher had given her, the dog-meat, the soup bones. The butcher in town, having been suddenly overcome with a feeling of pity, had loaded her grain bag heavily. It had been a big haul for the old woman. 48

It was a big haul for the dogs now. 49

IV

One of the Grimes dogs sprang suddenly out from among the others and began worrying the pack on the old woman's back. Had the dogs really been wolves that one would have been the leader of the pack. What he did, all the others did. 50

All of them sank their teeth into the grain bag the old woman had fastened with ropes to her back. 51

They dragged the old woman's body out into the open clearing. The worn-out dress was quickly torn from her shoulders. When she was found, a day or two later, the dress had been torn from her body clear to the hips, 52 but the dogs had not touched her body. They had got the meat out of the grain bag, that was all. Her body was frozen stiff when it was found, and the shoulders were so narrow and the body so slight that in death it looked like the body of some charming young girl.

Such things happened in towns of the Middle West, on farms near town, when I was a boy. A hunter out after rabbits found the old woman's body and did not touch it. Something, the beaten round path in the little snow-covered clearing, the silence of the place, the place where the dogs had worried the body trying to pull the grain bag away or tear it open — something startled the man and he hurried off to town.

I was in Main street with one of my brothers who was town newsboy and who was taking the afternoon papers to the stores. It was almost night.

The hunter came into a grocery and told his story. Then he went to a hardware-shop and into a drugstore. Men began to gather on the sidewalks. Then they started out along the road to the place in the woods.

My brother should have gone on about his business of distributing papers but he didn't. Every one was going to the woods. The undertaker went and the town marshal. Several men got on a dray and rode out to where the path left the road and went into the woods, but the horses weren't very sharply shod and slid about on the slippery roads. They made no better time than those of us who walked.

The town marshal was a large man whose leg had been injured in the Civil War. He carried a heavy cane and limped rapidly along the road. My brother and I followed at his heels, and as we went other men and boys joined the crowd.

It had grown dark by the time we got to where the old woman had left the road but the moon had come out. The marshal was thinking there might have been a murder. He kept asking the hunter questions. The hunter went along with his gun across his shoulders, a dog following at his heels. It isn't often a rabbit hunter has a chance to be so conspicuous. He was taking full advantage of it, leading the procession with the town marshal. "I didn't see any wounds. She was a beautiful young girl. Her face was buried in the snow. No, I didn't know her." As a matter of fact, the hunter had not looked closely at the body. He had been frightened. She might have been murdered and some one might spring out from behind a tree and murder him. In a woods, in the late afternoon, when the trees are all bare and there is white snow on the ground, when all is silent, something creepy steals over the mind and body. If something strange or uncanny has happened in the neighborhood all you think about is getting away from there as fast as you can.

The crowd of men and boys had got to where the old woman had crossed the field and went, following the marshal and the hunter, up the slight incline and into the woods.

My brother and I were silent. He had his bundle of papers in a bag slung across his shoulder. When he got back to town he would have to go on distributing his papers before he went home to supper. If I went along, as he had no doubt already determined I should, we would both be late. Either mother or our older sister would have to warm our supper.

Well, we would have something to tell. A boy did not get such a 61
chance very often. It was lucky we just happened to go into the grocery when the hunter came in. The hunter was a country fellow. Neither of us had ever seen him before.

Now the crowd of men and boys had got to the clearing. Darkness 62
comes quickly on such Winter nights, but the full moon made everything clear. My brother and I stood near the tree, beneath which the old woman had died.

She did not look old, lying there in that light, frozen and still. One of 63
the men turned her over in the snow and I saw everything. My body trembled with some strange mystical feeling and so did my brother's. It might have been the cold.

Neither of us had even seen a woman's body before. It may have been 64
the snow, clinging to the frozen flesh, that made it look so white and lovely, so like marble. No woman had come with the party from town; but one of the men, he was the town blacksmith, took off his overcoat and spread it over her. Then he gathered her into his arms and started off to town, all the others following silently. At that time no one knew who she was.

V

I had seen everything, had seen the oval in the snow, like a miniature race- 65
track, where the dogs had run, had seen how the men were mystified, had seen the white bare young-looking shoulders, had heard the whispered comments of the men.

The men were simply mystified. They took the body to the under- 66
taker's, and when the blacksmith, the hunter, the marshal and several others had got inside they closed the door. If father had been there perhaps he could have got in, but we boys couldn't.

I went with my brother to distribute the rest of his papers and when 67
we got home it was my brother who told the story.

I kept silent and went to bed early. It may have been I was not satis- 68
fied with the way he told it.

Later, in the town, I must have heard other fragments of the old 69
woman's story. She was recognized the next day and there was an investigation.

The husband and son were found somewhere and brought to town and 70
there was an attempt to connect them with the woman's death, but it did not work. They had perfect enough alibis.

However, the town was against them. They had to get out. Where they   71
went I never heard.

I remember only the picture there in the forest, the men standing   72
about, the naked girlish-looking figure, face down in the snow, the tracks
made by the running dogs and the clear cold Winter sky above. White fragments of clouds were drifting across the sky. They went racing across the
little open space among the trees.

The scene in the forest had become for me, without my knowing it, the   73
foundation for the real story I am now trying to tell. The fragments, you see,
had to be picked up slowly, long afterwards.

Things happened. When I was a young man I worked on the farm of a   74
German. The hired-girl was afraid of her employer. The farmer's wife hated
her.

I saw things at that place. Once later, I had a half-uncanny, mystical   75
adventure with dogs in an Illinois forest on a clear, moon-lit Winter night.
When I was a schoolboy, and on a Summer day, I went with a boy friend out
along a creek some miles from town and came to the house where the old
woman had lived. No one had lived in the house since her death. The doors
were broken from the hinges; the window lights were all broken. As the boy
and I stood in the road outside, two dogs, just roving farm dogs no doubt,
came running around the corner of the house. The dogs were tall, gaunt
fellows and came down to the fence and glared through at us, standing in the
road.

The whole thing, the story of the old woman's death, was to me as I   76
grew older like music heard from far off. The notes had to be picked up
slowly one at a time. Something had to be understood.

The woman who died was one destined to feed animal life. Anyway,   77
that is all she ever did. She was feeding animal life before she was born, as a
child, as a young woman working on the farm of the German, after she married, when she grew old and when she died. She fed animal life in cows, in
chickens, in pigs, in horses, in dogs, in men. Her daughter had died in
childhood and with her one son she had no articulate relations. On the night
when she died she was hurrying homeward, bearing on her body food for
animal life.

She died in the clearing in the woods and even after her death con-   78
tinued feeding animal life.

You see it is likely that, when my brother told the story, that night   79
when we got home and my mother and sister sat listening, I did not think he
got the point. He was too young and so was I. A thing so complete has its
own beauty.

I shall not try to emphasize the point. I am only explaining why I was   80
dissatisfied then and have been ever since. I speak of that only that you may
understand why I have been impelled to try to tell the simple story over
again.

SUBJECT QUESTIONS

1. Why is the story teller so careful to explain how he came by his facts and pieced the story together? (This is a short story; is "documentation" necessary?)
2. If we take a common definition of "the main character" as the one who undergoes a change in mental attitude as a result of some important event in his life, who is the main character in this story?
3. What kind of beauty does the boy find in the story of Mrs. Grimes?
4. Mrs. Grimes's dress is torn twice in the story. Is there any relation between those two events?
5. What do the dogs have to do with the story? Why does Anderson devote so much time to them?
6. Is there any significance to the fact that the hunter failed to recognize Mrs. Grimes, thinking her a beautiful young girl instead?
7. What does the story tell you about the moral attitudes of the townspeople?
8. What does it tell you about Anderson's view of art?

STRUCTURE QUESTIONS

1. Would you say that this story has unity or that it contains too much irrelevant detail? (Your answer may depend on who you decide is the main character.)
2. Did you find the concrete detail (the whole calf's liver, for example) interesting or annoying? Was it convincing (that is, did you sometimes think of this as autobiography rather than fiction)?
3. What devices other than concrete detail does Anderson employ to give a sense of realism to his story? Which part seems least realistic? Might Anderson have a reason for making certain parts less realistic than others?
4. Does Anderson seem to have overemphasized the importance of such an event as the death of Mrs. Grimes on the life of a boy? (That is, the description of events may be true to life at the same time the impression made on the boy is untrue to experience.)
5. Comment on the organization of the story: would it have been more, or less, effective had Anderson told it straight through without skipping back and forth in time?

SUGGESTION FOR WRITING

Describe an experience from your childhood that you did not fully understand until age and experience gave you added insight. (This does not need to be anything as traumatic as a death in the woods. It might just be something, for instance, that you did in all seriousness but which caused adults to laugh and unintentionally hurt your feelings.)

Acquainted with the Night

Robert Frost

Robert Frost (1874–1963) was one of America's most successful poets, winner of countless awards and honors, and often considered the unofficial poet laureate. He was the honored poet at President Kennedy's inauguration in 1961.

I have been one acquainted with the night.
I have walked out in rain — and back in rain.
I have outwalked the furthest city light.

I have looked down the saddest city lane.
I have passed by the watchman on his beat   5
And dropped my eyes, unwilling to explain.

I have stood still and stopped the sound of feet
When far away an interrupted cry
Came over houses from another street,

But not to call me back or say good-by;   10
And further still at an unearthly height
One luminary clock against the sky

Proclaimed the time was neither wrong nor right.
I have been one acquainted with the night.

SUBJECT QUESTIONS

1. The statement "I have been one acquainted with the night" is in the nature of a confession rather than a statement of fact or a boast. To what failing or weakness is the poet admitting?
2. Do you think Frost is using "night" with a symbolic meaning? If so, is it an appropriate symbol?

3. The poet seems to be looking — and listening — for something. Can you tell what? Should Frost have been more specific?
4. For what is the time "neither wrong nor right"? Is it possible that Frost himself doesn't know?

STRUCTURE QUESTIONS

1. The form of this poem is that used by Shelley in "Ode to the West Wind": a sonnet in "terza rima" with a concluding couplet. Analyze the rhyme scheme and meter. Does the tighter structure give the poem any advantages over free verse?
2. Is it possible that Frost has been too concrete in his choice of words? Might his meaning be clearer if he gave an abstract statement of it? Why would he avoid doing so? Would you say that it is possible to express ideas in concrete language that cannot be put into abstract language?
3. What is the pervading mood of this poem? How does Frost create the mood?
4. Far more than does a prose writer, the poet suggests meanings through images and accumulated connotations; thus, his approach is much more subjective. But he must still try to see and interpret accurately. Does Frost try to be honest with his reader? with himself?
5. The personal lyric is the most concentrated and powerful form of written expression. It is also the most difficult to write. If you have never tried your hand at one, you will find the experience enlightening — and perhaps a bit humiliating. Why is honesty so difficult to achieve in the short lyric?

SUGGESTION FOR WRITING

Write a description of a college scene in which you indicate by the details you select the mood of the scene or your judgment upon it. Use specific details rather than such interpretive words as "confusing," "depressing," and so on. Some suggestions:

a. The student union at 10 A.M.
b. A formal reception or dinner
c. The shower room on date night
d. The library on the afternoon of a home football game

The Abortion

Anne Sexton

Anne Sexton's first book of poems, To Bedlam and Part Way Back, was
published in 1960. In the years that followed she completed a number
of other volumes, one of which, Live or Die (1966), won a Pultizer Prize.
She married and lived in Weston, Massachusetts, before her death in
1974.

Somebody who should have been born
is gone.

Just as the earth puckered its mouth,
each bud puffing out from its knot,
I changed my shoes, and then drove south.   5

Up past the Blue Mountains, where
Pennsylvania humps on endlessly,
wearing, like a crayoned cat, its green hair,

its roads sunken in like a gray washboard;
where, in truth, the ground cracks evilly,   10
a dark socket from which the coal has poured,

Somebody who should have been born
is gone

the grass as bristly and stout as chives,
and me wondering when the ground would break,   15
and me wondering how anything fragile survives;

up in Pennsylvania, I met a little man,
not Rumpelstiltskin, at all, at all . . .
he took the fullness that love began.

Returning north, even the sky grew thin   20
like a high window looking nowhere.
The road was as flat as a sheet of tin.

Somebody who should have been born
is gone.

Yes, woman, such logic will lead   25
to loss without death. Or say what you meant,
you coward . . . this baby that I bleed.

SUBJECT QUESTIONS

1. Whether the experience related here was real or imaginary, the poet
   has used it as an example of a fairly common occurrence. Does she
   depend on the reader's knowledge of such experiences, or does the
   poem itself imply more universal extension?
2. Judging by this one poem only, what side would you expect Ms. Sexton to take in a debate over birth control legislation?
3. If the man she met was not at all like Rumpelstiltskin, why does she
   bother to drag in a fairy-tale character? In what ways might Rumpelstiltskin be constrasted with the abortionist? (The phrase "at all, at
   all" seems to imply that more than one point of contrast is intended.) What about the one point of comparison, that both men
   were "little"?
4. Do you find the nature description distracting from the "story"? Why
   do you suppose it is included?

STRUCTURE QUESTIONS

1. The refrain line, though a familiar device in folk ballads of lamenta-
   ble love affairs, usually occurs after a stanza or series of stanzas;
   what does the poet accomplish by putting her refrain first? Would
   the last refrain be more effective at the end of the poem?
2. Consider the images in the nature description ("the earth puckered
   its mouth," "like a crayoned cat," etc.). How does each relate to the
   meaning of the poem?
3. What effect does the imagery have on the tone or mood of the
   poem? Does the attitude toward nature remain constant?
4. Until the final stanza the poet has carefully controlled — perhaps
   even disguised — her feelings; but the last two lines are shockingly
   blunt. Does this sudden switch give added impact, or spoil the
   poem's integrity? On looking back, can you say that the bitterness
   was in the poem from the beginning?

SUGGESTION FOR WRITING

Recall an experience you faced with happy anticipation but which turned out a disappointment. Write two brief but concrete descriptions of the incident: one as you saw it when it happened, the other as you reflect back on it. Try to let the facts speak for themselves; the difference in points of view should produce a difference in the results without use of interpretive adjectives.

2

THE WORLD ABOUT US

Description

In some ways description is an extension of the use of personal example discussed in the preceding section. It is an extension from writers' selves to the places and people they have observed. If written properly, description conveys the same sense of immediacy, vividness, and interest. And it makes the same demand that writers keep their eyes and ears open to the world around them. There are differences too, of course. For one thing, the personal experience is usually presented in a narrative framework rather than a purely descriptive one. For another, description has numerous uses other than to provide a concrete illustration of a general principle.

Except in very short pieces, description is seldom found isolated from some other method of developing ideas. Yet it is an essential tool for virtually every kind of writer; a botanist can get along without it no better than a novelist can. For description is normally a means to an end rather than an end in itself — and the possible uses to which it can be put are infinite. The writer of a Boy Scout manual may carefully describe poison ivy so that readers will be able to avoid it. A public relations woman may want to describe a tract of New Mexico scabland in such a way that her readers will want to purchase an acre of it. A playwright describes his protagonist so that an actress will have a better idea of how to play that role. A novelist may describe the setting for action to give a sense of realism to her fiction — or she may use the description to create a mood of cheerfulness or desolation or foreboding. Compare Juliet's description of night as she awaits her new husband:

Gallop apace, you fiery-footed steeds,
Towards Phoebus' lodging: such a waggoner
As Phaethon would whip you to the west,
And bring in cloudy night immediately.
Spread thy close curtain, love-performing night,   5
That runaways' eyes may wink, and Romeo
Leap to these arms, untalk'd of and unseen.
Lovers can see to do their amorous rites
By their own beauties; or, if love be blind,
It best agrees with night. Come, civil night,   10
Thou sober-suited matron, all in black,
And learn me how to lose a winning match,
Play'd for a pair of stainless maidenhoods:
Hood my unmann'd blood, bating in my cheeks,
With thy black mantle; till strange love, grown bold,   15
Think true love acted simple modesty.
Come, night; come, Romeo; come, thou day in night;
For thou wilt lie upon the wings of night
Whiter than new snow on a raven's back.
Come, gentle night, come, loving, black-brow'd night,   20
Give me my Romeo; and, when he shall die,
Take him and cut him out in little stars,
And he will make the face of heaven so fine
That all the world will be in love with night
And pay no worship to the garish sun.   25

with Macbeth's description as he prepares to murder Duncan:

Now o'er the one half-world
Nature seems dead, and wicked dreams abuse
The curtain'd sleep; witchcraft celebrates
Pale Hecate's offerings, and wither'd murder,
Alarum'd by his sentinel, the wolf,   5
Whose howl's his watch, thus with his stealthy pace,
With Tarquin's ravishing strides, towards his design
Moves like a ghost.

Regardless of their purposes, what writers are after in description is the "essential nature" of the thing described — the special characteristics of poison ivy which will allow one to distinguish it from other forest plants. The problem is that a thing may have many "essences," and writers must decide which one best fits their purposes. What is the "essential nature" of a harmless drop of water, for instance? Much depends on the context in which it occurs. Obviously there is a considerable difference between a glistening drop of dew on a rose petal at sunrise and the first drop of rain spattering in the dust at second base during a World Series game. And writers' attitudes toward what they describe are also important: the baseball fan may be dismayed by that drop of rain and see it as an agent of evil; but if the pitcher is in a jam, that lovely mud-producing raindrop may to him seem sent from heaven.

Writers of description, then, must keep in mind both the occasion for which they are writing and the attitude toward their subjects which they want to re-create in their readers. In college writing, the nature of an assignment will frequently suggest the proper approach. (If the biology professor wants you to describe a drop of water as seen under a microscope, it is best to describe as accurately and objectively as possible, leaving your feelings out of it.) But when you are on your own, remember that, important as *accuracy of detail* is, just as crucial is proper *selection of detail*. You cannot describe everything about your subject, nor should you wish to. For many details, perhaps even obvious ones, may be irrelevant to the dominant impression you wish to convey. If you were describing Albert Einstein, you probably would not mention his height and weight. On the other hand, in a description of Abraham Lincoln, you might very well employ vivid physical details — the long loose frame, the huge floppy hands, the intense eyes — as outward manifestations of his inner personality. Surely the fact that Lincoln wore formal clothing uncomfortably is revealing of the man. Or what was the significance of Einstein's wild long hair? Was he setting a fashion trend for hippies, was he so modest that careful grooming seemed affectatious, was he so busy that haircuts were a waste of time? The details you select and the way in which you describe them should imply answers to such questions and thus convey a coherent impression of the subject.

The suggestions made in the introduction to the preceding section on proper word choice for personal example apply as well to description; review those pages before attempting to write a description. But a few other suggestions need to be added here. Be sure to evaluate the relevance of descriptive details before you include them. Abraham Lincoln may have had a prominent mole on his cheek, but how does that information contribute to the impression you wish to convey? Will a description of poison ivy's root system be useful in avoiding the itch? If not, leave it out.

One danger in writing description is the temptation to control the reader's attitude by using strings of interpretive adjectives — adjectives which really tell how you feel rather than what the subject looked like. "The speaker was quite impressive" or

"It was a really beautiful day" tell us little. Was it warm and sunny, or was there a fresh snowfall? Was it still snowing, or had the sun come out? Such details are what the reader needs to know. Not only are readers quite capable of inferring the effect you want — provided you supply the right details — but their impression will be much deeper if you let them draw the conclusion themselves. Cantankerous creatures that they are, readers have a natural resistance to being *told* how to feel, but a pliant willingness to feel anything you want them to if you simply provide the relevant details:

> For all the history of grief,
> An empty doorway and a maple leaf.

Let us go back to that harmless drop of water one more time. Suppose you had written for the biology professor an objective account of what you had seen under the microscope; but then you wanted to convey to some friends your repulsion at the sight of so many "animals" in your drinking water. If you wrote something like this:

> It was just ghastly; I can't tell you how ill the sight of that horrible water drop made me,

you would neither be telling your friends what you saw nor making them feel what you felt. They would only understand that *you* felt revulsion. But if you left out the "ghastly" and the "horrible," you could describe with vivid details which would re-create your feelings. A beginning of this sort might do:

> Although it was a drop of ordinary tap water — drinking water — under the microscope it came alive. Great green eels squirmed and slithered through it. Purple creatures like tadpoles, all head and tail, thrashed and churned blindly, colliding with other more sluggish monsters. A few blobs without tails for propulsion bobbed in the wake, expanding and contracting like lungs. . . .

Finally, you should remember that to describe what you have experienced, all the senses should be appealed to which were involved in your original experience, not just the sense of sight, which inexperienced writers rely on almost exclusively. For the qualities perceived by sight, such as color, shape, size, and movement, are probably not the only "essential" characteristics of a person or a landscape. It might be possible, in fact, to write a vivid description — say of a wharf on a pitch black night — without once appealing to the sense of sight. Sounds would be important: the water lapping, unseen gulls screeching, the rubbing of a boat against the dock. And the sense of touch: the night breeze, the chill moisture in the air, the spongy give of old boards underfoot. Perhaps even taste and smell: the odor of fish, the slight salt taste on the lips. For most descriptions, probably you will rely mainly on the sense of sight, but do not neglect the others; they can bring to life a "photographic" description.

The best way to organize materials for description depends both on what is being described and the impression of it you wish to convey. In describing a person, you might want to go from a photographic impression — physical features, clothing — to characterizing movements, to deeds and statements which reveal the inner person. In describing a scene, you might move like a movie camera from left to right, or from a long-range view to a close-up, or from the outside (of a building, for instance) to the inside. Or your purpose might better be served by proceeding from a broad view — snow-capped mountains and sparkling streams — to sharper details — hot dog wrappers, broken beer bottles, and the rusted car fender on the sand bar. But whatever method of organization you decide on, stick with it. The rapid alternation of long shot and zoom, or flashes of the past stuck into the present, may be all right for experimental movies, but they are difficult to handle in written description.

Seeing

Annie Dillard

Annie Dillard grew up in Pittsburgh and attended Hollins College. She is a contributing editor to Harper's *magazine and a columnist for* The Wilderness Society *magazine. Her first book of poems,* Tickets for a Prayer Wheel *(1973), was published at the University of Missouri. The following passage is from her first book of nature writing,* Pilgrim at Tinker Creek *(1974). Most of the book is a description of what she sees at her farm on Tinker Creek; here she discusses the problem of learning how to "see."*

When I was six or seven years old, growing up in Pittsburgh, I used to take   1
a precious penny of my own and hide it for someone else to find. It was a
curious compulsion; sadly, I've never been seized by it since. For some
reason I always "hid" the penny along the same stretch of sidewalk up the
street. I would cradle it at the roots of a sycamore, say, or in a hole left by a
chipped-off piece of sidewalk. Then I would take a piece of chalk, and,
starting at either end of the block, draw huge arrows leading up to the
penny from both directions. After I learned to write I labeled the arrows:
SURPRISE AHEAD or MONEY THIS WAY. I was greatly excited, during all this
arrow-drawing, at the thought of the first lucky passer-by who would receive in this way, regardless of merit, a free gift from the universe. But I
never lurked about. I would go straight home and not give the matter
another thought, until, some months later, I would be gripped again by the
impulse to hide another penny.

It is still the first week in January, and I've got great plans. I've been   2
thinking about seeing. There are lots of things to see, unwrapped gifts and
free surprises. The world is fairly studded and strewn with pennies cast
broadside from a generous hand. But — and this is the point — who gets
excited by a mere penny? If you follow one arrow, if you crouch motionless
on a bank to watch a tremulous ripple thrill on the water and are rewarded
by the sight of a muskrat kit paddling from its den, will you count that sight
a chip of copper only, and go your rueful way? It is dire poverty indeed
when a man is so malnourished and fatigued that he won't stoop to pick up

a penny. But if you cultivate a healthy poverty and simplicity, so that finding a penny will literally make your day, then, since the world is in fact planted in pennies, you have with your poverty bought a lifetime of days. It is that simple. What you see is what you get.

I used to be able to see flying insects in the air. I'd look ahead and see, not the row of hemlocks across the road, but the air in front of it. My eyes would focus along that column of air, picking out flying insects. But I lost interest, I guess, for I dropped the habit. Now I can see birds. Probably some people can look at the grass at their feet and discover all the crawling creatures. I would like to know grasses and sedges — and care. Then my least journey into the world would be a field trip, a series of happy recognitions. Thoreau, in an expansive mood, exulted, "What a rich book might be made about buds, including, perhaps, sprouts!" It would be nice to think so. I cherish mental images I have of three perfectly happy people. One collects stones. Another — an Englishman, say — watches clouds. The third lives on a coast and collects drops of seawater which he examines microscopically and mounts. But I don't see what the specialist sees, and so I cut myself off, not only from the total picture, but from the various forms of happiness.

Unfortunately, nature is very much a now-you-see-it, now-you-don't affair. A fish flashes, then dissolves in the water before my eyes like so much salt. Deer apparently ascend bodily into heaven; the brightest oriole fades into leaves. These disappearances stun me into stillness and concentration; they say of nature that it conceals with a grand nonchalance, and they say of vision that it is a deliberate gift, the revelation of a dancer who for my eyes only flings away her seven veils. For nature does reveal as well as conceal: now-you-don't-see-it, now-you-do. For a week last September migrating red-winged blackbirds were feeding heavily down by the creek at the back of the house. One day I went out to investigate the racket; I walked up to a tree, an Osage orange, and a hundred birds flew away. They simply materialized out of the tree. I saw a tree, then a whisk of color, then a tree again. I walked closer and another hundred blackbirds took flight. Not a branch, not a twig budged: the birds were apparently weightless as well as invisible. Or, it was as if the leaves of the Osage orange had been freed from a spell in the form of red-winged blackbirds; they flew from the tree, caught my eye in the sky, and vanished. When I looked again at the tree the leaves had reassembled as if nothing had happened. Finally I walked directly to the trunk of the tree and a final hundred, the real diehards, appeared, spread, and vanished. How could so many hide in the tree without my seeing them? The Osage orange, unruffled, looked just as it had looked from the house, when three hundred red-winged blackbirds cried from its crown. I looked downstream where they flew, and they were gone. Searching, I couldn't spot one. I wandered downstream to force

3

4

them to play their hand, but they'd crossed the creek and scattered. One show to a customer. These appearances catch at my throat; they are the free gifts, the bright coppers at the roots of trees.

It's all a matter of keeping my eyes open. Nature is like one of those 5 line drawings of a tree that are puzzles for children: Can you find hidden in the leaves a duck, a house, a boy, a bucket, a zebra, and a boot? Specialists can find the most incredibly well-hidden things. A book I read when I was young recommended an easy way to find caterpillars to rear: you simply find some fresh caterpillar droppings, look up, and there's your caterpillar. More recently an author advised me to set my mind at ease about those piles of cut stems on the ground in grassy fields. Field mice make them; they cut the grass down by degrees to reach the seeds at the head. It seems that when the grass is tightly packed, as in a field of ripe grain, the blade won't topple at a single cut through the stem; instead, the cut stem simply drops vertically, held in the crush of grain. The mouse severs the bottom again and again, the stem keeps dropping an inch at a time, and finally the head is low enough for the mouse to reach the seeds. Meanwhile, the mouse is positively littering the field with its little piles of cut stems into which, presumably, the author of the book is constantly stumbling.

If I can't see these minutiae, I still try to keep my eyes open. I'm 6 always on the lookout for antlion traps in sandy soil, monarch pupae near milkweed, skipper larvae in locust leaves. These things are utterly common, and I've not seen one. I bang on hollow trees near water, but so far no flying squirrels have appeared. In flat country I watch every sunset in hopes of seeing the green ray. The green ray is a seldom-seen streak of light that rises from the sun like a spurting fountain at the moment of sunset; it throbs into the sky for two seconds and disappears. One more reason to keep my eyes open. A photography professor at the University of Florida just happened to see a bird die in midflight; it jerked, died, dropped, and smashed on the ground. I squint at the wind because I read Stewart Edward White: "I have always maintained that if you looked closely enough you could *see* the wind — the dim, hardly-made-out, fine débris fleeing high in the air." White was an excellent observer, and devoted an entire chapter of *The Mountains* to the subject of seeing deer: "As soon as you can forget the naturally obvious and construct an artificial obvious, then you too will see deer."

But the artificial obvious is hard to see. My eyes account for less than 7 one percent of the weight of my head; I'm bony and dense; I see what I expect. I once spent a full three minutes looking at a bullfrog that was so unexpectedly large I couldn't see it even though a dozen enthusiastic campers were shouting directions. Finally I asked, "What color am I looking for?" and a fellow said, "Green." When at last I picked out the frog, I saw what painters are up against: the thing wasn't green at all, but the color of wet hickory bark.

The lover can see, and the knowledgeable. I visited an aunt and uncle at a quarter-horse ranch in Cody, Wyoming. I couldn't do much of anything useful, but I could, I thought, draw. So, as we all sat around the kitchen table after supper, I produced a sheet of paper and drew a horse. "That's one lame horse," my aunt volunteered. The rest of the family joined in: "Only place to saddle that one is his neck"; "Looks like we better shoot the poor thing, on account of those terrible growths." Meekly, I slid the pencil and paper down the table. Everyone in that family, including my three young cousins, could draw a horse. Beautifully. When the paper came back it looked as though five shining, real quarter horses had been corraled by mistake with a papier-mâché moose; the real horses seemed to gaze at the monster with a steady, puzzled air. I stay away from horses now, but I can do a creditable goldfish. The point is that I just don't know what the lover knows; I just can't see the artificial obvious that those in the know construct. The herpetologist asks the native, "Are there snakes in that ravine?" "Nosir." And the herpetologist comes home with, yessir, three bags full. Are there butterflies on that mountain? Are the bluets in bloom, are there arrowheads here, or fossil shells in the shale?

Peeping through my keyhole I see within the range of only about thirty percent of the light that comes from the sun; the rest is infrared and some little ultraviolet, perfectly apparent to many animals, but invisible to me. A nightmare network of ganglia, charged and firing without my knowledge, cuts and splices what I do see, editing it for my brain. Donald E. Carr points out that the sense impressions of one-celled animals are *not* edited for the brain: "This is philosophically interesting in a rather mournful way, since it means that only the simplest animals perceive the universe as it is."

A fog that won't burn away drifts and flows across my field of vision. When you see fog move against a backdrop of deep pines, you don't see the fog itself, but streaks of clearness floating across the air in dark shreds. So I see only tatters of clearness through a pervading obscurity. I can't distinguish the fog from the overcast sky; I can't be sure if the light is direct or reflected. Everywhere darkness and the presence of the unseen appalls. We estimate now that only one atom dances alone in every cubic meter of intergalactic space. I blink and squint. What planet or power yanks Halley's Comet out of orbit? We haven't seen that force yet; it's a question of distance, density, and the pallor of reflected light. We rock, cradled in the swaddling band of darkness. Even the simple darkness of night whispers suggestions to the mind. . . .

SUBJECT QUESTIONS

1. Annie Dillard complains that she fails to see most of what goes on around her. What evidence is there that she does in fact notice more than the average person might? Why does she complain, then, about her limitations?
2. The examples Dillard cites are natural phenomena that one might go a lifetime without noticing. Is there any value in even bothering to see them? Examine her argument toward the end of paragraph 2.
3. Because Dillard does "see" better than most of us, do you think there is an element of false modesty in her attitude here? What purpose is served by her lumping herself with the rest of us? Consider the point of her story about drawing pictures of horses in Wyoming (paragraph 8).
4. Would you say that her chief aim is to make us interested in what she sees, in the "problem of seeing" itself, or in improving our own vision?

STRUCTURE QUESTIONS

1. The opening anecdote about hiding pennies for others to find seems at first to have little to do with the subject of appreciating nature; how does Dillard relate it to her subject? Is use of the anecdote an effective way to open the essay?
2. The examples of phenomena to be seen by a careful observer are not very startling. Should she have included some more spectacular occurrences — tornadoes, or volcanic eruptions, perhaps? Would the point of the essay have been altered had she selected more thrilling examples?
3. By what techniques does Dillard make her personal experience an example to others? (Remember that no two people will see life in quite the same ways.)
4. Does Dillard's frequent citing of previous nature writers give this informal essay too much the look of a research paper? What does she achieve by these references to Thoreau, Donald Carr, the expert on caterpillars, and others?
5. Consider the ways in which Dillard makes her descriptions of ordinary events vivid without destroying (with exotic, overly poetic language) the very common quality she wants to emphasize. Does she balance the workload among verbs, adjectives, and nouns, or does she depend too heavily on one part of speech?
6. Although the tone of this essay is generally informal, Dillard often uses uncommon words where ordinary ones might do — "malnourished and fatigued" instead of "hungry and tired," for instance. Examine a few of these choices, and decide whether or

not they confuse the tone of the essay, and whether their specific purpose justifies their inclusion.

SUGGESTIONS FOR WRITING

1. Write a brief but detailed description of something you pass daily but have hardly noticed before — a leaf, the bark of a tree, a section of sidewalk. (The aim here is to describe accurately, not to think up some artificial way to "make it exciting.")
2. Describe something in motion — a cat, a caterpillar, a combine harvester, a weeping willow in the wind. You will need to find ways to convey the sense of motion: a snapshot is not a movie.
3. Select a site — student union, dormitory, library — and write an essay on "the sounds around me" in which you concentrate almost wholly on what you can hear rather than see.
4. Describe an object using as many facets of the sense of sight as are appropriate: color, shape, size, motion, light and shadow, texture, and so on.

The Death of a Moth

Annie Dillard

Annie Dillard (see preceding essay) is currently artist-in-residence at Western Washington State University. Previously, she lived for ten years in the Roanoke Valley of Virginia, near the site of the death of the moth which she describes here. This essay was written several years after "Seeing"; decide whether or not Dillard did in fact learn to "see" nature.

I live alone with two cats, who sleep on my legs. There is a yellow one, and a black one whose name is Small. In the morning I joke to the black one, Do you remember last night? Do you remember? I throw them both out before breakfast, so I can eat.

There is a spider, too, in the bathroom, of uncertain lineage, bulbous at the abdomen and drab, whose six-inch mess of web works, works somehow, works miraculously, to keep her alive and me amazed. The web is in a corner behind the toilet, connecting tile wall to tile wall. The house is new, the bathroom immaculate, save for the spider, her web, and the sixteen or so corpses she's tossed to the floor.

The corpses appear to be mostly sow bugs, those little armadillo creatures who live to travel flat out in houses, and die round. In addition to sow-bug husks, hollow and sipped empty of color, there are what seem to be two or three wingless moth bodies, one new flake of earwig, and three spider carcasses crinkled and clenched.

I wonder on what fool's errand an earwig, or a moth, or a sow bug, would visit that clean corner of the house behind the toilet; I have not noticed any blind parades of sow bugs blundering into corners. Yet they do hazard there, at a rate of more than one a week, and the spider thrives. Yesterday she was working on the earwig, mouth on gut; today he's on the floor. It must take a certain genius to throw things away from there, to find a straight line through that sticky tangle to the floor.

Today the earwig shines darkly, and gleams, what there is of him: a dorsal curve of thorax and abdomen, and a smooth pair of pincers by which I knew his name. Next week, if the other bodies are any indication, he'll be shrunk and gray, webbed to the floor with dust. The sow bugs beside him are curled and empty, fragile, a breath away from brittle fluff. The spiders lie on their sides, translucent and ragged, their legs drying in knots. The moths stagger against each other, headless, in a confusion of arcing strips of chitin like peeling varnish, like a jumble of buttresses for cathedral vaults, like nothing resembling moths, so that I would hesitate to call them moths, except that I have had some experience with the figure Moth reduced to a nub.

Two summers ago I was camped alone in the Blue Ridge Mountains of Virginia. I had hauled myself and gear up there to read, among other things, *The Day on Fire*, by James Ullman, a novel about Rimbaud that had made me want to be a writer when I was sixteen; I was hoping it would do it again. So I read every day sitting under a tree by my tent, while warblers sang in the leaves overhead and bristle worms trailed their inches over the twiggy dirt at my feet; and I read every night by candlelight, while barred owls called in the forest and pale moths seeking mates massed round my head in the clearing, where my light made a ring. [6]

Moths kept flying into the candle. They would hiss and recoil, reeling upside down in the shadows among my cooking pans. Or they would singe their wings and fall, and their hot wings, as if melted, would stick to the first thing they touched — a pan, a lid, a spoon — so that the snagged moths could struggle only in tiny arcs, unable to flutter free. These I could release by a quick flip with a stick; in the morning I would find my cooking stuff decorated with torn flecks of moth wings, ghostly triangles of shiny dust here and there on the aluminum. So I read, and boiled water, and replenished candles, and read on. [7]

One night a moth flew into the candle, was caught, burnt dry, and held. I must have been staring at the candle, or maybe I looked up when a shadow crossed my page; at any rate, I saw it all. A golden female moth, a biggish one with a two-inch wingspread, flapped into the fire, dropped abdomen into the wet wax, stuck, flamed, and frazzled in a second. Her moving wings ignited like tissue paper, like angels' wings, enlarging the circle of light in the clearing and creating out of the darkness the sudden blue sleeves of my sweater, the green leaves of jewelweed by my side, the ragged red trunk of a pine; at once the light contracted again and the moth's wings vanished in a fine, foul smoke. At the same time, her six legs clawed, curled, blackened, and ceased, disappearing utterly. And her head jerked in spasms, making a spattering noise; her antennae crisped and burnt away and her heaving mouthparts cracked like pistol fire. When it was all over, her head [8] was, so far as I could determine, gone, gone the long way of her wings and legs. Her head was a hole lost to time. All that was left was the glowing horn shell of her abdomen and thorax — a fraying, partially collapsed gold tube jammed upright in the candle's round pool.

And then this moth-essence, this spectacular skeleton, began to act as a   9 wick. She kept burning. The wax rose in the moth's body from her soaking abdomen to her thorax to the shattered hole where her head should have been, and widened into flame, a saffron-yellow flame that robed her to the ground like an immolating monk. That candle had two wicks, two winding flames of identical light, side by side. The moth's head was fire. She burned for two hours, until I blew her out.

She burned for two hours without changing, without swaying or kneel-   10 ing — only glowing within, like a building fire glimpsed through silhouetted walls, like a hollow saint, like a flame-faced virgin gone to God, while I read by her light, kindled, while Rimbaud in Paris burnt out his brain in a thousand poems, while night pooled wetly at my feet.

So. That is why I think those hollow shreds on the bathroom floor are moths.   11 I believe I know what moths look like, in any state.

I have three candles here on the table which I disentangle from the   12 plants and light when visitors come. The cats avoid them, although Small's tail caught fire once; I rubbed it out before she noticed. I don't mind living alone. I like eating alone and reading. I don't mind sleeping alone. The only time I mind being alone is when something is funny; then, when I am laughing at something funny, I wish someone were around. Sometimes I think it is pretty funny that I sleep alone.

SUBJECT QUESTIONS

1. Can you tell from this description whether or not Dillard has improved her ability to "see" since she wrote "Seeing"? What does she see in this essay that most of us would have missed?
2. What does the fact that the bathroom is immaculate except for the spider's web tell you about the author? Are spiders as repugnant to her as they are to most people?
3. What is there about the moth's death that makes Dillard wish to tell the story?
4. Does Dillard give enough descriptive details for the reader to form a mental picture of the moth? Can you visualize its skeleton acting as a candlewick?
5. Dillard uses the term "moth-essence" in paragraph 9. What is the essence of the moth from the author's point of view?

6. Is the mountain setting of any importance to Dillard's description? What function does it serve in the essay?

STRUCTURE QUESTIONS

1. How does the author get from the spider in the bathroom to the moth on the mountain? In which description does she seem most interested? Does the essay as a whole suggest any continuity between her life in the woods and her life in town?
2. Note that the visual description on the mountain is limited to the circle of light thrown by the candle. What happens when the amount of light changes? How does Dillard describe things outside the circle of light?
3. What is the ratio of action verbs to passive and linking verbs in this essay? Could the author profitably have substituted action verbs for some of the linking verbs? (Try rewriting two or three sentences to test the difference.)
4. How many interpretive adjectives can you find in this passage? Do you think Dillard has no feelings about the moth? What clues are there that she respects life and does care?
5. What appeals do you find to the senses other than sight in the description of the moth?
6. At crucial points in the description (paragraphs 8 and 10) Dillard resorts to similes rather than direct description. Does the effectiveness of the similes compensate for the somewhat artificial distraction to things not actually present in the scene (tissue paper, angels' wings, etc.)?

SUGGESTION FOR WRITING

Write two brief descriptions of just one object or event. In the first, keep the description as objective as possible. In the second, try to convey an attitude toward what you are describing without directly telling the reader what your attitude is ("I felt horrible," "It was very sad," etc.).

The Turtle

John Steinbeck

John Steinbeck (1902–1968) attended Stanford for one year, in 1919, then dropped out and became a reporter. His first novel, Cup of Gold, *was published in 1929. During World War II, Steinbeck was an overseas war correspondent. He won the Pulitzer Prize (1940), the Nobel Prize for Literature (1962), and the President's Freedom Medal (1964). Among his many best-sellers were* Tortilla Flat *(1935),* Of Mice and Men *(1937),* Cannery Row *(1945), and* East of Eden *(1952). The description of the turtle that follows is from an early chapter of his most famous novel,* The Grapes of Wrath *(1939). Steinbeck uses the painful progress of the turtle as an allegory of the struggle for survival, which is the theme of the novel.*

The concrete highway was edged with a mat of tangled, broken, dry grass, and the grass heads were heavy with oat beards to catch on a dog's coat, and foxtails to tangle in a horse's fetlocks, and clover burrs to fasten in sheep's wool; sleeping life waiting to be spread and dispersed, every seed armed with an appliance of dispersal, twisting darts and parachutes for the wind, little spears and balls of tiny thorns, and all waiting for animals and for the wind, for a man's trouser cuff or the hem of a woman's skirt, all passive but armed with appliances of activity, still, but each possessed of the anlage of movement. 1

The sun lay on the grass and warmed it, and in the shade under the grass the insects moved, ants and ant lions to set traps for them, grasshoppers to jump into the air and flick their yellow wings for a second, sow bugs like little armadillos, plodding restlessly on many tender feet. And over the grass at the roadside a land turtle crawled, turning aside for nothing, dragging his high-domed shell over the grass. His hard legs and yellow-nailed feet threshed slowly through the grass, not really walking, but boosting and dragging his shell along. The barley beards slid off his shell, and the cover burrs fell on him and rolled to the ground. His horny beak was partly open, and his fierce, humorous eyes, under brows like fingernails, stared straight ahead. He came over the grass leaving a beaten trail behind him, and the hill, which was the highway embankment, reared up ahead of him. For a 2 moment he stopped, his head held high. He blinked and looked up and down. At last he started to climb the embankment. Front clawed feet reached forward but did not touch. The hind feet kicked his shell along, and it scraped on the grass, and on the gravel. As the embankment grew steeper and steeper, the more frantic were the efforts of the land turtle. Pushing hind legs strained and slipped, boosting the shell along, and the horny head protruded as far as the neck could stretch. Little by little the shell slid up the embankment until at last a parapet cut straight across its line of march, the shoulder of the road, a concrete wall four inches high. As though they worked independently the hind legs pushed the shell against the wall. The head upraised and peered over the wall to the broad smooth plain of cement. Now the hands, braced on top of the wall, strained and lifted, and the shell came slowly up and rested its front end on the wall. For a moment the turtle rested. A red ant ran into the shell, into the soft skin inside the shell, and suddenly head and legs snapped in, and the armored tail clamped in sideways. The red ant was crushed between body and legs. And one head of wild oats was clamped into the shell by a front leg. For a long moment the turtle lay still, and then the neck crept out and the old humorous frowning eyes looked about and the legs and tail came out. The back legs went to work, straining like elephant legs, and the shell tipped to an angle so that the front legs could not reach the level cement plain. But higher and higher the hind legs boosted it, until at last the center of balance was reached, the front tipped down, the front legs scratched at the pavement, and it was up. But the head of wild oats was held by its stem around the front legs.

Now the going was easy, and all the legs worked, and the shell boosted along, waggling from side to side. A sedan driven by a forty-year-old woman approached. She saw the turtle and swung to the right, off the highway, the wheels screamed and a cloud of dust boiled up. Two wheels lifted for a moment and then settled. The car skidded back onto the road, and went on, but more slowly. The turtle had jerked into its shell, but now it hurried on, for the highway was burning hot.

And now a light truck approached, and as it came near the driver saw the turtle and swerved to hit it. His front wheel struck the edge of the shell, flipped the turtle like a tiddly-wink, spun it like a coin, and rolled it off the highway. The truck went back to its course along the right side. Lying on its back, the turtle was tight in its shell for a long time. But at last its legs waved in the air, reaching for something to pull it over. Its front foot caught a piece of quartz and little by little the shell pulled over and flopped upright. The wild oat head fell out and three of the spearhead seeds stuck in the ground. And as the turtle crawled on down the embankment, its shell dragged dirt over the seeds. The turtle entered a dust road and jerked itself along, drawing a wavy shallow trench in the dust with its shell. The old humorous eyes looked ahead, and the horny beak opened a little. His yellow toe nails slipped a fraction in the dust.

SUBJECT QUESTIONS

1. What justification can you see for Steinbeck's including this description in *The Grapes of Wrath,* a novel not about turtles but about the migration of the Joad family from the dust bowl of Oklahoma to California and of their struggle for existence?
2. Do you think Steinbeck is ultimately more interested in the turtle or in the wild oat seeds? What difference does your decision make to an interpretation of the passage?
3. Steinbeck has added to his nature description two very different kinds of motorists. Are these drivers atypical, or do they represent a significant proportion of all drivers? Why has Steinbeck bothered to include them?
4. Would you say that Steinbeck's attitude toward the natural processes he describes is basically optimistic, pessimistic, or simply mechanistic?

STRUCTURE QUESTIONS

1. Clearly Steinbeck has not tried to "psychoanalyze" the turtle. Would you say that the descriptive passages are also from the point of view of a detached observer, or does Steinbeck try to see what the turtle might see? (Consider, for instance, the passage in the middle of paragraph 2 describing the turtle's getting up onto the highway.)
2. Most writers of description overuse linking verbs and depend for descriptive force on their adjectives. ("The study desk was old and wobbly; its surface was uneven from the carved initials of two generations of students.") Steinbeck's first paragraph also uses two linking verbs, "was" and "were"; how many do you find thereafter? Consider how Steinbeck uses verbs to get action and drama into a virtually static scene.
3. Near the end of paragraph 2, Steinbeck shifts from active to passive voice in three sentences: "The red ant was crushed between body and legs. And one head of wild oats was clamped into the shell by a front leg. . . . But the head of wild oats was held by its stem around the front legs." Turn the sentences into active voice to see why Steinbeck made this shift.
4. Like all descriptions, Steinbeck's must be selective. Do his descriptive details create a consistent impression, an "essence" he wants to convey?

5. Which details best convey a sense of authenticity? Do they seem to be gratuitous details, or integral to the description? (Consider the age of the woman driver, for instance.)
6. One phrase is repeated like a refrain in the passage — reference to the old turtle's "humorous eyes." The phrase is ambiguous: the eyes might be funny to look at, the turtle might have a sense of humor, or in the archaic sense of "humour," his eyes could be dripping matter. Why do you think Steinbeck uses, and repeats, the phrase?

SUGGESTIONS FOR WRITING

1. Write a description of a natural setting dominated by some climatic condition — burning sun, wind, snow, etc.
2. Write a description in which you concentrate on the play of light and shadow rather than color, shape, or motion.
3. Describe a setting you experienced in total darkness — lying awake in a sleeping bag on a camping trip, for instance, or lying in bed listening for burglars or to a party next door. Use sound, touch, and smell, but not sight.

East Harlem

Patricia Cayo Sexton

Patricia Cayo Sexton has been an assembly-line worker and union official at a Detroit factory. She received her Ph.D. in 1960 from Wayne State University and is now a professor of sociology at New York University. Most of her professional interest has been with the working classes and the poverty-stricken. Her books include Education and Income, The American School, *and* Blue Collars and Hard Hats. *The following selection is the opening description which sets the scene for her study* Spanish Harlem: An Anatomy of Poverty *(1965).*

At 6:30 A.M., while silk-stocking Manhattan is asleep, East Harlem is starting to bustle. The poor are early risers. They have the jobs others don't want: the early-hour jobs, the late-hour jobs. Many rise early because it is a rural habit.

Along about 7:30 the streets are filled with fast-moving people: men, women, and swarms of children of all sizes. The parochial school children can be seen in clusters, with their togetherness identity tag — a school hat, a blouse, a uniform.

You may be able to buy a *New York Times* at the corner newsstand in the morning, but you probably will not be able to buy a cup of coffee. The poor drink their coffee and eat their breakfasts, such as they are, at home. Few eat out.

Some will stand at the bus stops, but most will crowd into the downtown subways that speed them to jobs in commercial or silk-stocking areas: to serve the affluent, or work in their stores or small industrial shops. Many of the Negro women will go to domestic service; and the Puerto Rican women, to their sewing machines in the garment shops.

Later in the day, if it is warm, the men who have no jobs will come out and stand on the sidewalks and talk together. They will watch the street and the passers-by and kibitz with one another. The old people, and from time to time the housewives, will sit at the window and join the watchers. And those with leisure may call them idle. Later, when the children return from school, the sidewalks and streets will jump with activity. Clusters of men, sitting on orange crates on the sidewalks, will play checkers or cards. The women will sit on the stoop, arms folded, and watch the young at play; and the young men, flexing their muscles, will look for some adventure. Vendors, ringing their bells, will hawk hot dogs, orange drinks, ice cream; and the caressing but often jarring noise of honking horns, music, children's games, and casual quarrels, whistles, singing, will go on late into the night. When you are in it you don't notice the noise, but when you stand away and listen to a taped conversation, the sound suddenly appears as a background roar. This loud stimulation of the senses may produce some of the emotionalism of the poor.

East Harlem is a busy place, night and day, filled with the joyous and troubled lives of residents — rather than the heavy commercial traffic of mid-Manhattan. New York's street life is unique. So much action, so much togetherness. The critics who lament its passing have a point. The middle class who disdain life conducted so openly in the streets might compare its satisfactions to the sometimes parched and estranged quality of their own backyards.

6

SUBJECT QUESTIONS

1. On which one part of life in East Harlem does the author focus in this brief passage? Her intention is to provide a setting for a study of life at the poverty level; does the description serve this purpose?
2. What is the "essential characteristic" of the East Harlem streets? Is this a "unique" characteristic, as the author claims?
3. Suggest some problems which might arise if the residents of East Harlem were transferred to high-rise apartments.
4. If the residents of East Harlem had "their own backyards," do you suppose the contrast made with the middle class in the final sentence would disappear?

STRUCTURE QUESTIONS

1. Comment on the author's use of future tense ("will stand," "will crowd," "will watch," and so on). Would present tense serve as well?
2. What is the organizing principle of this description? Is it a useful one?
3. This description is necessarily a generalized one — what you can see on almost any street in East Harlem; how does the author keep it from being vague?
4. Upper-class residential areas are twice referred to as "silk-stocking areas"; why does the author employ this old-fashioned phrase?
5. The final paragraph is more a commentary than part of the description. Is it a useful way to end the essay? Is it appropriate to draw the

final contrast between East Harlem streets and middle-class back-yards, rather than middle-class streets?

SUGGESTIONS FOR WRITING

1. Describe a street with which you are familiar — in a downtown shopping area, in a residential neighborhood, in fraternity row, or a country lane if you wish. Try by your selection of details to convey the "essence" of the street. Remember that words such as "busy" or "peaceful" are interpretive, not descriptive.
2. Describe a group of people, whether on a commuter train, at a football game, at a disco, Christmas shopping, and so on. Allow for individual differences, at the same time identifying what makes them a "group."

City Walking

Edward Hoagland

*Edward Hoagland (b. 1932) is a novelist, short story writer, and writer of
nature studies. He has been a teacher at the New School for Social Research and at Rutgers University, and he has won numerous writing
awards and fellowships including the Prix de Rome and a Guggenheim
Fellowship. Among his novels are* Cat Man *(1956),* The Circle Home
(1960), and The Peacock's Tail *(1965). The essay below, from* Red Wolves
and Black Bears, *first appeared in* The New York Times Book Review
(1975).

There is a time of life somewhere between the sullen fugues of adolescence   1
and the retrenchments of middle age when human nature becomes so absolutely absorbing one wants to be in the city constantly, even at the height
of the summer — Nature can't seem to hold a candle to it. One gobbles the
blocks, and if the weather is sweaty, so much the better; it brings everybody else out too. To the enthusiast's eye, what might later look to be
human avarice is simply energy, brutality is strength, ambition is not
wearisome or repellent or even alarming. In my own case, aiming to be a
writer, I knew that every mile I walked, the better writer I'd be; and I
went to 20th Street and the Hudson River to smell the yeasty redolence of
the Nabisco factory, and to West 12th Street to sniff the police stables. In
the meat market district nearby, if a tyro complained that his back ached,
the saying was, "Don't bleed on me!"

Down close to the Battery the banana boats used to unload (now they   2
are processed in Albany). Banana boats were the very definition of seagoing
grubbiness, but bejeweled snakes could be discovered aboard which had
arrived from the tropics as stowaways. On Bleecker Street you could get a
dozen clams on the half shell for fifty cents if you ate them outdoors; and on
Avenue A, piroshki, kielbasa and suchlike. Kids still swam from piers west
of the theater district in the Hudson and under Brooklyn Bridge, and I was
on the lookout among them for Huckleberry Finn. He was there, all right,
diving in, then scrambling up a piling, spitting water because he hadn't
quite learned how to swim. In the evening I saw him again on Delancey
Street, caught by the ear by a storekeeper for pilfering.

Oh yes, oh yes! one says, revisiting these old walking neighborhoods.   3
Yorkville, Inwood, Columbus Avenue. Our New York sky is not muscular
with cloud formations as is San Francisco's, or as green-smelling as
London's, and rounding a corner here, one doesn't stop stock-still to gaze
at the buildings as in Venice. The bartenders like to boast that in this city
we have "the best and worst," yet intelligent conversation, for example, is
mostly ad-libbed and comes in fits and starts, anywhere or nowhere; one
cannot trot out of an evening and go looking for it. We have our famous
New York energy instead, as well as its reverse, which is the keening misery, the special New York craziness, as if every thirteenth person standing
on the street is wearing a gauzy hospital smock and paper shower slippers.

Edmund G. Love wrote a good city walker's book some years ago   4
called *Subways Are for Sleeping*. Indeed they were, but now if the transit
police didn't prevent old bums from snoozing the night away while rum-
bling back and forth from Brooklyn to the Bronx, somebody would set them
on fire. Up on the street hunting parties are abroad, whom the walker must
take cognizance of; it's not enough to have your historical guidebook and go
maundering about to the Old Merchant's House on East 4th Street. A pair
of bravos will ask you for a light and want a light; another pair, when your
hands are in your pockets, will slug you. If you're lucky they will slug you;
the old bar fighters complain about how risky fighting has become. You
must have a considerable feel for these things, an extra sense, eyes in the
back of your head: or call it a walker's *emotional range*. You must know
when a pistol pointed at you playfully by a ten-year-old is a cap pistol and
when it's not; whether someone coming toward you with a broken bottle is
really going for you or not. We have grown to be students of police
work — watching a bank robber scram as the squad cars converge, watching a burglar tackled, watching four hoodlums unmercifully beating a cop
until four patrol cars scream to a halt and eight policemen club down the
hoods.

Nevertheless, if you ask people who have some choice in the matter   5
why they live in a particular neighborhood, one answer they will give is
that they "like to walk." Walking is a universal form of exercise, not age-
oriented or bound to any national heritage, and costs and implies nothing
except maybe a tolerant heart. Like other sports, it calls for a good eye as
well as cheerful legs — those chunky gluteus muscles that are the butt of
mankind's oldest jokes — because the rhythm of walking is in the sights
and one's response as much as simply in how one steps. In America at the
moment it may seem like something of a reader's or an individualist's sport,
because we are becoming suburban, and the suburbs have not adjusted to
the avocation of walking yet. But they will.

And yet times do change. Only this spring I was in a river town on   6
the Mississippi, loafing on a dock the barges tie to, on the lookout for

Huckleberry Finn once again. He was there, all right, with a barefoot, red-headed, tow-headed gang. They had sandy freckles and wore torn pants; Miss Watson still cut their hair. They were carrying a pailful of red-eared turtles and green frogs from the borrow pit behind the levee, and were boasting about the garfish they had noosed with a piece of piano wire. They began daring each other, and what the dare turned out to be — the best they could think of — was which of them had nerve enough to reach down and taste the Mississippi!

Now, muggers are herd creatures like the rest of us; they too have a "rush hour." So if a walker is indeed an individualist there is nowhere he can't go at dawn and not many places he can't go at noon. But just as it demeans life alongside a great river you can no longer swim in or drink from, to be crowded into the safer areas and hours takes much of the gloss off walking — one sport you shouldn't have to reserve a time and a court for.

SUBJECT QUESTIONS

1. What are some differences between city walking now and a few years ago?
2. Does Hoagland make clear how walking in New York is different from walking in other cities?
3. What does attitude have to do with what one sees? (See especially paragraph 1.)
4. Does the presence of muggers dampen Hoagland's enthusiasm for walking? What differences do they make in his walking habits?
5. Can you say why Hoagland keeps looking for a "Huckleberry Finn"? What might such a figure mean to him?

STRUCTURE QUESTIONS

1. In "Politics and the English Language" George Orwell gives writers this advice: "Never use a long word where a short one will do." Examine some of Hoagland's long or unfamiliar words, and decide whether shorter words would have done as well.
2. As Hoagland is describing walks throughout New York City, he can hardly give a concentrated, detailed description. Does he at least give a series of "snapshots" of the city? Would the description be as meaningful to a reader who does not know the city as to one who does?
3. Should Hoagland have included the paragraph about the unnamed "river town on the Mississippi"? Is it a distraction from the main subject? Does it serve a useful purpose?
4. Do the details selected contribute to the essential qualities of

"energy" and "keening misery"? What is the "keening misery"?
(Look up the verb "to keen" in your dictionary.)
5. Does Hoagland maintain a consistent attitude toward city walking?
Does his attitude jibe with the description of mugging and violence
in the city?

SUGGESTIONS FOR WRITING

1. Describe a familiar distance between two places as you would experience it by walking, by car, or by any other mode of transportation (running a stretch of rapids by canoe, for instance). Where appropriate, appeal to senses other than sight. Try to find a way
around a repetitious "next . . . then" method of organization.
2. Write a description of something moving past a fixed viewpoint — a
parade, a passing freight train, students going to class. Include details of sound as well as sight, if appropriate, but concentrate especially on motion.

Uncle John's Farm

Mark Twain

Samuel Langhorne Clemens (1835–1910), better known by his pen name, Mark Twain, preferred to be thought of as a philosopher and social critic rather than as a humorist. We know him best today, of course, as the author of Tom Sawyer *and* Huckleberry Finn. *In all his writing, however, his real genius lay in his ability to make use of the everyday materials from his own experience, to recreate them vividly and concretely, even if that entailed moving his uncle's farm several hundred miles down river. The excerpt reprinted here is from his* Autobiography (1924).

For many years I believed that I remembered helping my grandfather drink his whisky toddy when I was six weeks old, but I do not tell about that any more, now; I am grown old and my memory is not as active as it used to be. When I was younger I could remember anything, whether it had happened or not; but my faculties are decaying now, and soon I shall be so I cannot remember any but the things that never happened. It is sad to go to pieces like this, but we all have to do it.

My uncle, John A. Quarles, was a farmer, and his place was in the country four miles from Florida. He had eight children and fifteen or twenty negroes, and was also fortunate in other ways, particularly in his character. I have not come across a better man than he was. I was his guest for two or three months every year, from the fourth year after we removed to Hannibal till I was eleven or twelve years old. I have never consciously used him or his wife in a book, but his farm has come very handy to me in literature once or twice. In *Huck Finn* and in *Tom Sawyer, Detective* I moved it down to Arkansas. It was all of six hundred miles, but it was no trouble; it was not a very large farm — five hundred acres, perhaps — but I could have done it if it had been twice as large. And as for the morality of it, I cared nothing for that; I would move a state if the exigencies of literature required it.

It was a heavenly place for a boy, that farm of my uncle John's. The house was a double log one, with a spacious floor (roofed in) connecting it with the kitchen. In the summer the table was set in the middle of that shady and breezy floor, and the sumptuous meals — well, it makes me cry to think of them. Fried chicken, roast pig; wild and tame turkeys, ducks, and geese; venison just killed; squirrels, rabbits, pheasants, partridges, prairie-

Abridged from pp. 96–100, 102–104, 106, 109 and 115 in *The Autobiography of Mark Twain* Vol. 1 by Mark Twain. Copyright 1924 by Clara Gabrilowitsch; renewed 1952 by Clara Clemens Samossoud. Reprinted by permission of Harper & Row, Publishers, Inc.

chickens; biscuits, hot batter cakes, hot buckwheat cakes, hot "wheat bread," hot rolls, hot corn pone; fresh corn boiled on the ear, succotash, butter-beans, stringbeans, tomatoes, peas, Irish potatoes, sweet potatoes; butter-milk, sweet milk, "clabber"; watermelons, muskmelons, cantaloupes — all fresh from the garden; apple pie, peach pie, pumpkin pie, apple dumplings, peach cobbler — I can't remember the rest. . . .

The farmhouse stood in the middle of a very large yard, and the yard was fenced on three sides with rails and on the rear side with high palings; against these stood the smoke-house; beyond the palings was the orchard; beyond the orchard were the negro quarters and the tobacco fields. The front yard was entered over a stile made of sawed-off logs of graduated heights; I do not remember any gate. In a corner of the front yard were a dozen lofty hickory trees and a dozen black walnuts, and in the nutting season riches were to be gathered there. 4

Down a piece, abreast the house, stood a little log cabin against the rail fence; and there the woody hill fell sharply away, past the barns, the corn-crib, the stables, and the tobacco-curing house, to a limpid brook which sang along over its gravelly bed and curved and frisked in and out and here and there and yonder in the deep shade of overhanging foliage and vines — a divine place for wading, and it had swimming pools, too, which were forbid-den to us and therefore much frequented by us. For we were little Christian children and had early been taught the value of forbidden fruit. 5

In the little log cabin lived a bedridden white-headed slave woman whom we visited daily and looked upon with awe, for we believed she was upward of a thousand years old and had talked with Moses. The younger negroes credited these statistics and had furnished them to us in good faith. We accommodated all the details which came to us about her; and so we believed that she had lost her health in the long desert trip coming out of Egypt, and had never been able to get it back again. She had a round bald place on the crown of her head, and we used to creep around and gaze at it in reverent silence, and reflect that it was caused by fright through seeing Pharaoh drowned. We called her "Aunt" Hannah, Southern fashion. She was superstitious, like the other negroes; also, like them, she was deeply re-ligious. Like them, she had great faith in prayer and employed it in all ordi-nary exigencies, but not in cases where a dead certainty of result was urgent. Whenever witches were around she tied up the remnant of her wool in little tufts, with white thread, and this promptly made the witches impo-tent. . . . 6

I can see the farm yet, with perfect clearness. I can see all its belong-ings, all its details; the family room of the house, with a "trundle" bed in one corner and a spinning-wheel in another — a wheel whose rising and falling wail, heard from a distance, was the mournfulest of all sounds to me, and 7 made me homesick and low spirited, and filled my atmosphere with the wandering spirits of the dead; the vast fireplace, piled high, on winter nights, with flaming hickory logs from whose ends a sugary sap bubbled out, but did not go to waste, for we scraped it off and ate it; the lazy cat spread out on the rough hearthstones; the drowsy dogs braced against the jambs and blinking; my aunt in one chimney corner, knitting; my uncle in the other, smoking his corn-cob pipe; the slick and carpetless oak floor faintly mirroring the dancing flame tongues and freckled with black indentations where fire coals had popped out and died a leisurely death; half a dozen children romping in the background twilight; "split"-bottomed chairs here and there, some with rockers; a cradle — out of service, but waiting, with confidence; in the early cold mornings a snuggle of children, in shirts and chemises, occupying the hearthstone and procrastinating — they could not bear to leave that comfortable place and go out on the wind-swept floor space between the house and kitchen where the general tin basin stood, and wash.

Along outside of the front fence ran the country road, dusty in the summertime, and a good place for snakes — they liked to lie in it and sun themselves; when they were rattlesnakes or puff adders, we killed them; when they were black snakes, or racers, or belonged to the fabled "hoop" breed, we fled, without shame; when they were "house snakes," or "garters," we carried them home and put them in Aunt Patsy's work basket for a surprise; for she was prejudiced against snakes, and always when she took the basket in her lap and they began to climb out of it it disordered her mind. She never could seem to get used to them; her opportunities went for nothing. And she was always cold toward bats, too, and could not bear them; and yet I think a bat is as friendly a bird as there is. My mother was Aunt Patsy's sister and had the same wild superstitions. A bat is beautifully soft and silky; I do not know any creature that is pleasanter to the touch or is more grateful for caressings, if offered in the right spirit. I know all about these coleoptera, because our great cave, three miles below Hannibal, was multitudinously stocked with them, and often I brought them home to amuse my mother with. It was easy to manage if it was a school day, because then I had ostensibly been to school and hadn't any bats. She was not a suspicious person, but full of trust and confidence; and when I said, "There's something in my coat pocket for you," she would put her hand in. But she always took it out again, herself; I didn't have to tell her. It was remarkable, the way she couldn't learn to like private bats. The more experience she had, the more she could not change her views. . . .

Beyond the road where the snakes sunned themselves was a dense young thicket, and through it a dim-lighted path led a quarter of a mile; then out of the dimness one emerged abruptly upon a level great prairie which was covered with wild strawberry plants, vividly starred with prairie pinks, and walled in on all sides by forests. The strawberries were fragrant and fine, and in the season we were generally there in the crisp freshness of the early morning, while the dew beads still sparkled upon the grass and the woods were ringing with the first songs of the birds.

Down the forest slopes to the left were the swings. They were made of   10
bark stripped from hickory saplings. When they became dry they were dangerous. They usually broke when a child was forty feet in the air, and this was why so many bones had to be mended every year. I had no ill luck myself, but none of my cousins escaped. There were eight of them, and at one time and another they broke fourteen arms among them. But it cost next to nothing, for the doctor worked by the year — twenty-five dollars for the whole family. I remember two of the Florida doctors, Chowning and Meredith. They not only tended an entire family for twenty-five dollars a year, but furnished the medicines themselves. Good measure, too. Only the largest persons could hold a whole dose. Castor oil was the principal beverage. . . .

The country schoolhouse was three miles from my uncle's farm. It   11
stood in a clearing in the woods and would hold about twenty-five boys and girls. We attended the school with more or less regularity once or twice a week, in summer, walking to it in the cool of the morning by the forest paths, and back in the gloaming at the end of the day. All the pupils brought their dinners in baskets — corn dodger, buttermilk, and other good things — and sat in the shade of the trees at noon and ate them. It is the part of my education which I look back upon with the most satisfaction. My first visit to the school was when I was seven. A strapping girl of fifteen, in the customary sunbonnet and calico dress, asked me if I "used tobacco" — meaning did I chew it. I said no. It roused her scorn. She reported me to all the crowd, and said:

"Here is a boy seven years old who can't chew tobacco."   12

By the looks and comments which this produced I realized that I was a   13
degraded object, and was cruelly ashamed of myself. I determined to reform. But I only made myself sick; I was not able to learn to chew tobacco. I learned to smoke fairly well, but that did not conciliate anybody and I remained a poor thing, and characterless. I longed to be respected, but I never was able to rise. Children have but little charity for one another's defects.

As I have said, I spent some part of every year at the farm until I was   14
twelve or thirteen years old. The life which I led there with my cousins was full of charm, and so is the memory of it yet. I can call back the solemn twilight and mystery of the deep woods, the earthy smells, the faint odors of the wild flowers, the sheen of rain-washed foliage, the rattling clatter of

drops when the wind shook the trees, the far-off hammering of woodpeckers and the muffled drumming of wood pheasants in the remoteness of the forest, the snapshot glimpses of disturbed wild creatures scurrying through the grass — I can call it all back and make it as real as it ever was, and as blessed. I can call back the prairie, and its loneliness and peace, and a vast hawk hanging motionless in the sky, with his wings spread wide and the blue of the vault showing through the fringe of their end feathers. I can see the woods in their autumn dress, the oaks purple, the hickories washed with gold, the maples and the sumachs luminous with crimson fires, and I can hear the rustle made by the fallen leaves as we plowed through them. I can see the blue clusters of wild grapes hanging among the foliage of the sap-lings, and I remember the taste of them and the smell. I know how the wild blackberries looked, and how they tasted, and the same with the pawpaws, the hazelnuts, and the persimmons; and I can feel the thumping rain, upon my head, of hickory nuts and walnuts when we were out in the frosty dawn to scramble for them with the pigs, and the gusts of wind loosed them and sent them down. I know the stain of blackberries, and how pretty it is, and I know the stain of walnut hulls, and how little it minds soap and water, also what grudged experience it had of either of them. I know the taste of maple sap, and when to gather it, and how to arrange the troughs and the delivery tubes, and how to boil down the juice, and how to hook the sugar after it is made, also how much better hooked sugar tastes than any that is honestly come by, let bigots say what they will. I know how a prize watermelon looks when it is sunning its fat rotundity among pumpkin vines and "simblins"; I know how to tell when it is ripe without "plugging" it; I know how inviting it looks when it is cooling itself in a tub of water under the bed, waiting; I know how it looks when it lies on the table in the sheltered great floor space between house and kitchen, and the children gathered for the sacrifice and their mouths watering; I know the crackling sound it makes when the carv-ing knife enters its end, and I can see the split fly along in front of the blade as the knife cleaves its way to the other end; I can see its halves fall apart and display the rich red meat and the black seeds, and the heart standing up, a luxury fit for the elect; I know how a boy looks behind a yard-long slice of that melon, and I know how he feels; for I have been there. I know the taste of the watermelon which has been honestly come by, and I know the taste of the watermelon which has been acquired by art. Both taste good, but the ex-perienced know which tastes best. I know the look of green apples and peaches and pears on the trees, and I know how entertaining they are when they are inside of a person. I know how ripe ones look when they are piled in pyramids under the trees, and how pretty they are and how vivid their colors. I know how a frozen apple looks, in a barrel down cellar in the win-tertime, and how hard it is to bite, and how the frost makes the teeth ache, and yet how good it is, notwithstanding. I know the disposition of elderly people to select the specked apples for the children, and I once knew ways to beat the game. I know the look of an apple that is roasting and sizzling on a hearth on a winter's evening, and I know the comfort that comes of eating it hot, along with some sugar and a drench of cream. I know the delicate art and mystery of so cracking hickory nuts and walnuts on a flatiron with a hammer that the kernels will be delivered whole, and I know how the nuts, taken in conjunction with winter apples, cider, and doughnuts, make old people's old tales and old jokes sound fresh and crisp and enchanting, and juggle an evening away before you know what went with the time. I know the look of Uncle Dan'l's kitchen as it was on the privileged nights, when I was a child, and I can see the white and black children grouped on the hearth, with the firelight playing on their faces and the shadows flickering upon the walls, clear back toward the cavernous gloom of the rear, and I can hear Uncle Dan'l telling the immortal tales which Uncle Remus Harris was to gather into his book and charm the world with, by and by; and I can feel again the creepy joy which quivered through me when the time for the ghost story was reached — and the sense of regret, too, which came over me, for it was always the last story of the evening and there was nothing between it and the unwelcome bed.

I can remember the bare wooden stairway in my uncle's house, and   15
the turn to the left above the landing, and the rafters and the slanting roof over my bed, and the squares of moonlight on the floor, and the white cold world of snow outside, seen through the curtainless window. I can remember the howling of the wind and the quaking of the house on stormy nights, and how snug and cozy one felt, under the blankets, listening; and how the powdery snow used to sift in, around the sashes, and lie in little ridges on the floor and make the place look chilly in the morning and curb the wild desire to get up — in case there was any. I can remember how very dark that room was, in the dark of the moon, and how packed it was with ghostly stillness when one woke up by accident away in the night, and forgotten sins came flocking out of the secret chambers of the memory and wanted a hearing; and how ill chosen the time seemed for this kind of business; and how dismal was the hoo-hooing of the owl and the wailing of the wolf, sent mourning by on the night wind.

I remember the raging of the rain on that roof, summer nights, and   16
how pleasant it was to lie and listen to it, and enjoy the white splendor of the lightning and the majestic booming and crashing of the thunder. It was a very satisfactory room, and there was a lightning rod which was reachable from the window, an adorable and skittish thing to climb up and down, summer nights, when there were duties on hand of a sort to make privacy desirable.

I remember the 'coon and 'possum hunts, nights, with the negroes, 17
and the long marches through the black gloom of the woods, and the excitement which fired everybody when the distant bay of an experienced dog announced that the game was treed; then the wild scramblings and stumblings
through briers and bushes and over roots to get to the spot; then the lighting
of a fire and the felling of the tree, the joyful frenzy of the dogs and the
negroes, and the weird picture it all made in the red glare — I remember it
all well, and the delight that everyone got out of it, except the 'coon.

I remember the pigeon seasons, when the birds would come in mil- 18
lions and cover the trees and by their weight break down the branches. They
were clubbed to death with sticks; guns were not necessary and were not
used. I remember the squirrel hunts, and prairie-chicken hunts, and wild-
turkey hunts, and all that; and how we turned out, mornings, while it was
still dark, to go on these expeditions, and how chilly and dismal it was, and
how often I regretted that I was well enough to go. A toot on a tin horn
brought twice as many dogs as were needed, and in their happiness they
raced and scampered about, and knocked small people down, and made no
end of unnecessary noise. At the word, they vanished away toward the
woods, and we drifted silently after them in the melancholy gloom. But
presently the gray dawn stole over the world, the birds piped up, then the
sun rose and poured light and comfort all around, everything was fresh and
dewy and fragrant, and life was a boon again. After three hours of tramping
we arrived back wholesomely tired, overladen with game, very hungry, and
just in time for breakfast.

SUBJECT QUESTIONS

1. In the opening paragraph, Twain says he can better remember things
   that did not happen than those that did. Does his apology seem necessary considering what he remembers of his uncle's farm? Why
   would he include such an apology? Do you have any "memories" of
   things you know never really happened?
2. Twain is attempting to describe far more than are the other essayists
   in this section. Can you discern any principle of selection, any essence he wants to capture, or does he seem to be putting down everything he can recall?
3. List the activities Twain says he engaged in as a boy. Does his sound
   like an ideal upbringing? Does it sound like fun?
4. The only incident Twain relates from his school days was an embarrassing one. Can you tell why he views this country schooling as the
   most satisfying part of his education?
5. What kind of relationship seems to have existed between the white
   children and the slave children? (In a passage of his autobiography
   omitted here, Twain explains that relationship more explicitly.)

STRUCTURE QUESTIONS

1. Note that Twain includes descriptive details that appeal to all five senses. What are some of the more memorable nonvisual details?
2. Twain does not hesitate to use interpretive adjectives (sumptuous, divine, mournful, etc.). These, of course, do not describe. What do they do for the essay? Could Twain have achieved the same effects without them? Given so many authentic details already, can the reader accept and trust these interpretive shortcuts?
3. Examine the passage (paragraph 8) in which Twain tells about his tricks with snakes and bats. How does he manage to tell those anecdotes from a child's point of view without resorting to childish vocabulary?
4. In paragraph 14, Twain shifts to much longer paragraphs with many sentences beginning in parallel form: "I can call back," "I know," "I can remember," and "I remember." Is this use of parallel structure effective or has he overworked a rhetorical device? Given the content of those paragraphs, can you see why he has resorted to parallel construction?
5. Before he has finished, Twain has given us the events of a typical day on the farm, from getting out of bed in the morning to hearing ghost stories at night. Would there have been any advantage in organizing his material on the order of "One Day in the Life of Mark Twain"? Why do you suppose he doesn't structure it this way, considering that he does have problems with organizing a mass of recollections?

SUGGESTION FOR WRITING

Select some place having strong past associations for you — a house where you used to live, grandmother's kitchen, a favorite vacation spot — and describe it with appeals to as many of the five senses as are pertinent to the reader's experiencing vicariously your memories of it. (A beach, for instance, could hardly be described properly without appeals to sounds and smells, nor would a kitchen be devoid of smells and tastes.)

The Big Two-Hearted River
Part I

Ernest Hemingway

Ernest Hemingway (1899–1961) was an American novelist, journalist, and short story writer. His important novels include The Sun Also Rises *(1926),* A Farewell to Arms *(1929), and* For Whom the Bell Tolls *(1940). In the Nick Adams stories, Hemingway traces (though not in chronological order) the disillusionment of a young wounded veteran of World War I and his attempts after the war to come to terms with himself and his environment. In "The Big Two-Hearted River," he is trying to recapture the peace he had known in nature before the war. One senses that he is being almost too careful not to let anything upset him.*

The train went on up the track out of sight, around one of the hills of burnt timber. Nick sat down on the bundle of canvas and bedding the baggage man had pitched out of the door of the baggage car. There was no town, nothing but the rails and the burned-over country. The thirteen saloons that had lined the one street of Seney had not left a trace. The foundation of the Mansion House hotel stuck up above the ground. The stone was chipped and split by the fire. It was all that was left of the town of Seney. Even the surface had been burned off the ground.

Nick looked at the burned-over stretch of hillside, where he had expected to find the scattered houses of the town and then walked down the railroad track to the bridge over the river. The river was there. It swirled against the log spiles of the bridge. Nick looked down into the clear, brown water, colored from the pebbly bottom, and watched the trout keeping themselves steady in the current with wavering fins. As he watched them they changed their positions by quick angles, only to hold steady in the fast water again. Nick watched them a long time.

He watched them holding themselves with their noses into the current, many trout in deep, fast moving water, slightly distorted as he watched far down through the glassy convex surface of the pool, its surface pushing and swelling smooth against the resistance of the log-driven piles of the bridge. At the bottom of the pool were the big trout. Nick did not see them at first. Then he saw them at the bottom of the pool, big trout looking to hold themselves on the gravel bottom in a varying mist of gravel and sand, raised in spurts by the current.

Nick looked down into the pool from the bridge. It was a hot day. A   4
kingfisher flew up the stream. It was a long time since Nick had looked into a
stream and seen trout. They were very satisfactory. As the shadow of the
kingfisher moved up the stream, a big trout shot upstream in a long angle,
only his shadow marking the angle, then lost his shadow as he came through
the surface of the water, caught the sun, and then, as he went back into the
stream under the surface, his shadow seemed to float down the stream with
the current, unresisting, to his post under the bridge where he tightened
facing up into the current.

Nick's heart tightened as the trout moved. He felt all the old feeling.   5

He turned and looked down the stream. It stretched away, pebbly-   6
bottomed with shallows and big boulders and a deep pool as it curved away
around the foot of a bluff.

Nick walked back up the ties to where his pack lay in the cinders be-   7
side the railway track. He was happy. He adjusted the pack harness around
the bundle, pulling straps tight, slung the pack on his back, got his arms
through the shoulder straps and took some of the pull off his shoulders by
leaning his forehead against the wide band of the tumpline. Still, it was too
heavy. It was much too heavy. He had his leather rod-case in his hand and
leaning forward to keep the weight of the pack high on his shoulders he
walked along the road that paralleled the railway track, leaving the burned
town behind in the heat, and then turned off around a hill with a high, fire-
scarred hill on either side onto a road that went back into the country. He
walked along the road feeling the ache from the pull of the heavy pack. The
road climbed steadily. It was hard work walking up-hill. His muscles ached
and the day was hot, but Nick felt happy. He felt he had left everything
behind, the need for thinking, the need to write, other needs. It was all back
of him.

From the time he had gotten down off the train and the baggage man   8
had thrown his pack out of the open car door things had been different.
Seney was burned, the country was burned over and changed, but it did not
matter. It could not all be burned. He knew that. He hiked along the road,
sweating in the sun, climbing to cross the range of hills that separated the
railway from the pine plains.

The road ran on, dipping occasionally, but always climbing. Nick went   9
on up. Finally the road after going parallel to the burnt hillside reached the
top. Nick leaned back against a stump and slipped out of the pack harness.
Ahead of him, as far as he could see, was the pine plain. The burned country
stopped off at the left with the range of hills. On ahead islands of dark pine
trees rose out of the plain. Far off to the left was the line of the river. Nick
followed it with his eye and caught glints of the water in the sun.

There was nothing but the pine plain ahead of him, until the far blue   10 hills that marked the Lake Superior height of land. He could hardly see them, faint and far away in the heat-light over the plain. If he looked too steadily they were gone. But if he only half-looked they were there, the far-off hills of the height of land.

Nick sat down against the charred stump and smoked a cigarette. His pack balanced on the top of the stump, harness holding ready, a hollow molded in it from his back. Nick sat smoking, looking out over the country. He did not need to get his map out. He knew where he was from the position of the river. 11

As he smoked, his legs stretched out in front of him, he noticed a grasshopper walk along the ground and up onto his woolen sock. The grasshopper was black. As he had walked along the road, climbing, he had started many grasshoppers from the dust. They were all black. They were not the big grasshoppers with yellow and black or red and black wings whirring out from their black wing sheathing as they fly up. These were just ordinary hoppers, but all a sooty black in color. Nick had wondered about them as he walked, without really thinking about them. Now, as he watched the black hopper that was nibbling at the wool of his sock with its fourway lip, he realized that they had all turned black from living in the burned-over land. He realized that the fire must have come the year before, but the grasshoppers were all black now. He wondered how long they would stay that way. 12

Carefully he reached his hand down and took hold of the hopper by the wings. He turned him up, all his legs walking in the air, and looked at his jointed belly. Yes, it was black too, iridescent where the back and head were dusty. 13

"Go on, hopper," Nick said, speaking out loud for the first time. "Fly away somewhere." 14

He tossed the grasshopper up into the air and watched him sail away to a charcoal stump across the road. 15

Nick stood up. He leaned his back against the weight of his pack where it rested upright on the stump and got his arms through the shoulder straps. He stood with the pack on his back on the brow of the hill looking out across the country, toward the distant river and then struck down the hillside away from the road. Underfoot the ground was good walking. Two hundred yards down the hillside the fire line stopped. Then it was sweet fern, growing ankle high, to walk through, and clumps of jack pines; a long undulating country with frequent rises and descents, sandy underfoot and the country alive again. 16

Nick kept his direction by the sun. He knew where he wanted to strike the river and he kept on through the pine plain, mounting small rises to see other rises ahead of him and sometimes from the top of a rise a great solid island of pines off to his right or his left. He broke off some sprigs of the 17 heathery sweet fern, and put them under his pack straps. The chafing crushed it and he smelled it as he walked.

He was tired and very hot, walking across the uneven, shadeless pine plain. At any time he knew he could strike the river by turning off to his left. It could not be more than a mile away. But he kept on toward the north to hit the river as far upstream as he could go in one day's walking.   18

For some time as he walked Nick had been in sight of one of the big islands of pine standing out above the rolling high ground he was crossing. He dipped down and then as he came slowly up to the crest of the ridge he turned and made toward the pine trees.   19

There was no underbrush in the island of pine trees. The trunks of the trees went straight up or slanted toward each other. The trunks were straight and brown without branches. The branches were high above. Some interlocked to make a solid shadow on the brown forest floor. Around the grove of trees was a bare space. It was brown and soft underfoot as Nick walked on it. This was the over-lapping of the pine needle floor, extending out beyond the width of the high branches. The trees had grown tall and the branches moved high, leaving in the sun this bare space they had once covered with shadow. Sharp at the edge of this extension of the forest floor commenced the sweet fern.   20

Nick slipped off his pack and lay down in the shade. He lay on his back and looked up into the pine trees. His neck and back and the small of his back rested as he stretched. The earth felt good against his back. He looked up at the sky, through the branches, and then shut his eyes. He opened them and looked up again. There was a wind high up in the branches. He shut his eyes again and went to sleep.   21

Nick woke stiff and cramped. The sun was nearly down. His pack was heavy and the straps painful as he lifted it on. He leaned over with the pack on and picked up the leather rod-case and started out from the pine trees across the sweet fern swale, toward the river. He knew it could not be more than a mile.   22

He came down a hillside covered with stumps into a meadow. At the edge of the meadow flowed the river. Nick was glad to get to the river. He walked upstream through the meadow. His trousers were soaked with the dew as he walked. After the hot day, the dew had come quickly and heavily. The river made no sound. It was too fast and smooth. At the edge of the meadow, before he mounted to a piece of high ground to make camp, Nick looked down the river at the trout rising. They were rising to insects come from the swamp on the other side of the stream when the sun went down. The trout jumped out of water to take them. While Nick walked through the little stretch of meadow alongside the stream, trout had jumped high out of water. Now as he looked down the river, the insects must be settling on the surface, for the trout were feeding steadily all down the stream. As far down   23 the long stretch as he could see, the trout were rising, making circles all down the surface of the water, as though it were starting to rain.

The ground rose, wooded, and sandy, to overlook the meadow, the stretch of river and the swamp. Nick dropped his pack and rod-case and looked for a level piece of ground. He was very hungry and he wanted to make his camp before he cooked. Between two jack pines, the ground was quite level. He took the ax out of the pack and chopped out two projecting roots. That leveled a piece of ground large enough to sleep on. He smoothed out the sandy soil with his hand and pulled the sweet fern bushes by their roots. His hands smelled good from the sweet fern. He smoothed the uprooted earth. He did not want anything making lumps under the blankets. When he had the ground smooth, he spread his three blankets. One he folded double, next to the ground. The other two he spread on top.

With the ax he slit off a bright slab of pine from one of the stumps and split it into pegs for the tent. He wanted them long and solid to hold in the ground. With the tent unpacked and spread on the ground, the pack, leaning against a jack pine, looked much smaller. Nick tied the rope that served the tent for a ridge-pole to the trunk of one of the pine trees and pulled the tent up off the ground with the other end of the rope and tied it to the other pine. The tent hung on the rope like a canvas blanket on a clothesline. Nick poked a pole he had cut up under the back peak of the canvas and then made it a tent by pegging out the sides. He pegged the sides out taut and drove the pegs deep, hitting them down into the ground with the flat of the ax until the rope loops were buried and the canvas was drum tight.

Across the open mouth of the tent Nick fixed cheesecloth to keep out mosquitoes. He crawled inside under the mosquito bar with various things from the pack to put at the head of the bed under the slant of the canvas. Inside the tent the light came through the brown canvas. It smelled pleasantly of canvas. Already there was something mysterious and homelike. Nick was happy as he crawled inside the tent. He had not been unhappy all day. This was different though. Now things were done. There had been this to do. Now it was done. It had been a hard trip. He was very tired. That was done. He had made his camp. He was settled. Nothing could touch him. It was a good place to camp. He was there, in the good place. He was in his home where he had made it. Now he was hungry.

He came out, crawling under the cheesecloth. It was quite dark outside. It was lighter in the tent.

Nick went over to the pack and found, with his fingers, a long nail in a paper sack of nails, in the bottom of the pack. He drove it into the pine tree, holding it close and hitting it gently with the flat of the ax. He hung the pack up on the nail. All his supplies were in the pack. They were off the ground and sheltered now.

Nick was hungry. He did not believe he had ever been hungrier. He opened and emptied a can of pork and beans and a can of spaghetti into the frying pan.

"I've got a right to eat this kind of stuff, if I'm willing to carry it," Nick   30
said. His voice sounded strange in the darkening woods. He did not speak again.

He started a fire with some chunks of pine he got with the ax from a   31
stump. Over the fire he stuck a wire grill, pushing the four legs down into the ground with his boot. Nick put the frying pan on the grill over the flames. He was hungrier. The beans and spaghetti warmed. Nick stirred them and mixed them together. They began to bubble, making little bubbles that rose with difficulty to the surface. There was a good smell. Nick got out a bottle of tomato catchup and cut four slices of bread. The little bubbles were coming faster now. Nick sat down beside the fire and lifted the frying pan off. He poured about half the contents out into the tin plate. It spread slowly on the plate. Nick knew it was too hot. He poured on some tomato catchup. He knew the beans and spaghetti were still too hot. He looked at the fire, then at the tent, he was not going to spoil it all by burning his tongue. For years he had never enjoyed fried bananas because he had never been able to wait for them to cool. His tongue was very sensitive. He was very hungry. Across the river in the swamp, in the almost dark, he saw a mist rising. He looked at the tent once more. All right. He took a full spoonful from the plate.

"Chrise," Nick said. "Geezus Chrise," he said happily.   32

He ate the whole plateful before he remembered the bread. Nick fin-   33
ished the second plateful with the bread, mopping the plate shiny. He had not eaten since a cup of coffee and a ham sandwich in the station restaurant at St. Ignace. It had been a very fine experience. He had been that hungry before, but had not been able to satisfy it. He could have made camp hours before if he had wanted to. There were plenty of good places to camp on the river. But this was good.

Nick tucked two big chips of pine under the grill. The fire flared up.   34
He had forgotten to get water for the coffee. Out of the pack he got a folding canvas bucket and walked down the hill, across the edge of the meadow, to the stream. The other bank was in the white mist. The grass was wet and cold as he knelt on the bank and dipped the canvas bucket into the stream. It bellied and pulled hard in the current. The water was ice cold. Nick rinsed the bucket and carried it full up to the camp. Up away from the stream it was not so cold.

Nick drove another big nail and hung up the bucket full of water. He   35
dipped the coffee pot half full, put some more chips under the grill onto the fire and put the pot on. He could not remember which way he made coffee. He could remember an argument about it with Hopkins, but not which side he had taken. He decided to bring it to a boil. He remembered now that was Hopkins's way. He had once argued about everything with Hopkins. While

he waited for the coffee to boil, he opened a small can of apricots. He liked to open cans. He emptied the can of apricots out into a tin cup. While he watched the coffee on the fire, he drank the juice syrup of the apricots, carefully at first to keep from spilling, then meditatively sucking the apricots down. They were better than fresh apricots.

The coffee boiled as he watched. The lid came up and coffee and grounds ran down the side of the pot. Nick took it off the grill. It was a triumph for Hopkins. He put sugar in the empty apricot cup and poured some of the coffee out to cool. It was too hot to pour and he used his hat to hold the handle of the coffee pot. He would not let it steep in the pot at all. Not the first cup. It should be straight Hopkins all the way. Hop deserved that. He was a very serious coffee drinker. He was the most serious man Nick had ever known. Not heavy, serious. That was a long time ago. Hopkins spoke without moving his lips. He had played polo. He made millions of dollars in Texas. He had borrowed carfare to go to Chicago, when the wire came that his first big well had come in. He could have wired for money. That would have been too slow. They called Hop's girl the Blonde Venus. Hop did not mind because she was not his real girl. Hopkins said very confidently that none of them would make fun of his real girl. He was right. Hopkins went away when the telegram came. That was on the Black River. It took eight days for the telegram to reach him. Hopkins gave away his .22 caliber Colt automatic pistol to Nick. He gave his camera to Bill. It was to remember him always by. They were all going fishing again next summer. The Hop Head was rich. He would get a yacht and they would all cruise along the north shore of Lake Superior. He was excited but serious. They said good-bye and all felt bad. It broke up the trip. They never saw Hopkins again. That was a long time ago on the Black River.

Nick drank the coffee, the coffee according to Hopkins. The coffee was bitter. Nick laughed. It made a good ending to the story. His mind was starting to work. He knew he could choke it because he was tired enough. He spilled the coffee out of the pot and shook the grounds loose into the fire. He lit a cigarette and went inside the tent. He took off his shoes and trousers, sitting on the blankets, rolled the shoes up inside the trousers for a pillow and got in between the blankets.

Out through the front of the tent he watched the glow of the fire, when the night wind blew on it. It was a quiet night. The swamp was perfectly quiet. Nick stretched under the blanket comfortably. A mosquito hummed close to his ear. Nick sat up and lit a match. The mosquito was on the canvas, over his head. Nick moved the match quickly up to it. The mosquito made a satisfactory hiss in the flame. The match went out. Nick lay down again under the blanket. He turned on his side and shut his eyes. He was sleepy. He felt sleep coming. He curled up under the blanket and went to sleep.

SUBJECT QUESTIONS

1. Can you form a visual "map" of Nick's route from the burned town to his campsite? Is it important that we have such a map? Why do you think Hemingway bothers telling us, for instance, that as Nick hiked north the river was to his left?
2. What does the sentence "He could not remember which way he made coffee" tell you about Nick Adams (he clearly is not an amateur at camping)?
3. Do you see any reason for including at the end the reminiscence about Hopkins?
4. Most modern short stories examine a change in mental attitude as a result of a traumatic experience. Clearly there is no such experience in this story. What is Nick Adams's mental attitude? What clues do you have that he is trying not to think too much?
5. Most of the descriptive passages occur when Nick stops to rest and looks around. Do these passages produce clear pictures for the reader?

STRUCTURE QUESTIONS

1. Discuss some of the devices by which Hemingway gives a sense of authenticity to his fictional account. Does the reader feel that Hemingway himself must have visited the area described?
2. Clearly, Hemingway is capable of writing properly subordinated, complex sentences; yet characteristic of his style is heavy use of simple sentences, bordering sometimes on primer prose. Do you think that style serves any particular purpose in this story? Is it distracting? Perhaps the most noteworthy series of simple sentences occurs in paragraph 26. Is there any relationship between the subject and the style in that paragraph?
3. Taste and smell are the senses most frequently neglected by writers of description. Point out some of Hemingway's more effective appeals to these senses.
4. Point out several places where Hemingway changes his "camera focus" from panoramic to extreme close-up. These wide variations might reflect Hemingway's interest in nature or his desire for authenticity; or perhaps he wants to tell us something about Nick Adams. Nick's watching the trout might reflect the interest of any fisherman, but what might his examining the grasshopper in paragraphs 12 and 13 indicate?

SUGGESTIONS FOR WRITING

1. Describe a common creature through close observation — a housefly on your table, a cat trying to creep up on a bird, or the bird itself, for example. Birds are particularly interesting because of their high body temperature, which keeps them in a state approaching delirium; they make unexpected, quick movements, and have sudden changes in mood and attention.

2. Describe an event that occurs daily but which goes almost unobserved — your roommate getting dressed or eating breakfast, for instance. Or simply watch someone "studying" for half an hour. You may find that he smokes two cigarettes, gets up for a drink, stares out the window, puts a different cassette into the player, perhaps even reads a page or two of his psychology text.

Traveling Through the Dark

William Stafford

William E. Stafford (b. 1914) graduated from the University of Kansas and received his Ph.D. from the State University of Iowa. Most of his teaching career has been spent at Lewis and Clark College in Oregon. Stafford has published many volumes of poetry and won numerous awards, including the National Book Award for Poetry in 1962, for the volume from which the poem below is taken, Traveling Through the Dark. *In addition to his professional interests as poet and teacher, he has devoted much of his time to peace churches and other pacifist organizations, and he has worked in soil conservation with the U.S. Forest Service. His first book,* Down in My Heart *(1947), was not poetry but a book concerning his experiences as a conscientious objector during World War II. Stafford is best appreciated by critics for his descriptive poetry, an example of which follows.*

Traveling through the dark I found a deer
dead on the edge of the Wilson River road.
It is usually best to roll them into the canyon:
that road is narrow; to swerve might make more dead.

By glow of the tail-light I stumbled back of the car   5
and stood by the heap, a doe, a recent killing;
she had stiffened already, almost cold.
I dragged her off; she was large in the belly.

My fingers touching her side brought me the reason —
her side was warm; her fawn lay there waiting,   10
alive, still, never to be born.
Beside that mountain road I hesitated.

The car aimed ahead its lowered parking lights;
under the hood purred the steady engine.
I stood in the glare of the warm exhaust turning red;   15
around our group I could hear the wilderness listen.

I thought hard for us all — my only swerving —
then pushed her over the edge into the river.

SUBJECT QUESTIONS

1. The title seems to refer to a particular action at a particular time; given what happens in the poem, might the title have more general implications?
2. What clues do you have that this is not the driver's first experience with a slain deer?
3. There are unidentified passengers in the car; what is the effect of calling them "our group" instead of "my friends" or "my wife and children"?
4. To whom is the driver referring in the clause "I thought hard for us all"? Can you tell what he thought?
5. The driver could not literally "hear the wilderness listen." Should Stafford have used a different verb — "imagined," or "sensed," perhaps? Is anything implied about the relation between human beings and wilderness? Does the preceding description of the car in stanza 4 point to an alienation of people from nature?

STRUCTURE QUESTIONS

1. Although Stafford does divide this poem into stanzas, he uses neither rhyme nor a regular metrical "beat." Do you see a relationship between the structure and the subject of this poem? Does Stafford use any "poetic devices" — assonance, alliteration, and so on?
2. We do not know where or when this incident takes place; what is the point (or effect) of identifying the location as "the Wilson River road"?
3. How much of the setting is described in the poem? Does the reader get a clear picture? What is the basis for selection of details? Should Stafford have given some description of the surrounding wilderness?
4. Identify descriptive details which appeal to senses other than sight.
5. Stafford would not have bothered to write this poem if he did not have strong feelings about the subject. Why does he not express those feelings in the poem? Can you draw any conclusions about the relative effects of presenting facts vividly and of telling the reader how you felt about them ("I felt just dreadful about that poor little fawn, so utterly helpless and sad")?

SUGGESTIONS FOR WRITING

1. Most of us have thoughtlessly or carelessly destroyed life, and afterwards wondered why we had done so — purposely stepped on a

beetle on the sidewalk, picked wildflowers only to let them wither on the dashboard, perhaps even shot a sparrow with a BB gun. Recount such as experience, concentrating on the description rather than on how you felt.

2. Describe an emotional experience without telling the reader how you felt. Select descriptive details which will cause the reader to have the same emotional response you had. (This need not be an earth-shaking experience — your first attempt to put a worm on a hook will do.)

3

PLAYSCHOOLS AND COLLEGES

Comparison and Contrast

Comparison and contrast are perhaps the most natural of all methods of establishing or clarifying an attitude. They are the product of the important human ability to see relationships and differences where none would be apparent to other animals. All of us utilize this ability daily, sometimes in making important decisions, sometimes in situations so insignificant that we are not even aware of employing comparison and contrast. We use it in deciding whether to sleep late or get up in time for breakfast, whether to sign up for biology or chemistry. But this ability to see likenesses and differences is the basis of what may be our most significant capacity, evaluation. Before one can say, "Professor X is a better teacher than Professor Z," one must, of course, recognize that important differences exist between the two professors or between their methods of presenting material.

Frequently in writing expository prose, students find it necessary to employ the methods of comparison and contrast in order to clarify either their subjects or their attitudes toward them. If they were writing papers on socialism, for instance, they would almost surely want to point out the similarities and differences between socialism and communism. They would probably also want to compare and contrast two or more existing types of socialism — English, French, and Mexican, perhaps. Although writing comparison and contrast is not as difficult as some other writing assignments, it does require meticulous care, and the student should remember a few basic rules.

In the first place, writers must *establish clear bases for comparison*. Particularly in dealing with broad concepts or with groups of people, they may have to choose from a number of possible bases for comparison, and it would not do for them to confuse those bases or switch from one to another without warning. Suppose a writer wishes to compare socialism and communism; to consider and cover all possible bases for comparison would require a large volume. If the paper is to be a short one, the writer will probably have to limit the investigation to only one area — the extent of arbitrary political control by the government in power, perhaps, or the similarities and differences in economic theory and practice, the use of secret police and other methods of coercion to prevent internal resistance, or the degree of control over communications media. Once the basis of comparison is selected, the writer should stick with it, developing it fully and clearly through both sides of the comparison. It would hardly be cricket, for instance, to discuss communism's totalitarian political system and then switch to socialism's economic system.

If the topic on which the student is writing is sufficiently limited, there is, of course, no reason that the student can't utilize several bases of comparison in the same essay — being sure to treat each one separately and fully before going on to the next. In a paper on the adequacy of preparation for the academic work of college given by public high schools and private preparatory schools, the writer would probably consider outside reading assignments, research paper writing, and intellectual stimulation from fellow students as well as actual classroom preparation. But there would be no point in dragging in other comparisons which might occur to the writer — social life, or athletic programs, for instance.

A second rule is that writers must *observe accurately*. Quite often minute details will be the most important, particularly since they are the ones an average observer is likely to miss. Good writers will never dismiss distinctions without examining them or be so careless as to claim, for instance, that "communism and fascism are really just two names for the same thing." Both terms may imply totalitarian governments and police states, but there must be some reason for the mutual hatred between fascist and communist. A closer examination would reveal such vital differences as the attitudes toward class structure and toward racial integration.

Obviously, then, writers must also have an *adequate knowledge* of their subject. A passing acquaintance, half-hearted guesswork, or simply a vivid imagination will not do: the really important similarities and differences between two types of skin rash will be apparent only to a person trained in dermatology. Students who try to write comparison and contrast without familiarizing themselves with their subject are merely wasting their readers' time as well as their own. A student who has an interest in the subject but not full knowledge of it can make good use of the college library.

The preceding three rules, though applicable to all comparison, are virtually useless without a fourth. Far more frequently than chance would justify, composition teachers are disappointed by students who hand in "comparison" papers somewhat like the one on which the following summary is based:

> As I look out my window I cannot help noticing the staunch old oak tree which stands so majestically beside the dormitory. . . . In many ways, it seems to me that this oak tree is very like my religion. . . .
>
> In the first place, the oak has its roots deep in a firm foundation, from which it receives material sustenance. The roots of my religion, too, are deep. . . .
>
> Secondly, the oak has a mighty trunk which is not shaken by the winds of chance. In the same way, my faith is unshakable. . . .
>
> And finally, the branches of the tree reach up to heaven, whence comes eternal light. The aim of my religion, similarly, is to reach up to heaven. . . .

Such a "comparison" may give a connotative indication of the firmness of the writer's faith and perhaps an appreciation of the ingenuity. But it does not give the reader any specific information about trees, about the exact nature of the writer's religious beliefs, or about any real relationship between the two. It is, in short, not true comparison at all, but analogy.

Comparison shows likeness between things in the same class, where analogy points out a similarity between things in different classes. "The cloud from an atomic blast is shaped like a mushroom" is an analogy, because atomic clouds and mushrooms have little in common except shape. Analogy usually compares the unfamiliar with the familiar, not to establish relationships but to clarify the less familiar. Comparison, on the other hand, seeks both to clarify and to demonstrate relations. In other words, something is said about both objects or ideas being compared, and the points of comparison, though generally more subtle than those in analogy, are at the same time more significant. "Jeffersonian democracy was similar to modern liberal Republicanism" is the beginning of a comparison, for the two concepts are in the same general class. Clearly such a comparison, to be worthwhile, must be developed much more carefully than a simple analogy. And something must be said about both Jeffersonian Democrats and liberal Republicans if the comparison is to be meaningful. Would they have the same views on states' rights, or on civil liberties, for instance? It is not enough to say merely that both are "mildly conservative" by modern standards.

In comparing two concepts writers should remember to look for significant points of comparison that are not commonly recognized. To dwell on the obvious would be a waste of time for reader and writer alike. On the other hand, writers should not strain for comparison where there is only a remote and unimportant similarity, if any. Comparison should never be merely an exercise in ingenuity.

Most of the rules for comparison also apply to its opposite, contrast: the things or ideas must be in the same class, the differences developed at length should be significant but not boringly obvious, and the writer should never search for differences for their own sake, regardless of whether or not they are worth mentioning. It is possible, however, to develop fully only one side of a contrast if the writer can assume that the reader is already familiar with the other side.

Because contrast is useful only if the concepts being contrasted have many aspects in common or are frequently confused, comparison and contrast are usually employed in the same essay. A student who was to write a paper on "My High School and College Math Classes" would want to point out both similarities and differences. The student would not dwell on such obvious distinctions as "College courses are harder than the ones I had in high school," but would concentrate on similarities in methods of explaining abstract laws, perhaps, or differences in methods of integrating algebra and trigonometry.

Combining comparison and contrast is likely to be a matter of intellectual honesty. A writer who devotes a paper to proving that "Democracy and communism are in *all* respects unalterably opposed" or that "Democrats and Republicans really have identical beliefs" is either misguided or dishonest. Democracy and communism are not "unalterably opposed" on such issues as the liberation of African colonies from European domination or foreign aid for underdeveloped countries; and Democrats and Republicans hardly agree *en masse* on excess profits taxes or federal power projects.

Students who intend to write a comparison and contrast paper must first limit their subject to something they can treat in depth and with some insight. The title "High School and College Compared" would probably be much too broad for a short paper: the writer would be tempted to dwell on obvious differences — "College is harder than high school," "Students at college are more serious," "Most college students live away from home for the first time." A more useful subject might be "Using the Library: High School and College" or "Classroom Discussion in High School and College."

Remember that writing should never be a mere exercise: writers should learn something, at least by clarifying their views, and readers should gain insight into both the subject and the ways in which different people view the same subject.

Comparison and contrast may be employed both as the chief method of development and as the primary aim of an essay, or they may be used to furnish background information necessary for some further purpose. But in either case, certain basic principles are observed: the basis of the comparison is made clear, and distinctions and similarities pointed out are real and significant, neither blatantly obvious nor merely clever.

Writers will encounter some problems in organizing comparison and contrast papers, for they must organize their materials in two ways at once — by the divisions of the subject matter and by the two concepts being compared. Depending on the length of the paper and the complexity of the subject, writers can select from three possible methods of organization: (1) present all the points about one side of the comparison, and then in the same order all the points about the other side; (2) alternate paragraphs about side A and side B according to subject divisions; or (3) alternate sentences about side A and side B within a paragraph. Suppose a writer were comparing and contrasting public high schools with private preparatory schools. If the paper were fairly short, so that the reader could keep the first half in mind while reading the second half, the outline might look something like this:

I. High Schools
   A. Classroom preparation
   B. Library assignments
   C. Research paper writing
   D. Intellectual environment
II. Private Schools
   A. Classroom preparation
   B. Library assignments
   C. Research paper writing
   D. Intellectual environment

If, on the other hand, the paper were to be rather long and the writer had a number of facts on each basis for comparison, alternating paragraphs probably would be the best approach. The outline would then look like this:

I. Classroom Preparation
   A. High schools
   B. Private schools

II. Library Assignments
   A. High schools
   B. Private schools
III. Research Paper Writing
   A. High schools
   B. Private schools
IV. Intellectual Environment
   A. High schools
   B. Private schools

The third possibility, alternating sentences about high school and preparatory school within a paragraph on classroom preparation, and so on, though sometimes employed, is generally satisfactory only for very brief and relatively simple papers or when time is a factor — as in essay examinations or in-class themes. But regardless of which method is chosen, the writer should employ it consistently throughout the paper. Careful planning always pays in better grades and time saved; the writer who "waits for an inspiration" will waste hours and perhaps never get that inspiration.

Education

E. B. White

E. B. White (b. 1899) is an essayist and fiction writer. He began as a reporter, and was later an editor at The New Yorker *and a regular contributor to* Harper's. *This extract is from* One Man's Meat *(1944), an account of White's move away from crowded city life.*

I have an increasing admiration for the teacher in the country school where we have a third-grade scholar in attendance. She not only undertakes to instruct her charges in all the subjects of the first three grades, but she manages to function quietly and effectively as a guardian of their health, their clothes, their habits, their mothers, and their snowball engagements. She has been doing this sort of Augean task for twenty years, and is both kind and wise. She cooks for the children on the stove that heats the room, and she can cool their passions or warm their soup with equal competence. She conceives their costumes, cleans up their messes, and shares their confidences. My boy already regards his teacher as his great friend, and I think tells her a great deal more than he tells us.

The shift from city school to country school was something we worried about quietly all last summer. I have always rather favored public school over private school, if only because in public school you meet a greater variety of children. This bias of mine, I suspect, is partly an attempt to justify my own past (I never knew anything but public schools) and partly an involuntary defense against getting kicked in the shins by a young ceramist on his way to the kiln. My wife was unacquainted with public schools, never having been exposed (in her early life) to anything more public than the washroom of Miss Winsor's. Regardless of our backgrounds, we both knew that the change in schools was something that concerned not us but the scholar himself. We hoped it would work out all right. In New York our son went to a medium-priced private institution with semi-progressive ideas of education, and modern plumbing. He learned fast, kept well, and we were satisfied. It was an electric, colorful, regimented existence with moments of pleasurable pause and giddy incident. The day the Christmas angel fainted and had to be carried out by one of the Wise Men was educational in the highest sense of the term. Our scholar gave imitations of it around the house for weeks afterward, and I doubt if it ever goes completely out of his mind.

His days were rich in formal experience. Wearing overalls and an old   3
sweater (the accepted uniform of the private seminary), he sallied forth at morn accompanied by a nurse or a parent and walked (or was pulled) two blocks to a corner where the school bus made a flag stop. This flashy vehicle was as punctual as death: seeing us waiting at the cold curb, it would sweep to a halt, open its mouth, suck the boy in, and spring away with an angry growl. It was a good deal like a train picking up a bag of mail. At school the scholar was worked on for six or seven hours by half a dozen teachers and a nurse, and was revived on orange juice in mid-morning. In a cinder court he played games supervised by an athletic instructor, and in a cafeteria he ate lunch worked out by a dietitian. He soon learned to read with gratifying facility and discernment and to make Indian weapons of a semi-deadly nature. Whenever one of his classmates fell low of a fever the news was put on the wires and there were breathless phone calls to physicians, discussing periods of incubation and allied magic.

In the country all one can say is that the situation is different, and   4
somehow more casual. Dressed in corduroys, sweatshirt, and short rubber boots, and carrying a tin dinner-pail, our scholar departs at crack of dawn for the village school, two and a half miles down the road, next to the cemetery. When the road is open and the car will start, he makes the journey by motor, courtesy of his old man. When the snow is deep or the motor is dead or both, he makes it on the hoof. In the afternoons he walks or hitches all or part of the way home in fair weather, gets transported in foul. The schoolhouse is a two-room frame building, bungalow type, shingles stained a burnt brown with weather-resistant stain. It has a chemical toilet in the basement and two teachers above stairs. One takes the first three grades, the other the fourth, fifth, and sixth. They have little or no time for individual instruction, and no time at all for the esoteric. They teach what they know themselves, just as fast and as hard as they can manage. The pupils sit still at their desks in class, and do their milling around outdoors during recess.

There is no supervised play. They play cops and robbers (only they call   5
it "Jail") and throw things at one another — snowballs in winter, rose hips in fall. It seems to satisfy them. They also construct darts, pinwheels, and "pick-up sticks" (jackstraws), and the school itself does a brisk trade in penny candy, which is for sale right in the classroom and which contains "surprises." The most highly prized surprise is a fake cigarette, made of cardboard, fiendishly lifelike.

The memory of how apprehensive we were at the beginning is still   6
strong. The boy was nervous about the change too. The tension, on that first fair morning in September when we drove him to school, almost blew the windows out of the sedan. And when later we picked him up on the road,

wandering along with his little blue lunch-pail, and got his laconic report "All right" in answer to our inquiry about how the day had gone, our relief was vast. Now, after almost a year of it, the only difference we can discover in the two school experiences is that in the country he sleeps better at night — and *that* probably is more the air than the education. When grilled on the subject of school-in-country *vs.* school-in-city, he replied that the chief difference is that the day seems to go so much quicker in the country. "Just like lightning," he reported.

SUBJECT QUESTIONS

1. Which of the two schools does White seem to prefer? Which does the boy prefer? Do the conclusions given in the last paragraph support, or alter, your impressions before that point? Might White want the reader to draw stronger conclusions of his own?
2. White says that the boy's sleeping better is probably due to the air rather than the education. Does the very inclusion of the statement imply any connection between sleeping and education?
3. How much significance is there in the apparently simple difference that the boy himself finds? (See the last two sentences.)
4. The differences in the clothing worn at the private school, overalls and old sweater, and at the country school, corduroys and sweatshirt, is not very great. Why does White bother to mention it at all? Examine the two sentences in which we are given this information.
5. White says very little about the actual course work at the two schools. Does he seem to consider this unimportant? Can the reader guess from the information given what the probable differences in schoolwork are?

STRUCTURE QUESTIONS

1. List the different bases of comparison and contrast which White employs. Are these adequate to characterize the two schools? Could White profitably have omitted any of these — or included others?
2. Which of the three general methods of organization discussed in the introduction to this section does White employ? How rigidly does he follow this organization?
3. White points out differences between the two schools not only by the facts he gives, but by the very language he uses to relate these facts. Contrast, for example, the highly metaphoric description of the boy's transportation to the private school with the more casual account of transportation in the country. How does the language affect the reader's attitude toward the two schools?
4. E. B. White's essays are models of prose style which is informal and honest, never stiff or pretentious. The reader is encouraged to study

the organization, word choice, and sentence construction of this brief essay to discover how White achieves a style which is clear and interesting — and which establishes a bond of trust between reader and writer.

SUGGESTIONS FOR WRITING

1. Write a paper comparing and contrasting two schools which you attended as a result of a move or transfer, or when you progressed from junior high to high school. Before you write, select a consistent method of organizing your material and decide on the most significant bases of comparison and contrast.
2. Contrast one of the courses you are taking in college with one on the same subject which you had in high school.
3. Probably one difference you have found between high school and college is that in college there is more control *in* class and less regimentation *outside* class. Contrast the two educational experiences from this point of view.

Pedestrian Students and High-Flying Squirrels

Liane Ellison Norman

Liane Ellison Norman teaches journalism and literature at the University of Pittsburgh. After the radical movements and student riots of the 1960s, the late 1970s saw a swing to a much more cautious generation of students. While the serious recognition on the part of these more careful students that after college lies the shadow of an uncertain job market may be a commendable change from the antiestablishment attitudes of earlier students, the author here finds some disturbing disadvantages to their "pedestrian" views. The essay first appeared in 1978.

The squirrel is curious. He darts and edges, profile first, one bright black eye on me, the other alert for enemies on the other side. Like a fencer, he faces both ways, for every impulse toward me, an impulse away. His tail is airy. He flicks and flourishes it, taking readings of some subtle kind. 1

I am enjoying a reprieve of warm sun in a season of rain and impending frost. Around me today is the wine of the garden's final ripening. On the zucchini, planted late, the flagrant blossoms flare and decline in a day's time. 2

I am sitting on the front porch thinking about my students. Many of them earnestly and ardently want me to teach them to be hacks. Give us ten tricks, they plead, ten nifty fail-safe ways to write a news story. Don't make us think our way through these problems, they storm (and when I am insistent that thinking *is* the trick, "You never listen to us," they complain). Who cares about the First Amendment? they sneer. What are John Peter Zenger and Hugo Black to us? Teach us how to earn a living. They will be content, they explain, with know-how and jobs, satisfied to do no more than cover the tedium of school board and weather. 3

Under the rebellion, there is a plaintive panic. What if, on the job — assuming there is a job to be on — they fearlessly defend the free press against government, grand jury, and media monopoly, but don't know how to write an obituary. Shouldn't obituaries come first? 4

I hope not, but even obituaries need good information and firm prose, and both, I say, require clear thought. 5

The squirrel does not share my meditation. He grows tired of inquiring into me. His dismissive tail floats out behind as he takes a running leap 6

First published in *The Center Magazine*. Reprinted by permission from the author.

into the tree. Up the bark he goes and onto a branch, where he crashes
through the leaves. He soars from slender perch to slender perch, shaking
up the tree as if he were the west wind. What a madcap he is, to go racing
from one twig that dips under him to another at those heights!

His acrobatic clamor loosens buckeyes in their prickly armor. They 7
drop, break open, and he is down the tree in a twinkling, picking, choosing. He finds what he wants and carries it, an outsize nut which is bur-
nished like a fine cello, across the lawn, up a pole, and across the tightrope
telephone line to the other side, where he disappears in maple foliage.

Some inner clock or calendar tells him to stock his larder against the 8
deep snows and hard times that are coming. I have heard that squirrels are
fuzzy-minded, that they collect their winter groceries and store them, and
then forget where they are cached. But this squirrel is purposeful; he appears to know he'd better look ahead. Faced with necessity, he is prudent,
but not fearful. He prances and flies as he goes about his task of preparation, and he never fails to look into whatever startles his attention.

Though he is not an ordinary pedestrian, crossing the street far 9
above, I sometimes see the mangled fur of a squirrel on the street, with no
flirtation left. Even a high-flying squirrel may zap himself on an aerial live
wire. His days are dangerous and his winters are lean, but still he lays in
provisions the way a trapeze artist goes about his work, with daring and
dash.

For the squirrel, there is no work but living. He gathers food, repro- 10
duces, tends the children for a while, and stays out of danger. Doing these
things with style is what distinguishes him. But for my students, unemployment looms as large as the horizon itself. Their anxiety has cause. And
yet, what good is it? Ten tricks or no ten tricks, there are not enough jobs.
The well-trained, well-educated stand in line for unemployment checks
with the unfortunates and the drifters. Neither skill nor virtue holds certain
promise. This being so, I wonder, why should these students not demand,
for the well-being of their souls, the liberation of their minds?

It grieves me that they want to be pedestrians, earthbound and al- 11
ways careful. You ask too much, they say. What you want is painful and
unfair. There are a multitude of pressures that instruct them to train, not
free, themselves.

Many of them are the first generation to go to college; family aspira- 12
tions are in their trust. Advisers and models tell them to be doctors,
lawyers, engineers, cops, and public-relations people; no one ever tells
them they can be poets, philosophers, farmers, inventors, or wizards.
Their elders are anxious too; they reject the eccentric and the novel. And,
realism notwithstanding, they cling to talismanic determination; play it safe
and do things right and I, each one thinks, will get a job even though
others won't.

I tell them fondly of my college days, which were a dizzy time (as I 13 think the squirrel's time must be), as I let loose and pitched from fairly firm stands into the space of intellect and imagination, never quite sure what solid branch I would light on. That was the most useful thing I learned, the practical advantage (not to mention the exhilaration) of launching out to find where my propellant mind could take me.

A luxury? one student ponders, a little wistfully. 14

Yes, luxury, and yet necessity, and it aroused that flight, a fierce 15 unappeasable appetite to know and to essay. The luxury I speak of is not like other privileges of wealth and power that must be hoarded to be had. If jobs are scarce, the heady regions of treetop adventure are not. Flight and gaiety cost nothing, though of course they may cost everything.

The squirrel, my frisky analogue, is not perfectly free. He must go on 16 all fours, however nimbly he does it. Dogs are always after him, and when he barely escapes, they rant up the tree as he dodges among the branches that give under his small weight. He feeds on summer's plenty and pays the price of strontium in his bones. He is no freer of industrial ordure than I am. He lives, mates, and dies (no obituary, first or last, for him), but still he plunges and balances, risking his neck because it is his nature.

I like the little squirrel for his simplicity and bravery. He will never 17 get ahead in life, never find a good job, never settle down, never be safe. There are no sure-fire tricks to make it as a squirrel.

SUBJECT QUESTIONS

1. What do the author's students want from their journalism class? What does the author want them to learn?
2. When jobs are scarce, does it seems safer to be a pedestrian student than a high-flying squirrel? Does Norman suggest any practical advantages to the latter course?
3. The author seems to imply in paragraph 3 that "high flying " is the way to become good journalists, but in paragraph 10 that if students can't be sure of getting a job, they might as well "liberate their minds" in college. Is there a contradiction in her argument?
4. Why does the author include the sober reminder in paragraph 16 that squirrels, like pedestrians, have a hard life? Does admitting this weaken her position?
5. Given the pressures of family and job future, what inducements are there to forsake the safe, pedestrian path? Can a pedestrian become a "high-flying squirrel" simply by deciding to be one? What changes are necessary?

STRUCTURE QUESTIONS

1. This essay develops both an analogy between students and squirrels and a contrast between two kinds of students. Is the issue clarified or confused by this dual focus?
2. What are the points of similarity between squirrels and "high-flying" students? Keeping in mind that analogy only points out similarity between two classes of things for purposes of clarification, does this analogy achieve its desired effect?
3. The opening two paragraphs first describe the squirrel and then the autumn setting. Is this beginning defensible, or should the author have gone directly to the crucial issue of paragraph 3? Consider carefully what those first two paragraphs accomplish.
4. Considerably more space is devoted to description of the squirrel (about half the essay) than is necessary to establish the analogy with students. Do you see any way in which this description illustrates the point the author is trying to make about journalism students? How does the description differ from "pedestrian" journalism?
5. What useful purpose is served by the introduction of the personal example at paragraph 13? Is it strategically placed in the essay? (Consider the effect if it followed paragraph 3, which it could do logically.)

SUGGESTIONS FOR WRITING

1. Develop a comparison and contrast paper between a "pedestrian" and a "high-flying" student in a course you are currently taking. This exercise will be more profitable if you can find actual rather than hypothetical students to compare.
2. Write a comparison and contrast between "pedestrian" and "high-flying" essay writing; make your descriptions illustrative of each type of writing. (The simplest method of organization would be to develop one side of the contrast completely before going on to the next, but if you can keep the two writing styles distinct, you might work out an ingenious alternating method of organization.)

Summerhill Education vs. Standard Education

A. S. Neill

Alexander S. Neill (1883–1973) was born in Scotland and educated in Edinburgh. A prolific writer, educator, and child psychologist, Neill founded, in Suffolk, England, the famous Summerhill School, an experimental school aimed at freeing the child's creative imagination from the restrictions of conventional education. Besides Summerhill, *from which the following extract comes, Neill's books on unregimented education are* The Problem Child, The Problem Parent, The Problem Teacher, *and* The Problem Family.

I hold that the aim of life is to find happiness, which means to find interest. Education should be a preparation for life. Our culture has not been very successful. Our education, politics, and economics lead to war. Our medicines have not done away with disease. Our religion has not abolished usury and robbery. Our boasted humanitarianism still allows public opinion to approve of the barbaric sport of hunting. The advances of the age are advances in mechanism — in radio and television, in electronics, in jet planes. New world wars threaten, for the world's social conscience is still primitive. 1

If we feel like questioning today, we can pose a few awkward questions. Why does man seem to have many more diseases than animals have? Why does man hate and kill in war when animals do not? Why does cancer increase? Why are there so many suicides? So many insane sex crimes? Why the hate that is anti-Semitism? Why Negro hating and lynching? Why backbiting and spite? Why is sex obscene and a leering joke? Why is being a bastard a social disgrace? Why the continuance of religions that have long ago lost their love and hope and charity? Why, a thousand whys about our vaunted state of civilized eminence! 2

I ask these questions because I am by profession a teacher, one who deals with the young. I ask these questions because those so often asked by teachers are the unimportant ones, the ones about school subjects. I ask what earthly good can come out of discussions about French or ancient history or what not when these subjects don't matter a jot compared to the larger question of life's natural fulfillment — of man's inner happiness. 3

How much of our education is real doing, real self-expression? Handi- 4 work is too often the making of a pin tray under the eye of an expert. Even the Montessori system, well-known as a system of directed play, is an artificial way of making the child learn by doing. It has nothing creative about it.

In the home, the child is always being taught. In almost every home, there is always at least one ungrown-up grownup who rushes to show Tommy how his new engine works. There is always someone to lift the baby up on a chair when baby wants to examine something on the wall. Every time we show Tommy how his engine works we are stealing from that child the joy of life — the joy of discovery — the joy of overcoming an obstacle. Worse! We make that child come to believe that he is inferior, and must depend on help.

Parents are slow in realizing how unimportant the learning side of school is. Children, like adults, learn what they want to learn. All prize-giving and marks and exams sidetrack proper personality development. Only pedants claim that learning from books is education.

Books are the least important apparatus in a school. All that any child needs is the three R's; the rest should be tools and clay and sports and theater and paint and freedom.

Most of the school work that adolescents do is simply a waste of time, of energy, of patience. It robs youth of its right to play and play and play; it puts old heads on young shoulders.

When I lecture to students at teacher training colleges and universities, I am often shocked at the ungrownupness of these lads and lasses stuffed with useless knowledge. They know a lot; they shine in dialectics; they can quote the classics — but in their outlook on life many of them are infants. For they have been taught *to know*, but have not been allowed *to feel*. These students are friendly, pleasant, eager, but something is lacking — the emotional factor, the power to subordinate thinking to feeling. I talk to these of a world they have missed and go on missing. Their textbooks do not deal with human character, or with love, or with freedom, or with self-determination. And so the system goes on, aiming only at standards of book learning — goes on separating the head from the heart.

It is time that we were challenging the school's notion of work. It is taken for granted that every child should learn mathematics, history, geography, some science, a little art, and certainly literature. It is time we realized that the average young child is not much interested in any of these subjects.

I prove this with every new pupil. When told that the school is free, every new pupil cries, "Hurrah! You won't catch me doing dull arithmetic and things!"

I am not decrying learning. But learning should come after play. And learning should not be deliberately seasoned with play to make it palatable.

Learning is important — but not to everyone. Nijinsky could not pass his school exams in St. Petersburg, and he could not enter the State Ballet without passing those exams. He simply could not learn school subjects — his mind was elsewhere. They faked an exam for him, giving him the answers with the papers — so a biography says. What a loss to the world if Nijinsky had had to really pass those exams!

Creators learn what they want to learn in order to have the tools that 14 their originality and genius demand. We do not know how much creation is killed in the classroom with its emphasis on learning.

I have seen a girl weep nightly over her geometry. Her mother wanted 15 her to go to the university, but the girl's whole soul was artistic. I was delighted when I heard that she had failed her college entrance exams for the seventh time. Possibly, the mother would now allow her to go on the stage as she longed to do.

Some time ago, I met a girl of fourteen in Copenhagen who had spent 16 three years in Summerhill and had spoken perfect English here. "I suppose you are at the top of your class in English," I said.

She grimaced ruefully. "No, I'm at the bottom of my class, because I 17 don't know English grammar," she said. I think that disclosure is about the best commentary on what adults consider education.

Indifferent scholars who, under discipline, scrape through college or 18 university and become unimaginative teachers, mediocre doctors, and incompetent lawyers would possibly be good mechanics or excellent bricklayers or first-rate policemen.

We have found that the boy who cannot or will not learn to read until 19 he is, say, fifteen is always a boy with a mechanical bent who later on becomes a good engineer or electrician. I should not dare dogmatize about girls who never go to lessons, especially to mathematics and physics. Often such girls spend much time with needlework, and some, later on in life, take up dressmaking and designing. It is an absurd curriculum that makes a prospective dressmaker study quadratic equations or Boyle's Law.

Caldwell Cook wrote a book called *The Play Way,* in which he told 20 how he taught English by means of play. It was a fascinating book, full of good things, yet I think it was only a new way of bolstering the theory that learning is of the utmost importance. Cook held that learning was so important that the pill should be sugared with play. This notion that unless a child is learning something the child is wasting his time is nothing less than a curse — a curse that blinds thousands of teachers and most school inspectors. Fifty years ago the watchword was "Learn through doing." Today the watchword is "Learn through playing." Play is thus used only as a means to an end, but to what good end I do not really know.

If a teacher sees children playing with mud, and he thereupon im- 21 proves the shining moment by holding forth about river-bank erosion, what end has he in view? What child cares about river erosion? Many so-called educators believe that it does not matter what a child learns as long as he is *taught* something. And, of course, with schools as they are — just mass-production factories — what can a teacher do but teach something and come to believe that teaching, in itself, matters most of all?

When I lecture to a group of teachers, I commence by saying that I am   22
not going to speak about school subjects or discipline or classes. For an hour my audience listens in rapt silence; and after the sincere applause, the chairman announces that I am ready to answer questions. At least three-quarters of the questions deal with subjects and teaching.

I do not tell this in any superior way. I tell it sadly to show how the   23
classroom walls and the prisonlike buildings narrow the teacher's outlook, and prevent him from seeing the true essentials of education. His work deals with the part of a child that is above the neck; and perforce, the emotional, vital part of the child is foreign territory to him.

I wish I could see a bigger movement of rebellion among our younger   24
teachers. Higher education and university degrees do not make a scrap of difference in confronting the evils of society. A learned neurotic is not any different than an unlearned neurotic.

In all countries, capitalist, socialist, or communist, elaborate schools   25
are built to educate the young. But all the wonderful labs and workshops do nothing to help John or Peter or Ivan surmount the emotional damage and the social evils bred by the pressure on him from his parents, his school-teachers, and the pressure of the coercive quality of our civilization.

SUBJECT QUESTIONS

1. If the aim of life is happiness and the aim of education is preparation for life, does it follow that the goal of education is happiness?
2. Neill asks a number of embarrassing questions in paragraph 2. Does he demonstrate that his brand of education would eliminate the need for such questions? Does he mean to imply that standard education is the source of these problems or that it ignores them?
3. How, according to Neill, does his system of education differ from the Montessori system and from "learn through playing"?
4. Neill asserts, perhaps correctly, that the average child is "not much interested" in the standard subjects taught in school. Does it follow that such subjects should not be taught?
5. Would you agree that creative people will learn what they need without being taught and that noncreative people would be better off without being taught things they will never use? Does emphasis on learning kill creativity? Does a student learn anything from a standard curriculum besides "knowledge"?
6. What do you think might be the chief advantages of attending a school like Summerhill? What might be the disadvantages?

STRUCTURE QUESTIONS

1. Do you see any problem in transition between the subject of the first three paragraphs and the remainder of the essay?
2. What is the basis of contrast between Summerhill education and standard education?
3. Criticize the division of materials into paragraphs, especially in paragraphs 5 through 8 and 10 through 14. Can you suggest more logical paragraphs?
4. Comment on Neill's use of specific examples. Do they provide effective support for his position? Do they seem typical rather than "loaded"? (That is, could one find examples of people who "failed" in life because they didn't learn enough in school? Keep in mind that Neill's definition of success is not getting a high-paying job.)
5. Does Neill's complete commitment to his own system interfere with the drawing of a valid contrast with the standard system? (It need not interfere, of course; most contrasts imply a value judgment one way or the other.)

SUGGESTIONS FOR WRITING

1. Write a comparison and contrast paper in which you point out the advantages and disadvantages of learning by doing and of learning in the classroom. Select an area with which you are familiar, whether auto mechanics or poetry.
2. Write an essay contrasting the kind of learning experience which takes place in two different types of courses — composition and calculus, for example, or interior design and botany.

Confessions of
a Misspent Youth

Mara Wolynski

Mara Wolynski is a free-lance writer who began her career in 1975. Her articles have appeared in Vogue *and* Mademoiselle. *The following essay was first published in* Newsweek.

The idea of permissive education appealed to my mother in 1956 when she   1
was a Bohemian and I was four. In Greenwich Village, she found a small
private school whose beliefs were hers and happily enrolled me. I know it
was an act of motherly love but it might have been the worst thing she ever
did to me. This school — I'll call it Sand and Sea — attracted other such
parents, upper-middle-class professionals who were determined not to have
their children pressured the way they had been. Sand and Sea was the
school without pain. And it was the kind of school that the back-to-basics
people rightly fear most. At Sand and Sea, I soon became an exemplar of educational freedom — the freedom not to learn.

Sand and Sea was run by fifteen women and one man who taught   2
"science." They were decent people, some old, some young, and all devoted
to cultivating the innate creativity they were convinced we had. There was a
tremendous emphasis on the arts. We weren't taught techniques, however,
because any kind of organization stunted creativity.

Happiness and Hieroglyphics

We had certain hours allotted to various subjects but we were free to dismiss   3
anything that bored us. In fact, it was school policy that we were forbidden
to be bored or miserable or made to compete with one another. There were
no tests and no hard times. When I was bored with math, I was excused and
allowed to write short stories in the library. The way we learned history was
by trying to re-create its least important elements. One year, we pounded
corn, made tepees, ate buffalo meat and learned two Indian words. That was
early American history. Another year we made elaborate costumes, clay
pots, and papier-mâché gods. That was Greek culture. Another year we were
all maidens and knights in armor because it was time to learn about the

Middle Ages. We drank our orange juice from tin-foil goblets but never found out what the Middle Ages were. They were just "The Middle Ages."

I knew that the Huns pegged their horses and drank a quart of blood 4 before going to war but no one ever told us who the Huns were or why we should know who they were. And one year, the year of ancient Egypt, when we were building our pyramids, I did a thirty-foot-long mural for which I laboriously copied hieroglyphics onto the sheet of brown paper. But no one ever told me what they stood for. They were just there and beautiful.

Ignorance Is Not Bliss

We spent great amounts of time being creative because we had been told by 5 our incurably optimistic mentors that the way to be happy in life was to create. Thus, we didn't learn to read until we were in the third grade because early reading was thought to discourage creative spontaneity. The one thing they taught us very well was to hate intellectuality and anything connected with it. Accordingly, we were forced to be creative for nine years. And yet Sand and Sea has failed to turn out a good artist. What we did do was to continually form and re-form interpersonal relationships and that's what we thought learning was all about and we were happy. At ten, for example, most of us were functionally illiterate but we could tell that Raymond was "acting out" when, in the middle of what passed for English, he did the twist on top of his desk. Or that Nina was "introverted" because she always cowered in the corner.

When we finally were graduated from Canaan, however, all the happy 6 little children fell down the hill. We felt a profound sense of abandonment. So did our parents. After all that tuition money, let alone the loving freedom, their children faced high school with all the glorious prospects of the poorest slum-school kids. And so it came to be. No matter what school we went to, *we* were the underachievers and the culturally disadvantaged.

For some of us, real life was too much — one of my oldest friends from 7 Sand and Sea killed himself two years ago after flunking out of the worst high school in New York at twenty. Various others have put in time in mental institutions where they were free, once again, to create during occupational therapy.

During my own high-school years, the school psychologist was baffled 8 by my lack of substantive knowledge. He suggested to my mother that I be given a battery of psychological tests to find out why I was blocking out information. The thing was, I wasn't blocking because I had no information to block. Most of my Sand and Sea classmates were also enduring the same kinds of hardships that accompany severe handicaps. My own reading comprehension was in the lowest eighth percentile, not surprisingly. I was often asked by teachers how I had gotten into high school. However, I did manage to stumble *not* only through high school but also through college (first junior college — rejected by all four-year colleges, and then New York University), hating it all the way as I had been taught to. I am still amazed that I have a B.A., but think of it as a B.S.

The Lure of Learning

The parents of my former classmates can't figure out what went wrong. They had sent in bright curious children and gotten back, nine years later, help-less adolescents. Some might say that those of us who freaked out would have freaked out anywhere, but when you see the same bizarre behavior pattern in succeeding graduating classes, you can draw certain terrifying conclusions.   9

Now I see my twelve-year-old brother (who is in a traditional school) doing college-level math and I know that he knows more about many other things besides math than I do. And I also see traditional education working in the case of my fifteen-year-old brother (who was summarily yanked from Sand and Sea, by my reformed mother, when he was eight so that he wouldn't become like me). Now, after seven years of real education, he is making impressive film documentaries for a project on the Bicentennial. A better learning experience than playing Pilgrim for four and a half months, and Indian for four and a half months, which is how I imagine they spent this year at Sand and Sea.   10

And now I've come to see that the real job of school is to entice the student into the web of knowledge and then, if he's not enticed, to drag him in. I wish I had been.   11

SUBJECT QUESTIONS

1. If the aim of Sand and Sea was to encourage freedom and creativity, did it go against its own doctrine by forbidding boredom and compe-tition, or by teaching students to "hate intellectuality," or by forcing them to be creative?
2. Wolynski's picture of the school is not a flattering one; yet she says "we were happy." Would the students' later problems have been solved if Sand and Sea had also included a high school and college? (That is, might one argue that the trouble was not with the educa-tion but in the fact the students were required to continue in con-ventional high schools?)
3. Why do you think, despite all the emphasis on creativity, Sand and Sea failed to turn out a good artist? Do freedom and creativity require training and discipline in the same way that English composi-tion and mathematics do?
4. Wolynski suggests that traditional subjects were available if a child

pursued the opportunity to study them. Why didn't she learn anything in these courses?
5. Would you agree with Wolynski's conclusion in the last paragraph? Is she overreacting to a bad experience?

STRUCTURE QUESTIONS

1. Wolynski does not use one of the methods of organization suggested in the introduction to this section. Do you see why not? Is her own principle of organization satisfactory for her purpose in this essay?
2. Except near the end, Wolynski spends most of her time developing only one side of the contrast. Should she have given parallel details about standard schools? Is the difference between the two types of schools clear?
3. What is the basis of the contrast? Would it have been fairer to contrast the degrees of creativity inspired by the two school systems?
4. How does Wolynski avoid the charge of "sour grapes from an unsuccessful student"? Does her own experience seem typical?
5. Why is the use of her two brothers for contrast at the end a particularly effective choice?
6. Most of Wolynski's specific examples of schoolwork are drawn from the teaching of history. Should she have given examples of how other courses were taught or are the passing references to reading and English enough?

SUGGESTIONS FOR WRITING

1. Contrast the ideal of a "free" education as suggested by A. S. Neill with the reality as experienced by Wolynski and her classmates.
2. Contrast the education Wolynski received with your own grade-school education.

Universities and Their Function

Alfred North Whitehead

Alfred North Whitehead (1861–1947) was an English mathematician and philosopher. He taught mathematics at Cambridge University and the University of London, and later philosophy at Harvard University. With Bertrand Russell he wrote the great Principia Mathematica *(1910). Later he wrote many books of philosophy, the best-known and most frequently reprinted being* Science and the Modern World *(1925). Although the essay which follows was written over fifty years ago, its concern seems curiously modern and not far from the concern of the preceding "Pedestrian Students and High-Flying Squirrels."*

The universities are schools of education, and schools of research. But the primary reason for their existence is not to be found either in the mere knowledge conveyed to the students or in the mere opportunities for research afforded to the members of the faculty. 1

The justification for a university is that it preserves the connection between knowledge and the zest of life, by uniting the young and the old in the imaginative consideration of learning. The university imparts information, but it imparts it imaginatively. At least, this is the function which it should perform for society. A university which fails in this respect has no reason for existence. This atmosphere of excitement, arising from imaginative consideration, transforms knowledge. A fact is no longer a bare fact: it is invested with all its possibilities. It is no longer a burden on the memory: it is energizing as the poet of our dreams, and as the architect of our purposes. 2

Imagination is not to be divorced from the facts: it is a way of illuminating the facts. It works by eliciting the general principles which apply to the facts, as they exist, and then by an intellectual survey of alternative possibilities which are consistent with those principles. It enables men to construct an intellectual vision of a new world, and it preserves the zest of life by the suggestion of satisfying purposes. 3

Youth is imaginative, and if the imagination be strengthened by discipline this energy of imagination can in great measure be preserved 4 through life. The tragedy of the world is that those who are imaginative have but slight experience, and those who are experienced have feeble imaginations. Fools act on imagination without knowledge; pedants act on knowledge without imagination. The task of a university is to weld together imagination and experience.

These reflections upon the general functions of a university can be at once translated in terms of the particular functions of a business school. We need not flinch from the assertion that the main function of such a school is to produce men with a greater zest for business.

In a simpler world, business relations were simpler, being based on the immediate contact of man with man and on immediate confrontation with all relevant material circumstances. To-day business organization requires an imaginative grasp of the psychologies of populations engaged in differing modes of occupation; of populations scattered through cities, through mountains, through plains; of populations on the ocean, and of populations in mines, and of populations in forests. It requires an imaginative grasp of conditions in the tropics, and of conditions in temperate zones. It requires an imaginative grasp of the interlocking interests of great organizations, and of the reactions of the whole complex to any change in one of its elements. It requires an imaginative understanding of laws of political economy, not merely in the abstract, but also with the power to construe them in terms of the particular circumstances of a concrete business. It requires some knowledge of the habits of government, and of the variations of those habits under diverse conditions. It requires an imaginative vision of the binding forces of any human organization, a sympathetic vision of the limits of human nature and of the conditions which evoke loyalty of service. It requires some knowledge of the laws of health, and of the laws of fatigue, and of the conditions for sustained reliability. It requires an imaginative understanding of the social effects of the conditions of factories. It requires a sufficient conception of the role of applied science in modern society. It requires that discipline of character which can say "yes" and "no" to other men, not by reason of blind obstinacy, but with firmness derived from a conscious evaluation of relevant alternatives.

The universities have trained the intellectual pioneers of our civilization — the priests, the lawyers, the statesmen, the doctors, the men of science, and the men of letters. The conduct of business now requires intellectual imagination of the same type as that which in former times has mainly passed into those other occupations.

There is one great difficulty which hampers all the higher types of human endeavor. In modern times this difficulty has even increased in its possibilities for evil. In any large organization the younger men, who are novices, must be set to jobs which consist in carrying out fixed duties in obedience to orders. No president of a large corporation meets his youngest employee at his office door with the offer of the most responsible job which the work of that corporation includes. The young men are set to work at a fixed routine, and only occasionally even see the president as he passes in and out of the building. Such work is a great discipline. It imparts knowledge, and it produces reliability of character; also it is the only work for which the young men, in that novice stage, are fit, and it is the work for which they are hired. There can be no criticism of the custom, but there may be an unfortunate effect — prolonged routine work dulls the imagination.

The way in which a university should function in the preparation for   9
an intellectual career, such as modern business or one of the older professions, is by promoting the imaginative consideration of the various general principles underlying that career. Its students thus pass into their period of technical apprenticeship with their imaginations already practised in connecting details with general principles. The routine then receives its meaning, and also illuminates the principles which give it that meaning. Hence, instead of a drudgery issuing in a blind rule of thumb, the properly trained man has some hope of obtaining an imagination disciplined by detailed facts and by necessary habits.

Thus the proper function of a university is the imaginative acquisition   10
of knowledge. Apart from this importance of the imagination, there is no reason why business men, and other professional men, should not pick up their facts bit by bit as they want them for particular occasions. A university is imaginative or it is nothing — at least nothing useful.

SUBJECT QUESTIONS

1. What does Whitehead see as the chief function of a university? Why is a university an ideal place to develop this talent?
2. If education and research are not the main functions of a university, why do you suppose university catalogues and presidents stress them heavily?
3. Why do you think Whitehead chose business administration as his primary example rather than some more "speculative" study such as philosophy?
4. Is Whitehead arguing for the same kind of education as Liane Norman in "Pedestrian Students and High-Flying Squirrels"? Do you see any important differences? Would A. S. Neill approve of Whitehead's view?
5. In paragraph 8, does Whitehead mean that young people in business should be given the imaginative jobs and the older employees assigned to "drudgery"? Are new employees usually assigned to dreary tasks? If college stimulates the imagination, will not new graduates be disappointed with the dull tasks given them in busi-

ness? Should the university teach business majors to be satisfied with dreary jobs?

6. Do you agree that "Fools act on imagination without knowledge; pedants act on knowledge without imagination"?

STRUCTURE QUESTIONS

1. Does Whitehead make clear the difference between a "fact" and a "fact imaginatively considered"? Should he have included examples to support his generalizations in paragraphs 2 and 3?
2. In his contrast between modern business and "a simpler world," Whitehead writes mostly about new developments. Is he correct in assuming that he need not develop the other side of the contrast fully? Does his discussion of modern requirements imply a fuller contrast?
3. In this short essay, Whitehead is dealing primarily in generalizations. The best way to avoid fuzziness in this kind of writing is to employ "action" verbs and concrete nouns. Does Whitehead do this?
4. Examine Whitehead's transitions from one paragraph to the next (repeated key words, pronouns with antecedents in the earlier paragraphs, conjunctive adverbs, etc.) Is there any point at which a better transition is needed?
5. The final paragraph says nothing which has not already been said; is there any excuse for its inclusion?

SUGGESTION FOR WRITING

Compare and contrast the approach to education which you expected or wanted from college with that which you have in fact thus far encountered; concentrate on what Whitehead calls "imaginative consideration" of knowledge. Use specific courses as illustration.

Of This Time, of That Place

Lionel Trilling

*Lionel Trilling (1905–1975), was professor of English at Columbia. He
wrote several scholarly studies and important books of criticism as well
as short stories. "Of This Time, of That Place" (1943) is considered to be
one of the finest of modern short stories. It first appeared in the* Partisan
Review.

*The primary aim of this story, of course, is not merely comparison
and contrast. It is included here to illustrate the fact that comparison
and contrast can be usefully employed in other forms of writing and do
not exist solely in isolated form as comparison-and-contrast essays.*

It was a fine September day. By noon it would be summer again, but now it   1
was true autumn with a touch of chill in the air. As Joseph Howe stood on
the porch of the house in which he lodged, ready to leave for his first class of
the year, he thought with pleasure of the long indoor days that were coming.
It was a moment when he could feel glad of his profession.

On the lawn the peach tree was still in fruit and young Hilda Aiken was   2
taking a picture of it. She held the camera tight against her chest. She
wanted the sun behind her, but she did not want her own long morning
shadow in the foreground. She raised the camera, but that did not help, and
she lowered it, but that made things worse. She twisted her body to the left,
then to the right. In the end she had to step out of the direct line of the sun.
At last she snapped the shutter and wound the film with intense care.

Howe, watching her from the porch, waited for her to finish and called   3
good morning. She turned, startled, and almost sullenly lowered her glance.
In the year Howe had lived at the Aikens', Hilda had accepted him as one of
her family, but since his absence of the summer she had grown shy. Then
suddenly she lifted her head and smiled at him, and the humorous smile
confirmed his pleasure in the day. She picked up her bookbag and set off for
school.

The handsome houses on the streets to the college were not yet fully   4
awake, but they looked very friendly. Howe went by the Bradby house
where he would be a guest this evening at the first dinner party of the year.
When he had gone the length of the picket fence, the whitest in town, he

Copyright 1943, 1971 by Lionel Trilling. Reprinted from his volume *Of This Time, of That
Place and Other Stories* by permission of Harcourt Brace Jovanovich, Inc.

turned back. Along the path there was a fine row of asters and he went through the gate and picked one for his buttonhole. The Bradbys would be pleased if they happened to see him invading their lawn and the knowledge of this made him even more comfortable.

He reached the campus as the hour was striking. The students were hurrying to their classes. He himself was in no hurry. He stopped at his dim cubicle of an office and lit a cigarette. The prospect of facing his class had suddenly presented itself to him and his hands were cold; the lawful seizure of power he was about to make seemed momentous. Waiting did not help. He put out his cigarette, picked up a pad of theme paper, and went to his classroom.

As he entered, the rattle of voices ceased, and the twenty-odd fresh-men settled themselves and looked at him appraisingly. Their faces seemed gross, his heart sank at their massed impassivity, but he spoke briskly.

"My name is Howe," he said, and turned and wrote it on the black-board. The carelessness of the scrawl confirmed his authority. He went on, "My office is 412 Slemp Hall, and my office-hours are Monday, Wednesday and Friday from eleven-thirty to twelve-thirty."

He wrote, "M., W., F., 11:30-12:30." He said, "I'll be very glad to see any of you at that time. Or if you can't come then, you can arrange with me for some other time."

He turned again to the blackboard and spoke over his shoulder. "The text for the course is Jarman's *Modern Plays,* revised edition. The Co-op has it in stock." He wrote the name, underlined "revised edition" and waited for it to be taken down in the new notebooks.

When the bent heads were raised again he began his speech of pro-spectus. "It is hard to explain — " he said, and paused as they composed themselves. "It is hard to explain what a course like this is intended to do. We are going to try to learn something about modern literature and some-thing about prose composition."

As he spoke, his hands warmed and he was able to look directly at the class. Last year on the first day the faces had seemed just as cloddish, but as the term wore on they became gradually alive and quite likable. It did not seem possible that the same thing could happen again.

"I shall not lecture in this course," he continued. "Our work will be carried on by discussion and we will try to learn by an exchange of opinion. But you will soon recognize that my opinion is worth more than anyone else's here."

He remained grave as he said it, but two boys understood and laughed. The rest took permission from them and laughed too. All Howe's private ironies protested the vulgarity of the joke, but the laughter made him feel benign and powerful.

When the little speech was finished, Howe picked up the pad of paper he had brought. He announced that they would write an extemporaneous theme. Its subject was traditional, "Who I am and why I came to Dwight College." By now the class was more at ease and it gave a ritualistic groan of protest. Then there was stir as fountain pens were brought out and the writing-arms of the chairs were cleared, and the paper was passed about. At last, all the heads bent to work, and the room became still.

Howe sat idly at his desk. The sun shone through the tall clumsy windows. The cool of the morning was already passing. There was a scent of autumn and of varnish and the stillness of the room was deep and oddly touching. Now and then a student's head was raised and scratched in the old, elaborate students' pantomime that calls the teacher to witness honest intellectual effort. **15**

Suddenly a tall boy stood within the frame of the open door. "Is this," he said, and thrust a large nose into a college catalogue, "is this the meeting place of English 1A? The section instructed by Dr. Joseph Howe?" **16**

He stood on the very sill of the door, as if refusing to enter until he was perfectly sure of all his rights. The class looked up from work, found him absurd and gave a low mocking cheer. **17**

The teacher and the new student, with equal pointedness, ignored the disturbance. Howe nodded to the boy, who pushed his head forward and then jerked it back in a wide elaborate arc to clear his brow of a heavy lock of hair. He advanced into the room and halted before Howe, almost at attention. In a loud, clear voice he announced, "I am Tertan, Ferdinand R., reporting at the direction of Head of Department Vincent." **18**

The heraldic formality of this statement brought forth another cheer. Howe looked at the class with a sternness he could not really feel, for there was indeed something ridiculous about this boy. Under his displeased regard the rows of heads dropped to work again. Then he touched Tertan's elbow, led him up to the desk and stood so as to shield their conversation from the class. **19**

"We are writing an extemporaneous theme," he said. "The subject is, 'Who I am and why I came to Dwight College.' " **20**

He stripped a few sheets from the pad and offered them to the boy. Tertan hesitated and then took the paper, but he held it only tentatively. As if with the effort of making something clear, he gulped, and a slow smile fixed itself on his face. It was at once knowing and shy. **21**

"Professor," he said, "to be perfectly fair to my classmates" — he made a large gesture over the room — "and to you" — he inclined his head to Howe — "this would not be for me an extemporaneous subject." **22**

Howe tried to understand. "You mean you've already thought about it — you've heard we always give the same subject? That doesn't matter." **23**

Again the boy ducked his head and gulped. It was the gesture of one who wishes to make a difficult explanation with perfect candor. "Sir," he **24** said, and made the distinction with great care, "the topic I did not expect, but I have given much ratiocination to the subject."

Howe smiled and said, "I don't think that's an unfair advantage. Just go ahead and write." 25

Tertan narrowed his eyes and glanced sidewise at Howe. His strange mouth smiled. Then in quizzical acceptance, he ducked his head, threw back the heavy, dank lock, dropped into a seat with a great loose noise and began to write rapidly. 26

The room fell silent again and Howe resumed his idleness. When the bell rang, the students who had groaned when the task had been set now groaned again because they had not finished. Howe took up the papers, and held the class while he made the first assignment. When he dismissed it, Tertan bore down on him, his slack mouth held ready for speech. 27

"Some professors," he said, "are pedants. They are Dryasdusts. However, some professors are free souls and creative spirits. Kant, Hegel and Nietzsche were all professors." With this pronouncement he paused. "It is my opinion," he continued, "that you occupy the second category." 28

Howe looked at the boy in surprise and said with good-natured irony, "With Kant, Hegel and Nietzsche?" 29

Not only Tertan's hand and head but his whole awkward body waved away the stupidity. "It is the kind and not the quantity of the kind," he said sternly. 30

Rebuked, Howe said as simply and seriously as he could, "It would be nice to think so." He added, "Of course I am not a professor." 31

This was clearly a disappointment but Tertan met it. "In the French sense," he said with composure. "Generically, a teacher." 32

Suddenly he bowed. It was such a bow, Howe fancied, as a stage-director might teach an actor playing a medieval student who takes leave of Abelard — stiff, solemn, with elbows close to the body and feet together. Then, quite as suddenly, he turned and left. 33

A queer fish, and as soon as Howe reached his office, he shifted through the batch of themes and drew out Tertan's. The boy had filled many sheets with his unformed headlong scrawl. "Who am I?" he had begun. "Here, in a mundane, not to say commercialized academe, is asked the question which from time long immemorially out of mind has accreted doubts and thoughts in the psyche of man to pester him as a nuisance. Whether in St. Augustine (or Austin as sometimes called) or Miss Bashkirtsieff or Frederic Amiel or Empedocles, or in less lights of the intellect than these, this posed question has been ineluctable." 34

Howe took out his pencil. He circled "academe" and wrote "vocab." in the margin. He underlined "time long immemorially out of mind" and wrote "Diction!" But this seemed inadequate for what was wrong. He put down his pencil and read ahead to discover the principle of error in the theme. "Today 35 as ever, in spite of gloomy prophets of the dismal science (economics) the question is uninvalidated. Out of the starry depths of heaven hurtles this spear of query demanding to be caught on the shield of the mind ere it pierces the skull and the limbs be unstrung."

Baffled but quite caught, Howe read on. "Materialism, by which is   36
meant the philosophic concept and not the moral idea, provides no aegis against the question which lies beyond the tangible (metaphysics). Existence without alloy is the question presented. Environment and heredity relegated aside, the rags and old clothes of practical life discarded, the name and the instrumentality of livelihood do not, as the prophets of the dismal science insist on in this connection, give solution to the interrogation which not from the professor merely but veritably from the cosmos is given. I think, therefore I am (cogito etc.) but who am I? Tertan I am, but what is Tertan? Of this time, of that place, of some parentage, what does it matter?"

Existence without alloy: the phrase established itself. Howe put aside   37
Tertan's paper and at random picked up another. "I am Arthur J. Casebeer, Jr.," he read. "My father is Arthur J. Casebeer and my grandfather was Arthur J. Casebeer before him. My mother is Nina Wimble Casebeer. Both of them are college graduates and my father is in insurance. I was born in St. Louis eighteen years ago and we still make our residence there."

Arthur J. Casebeer, who knew who he was, was less interesting than   38
Tertan, but more coherent. Howe picked up Tertan's paper again. It was clear that none of the routine marginal comments, no "sent. str." or "punct." or "vocab." could cope with this torrential rhetoric. He read ahead, contenting himself with underscoring the errors against the time when he should have the necessary "conference" with Tertan.

It was a busy and official day of cards and sheets, arrangements and   39
small decisions, and it gave Howe pleasure. Even when it was time to attend the first of the weekly Convocations he felt the charm of the beginning of things when intention is still innocent and uncorrupted by effort. He sat among the young instructors on the platform, and joined in their humorous complaints at having to assist at the ceremony, but actually he got a clear satisfaction from the ritual of prayer, and prosy speech, and even from wearing his academic gown. And when the Convocation was over the pleasure continued as he crossed the campus, exchanging greetings with men he had not seen since the spring. They were people who did not yet, and perhaps never would, mean much to him, but in a year they had grown amiably to be part of his life. They were his fellow-townsmen.

The day had cooled again at sunset, and there was a bright chill in the   40
September twilight. Howe carried his voluminous gown over his arm, he swung his doctoral hood by its purple neckpiece, and on his head he wore his mortarboard with its heavy gold tassel bobbing just over his eye. These

were the weighty and absurd symbols of his new profession and they pleased him. At twenty-six Joseph Howe had discovered that he was neither so well off nor so bohemian as he had once thought. A small income, adequate when supplemented by a sizable cash legacy, was genteel poverty when the cash was all spent. And the literary life — the room at the Lafayette, or the small apartment without a lease, the long summers on the Cape, the long afternoons and the social evenings — began to weary him. His writing filled his mornings, and should perhaps have filled his life, yet it did not. To the amusement of his friends, and with a certain sense that he was betraying his own freedom, he had used the last of his legacy for a year at Harvard. The small but respectable reputation of his two volumes of verse had proved useful — he continued at Harvard on a fellowship and when he emerged as Doctor Howe he received an excellent appointment, with prospects, at Dwight.

He had his moments of fear when all that had ever been said of the dangers of the academic life had occurred to him. But after a year in which he had tested every possibility of corruption and seduction he was ready to rest easy. His third volume of verse, most of it written in his first years of teaching, was not only ampler but, he thought, better than its predecessors. 41

There was a clear hour before the Bradby dinner party, and Howe looked forward to it. But he was not to enjoy it, for lying with his mail on the hall table was a copy of this quarter's issues of *Life and Letters*, to which his landlord subscribed. Its severe cover announced that its editor, Frederic Woolley, had this month contributed an essay called "Two Poets," and Howe, picking it up, curious to see who the two poets might be, felt his own name start out at him with cabalistic power — Joseph Howe. As he continued to turn the pages his hand trembled. 42

Standing in the dark hall, holding the neat little magazine, Howe knew that his literary contempt for Frederic Woolley meant nothing, for he suddenly understood how he respected Woolley in the way of the world. He knew this by the trembling of his hand. And of the little world as well as the great, for although the literary groups of New York might dismiss Woolley, his name carried high authority in the academic world. At Dwight it was even a revered name, for it had been here at the college that Frederic Woolley had made the distinguished scholarly career from which he had gone on to literary journalism. In middle life he had been induced to take the editorship of *Life and Letters,* a literary monthly not widely read but heavily endowed, and in its pages he had carried on the defense of what he sometimes called the older values. He was not without wit, he had great knowledge and considerable taste, and even in the full movement of the "new" literature he had won a certain respect for his refusal to accept it. In France, even in England, he would have been connected with a more robust 43 tradition of conservatism, but America gave him an audience not much better than genteel. It was known in the college that to the subsidy of *Life and Letters* the Bradbys contributed a great part.

As Howe read, he saw that he was involved in nothing less than an event. When the Fifth Series of *Studies in Order and Value* came to be collected, this latest of Frederic Woolley's essays would not be merely another step in the old direction. Clearly and unmistakably, it was a turning point. All his literary life Woolley had been concerned with the relation of literature to morality, religion, and the private and delicate pieties, and he had been unalterably opposed to all that he had called "inhuman humanitarianism." But here, suddenly, dramatically late, he had made an about-face, turning to the public life and to the humanitarian politics he had so long despised. This was the kind of incident the histories of literature make much of. Frederic Woolley was opening for himself a new career and winning a kind of new youth. He contrasted the two poets, Thomas Wormser, who was admirable, Joseph Howe, who was almost dangerous. He spoke of the "precious subjectivism" of Howe's verse. "In times like ours," he wrote, "with millions facing penury and want, one feels that the qualities of the *tour d'ivoire* are well-nigh inhuman, nearly insulting. The *tour d'ivoire* becomes the *tour d'ivresse*, and it is not self-intoxicated poets that our people need." The essay said more: "The problem is one of meaning. I am not ignorant that the creed of the esoteric poets declares that a poem does not and should not *mean* anything, that it *is* something. But poetry is what the poet makes it, and if he is a true poet he makes what his society needs. And what is needed now is the tradition in which Mr. Wormser writes, the true tradition of poetry. The Howes do no harm, but they do no good when positive good is demanded of all responsible men. Or do the Howes indeed do no harm? Perhaps Plato would have said they do, that in some ways theirs is the Phrygian music that turns men's minds from the struggle. Certainly it is true that Thomas Wormser writes in the lucid Dorian mode which sends men into battle with evil."

It was easy to understand why Woolley had chosen to praise Thomas Wormser. The long, lilting lines of *Corn Under Willows* hymned, as Woolley put it, the struggle for wheat in the Iowa fields, and expressed the real lives of real people. But why out of the dozen more notable examples he had chosen Howe's little volume as the example of "precious subjectivism" was hard to guess. In a way it was funny, this multiplication of himself into "the Howes." And yet this becoming the multiform political symbol by whose creation Frederic Woolley gave the sign of a sudden new life, this use of him as a sacrifice whose blood was necessary for the rites of rejuvenation, made him feel oddly unclean.

Nor could Howe get rid of a certain practical resentment. As a poet he had a special and respectable place in the college life. But it might be another thing to be marked as the poet of a wilful and selfish obscurity.

As he walked to the Bradbys', Howe was a little tense and defensive. It seemed to him that all the world knew of the "attack" and agreed with it. And, indeed, the Bradbys had read the essay but Professor Bradby, a kind and pretentious man, said, "I see my old friend knocked you about a bit, my boy," and his wife Eugenia looked at Howe with her childlike blue eyes and said, "I shall *scold* Frederic for the untrue things he wrote about you. You aren't the least obscure." They beamed at him. In their genial snobbery they seemed to feel that he had distinguished himself. He was the leader of Howeism. He enjoyed the dinner party as much as he had thought he would.

And in the following days, as he was more preoccupied with his duties, the incident was forgotten. His classes had ceased to be mere groups. Student after student detached himself from the mass and required or claimed a place in Howe's awareness. Of them all it was Tertan who first and most violently signaled his separate existence. A week after classes had begun Howe saw his silhouette on the frosted glass of his office door. It was motionless for a long time, perhaps stopped by the problem of whether or not to knock before entering. Howe called "Come in!" and Tertan entered with his shambling stride.

He stood beside the desk, silent and at attention. When Howe asked him to sit down, he responded with a gesture of head and hand, as if to say that such amenities were beside the point. Nevertheless, he did take the chair. He put his ragged, crammed briefcase between his legs. His face, which Howe now observed fully for the first time, was confusing, for it was made up of florid curves, the nose arched in the bone and voluted in the nostril, the mouth loose and soft and rather moist. Yet the face was so thin and narrow as to seem the very type of asceticism. Lashes of unusual length veiled the eyes and, indeed, it seemed as if there were a veil over the whole countenance. Before the words actually came, the face screwed itself into an attitude of preparation for them.

"You can confer with me now?" Tertan said.

"Yes, I'd be glad to. There are several things in your two themes I want to talk to you about." Howe reached for the packet of themes on his desk and sought for Tertan's. But the boy was waving them away.

"These are done perforce," he said. "Under the pressure of your requirement. They are not significant; mere duties." Again his great hand flapped vaguely to dismiss his themes. He leaned forward and gazed at his teacher.

"You are," he said, "a man of letters? You are a poet?" It was more declaration than question.

"I should like to think so," Howe said.   54

At first Tertan accepted the answer with a show of appreciation, as   55
though the understatement made a secret between himself and Howe. Then
he chose to misunderstand. With his shrewd and disconcerting control of
expression, he presented to Howe a puzzled grimace. "What does that
mean?" he said.

Howe retracted the irony. "Yes. I am a poet." It sounded strange to   56
say.

"That," Tertan said, "is a wonder." He corrected himself with his duck-   57
ing head. "I mean that is wonderful."

Suddenly, he dived at the miserable briefcase between his legs, put it   58
on his knees, and began to fumble with the catch, all intent on the difficulty
it presented. Howe noted that his suit was worn thin, his shirt almost unclean. He became aware, even, of a vague and musty odor of garments worn
too long in unaired rooms. Tertan conquered the lock and began to concentrate upon a search into the interior. At last he held in his hand what he was
after, a torn and crumpled copy of *Life and Letters*.

"I learned it from here," he said, holding it out.   59

Howe looked at him sharply, his hackles a little up. But the boy's face   60
was not only perfectly innocent, it even shone with a conscious admiration.
Apparently nothing of the import of the essay had touched him except the
wonderful fact that his teacher was a "man of letters." Yet this seemed too
stupid, and Howe, to test it, said, "The man who wrote that doesn't think it's
wonderful."

Tertan made a moist hissing sound as he cleared his mouth of saliva.   61
His head, oddly loose on his neck, wove a pattern of contempt in the air. "A
critic," he said, "who admits *prima facie* that he does not understand." Then
he said grandly, "It is the inevitable fate."

It was absurd, yet, Howe was not only aware of the absurdity but of a   62
tension suddenly and wonderfully relaxed. Now that the "attack" was on the
table between himself and this strange boy, and subject to the boy's funny
and absolutely certain contempt, the hidden force of his feeling was revealed
to him in the very moment that it vanished. All unsuspected, there had been
a film over the world, a transparent but discoloring haze of danger. But he
had no time to stop over the brightened aspect of things. Tertan was going
on. "I also am a man of letters. Putative."

"You have written a good deal?" Howe meant to be no more than   63
polite, and he was surprised at the tenderness he heard in his words.

Solemnly the boy nodded, threw back the dank lock, and sucked in a   64
deep, anticipatory breath. "First, a work of homiletics, which is a defense of
the principles of religious optimism against the pessimism of Schopenhauer
and the humanism of Nietzsche."

"Humanism? Why do you call it humanism?"   65

"It is my nomenclature for making a deity of man," Tertan replied   66
negligently. "Then three fictional works, novels. And numerous essays in
science, combating materialism. Is it your duty to read these if I bring them
to you?"

Howe answered simply, "No, it isn't exactly my duty, but I shall be   67
happy to read them."

Tertan stood up and remained silent. His rested his bag on the chair.   68
With a certain compunction — for it did not seem entirely proper that, for
two men of letters, one should have the right to blue-pencil the other, to
grade him or to question the quality of his "sentence structure" — Howe
reached for Tertan's papers. But before he could take them up, the boy suddenly made his bow-to-Abelard, the stiff inclination of the body with the
hands seeming to emerge from the scholar's gown. Then he was gone.

But after his departure something was still left of him. The timbre of   69
his curious sentences, the downright finality of so quaint a phrase as "It is
the inevitable fate" still rang in the air. Howe gave the warmth of his feeling
to the new visitor who stood at the door announcing himself with a genteel
clearing of the throat.

"Doctor Howe, I believe?" the student said. A large hand advanced   70
into the room and grasped Howe's hand. "Blackburn, sir, Theodore Blackburn, vice-president of the Student Council. A great pleasure, sir."

Out of a pair of ruddy cheeks a pair of small eyes twinkled good-na-   71
turedly. The large face, the large body were not so much fat as beefy and
suggested something "typical" — monk, politician, or innkeeper.

Blackburn took the seat beside Howe's desk. "I may have seemed to   72
introduce myself in my public capacity, sir," he said. "But it is really as an
individual that I came to see you. That is to say, as one of your students to
be."

He spoke with an English intonation and he went on, "I was once an   73
English major, sir."

For a moment Howe was startled, for the roast-beef look of the boy   74
and the manner of his speech gave a second's credibility to one sense of his
statement. Then the collegiate meaning of the phrase asserted itself, but
some perversity made Howe say what was not really in good taste even with
so forward a student, "Indeed? What regiment?"

Blackburn stared and then gave a little pouf-pouf of laughter. He   75
waved the misapprehension away. "*Very* good, sir. It certainly is an ambiguous term." He chuckled in appreciation of Howe's joke, then cleared his
throat to put it aside. "I look forward to taking your course in the romantic
poets, sir," he said earnestly. "To me the romantic poets are the very crown
of English literature."

Howe made a dry sound, and the boy, catching some meaning in it,   76
said, "Little as I know them, of course. But even Shakespeare who is so dear

to us of the Anglo-Saxon tradition is in a sense but the preparation for
Shelley, Keats and Byron. And Wadsworth."

Almost sorry for him, Howe dropped his eyes. With some embarrass- 77
ment, for the boy was not actually his student, he said softly, "Wordsworth."

"Sir?" 78

"Wordsworth, not Wadsworth. You said Wadsworth." 79

"Did I, sir?" Gravely he shook his head to rebuke himself for the error. 80
"Wordsworth, of course — slip of the tongue." Then, quite in command
again, he went on. "I have a favor to ask of you, Doctor Howe. You see, I
began my college course as an English major," — he smiled — "as I said."

"Yes?" 81

"But after my first year I shifted. I shifted to the social sciences. Sociol- 82
ogy and government — I find them stimulating and very *real*." He paused,
out of respect for reality. "But now I find that perhaps I have neglected the
other side."

"The other side?" Howe said. 83

"Imagination, fancy, culture. A well-rounded man." He trailed off as if 84
there were perfect understanding between them. "And so, sir, I have decided to end my senior year with your course in the romantic poets."

His voice was filled with an indulgence which Howe ignored as he said 85
flatly and gravely, "But that course isn't given until the spring term."

"Yes, sir, and that is where the favor comes in. Would you let me take 86
your romantic prose course? I can't take it for credit, sir, my program is full,
but just for background it seems to me that I ought to take it. I do hope," he
concluded in a manly way, "that you will consent."

"Well, it's no great favor, Mr. Blackburn. You can come if you wish, 87
though there's not much point in it if you don't do the reading."

The bell rang for the hour and Howe got up. 88

"May I begin with this class, sir?" Blackburn's smile was candid and 89
boyish.

Howe nodded carelessly and together, silently, they walked to the 90
classroom down the hall. When they reached the door Howe stood back to
let his student enter, but Blackburn moved adroitly behind him and grasped
him by the arm to urge him over the threshold. They entered together with
Blackburn's hand firmly on Howe's biceps, the student inducting the teacher
into his own room. Howe felt a surge of temper rise in him and almost
violently he disengaged his arm and walked to the desk, while Blackburn
found a seat in the front row and smiled at him.

II

The question was, At whose door must the tragedy be laid? 91

All night the snow had fallen heavily and only now was abating in 92 sparse little flurries. The windows were valanced high with white. It was very quiet; something of the quiet of the world had reached the class, and Howe found that everyone was glad to talk or listen. In the room there was a comfortable sense of pleasure in being human.

Casebeer believed that the blame for the tragedy rested with heredity. Picking up the book he read, "The sins of the fathers are visited on their children." This opinion was received with general favor. Nevertheless, Johnson ventured to say that the fault was all Pastor Manders' because the Pastor had made Mrs. Alving go back to her husband and was always hiding the truth. To this Hibbard objected with logic enough, "Well then, it was really all her husband's fault. He *did* all the bad things." De Witt, his face bright with an impatient idea, said that the fault was all society's. "By society I don't mean upper-crust society," he said. He looked around a little defiantly, taking in any members of the class who might be members of upper-crust society. "Not in that sense. I mean the social unit."

Howe nodded and said, "Yes, of course."

"If the society of the time had progressed far enough in science," De Witt went on, "then there would be no problem for Mr. Ibsen to write about. Captain Alving plays around a little, gives way to perfectly natural biological urges, and he gets a social disease, a venereal disease. If the disease is cured, no problem. Invent salvarsan and the disease is cured. The problem of heredity disappears and li'l Oswald just doesn't get paresis. No paresis, no problem — no problem, no play."

This was carrying the ark into battle, and the class looked at De Witt with respectful curiosity. It was his usual way and on the whole they were sympathetic with his struggle to prove to Howe that science was better than literature. Still, there was something in his reckless manner that alienated them a little.

"Or take birth-control, for instance," De Witt went on. "If Mrs. Alving had some knowledge of contraception, she wouldn't have had to have li'l Oswald at all. No li'l Oswald, no play."

The class was suddenly quieter. In the back row Stettenhover swung his great football shoulders in a righteous sulking gesture, first to the right, then to the left. He puckered his mouth ostentatiously. Intellect was always ending up by talking dirty.

Tertan's hand went up, and Howe said, "Mr. Tertan." The boy shambled to his feet and began his long characteristic gulp. Howe made a motion with his fingers, as small as possible, and Tertan ducked his head and smiled in apology. He sat down. The class laughed. With more than half the term gone, Tertan had not been able to remember that one did not rise to speak. He seemed unable to carry on the life of the intellect without this mark of respect for it. To Howe the boy's habit of rising seemed to accord with the formal shabbiness of his dress. He never wore the casual sweaters and jackets of his classmates. Into the free and comfortable air of the college classroom he brought the stuffy sordid strictness of some crowded, metropolitan high school.

"Speaking from one sense," Tertan began slowly, "there is no blame 100 ascribable. From the sense of determinism, who can say where the blame lies? The preordained is the preordained and it cannot be said without rebellion against the universe, a palpable absurdity."

In the back row Stettenhover slumped suddenly in his seat, his heels 101 held out before him, making a loud, dry, disgusted sound. His body sank until his neck rested on the back of his chair. He folded his hands across his belly and looked significantly out of the window, exasperated not only with Tertan, but with Howe, with the class, with the whole system designed to encourage this kind of thing. There was a certain insolence in the movement and Howe flushed. As Tertan continued to speak, Howe stalked casually toward the window and placed himself in the line of Stettenhover's vision. He stared at the great fellow, who pretended not to see him. There was so much power in the big body, so much contempt in the Greek-athlete face under the crisp Greek-athlete curls, that Howe felt almost physical fear. But at last Stettenhover admitted him to focus and under his disapproving gaze sat up with slow indifference. His eyebrows raised high in resignation, he began to examine his hands. Howe relaxed and turned his attention back to Tertan.

"Flux of existence," Tertan was saying, "produces all things, so that 102 judgment wavers. Beyond the phenomena, what? But phenomena are adumbrated and to them we are limited."

Howe saw it for a moment as perhaps it existed in the boy's mind — 103 the world of shadows which are cast by a great light upon a hidden reality as in the old myth of the Cave. But the little brush with Stettenhover had tired him, and he said irritably, "But come to the point, Mr. Tertan."

He said it so sharply that some of the class looked at him curiously. For 104 three months he had gently carried Tertan through his verbosities, to the vaguely respectful surprise of the other students, who seemed to conceive that there existed between this strange classmate and their teacher some special understanding from which they were content to be excluded. Tertan looked at him mildly, and at once came brilliantly to the point. "This is the summation of the play," he said and took up his book and read, " 'Your poor father never found any outlet for the overmastering joy of life that was in him. And I brought no holiday into his home, either. Everything seemed to turn upon duty and I am afraid I made your poor father's home unbearable to him, Oswald.' Spoken by Mrs. Alving."

Yes that was surely the "summation" of the play and Tertan had hit it, 105 as he hit, deviously and eventually, the literary point of almost everything. But now, as always, he was wrapping it away from sight. "For most mortals," he said, "there are only joys of biological urgings, gross and crass, such as the sensuous Captain Alving. For certain few there are the transmutations beyond these to a contemplation of the utter whole."

Oh, the boy was mad. And suddenly the word, used in hyperbole, in-   106
tended almost for the expression of exasperated admiration, became literal. Now that the word was used, it became simply apparent to Howe that Tertan was mad.

It was a monstrous word and stood like a bestial thing in the room. Yet   107
it so completely comprehended everything that had puzzled Howe, it so arranged and explained what for three months had been perplexing him that almost at once its horror became domesticated. With this word Howe was able to understand why he had never been able to communicate to Tertan the value of a single criticism or correction of his wild, verbose themes. Their conferences had been frequent and long but had done nothing to reduce to order the splendid confusion of the boy's ideas. Yet, impossible though its expression was, Tertan's incandescent mind could always strike for a moment into some dark corner of thought.

And now it was suddenly apparent that it was not a faulty rhetoric that   108
Howe had to contend with. With his new knowledge he looked at Tertan's face and wondered how he could have so long deceived himself. Tertan was still talking, and the class had lapsed into a kind of patient unconsciousness, a coma of respect for words which, for all that most of them knew, might be profound. Almost with a suffusion of shame, Howe believed that in some dim way the class had long ago had some intimation of Tertan's madness. He reached out as decisively as he could to seize the thread of Tertan's discourse before it should be entangled further.

"Mr. Tertan says that the blame must be put upon whoever kills the   109
joy of living in another. We have been assuming that Captain Alving was a wholly bad man, but what if we assume that he became bad only because Mrs. Alving, when they were first married, acted toward him in the prudish way she says she did?"

It was a ticklish idea to advance to freshmen and perhaps not profit-   110
able. Not all of them were following.

"That would put the blame on Mrs. Alving herself, whom most of you   111
admire. And she herself seems to think so." He glanced at his watch. The hour was nearly over. "What do you think, Mr. De Witt?"

De Witt rose to the idea; he wanted to know if society couldn't be   112
blamed for educating Mrs. Alving's temperament in the wrong way. Casebeer was puzzled, Stettenhover continued to look at his hands until the bell rang.

Tertan, his brows louring in thought, was making as always for a pri-   113
vate word. Howe gathered his books and papers to leave quickly. At this moment of his discovery and with the knowledge still raw, he could not

engage himself with Tertan. Tertan sucked in his breath to prepare for speech and Howe made ready for the pain and confusion. But at that moment Casebeer detached himself from the group with which he had been conferring and which he seemed to represent. His constituency remained at a tactful distance. The mission involved the time of an assigned essay. Casebeer's presentation of the plea — it was based on the freshmen's heavy duties at the fraternities during Carnival Week — cut across Tertan's preparations for speech. "And so some of us fellows thought," Casebeer concluded with heavy solemnity, "that we could do a better job, give our minds to it more, if we had more time."

Tertan regarded Casebeer with mingled curiosity and revulsion. Howe   114
not only said that he would postpone the assignment but went on to talk about the Carnival, and even drew the waiting constituency into the conversation. He was conscious of Tertan's stern and astonished stare, then of his sudden departure.

Now that the fact was clear, Howe knew that he must act on it. His   115
course was simple enough. He must lay the case before the Dean. Yet he hesitated. His feeling for Tertan must now, certainly, be in some way invalidated. Yet could he, because of a word, hurry to assign to official and reasonable solicitude what had been, until this moment, so various and warm? He could at least delay and, by moving slowly, lend a poor grace to the necessary, ugly act of making his report.

It was with some notion of keeping the matter in his own hands that he   116
went to the Dean's office to look up Tertan's records. In the outer office the Dean's secretary greeted him brightly, and at his request brought him the manila folder with the small identifying photograph pasted in the corner. She laughed. "He was looking for the birdie in the wrong place," she said.

Howe leaned over her shoulder to look at the picture. It was as bad as   117
all the Dean's office photographs were, but it differed from all that Howe had ever seen. Tertan, instead of looking into the camera, as no doubt he had been bidden, had, at the moment of exposure, turned his eyes upward. His mouth, as though conscious of the trick played on the photographer, had the sly superior look that Howe knew.

The secretary was fascinated by the picture. "What a funny boy," she   118
said. "He looks like Tartuffe!"

And so he did, with the absurd piety of the eyes and the conscious   119
slyness of the mouth and the whole face bloated by the bad lens.

"Is he *like* that?" the secretary said.   120

"Like Tartuffe? No."   121

From the photograph there was little enough comfort to be had. The   122
records themselves gave no clue to madness, though they suggested sadness enough. Howe read of a father, Stanislaus Tertan, born in Budapest and trained in engineering in Berlin, once employed by the Hercules Chemical

Corporation — this was one of the factories that dominated the sound end of the town — but now without employment. He read of a mother Erminie (Youngfellow) Tertan, born in Manchester, educated at a Normal School at Leeds, now housewife by profession. The family lived on Greenbriar Street which Howe knew as a row of once elegant homes near what was now the factory district. The old mansion had long ago been divided into small and primitive apartments. Of Ferdinand himself there was little to learn. He lived with his parents, had attended a Detroit high school and had transferred to the local school in his last year. His rating for intelligence, as expressed in numbers, was high, his scholastic record was remarkable, he held a college scholarship for his tuition.

Howe laid the folder on the secretary's desk. "Did you find what you wanted to know?" she asked. 123

The phrases from Tertan's momentous first theme came back to him. "Tertan I am, but what is Tertan? Of this time, of that place, of some parentage, what does it matter?" 124

"No, I didn't find it," he said. 125

Now that he had consulted the sad, half-meaningless record he knew all the more firmly that he must not give the matter out of his own hands. He must not release Tertan to authority. Not that he anticipated from the Dean anything but the greatest kindness for Tertan. The Dean would have the experience and skill which he himself could not have. One way or another the Dean could answer the question, "What is Tertan?" Yet this was precisely what he feared. He alone could keep alive — not forever but for a somehow important time — the question, "What is Tertan?" He alone could keep it still a question. Some sure instinct told him that he must not surrender the question to a clean official desk in a clear official light to be dealt with, settled and closed. 126

He heard himself saying, "Is the Dean busy at the moment? I'd like to see him." 127

His request came thus unbidden, even forbidden, and it was one of the surprising and startling incidents of his life. Later when he reviewed the events, so disconnected in themselves, or so merely odd, of the story that unfolded for him that year, it was over this moment, on its face the least notable, that he paused longest. It was frequently to be with fear and never without a certainty of its meaning in his own knowledge of himself that he would recall this simple, routine request, and the feeling of shame and freedom it gave him as he sent everything down the official chute. In the end, of course, no matter what he did to "protect" Tertan, he would have had to make the same request and lay the matter on the Dean's clean desk. But it would always be a landmark of his life that, at the very moment when he was rejecting the official way, he had been, without will or intention, so gladly drawn to it. 128

After the storm's last delicate flurry, the sun had come out. Reflected   129
by the new snow, it filled the office with a golden light which was almost
musical in the way it made all the commonplace objects of efficiency shine
with a sudden sad and noble significance. And the light, now that he noticed
it, made the utterance of his perverse and unwanted request even more
momentous.

The secretary consulted the engagement pad. "He'll be free any min-   130
ute. Don't you want to wait in the parlor?"

She threw open the door of the large and pleasant room in which the   131
Dean held his Committee meetings, and in which his visitors waited. It was
designed with a homely elegance on the masculine side of the eighteenth-
century manner. There was a small coal fire in the grate and the handsome
mahogany table was strewn with books and magazines. The large windows
gave on the snowy lawn, and there was such a fine width of window that the
white casements and walls seemed at this moment but a continuation of the
snow, the snow but an extension of casement and walls. The outdoors
seemed taken in and made safe, the indoors seemed luxuriously freshened
and expanded.

Howe sat down by the fire and lighted a cigarette. The room had its in-   132
tended effect upon him. He felt comfortable and relaxed, yet nicely organized, some young diplomatic agent of the eighteenth century, the newly
fledged Swift carrying out Sir William Temple's business. The rawness of
Tertan's case quite vanished. He crossed his legs and reached for a
magazine.

It was that famous issue of *Life and Letters* that his idle hand had found   133
and his blood raced as he sifted through it, and the shape of his own name,
Joseph Howe, sprang out at him, still cabalistic in its power. He tossed the
magazine back on the table as the door of the Dean's office opened and the
Dean ushered out Theodore Blackburn.

"Ah, Joseph!" the Dean said.   134

Blackburn said. "Good morning, Doctor." Howe winced at the title   135
and caught the flicker of amusement over the Dean's face. The Dean stood
with his hand high on the door-jamb and Blackburn, still in the doorway,
remained standing almost under the long arm.

Howe nodded briefly to Blackburn, snubbing his eager deference.   136
"Can you give me a few minutes?" he said to the Dean.

"All the time you want. Come in." Before the two men could enter the   137
office, Blackburn claimed their attention with a long full "er." As they turned
to him, Blackburn said, "Can *you* give *me* a few minutes, Doctor Howe?"
His eyes sparkled at the little audacity he had committed, the slightly im-
pudent play with hierarchy. Of the three of them Blackburn kept himself the
lowest, but he reminded Howe of his subaltern relation to the Dean..

"I mean, of course," Blackburn went on easily, "when you've finished   138
with the Dean."

"I'll be in my office shortly," Howe said, turned his back on the ready   139
"Thank you, sir," and followed the Dean into the inner room.

"Energetic boy," said the Dean. "A bit beyond himself but very ener-   140
getic. Sit down."

The Dean lighted a cigarette, leaned back in his chair, sat easy and   141
silent for a moment, giving Howe no signal to go ahead with business. He
was a young Dean, not much beyond forty, a tall handsome man with sad,
ambitious eyes. He had been a Rhodes scholar. His friends looked for great
things from him, and it was generally said that he had notions of education
which he was not yet ready to try to put into practice.

His relaxed silence was meant as a compliment to Howe. He smiled   142
and said, "What's the business, Joseph?"

"Do you know Tertan — Ferdinand Tertan, a freshman?"   143

The Dean's cigarette was in his mouth and his hands were clasped   144
behind his head. He did not seem to search his memory for the name. He
said, "What about him?"

Clearly the Dean knew something, and he was waiting for Howe to tell   145
him more. Howe moved only tentatively. Now that he was doing what he
had resolved not to do, he felt more guilty at having been so long deceived
by Tertan and more need to be loyal to his error.

"He's a strange fellow," he ventured. He said stubbornly, "In a strange   146
way he's very brilliant." He concluded, "But very strange."

The springs of the Dean's swivel chair creaked as he came out of his   147
sprawl and leaned forward to Howe. "Do you mean he's so strange that it's
something you could give a name to?"

Howe looked at him stupidly. "What do you mean?" he said.   148

"What's his trouble?" the Dean said more neutrally.   149

"He's very brilliant, in a way. I looked him up and he has a top in-   150
telligence rating. But somehow, and it's hard to explain just how, what he
says is always on the edge of sense and doesn't quite make it."

The Dean looked at him and Howe flushed up. The Dean had surely   151
read Woolley on the subject of "the Howes" and the *tour d'ivresse*. Was that
quick glance ironical?

The Dean picked up some papers from his desk, and Howe could see   152
that they were in Tertan's impatient scrawl. Perhaps the little gleam in the
Dean's glance had come only from putting facts together.

"He sent me this yesterday," the Dean said. "After an interview I had   153
with him. I haven't been able to do more than glance at it. When you said
what you did, I realized there was something wrong."

Twisting his mouth, the Dean looked over the letter. "You seem to be   154 involved," he said without looking up. "By the way, what did you give him at mid-term?"

Flushing, setting his shoulders, Howe said firmly, "I gave him A-minus."   155

The Dean chuckled. "Might be a good idea if some of our nicer boys   156 went crazy — just a little." He said, "Well," to conclude the matter and handed the papers to Howe. "See if this is the same thing you've been finding. Then we can go into the matter again."

Before the fire in the parlor, in the chair that Howe had been occupy-   157 ing, sat Blackburn. He sprang to his feet as Howe entered.

"I said my office, Mr. Blackburn." Howe's voice was sharp. Then he   158 was almost sorry for the rebuke, so clearly and naively did Blackburn seem to relish his stay in the parlor, close to authority.

"I'm in a bit of a hurry, sir," he said, "and I did want to be sure to   159 speak to you, sir."

He was really absurd, yet fifteen years from now he would have grown   160 up to himself, to the assurance and mature beefiness. In banks, in consular offices, in brokerage firms, on the bench, more seriously affable, a little sterner, he would make use of his ability to be administered by his job. It was almost reassuring. Now he was exercising his too-great skill on Howe. "I owe you an apology, sir," he said.

Howe knew that he did, but he showed surprise.   161

"I mean, Doctor, after your having been so kind about letting me at-   162 tend your class, I stopped coming." He smiled in deprecation. "Extracurricular activities take up so much of my time. I'm afraid I undertook more than I could perform."

Howe had noticed the absence and had been a little irritated by it after   163 Blackburn's elaborate plea. It was an absence that might be interpreted as a comment on the teacher. But there was only one way for him to answer. "You've no need to apologize," he said. "It's wholly your affair."

Blackburn beamed. "I'm so glad you feel that way about it, sir. I was   164 worried you might think I had stayed away because I was influenced by — " he stopped and lowered his eyes.

Astonished, Howe said, "Influenced by what?"   165

"Well, by — " Blackburn hesitated and for answer pointed to the table   166 on which lay the copy of *Life and Letters*. Without looking at it, he knew where to direct his hand. "By the unfavorable publicity, sir." He hurried on. "And that brings me to another point, sir. I am secretary of Quill and Scroll, sir, the student literary society, and I wonder if you would address us. You could read your own poetry, sir, and defend your own point of view. It would be very interesting."

It was truly amazing. Howe looked long and cruelly into Blackburn's   167 face, trying to catch the secret of the mind that could have conceived this way of manipulating him, this way so daring and inept — but not entirely inept — with its malice so without malignity. The face did not yield its secret. Howe smiled broadly and said, "Of course I don't think you were influenced by the unfavorable publicity."

"I'm still going to take — regularly, for credit — your romantic poets course next term," Blackburn said. 168

"Don't worry, my dear fellow, don't worry about it." 169

Howe started to leave and Blackburn stopped him with, "But about Quill, sir?" 170

"Suppose we wait until next term? I'll be less busy then." 171

And Blackburn said, "Very good, sir, and thank you." 172

In his office the little encounter seemed less funny to Howe, was even in some indeterminate way disturbing. He made an effort to put it from his mind by turning to what was sure to disturb him more, the Tertan letter read in the new interpretation. He found what he had always found, the same florid leaps beyond fact and meaning, the same headlong certainty. But as his eye passed over the familiar scrawl it caught his own name, and for the second time that hour he felt the race of his blood. 173

"The Paraclete," Tertan had written to the Dean, "from a Greek word meaning to stand in place of, but going beyond the primitive idea to mean traditionally the helper, the one who comforts and assists, cannot without fundamental loss be jettisoned. Even if taken no longer in the supernatural sense, the concept remains deeply in the human consciousness inevitably. Humanitarianism is no reply, for not every man stands in the place of every other man for this other comrade's comfort. But certain are chosen out of the human race to be the consoler of some other. Of these, for example, is Joseph Barker Howe, Ph.D. Of intellects not the first yet of true intellect and lambent instructions, given to that which is intuitive and irrational, not to what is logical in the strict word, what is judged by him is of the heart and not the head. Here is one chosen, in that he chooses himself to stand in the place of another for comfort and consolation. To him more than another I give my gratitude, with all respect to our Dean who reads this, a noble man, but merely dedicated, not consecrated. But not in the aspect of the Paraclete only is Dr. Joseph Barker Howe established, for he must be the Paraclete to another aspect of himself, that which is driven and persecuted by the lack of understanding in the world at large, so that he in himself embodies the full history of man's tribulations and, overflowing upon others, notably the present writer, is the ultimate end." 174

This was love. There was no escape from it. Try as Howe might to remember that Tertan was mad and all his emotions invalidated, he could not destroy the effect upon him of his student's stern, affectionate regard. He had betrayed not only a power of mind but a power of love. And, however firmly he held before his attention the fact of Tertan's madness, 175 he could do nothing to banish the physical sensation of gratitude he felt. He had never thought of himself as "driven and persecuted" and he did not now. But still he could not make meaningless his sensation of gratitude. The pitiable Tertan sternly pitied him, and comfort came from Tertan's never-to-be-comforted mind.

III

In an academic community, even an efficient one, official matters move   176
slowly. The term drew to a close with no action in the case of Tertan, and Joseph Howe had to confront a curious problem. How should he grade his strange student, Tertan?

Tertan's final examination had been no different from all his other writ-   177
ing, and what did one "give" such a student? De Witt must have his A, that was clear. Johnson would get a B. With Casebeer it was a question of a B-minus or a C-plus, and Stettenhover, who had been crammed by the team tutor to fill half a blue-book with his thin feminine scrawl, would have his C-minus which he would accept with mingled indifference and resentment. But with Tertan it was not so easy.

The boy was still in the college process and his name could not be   178
omitted from the grade sheet. Yet what should a mind under suspicion of madness be graded? Until the medical verdict was given, it was for Howe to continue as Tertan's teacher and to keep his judgment pedagogical. Impossible to give him an F: he had not failed. B was for Johnson's stolid mediocrity. He could not be put on the edge of passing with Stettenhover, for he exactly did not pass. In energy and richness of intellect he was perhaps even De Witt's superior, and Howe toyed grimly with the notion of giving him an A, but that would lower the value of the A De Witt had won with his beautiful and clear, if still arrogant, mind. There was a notation which the Registrar recognized — Inc., for Incomplete, and in the horrible comedy of the situation, Howe considered that. But really only a mark of M for Mad would serve.

In his perplexity, Howe sought the Dean, but the Dean was out of   179
town. In the end, he decided to maintain the A-minus he had given Tertan at mid-term. After all, there had been no falling away from that quality. He entered it on the grade sheet with something like bravado.

Academic time moves quickly. A college year is not really a year, lack-   180
ing as it does three months. And it is endlessly divided into units which, at their beginning, appear larger than they are — terms, half-terms, months, weeks. And the ultimate unit, the hour, is not really an hour, lacking as it does ten minutes. And so the new term advanced rapidly, and one day the fields about the town were all brown, cleared of even the few thin patches of snow which had lingered so long.

Howe, as he lectured on the romantic poets, became conscious of   181

Blackburn emanating wrath. Blackburn did it well, did it with enormous dignity. He did not stir in his seat, he kept his eyes fixed on Howe in perfect attention, but he abstained from using his notebook, there was no mistaking what he proposed to himself as an attitude. His elbow on the writing-wing of the chair, his chin on the curled fingers of his hand, he was the embodiment of intellectual indignation. He was thinking his own thoughts, would give no public offense, yet would claim his due, was not to be intimidated. Howe knew that he would present himself at the end of the hour.

Blackburn entered the office without invitation. He did not smile; there was no cajolery about him. Without invitation he sat down beside Howe's desk. He did not speak until he had taken the blue-book from his pocket. He said, "What does this mean, sir?" 182

It was a sound and conservative student tactic. Said in the usual way it meant. "How could you have so misunderstood me?" or "What does this mean for my future in the course?" But there were none of the humbler tones in Blackburn's way of saying it. 183

Howe made the established reply, "I think that's for you to tell me." 184

Blackburn continued icy. "I'm sure I can't, sir." 185

There was a silence between them. Both dropped their eyes to the blue-book on the desk. On its cover Howe had penciled: "F. This is very poor work." 186

Howe picked up the blue-book. There was always the possibility of injustice. The teacher may be bored by the mass of papers and not wholly attentive. A phrase, even the student's handwriting, may irritate him unreasonably. "Well," said Howe. "Let's go through it." 187

He opened the first page. "Now here: you write, 'In *The Ancient Mariner,* Coleridge lives in and transports us to a honey-sweet world where all is rich and strange, a world of charm to which we can escape from the humdrum existence of our daily lives, the world of romance. Here, in this warm and honey-sweet land of charming dreams we can relax and enjoy ourselves.' " 188

Howe lowered the paper and waited with a neutral look for Blackburn to speak. Blackburn returned the look boldly, did not speak, sat stolid and lofty. At last Howe said, speaking gently, "Did you mean that, or were you just at a loss for something to say?" 189

"You imply that I was just 'bluffing'?" The quotation marks hung palpable in the air about the word. 190

"I'd like to know. I'd prefer believing that you were bluffing to believing that you really thought this." 191

Blackburn's eyebrows went up. From the height of a great and firm-based idea he looked at his teacher. He clasped the crags for a moment and then pounced, craftily suavely. "Do you mean, Doctor Howe, that there aren't two opinions possible?" 192

It was superbly done in its air of putting all of Howe's intellectual life 193 into the balance. Howe remained patient and simple. "Yes, many opinions are possible, but not this one. Whatever anyone believes of *The Ancient Mariner*, no one can in reason believe that it represents a — a honey-sweet world in which we can relax."

"But that is what I *feel*, sir."   194

This was well-done, too. Howe said, "Look, Mr. Blackburn. Do you   195 really relax with hunger and thirst, the heat and the sea-serpents, the dead men with staring eyes, Life in Death and the skeletons? Come now, Mr. Blackburn."

Blackburn made no answer, and Howe pressed forward. "Now, you say   196 of Wordsworth, 'Of peasant stock himself, he turned from the effete life of the salons and found in the peasant the hope of a flaming revolution which would sweep away all the old ideas. This is the subject of his best poems.' "

Beaming at his teacher with youthful eagerness, Blackburn said, "Yes,   197 sir, a rebel, a bringer of light to suffering mankind. I see him as a kind of Prothemeus."

"A kind of what?"   198

"Prothemeus, sir."   199

"Think, Mr. Blackburn. We were talking about him only today and I   200 mentioned his name a dozen times. You don't mean Prothemeus. You mean — " Howe waited, but there was no response.

"You mean Prometheus."   201

Blackburn gave no assent, and Howe took the reins. "You've done a   202 bad job here, Mr. Blackburn, about as bad as could be done." He saw Blackburn stiffen and his genial face harden again. "It shows either a lack of preparation or a complete lack of understanding." He saw Blackburn's face begin to go to pieces and he stopped.

"Oh, sir," Blackburn burst out, "I've never had a mark like this before,   203 never anything below a B, never. A thing like this has never happened to me before."

It must be true, it was a statement too easily verified. Could it be that   204 other instructors accepted such flaunting nonsense? Howe wanted to end the interview. "I'll set it down to lack of preparation," he said. "I know you're busy. That's not an excuse, but it's an explanation. Now, suppose you really prepare, and then take another quiz in two weeks. We'll forget this one and count the other."

Blackburn squirmed with pleasure and gratitude. "Thank you, sir.   205 You're really very kind, very kind."

Howe rose to conclude the visit. "All right, then — in two weeks."   206

It was that day that the Dean imparted to Howe the conclusion of the   207 case of Tertan. It was simple and a little anti-climactic. A physician had been called in, and had said the word, given the name.

"A classic case, he called it," the Dean said. "Not a doubt in the   208 world," he said. His eyes were full of miserable pity, and he clutched at a word. "A classic case, a classic case." To his aid and to Howe's there came the Parthenon and the form of the Greek drama, the Aristotelian logic, Racine and the Well-Tempered Clavichord, the blueness of the Aegean and its clear sky. Classic — that is to say, without a doubt, perfect in its way, a veritable model, and, as the Dean had been told, sure to take a perfectly predictable and inevitable course to a foreknown conclusion.

It was not only pity that stood in the Dean's eyes. For a moment there was fear too. "Terrible," he said, "it is simply terrible." 209

Then he went on briskly. "Naturally, we've told the boy nothing. And, naturally, we won't. His tuition's paid by his scholarship, and we'll continue him on the rolls until the end of the year. That will be the kindest. After that the matter will be out of our control. We'll see, of course, that he gets into the proper hands. I'm told there will be no change, he'll go on like this, be as good as this, for four to six months. And so we'll just go along as usual." 210

So Tertan continued to sit in Section 5 of English 1A, to his classmates still a figure of curiously dignified fun, symbol to most of them of the respectable but absurd intellectual life. But to his teacher he was now very different. He had not changed — he was still the greyhound casting for the scent of ideas, and Howe could see that he was still the same Tertan, but he could not feel it. What he felt as he looked at the boy sitting in his accustomed place was the hard blank of a fact. The fact itself was formidable and depressing. But what Howe was chiefly aware of was that he had permitted the metamorphosis of Tertan from person to fact. 211

As much as possible he avoided seeing Tertan's upraised hand and eager eye. But the fact did not know of its mere factuality, it continued its existence as if it were Tertan, hand up and eye questioning, and one day it appeared in Howe's office with a document. 212

"Even the spirit who lives egregiously, above the herd, must have its relations with the fellowman," Tertan declared. He laid the document on Howe's desk. It was headed "Quill and Scroll Society of Dwight College. Application for Membership." 213

"In most ways these are crass minds," Tertan said, touching the paper. "Yet as a whole, bound together in their common love of letters, they transcend their intellectual lacks since it is not a paradox that the whole is greater than the sum of its parts." 214

"When are the elections?" Howe asked. 215

"They take place tomorrow." 216

"I certainly hope you will be successful." 217

"Thank you. Would you wish to implement that hope?" A rather dirty finger pointed to the bottom of the sheet. "A faculty recommender is necessary," Tertan said stiffly, and waited. 218

"And you wish me to recommend you?" 219

"It would be an honor."   220

"You may use my name."   221

Tertan's finger pointed again. "It must be a written sponsorship, signed   222
by the sponsor." There was a large blank space on the form under the heading, "Opinion of Faculty Sponsor."

This was almost another thing and Howe hesitated. Yet there was   223
nothing else to do and he took out his fountain pen. He wrote, "Mr. Ferdinand Tertan is marked by his intense devotion to letters and by his excep-
tional love of all things of the mind." To this he signed his name, which
looked bold and assertive on the white page. It disturbed him, the strange
affirming power of a name. With a businesslike air, Tertan whipped up the
paper, folding it with decision, and put it into his pocket. He bowed and
took his departure, leaving Howe with the sense of having done something
oddly momentous.

And so much now seemed odd and momentous to Howe that should   224
not have seemed so. It was odd and momentous, he felt, when he sat with
Blackburn's second quiz before him, and wrote in an excessively firm hand
the grade of C-minus. The paper was a clear, an indisputable failure. He was
carefully and consciously committing a cowardice. Blackburn had told the
truth when he had pleaded his past record. Howe had consulted it in the
Dean's office. It showed no grade lower than a B-minus. A canvass of some
of Blackburn's previous instructors had brought vague attestations to the adequate powers of a student imperfectly remembered, and sometimes surprise
that his abilities could be questioned at all.

As he wrote the grade, Howe told himself that his cowardice sprang   225
from an unwillingness to have more dealings with a student he disliked. He
knew it was simpler than that. He knew he feared Blackburn; that was the
absurd truth. And cowardice did not solve the matter after all. Blackburn,
flushed with a first success, attacked at once. The minimal passing grade had
not assuaged his feelings and he sat at Howe's desk and again the blue-book
lay between them. Blackburn said nothing. With an enormous impudence,
he was waiting for Howe to speak and explain himself.

At last Howe said sharply and rudely, "Well?" His throat was tense and   226
the blood was hammering in his head. His mouth was tight with anger at
himself for his disturbance.

Blackburn's glance was almost baleful. "This is impossible, sir."   227

"But there it is," Howe answered.   228

"Sir?" Blackburn had not caught the meaning but his tone was still   229
haughty.

Impatiently Howe said, "There it is, plain as day. Are you here to   230
complain again?"

"Indeed I am, sir." There was surprise in Blackburn's voice that Howe   231
should ask the question.

"I shouldn't complain if I were you. You did a thoroughly bad job on   232
your first quiz. This one is a little, only a very little, better." This was not
true. If anything, it was worse.

"That might be a matter of opinion, sir."   233

"It is a matter of opinion. Of my opinion."   234

"Another opinion might be different, sir."   235

"You really believe that?" Howe said.   236

"Yes." The omission of the "sir" was monumental.   237

"Whose, for example?"   238

"The Dean's, for example." Then the fleshy jaw came forward a little.   239
"Or a certain literary critic's, for example."

It was colossal and almost too much for Blackburn himself to handle.   240
The solidity of his face almost crumpled under it. But he withstood his own
audacity and went on. "And the Dean's opinion might be guided by the
knowledge that the person who gave me this mark is the man whom a
famous critic, the most eminent judge of literature in this country, called a
drunken man. The Dean might think twice about whether such a man is fit
to teach Dwight students."

Howe said in quiet admonition, "Blackburn, you're mad," meaning no   241
more than to check the boy's extravagance.

But Blackburn paid no heed. He had another shot in the locker. "And   242
the Dean might be guided by the information, of which I have evidence,
documentary evidence," — he slapped his breast pocket twice — "that this
same person personally recommended to the college literary society, the oldest in the country, that he personally recommended a student who is crazy,
who threw the meeting into an uproar — a psychiatric case. The Dean might
take that into account."

Howe was never to learn the details of that "uproar." He had always to   243
content himself with the dim but passionate picture which at that moment
sprang into his mind, of Tertan standing on some abstract height and madly
denouncing the multitude of Quill and Scroll who howled him down.

He sat quiet a moment and looked at Blackburn. The ferocity had en-   244
tirely gone from the student's face. He sat regarding his teacher almost be-
nevolently. He had played a good card and now, scarcely at all unfriendly,
he was waiting to see the effect. Howe took up the blue-book and negligently sifted through it. He read a page, closed the book, struck out the
C-minus and wrote an F.

"Now you may take the paper to the Dean," he said. "You may tell him   245
that after reconsidering it, I lowered the grade."

The gasp was audible. "Oh, sir!" Blackburn cried. "Please!" His face   246
was agonized. "It means my graduation, my livelihood, my future. Don't do
this to me."

"It's done already."   247

Blackburn stood up. "I spoke rashly, sir, hastily. I had no intention, no   248
real intention, of seeing the Dean. It rests with you — entirely, entirely. I
hope you will restore the first mark."

"Take the matter to the Dean or not, just as you choose. The grade is   249
what you deserve and it stands."

Blackburn's head dropped. "And will I be failed at mid-term, sir?"   250
"Of course."   251

From deep out of Blackburn's great chest rose a cry of anguish. "Oh,   252
sir, if you want me to go down on my knees to you, I will, I will."

Howe looked at him in amazement.   253

"I will, I will. On my knees, sir. This mustn't, mustn't happen."   254

He spoke so literally, meaning so very truly that his knees and exactly   255
his knees were involved and seeming to think that he was offering something
of tangible value to his teacher, that Howe, whose head had become icy
clear in the nonsensical drama, thought, "The boy is mad," and began to
speculate fantastically whether something in himself attracted or developed
aberration. He could see himself standing absurdly before the Dean and saying, "I've found another. This time it's the vice-president of the Council, the
manager of the debating team and secretary of Quill and Scroll."

One more such discovery, he thought, and he himself would be discov-   256
ered! And there, suddenly, Blackburn was on his knees with a thump, his
huge thighs straining his trousers, his hand outstretched in a great gesture of
supplication.

With a cry, Howe shoved back his swivel chair and it rolled away on its   257
casters half across the little room. Blackburn knelt for a moment to nothing
at all, then got to his feet.

Howe rose abruptly. He said, "Blackburn, you will stop acting like an   258
idiot. Dust your knees off, take your paper and get out. You've behaved like
a fool and a malicious person. You have half a term to do a decent job. Keep
your silly mouth shut and try to do it. Now get out."

Blackburn's head was low. He raised it and there was a pious light in   259
his eyes. "Will you shake hands, sir?" he said. He thrust out his hand.

"I will not," Howe said.   260

Head and hand sank together. Blackburn picked up his blue-book and   261
walked to the door. He turned and said, "Thank you, sir." His back, as he
departed, was heavy with tragedy and stateliness.

IV

After years of bad luck with the weather, the College had a perfect day for   262
Commencement. It was wonderfully bright, the air so transparent, the wind
so brisk that no one could resist talking about it.

As Howe set out for the campus he heard Hilda calling from the back   263
yard. She called, "Professor, professor," and came running to him.

Howe said, "What's this 'professor' business?"   264

"Mother told me," Hilda said. "You've been promoted. And I want to   265
take your picture."

"Next year," said Howe. "I won't be a professor until next year. And   266
you know better than to call anybody 'professor.'"

"It was just in fun," Hilda said. She seemed disappointed.   267

"But you can take my picture if you want. I won't look much different   268
next year." Still, it was frightening. It might mean that he was to stay in this
town all his life.

Hilda brightened. "Can I take it in this?" she said, and touched the   269
gown he carried over his arm.

Howe laughed. "Yes, you can take it in this."   270

"I'll get my things and meet you in front of Otis," Hilda said. "I have   271
the background all picked out."

On the campus the Commencement crowd was already large. It stood   272
about in eager, nervous little family groups. As he crossed, Howe was
greeted by a student, capped and gowned, glad of the chance to make an
event for his parents by introducing one of his teachers. It was while Howe
stood there chatting that he saw Tertan.

He had never seen anyone quite so alone, as though a circle had been   273
woven about him to separate him from the gay crowd on the campus. Not
that Tertan was not gay, he was the gayest of all. Three weeks had passed
since Howe had last seen him, the weeks of examination, the lazy week
before Commencement, and this was now a different Tertan. On his head he
wore a panama hat, broad-brimmed and fine, of the shape associated with
South American planters. He wore a suit of raw silk, luxurious, but yellowed
with age and much too tight, and he sported a whangee cane. He walked
sedately, the hat tilted at a devastating angle, the stick coming up and down
in time to his measured tread. He had, Howe guessed, outfitted himself to
greet the day in the clothes of that ruined father whose existence was on
record in the Dean's office. Gravely and arrogantly he surveyed the scene —
in it, his whole bearing seemed to say, but not of it. With haughty step,
with his flashing eye, Tertan was coming nearer. Howe did not wish to be
seen. He shifted his position slightly. When he looked again, Tertan was not
in sight.

The chapel clock struck the quarter hour. Howe detached himself from   274
his chat and hurried to Otis Hall at the far end of the campus. Hilda had not
yet come. He went up into the high portico and, using the glass of the door
for a mirror, put on his gown, adjusted the hood on his shoulders and set the
mortarboard on his head. When he came down the steps, Hilda had arrived.

Nothing could have told him more forcibly that a year had passed than   275
the development of Hilda's photographic possessions from the box camera of
the previous fall. By a strap about her neck was hung a leather case, so thick
and strong, so carefully stitched and so molded to its contents that it could

only hold a costly camera. The appearance was deceptive, Howe knew, for he had been present at the Aikens' pre-Christmas conference about its purchase. It was only a fairly good domestic camera. Still, it looked very impressive. Hilda carried another leather case from which she drew a collapsible tripod. Decisively she extended each of its gleaming legs and set it up on the path. She removed the camera from its case and fixed it to the tripod. In its compact efficiency the camera almost had a life of its own, but Hilda treated it with easy familiarity, looked into its eye, glanced casually at its gauges. Then from a pocket she took still another leather case and drew from it a small instrument through which she looked first at Howe, who began to feel inanimate and lost, and then at the sky. She made some adjustment on the instrument, then some adjustment on the camera. She swept the scene with her eye, found a spot and pointed the camera in its direction. She walked to the spot, stood on it and beckoned to Howe. With each new leather case, with each new instrument, and with each new adjustment she had grown in ease and now she said, "Joe, will you stand here?"

Obediently Howe stood where he was bidden. She had yet another instrument. She took out a tape-measure on a mechanical spool. Kneeling down before Howe, she put the little metal ring of the tape under the tip of his shoe. At her request, Howe pressed it with his toe. When she had measured her distance, she nodded to Howe who released the tape. At a touch, it sprang back into the spool. "You have to be careful if you're going to get what you want," Hilda said. "I don't believe in all this snap-snap-snapping," she remarked loftily. Howe nodded in agreement, although he was beginning to think Hilda's care excessive.

Now at last the moment had come. Hilda squinted into the camera, moved the tripod slightly. She stood to the side, holding the plunger of the shutter-cable. "Ready," she said. "Will you relax, Joseph, please?" Howe realized that he was standing frozen. Hilda stood poised and precise as a setter, one hand holding the little cable, the other extended with curled dainty fingers like a dancer's, as if expressing to her subject the precarious delicacy of the moment. She pressed the plunger and there was the click. At once she stirred to action, got behind the camera, turned a new exposure. "Thank you," she said. "Would you stand under that tree and let me do a character study with light and shade?"

The childish absurdity of the remark restored Howe's ease. He went to the little tree. The pattern the leaves made on his gown was what Hilda was after. He had just taken a satisfactory position when he heard in the unmistakable voice. "Ah, Doctor! Having your picture taken?"

Howe gave up the pose and turned to Blackburn who stood on the walk, his hands behind his back, a little too large for his bachelor's gown. Annoyed that Blackburn should see him posing for a character study in light and shade, Howe said irritably, "Yes, having my picture taken."

Blackburn beamed at Hilda. "And the little photographer?" he said. 280 Hilda fixed her eyes on the ground and stood closer to her brilliant and aggressive camera. Blackburn, teetering on his heels, his hands behind his back, wholly prelatical and benignly patient, was not abashed at the silence. At last Howe said, "If you'll excuse us, Mr. Blackburn, we'll go on with the picture."

"Go right ahead, sir. I'm running along." But he only came closer. 281 "Doctor Howe," he said fervently, "I want to tell you how glad I am that I was able to satisfy your standards at last."

Howe was surprised at the hard, insulting brightness of his own voice, 282 and even Hilda looked up curiously as he said, "Nothing you have ever done has satisfied me, and nothing you could ever do would satisfy me, Blackburn."

With a glance at Hilda, Blackburn made a gesture as if to hush 283 Howe — as though all his former bold malice had taken for granted a kind of understanding between himself and his teacher, a secret which must not be betrayed to a third person. "I only meant, sir," he said, "that I was able to pass your course after all."

Howe said, "You didn't pass my course, I passed you out of my course. 284 I passed you without even reading your paper. I wanted to be sure the college would be rid of you. And when all the grades were in and I did read your paper, I saw I was right not to have read it first."

Blackburn presented a stricken face. "It was very bad, sir?" 285

But Howe had turned away. The paper had been fantastic. The paper 286 had been, if he wished to see it so, mad. It was at this moment that the Dean came up behind Howe and caught his arm. "Hello, Joseph," he said. "We'd better be getting along, it's almost late."

He was not a familiar man, but when he saw Blackburn, who ap- 287 proached to greet him, he took Blackburn's arm, too. "Hello, Theodore," he said. Leaning forward on Howe's arm and on Blackburn's, he said, "Hello, Hilda dear." Hilda replied quietly, "Hello, Uncle George."

Still clinging to their arms, still linking Howe and Blackburn, the Dean 288 said, "Another year gone, Joe, and we've turned out another crop. After you've been here a few years, you'll find it reasonably upsetting — you wonder how there can be so many graduating classes while you stay the same. But of course you don't stay the same." Then he said, "Well," sharply, to dismiss the thought. He pulled Blackburn's arm and swung him around to Howe. "Have you heard about Teddy Blackburn?" he asked. "He has a job already, before graduation — the first man of his class to be placed." Expectant of congratulations, Blackburn beamed at Howe. Howe remained silent.

"Isn't that good?" the Dean said. Still Howe did not answer and the 289 Dean, puzzled and put out, turned to Hilda. "That's a very fine-looking camera, Hilda." She touched it with affectionate pride.

"Instruments of precision," said a voice. "Instruments of precision." Of 290 the three with joined arms, Howe was the nearest to Tertan, whose gaze took in all the scene except the smile and the nod which Howe gave him. The boy leaned on his cane. The broad-brimmed hat, canting jauntily over his eye, confused the image of his face that Howe had established, suppressed the rigid lines of the ascetic and brought out the baroque curves. It made an effect of perverse majesty.

"Instruments of precision," said Tertan for the last time, addressing no 291 one, making a casual comment to the universe. And it occurred to Howe that Tertan might not be referring to Hilda's equipment. The sense of the thrice-woven circle of the boy's loneliness smote him fiercely. Tertan stood in majestic jauntiness, superior to all the scene, but his isolation made Howe ache with a pity of which Tertan was more the cause than the object, so general and indiscriminate was it.

Whether in his sorrow he made some unintended movement toward 292 Tertan which the Dean checked, or whether the suddenly tightened grip on his arm was the Dean's own sorrow and fear, he did not know. Tertan watched them in the incurious way people watch a photograph being taken, and suddenly the thought that, to the boy, it must seem that the three were posing for a picture together made Howe detach himself almost rudely from the Dean's grasp.

"I promised Hilda another picture," he announced — needlessly, for 293 Tertan was no longer there, he had vanished in the last sudden flux of visitors who, now that the band had struck up, were rushing nervously to find seats.

"You'd better hurry," the Dean said. "I'll go along, it's getting late for 294 me." He departed and Blackburn walked stately by his side.

Howe again took his position under the little tree which cast its shadow 295 over his face and gown. "Just hurry, Hilda, won't you?" he said. Hilda held the cable at arm's length, her other arm crooked and her fingers crisped. She rose on her toes and said "Ready," and pressed the release. "Thank you," she said gravely and began to dismantle her camera as he hurried off to join the procession.

SUBJECT QUESTIONS

1. Disregarding for the moment the differences in the two boys' characters, what is the major difference between the two situations that face Dr. Howe? Consider the attitudes of the other faculty members. How do these attitudes influence Dr. Howe?
2. Put yourself in Dr. Howe's position: What would you have done about Tertan? Dr. Howe makes one decision in the dean's waiting room but immediately follows an alternative course. Why? Would you have recommended Tertan to the writer's club?

3. What would you have done about Blackburn? What reason does Dr. Howe give for passing Blackburn? Do you think this is his real reason?

4. Could you say that in the one area of literary interpretation Blackburn was less "sane" than Tertan? If so, shouldn't Dr. Howe have reported Blackburn to the dean? Had he done so, what do you suppose the result would have been?

5. Although he is mentally deranged, Tertan is believable as a character. What about Blackburn? Could a student with a B average, a former English major, be so inept in a literature course? (Dr. Howe himself finds this difficult to believe; does his disbelief make the situation more acceptable to the reader?) Might it be possible for a person like Blackburn to slide through four years of college by bluffing?

6. Why is the incident of Woolley's essay included in the story? Does it have any effect on the outcome? Why should Dr. Howe pay any attention to a critic he despises? Contrast the ways in which Tertan and Blackburn react to Woolley's criticism of Howe.

7. If "insanity" is determined by "abnormal" behavior, does it follow that if normal behavior changed, we might judge people insane who still conformed to the original norms?

STRUCTURE QUESTIONS

1. Although we see Tertan and Blackburn only from Dr. Howe's point of view, does Trilling adequately differentiate them? What is the primary basis of comparison between the two students?

2. Trilling also employs lesser bases of comparison, such as dress. What, if anything, do these add?

3. Why do you suppose Trilling introduces other students — Casebeer, De Witt, and the football player Stettenhover — as well as the girl Hilda when they have so little to do with the central issue? Are Dr. Howe's relations with these people unusual? What significance do the students' names have?

4. Is the contrast which the critic Frederic Woolley makes between the poetry of Dr. Howe and Thomas Wormser sufficiently clear? Should Trilling have gone into more detail on this difference? What does the choice of names for the critic and rival poet tell the reader?

SUGGESTION FOR WRITING

Compare and contrast two of your college acquaintances *as students*. Make accurate and significant observations, but do not attempt to psychoanalyze them. Set up such bases of comparison as study habits, intellectual activities, and class participation.

In a Spring
Still Not Written of

Robert Wallace

Robert Wallace (b. 1932) is a poet, novelist, and educator. Trained at Harvard and Cambridge, he has published widely and has won numerous poetry awards. Wallace has taught at Bryn Mawr and at Vassar, where the experience related in this poem took place. He is now professor of English at Case Western Reserve University in Cleveland.

This morning
with a class of girls outdoors, I saw
how frail poems are
in a world burning up with flowers,
in which, overhead,
the great elms   5
— green, and tall —
stood carrying leaves in their arms.

The girls listened equally
to my drone, and to the bees'
ricocheting   10
among them for the blossom on the bone,
or gazed off at a distant mower's
astronomies of green
and clover, flashing,
threshing in the new, untarnished sunlight.   15

And all the while, dwindling,
tinier, the voices — Yeats, Marvell, Donne —
sank drowning
in a spring still not written of,
as only the sky   20
clear above the brick bell tower
— blue, and white —
was shifting toward the hour.

Calm, indifferent, cross-legged   25
or on elbows half-lying in the grass —
how should the great dead
tell them of dying?
They will come to time for poems at last,
when they have found they are no more   30
the beautiful and young
all poems are for.

SUBJECT QUESTIONS

1. Why would poems seem more "frail" outdoors on a spring morning than they would in a classroom?
2. Have you found that any subject — not just poetry — seems less important when the teacher holds class outside?
3. Do you agree with the girls in Wallace's class that directly experiencing life is more meaningful than reading about someone else's experiences? If so, how does one justify the reading of poetry?
4. In what sense are all poems for "the beautiful and young"? Why don't the beautiful and young appreciate them?
5. What do you suppose the reaction might be if Wallace read this poem to the class of girls outdoors?

STRUCTURE QUESTIONS

1. In this lyric poem, the contrast is developed more by suggestion, by connotation, than by denotation; hence, the reader should be able to understand the difference between the appeals of reality and of poetry without, perhaps, being expected to write a prose paraphrase of the contrast. Is this the case?
2. The poem is divided into four stanzas of eight lines each. Are these divisions artificial, or do they reflect logical progressions in the thought?
3. Does Wallace use any rhyme and regular meter? What chiefly distinguishes this writing as poetry? (That is, if it were printed simply as five prose sentences in a paragraph, would it "read" like prose?)
4. In the second stanza, why is "drone" a better choice than a word with roughly equivalent meaning, such as "monotone"? Why does "bees" end that line instead of "ricocheting"?
5. Not many of the images in this poem are particularly unusual, describing as they do the scene on a typical college campus. Do the few unusual images ("blossom on the bone" or "astronomies of

green,'' for instance) seem out of place, or does there appear to be a special reason for including them?

6. What is the subject of the poems Wallace has been reading to his class? Why is this subject more appropriate than, say, love to the contrast Wallace is establishing?

SUGGESTION FOR WRITING

Select two essays from the text, one of which you found interesting and meaningful and the other unappealing. Compare and contrast the two, making clear the bases upon which you prefer one over the other.

4

THE PROGRAMMED CITIZEN

Process

Probably ninety percent of scientific — and research paper — writing employs two methods of presentation: analysis of cause and effect and of process. The two can be distinguished quite easily: cause and effect analysis answers the question, *"Why* does something work or happen?" and process analysis answers the question, *"How* does it work or happen?" A study of the principles of physics which cause an internal combustion engine to operate would be analysis of cause and effect; an explanation of how an engine is constructed would be process analysis. The reason so much writing is of these two types is probably apparent. Although the first duty of scientists is to observe accurately, the isolated facts they collect are meaningless until some relationships or applications are worked out. Cause and effect and process analysis show these relations and applications.

Process refers to the explanation, step by step, of the way in which something happens or operates. It does not, like cause and effect, have to tell *why* the phenomenon occurs, but only *how* it happens. Thus a recipe for devil's food cake is a simple process analysis. Such questions as "Why does yeast make dough rise?" do not need to be answered (although cause and effect analysis is frequently combined with process). If the process is followed correctly, the dough *will* rise, whether or not we understand why it does.

Generally speaking, there are two kinds of process analysis, mechanical and historical, though such a division overlaps to some degree. Mechanical process explains the steps by which a thing is put together or operates. The instructions for setting up an experiment in chemistry lab are an example of mechanical process; so, in coded form, is the score for playing Mozart's *Jupiter* Symphony. More complicated mechanical processes would be an analysis of how sea gulls fly and an explanation of how a linear accelerator is constructed.

Historical process analysis is the same sort of procedure, except that it represents a description of the steps by which an event or series of events took place historically. Of this type would be a logistical account of the Battle of Bull Run — the deployment of troops, position of artillery, steps in the attack procedure, and so on. A geological account of the formation of the Hawaiian Islands would also be an historical process, as would a description of the way in which Macbeth attained the throne.

Writing process papers is ordinarily somewhat easier than is analysis of cause and effect. Some processes, of course, are extremely complicated, but even so you do not have to worry about such problems as multiplicity of causes. If you understand the process clearly, then you have only to worry about writing carefully.

There are two important rules to keep in mind when writing a process paper. In the first place, the steps in any process must be kept in exact order. If you do not do this, a simple chemistry experiment can destroy both laboratory and experimenter. If you reverse the steps "add ⅔ cup milk" and "simmer 20 minutes," the result can be a plate of fudge best attacked with hammer and chisel.

This rule of exact order is obvious and hardly needs to be dwelled upon. More important for a writer to remember is the rule of clarity; if one step in a process involving fifty steps is not clearly explained, the whole process is useless to the reader. Forty-nine clear explanations out of fifty is a good average, but in process it will not do. Anyone who has made clothes probably knows the frustration of trying to decipher a step not clearly explained on the pattern, as does anyone who has built a radio from a foreign-made kit with directions written by an unskilled translator. Even the simplest process demands clarity in each step; the more complicated ones which you will have to write as a college student — lab reports, research papers, case histories, and engineering reports — require even closer attention to clarity.

Many of these processes are of the least complicated variety, simple sets of directions. But the processes you will write in college frequently will not allow an explanation of steps in uninterrupted 1-2-3-4 order. One problem is that the subject is likely to demand descriptions and explanations which are not part of the process itself. Another is that in a complicated process several things may be happening simultaneously. Consequently, you may have to proceed by stages or subdivisions. Even in a purely mechanical process like the operation of an automobile engine, subdivisions would be necessary: the carburetion system; the ignition system, the piston, rod, and valve assembly and operation; and the transmission. (The steps in each subdivision, of course, must still be kept in order.) In such fields as biology and psychology, the processes may be even more complicated. Your problem then will be to find a way of organizing the material in such a way that the reader can understand all the factors involved and still see clearly the steps or stages of the process.

It is because of the absolute necessity for clarity that process writing is such useful practice for students in college composition. Process analysis can develop the habit of making certain that your reader will understand what you are trying to communicate. When you write a process paper, you should test your explanations by reading the first draft to someone who is not familiar with the process being explained. Any steps which your listener does not understand you can then rewrite and explain in greater detail. In extremely complicated processes, you may find diagrams useful in explaining some of the steps.

Choosing the Class of '83

Evan Thomas

A few minutes after midnight on April 14, some 2,500 thick letters and 1
*9,000 thin ones will leave the Providence post office. The thick letters offer
admission to Brown, a highly selective Ivy League university. The thin letters say no or relegate applicants to the limbo of the waiting list. Those who
go through thick and thin are participating in a process that mixes careful
weighing, educated guesswork and plain horse trading. Time's Evan
Thomas sat in on the admissions committee. His report:*

On a rainy Sunday morning in March, Brown Admissions Director Jim 2
Rogers and three committee members contemplate a fat computer print-
out. It measures, in code, the credentials of the 11,421 high school seniors
who have applied to Brown. Next to each applicant's name, a long string of
numbers and cryptic abbreviations shows college board scores, class rank,
grade-point average and a preliminary rating for academic promise and
personal quality on a scale of 1 to 6. Other symbols reveal more: "LEG 1"
is a legacy, the son of a Brown alumnus. "M1" is a black; "M8" a Chicano.
"50" means the Brown football coach is interested, "70" that Brown's development office has marked the candidate's parents as potential benefac-
tors.

Rogers and his committee begin with 25 applicants from a high- 3
pressure high school in a prosperous Midwestern suburb. They rapidly reject a dozen students with mediocre grades and below-550 board scores,
then slow down. The prospects begin to look alike: board scores in the
600s, class rank in the top fifth. Many applicants from competitive schools
realize this and mail in poems, photo albums, homemade cookies, anything
to stand out. One student has sent an 8-by-10 glossy of himself water-skiing
at a 30° angle, spray flying, muscles rippling. Others have mailed in serious
portfolios, evaluated by the art department.

The committee passes around a thick application folder from "Mary." 4
"Whoops!" says Rogers. "A 'Pinocchio'!" In Brown admissions jargon, that
means her guidance counselor has checked off boxes rating her excellent
for academic ability but only good or average for humor, imagination and

character. On the printed recommendation form, the low checks stick out from the high ones like a long, thin nose. "A rating of average usually means the guidance counselor thinks there is something seriously wrong," explains Admissions Officer Paulo de Oliveira. Mary's interview with a Brown alumnus was also lukewarm, and worse, she has written a "jock essay," *i.e.*, a very short one. Rogers scrawls a Z, the code for rejection, on her folder.

"Peter" is a "double leg" — both his mother and father went to   5
Brown. He is unexciting but unobjectionable, and his grades and scores are good. "We're trapped," sighs a committee member. There is laughter around the table, but no one doubts that keeping the alumni happy is worth it. After all, they pay for Brown's quality. Peter gets an "A 83" — A for admit; the 83 warns that a lop-off is still possible when Rogers re-examines legacy applications in April. The committee moves on to "John": "Third in his class, 730 verbal, a genuine interest in history," says Committee Member Steve Coon, "and he can hit the long ball."

Brown may stress academics, but it likes jocks, too, especially after suffer-   6
ing with a football team that went 9-58-2 in the Ivy League during the '60s. At Rogers' elbow are "depth charts" listing athletes by sport, the position they play and ranking by Brown coaches, usually on a scale of 1 to 6. There are also depth charts for alumni children, music, art, theater. The music department, for instance, rates oboists and violinists by ability and the orchestra's need for them.

That evening Rogers meets with the hockey coach to review 82 pros-   7
pects. Picking up the application of a defenseman from Canada, Rogers reads his courses aloud: "English, auto mechanics, consumer math, shop . . ." He looks for the essay. There is none; instead, the candidate has enclosed his team's player program, listing goals, assists, penalty minutes. Rogers shakes his head and starts reading another folder. "Bingo!" he cries. "A's and B's, 600 boards. You've got him." Several "weak but still breathing" candidates later, the coach anxiously states his need for ten forwards, five defensemen and two goalies. Rogers is good-natured about it, but he makes no promises.

The next morning the admissions committee scans applications from a   8
small rural high school in the Southwest. It is searching for prized specimens known as "neat small-town kids." "Amy" is near the top of her class, with mid-500 verbals, high-600 math and science. She is also poor, white and "geo" — she would add to the geographic and economic diversity that saves Brown from becoming a postgraduate New England prep school. While just over 20% of the New York State applicants will get in, almost 40% will be admitted from Region 7 — Oklahoma, Texas, Arkansas and

Louisiana. Amy's high school loves her, and she wants to study engineering. Brown badly wants engineering students; unfortunately, Amy spells *engineering* wrong. "Dyslexia," says Jimmy Wrenn, a linguistics professor. After some debate, the committee puts her on the waiting list. Argues Member Betts Howes: "She's 'B for B.'"

"B for B" means "Burning for Brown," and it counts. Until now, because of the almost immutable pecking order of colleges, only about half the students admitted actually enrolled at Brown. The rest went to schools like Princeton, Yale and Harvard, which has about a 75% "yield." But lately Brown has become very popular. At a time when the end of the baby boom spells a declining applicant pool, the school's applications have jumped 25% in two years. With good reason. Brown works hard to sell itself. The 16 members of the admissions committee are young, diverse, impressive — the kind of mix Brown wants to enroll. The group visits almost 1,000 high schools in the fall. A network of 2,900 loyal alumni follow up with interviewing and more recruiting. They tell high school students that Brown is remarkably relaxed in an era of grade grubbing; that Brown has a beautiful campus; that Providence is not as blighted as it looks from Interstate 95; that nearly every Brown student who applies to grad school gets in. They are telling the truth, and Brown students confirm it on the college-high school grapevine.

As do other schools, Brown automatically sends a letter to everyone with board scores over 650 in selected zip-code areas, many of them urban ghettos. The competition for top minority students is fierce. "A black with 650 verbals can heat his house for the winter with college catalogues," says Rogers. Brown's black applicant pool steadily declined from a high of over 700 in 1971 to 374 two years ago. Thanks to a recruiting push, more than 500 applied this year; of them about 200 will get in. Some will be risks: "Elaine," for instance, has board scores below 400. But she is near the top of her class at a tough inner-city school, and she has been getting up at 6 a.m. to take courses at a nearby college. Her mother is a maid, and she has six siblings, including a brother at Yale. Her essay radiates energy and will. She gets an A 83 — admitted, unless Rogers has second thoughts at "minority review": "If we take her, I'm going to grab that grade book a year from now and see how she's doing."

This week the committee makes its last and hardest choices. On Sunday Rogers conducts "athletic review." "It does no good to take 48 split ends and no linebackers," he explains. The director of athletics invariably appears and nervously paces the hallway outside the committee's meeting room. Sunday afternoon is set aside for "legacy review" to make sure the alumni have not been slighted. Monday morning is "geographic review," to make sure the regional mix is right. Then a waiting list of some 500 candidates must be drawn up; for most, it is Brown's polite way of saying that they came close but could not be squeezed in. Rogers will also look at the ratio of males to females. Last year Brown took more women than men, although more men than women applied. This year the ratio will be about fifty-fifty.

Similar trade-offs are being made in admissions offices around the Ivy 12
League. The bartering is purely intramural. Contrary to rumor, the Ivy schools are not involved in a conspiracy. They get together only to make certain that financial-aid applicants are offered the same tuition reductions at every school. If Brown's admissions committee has given A's to more needy students than the college can afford with its $1.25 million financial-aid budget, a few A's will become Z's, a cutback Brown has been forced to make only twice in ten years.

By Wednesday night it should all be over. A weary Rogers will hear 13
last appeals. The next morning he will get on the telephone and start apologizing to certain loyal alumni whose children have been rejected. "It's an exciting time," he says, working up a smile. It is an expression familiar to anyone who has watched baseball managers approaching the cut-off date, politicians on the stump and admissions directors in the spring.

SUBJECT QUESTIONS

1. Of the standards by which candidates are selected, which seem to be essential and which are "added advantages" to the candidate?
2. Judging by the examples given, what kinds of tactics by candidates almost guarantee rejection?
3. Selection by race, geography, or parental background seems discriminatory against otherwise qualified candidates; on what bases could you defend such principles of selection?
4. Would it be easier for a college simply to accept the best-qualified candidates without worrying about a proper "mix"? What difficulties would be inherent in this simpler policy?
5. Being one among eleven thousand entries on a computer print-out seems rather dehumanizing. Does the admissions committee described here take acceptable account of individual differences and qualities?

STRUCTURE QUESTIONS

1. Would this analysis enable a reader to duplicate the process described? Does it help the reader to understand how admissions are decided?

2. Which parts of the process are presented in 1–2–3 order? Would it be possible to analyze the entire process in this way?
3. Are the various facts, figures, and code words illuminating, or do they make parts of the process seem mysterious? Do you suppose the writer intended to convey at times a sense of indescribable complication?
4. Are the numerous brief examples helpful in understanding the process as a whole? (Consider the effect if "Amy" and the others had been omitted.)
5. Is it possible to tell from the tone of this essay whether or not the writer approves of Brown's selection process? Is he trying to be fair and objective? What might he have done to alter the reader's view had he wished to do so?
6. The final paragraph brings the process to a logical conclusion. What is the point of the comparison in the last sentence? Does it seem a good — or clever — way to end the essay?

SUGGESTIONS FOR WRITING

1. Describe the process by which you selected the college or colleges you wanted to attend.
2. Analyze the process by which you actually applied for admission. Include any unusual tactics you employed. (Or you may wish to emphasize the depersonalizing effect of the admissions forms, if they did not allow scope for individual traits and abilities.)
3. Describe the process of orientation for new students at your college. (If your college has no orientation program, you may want to describe your first week as a comedy of errors.)

The Peter Principle
Raymond Hull

Raymond Hull is the collaborator with Dr. Laurence J. Peter on the book
The Peter Principle *(1969).*

Bunglers are always with us and always have been. Winston Churchill tells   1
us, in his history of World War II, that in August, 1940, he had to take
charge personally of the Armed Forces' Joint Planning Committee because,
after almost twelve months of war, the Committee had not originated a
single plan.

In the 1948 Presidential election, the advance public-opinion polls   2
awarded an easy victory to Thomas E. Dewey. In the Fifties, there was the
Edsel bungle. In 1965, Houston's domed baseball stadium opened and was
so ill-suited to baseball that, on sunny days, fielders could not see fly balls
against the blinding glare from the skylight.

We have come to expect incompetence as a necessary feature of civili-   3
zation. We may be irked, but we are no longer amazed, when our bosses
make idiotic decisions, when automobile makers take back thousands of new
cars for repairs, when store clerks are insolent, when law reforms fail to
check crime, when moon rockets can't get off the ground, when widely used
medicines are found to be poisons, when universities must teach freshmen to
read, or when a hundred-ton airliner is brought down by a duck.

We see these malpractices and mishaps as unconnected accidents, in-   4
evitable results of human fallibility.

But one man says, "These occurrences are not accidents; they are sim-   5
ply the fruits of a system which, as I have shown, *develops, perpetuates and
rewards incompetence."*

The Newton of incompetence theory is a burly, black-haired, slow-   6
spoken Canadian philosopher and iconoclast, Dr. Laurence J. Peter, who
made his living as Assistant Professor of Education at the University of
British Columbia until recently, when he moved down the coast to become a
Professor of Education at the University of Southern California.

There is nothing incompetent about Dr. Peter. He is a successful au-   7
thor: his *Prescriptive Teaching* is a widely used text on the education of
problem children. He built a house with his own hands, makes his own

wine, is an expert cook, a skilled woodcarver, and an inventor. (He created a new tool rack for school woodwork shops and perfected an apparatus for marking fifty exam papers at once.) Yet his chief claim to fame may be his founding of the science of hierarchiology.

Hierarchiology [he says,] is the study of hierarchies. "Hierarchy" originally meant "church government by clergy graded into ranks." The term now includes any organization whose members or employees are arranged by rank or grade.

Early in life, I faced the problem of occupational incompetence. As a young schoolteacher I was shocked, baffled, to see so many knotheads as principals, inspectors and superintendents.

I questioned older teachers. All I could find was that the knotheads, earlier in their career, had been capable, and that was why they had been promoted.

Eventually I realized that the same phenomenon occurs in all trades and professions, because the same basic rule governs the climb through every hierarchy. A competent employee is eligible for promotion, but incompetence is a bar to promotion. So an employee's final position must be one for which he is incompetent!

Suppose you own a drug-manufacturing firm, Perfect Pill Incorporated. Your foreman pill-roller dies of a perforated ulcer; you seek a replacement among the rank-and-file pill-rollers. Miss Cylinder, Mrs. Ellipse and Mr. Cube are variously incompetent and so don't qualify. You pick the best pill-roller, Mr. Sphere, and promote him to foreman.

Suppose Sphere proves highly competent in this new job: later, when deputy-works-manager Legree moves up one step, Sphere will take his place.

But if Sphere is incompetent as foreman, he won't be promoted again. He has reached what I call his *level of incompetence* and there he will stay till he retires.

An employee may, like Mr. Cube, reach his level of incompetence at the lowest rank: he is never promoted. It may take one promotion to place him at his level of incompetence; it may take a dozen. But, sooner or later, he does attain it.

Dr. Peter cites the case of the late General A. Jacks.* His hearty manner, informal dress, scorn for petty regulations and disregard for personal safety made him the idol of his men. He led them from victory to victory.

Had the war ended sooner, Jacks might have retired, covered in glory. But he was promoted to the rank of field marshal. Now he had to deal, not with fighting men, but with politicians of his own country, and with two punctilious Allied field marshals.

He quarreled with them all and took to spending whole days drunk, sulking in his trailer. The conduct of the war slipped out of his hands and into those of his subordinates.

The final promotion had brought him from doing what he *could* do, to attempting what he could not do. He had reached his level of incompetence.

* It is Dr. Peter's usual practice to employ fictitious names in his case histories.

The Jacks' case exemplifies the Peter Principle, the basic theorem of hierarchiology. *In a hierarchy each employee tends to rise to his level of incompetence: every post tends to be occupied by an employee incompetent to execute its duties.* ₁₀

How is it, then, that any work is done at all? Peter says, "Work is done by people who have not yet attained final placement at their level of incompetence." ₁₁

And how is it that we occasionally see a competent person at the very top of the hierarchy? "Simply because there are not enough ranks for him to have reached his level of incompetence: in other words, *in that hierarchy* there is no task beyond his abilities." ₁₂

As a rule, such a prodigy of competence eventually sidesteps into another hierarchy — say from the Armed Forces into industry, from law to politics, from business to government — and there finds his level of incompetence. A well-known example is Macbeth, a successful general, but an incompetent king.

In an unpublished monograph, *The Pathology of Success: Morbidity and Mortality at the Level of Incompetence,* Peter expands his theory to take in matters of health. ₁₃

Certain physical conditions are associated with the final placement: peptic ulcers, high blood pressure, nervous disorders, migraine headaches, alcoholism, insomnia, obesity and cardiovascular complaints. Obviously such symptoms indicate the patient's constitutional incompetence for his level of responsibility.

Edgar Allan Poe, a highly competent writer, proved incompetent when raised to the rank of editor. He became "nervous in a very unusual degree," took to drink and then to drugs in a vain search for relief.

Such ailments, usually appearing two or more together, constitute the Final Placement Syndrome.

Medication and surgery are often prescribed for F.P.S. patients, but they miss the root cause of the condition. Psychoanalysis fails for the same reason. The analyst is probing into the patient's subconscious for Oedipus complex, castration-complex, penis-envy or whatnot, when the trouble really lies outside, in the patient's hierarchal placement.

Is there no escape? Must every worker reach his level of incompetence, suffer the miseries of Final Placement Syndrome and become a laughing stock for his behavioral or temperamental symptoms? ₁₄

Peter describes two escape routes. The first is for a man who realizes that he has reached his level of incompetence, yet still wants to preserve health, self-respect and sanity. ₁₅

Many an employee adjusts to final placement by the process of Substitution. Instead of executing his proper duties, he substitutes a set of irrelevant duties, and these self-imposed tasks he carries out to perfection.

A. L. Tredwell, assistant principal of a secondary school, was intellectually competent and maintained good relationships with teachers, students, and parents. He was promoted to principal. Soon it became clear that he lacked the finesse to deal with newspaper reporters, school-board members, and the district superintendent. He fell out of favor with the officials, and his school lost community support. Realizing consciously or subconsciously — it doesn't matter which — that he was incompetent for the proper duties of a principal, Tredwell *Substituted*. He developed an obsessive concern with the movement of students and staff about the school.

He drew complex plans of traffic-flow, had white lines painted on floors and arrows on walls, spent hours prowling the building looking for violations of his rules, and bombarded professional journals with articles about his scheme.

Tredwell's Substitution is a great success. He is active and contented now, and shows no sign of the Final Placement Syndrome.

Peter's alternate escape route is for the employee who is capably and happily doing his work and who wants to avoid ever reaching his level of incompetence. [16]

Merely to *refuse* promotion seldom leads to happiness. It annoys one's superiors, rouses suspicion among one's peers, and shames one's wife and children. Few people can endure all that. So one must contrive never to be offered promotion. [17]

The first step is to avoid asking, or seeming to ask, for it. The oft-heard complaint, "My job lacks challenge," is usually understood as showing desire for promotion. So don't give voice to such complaints! [18]

The second step is described by Peter in his lecture, Creative Incompetence: "I have found some employees who are contented in their work, and who seem to be using effective means of maintaining their position." [19]

Adam Greenaway, a gardener, happily tends the landscaped grounds of the Ideal Trivet Company. He is competent in all aspects of his work but one: He keeps losing delivery slips for goods received. He gives vague explanations such as "I must have planted the papers with the shrubs." Most important, he concealed the fact that he wanted to avoid promotion.

Lack of delivery slips so upset the accounting department that, when a new maintenance foreman was needed, Greenaway was not considered for the post.

Thus he could stay indefinitely at a level of competence and enjoy the keen personal satisfaction of regularly accomplishing useful work. Surely this offers as great a challenge as the traditional drive for higher ranks!

By his Darwinian Extension Theorem, Peter applies his Principle to the whole human race. Man may go the way of the dinosaur and the sabre-tooth tiger. Those beasts were destroyed by excessive development of the qualities — bulk and fangs — that had originally favored their survival. Man's cleverness was originally a survival characteristic, but now he has become clever enough to destroy himself. If he takes that step, he will achieve his ultimate level of incompetence, in proving himself unfit to live. [20]

"Man's one hope," says Peter, "lies in hierarchiology. I feel that it will [21] soon be recognized as the supreme science. Earlier sociological studies have insufficiently recognized man's hierarchal nature."

A knowledge of the Peter Principle becomes more and more important as hierarchal systems become stronger. Government and education are prime examples. Both already swollen, both expanding their demands for money and manpower, both extending their influence as more people stay longer in school, and as government controls more functions of life. Even industry, once a stronghold of individualism, is largely an aggregation of hierarchies. My point is that man ought to be using the hierarchal system for his benefit. But he can't possibly use it unless he understands it, and to do that he must understand the Peter Principle. Failing such understanding, the system will destroy the individuals who comprise it.

Many people accept the Peter Principle on first hearing. It sounds so   22
obvious, so like common sense; it explains so aptly a group of hitherto mystifying phenomena.

In academic circles, however, the Principle has made little impression.   23
A few of Peter's subordinates when he was at the University of British Columbia grasped it, but none of his superiors. Some of them saw it as a humorous trifle, others as sociological heresy. Said Peter at the time: "I'm neither primarily funny or unfunny. I study society scientifically because I must live in it. I present my findings to you because they describe the world you live in."

Anyway, I'm too busy to worry much about what others think of me. I teach future schoolteachers how to work with handicapped and disturbed children. I'm pursuing two fascinating lines of research: into autism, a profound emotional disorder in which children have no sense of self, and no ability to learn by experience; and into developmental dyslexia, an inability to recognize printed words that often, tragically, pins a "mentally retarded" label on a genuinely intelligent child. It's all deeply satisfying: I'm about as happy in my work as anyone I know.

The thought then occurred that Peter's hierarchiology might, just   24
might, be *his* form of Creative Incompetence — a means of making himself slightly suspect, and so avoiding an unwanted academic promotion.

"No, no! Of course not!" said the doctor. "But even if it were, of course   25
I wouldn't admit it!"

SUBJECT QUESTIONS

1. Test your understanding of the Peter Principle by applying it to a hierarchy not considered in detail in this essay.
2. Do you agree that the Peter Principle operates in every organization having a hierarchal structure? Can you think of any in which it does not apply?
3. If Peter believes that his principle applies to all organizations, why doesn't he advocate the abolition of hierarchies?

4. Criticize the following application of the Peter Principle: "The United Nations General Assembly accomplishes little because it is composed of formerly able statesmen who were promoted to their level of incompetence."
5. How, according to Peter, can a person avoid reaching his level of incompetence? How has Peter himself avoided it?
6. Can you suggest ways by which a hierarchy — say a school system or a business corporation — could avoid filling all its executive positions with incompetents?
7. Does the process which Peter calls "Substitution" strike you as a satisfactory way to avoid "Final Placement Syndrome"? Is it prevalent, judging from your own observation?

STRUCTURE QUESTIONS

1. Several separate processes are explained in this essay, including the historical process of how Peter arrived at his principle. Does including more than one process in the same article cause any confusion? Do they all belong here?
2. Professor Peter explains his principle with two illustrations, the cases of Mr. Sphere and General A. Jacks. Does this procedure give a clear idea of the process? Why must Peter resort to particular examples instead of outlining the steps in general?
3. Do you think Hull created a structural problem for himself by trying to tell his readers about Professor Peter and about the Peter Principle both in the same essay? Does one lead naturally into the other? How does Hull tie them together at the end?
4. Peter says that "man ought to be using the hierarchal system for his benefit." Does this essay make clear how man can do this, considering Peter's contention that his principle invariably operates at present? Should the essay have been expanded at this point? Or should the statement have been omitted?

SUGGESTION FOR WRITING

Write a process paper in which you explain more carefully than Hull how the Peter Principle works. Use examples drawn from some hierarchy you are familiar with (the business of one of your parents, the educational system, fraternity organization, and so on).

The Art of
the Memorandum

Joseph Porter Clerk, Jr.

"Joseph Porter Clerk, Jr." is a pseudonym. At the time the essay was written, the author worked for the federal government and for obvious reasons wished to remain anonymous. The article was one of a series on government red tape which appeared in The Washington Monthly.

Armies move on their stomachs, governments on their memoranda. 1
Memoranda are the devices by which bureaucrats communicate, make decisions, and record what has happened. You cannot succeed in government without mastering the art. Nor is it easy to come by. After seven years in government, I am just gaining a beginner's command over this indispensable tool of deceptively simple appearance.

When I entered government, I assumed a memorandum was an 2
official document that bureaucrat A wrote to bureaucrat B when A wanted B to do something. This was naive. B's usual response is to do nothing.

This may be because B is too busy writing his own memoranda or, 3
more likely, because B is one of those public servants whose impulses to action are thoroughly controlled by their awareness of the accompanying risks.

In either event, the primary rule of the memorandum is to expect no 4
action from its recipient.

This rule, when first learned, tends to be dispiriting, but its advan- 5
tages soon become apparent. Other men's inertia can be the secret of your power to act and to influence policy.

Consider a simple example. As a novice you would have written to 6
your superior asking his permission to do such and such. You would have received no answer and therefore not had the authority to do what you had proposed doing. You now know that your memo should say, "Next Tuesday I plan to. . . ." No answer constitutes your authority to act. (The Navy has honored this tactic with the acronym UNODIR — "unless otherwise directed.")

This sort of thing won't work if there is the slightest hint of anything 7
unusual about your proposal. The memorandum must imply, "I'm probably wasting your time to ask you to read what is obviously a matter of course,

Reprinted with permission from *The Washington Monthly*. Copyright 1969 by The Washington Monthly Co., 1611 Connecticut Ave., N.W., Washington, DC 20009.

but I feel I should always lean over backwards to keep you fully informed."

You may, in fact, propose a revolutionary change in policy, but it   8
should always be stated as an interpretation of present policy — an ex-
egesis on scripture in the absence of new revelation.

New ideas are fragile in a bureaucracy. And their chances of survival   9
usually diminish when they are proclaimed as new ideas. Instead, say that
you are merely examining the assumptions underlying the status quo.
While your reputation for liveliness may suffer, your ideas may succeed.

Occasionally, however, you should advertise the novelty of your   10
proposal. There are some government officials who take great pride in
being "open to new approaches." The hazard in dealing with them is that
some mean it and some don't. Thus it is crucially important to know your
readers. Not only must you know the identity of those few lovers of new
ideas for whose benefit you can speak out boldly, but also of that other (not
always mutually exclusive) minority, the officials who actually do something
when they receive a memorandum.

But you can be assured that most of your readership will be the non-   11
responders. The key fact to realize about them is that everyone who reads
your memo and does nothing is to some degree implicated in the action
you propose or the policy interpretation you make.

Therefore you want to address the memo to (or at least note "copy   12
to") everyone whose assent you need. Since some of them are likely to be
busy and important people who might be able to claim they never read
your message in the event its result proves unpopular, you must make sure
that they do, in fact, read it.

One device that practically guarantees that B will read it is to add as   13
another addressee someone who is important to B — his superior, perhaps, or the man who controls his budget or his personnel allotment.

Mark the message "Secret" or "Confidential" or "For President's   14
Eyes Only." Security classifications were not devised for their value in
catching attention, but that only makes them more useful for the purpose.

Make your message stand out from the others. If blue paper is re-   15
quired for memos, use pink. If most messages are in the form of official
cables (as is the case in U.S. embassies overseas), use a commercial cable
or write a letter. If messages are in letter form (as is generally true in
domestic agencies), send a telegram.

Another way to gain attention is to use concise English. However,   16
there is a risk here: you may be regarded as a dangerous eccentric. It
should never be tried by a new man, for he will be looked upon with pity
as a novice who simply lacks the appropriate vocabulary.

Sometimes you will want to make sure that a recipient does *not* read   17
your memorandum. He may be one of those unpredictable action-takers
mentioned earlier, or he may be a man you know to be totally dedicated to

shooting down any idea of yours. Nevertheless, you need to have him implicated in this one. How do you manage it without having him read the memorandum? Make it long and dull. Make the subject sound highly technical. Send a faint carbon or a bad Xerox. See that it is delivered late Friday afternoon. It will join large piles of written material behind the executive's desk, where it will testify to his good intentions until the day of his retirement. Or it will travel thousands of miles in the bottom of his briefcase waiting for a moment that will never come.

When I was working in the General Counsel's office at AID, I once 18 recommended that we send a complaint against a construction firm to the Department of Justice for suit. The firm had built a road in Southeast Asia which collapsed. It was important to get the case to the Department of Justice not so much because several million dollars of taxpayers' money was involved, but because once the problem was at Justice we could stop wasting our time answering inquiries from Congress and the General Accounting Office. We could simply reply that Justice was considering suit and that we had been asked not to comment.

My memorandum recommending suit had to do with the kind of de- 19 cision that the General Counsel would feel he should make himself but would never find time for. To get my memorandum through him I knew that I would have to persuade him at the outset that he would never study the matter. Assembling the relevant (and not so relevant) papers having to do with the case and labeling them exhibit 1, 2, 3, etc., I piled the whole mass in a shopping cart borrowed from the General Services Administration and wheeled it into his office, with my memo on top. I urged a personal study of the problem. I got his initials in three minutes.

Success with the memorandum can depend just as much on your fel- 20 low senders as on the recipients. Mustering others to join in sending a memorandum accomplishes two things: it displays wider support for the message and, more important, it diffuses responsibility for it. The desirability of the latter becomes clear when the memorandum outrages a higher official.

Multiple authorship is ordinarily effected by a device known as 21 "clearance." This process consists of obtaining on the yellow copy of the memorandum the signatures or initials of persons other than the nominal sender of the memorandum. The most extraordinary thing about the process is that one knows exactly what "clearance" means. Some degree of affirmation is presumed to be involved. The vagueness of that affirmation may make it easier to get B to clear a memorandum than to act upon it. He can mean "yes, in principle" without assuming an obligation to do anything. An additional advantage is that you can more easily pressure for a quick initialling, so as not to "hold up the memo."

Of course the reverse may also be a good tactic. Instead of asking 22 such known sympathizers as P and Q to clear the memorandum, put them down as addressees. This places them in the position of being able to initiate a favorable response. This device can even be extended to having someone else send to you the memorandum you would have liked to write (or maybe did in fact write) so that you can respond favorably. This is the only sure-fire method of assuring prompt action by the addressee.

Suppose all this art has been directed at you and there is now a   23
memorandum on your desk from someone else proposing an action or supporting a policy about which you are doubtful but don't wish to commit yourself, even by implication.

Reply that the proposal is so interesting that it deserves to be the   24
subject of a large task force study. This will guarantee a six-month delay at the very least.

SUBJECT QUESTIONS

1. The aim of this essay is clearly satiric; does that fact negate the validity of the process it describes?
2. Judging by this process, what would be the usual fate of a new idea?
3. If all bureaucrats actually used Clerk's technique, quite a bit might be accomplished. How can you know that they don't use it?
4. The author gives only one concrete example. Is it helpful? Should he have included more?

STRUCTURE QUESTIONS

1. Are the steps in the process clearly described?
2. Do you have any difficulty with the order of those steps? Are too many alternative procedures inserted?
3. Would it be possible for a reader to follow the directions given and get desired results without further information?
4. Does the counter-process offered in the final two paragraphs destroy the essay's unity, or does it form a suitable conclusion?

SUGGESTIONS FOR WRITING

1. Offer in clear process form your proposed solution to some perennial campus problem such as student parking regulations, enrollment procedures, or new student orientation. As the assignment is concerned with process, not argument, concentrate on how your system would work or how it could be implemented rather than on why it is a better idea than the existing sytem.
2. Explain as clearly as you can the workings of a system on campus

with which you have had recent contact — fraternity rush, procedures for checking out reserve material in the library, procedures for
obtaining advanced placement, and so on. (Note: If the instructor
allows, this assignment offers possibilities for combining satire with
practice in process analysis. One can imagine analyses of impossibly
fouled-up processes on a college campus — how to make section
changes in English composition, for instance.)

Jesse Jackson's Revolutionary Message

Harry S. Ashmore

Harry Scott Ashmore (b. 1916) graduated from Clemson University and was a Nieman Fellow at Harvard University. He began his career as a newspaper reporter and eventually became editor of The Arkansas Gazette. *He was an assistant on Adlai Stevenson's campaign committee, editor-in-chief of the* Encyclopaedia Britannica, *and director of the Fund for the Republic. Ashmore has won the Pulitzer Prize for Editorial Writing and has published numerous books, including* The Negro and the Schools *(1954),* An Epitaph for Dixie *(1958), and* Mission to Hanoi *(1968).*

The walling off of racial minorities in decaying center cities is not the cause of the national urban crisis, only its most visible symptom. If, as the California Supreme Court held in *Serrano,* equality of financial support is impossible within the limits of existing school taxing units, it may follow that equality of opportunity will require attendance in areas outside those now imposed by district lines. 1

Yet, even if the courts should move in that precedent-breaking direction, the demographic facts of life still will have to be dealt with. There is no prospect in Washington or Sacramento of the massive infusion of public funds that would be required to make any significant change in the residential patterns of, say, Los Angeles. This means that the present generation of minority school children will be conditioned primarily by the prevailing culture of the ghettos where they live, even if some get their schooling elsewhere. And it means, too, that the ghetto schools, to which white children must be assigned, also will be conditioned by their surroundings. In many inner-city schools, that conditioning has produced patterns of decadence, disorder, and outright violence that are a legitimate concern of parents of any color who find their children assigned to them. 2

The only black leader of the first rank who has faced this issue squarely is the Reverend Jesse Jackson, the dynamic disciple of Martin Luther King, who leads a community-action organization based on Chicago's south side. For more than a year Jackson has been appearing in inner-city schools across the country calling upon students, teachers, and parents to join in a program of moral regeneration. He calls his project 3

Reprinted with permission from *The Center Magazine,* a publication of the Robert Maynard Hutchins Center for the Study of Democratic Institutions, Santa Barbara, California.

EXCEL, for excellence, and preaches a gospel of self-discipline as essential to the restoration of academic standards. From coast to coast the self-styled "country preacher" has galvanized his audiences, with results described by the *National Observer:*

> To the surprise of many and the chargrin of some, and to the utter delight of Jesse Jackson, the response to his impassioned, austere, and — his critics say — reactionary message has been almost uniformly the same: wild enthusiasm. Students stamp, cheer, and shout. Parents applaud, clergymen shout 'Hallelujah!' and school administrators and teachers add a loud 'Amen!'   4

EXCEL is a sophisticated community-organization plan designed to center around the high school. Internally it seeks to generate student peer-group pressure behind academic achievement as an offset to the drug- and sex-oriented hedonism that characterizes the contemporary "youth culture." Externally it seeks to organize parents and community leaders to support the drive for academic excellence with the fervor they now accord a winning athletic team.   5

The Chicago Vocational School, where Jackson first began to apply his self-help doctrine, provided the model that has prompted the Chicago Board of Education to assign a task force of its own personnel to initiate EXCEL in ten other high schools. Last spring I spent some time at the Chicago Vocational School [C.V.S.] going over the results with its highly pragmatic principal, Reginald Brown.   6

By applying the principles embodied in EXCEL, Brown says, C.V.S. has been brought back from near collapse after suffering a decade of recurrent riots, rampant vandalism, and regular raids by the narcotics squad. Enrollment has risen to 4,460 from a low of 3,300. The drop-out rate is down to less than four per cent, ranking the school fifteenth among the seventy high schools in the Chicago system. Academic standards are such that last June seventy-two seniors were denied diplomas when 753 of their classmates were graduated. That, Brown says, reverses the practice of previous years when C.V.S. handed a certificate to "anybody who turned up at commencement." Community support is evidenced by more than $160,000 contributed last year by neighborhood merchants to finance social and cultural activities for students too poor to pay their own way.   7

Everything I saw at C.V.S. supported Brown's claim that there is no violence within the school other than the usual teenage skirmishing, which is dealt with through an EXCEL-shaped disciplinary system with student involvement at all levels. Not a single hard-drug incident was recorded at C.V.S. last year, and Brown says that if any pot is being smoked, it is no nearer to the monitors than the parking lot.   8

It is true that the EXCEL program can make little claim to trailblazing originality. Jesse Jackson, as Eric Sevareid observed, "is propagating an   9 idea that is so old that it is new. He is saying, in effect, that all revolutions, including the black revolution, get to the point where further progress depends not on social forces but on the personal behavior of the revolutionaries."

"You can talk black and be popular," Jesse Jackson says to the dissi-   10
dents among his own people. "You can argue for a bigger share of what's being passed out and be politic. Or you can be prophetic and say what needs to be said." He was surely wearing his prophet's robes when he addressed these words to his white brethren:

"We have demonstrated that we can revive the hope of black children who   11
live in a ravaged culture most whites cannot even imagine. Now we have to find out whether the community will give them the opportunity to carry out their commitment to better themselves. That's the demand for excellence our time lays on each of us. If we fail in this, the civil-rights struggle has come to a dead end — and the community as a whole will pay a terrible price. We are not seeking charity for the black minority. We are asking you to face up to the minimum requirements for the survival of civilization as it has emerged in these United States."

SUBJECT QUESTIONS

1. What have the opening two paragraphs about busing to do with the chief concern of the essay, project EXCEL?
2. How does Reverend Jackson motivate ghetto schoolchildren to cooperate in the EXCEL project? Why would students want to make high school harder? Would you have preferred more rigid standards of excellence?
3. What would be the motivation for neighborhood merchants, who may have no children in school, to contribute to EXCEL?
4. Excellent public speakers like Jesse Jackson might well be able to make listeners enthusiastic about EXCEL; do you see anything in the program which would keep it going once this original motivation was gone?
5. Is there any contradiction between Eric Sevareid's summary of Reverend Jackson's position (paragraph 9) and the challenge to the community in the last paragraph?

STRUCTURE QUESTIONS

1. A high school principal could hardly institute an EXCEL project with the process as described in this brief essay; does Ashmore give the casual reader a reasonably clear idea of how the project works? What kinds of information might he have added?
2. Granting that Ashmore needs an introduction to the general prob-

lems which Reverend Jackson is trying to solve, what has gone wrong, stylistically, with the two introductory paragraphs of this essay? (You may want to glance back at the advice given on pages 153–55 of this text.)

3. To avoid a style like a patchwork quilt, it is normally better to paraphrase than to quote the authorities directly. About one-third of this essay, however, is direct quotation. Does Ashmore introduce these quotations smoothly and naturally?

4. Can you tell by this essay whether the EXCEL project is a process whose steps must be introduced in sequence, or one in which the parts must function simultaneously? Should Ashmore have been clearer on this score?

5. The example of Chicago Vocational School aims to show the results of the process, not the process itself; does it also illuminate the way in which the project actually works? Is this example needed?

SUGGESTIONS FOR WRITING

1. If you have participated in one of the many educational experiments in which part of the class is taught one way and part another way, describe how the project was conducted.

2. Describe a civic project with which you are familiar or in which you participated (city beautification, clean-up of a beach after an oil-spill, setting up a recycling center or youth recreation center, and so on) and explain how the project was carried out.

3. Analyze the process of organizing a fund-raising drive with which you are familiar.

To Bid the World Farewell

Jessica Mitford

Jessica Mitford was born in England in 1917. She came to America in 1939 and is now Distinguished Professor at San Jose State University. She attained national attention with her best-seller, The American Way of Death *(1963), from which the essay below is taken. Her more recent books are* The Trial of Dr. Spock *(1970) and* Kind and Usual Punishment *(1973). Miss Mitford lectures widely at campuses across America.*

Embalming is indeed a most extraordinary procedure, and one must wonder at the docility of Americans who each year pay hundreds of millions of dollars for its perpetuation, blissfully ignorant of what it is all about, what is done, how it is done. Not one in ten thousand has any idea of what actually takes place. Books on the subject are extremely hard to come by. They are not to be found in most libraries or bookshops.   1

In an era when huge television audiences watch surgical operations in the comfort of their living rooms, when, thanks to the animated cartoon, the geography of the digestive system has become familiar territory even to the nursery school set, in a land where the satisfaction of curiosity about almost all matters is a national pastime, the secrecy surrounding embalming can, surely, hardly be attributed to the inherent gruesomeness of the subject. Custom in this regard has within this century suffered a complete reversal. In the early days of American embalming, when it was performed in the home of the deceased, it was almost mandatory for some relative to stay by the embalmer's side and witness the procedure. Today, family members who might wish to be in attendance would certainly be dissuaded by the funeral director. All others, except apprentices, are excluded by law from the preparation room.   2

A close look at what does actually take place may explain in large measure the undertaker's intractable reticence concerning a procedure that has become his major *raison d'être.* Is it possible he fears that public information about embalming might lead patrons to wonder if they really want this service? If the funeral men are loath to discuss the subject outside the trade, the reader may, understandably, be equally loath to go on reading at this point. For those who have the stomach for it, let us part the formaldehyde curtain. . . .   3

The body is first laid out in the undertaker's morgue — or rather, Mr. 4
Jones is reposing in the preparation room — to be readied to bid the world
farewell.

The preparation room in any of the better funeral establishments has 5
the tiled and sterile look of a surgery, and indeed the embalmer-restorative
artist who does his chores there is beginning to adopt the term "der-
masurgeon" (appropriately corrupted by some mortician-writers as "demi-
surgeon") to describe his calling. His equipment, consisting of scalpels, scis-
sors, augers, forceps, clamps, needles, pumps, tubes, bowls and basins, is
crudely imitative of the surgeon's, as is his technique, acquired in a nine- or
twelve-month post-high-school course in an embalming school. He is supplied by an advanced chemical industry with a bewildering array of fluids,
sprays, pastes, oils, powders, creams, to fix or soften tissue, shrink or distend
it as needed, dry it here, restore the moisture there. There are cosmetics,
waxes and paints to fill and cover features, even plaster of Paris to replace
entire limbs. There are ingenious aids to prop and stabilize the cadaver: a
Vari-Pose Head Rest, the Edwards Arm and Hand Positioner, the Repose
Block (to support the shoulders during the embalming), and the Throop Foot
Positioner, which resembles an old-fashioned stocks.

Mr. John H. Eckels, president of the Eckels College of Mortuary 6
Science, thus describes the first part of the embalming procedure: "In the
hands of a skilled practitioner, this work may be done in a comparatively
short time and without mutilating the body other than by slight incision — so
slight that it scarcely would cause serious inconvenience if made upon a living person. It is necessary to remove the blood, and doing this not only helps
in the disinfecting, but removes the principal cause of disfigurements due to
discoloration."

Another textbook discusses the all-important time element: "The ear- 7
lier this is done, the better, for every hour that elapses between death and
embalming will add to the problems and complications encountered. . . ."
Just how soon should one get going on the embalming? The author tells us,
"On the basis of such scanty information made available to this profession
through its rudimentary and haphazard system of technical research, we
must conclude that the best results are to be obtained if the subject is embalmed before life is completely extinct — that is, before cellular death has
occurred. In the average case, this would mean within an hour after somatic
death." For those who feel that there is something a little rudimentary, not
to say haphazard, about this advice, a comforting thought is offered by another writer. Speaking of fears entertained in early days of premature burial,
he points out, "One of the effects of embalming by chemical injection, however, has been to dispel fears of live burial." How true; once the blood is removed, chances of live burial are indeed remote.

To return to Mr. Jones, the blood is drained out through the veins and 8
replaced by embalming fluid pumped in through the arteries. As noted in

The Principles and Practices of Embalming, "Every operator has a favorite injection and drainage point — a fact which becomes a handicap only if he fails or refuses to forsake his favorites when conditions demand it." Typical favorites are the carotid artery, femoral artery, jugular vein, subclavian vein. There are various choices of embalming fluid. If Flextone is used, it will produce a "mild, flexible rigidity. The skin retains a velvety softness, the tissues are rubbery and pliable. Ideal for women and children." It may be blended with B. and G. Products Company's Lyf-Lyk tint, which is guaranteed to reproduce "nature's own skin texture . . . the velvety appearance of living tissue." Suntone comes in three separate tints: Suntan; Special Cosmetic Tint, a pink shade "especially indicated for young female subjects"; and Regular Cosmetic Tint, moderately pink.

About three to six gallons of a dyed and perfumed solution of formaldehyde, glycerin, borax, phenol, alcohol and water is soon circulating through Mr. Jones, whose mouth has been sewn together with a "needle directed upward between the upper lip and gum and brought out through the left nostril," with the corners raised slightly "for a more pleasant expression." If he should be bucktoothed, his teeth are cleaned with Bon Ami and coated with colorless nail polish. His eyes, meanwhile, are closed with flesh-tinted eye caps and eye cement.   9

The next step is to have at Mr. Jones with a thing called a trocar. This is a long, hollow needle attached to a tube. It is jabbed into the abdomen, poked around the entrails and chest cavity, the contents of which are pumped out and replaced with "cavity fluid." This done, and the hole in the abdomen sewn up, Mr. Jones's face is heavily creamed (to protect the skin from burns which may be caused by leakage of the chemicals), and he is covered with a sheet and left unmolested for a while. But not for long — there is more, much more, in store for him. He has been embalmed, but not yet restored, and the best time to start the restorative work is eight to ten hours after embalming, when the tissues have become firm and dry.   10

The object of all this attention to the corpse, it must be remembered, is to make it presentable for viewing in an attitude of healthy repose. "Our customs require the presentation of our dead in the semblance of normality . . . unmarred by the ravages of illness, disease or mutilation," says Mr. J. Sheridan Mayer in his *Restorative Art.* This is rather a large order since few people die in the full bloom of health, unravaged by illness and unmarked by some disfigurement. The funeral industry is equal to the challenge: "In some cases the gruesome appearance of a mutilated or disease-ridden subject may be quite discouraging. The task of restoration may seem impossible and shake the confidence of the embalmer. This is the time for intestinal fortitude and determination. Once the formative work is begun and affected tissues are cleaned or removed, all doubts of success vanish. It is surprising and gratifying to discover the results which may be obtained."   11

The embalmer, having allowed an appropriate interval to elapse, re-   12 turns to the attack, but now he brings into play the skill and equipment of sculptor and cosmetician. Is a hand missing? Casting one in plaster of Paris is a simple matter. "For replacement purposes, only a cast of the back of the hand is necessary; this is within the ability of the average operator and is quite adequate." If a lip or two, a nose or an ear should be missing, the embalmer has at hand a variety of restorative waxes with which to model replacements. Pores and skin texture are simulated by stippling with a little brush, and over this cosmetics are laid on. Head off? Decapitation cases are rather routinely handled. Ragged edges are trimmed, and head joined to torso with a series of splints, wires and sutures. It is a good idea to have a little something at the neck — a scarf or high collar — when time for viewing comes. Swollen mouth? Cut out tissue as needed from inside the lips. If too much is removed, the surface contour can easily be restored by padding with cotton. Swollen necks and cheeks are reduced by removing tissue through vertical incisions made down each side of the neck. "When the deceased is casketed, the pillow will hide the suture incisions . . . as an extra precaution against leakage, the suture may be painted with liquid sealer."

The opposite condition is more likely to be present itself — that of emaciation. His hypodermic syringe now loaded with massage cream, the embalmer seeks out and fills the hollowed and sunken areas by injection. In this procedure the backs of the hands and fingers and the under-chin area should not be neglected. 13

Positioning the lips is a problem that recurrently challenges the ingenuity of the embalmer. Closed too tightly, they tend to give a stern, even disapproving expression. Ideally, embalmers feel, the lips should give the impression of being ever so slightly parted, the upper lip protruding slightly for a more youthful appearance. This takes some engineering, however, as the lips tend to drift apart. Lip drift can sometimes be remedied by pushing one or two straight pins through the inner margin of the lower lip and then inserting them between the two front upper teeth. If Mr. Jones happens to have no teeth, the pins can just as easily be anchored in his Armstrong Face Former and Denture Replacer. Another method to maintain lip closure is to dislocate the lower jaw, which is then held in its new position by a wire run through holes which have been drilled through the upper and lower jaws at the midline. As the French are fond of saying, *il faut souffrir pour être belle.*[1] 14

If Mr. Jones has died of jaundice, the embalming fluid will very likely turn him green. Does this deter the embalmer? Not if he has intestinal fortitude. Masking pastes and cosmetics are heavily laid on, burial garments and casket interiors are color-correlated with particular care, and Jones is displayed beneath rose-colored lights. Friends will say, "How *well* he looks." 15

[1] "One must suffer in order to be beautiful."

Death by carbon monoxide, on the other hand, can be rather a good thing from the embalmer's viewpoint: "One advantage is the fact that this type of discoloration is an exaggerated form of a natural pink coloration." This is nice because the healthy glow is already present and needs but little attention.

The patching and filling are completed, Mr. Jones is now shaved, washed and dressed. Cream-based cosmetic, available in pink, flesh, suntan, brunette and blond, is applied to his hands and face, his hair is shampooed and combed (and, in the case of Mrs. Jones, set), his hands manicured. For the horny-handed son of toil special care must be taken; cream should be applied to remove ingrained grime, and the nails cleaned. "If he were not in the habit of having them manicured in life, trimming and shaping is advised for better appearance — never questioned by kin." 16

Jones is now ready for casketing (this is the present participle of the verb "to casket"). In this operation his right shoulder should be depressed slightly "to turn the body a bit to the right and soften the appearance of lying flat on the back." Positioning the hands is a matter of importance, and special rubber positioning blocks may be used. The hands should be cupped slightly for a more lifelike, relaxed appearance. Proper placement of the body requires a delicate sense of balance. It should lie as high as possible in the casket, yet not so high that the lid, when lowered, will hit the nose. On the other hand, we are cautioned, placing the body too low "creates the impression that the body is in a box." 17

Jones is next wheeled into the appointed slumber room where a few last touches may be added — his favorite pipe placed in his hand or, if he was a great reader, a book propped into position. (In the case of little Master Jones a Teddy bear may be clutched.) Here he will hold open house for a few days, visiting hours 10 A.M. to 9 P.M. 18

SUBJECT QUESTIONS

1. What reason does Mitford offer for the public's ignorance about what goes on in an embalming room? Are there some things people prefer not to know about?
2. In paragraph 3, Mitford invites the reader with no "stomach" to stop reading at this point. What is the effect of this warning? Does it make you prefer to stop reading, is it a challenge to be brave and read on, or does it excite your curiosity about what is coming?
3. In her description of the preparation room (paragraph 5), why do you think Mitford inserts the comment about the education necessary to be a mortician?
4. Mitford's immediate end is to analyze the process of preparing a body. What seems to be her ultimate aim?

5. The whole art of the mortician seems to be devoted to the purpose of making the body appear lifelike, as though only asleep, for the comfort of the bereaved. Would this comfort continue when the casket is lowered into the ground? Might not the bereaved be more willing to part with a very dead-looking body?

STRUCTURE QUESTIONS

1. The "preparation" process does not begin until paragraph 4. What purpose do the first three paragraphs serve?
2. Why does Mitford correct herself in paragraph 4? What is a euphemism? Would your expect to find an exorbitant number of euphemisms in the vocabulary of an undertaker?
3. Point out some of the ways Mitford controls the reader's response to the process she is describing. Would a less repugnant description be possible? Would it be a falsification of the process? Consider the wording in paragraph 1, for instance.
4. Is each step in the process described clearly — or at least clearly enough for the stomach of the average reader? Why do you think Mitford includes considerable detail about some steps — positioning the lips, for instance — and very little about pumping out the stomach cavity?

SUGGESTION FOR WRITING

Describe a process with which you are familiar. Try to influence the reader's attitude toward the process by your choice of descriptive detail. Avoid interpretive words.

The Gentleman's
Guide to Suicide

J. P. Donleavy

James Patrick Donleavy was born in New York in 1926 and educated at Trinity College, Dublin. He has won many awards, both as a novelist and as a playwright, despite the fact that he is unconventional and difficult to characterize or criticize. Among his novels are The Beastly Beatitudes of Balthazar B *(1968) and* The Onion Eaters *(1971). The following essay is taken from a curious book,* The Unexpurgated Code: A Complete Manual of Survival and Manners *(1975).*

Be neat when ending it all. It is exceedingly perverse to leave one's remains in an unlovely condition or where your corpse is likely to cause distressing nuisance. Even if it means an irritating postponement or inconvenience, always plan an appropriate time and place to kill yourself. Especially avoid any impromptu on the spur of the moment leavetakings involving rail tracks. These often become impulse sites for a permanent departure, thereby causing disquieting delays for others who with urgent deals or love trysts pending may still have a lot to live for. 1

On no account can it be accepted as thoroughbred to use shotgun blasts at close range particularly upon the skull where it knocks hell out of your afterlife phosphorescence.[1] There exists a wide range of other suitable weapons and vulnerable body sites which can achieve the desired dispatch. An elegantly embellished revolver firing straight into your heart a platinum plated bullet engraved with your armorial bearings is a stylish and dignified finishing stroke. A chaise longue is a markedly suitable setting for this type of exit. 2

It is seemly if your method of death is in keeping with your qualities as a person. But not, however, if you are a bit of a bungler and botcher. There is nothing more dumb brained than taking a jump to hang yourself and ending up suspended under the armpits half strangling on some coat hook without a hope of dying. If this is the kind of carnival joke you're likely to perform, try free fall bridge departure over open waters. There are many architecturally fine high spans offering this opportunity but as they were not designed for this purpose make sure you're not impeded by an embellish- 3

[1] Donleavy's term for the soul.

ment before hitting pay dirt or water. Additionally, some bridge sites offer the presence of sharks which make away with remains and this especially assists those without previous disposal arrangements with a reputable undertaker. However, if inadvertently you should execute a perfect olympic dive be prepared for bobbing back up in the water alive. Although a good punch on the nose is supposed to scare sharks away, these fish are notoriously unpredictable. And you may be suddenly glad also to be an olympic sprint swimmer.

Building jumping is most appropriately done from high up in the best financial districts where pedestrians are used to that kind of thing. It is really déclassé in other areas where it may attract a large gathering. The sense of power it incites in one is particularly unbecoming as you stand up there looking down on a sea of spellbound faces with the peanut and pretzel vendors making sales on the edge of the crowd. Even though your performance is without fee it is simply quite unchic to loll around toying with the public's attention, making yourself a socially diminished spectacle of conceit. Especially when leaning poised but teetering just that little bit extra out over the parapet with the crowd absolutely going out of its mind with gasps of suspense. Followed then by their groans of disappointment as you sway backwards to safety again. Instead of finally jumping you should join a circus.

In cases where your desire to exit this world has been provoked by many months of low down shabby treatment from the boys in the office, building jumping is permissible from your place of work. As this is your own little way of getting back at these horrid types, you may indulge to the full any parapet tricks you may have up your sleeve. And departing on your last wingless flight, be assured that it really does throw an incredible pall over the staff which can easily persist for hours on end. Although you may not be around to see it after you've been scraped up, many will descend on the elevator more slowly than you did in free flight to examine where you collided with the pavement. And they will express their surprise at how perfectly clean the spot is where hardly a trace of you now remains.

Poisons, usually of the old-fashioned variety, which disfigure the facial expression, must be rated as an ungraceful leavetaking. On the whole, they make for a rather contorted goodbye. So too do the various methods of strangling which cause eye-bulging and ghastly grimace. Crushing and squashing in spite of erasing one's expression should also be avoided as they leave a diabolically shocking flatness to be scratched up. Self-destruction by suttee and disembowling are dramatic but go unappreciated except in the countries where these are an accepted means of attaining your higher graduation. Although not disclosing that it is planned for this purpose, your local travel agent will be glad to arrange a leisurely trip and your heirs should be entitled to claim reimbursement for the return journey.

Requiring some self-control, holding your head under water is not an unpleasant way to go. Once the first thirst quenching lungful is aboard, this initial gulp and gasp relaxes the synapses rapidly into a rather pleasant swirling sleep. Gas is another method affording some peaceful reverie before drifting off. Except of course where certain vapors in contact with a spark can incite a condition which can make your and maybe a few of the neighbors' ascent into the last darkness take place with amazing velocity.

Although of classical significance heinous procedures such as the holding of one's nose and jumping into a den of rattlers, gaboon vipers or mambas is certain to make decent-minded people in a free society wonder what the hell kind of perverted problems you are trying to tear yourself permanently away from. Dispatch in the industrial manner known as the Scandinavian blast must also be considered outré, involving as it does a stroll down the boulevard smoking a stick of dynamite disguised as a cigar usually carrying an excellent brand name. Although sending you in a lot of simultaneous directions it is an extremely unchic way of heading for the happy humping ground.

For the connoisseur, ending it all at sea is the height of particularity. A late autumn westward sailing from the old to the new world with a trunkload of tweed suitings for hurricane deck constitutionals is your man. Your moment of adieu should be chosen as that least objectionable to one's fellow first class passengers and should always be taken in black tie from the lonelier starboard side. Imbibe your usual amounts of snuff and after-dinner port. Don't be afraid of enjoying these last days. They can be the happiest of your life. However do not accept an invitation to sit at the captain's table and beware of getting totally caught up in shipboard activities, especially ping-pong tournaments and games, the outcome of which may delay your earthly exit till it's time to dock. Romance too should be avoided unless it is one of those heart palpitating wild mad grabbing one night stands tumbling and crashing in various frissonic crescendos all over the state room. These fleshy shenanigans often add an aura of tender poignancy to your last goodbye as well as to your brief partner's memory of you. But do avoid inciting gossip which will make your gymnastic companion, left behind, the subject of speculation as to what the hell she did to make you go over the side.

As your remaining shipboard days unfold with your grave just a jump away, continue your brisk morning walks on deck before breakfast. The salt ocean spray on your cheeks and fresh air in your lungs will raise a marvelous appetite. Afternoons in your deck chair read from the minor to the great poets and contemplate that the sea will soon be your own private memorial. But don't allow this to make you eerie. Nor take your dive too early in the voyage to depress everyone for the rest of the trip.

On the edge of the Gulf Stream about three hundred miles south of

Nova Scotia is the best spot. The sea temperature will be about ten degrees centigrade and the depth plenty deep at thirteen thousand feet. Then following a simple but nourishing champagne meal of caviar, pressed duck, and asparagus, ending with strawberries and cream, take a final blast of cognac, round off with a few turns on the dance floor with your companion pal provided you have the self-control to avoid being tugged down to her state room for another blazing event. If she persists in hugging you excuse yourself for a series of long distance telephone calls and take a running hurdle at the railings just before three A.M.

Tips for your cabin steward and others who have rendered signal service should be left placed prominently in your state room. It is sporting to leave an amount covering the full journey. But make sure your steward has retired for the night as it is essential your premature gratuities do not result in the raising of the man overboard alarm. It really is embarrassing to be rescued and fished out amid all the searchlights with the remainder of the trip a nightmare of whispers and pointings every time you want a breath of fresh air at the ship's rails.

With your departure succeeding unnoticed you will land up to your scalp in the ocean. If you have avoided testicular concussion by means of cupped hands you will at first feel a pain free clutching sensation as you watch the liner make its way away like an illuminated fairy tale city trailing a great boiling white wake on the midnight depths. You may also think you hear the fading strains of the dance band. This is extremely unlikely but indeed you may count upon sniffing a fume or two from the vessel's turbines. In any event an awesome sense of peace will be yours paddling there in the extremely chilly water and you will be astonished as you come to profound terms with yourself at how much pleasure your own company will give you at this time.

Parting Words, Gestures, Apparel and Conversations

Proper care should be given to one's clothing at the time of one's deliberate demise. Informality is permissible for gassing and poisoning. For jumping and hanging, stick with sports apparel. Nudity, unless for drowning in the privacy of one's bath, always denotes an unpleasant characteristic in the deceased.

Final letters should be brief, unapologetic and neither sad nor glad. If you happen to have been a politically important personage in life "No comment" is proper. Most other sentiments sound forced when they are your very last utterances. But especially sidestep the one,

"It was a good life while it lasted."

That really is a remark of the bootless and unhorsed. Anyone speaking   16
straight from the bowels knows that life is mostly a pain in the arse. Therefore confine yourself to notes concerning various domestic matters, especially
those regarding household pets who may have been your only living solace.

"Please leave milk for Esme the cat and feed Putsie my piranha."

Political gestures, sentiments and shouts of "Up the Republic" and   17
"Long live liberty" and other remarks are strictly déclassé unless you are
aboard a liner traveling and jumping tourist class. Obscene gestures are also
out of place except in the case of the boys at the office. To make them really
smitten with your demise, an impassioned shout accompanied by a shaking
of the fist is in order.

"You really dirty lousy bunch of rotten guys."

However, one last warning concerning parting conversations. While on   18
deck leaning, expectantly over the rails, some previous pomposity may approach attempting to challenge you by first pretending to ask for a light.

"I say there old man, got a light."
"Sorry left my solid platinum lighter in my suite."
"Sir are you merely being painfully pretentious or have you left your
vulgar valuables behind because you are jumping."
"I beg your brazen pardon."
"Look here old man, I saw you standing well back as if to vault the rails
just as I came out on deck from the first class smoking room."
"I was merely exercising my thighs and calves having missed my after-
noon game of quoits."
"Sir, upon my monocle I regard that as monstrous twaddle, rot, bosh
and figs."
"How dare you accuse me of arrant poppycock."
"Of course sir, I dare. Just as I dare notice your one red and one green
sock. Witnessing such sartorial black tie blasphemy in first class is heinous,
sir."
"Those hues happen to be, if you don't mind, my racing colors, you
ruddy commoner you."
"Ha ha. If you think sir, by that remark that I would mistake you for a
member of the titled classes you have another transatlantic trip coming."
"I am a prince."
"I venture to suggest that that is more bull, pish, tush and mummery,
sir, and I would request you take your royal nonsense and person to another
shipping line. Because if you think that for one muffin you are going to deliberately delay this vessel for two hours in a rescue attempt of your plebeian
remains you have another jump coming."

This is extremely irritating behavior especially at a time during which   19
you are tasting the last of this life. This chap has quite obviously let his
monocled pomposity go to his head where clearly he intends it should set his
course in history. Short of calling for ping-pong paddles at dawn, a light pep-
pering of your chamois gloves about your chap's jowls should suffice a challenge to a duel. Naturally you don't want to delay your higher graduation by
getting hurt. Plus it's always difficult to jump as a cripple.

But if this son of a bitch persists in unpleasant testiness, take him by   20
his satin lapels or cummerbund and tug, tip and twist him over the rails with
you. He'll yell bloody murder and you may have to sock him unconscious
but at least you won't have to book another ocean passage. However it does
mean a gross lack of privacy down in the waves. Especially with an opinion-
ated prig who is likely to die like a commoner instead of a prince. . . .

SUBJECT QUESTIONS

1. Donleavy's advice is supposedly intended for the very rich. Is it inappropriate for other classes?
2. Why do you suppose Donleavy would write an article like this? Is a
   person seriously intent on suicide likely to follow Donleavy's suggested procedure?
3. What special warnings does he give about jumping from buildings?
4. Which method of suicide does Donleavy particularly recommend?
   Does it seem most fitting for the connoisseur?
5. Which methods are especially to be avoided by the true gentleman?
6. Does it seem appropriate that on a social level where everything else
   is done "by the book," Donleavy should give "the book" on suicide?

STRUCTURE QUESTIONS

1. Because Donleavy is discussing various types of suicide, all of his instructions cannot apply to any one type. Can you isolate steps generally applicable in the process? Are these presented in order?
2. Has the author observed the rule of clarity in explaining his process?
   Do any points need further explanation?
3. Why has Donleavy resorted to such French phrases as chic, déclassé,
   and outré? Are there no satisfactory English translations?
4. As a novelist, Donleavy may be less concerned with mechanical correctness than would a good expository prose writer. Do you notice
   any passages where attention to correctness might have improved
   the writing?
5. In general, does the style seem proper for the "gentleman" reader?
   Are there any notable deviations from this style? Are they lapses or
   do they serve a purpose?

SUGGESTION FOR WRITING

Write a process paper detailing correct behavior at some social event — how to conduct yourself at a dress dinner or at a football game, how to impress your teacher in the classroom. You may want to try a satirical approach if you think you can handle the required subtlety. If necessary, be prepared to describe what should not be done as well as what should be done.

Computers Don't Argue

Gordon R. Dickson

Gordon R. Dickson was born in Edmonton, Alberta, in 1923. He is best known as a mystery and science fiction writer. Dickson has published hundreds of short stories and novelettes, and a great many novels have followed his first science fiction book, Alien from Arcturus *(1956). Recently Dickson has been writing juvenile historical fiction as well as science fiction.*

Treasure Book Club   1
PLEASE DO NOT FOLD, SPINDLE OR MUTILATE THIS CARD
Mr: Walter A. Child Balance: $4.98
Dear Customer: Enclosed is your latest book selection. "Kidnapped,"
by Robert Louis Stevenson.

437 Woodlawn Drive   2
Panduk, Michigan
Nov. 16, 1965

Treasure Book Club
1823 Mandy Street
Chicago, Illinois

Dear Sirs:
I wrote you recently about the computer punch card you sent, billing me for "Kim," by Rudyard Kipling. I did not open the package containing it until I had already mailed you my check for the amount on the card. On opening the package, I found the book missing half its pages. I sent it back to you, requesting either another copy or my money back. Instead, you have sent me a copy of "Kidnapped," by Robert Louis Stevenson. Will you please straighten this out?
I hereby return the copy of "Kidnapped."

Sincerely yours,
Walter A. Child

Treasure Book Club   3
SECOND NOTICE
PLEASE DO NOT FOLD, SPINDLE OR MUTILATE THIS CARD
Mr. Walter A. Child Balance: $4.98
For "Kidnapped," by Robert Louis Stevenson
(If remittance has been made for the above, please disregard this notice)

                                            437 Woodlawn Drive   4
                                            Panduk, Michigan
                                            Jan. 21, 1966
Treasure Book Club
1823 Mandy Street
Chicago, Illinois

Dear Sirs:
May I direct your attention to my letter of November 16, 1965? You are still
continuing to dun me with computer punch cards for a book I did not order.
Whereas, actually, it is your company that owes *me* money.
                                            Sincerely yours,
                                            Walter A. Child

                                            Treasure Book Club   5
                                            1823 Mandy Street
                                            Chicago, Illinois
                                            Feb. 1, 1966
Mr. Walter A. Child
437 Woodlawn Drive
Panduk, Michigan

Dear Mr. Child:
We have sent you a number of reminders concerning an amount owing to us
as a result of book purchases you have made from us. This amount, which is
$4.98 is now long overdue.
    This situation is disappointing to us, particularly since there was no hesi-
tation on our part in extending you credit at the time original arrangements
for these purchases were made by you. If we do not receive payment in
full by return mail, we will be forced to turn the matter over to a collection
agency.
                                            Very truly yours,
                                            Samuel P. Grimes
                                            Collection Mgr.

437 Woodlawn Drive   6
Panduk, Michigan
Feb. 5, 1966

Dear Mr. Grimes:

Will you stop sending me punch cards and form letters and make me some kind of a direct answer from a human being?

I don't owe you money. *You* owe me money. Maybe I should turn your company over to a collection agency.

Walter A. Child

FEDERAL COLLECTION OUTFIT   88 Prince Street   7
Chicago, Illinois
Feb. 28, 1966

Mr. Walter A. Child
437 Woodlawn Drive
Panduk, Michigan

Dear Mr. Child:

Your account with the Treasure Book Club, of $4.98 plus interest and charges has been turned over to our agency for collection. The amount due is now $6.83. Please send your check for this amount or we shall be forced to take immediate action.

Jacob N. Harshe
Vice President

FEDERAL COLLECTION OUTFIT   88 Prince Street   8
Chicago, Illinois
April 8, 1966

Mr. Walter A. Child
437 Woodlawn Drive
Panduk, Michigan

Dear Mr. Child:

You have seen fit to ignore our courteous requests to settle your long overdue account with Treasure Book Club, which is now, with accumulated interest and charges, in the amount of $7.51.

If payment in full is not forthcoming by April 11, 1966 we will be forced to turn the matter over to our attorneys for immediate court action.

Ezekiel B. Harshe
President

MALONEY, MAHONEY, MACNAMARA and PRUITT   9
    Attorneys

                                                    89 Prince Street
                                                    Chicago, Illinois
                                                    April 29, 1966

Mr. Walter A. Child
437 Woodlawn Drive
Panduk, Michigan

Dear Mr. Child:
Your indebtedness to the Treasure Book Club has been referred to us for
legal action to collect.
        This indebtedness is now in the amount of $10.01. If you will send us
this amount so that we may receive it before May 5, 1966, the matter may be
satisfied. However, if we do not receive satisfaction in full by that date, we
will take steps to collect through the courts.
        I am sure you will see the advantage of avoiding a judgment against
you, which as a matter of record would do lasting harm to your credit rating.
                                            Very truly yours,
                                            Hagthorpe M. Pruitt, Jr.
                                            Attorney-at-law

                                                    437 Woodlawn Drive   10
                                                    Panduk, Michigan
                                                    May 4, 1966

Mr. Hagthorpe M. Pruitt, Jr.
Maloney, Mahoney, MacNamara and Pruitt
89 Prince Street
Chicago, Illinois

Dear Mr. Pruitt:
You don't know what a pleasure it is to me in this matter to get a letter from
a live human being to whom I can explain the situation.
        This whole matter is silly. I explained it fully in my letters to the
Treasure Book Company. But I might as well have been trying to explain to
the computer that puts out their punch cards, for all the good it seemed to
do. Briefly, what happened was I ordered a copy of "Kim," by Rudyard
Kipling, for $4.98. When I opened the package they sent me, I found the
book had only half its pages, but I'd previously mailed a check to pay them
for the book.
        I sent the book back to them, asking either for a whole copy or my

money back. Instead, they sent me a copy of "Kidnapped," by Robert Louis Stevenson — which I had not ordered; and for which they have been trying to collect from me.

Meanwhile, I am still waiting for the money back that they owe me for the copy of "Kim" that I didn't get. That's the whole story. Maybe you can help me straighten them out.

Relievedly yours,
Walter A. Child

P.S.: I also sent them back their copy of "Kidnapped," as soon as I got it, but it hasn't seemed to help. They have never even acknowledged getting it back.

MALONEY, MAHONEY, MACNAMARA and PRUITT   11
    Attorneys

89 Prince Street
Chicago, Illinois
May 9, 1966

Mr. Walter A. Child
437 Woodlawn Drive
Panduk, Michigan

Dear Mr. Child:
I am in possession of no information indicating that any item purchased by you from the Treasure Book Club has been returned.

I would hardly think that, if the case had been as you stated, the Treasure Book Club would have retained us to collect the amount owing from you.

If I do not receive your payment in full within three days, by May 12, 1966, we will be forced to take legal action.

Very truly yours,
Hagthorpe M. Pruitt, Jr.

COURT OF MINOR CLAIMS   12
    Chicago, Illinois

Mr. Walter A. Child
437 Woodlawn Drive
Panduk, Michigan

Be informed that a judgment was taken and entered against you in this court this day of May 26, 1966 in the amount of $15.66 including court costs.

Payment in satisfaction of this judgment may be made to this court or to the adjudged creditor. In the case of payment being made to the creditor, a release should be obtained from the creditor and filed with this court in order to free you of legal obligation in connection with this judgment.

Under the recent Reciprocal Claims Act, if you are a citizen of a different state, a duplicate claim may be automatically entered and judged against you in your own state so that collection may be made there as well as in the State of Illinois.

COURT OF MINOR CLAIMS   13
   Chicago, Illinois
PLEASE DO NOT FOLD, SPINDLE OR MUTILATE THIS CARD

Judgment was passed this day of May 27, 1966, under Statute $15.66
   Against: Child, Walter A. of 347 Woodlawn Drive, Panduk, Michigan.
Pray to enter a duplicate claim for judgment
     In: Picayune Court — Panduk, Michigan
     For amount: Statute 941

                                    437 Woodlawn Drive   14
                                    Panduk, Michigan
Samuel P. Grimes   May 31, 1966
Vice President, Treasure Book Club
1823 Mandy Street
Chicago, Illinois

Grimes:
This business has gone far enough. I've got to come down to Chicago on business of my own tomorrow. I'll see you then and we'll get this straightened out once and for all, about who owes what to whom, and how much!
                                    Yours,
                                    Walter A. Child

From the desk of the Clerk   15
   Picayune Court

                                    June 1, 1966
Harry:
The attached computer card from Chicago's Minor Claims Court against A. Walter has a 1500-series Statute number on it. That puts it over in Criminal with you, rather than Civil, with me. So I herewith submit it for your computer instead of mine. How's business?
                                      Joe

CRIMINAL RECORDS
  Panduk, Michigan
PLEASE DO NOT FOLD, SPINDLE OR MUTILATE THIS CARD

Convicted: (Child) A. Walter
On: May 26, 1966
Address: 437 Woodlawn Drive
Panduk, Mich.
Crim: Statute: 1566 (Corrected) 1567
Crime: Kidnap
Date: Nov. 16, 1965
Notes: At large. To be picked up at once.

POLICE DEPARTMENT, PANDUK, MICHIGAN. TO POLICE DEPARTMENT
CHICAGO ILLINOIS. CONVICTED SUBJECT A. (COMPLETE FIRST NAME UN-
KNOWN) WALTER, SOUGHT HERE IN CONNECTION REF. YOUR NOTIFICATION
OF JUDGMENT FOR KIDNAP OF CHILD NAMED ROBERT LOUIS STEVENSON, ON
NOV. 16, 1965. INFORMATION HERE INDICATES SUBJECT FLED HIS RESI-
DENCE, AT 437 WOODLAND DRIVE, PANDUK, AND MAY BE AGAIN IN YOUR
AREA.
      POSSIBLE CONTACT IN YOUR AREA: THE TREASURE BOOK CLUB, 1823
MANDY STREET, CHICAGO, ILLINOIS. SUBJECT NOT KNOWN TO BE DANGER-
OUS. PICK UP AND HOLD, ADVISING US OF CAPTURE . . .

TO POLICE DEPARTMENT, PANDUK, MICHIGAN. REFERENCE YOUR
REQUEST TO PICK UP AND HOLD A. (COMPLETE FIRST NAME UNKNOWN)
WALTER, WANTED IN PANDUK ON STATUTE 1567, CRIME OF KIDNAPPING.
      SUBJECT ARRESTED AT OFFICES OF TREASURE BOOK CLUB, OPERATING
THERE UNDER ALIAS WALTER ANTHONY CHILD AND ATTEMPTING TO COL-
LECT $4.98 FROM ONE SAMUEL P. GRIMES, EMPLOYEE OF THAT COMPANY.
      DISPOSAL: HOLDING FOR YOUR ADVICE.

POLICE DEPARTMENT PANDUK, MICHIGAN TO POLICE DEPARTMENT
CHICAGO, ILLINOIS
      REF. A. WALTER (ALIAS WALTER ANTHONY CHILD) SUBJECT WANTED
FOR CRIME OF KIDNAP, YOUR AREA, REF: YOUR COMPUTER PUNCH CARD
NOTIFICATION OF JUDGMENT, DATED MAY 27, 1966. COPY OUR CRIMINAL
RECORDS PUNCH CARD HEREWITH FORWARDED TO YOUR COMPUTER
SECTION.

CRIMINAL RECORDS
    Chicago, Illinois
PLEASE DO NOT FOLD, SPINDLE OR MUTILATE THIS CARD

SUBJECT (CORRECTION — OMITTED RECORD SUPPLIED)
APPLICABLE STATUTE NO. 1567
JUDGMENT NO. 456789
TRIAL RECORD: APPARENTLY MISFILED AND UNAVAILABLE
DIRECTION: TO APPEAR FOR SENTENCING BEFORE JUDGE JOHN ALEXANDER
MCDIVOT, COURTROOM A JUNE 9, 1966

From the Desk of   21
Judge Alexander J. McDivot

                                            June 2, 1966
Dear Tony:
I've got an adjudged criminal coming up before me for sentencing Thursday
morning — but the trial transcript is apparently misfiled.
    I need some kind of information (Ref: A. Walter — Judgment No.
456789, Criminal). For example, what about the victim of the kidnapping.
Was victim harmed?

                                            Jack McDivot

                                            June 3, 1966   22

Records Search Unit

Re: Ref: Judgment No. 456789 — was victim harmed?

                                            Tonio Malagasi
                                            Records Division

                                            June 3, 1966   23

To: United States Statistics Office
Attn.: Information Section
Subject: Robert Louis Stevenson
Query: Information concerning

                                            Records Search Unit
                                            Criminal Records Division
                                            Police Department
                                            Chicago, Ill.

June 5, 1966   ₂₄

To: Records Search Unit
Criminal Records Division
Police Department
Chicago, Illinois

Subject: Your query re Robert Louis Stevenson (File no. 189623)

Action: Subject deceased. Age at death, 44 yrs. Further information requested?

> A. K.
> Information Section
> U. S. Statistics Office

June 6, 1966   25

To: United States Statistics Office
Attn.: Information Division
Subject: RE: File no. 189623

No further information required.

> Thank you.
> Records Search Unit

> Criminal Records Division   26
> Police Department
> Chicago, Illinois
> June 7, 1966

To: Tonio Malagasi
Records Division
Re: Ref: judgment No. 456789 — victim is dead.

> Records Search Unit

June 7, 1966   27

To: Judge Alexander J. McDivot's Chambers

Dear Jack:
Ref: Judgment No. 456789. The victim in this kidnap case was apparently slain.

From the strange lack of background information on the killer and his victim, as well as the victim's age, this smells to me like a gangland killing. This for your information. Don't quote me. It seems to me, though, that Stevenson — the victim — has a name that rings a faint bell with me. Possibly, one of the East Coast Mob, since the association comes back to me as

something about pirates — possibly New York dockage hijackers — and
something about buried loot.

As I say, above is only speculation for your private guidance.

Any time I can help . . .

> Best,
> Tony Malagasi
> Records Division

MICHAEL R. REYNOLDS   28
   Attorney-at-law
                                              49 Water Street
                                              Chicago, Illinois
                                              June 8, 1966
Dear Tim:

Regrets: I can't make the fishing trip. I've been court-appointed here to
represent a man about to be sentenced tomorrow on a kidnapping
charge.

Ordinarily, I might have tried to beg off, and McDivot, who is doing
the sentencing, would probably have turned me loose. But this is the
damndest thing you ever heard of.

The man being sentenced has apparently been not only charged, but
adjuged guilty as a result of a comedy of errors too long to go into here. He
not only isn't guilty — he's got the best case I ever heard of for damages
against one of the larger Book Clubs headquartered here in Chicago. And
that's a case I wouldn't mind taking on.

It's inconceivable — but damnably possible, once you stop to think of
it in this day and age of machine-made records — that a completely innocent
man could be put in this position.

There shouldn't be much to it. I've asked to see McDivot tomorrow
before the time for sentencing, and it'll just be a matter of explaining to him.
Then I can discuss the damage suit with my freed client at his leisure.

Fishing next weekend?

> Yours,
> Mike

MICHAEL R. REYNOLDS   29
   Attorney-at-law
                                              49 Water Street
                                              Chicago, Illinois
                                              June 10
Dear Tim:

In haste —

No fishing this coming week either. Sorry.

You won't believe it. My innocent-as-a-lamb-and-I'm-not-kidding client has
just been sentenced to death for first-degree murder in connection with the
death of his kidnap victim.

Yes, I explained the whole thing to McDivot. And when he explained his situation to me, I nearly fell out of my chair.

It wasn't a matter of my not convincing him. It took less than three minutes to show him that my client should never have been within the walls of the County Jail for a second. But — get this — McDivot couldn't do a thing about it.

The point is, my man had already been judged guilty according to the computerized records. In the absence of a trial record — of course there never was one (but that's something I'm not free to explain to you now) — the judge has to go by what records are available. And in the case of an adjudged prisoner, McDivot's only legal choice was whether to sentence to life imprisonment, or execution.

The death of the kidnap victim, according to the statute, made the death penalty mandatory. Under the new laws governing length of time for appeal, which has been shortened because of the new system of computerizing records, to force an elimination of unfair delay and mental anguish to those condemned, I have five days in which to file an appeal, and ten to have it acted on.

Needless to say, I am not going to monkey with an appeal. I'm going directly to the Governor for a pardon — after which we will get this farce reversed. McDivot has already written the governor, also, explaining that his sentence was ridiculous, but that he had no choice. Between the two of us, we ought to have a pardon in short order.

Then, I'll make the fur fly . . .

And we'll get in some fishing.

Best,
Mike

OFFICE OF THE GOVERNOR OF ILLINOIS   June 17, 1966
Mr. Michael R. Reynolds
49 Water Street
Chicago, Illinois

Dear Mr. Reynolds:
In reply to your query about the request for pardon for Walter A. Child (A. Walter), may I inform you that the Governor is still on his trip with the Midwest Governors Committee, examining the Wall in Berlin. He should be back next Friday.

I will bring your request and letters to his attention the minute he returns.

Very truly yours,
Clara B. Jilks
Secretary to the Governor

June 27, 1966   31

Michael R. Reynolds
49 Water Street
Chicago, Illinois

Dear Mike:
Where is that pardon?
My execution date is only five days from now!

Walt

Walter A. Child (A. Walter)   June 29, 1966   32
Cell Block E
Illinois State Penitentiary
Joliet, Illinois

Dear Walt:
The Governor returned, but was called away immediately to the White
House in Washington to give his views on interstate sewage.
   I am camping on his doorstep and will be on him the moment he
arrives here.
   Meanwhile, I agree with you about the seriousness of the situation.
The warden at the prison there, Mr. Allen Magruder, will bring this letter to
you and have a private talk with you. I urge you to listen to what he has to
say; and I enclose letters from your family also urging you to listen to
Warden Magruder.

Yours,
Mike

Michael R. Reynolds   June 30, 1966   33
49 Water Street
Chicago, Illinois

Dear Mike: (This letter being smuggled out by Warden Magruder) As I was
talking to Warden Magruder in my cell, here, news was brought to him that
the Governor has at last returned for a while to Illinois, and will be in his
office early tomorrow morning, Friday. So you will have time to get the
pardon signed by him and delivered to the prison in time to stop my
execution on Saturday.
   Accordingly, I have turned down the Warden's kind offer of a chance
to escape; since he told me he could by no means guarantee to have all the

guards out of my way when I tried it; and there was a chance of my being killed escaping.

But now everything will straighten itself out. Actually, an experience as fantastic as this had to break down sometime under its own weight.

Best,
Walt

FOR THE SOVEREIGN STATE OF ILLINOIS   34

I, Hubert Daniel Willikens, Governor of the State of Illinois, and invested with the authority and powers appertaining thereto, including the power to pardon those in my judgement wrongfully convicted or otherwise deserving of executive mercy, do this day of July 1, 1966 announce and proclaim that Walter A. Child (A. Walter) now in custody as a consequence of erroneous conviction upon a crime of which he is entirely innocent, is fully and freely pardoned of said crime. And I do direct the necessary authorities having custody of the said Walter A. Child (A. Walter) in whatever place or places he may be held, to immediately free, release, and allow unhindered departure to him. . . .

Interdepartmental Routing Service   35
PLEASE DO NOT FOLD, MUTILATE, OR SPINDLE THIS CARD
Failure to route Document properly.
To: Governor Hubert Daniel Willikens
Re: Pardon issued to Walter A. Child, July 1, 1966

Dear State Employee:
You have failed to attach your Routing Number.
PLEASE: Resubmit document with this card and form 876, explaining your authority for placing a TOP RUSH category on this document. Form 876 must be signed by your Departmental Superior.

RESUBMIT ON: Earliest possible date ROUTING SERVICE office is open. In this case, Tuesday, July 5, 1966.

WARNING: Failure to submit form 876 WITH THE SIGNATURE OF YOUR SUPERIOR may make you liable to prosecution for misusing a Service of the State Government. A warrant may be issued for your arrest.

There are NO exceptions. YOU have been WARNED.

SUBJECT QUESTIONS

1. As a fiction writer, Dickson is less concerned with the *possible* than with the *probable*, to use Aristotle's terms. That is, even if we know that the events did not happen, we should be made to feel that they

might have happened. Does Dickson succeed in giving his story this probability?
2. Despite his title, Dickson is not likely to be attacking computers themselves (computers merely handle the information given them by humans). What is the object of Dickson's attack?
3. Perhaps the major step in the process by which Walter Child was executed is the switch in the charge against him from civil to criminal (kidnapping). Examine the text carefully to see how this came about.
4. On whom should the blame for the miscarriage of justice described here finally rest?
5. What does the final memo to the governor imply about "who's in charge"?

STRUCTURE QUESTIONS

1. Because Dickson has invented this process, we should be able to assume that the steps are in correct and necessary order. Are there in fact any places where the steps could be rearranged and still give the same result?
2. Are there any steps in the process that are not clearly explained? (As this is process rather than cause-and-effect analysis, *why* they happened need not be explained.)
3. As this story is composed of various communications, the style is not, and should not be, consistent throughout the story. Does the style of each letter or memorandum seem appropriate to the type of person (or computer) who sent it?
4. "Computers Don't Argue" is obviously not constructed in the way most short stories are; did you find Dickson's approach confusing? Should he have begun with an introduction or explanation? Would the effect have been the same had he done so?

SUGGESTIONS FOR WRITING

1. If you have had a running battle with a computer, write a process paper explaining the steps in that struggle and its outcome.
2. If your university has computerized registration, write a process paper on the subject, "How to Beat the Computer." Or you may wish to write a process paper explaining "How to Pass a Machine-Graded Examination."

The Unknown Citizen

W. H. Auden

Wystan Hugh Auden (1907–1973) was born in England. He published
some twenty-five volumes of poetry, five plays, five volumes of criticism, five translations, and edited twenty-seven other volumes. Auden
won numerous awards for poetry, including Pulitzer and Bollingen
prizes and the King's Gold Medal (1937). Although "The Unknown Citizen" should be judged primarily as a poem, it is also an interesting kind
of double process analysis: it shows how the unknown citizen "got processed" by his society, and it is a recipe for cooking up a model citizen
according to accepted standards. The poem was composed in 1940, but
Auden might have written something not very different today.

(To JS / 07 / M / 378
This Marble Monument
Is Erected by the State)

He was found by the Bureau of Statistics to be
One against whom there was no official complaint,
And all the reports on his conduct agree
That, in the modern sense of an old-fashioned word, he was a saint,
For in everything he did he served the Greater Community.   5
Except for the War till the day he retired
He worked in a factory and never got fired,
But satisfied his employers, Fudge Motors Inc.
Yet he wasn't a scab or odd in his views,
For his Union reports that he paid his dues,   10
(Our report on his Union shows it was sound)
And our Social Psychology workers found
That he was popular with his mates and liked a drink.
The Press are convinced that he bought a paper every day
And that his reactions to advertisements were normal in every way.   15
Policies taken out in his name prove that he was fully insured,

And his Health-card shows he was once in hospital but left it cured.
Both Producers Research and High-Grade Living declare
He was fully sensible to the advantages of the Instalment Plan
And had everything necessary to the Modern Man,   20
A phonograph, a radio, a car and a frigidaire.
Our researchers into Public Opinion are content
That he held the proper opinions for the time of year;
When there was peace, he was for peace; when there was war, he went.
He was married and added five children to the population,   25
Which our Eugenist says was the right number for a parent of his
    generation,
And our teachers report that he never interfered with their education.
Was he free? Was he happy? The question is absurd:
Had anything been wrong, we should certainly have heard.

SUBJECT QUESTIONS

1. Is there any way to tell whether the citizen acted from his own chosen values or because he had been perfectly programmed? (How
   does Auden make clear, in other words, that his intent is satire?)
2. In what sense can the citizen be called a "saint"? If he is a saint, why
   is he "unknown"?
3. "And our teachers report that he never interfered with their education"; what is implied by the choice of the pronoun "their"?
4. Do all the statistics on the unknown citizen add up to a coherent
   portrait? Is anything missing? (Note that his religion is not mentioned; should it be?)
5. Assuming that Auden's portrait is approximately what the establishment encourages — whether consciously or not — as a model, what
   would the result be if it succeeded in getting everyone to conform to
   that model? How would such a society differ from that pictured in
   Huxley's Brave New World?

STRUCTURE QUESTIONS

1. Try working out the rhyme scheme of the poem. Is there any regular
   rhythm (iambic pentameter, e.g.)? Do you think Auden was trying to
   write an "unpoetic poem"? Would there have been any advantage,
   given the subject, to making the meter and rhyme scheme monoto-
   nously regular?
2. The poem makes clear all the ingredients of the establishment's recipe for a model citizen; are they arranged in any logical order?
   Should they be?
3. Do you think the last two lines are really necessary to the poem?

What effect do they have? Are they out of character with the rest of the inscription on the monument?

SUGGESTION FOR WRITING

Write a process paper explaining how a social institution (church, family, school, fraternity) goes about "programming" its members to act in predictable ways. You need not imply that such training is necessarily bad. Just explain the process.

5

THE FAMILY UNDER STRESS

Cause and Effect

The immediate difficulty confronting the analyzer of cause and effect relations is the possibility of a "multiplicity of causes." Seldom in nature or in society does a one cause–one effect relationship occur; normally a number of factors contribute to any one result, and one cause such as the atom bomb can have any number of aftereffects. If a chemical reaction will not take place except under pressure, at a certain temperature, and in the presence of a catalyst, then pressure, temperature, and catalyst must be considered along with the chemicals actually involved in the reaction as "causes" of the reaction. In the social sciences the problems are even more complicated, and observers who fail to expect many causes or effects are almost certain to distort their analysis. Gibbon in his great work, *The Decline and Fall of the Roman Empire,* failed to see the multiplicity of economic and political causes involved when he tried to show that the Roman Empire fell primarily because of the rise of Christianity.

Another danger in cause and effect analysis is the possible presence of incidental factors which are not really a part of the cause but which may appear to be so because of their very presence. "This must be a good theme — I spent six hours on it" or "I knew he'd fail that test: he went off on a pledge trip the previous weekend" are common examples of too-hasty assumption of a cause and effect relationship. A less obvious example would be this: "No wonder I failed the test — I had a bad headache that day." The headache might, of course, have been a partial cause, but the student might also have done just as badly without the headache. Certainly it would be a mistake to assume a one cause–one effect relationship here.

In spite of these difficulties of false cause and multiplicity of causes, analysis of cause and effect can be a profitable endeavor, even by the student untrained in the intricacies of logical analysis. Take the question, "Why did I come to college?" Perhaps students have never really thought about an answer to this question, but if they consider it objectively they can probably discover the causes for their coming to college: pure interest in learning, desire for better jobs, parental pressure, desire to keep up with friends, unreadiness to face the world on their own, and so on. Although they may miss a few causes their answers are likely to tell them something about themselves which they hadn't realized before. Or take one more example: Jane asks herself, "Why do I love John?" Probably she will either invent a few likely sounding reasons (rationalize) or quickly put the question out of her head unanswered. But if she honestly and objectively tries to answer it, she may find that her love has a sounder basis than she suspected — or she may realize that she is being "taken."

At any rate, because students are constantly being called upon to analyze cause and effect relationships ("Why did Hamlet refuse to kill the king at prayers?" "Why does this painting seem to have more depth than that one?" "What factors influence juvenile delinquency rates?"), it is good to know some of the basic principles involved.

The primary requirement is an objective, unprejudiced approach. Analyzers must never make the mistake of assuming they know the cause beforehand and then look for supporting evidence. This is what happens when a tobacco company employs an "impartial" scientist to prove that there is no cause and effect relation between smoking and lung cancer. At best this investigator's chances of arriving at "truth" are cut in half before even beginning.

Another requirement, then, is that the analyzer gather all the facts available and consider all possible explanations, or causes, for an effect. If Joe asks Henrietta to go water skiing with him and she refuses, he cannot immediately conclude that Henrietta is either a snob or a fool. To arrive at the real cause or causes for this effect, Joe needs to collect as much pertinent evidence as he can, formulate various hypotheses from these facts, and then test each hypothesis to see if it might be the cause, or part of the cause, of Henrietta's refusal. Perhaps she doesn't like water skiing; she may have a cold; she may have several important tests coming up; she may be engaged to another man; or she may not like Joe. If Joe tests each of these possibilities and finds that Henrietta is healthy, loves water skiing, does not have another boyfriend but does date, then Joe may suspect — but not yet definitely conclude — that Henrietta does not like him.

But how can he find out for certain? His next step would be a controlled experiment to check his remaining hypothesis. He might try asking Henrietta to a different social function, say a concert, on a different day. If she accepts gladly, Joe must go back and check on other possible causes of the water skiing fiasco. If on the other hand she still refuses, he has further corroborating evidence for his hypothesis that Henrietta doesn't like him. But it may be that she doesn't like concerts and refused the second date on that account. So Joe must test a bit further. He might induce his friend Jim to ask Henrietta to go water skiing at the same time and place Joe had suggested to her. If she accepts, Joe can be fairly certain that *he* is at least partly the cause for Henrietta's refusal. As a final check, he could have a second friend ask Henrietta to the concert. If she accepts that date, too, Joe can start looking for greener pastures — or other girl friends.

But suppose Joe is interested only in Henrietta and wants to know *why* she doesn't like him. Then he must begin a whole new series of analyses. He must gather the facts about himself and Henrietta that might be pertinent to their relationship, and from these formulate hypotheses which could explain the effect. There may be a basic personality clash; she may be a foot taller than Joe; she may not like his taste in clothing; or perhaps he needs a better toothpaste. The point is that Joe must again employ the same principles of objective analysis and testing that he used in arriving at the first conclusion.

The same procedures apply for any analysis of cause and effect. Because the facts and circumstances will be different in different problems, no more specific advice than this can be given here. Tracking down cause and effect relations may sometimes seem frustrating, but it can be a fascinating search. It is what provides the excitement in almost any research project. If students who attempt cause and effect analyses will remember to be unprejudiced, to collect as many pertinent facts as possible, and to test each hypothesis, they should be able to make some significant contribution, at least to their own self-knowledge.

The Wrong Side of the Generation Gap

Ellen Goodman

Ellen Goodman writes a column for The Boston Globe *that is syndicated and appears in more than two hundred newspapers across the country. A cum laude graduate of Radcliffe College, Goodman was a Nieman Fellow at Harvard University. Her commentaries have been heard on television and radio, and she is the author of the book* Turning Points *(1979). She lives with her daughter not far from Boston. The following article is from a collection of her essays entitled* Close to Home *(1978).*

Last week, seventy-six-year-old Henry Jumping Bull complained in public   1
about the younger generation. Like every other older generation since his
grandpa, Sitting Bull, was knee-high to a buffalo, he lamented the fact that
"the kids these days" had lost the old values and were going to hell in
various and sundry handbaskets.

Well, I hate to take issue with him, but the fellow does seem to have   2
his sights on the wrong side of the generation gap. While in the sixties
middle-aged parents were appalled at the lifestyles of their children, in the
seventies midlife children are trying to cope with the changing lifestyles of
their parents' generation.

A friend of mine just experienced what could only be called genera-   3
tion shock. Her sixty-year-old widowed mother was coming up from her
Florida home for a two-week visit. This in itself presented no more than
the usual problems — "if she tells me once more to fork-split the English
muffins . . ." — but this time Mother was bringing the New Man in Her
Life.

The question before the house was (are you ready?), "Should I put   4
them in one bedroom or two?"

When I suggested that she ask her mother, this thirty-four-year-old   5
woman, who has read the collected works of Carlos Castaneda and medi-
tates with her husband and children twice a day, shrieked, "I can't ask my
mother *that!*"

It's all very confusing. A father in our crowd who regularly threatened   6
death and dismemberment to his children if they were out past midnight
is now widowed and having a "relationship," mind you, with a fifty-

From *Close to Home* by Ellen Goodman. Copyright © 1979 by The Washington Post Company. Reprinted by permission of Simon & Schuster, a Division of Gulf & Western Corporation.

eight-year-old divorcée on Cape Cod. His thirty-eight-year-old son was concerned that he may marry this woman despite the fact that they are not of the same faith. It is now the father who has to suggest to his boy, "Why? Are you afraid we will have conflicts bringing up the children?"

There are all kinds of symptoms of this role reversal going around. 7 There are "children" who find themselves listening to tales of their parents' dates. There are parents who find themselves worrying about whether they should bring their new friends home to meet the children. Not to mention the grandchildren.

Then, of course, there are growing numbers of so-called senior citi- 8 zens who are living together with more Social Security and less legality. Two widowed and/or retired singles find the cost of marriage very dear in terms of lost pensions or reduced Social Security, and so many don't marry.

This leads to a certain awkwardness around Thanksgiving, etc. About 9 a year ago, Jane Otten of Washington described her difficulty finding a way to talk about the woman her son was living with. "This is my son's uh . . ." Let me tell you, that's nothing compared with introducing your father's "uh."

The worst case of judgment reversal came from the husband of an old 10 roommate of mine who was visiting from Oregon. This man I once described as the only middle-aged junior at Harvard. He was tall, skinny and stuffy at twenty and still is. He informed me that he is not at all sure he will allow (sic) his children to visit with their grandmother and her "uh," because he is not sure he wants them exposed to such, and I quote, "immorality."

And the beat goes on. 11

It seems to be a lot easier to deal with change among our children 12 than our parents. We have come to expect that "kids will be kids," adolescent revolt and all that. But our parents are supposed to be the safe repositories of tradition against which we — not they — can revolt. They are supposed to go down the road of retirement life baking cookies, puttering in the garden and taking their grandchildren to the zoo.

"Remember when sixty-five was old?" my former roommate asked 13 me in a voice that I can only describe as wistful.

It would be terribly convenient, of course, if our parents would really 14 retire, would lead their lives according to the original life plan, beading Christmas skirts and refinishing rockers, without being touched by death, divorce, disaster, vulnerability, insecurity or, certainly, sexuality. After all, doesn't the generation in the middle have enough trouble with their children?

There are those of us who seem to insist that it is inconsiderate of our 15 parents to still be in a state of change after age fifty-five, or sixty at the latest. Especially when we want them to be our Parents, for heaven's sake, and they keep turning out to be people. The nerve of them.

I simply do not know what is happening to the older generation these days. 16

SUBJECT QUESTIONS

1. What seems to be the most disconcerting effect of changing attitudes among the older generation? Has Goodman selected atypical examples, or does the behavior she describes appear to be widespread?
2. Assuming that the younger generation regularly rejects many traditional behavior patterns, why would they object to the older generation's doing the same?
3. Could it be said that grandparents and grandchildren have, at least from Goodman's one concern here, more in common with one another than with the generation in the middle? Or does that middle generation indulge in the same behavior?
4. In this short essay, Goodman is mainly concerned with effects, not their causes. How would you account for the changing behavior of "grandpa's generation"?
5. Goodman says, "we want them to be our Parents," but "they keep turning out to be people." What is the implied difference between parents and people? Don't we normally consider our parents to be "people"?

STRUCTURE QUESTIONS

1. Goodman uses causal analysis both to entertain and to point out discrepancies between our attitudes toward ourselves and those toward our parents. Does one aim interfere with the other, or does Goodman achieve both?
2. Examine Goodman's use of slightly altered clichés to achieve ironic effect. How many of these can you find?
3. "Remember when sixty-five was old?" Is this question intended to suggest part of the cause for the effect Goodman is describing? Should she have developed it further? Does paragraph 8 suggest an economic cause?
4. Toward what age group is this essay directed? How can you tell? Would it need to be written differently if the readers were primarily teen-agers?
5. What is the point of opening with the anecdote about Henry Jumping Bull? How does the closing sentence relate to this beginning paragraph?

6. Count the number of concrete examples Goodman uses in this brief essay. Would she have done better to develop one at length rather than introduce a number of brief ones? Does each serve a different but related purpose?

SUGGESTIONS FOR WRITING

1. Describe, and try to account for, a particular behavior pattern in a grandparent or other elderly person you know well. Does this person behave as you would expect? Do you approve? You may want to write about the reasons for your own expectations.
2. In America, young people take full-time jobs very much later than previously (or than in Third World countries today), and more and more people are living past retirement age. Consider some of the effects of these two phenomena. You may want to concentrate on economic implications, social effects, or attitudes toward leisure.

Omnigamy: The New Kinship System

Lionel Tiger

Lionel Tiger (b. 1937) is a Canadian-born anthropologist, director of graduate programs at Rutgers University and research director at the H. F. Guggenheim Foundation. He is especially interested in the family as a social unit and modern attempts to find viable substitutes for it. Among his books in this area are Men in Groups *(1969) and* Women in the Kibbutz *(1975). His most recent book is* Optimism: The Biology of Hope *(1980). The essay which follows first appeared in* Psychology Today.

A hapless British cabinet minister responsible for the hapless UK telephone system once complained that the more phones installed in his country, the more there were to call, and so the demand for phones increased: supply creates demand. Somewhat the same thing is happening with marriage in America. The more divorces there are, the more experienced marriers exist, ready to remarry — and many do. The divorce rate has jumped 250 percent in the past 21 years; about 80 percent of the formerly married remarry. With each new marriage, the parents and children involved acquire a whole new set of relatives, friends, and associations — in effect, they stretch their kinship system. Many people are married to people who have been married to other people who are now married to still others to whom the first parties may not have been married, but to whom somebody has likely been married. Our society, once based on the principle of solid monogamy until death do us part, has shifted toward a pattern of serial polygamy, in which people experience more than one spouse, if only one at a time. Thus we appear to be moving to a new and imprecise system we might call omnigamy, in which each will be married to all.

People keep marrying, even though happy marriages are regarded as surprising and much-envied occurrences. The not-so-stately pageant of marriage goes on, heedless of the cautionary cries of pain and the clenched question: Why? Various responsible estimators expect that from a third to a half of the marriages formed in this decade will end in divorce sometime. That is astonishing. It is also astonishing that, under the circumstances, marriage is still legally allowed. If nearly half of anything else ended so disastrously, the government would surely ban it immediately. If half the tacos served in restaurants caused dysentery, if half the people learning karate broke their palms, if only 6 percent of people who went on roller-coasters damaged their middle ears, the public would be clamoring for action. Yet the most intimate of disasters — with consequences that may last a lifetime for both adults and children — happens over and over again. Marriage has not yet gone underground.

To an anthropologist, the emergence of a new kinship system should   3
be as exciting as the discovery of a new comet to an astronomer. But in the case of omnigamy, the developing pattern is still unclear, the forces shaping it unanalyzed, the final structure difficult to predict. We know the numbers of marriages and remarriages, but what about the apparent acceleration of the process? The new system permits — perhaps even demands — that its members repair themselves quickly after crises of vast personal proportion. In the slapdash, overpraised, and sentimental film *An Unmarried Woman*, Jill Clayburgh explains to her (quite nauseating) therapist how agonizing and lonely it was when her husband of umpteen years left her, and how she has been without sexual congress for such a long, long time. When the therapist hears this dreadful fact, she earnestly recommends that this casualty of a massive private accident return immediately to the sexual fray. It has, after all, been *seven weeks.*

The heroine subsequently decides to reject an offer to join an attrac-   4
tive and apparently quite suitable artist. Instead she chooses to lead an independent life as a part-time secretary in a SoHo art gallery, which makes her somewhat radical with respect to the omnigamous system. For her obligation seems clear: she must form some sturdy response, one way or the other, to the ambient fact of marriage and remarriage. To remain haunted by grief and inhibited by a sense of failure is taken as a mere expression of cowardice or restlessness.

When anthropology first started out, the difficult trick in studying any   5
culture was to discover just what the kinship system was — who was married to whom, and why, and what connections counted for inheritance, status, and authority. We found that marriage was the instrument for creating the extended family, which provided for most human needs in the tribal societies. If an anthropologist from the Trobriand Islands came here now, he or she could well conclude that by stimulating further marriages, divorce has come to be an important organizing principle in our society, since kinship alliances among divorced people are so extensive and complex.

When parents divorce and remarry, the new family connections ex-   6
tend the reach of family life to dimensions a Baganda or Trobriander or Hopi could well understand. Take an example: after the divorce of A and B, siblings A1 and B1 live with A and her new husband, C, but visit B and his new wife, D, on weekends. C's children, C1, C2, and C3, like to go to

basketball games with A1 and B1. D's children by her first marriage also enjoy the company of A1 and B1, and take them along on visits to their father, E, a former star athlete who becomes an important hero and role model to the children of A, who has never met him and probably never will.

Nor is it only marriage that binds. In a world where all Mom and Dad's companions are potential mates, Dad's live-in girl friend may turn up for parents' night at school when he's out of town. She also may have a brother — a kind of stepuncle to the kids — with a 40-foot sloop. (The spreading network can put children in touch with a dislocating variety of styles.)

What this means for children, and how it affects their sense of what is stable, what is optional, what is fast, slow, brisk, or stately, is, of course, difficult to say. The generation of children spawned by the Age of Omnigamy has not yet made its mark on the social system in any clear way; we cannot know whether they are immune, immunized, or carriers of the bug across generational lines. In the old days, people were titillated by the polygamous habits of Hollywood celebrities, but few were tempted to emulate them. Parents, grandparents, aunts, and uncles seem to be more important role models for children. When they keep changing partners, it will likely increase the child's sense of the tentativeness in all relations that the new system reflects.

While I am not implying that omnigamous parents set a bad example, they surely set some example. The consequences for their own children and for those others with whom they come in contact must be considerable. Divorce as a recurrent aspect of life may make it relatively easier for children to accept when they are young, but harder to avoid when they become adults. And who has calculated the effect of omnigamy on grandparents, whose connections with their grandchildren suddenly come to be mediated by strangers — stepparents who might even move them to some distant city?

I do not mean to be alarmist and implacably negative about all this. The existence of relatively civilized divorce options is as much a sign of human freedom as it is of sanctioned personal confusion and pain. Who, after all, would wish to confirm in their desperate plight the countless real-world descendants of Madame Bovary?

Surely, too, there is a value in the extension of personal experience to wider circles of people than strict and permanent monogamy permits. And there is presumably an enhancement of personal vividness, which the new, relatively unstructured world permits — if not coerces.

Omnigamy may have interesting economic implications as well. Adrienne Harris of York University in Toronto has pointed out that each marital separation stimulates the repurchase of those items left in one household and needed in the next. Like amoebas splitting, one dishwasher becomes two, one vacuum cleaner becomes two, one television becomes two; domestic purchases even become impetuous ("Why shouldn't I have *my* Cuisinart to do my fish mousse when he/she has *our* Cuisinart for hers/ his?"). One can't help speculating that the rapid increase in retail outlets selling cooking equipment reflects the doubled demands of the new kinship system.

And where would the real estate market be without house sales to 13 accommodate people who can no longer accommodate each other? And has anyone wondered why the garage sale has recently become so common? The economic shifts that depend on the breakup and re-forming of marital units are a form of internal colonialism: at the same time that the United States can no longer control foreign markets, it is expanding its internal ones. The family system, which both Engels and Marx saw as the stimulus for the development of capitalism, may even, in the new form, turn out to be one of its props. As with all colonialisms, however, many people come to be exploited. Taking up the options omnigamy offers strains the financial and emotional resources both.

Can it be said that these comments apply mostly to a small group of 14 self-involved persons inhabiting the Upper East and West Sides of Manhattan, where the production of novels and articles about marriage and anguished personal failure is a major cottage industry? No. If the divorce rates persist and cities continue to export their social patterns, as in the past, other communities still complacently conventional and relatively monogamous will make a gradual but perceptible shift to omnigamy. The pattern will broaden unless there is soon — and there could be — a renewed commitment to monogamous fidelity, and possibly even to the importance of virginity as a factor in marital choice (this possibility seems rather remote). What does seem clear is that many changes will derive from these many changes, perhaps even a return to notions of marriage based on economic convenience and an agreement to mount a common assault on loneliness. Marriage could be on its way to becoming a generalized corporate, if small-scale, experience capable of providing some sense of community and some prospect of continuity. But it may also become a relatively planless arrangement and rearrangement of fickle magnets inexplicably and episodically drawn into each other's orbits for varying purposes and periods.

SUBJECT QUESTIONS

1. If a high percentage of marriages end in failure, why do eighty percent of the divorcees get remarried? Are they simply gluttons for punishment?
2. In paragraph 2, Tiger points out that almost any practice other than

marriage would be outlawed if it had a failure rate of fifty percent. Is it "astonishing," then, that marriage is still legal? Should it be?

3. What seems to be the chief impact on children in the new system of "serial polygamy"? Does Tiger think the extended network of relations is good or bad?

4. What are the "economic implications" of omnigamy? Would it be in the interest of manufacturers to popularize divorce in their advertising?

5. Which of the possibilities offered in the final two sentences seems preferable? Does Tiger dismiss the possibility of a return to the "normal happy marriage" which film romances still hold up as the ideal culmination of a love affair?

6. A satirical popular song several years ago which commented on the new kinship system was called "I'm My Own Grandpa." Think of some complicated family relationships which could result from "serial polygamy" (e.g., the children of a man whose second marriage was to his first wife's sister).

STRUCTURE QUESTIONS

1. Does the opening analogy between remarriage and the British telephone system help to clarify what "is happening with marriage in America"? Is it a useful way to begin the essay?

2. What is the point of Tiger's summarizing the plot of the film *An Unmarried Woman* (in paragraphs 3 and 4)? How might Tiger have made its relevance clearer?

3. While the entire essay is devoted to cause and effect relations, Tiger does not fully analyze the effects of omnigamy; why doesn't he? Does he make clear that these effects are bound to be different from those of traditional monogamous marriages?

4. Several shorter causal analyses are developed within the framework of the general subject. Examine one of these — for example, the one on "economic implications." Given its brevity, does it conform to the rules set out in the introduction to this section?

5. Tiger is a professional anthropologist and sociologist. Does he manage to avoid the gobbledygook often associated with social scientists? What devices does he use to avoid writing "social scientese"? Are there passages which could be improved with less abstract writing?

SUGGESTIONS FOR WRITING

1. If you have first- or second-hand knowledge of a situation like one of those developed in paragraphs 6 and 7, analyze the effects of such remarriages on the children involved.

2. Analyze the causes or effects of the increasingly common practice of "trial marriage" or simply "living together" among college students.
3. Construct an essay on the possible advantages (or disadvantages) of widespread omnigamy. Or consider the differences in effects in a big city and in a small town.

Untying the Family
Bruno Bettelheim

Bruno Bettelheim is a retired professor of education, behavioral sciences, and psychiatry and Director Emeritus of the Orthogenic School at the University of Chicago. He has written a number of books, including A Home for the Heart *(1973),* Dialogues with Mothers *(1962),* Children of the Dream *(1969), and* The Uses of Enchantment *(1976). The following essay was written as the basis for a discussion by experts on marriage and the family. In the first half, not reprinted here, Bettelheim had pointed out that while there may still be valid psychological reasons for getting married, economic and social forces no longer make a necessity of marriage, as they did until the present century.*

All this is well known. What are not so well known are changes which have occurred during the last few generations due to advances in medical sciences and alterations in the life cycle of the individual.

Much has been written about the new sexual morality, or freedom, which no longer requires dependence on one marital partner for sexual satisfaction. But it was not a morality of sexual freedom which brought about the significant changes in our views of marriage and family relations. Rather, it was progress in the medical sciences: ease of contraception and control of venereal disease. Monogamy was most powerfully buttressed by the fear that satisfying — that is, completed — intercourse was likely to lead to pregnancy, and by anxiety about who would take care of the mother during and after pregnancy, and of the child after his birth, if marriage did not tie a male to his family.

In promiscuous relations there was the great danger of contracting venereal disease, a horrible and often lethal sickness. Only in sexual relations with one's marital partner could one feel reasonably protected against this danger.

Before the appearance of the pill and similar contraceptive devices and the ready availability of abortion, it was essentially up to the male to see to it that sexual relations did not result in pregnancy. The female's ability to protect herself against this danger was much more limited. If the male was the one who alone could protect the female against such danger — short of her

Reprinted with permission from the September/October 1976 issue of *The Center Magazine*, publication of The Center for the Study of Democratic Institutions, Santa Barbara, California.

giving up a normal sexual life — how understandable that such a socially and psychologically protective role often became tantamount to a dominating role. Often the survival of mother and child depended on the husband-father providing much of the livelihood, especially during the last stages of pregnancy and during the nursing period. This dependency was another reason for the male to assume and the female to accept his protective role, which again easily became one of dominance in important respects. Marital relations were built on this role of the male and on the female's catering to it through accepted or assumed submission.

Modern contraceptive devices have put the woman in control over her pregnancies. No longer does she have to rely either on foregoing normal and complete sex experiences or on the man acting with responsibility. It is she who now has full control over and responsibility for childbirth. This is a reversal of roles which necessarily must lead to far-reaching changes in marital relations. Changes are already taking place, since the person who carries major responsibility naturally becomes the more dominant in a relationship. If children make for the family, the person who decides whether, how many, and when children will be born has the final say in regard to family matters. This is today's reality. But, again, the expectations of both males and females are in many cases still the old ones: that the male should be the protector and the person who decides: that the female should be the one who is part of the decisions but should not make them on her own. These expectations fly in the face of what has become their basis for sexual reality.

With venereal disease readily curable, a much greater barrier against promiscuous relations has been removed than we are ready to realize. Our self-love and high opinion of ourselves suggest to us that modern sexual freedom is due to our greater enlightenment. Actually, it is largely due to the removal of fear of the consequences of promiscuity. Still, the fact remains that that fear was a powerful reinforcer of the marriage bond and that it helped strengthen the family. Now, the family will have to survive without being buttressed by fears often camouflaged as higher morality.

A consequence of effective contraception and ease of abortion is that having a child is truly the parents' free decision, most of all the mother's. It is a decision which is all the more difficult to make since foregoing having children no longer interferes with sexual pleasure. To become pregnant was viewed as an act of God. It is much easier to accept God's will than to have to live with the consequences of one's free decisions. The question, did I really want to have this child, when seriously raised, often becomes difficult to answer with certainty. The same goes for the spacing of children, which today is a difficult and often bothersome problem, whereas before it was due to the exigencies of nature.

Children, too, at a relatively early age, know that their parents had a choice in the matter of their being born. Today they can rightly throw into a

5

6

7

8

parent's face the fact that they had not asked to see the light of day. At a time when having children was much less of a choice, the child accepted implicitly that he could not expect his parents to forego sex so that he would not be born. Now the responsibility of having children weighs so much more heavily, since not having them no longer requires abstinence. It is a new and difficult responsibility being added to the burdens of marriage, and this at a time when there is much less compelling reason to engage in marriage.

There are other changes due to our living longer. For example, less than two   9
hundred years ago, the average length a couple remained living together was seventeen years, largely because so many women died as a consequence of pregnancies and because men on the average died much earlier than now. Despite the frequency of divorces, in 1960 the average duration of a middle-class marriage in the Western world was thirty-nine years. Obviously it is much more demanding of two persons to live together in a marriage for thirty-nine years than for less than half of that time. Thus, even in a good marriage the strains are much greater than ever before. Nevertheless, the current expectation is that a marriage lasting more than twice as long should be as smooth as was one of much shorter duration.

A consequence of longevity is that we live much longer not only with   10
each other, but also with our children. Two hundred years ago, the average age of a child on losing one parent through death was fourteen; in 1960 it was forty. Even today, very few parents run into serious troubles with their children before the age of fourteen. If only one parent remains alive, this poses hardship also for the child; but at least he cannot play one parent against the other, a frequent source of family difficulties. And difficulties in growing up and seeking independence could not arise between both of the parents and their child when one of the parents was no longer living.

Only a few generations ago, most children left their homes at the   11
beginning of puberty. Again, few serious conflicts occur between children and their parents before that time. When they were twelve years old, or a bit older, children were apprenticed out or they joined the labor force in some other form. They were no longer treated as children, although not yet necessarily viewed as fully grown up. It is something entirely new that most children are kept economically — hence also socially — dependent on their parents until they are twenty or older. Yet, again, the tacit expectation is that things should proceed as smoothly in today's family when children remain dependent up to the age of eighteen and beyond, as they did when the child remained part of the family only up to about the age of thirteen.

As if all this would not be sufficient to explain the tremendously greater   12
social and psychological strains from which the family suffers because so much more is expected of it — and this when it fulfills fewer necessary func-

tions — children also mature much sooner than ever before and, at the same time, they are kept dependent so much longer. At the end of the eighteenth century the average age of the girl at the onset of menarche was over seventeen. At the beginning of this century in the United States, it was over fourteen. Today it is just over twelve. Thus, children become physiologically and sexually mature five years earlier than some 150 years ago. At the same time they are kept dependent for at least five years longer.

SUBJECT QUESTIONS

1. What important changes in family relations have modern birth control methods caused?
2. Bettelheim suggests that the prudery of the past was less a result of morality than of fear of disease. Do you think the Victorians would have been more promiscuous if they had had penicillin?
3. What has the increase in life expectancy to do with modern marital problems?
4. Do you think early puberty has any effect on family relations? Does being dependent on parents some ten years after puberty make a difference to youths? Might parents treat their children differently if they knew those children would be leaving home at age twelve or thirteen?
5. In his discussions both of husband and wife living together and of parents and children living together, Bettelheim seems to assume that the longer these relationships last the more chance they have to go wrong. Isn't it likely that families would simply get used to each other after a while? Do many marriages break up after the seventeen years which used to be the average length of a marriage?

STRUCTURE QUESTIONS

1. The conclusions in paragraphs 4 and 5 have to do with the male's loss of dominance in the family; should Bettelheim have shown that this change has actually weakened family structure as a whole?
2. Bettelheim makes much of the changes wrought by modern birth control methods. Is it possible that use of the pill is an *effect* of changing social values rather than a cause of them?
3. Several rather delicate subjects are discussed in this essay (venereal disease, for instance). How has Bettelheim managed to discuss these without being offensive? Does he become too vague in places?
4. The essay was intended to introduce topics for discussion at a conference and perhaps cannot be expected to provide exhaustive causal analyses. Are there places where an average reader needs fuller analysis?

5. Has Bettelheim avoided the jargon of social scientists? Note that his sentences average considerably longer than those of most essays in this book; is their length justified by the complexity of thought? Did you notice that they were long?
6. Examine the final paragraph and decide whether it makes a fitting conclusion. Should there have been a summary paragraph?

SUGGESTION FOR WRITING

Bettelheim says that pressure on the family results from teen-agers maturing earlier but leaving home later. Analyze the effects of this situation on the individual teen-ager. (In your own case, you may conclude that the extra years at home are good rather than a source of pressure; treat the subject as honestly as you can.)

Do We Need the Family?

Eulah Laucks

Eulah Laucks is a social critic and author; she is also a member of the Board of Directors for the Center for the Study of Democratic Institutions. Here she takes a hard look at one of those institutions, marriage, a subject on which she has often written. This essay first appeared in The Center Report.

In an earlier study of the family, I took as given that in general a nation's family structure determines the kind of society it will have, and that any attempts to change or improve the society must begin with changing the family. Six years later now, I have come to feel that, paradoxically, although some kind of family structure may be indispensable to societal functioning, it is the *society* that determines what the family will be, and not the other way around. Whatever kind of family a given society *needs* is the kind of family it will have. Thus, any change or improvement in family forms may have to come as a result of changes in other societal structures. That means the whole web of political-economic institutions and leadership. [1]

I think of the family as being what we *are* and of society as being *how we act*. There is always a lag between what we are and what we are doing. Today, this lag is so great, and the pace at which we are going so fast, that we are not even comprehending the results of our actions, let alone discriminating as to what of it all we are letting form our national character. It's no wonder that as human beings and as members of families we are confused, adrift and almost totally alienated from the societal actions which overwhelm us. [2]

As to the statement that the family may be indispensable to societal function — this may *not* be true today. I think it is true only when a society is more or less homogeneous in nature. When society is fragmented, chaotic and seemingly beyond individual comprehension, as it is today, there may be no place for family in any form we might recognize from past experience. The traditional family as the hearthstone of society may now be an indulgence of our nostalgia. We are already well into an era of experimental transitional forms of group living. Perhaps we should give more than passing thought to whether we should accept and try to stabilize the better among [3]

Reprinted with permission from the October 1973 *Center Report,* a publication of the Robert Maynard Hutchins Center for the Study of Democratic Institutions, Santa Barbara, California.

them or let a runaway society impress its own unexamined needs upon us.

The traditional nuclear family came into being a couple of hundred years ago as the result of societal pressures during the shift from feudalism to industrialism. For a long time prior to that, societal structures in general were fairly rigid but family living was extended into the community and therefore was less confined. There was no work ethic as such. Sabbath and holy days were reserved for celebration. And since there were about a hundred and fifty saints' days in the year, there was plenty of rest and recreation for everyone. Children reached what was called "the age of reason" at seven and were then considered — to the extent their capacities allowed — adult. There were almost mandatory communal games and festivities that children and adults collectively celebrated. There was no generation gap of interests.

As the Industrial Revolution developed, however, activities of children and parents diverged. Schooling experience was taken out of the home and its time span lengthened. Families became more and more self-centered. The process of tracking children into careers of their parents' choosing developed. Individual private property became important.

Thus, as capitalism replaced feudalism, the nuclear family became the device for expanding and perpetuating private fortunes. People of lesser means became infected with the Horatio Alger syndrome, and the American Dream was born. During the Victorian age, when "children were seen and not heard," the family had solidified into strict separation of parents and children. In general, offspring were delegated to nannies and governesses, or — in the case of the impoverished — were largely left to fend for themselves. In the case of the upper classes, who set the styles, what was least annoying to parents was considered best for the children. Then along came Freud to shake parental guidelines with his dictum that "the child is father to the neurotic." As this was gradually but widely accepted by child-rearers, such unpleasantnesses as toilet-training, prohibitions against thumb-sucking and masturbation, and so on, were discarded in favor of "ego strengthening." Thus, permissiveness was ushered in and later reinforced by Spock and the followers of Dewey.

Not only the children, then, but the parents also, became neurotic. Parents, who were totally unequipped for the job, became psychiatrists to their children. The era of the guilt-ridden, anxious, ineffectual parent began; the seeds of disintegration were sown in the traditional family structure.

As Janet Malcolm stated in a recent issue of *The New Yorker:* "Children, unlike [psychiatric] patients, don't go away after fifty minutes." Parents faced the dilemma of the tension between doing what they felt was good for the development of the child and what they (the parents) could stand by way of undisciplined noise, sloppiness and destructiveness. The "togetherness" of the Fifties then gave rise to the total confusion of the Sixties when frustration followed disillusionment as ever-expanding technological forces closed in on the family, along with war, riots, student revolts and assassinations.

Today, with Women's Lib, the pill, permissive attitudes toward sex — in and out of marriage — with the rise in the use of babysitters and day care centers, and with the growing rate of single-parent families, the traditional nuclear family, where it hasn't altogether disintegrated, has become demoralized. Only thirty-five percent of families in this country are now nuclear — that is, with both mother and father and children comprising the unit. Three-fifths of the people on welfare are mothers without husbands.

We might say, in general, that at best these days the American family barely manages to hold together in some kind of nuclearity until the children are grown. In spite of protestations to the contrary of "square" families who often pray and stay together with gritted teeth, so help them God, the American family today is fast becoming merely a place for each member to hang his hat while he is doing his own thing or waiting for a better perch to hop to. This is the logical outgrowth of changing societal pressures.

It might be well here to list some of the pressures responsible for disintegration of the family over the past twenty-five years:

Government and other bureaucracies have developed to the point that they handle almost everything for the individual citizen from his conception to his interment. We are all fast losing personhood.

Society *in general* has become depersonalized. With the spread of television and other instant forms of communication — everything in the world happens right in our living rooms. Instant knowledge of remote real happenings has given rise to casual acceptance of them, as if they were only screen entertainment. This is true even of the killings of war.

Schools, to a great extent, have taken over the responsibilities of parenting — even as to health care.

Installment buying has provided instant gratification, which has led to the lessening of individual capacities for discipline and sacrifice, and has had a tattering effect on our moral fiber.

We have become a nomadic society. Twenty percent of Americans have moved annually for the past twenty years. Half the population does not live in its natal state. Neighborhoods and communities have ceased to be important as hubs for communal activities.

There has been homogenization of styles and ideas, mainly because of concentrated urbanization, television, radio, and easy access to travel.

There has been an increasingly wider scattering of interests and activities of individual family members. We have been segregated ever more sharply into age groups. Generation gaps have opened at five-year intervals.

As a result of Women's Liberation and the fact that forty percent of mothers work outside the home, we have moved into a time when baby-sitting and child care centers have become indispensable services along with laundry and milk deliveries.

Divorce has been made painless, quick, and is no longer a stigma. There are now sixteen million divorced people in the U.S. Extra-legal cohabitation, birth control, and abortion are generally accepted. First marriages have dropped sharply since the advent of the pill, and divorced people are not remarrying at as high a rate as formerly. Divorced status now may be said to be a normal permanent phenomenon in our culture.

Men have come to taking custody of children in divorce cases. It is no longer a stigma for women to give them up. And women now are often refusing to take on the *single* responsibility of raising children. In the last two years, the number of children living with divorced fathers has risen fifty percent. (One startling development in recent years is that often neither parent wants custody. John R. Evans, Chief Judge of Juvenile Court in Denver, stated recently that throughout the country there is wholesale abdication of parental responsibility.)

What we think of as the virtues that draw us to marriage — the yearning for routine, permanence and security — are, say some, the things that drive us to divorce.

The paradox is that in spite of all of the foregoing, we still seem to be thinking in terms of the traditional family. This, doggedly, is what we *are!* Yet we act — or are impelled by the pace and impingement of the technological environment — as if the traditional family really no longer has meaning for us. Hence the lag between family and society — between what we are and how we act — is very wide, indeed. [12]

What is the question to ask, then? *Not:* Do we, as individuals, *want* the family? (although I personally think that ought to be the real question), but: Does society *need* the family? Demographically, today's society does not need the family. We do not have to have a Paul Ehrlich to point out to us that the planet already has an oversupply of people. Technotronic society has no need for more children. We could get along from here on out with only a few strategically-placed breeding installations. [13]

Economically, society does not need the family. There is no longer need for great labor force concentrations or financial hierarchies. How about the self-serving needs of citizens — ego trips, name and gene survival? The [14] bio-programmed society which seems likely ahead not only could do without personalized needs — it would doubtless find them a hindrance.

Is it necessary to preserve the family in order to support *female* citizens? Women in general, and Women's Libbers in particular, are demonstrating in all sectors that they can earn their own livings and not necessarily be dependent on male support. Men could avoid taking financial responsibility for wives by hiring cooks and maids. Sex requirements for both men and women could be bureaucratized or otherwise programmed. 15

We might well ponder the advisability of reining in the societal horse that is running away with us — at least long enough to ask a hard question or two. Is the family an institution for the nurture and betterment of people, or is it a dispensable adjunct of our public actions gone wild? If we believe society *does* need the family, and that the family is a valuable human institution, we might consider what future forms — or transitional forms — it is taking or is likely to take, and prepare ourselves for them for the betterment of ourselves and posterity. 16

SUBJECT QUESTIONS

1. Can you explain Laucks's distinction between "what we *are*" and "*how we act*"?
2. Why, according to Laucks, did the nuclear family come into existence? What kind of social structure existed before the nuclear family?
3. On what grounds does Laucks suggest that the family may no longer be necessary? Would she prefer to do away with it as an anachronism?
4. Were you surprised at Laucks's statistic that only 35 percent of today's families are nuclear? What would the other 65 percent be?
5. Laucks lists eleven causes for the disintegration of the family. Is it clear how all of these have contributed to family disintegration? Is the list intended to be exhaustive?
6. Is it possible to have "homogenization of styles and ideas" simultaneously with a "wider scattering of interests and activities"?
7. If society "does not need the family," might there be reasons to preserve it anyway?

STRUCTURE QUESTIONS

1. What, if anything, does Laucks achieve by admitting at the beginning that she was mistaken in the past? Does the admission weaken the reader's confidence in her expertise?
2. Is Laucks's causal analysis limited to the list of eleven pressures halfway through the essay? Is it effective strategy to lump all these pres-

sures together instead of developing each spearately? Does Laucks make clear how each pressure is a contributing influence?

3. Obviously Laucks is aware of a multiplicity of causes; is she equally concerned about the possibility of "apparent, or false cause"? (See introduction.)

4. Sociologists tend to write for one another — that is, to use terminology which is understandable only by other sociologists. Has Laucks written her essay in language understandable to an educated nonspecialist?

5. Laucks seems intent on showing that the family has outlived its usefulness. Discuss the advisability of her saving until the final paragraph her suggestion that the family is worth saving. Would she have done better to make clear earlier how she feels personally?

SUGGESTIONS FOR WRITING

1. Write an analysis of the effects that inflation or unemployment or another current social problem has had on you or your family. The increasing costs of college education might be appropriate.

2. Select a parent or someone you know well and see if you can discover a relationship between the kind of work he does and his attitudes and values.

3. Select one of the eleven causes of family disintegration listed by Laucks and show that it is, or is not, a source of pressure on your own family.

The Cowards of Christmas Eve

Earl Shorris

Earl Shorris (b. 1936) is a free-lance writer on social conditions and problems. He has written a book on the problems of American Indians called The Death of the Great Spirit *(1971).*

December is the most violent month, the time of murder, robbery, assault, 1
suicide, and Christmas. While most of the world is gathering its breath to
sing, there is also a growing darkness, until on the night before Christmas
husbands and wives make war on each other, as on no other night of the
year. In New York City the number of murders and manslaughter cases on
December 24 is almost twice the daily average for the year.

Perhaps it has always been that way; we cannot know. There is evi- 2
dence only of the season and the way in which humans have responded to it,
evidence that we are a fearful species, revolving around the sun, weakest
during the long nights of winter. The ancient Mayans called the five extra
days at the end of their calendar "the days with no name," and they believed
that these were the unluckiest days. In France, Germany, Switzerland, Italy
and parts of Central Europe, the twelve days between Christmas and Epi-
phany were thought to be days of evil, full of witches and werewolves. Pine
resin was burned at night to drive the witches away, and on Christmas Eve
the fields and orchards were sprayed with gunfire to preserve them from the
work of witches. It was the custom among the English and the French to kill
a wren on Christmas Eve.

"It's the accounting time," says a psychiatrist in San Francisco, Dr. 3
Murray Persky. "People think of aging then. When you get older, you don't
count birthdays; the end of the year comes at Christmas."

A businessman in New York calls it "a time of moral guilt." In Detroit, 4
Lieutenant Donald Kolehmainen, who has spent most of his seventeen years
as a policeman working in ghetto areas, says, "People who've rejected Christ
during the past year get depressed by it. People look back on the year, what
they've accomplished. There's frustration, guilt feelings." Even doubt is sufficient to make a man feel guilty on a religious night, if he has heard the Reverend Billy Graham say, "He [God] never causes His children to doubt."

You better not shout,
You better not cry,
You better not pout,
I'm tellin' you why,
Santa Claus is coming to town.

On Christmas Eve the social pressure to be happy is everywhere: mag-   5
azines, newspapers and television networks have been making a din of happiness since Thanksgiving Day. Timothy Cadigan, a San Francisco policeman,
has often seen the result: "Here's a guy living in a project, he's got six kids,
they really haven't got enough for the kids, and on that tube in the next
room it's really supposed to be a better life. It's supposed to be a spiritual
time, a happy time, and then a guy says to himself, 'Hey, I'm not happy.' "

I'm dreaming of a white Christmas
Just like the ones I used to know.

The impossible demands of the media are also claimed by nostalgia.   6
What could be more wonderful to a man with no prospects than a childhood
Christmas remembered? This anxious moment edits out the anxieties of
Christmases past: secondhand bicycles are winged horses, stewed hens are
feasts of great-breasted turkeys, tenements have warm hearths giving off the
perfect odor of aged oak burning high. In the fall to nostalgia the edited past
becomes the incurable past, a mirror for the future.

"Hey, I'm not happy."   7
"This is it. That's all there is."   8

The Magi will not arrive with gifts. Dr. Persky and other psychiatrists   9
say this is a critical moment for many people, facing the fact that there is no
Santa Claus. It seems comic that adults should be so upset by it, but the loss
of Santa Claus is also a loss of parental protection, another end to innocence,
the sign of the loneliness of the world, proof that luck is but a dream.

Of all nights, it would seem that on Christmas Eve in a Christian na-   10
tion, those who find themselves suddenly conscious of the human predica-
ment would be able to make Kierkegaard's "leap to faith." Yet, it is so often
not the case; we do not live in an age of faith, and the profound courage
needed to live without faith occurs seldom. When the distresses of the night
bring about the agonized moment, the faithless, the profound cowards, kill
themselves or others, sometimes using guns or knives, but most often with
murderous words.

There are murders and suicides enough at the Christmas season; the   11
F.B.I. Uniform Crime Report documents the rise in violent crimes in the
month of December. But it is the violence wished and not done that concerns the clergy and the psychotherapists, for they know that the difference
between murder wished and murder done is very slim. From the beginning
of December the Sunday sermons try to deal with the problem, describing

the season of brotherly love, peace on earth, goodwill toward men, proclaiming the Advent season a time of quiet and joyous anticipation.

By Christmas Eve the season is anything but quiet. Inspector Arturo 12 Islas of the El Paso, Texas, Police Department says, "It's out there in the streets, that high nervous feeling. Everybody starts getting in a hurry, every nerve is up, then you have the drinking."

The tensions seem to affect everyone. The son of the pastor of a church 13 in Virginia says that by the time his father gets through the season to Christmas Eve he is tired and testy. A woman from Brooklyn says that everybody gets mad over the presents and spending too much. A man from Michigan claims that the only time he ever heard his parents fight was on Christmas Eve. Another man says he left his wife on Christmas Eve. The difficulty of the season crosses racial, religious, economic and ethnic bounds. The stress of the winter solstice is human, natural, and therefore unavoidable; it is also peculiarly urban.

In New Milford, Connecticut, where 16,500 people are spread over 14 sixty-four square miles, Police Sergeant Richard Hills reports only one family fight on Christmas Eve in the past fifteen years. The style of celebrating Christmas in that mill town is very different from the way it is in Detroit or San Francisco. Sergeant Hills says, "Christmas Eve is open house in New Milford. People go visiting, families get together."

Lieutenant Kolehmainen describes an opposite situation in Detroit — 15 people stay at home: "On Christmas Eve they're isolated one on one more than at any other time." Officer Cadigan says that in San Francisco "there's nowhere to go, they're stuck with each other. This thing just keeps building up until it explodes." Monsignor Cassidy of the Archdiocese of New York thinks that problems on Christmas Eve are a direct result of the shift from the extended family to the nuclear family unit. "Christmas," he says, "is meant to be shared. If you have a nuclear family, there's too much pressure. In the old family tradition they all worked together and lived together. No family can stand alone. Loneliness is the greatest suffering of mankind."

In his role as a psychologist and family counselor, Monsignor Cassidy 16 tries to prepare his patients for Christmas Eve by seeking to help them solve the problems of loneliness and isolation. "People should get together with their families," he says, "even if it means flying home to Milwaukee or something, using the money for that instead of Christmas gifts."

A portrait of the troubled family on Christmas Eve emerges: The set- 17 ting is a large city, where isolation of the family unit extends from the ghetto to the quiet streets of middle- and upper-middle-class neighborhoods. In almost every case the man has been drinking, and often both the husband and wife are drunk. Perhaps the woman and children ate dinner together while the man attended a party at his place of work. Or if the man came home early, the children and parents have moved into separate rooms. The children watch television programs that the parents have seen before: *Miracle on 34th Street* or *White Christmas*. There is nothing to attract or interest the parents. In some cities the bars are closed, in all cities they are empty. Bowling leagues and bridge games are suspended. Every avenue of escape is cut off. "You have to face your family," said Dr. Persky. "You don't have the right on Christmas Eve to go off and do the usual things that are the defenses against your spouse." A man and a woman sit together, usually in the kitchen, getting drunk, facing the nakedness of their lives, and the fight begins.

The police can do no more than put off a war, solve the moment. They   18
arrive in answer to a telephone call from the woman, make a show of authority, listen to both sides of the argument, find some means to a détente, and then they leave to answer another call. Sometimes they recommend marriage counseling or psychiatric help. Inspector Islas says he asks a priest to come to the house when he thinks a priest can help, but neither he nor any other policeman expects anything more than a momentary solution.

The ostensible cause of Christmas Eve fights is almost always   19
money — the lack of money, the waste of money, the failure to spend money, the choice of how or on whom to spend money. Here are three descriptions by three police officers who have between them sixty-three years of experience:

Lieutenant Kolehmainen (Detroit): "There's a sense of frustration on   20
the male's part for not providing a good Christmas for the kids. He has to have something to vent his frustrations on. A guy who feels that inadequate has to take it out on somebody. And his wife is usually closest."

Officer Cadigan (San Francisco): "In one room the kids are watching   21
TV — some Christmas show is on. There's a little three or four foot Christmas tree. And in the kitchen, the mother and father are hollering and swearing. It always seems to me it's about money. Not that they're not making enough, but the guy spent it on something else, gambling, a car they shouldn't have bought."

Inspector Islas (El Paso): "On Christmas Eve the fights are due to the   22
disappointments. You get the wife expecting a $900 fur coat and she gets a $10 radio, and there it goes. Or you find her saying to the husband, 'You spent fifty dollars on this no-good radio when we could have lived for two weeks on that.' You have more fights over money than anything else."

There is nothing spiritual in Santa's bag; it is full of gifts that cost   23
money; this is a Calvinist country. Max Weber pointed to the Calvinist thinking in Benjamin Franklin's maxims about hard work and frugality. R. H. Tawney found a hardened version of Calvinism in the works of early American clergymen. The cruel social theories of Herbert Spencer were popular in America until the early part of this century, and the aftermath of them lives on in conservative politics and in works like those of Billy Graham.

But if on the night before Christmas a man should survey his house   24
and find the meagerness of it more than he can bear, where will he turn?
From the Reverend Billy Graham, from Spencer and Cotton and Winthrop
and Calvin himself, he will have learned that the poor are not among the
elect of God. Then how will that man survive the night?

The pile of gifts beneath the tree is a judgment of the man who put   25
them there. If he is poor and there are no gifts, he is condemned. If he is
middle-class, the gifts are still less than they should have been. Even if a
man is rich enough, the giving of gifts causes problems. Monsignor Cassidy,
who understands the custom in its spiritual sense as symbolizing the gifts
that were given to Christ by the Magi, and thinks beyond that to Christ offering himself on the cross, giving a gift to mankind, says that most fights on
the night before Christmas begin over gifts. In his role as a family counselor
he has heard the aftermath of many such arguments, out of which he has developed a theory of the secular symbolism of Christmas gifts.

He begins with a game: "If my mother gives me a red tie and a blue tie   26
for Christmas, and I wear the red tie when I go to her house on Christmas
Day, she'll say that I don't like the blue tie." He laughs at the little paradox
and goes on to the more serious problems: "Very often a couple will have a
fight over the gift they gave his mother or her mother for Christmas. It's one
of the things that always comes up in marriage counseling.

"Giving a gift is unlike other things. You've got to show inner feelings   27
by words, but you show even more by giving a gift. People interpret a cheap
gift as meaning that you hold them cheaply. There's also the thing about
spending more money than you should, trying to buy people's affection. So if
the gift is too small, you're saying that you don't think much of them, and if
the gift is too big and you've spent too much money, you feel the pressure
on yourself.

"It's not how you give the gift that's important, but how I perceive it.   28
People just accept a gift, there's no social mechanism for discussing it. I may
think, 'You gave me a crappy gift,' but I can't say that."

Out of this mute game of I-think-you-think-about-me come many of the   29
family arguments. The game cannot be won. Since neither the giver nor the
receiver can know the other's position, no move can be countered. It's like
one of R. D. Laing's "Knots." In its simplest form the receiver perceives the
true feeling of the giver and is displeased. Or the receiver may mis-perceive
the true feeling of the giver and be displeased. Or the giver may mis-perceive the receiver's perception of the giver's true feeling and be displeased.
And so on.

Perhaps a mandatory gift is not a gift at all, since the form is not the in-   30
vention of the giver. Its only meaning is contained in the content; dollar values must be applied, for no motive can be assigned other than the hewing to
convention. The mandatory gift forces the giver to apply a monetary standard

to love and friendship. If he is unable to afford the gift he wishes to give then he is unable to give love or friendship. All of that in the natural season of reckoning.

Perhaps that is why family fights are common to both the rich and the poor on Christmas Eve. Timothy Cadigan, who worked for many years in a precinct that covered both the Fillmore ghetto and the rich Pacific Heights area in San Francisco, says that Christmas Eve is the one night of the year when family fights are as frequent among the rich as the poor. "Those are the worst fights," he says of the arguments among the rich. "Sometimes when I go into those houses, I look at the people and I can see the boredom boiling out of their eyes. Poor people have a better conception of life." 31

Monsignor Cassidy says, "In lower-class families there's always a sense of hope on Christmas Eve that things will be getting better. With middle- and upper-middle-class families there's a sense of frustration — things didn't go as well as they expected." 32

It is tempting to assign the blame to the customs of Christmas and have done with it, to say, like the Puritans, that the holiday has pagan origins and is therefore barbarous and should not be celebrated. But for all its flaws and perversions, Christmas cannot cause a dark side of man: peaceful people do not destroy each other on Christmas Eve, they laugh and practice joy; the calendrical worst is over, God or the sun is reborn, sing Hallelujah! 33

The poison is not in the scent of evergreens or the sound of bells, but in the histories that are unmasked by the pas de deux of the night before Christmas. The ritual moment calls for faith or courage. But the age of faith is long passed and cowards cannot be lovers. The times call for a messiah. 34

SUBJECT QUESTIONS

1. We have been accustomed to think of the "long, hot summer" as the time of riots and violence. Is there a significant difference between the crimes of summer and the violence of Christmas Eve?
2. Shorris is discussing violent people. Why does he call them cowards in his title?
3. Why, according to Shorris, are there so many family fights on Christmas Eve? Why doesn't the "Christmas spirit" alleviate the violence?
4. In what way does the "loss of Santa Claus" affect adults? Are childhood Christmases usually remembered as being better than they really were?
5. What effect does the Calvinist doctrine of hard work have on people who no longer have faith?
6. Would you agree with Shorris about the economic emphasis placed on gift-giving?

7. Why are Christmas fights worse among the rich than among the poor? Why are there more quarrels in the city than in rural areas?

STRUCTURE QUESTIONS

1. Criticize Shorris's method of organization. Could you make a reasonable outline of the essay?
2. Consider the effectiveness of the author's strategy in citing numerous opinions to support his generalizations. Do the quotations cause any stylistic or organizational difficulties? Do they help the causal analysis?
3. Shorris states in the opening paragraph the statistic with which he is concerned. Does the remainder of the essay satisfactorily explain the causes for the high number of Christmas Eve murders?
4. At one point Shorris says the chief cause of the problem is loneliness; a little later he says that the "ostensible cause of Christmas Eve fights is almost always money." Is he contradicting himself? How could he have indicated more clearly the relation between the chief cause and the ostensible cause?
5. How would you characterize the style of this essay? Judging from the style, do you think the author is likely to be a sociologist, a journalist, or a politician?

SUGGESTIONS FOR WRITING

1. Analyze the causes of the stress which often occurs among college roommates. In the course of your analysis you may wish to suggest ways to alleviate that stress.
2. If you have been in a class in which there was considerable friction between teacher and students, describe and analyze the causes for that friction.
3. Try to account for some curious but common social behavior, such as, for example, the excitement of a crowd at a college football game, or the trancelike state of people at a discotheque. (N.B.: Be sure to select some form of behavior you have observed and know something about.)

Counterparts

James Joyce

James Joyce (1882–1941) was an Irish poet and novelist whose stream-of-consciousness novels, Ulysses *and* Finnegans Wake, *have had a strong influence on young writers of our own day. The story below was taken from his first book,* Dubliners *(1914).*

The bell rang furiously and, when Miss Parker went to the tube, a furious voice called out in a piercing North of Ireland accent: 1

"Send Farrington here!" 2

Miss Parker returned to her machine, saying to a man who was writing at a desk: 3

"Mr. Alleyne wants you upstairs." 4

The man muttered *"Blast* him!" under his breath and pushed back his chair to stand up. When he stood up he was tall and of great bulk. He had a hanging face, dark wine-coloured, with fair eyebrows and moustache: his eyes bulged forward slightly and the whites of them were dirty. He lifted up the counter and, passing by the clients, went out of the office with a heavy step. 5

He went heavily upstairs until he came to the second landing, where a door bore a brass plate with the inscription *Mr. Alleyne.* Here he halted, puffing with labour and vexation, and knocked. The shrill voice cried: 6

"Come in!" 7

The man entered Mr. Alleyne's room. Simultaneously Mr. Alleyne, a little man wearing gold-rimmed glasses on a clean-shaven face, shot his head up over a pile of documents. The head itself was so pink and hairless it seemed like a large egg reposing on the papers. Mr. Alleyne did not lose a moment: 8

"Farrington? What is the meaning of this? Why have I always to complain of you? May I ask you why you haven't made a copy of that contract between Bodley and Kirwan? I told you it must be ready by four o'clock." 9

"But Mr. Shelley said, sir —" 10

"Mr. Shelley said, sir. . . . Kindly attend to what I say and not to what 11

Mr. Shelley says, sir. You have always some excuse or another for shirking work. Let me tell you that if the contract is not copied before this evening I'll lay the matter before Mr. Crosbie. . . . Do you hear me now?"

"Yes, sir." 12

"Do you hear me now? . . . Ay and another little matter! I might as 13 well be talking to the wall as talking to you. Understand once for all that you get a half an hour for your lunch and not an hour and a half. How many courses do you want, I'd like to know. . . . Do you mind me now?"

"Yes, sir." 14

Mr. Alleyne bent his head again upon his pile of papers. The man 15 stared fixedly at the polished skull which directed the affairs of Crosbie & Alleyne, gauging its fragility. A spasm of rage gripped his throat for a few moments and then passed, leaving after it a sharp sensation of thirst. The man recognised the sensation and felt that he must have a good night's drinking. The middle of the month was passed and, if he could get the copy done in time, Mr. Alleyne might give him an order on the cashier. He stood still, gazing fixedly at the head upon the pile of papers. Suddenly Mr. Alleyne began to upset all the papers, searching for something. Then, as if he had been unaware of the man's presence till that moment, he shot up his head again, saying:

"Eh? Are you going to stand there all day? Upon my word, Farrington, 16 you take things easy!"

"I was waiting to see . . ." 17

"Very good, you needn't wait to see. Go downstairs and do your work." 18

The man walked heavily towards the door and, as he went out of the 19 room, he heard Mr. Alleyne cry after him that if the contract was not copied by evening Mr. Crosbie would hear of the matter.

He returned to his desk in the lower office and counted the sheets 20 which remained to be copied. He took up his pen and dipped it in the ink but he continued to stare stupidly at the last words he had written: *In no case shall the said Bernard Bodley be* . . . The evening was falling and in a few minutes they would be lighting the gas: then he could write. He felt that he must slake the thirst in his throat. He stood up from his desk and, lifting the counter as before, passed out of the office. As he was passing out the chief clerk looked at him inquiringly.

"It's all right, Mr. Shelley," said the man, pointing with his finger to 21 indicate the objective of his journey.

The chief clerk glanced at the hat-rack, but, seeing the row complete, 22 offered no remark. As soon as he was on the landing the man pulled a shepherd's plaid cap out of his pocket, put it on his head and ran quickly down the rickety stairs. From the street door he walked on furtively on the inner side of the path towards the corner and all at once dived into a doorway. He was now safe in the dark snug of O'Neill's shop, and filling up the little window that looked into the bar with his inflamed face, the colour of dark wine or dark meat, he called out:

"Here, Pat, give us a g.p., like a good fellow."   23

The curate brought him a glass of plain porter. The man drank it at a   24 gulp and asked for a caraway seed. He put his penny on the counter and, leaving the curate to grope for it in the gloom, retreated out of the snug as furtively as he had entered it.

Darkness, accompanied by a thick fog, was gaining upon the dusk of   25 February and the lamps in Eustace Street had been lit. The man went up by the houses until he reached the door of the office, wondering whether he could finish his copy in time. On the stairs a moist pungent odour of perfumes saluted his nose: evidently Miss Delacour had come while he was out in O'Neill's. He crammed his cap back again into his pocket and re-entered the office, assuming an air of absent-mindedness.

"Mr. Alleyne has been calling for you," said the chief clerk severely.   26 "Where were you?"

The man glanced at the two clients who were standing at the counter   27 as if to intimate that their presence prevented him from answering. As the clients were both male the chief clerk allowed himself a laugh.

"I know that game," he said. "Five times in one day is a little bit. . . .   28 Well, you better look sharp and get a copy of our correspondence in the Delacour case for Mr. Alleyne."

This address in the presence of the public, his run upstairs and the   29 porter he had gulped down so hastily confused the man and, as he sat down at his desk to get what was required, he realised how hopeless was the task of finishing his copy of the contract before half past five. The dark damp night was coming and he longed to spend it in the bars, drinking with his friends amid the glare of gas and the clatter of glasses. He got out the Delacour correspondence and passed out of the office. He hoped that Mr. Alleyne would not discover that the last two letters were missing.

The moist pungent perfume lay all the way up to Mr. Alleyne's room.   30 Miss Delacour was a middle-aged woman of Jewish appearance. Mr. Alleyne was said to be sweet on her or on her money. She came to the office often and stayed a long time when she came. She was sitting beside his desk now in an aroma of perfumes, smoothing the handle of her umbrella and nodding the great black feather in her hat. Mr. Alleyne had swivelled his chair round to face her and thrown his right foot jauntily upon his left knee. The man put the correspondence on the desk and bowed respectfully but neither Mr. Alleyne nor Miss Delacour took any notice of his bow. Mr. Alleyne tapped a finger on the correspondence and then flicked it towards him as if to say: *"That's all right: you can go."*

The man returned to the lower office and sat down again at his desk.   31

He stared intently at the incomplete phrase: *In no case shall the said Bernard Bodley be* . . . and thought how strange it was that the last three words began with the same letter. The chief clerk began to hurry Miss Parker, saying she would never have the letters typed in time for post. The man listened to the clicking of the machine for a few minutes and then set to work to finish his copy. But his head was not clear and his mind wandered away to the glare and rattle of the public-house. It was a night for hot punches. He struggled on with his copy, but when the clock struck five he had still fourteen pages to write. Blast it! He couldn't finish it in time. He longed to execrate aloud, to bring his fist down on something violently. He was so enraged that he wrote *Bernard Bernard* instead of *Bernard Bodley* and had to begin again on a clean sheet.

He felt strong enough to clear out the whole office single-handed. His 32 body ached to do something, to rush out and revel in violence. All the indignities of his life enraged him. . . . Could he ask the cashier privately for an advance? No, the cashier was no good, no damn good: he wouldn't give an advance. . . . He knew where he would meet the boys: Leonard and O'Halloran and Nosey Flynn. The barometer of his emotional nature was set for a spell of riot.

His imagination had so abstracted him that his name was called twice 33 before he answered. Mr. Alleyne and Miss Delacour were standing outside the counter and all the clerks had turned round in anticipation of something. The man got up from his desk. Mr. Alleyne began a tirade of abuse, saying that two letters were missing. The man answered that he knew nothing about them, that he had made a faithful copy. The tirade continued: it was so bitter and violent that the man could hardly restrain his fist from descending upon the head of the manikin before him.

"I know nothing about any other two letters," he said stupidly. 34

"*You — know — nothing.* Of course you know nothing," said Mr. Al- 35 leyne. "Tell me," he added, glancing first for approval to the lady beside him, "do you take me for a fool? Do you think me an utter fool?"

The man glanced from the lady's face to the little egg-shaped head and 36 back again; and, almost before he was aware of it, his tongue had found a felicitous moment:

"I don't think, sir," he said, "that that's a fair question to put to me." 37

There was a pause in the very breathing of the clerks. Everyone was 38 astounded (the author of the witticism no less than his neighbours) and Miss Delacour, who was a stout amiable person, began to smile broadly. Mr. Alleyne flushed to the hue of a wild rose and his mouth twitched with a dwarf's passion. He shook his fist in the man's face till it seemed to vibrate like the knob of some electric machine:

"You impertinent ruffian! You impertinent ruffian! I'll make short work 39

of you! Wait till you see! You'll apologise to me for your impertinence or
you'll quit the office instanter! You'll quit this, I'm telling you, or you'll
apologise to me!"

He stood in a doorway opposite the office watching to see if the cashier   40
would come out alone. All the clerks passed out and finally the cashier came
out with the chief clerk. It was no use trying to say a word to him when he
was with the chief clerk. The man felt that his position was bad enough. He
had been obliged to offer an abject apology to Mr. Alleyne for his impertinence but he knew what a hornets' nest the office would be for him. He
could remember the way in which Mr. Alleyne had hounded little Peake out
of the office in order to make room for his own nephew. He felt savage and
thirsty and revengeful, annoyed with himself and with everyone else. Mr.
Alleyne would never give him an hour's rest; his life would be a hell to him.
He had made a proper fool of himself this time. Could he not keep his
tongue in his cheek? But they had never pulled together from the first, he
and Mr. Alleyne, ever since the day Mr. Alleyne had overheard him mim-
icking his North of Ireland accent to amuse Higgins and Miss Parker: that
had been the beginning of it. He might have tried Higgins for the money,
but sure Higgins never had anything for himself. A man with two establishments to keep up, of course he couldn't. . . .

He felt his great body again aching for the comfort of the public-house.   41
The fog had begun to chill him and he wondered could he touch Pat in
O'Neill's. He could not touch him for more than a bob — and a bob was no
use. Yet he must get money somewhere or other; he had spent his last
penny for the g.p. and soon it would be too late for getting money anywhere.
Suddenly, as he was fingering his watchchain, he thought of Terry Kelly's
pawn-office in Fleet Street. That was the dart! Why didn't he think of it
sooner?

He went through the narrow alley of Temple Bar quickly, muttering to   42
himself that they could all go to hell because he was going to have a good
night of it. The clerk in Terry Kelly's said A crown! but the consignor held out
for six shillings; and in the end the six shillings was allowed him literally. He
came out of the pawn-office joyfully, making a little cylinder of the coins between his thumb and fingers. In Westmoreland Street the footpaths were
crowded with young men and women returning from business and ragged
urchins ran here and there yelling out the names of the evening editions.
The man passed through the crowd, looking on the spectacle generally with
proud satisfaction and staring masterfully at the office-girls. His head was full
of the noises of tram-gongs and swishing trolleys and his nose already sniffed
the curling fumes of punch. As he walked on he preconsidered the terms in
which he would narrate the incident to the boys:

"So, I just looked at him — coolly, you know, and looked at her. Then   43

I looked back at him again — taking my time, you know. 'I don't think that that's a fair question to put to me,' says I."

Nosey Flynn was sitting up in his usual corner of Davy Byrne's and, when he heard the story, he stood Farrington a half-one, saying it was as smart a thing as ever he heard. Farrington stood a drink in his turn. After a while O'Halloran and Paddy Leonard came in and the story was repeated to them. O'Halloran stood tailors of malt, hot, all round and told the story of the retort he had made to the chief clerk when he was in Callan's of Frownes's Street; but, as the retort was after the manner of the liberal shepherds in the eclogues, he had to admit that it was not as clever as Farrington's retort. At this Farrington told the boys to polish off that and have another.

Just as they were naming their poisons who should come in but Higgins! Of course he had to join in with the others. The men asked him to give his version of it, and he did so with great vivacity for the sight of five small hot whiskies was very exhilarating. Everyone roared laughing when he showed the way in which Mr. Alleyne shook his fist in Farrington's face. Then he imitated Farrington, saying, "*And here was my nabs, as cool as you please,*" while Farrington looked at the company out of his heavy dirty eyes, smiling and at times drawing forth stray drops of liquor from his moustache with the aid of his lower lip.

When that round was over there was a pause. O'Halloran had money but neither of the other two seemed to have any; so the whole party left the shop somewhat regretfully. At the corner of Duke Street Higgins and Nosey Flynn bevelled off to the left while the other three turned back towards the city. Rain was drizzling down on the cold streets and, when they reached the Ballast Office, Farrington suggested the Scotch House. The bar was full of men and loud with the noise of tongues and glasses. The three men pushed past the whining match-sellers at the door and formed a little party at the corner of the counter. They began to exchange stories. Leonard introduced them to a young fellow named Weathers who was performing at the Tivoli as an acrobat and knockabout *artiste.* Farrington stood a drink all round. Weathers said he would take a small Irish and Apollinaris. Farrington, who had definite notions of what was what, asked the boys would they have an Apollinaris too; but the boys told Tim to make theirs hot. The talk became theatrical. O'Halloran stood a round and then Farrington stood another round, Weathers protesting that the hospitality was too Irish. He promised to get them in behind the scenes and introduce them to some nice girls. O'Halloran said that he and Leonard would go, but that Farrington wouldn't go because he was a married man; and Farrington's heavy dirty eyes leered at the company in token that he understood he was being chaffed. Weathers made them all have just one little tincture at his expense and promised to meet them later on at Mulligan's in Poolbeg Street.

When the Scotch House closed they went round to Mulligan's. They went into the parlour at the back and O'Halloran ordered small hot specials all around. They were all beginning to feel mellow. Farrington was just standing another round when Weathers came back. Much to Farrington's relief he drank a glass of bitter this time. Funds were getting low but they had enough to keep them going. Presently two young women with big hats and a young man in a check suit came in and sat at a table close by. Weathers saluted them and told the company that they were out of the Tivoli. Farrington's eyes wandered at every moment in the direction of one of the young women. There was something striking in her appearance. An immense scarf of peacock-blue muslin was wound around her hat and knotted in a great bow under her chin; and she wore bright yellow gloves, reaching to the elbow. Farrington gazed admiringly at the plump arm which she moved very often and with much grace; and when, after a little time, she answered his gaze he admired still more her large dark brown eyes. The oblique staring expression in them fascinated him. She glanced at him once or twice and, when the party was leaving the room, she brushed against his chair and said "*O pardon!*" in a London accent. He watched her leave the room in the hope that she would look back at him, but he was disappointed. He cursed his want of money and cursed all the rounds he had stood, particularly all the whiskies and Apollinaris which he had stood to Weathers. If there was one thing that he hated it was a sponge. He was so angry that he lost count of the conversation of his friends. 47

When Paddy Leonard called him he found that they were talking about feats of strength. Weathers was showing his biceps muscle to the company and boasting so much that the other two had called on Farrington to uphold the national honour. Farrington pulled up his sleeve accordingly and showed his biceps muscle to the company. The two arms were examined and compared and finally it was agreed to have a trial of strength. The table was cleared and the two men rested their elbows on it, clasping hands. When Paddy Leonard said "*Go!*" each was to try to bring down the other's hand on to the table. Farrington looked very serious and determined. 48

The trial began. After about thirty seconds Weathers brought his opponent's hand slowly down to the table. Farrington's dark wine-coloured face flushed darker still with anger and humiliation at having been defeated by such a stripling. 49

"You're not to put the weight of your body behind it. Play fair," he said. 50

"Who's not playing fair?" said the other. 51

"Come on again. The two best out of three." 52

The trial began again. The veins stood out on Farrington's forehead, and the pallor of Weathers' complexion changed to peony. Their hands and arms trembled under the stress. After a long struggle Weathers again 53 brought his opponent's hand slowly on to the table. There was a murmur of applause from the spectators. The curate, who was standing beside the table, nodded his red head towards the victor and said with stupid familiarity:

"Ah! that's the knack!"   54

"What the hell do you know about it?" said Farrington fiercely, turning   55 on the man. "What do you put in your gab for?"

"Sh, sh!" said O'Halloran, observing the violent expression of Farring-   56 ton's face. "Pony up, boys. We'll have just one little smahan more and then we'll be off."

A very sullen-faced man stood at the corner of O'Connell Bridge waiting   57 for the little Sandymount tram to take him home. He was full of smoul- dering anger and revengefulness. He felt humiliated and discontented; he did not even feel drunk; and he had only twopence in his pocket. He cursed everything. He had done for himself in the office, pawned his watch, spent all his money; and he had not even got drunk. He began to feel thirsty again and he longed to be back again in the hot reeking public-house. He had lost his reputation as a strong man, having been defeated twice by a mere boy. His heart swelled with fury and, when he thought of the woman in the big hat who had brushed against him and said *Pardon!* his fury nearly choked him.

His tram let him down at Shelbourne Road and he steered his great   58 body along in the shadow of the wall of the barracks. He loathed returning to his home. When he went in by the side-door he found the kitchen empty and the kitchen fire nearly out. He bawled upstairs:

"Ada! Ada!"   59

His wife was a little sharp-faced woman who bullied her husband when   60 he was sober and was bullied by him when he was drunk. They had five children. A little boy came running down the stairs.

"Who is that?" said the man peering through the darkness.   61

"Me, pa."   62

"Who are you? Charlie?"   63

"No, pa. Tom."   64

"Where's your mother?"   65

"She's out at the chapel."   66

"That's right. . . . Did she think of leaving any dinner for me?"   67

"Yes, pa. I — "   68

"Light the lamp. What do you mean by having the place in darkness?   69 Are the other children in bed?"

The man sat down heavily on one of the chairs while the little boy lit   70 the lamp. He began to mimic his son's flat accent, saying half to himself: "At *the chapel. At the chapel, if you please!*" When the lamp was lit he banged his fist on the table and shouted:

"What's for my dinner?" 71

"I'm going . . . to cook it, pa," said the little boy. 72

The man jumped up furiously and pointed to the fire. 73

"On that fire! You let the fire out! By God, I'll teach you to do that again!" 74

He took a step to the door and seized the walking-stick which was standing behind it. 75

"I'll teach you to let the fire out!" he said, rolling up his sleeve in order to give his arm free play. 76

The little boy cried "O, pa!" and ran whimpering round the table, but the man followed him and caught him by the coat. The little boy looked about him wildly but, seeing no way of escape, fell upon his knees. 77

"Now, you'll let the fire out the next time!" said the man, striking at him vigorously with the stick. "Take that, you little whelp!" 78

The boy uttered a squeal of pain as the stick cut his thigh. He clasped his hands together in the air and his voice shook with fright. 79

"O, pa!" he cried. "Don't beat me, pa! And I'll . . . I'll say a *Hail Mary* for you. . . . I'll say a *Hail Mary* for you, pa, if you don't beat me. . . . I'll say a *Hail Mary*. . . ." 80

SUBJECT QUESTIONS

1. What is a counterpart? There is only one central figure in this story; is "Counterparts" an inappropriate title, then?
2. Each incident in the story causes the same mental reaction on Farrington's part; what is it? Does this day seem to be a rare "bad" one in Farrington's life, or a typical day? What clues does Joyce give?
3. What would you say is Farrington's basic problem? Consider his attitude toward his boss. Why does he do more daydreaming than work?
4. Why does Farrington beat his innocent son at the end? Trace the chain of cause and effect that results in this violence.
5. Do you think it is coincidence that Farrington's wife is at church when he comes home? Does she seem to be an innocent victim of Farrington's fury, or part of the cause of it?

STRUCTURE QUESTIONS

1. Because "Counterparts" is a narrative rather than expository prose, the principle of organization is naturally time sequence. Still, Joyce must select the incidents to put into that sequence. Do all the incidents contribute to a thematic unity without being redundant?
2. Joyce several times stops the narrative to include brief passages of exposition on the state of Farrington's mind. Examine some of these;

are they an intrusion on the story? Are they necessary for a full understanding of the causes of Farrington's actions?
3. Does Joyce make clear and convincing the cause and effect relationships among the incidents narrated? Could he have been more explicit without damaging the story? Does he need to be more explicit?
4. How heavily does Joyce employ descriptive detail to bolster the effect of his narrative? Examine one of the incidents closely to see how much use is made of concrete detail.

SUGGESTION FOR WRITING

Write a cause and effect analysis, in narrative form, of some incident involving either yourself or a close acquaintance. As far as possible, make the narrative indicate the causal relations instead of stopping the story to explain them. Be sure to include sufficient descriptive detail to give a clear picture of what is happening. That is, let your narrative proceed by pictures instead of a bare "after that . . . then . . . next" formula.

Bloodstains

Joyce Carol Oates

Joyce Carol Oates was born in western New York in 1938. One of our most prolific young writers, she has already published three collections of short stories, By the North Gate (1963), Upon the Sweeping Flood (1965), and The Wheel of Love (1970); two volumes of poetry, Anonymous Sins (1969) and Love and Its Derangements (1970); two plays, and many novels, including With Shuddering Fall (1964), A Garden of Earthly Delights (1967), Expensive People (1968), and Them (1969). The latter, a kind of modern gothic novel, won the National Book Award for fiction in 1970. Miss Oates currently lives in Canada, where she is a professor of English at the University of Windsor. In her fiction, her chief interest seems to be in characters struggling in an environment they can neither understand nor control. As one critic, Alfred Kazin, puts it, "They are caught up in the social convulsion and move unheedingly, compulsively, blindly, through the paces assigned to them by the power god." "Bloodstains" first appeared in Harper's (August, 1971).

He sat. He turned to see that he was sharing the bench with a young mother 1
who did not glance around at him. The park they were in was a small noisy
island around which traffic moved in a continual stream. Aged, listless men
sat on other benches — a few women shoppers, pausing to rest, their eyes
eagle-bright and their gloved fingers tugging at the straps of shoes or at
hemlines — a few children, Negro and white, urchins from the tenement
homes a few blocks off this wide main street. Great untidy flocks of pigeons
rose and settled again and rose, startled, scattering. Lawrence Pryor looked
at everything keenly. He knew that he was out of place here; he had come
down from his office because his eleven o'clock appointment had canceled
out; he was free for half an hour. The only place to sit had been beside this
pretty young mother, who held her baby up to her face and took no interest
at all in the pigeons or the chattering children or Lawrence himself. He was
sitting in a patch of sunlight that fell upon him through the narrow channel
between two tall buildings, as if singling him out for a blessing.

All these women shoppers! He watched them cross quickly to the 2
island, and quickly over to the other curb, for they rarely had the time to sit

248

and rest. They were in a hurry. Because of them, hurrying across the street, traffic was backed up waiting to make right-hand turns. Out of the crowd of shoppers he saw a blond woman appear, walking briskly and confidently. She hurried against a red light and a horn sounded. How American she was, how well-dressed and sure of herself! Lawrence found himself staring at her, imagining the face that might reveal itself to him if he were to approach her — startled and elegant and composed, seeing by his face that he was no danger to her, no danger.

She did not cross the little park but took the sidewalk that led around   3
it. Avoiding the benchsitters and the pigeons. Lawrence was disappointed. And then, watching her, he saw that the woman was familiar — her brisk, impatient walk, her trim blue coat — and, indeed, he knew her well, the woman was his own wife! He tapped his jaw with the tips of his fingers in a gesture of amused surprise. Of course! Beverly! As if acting out embarrassment for an audience, he smiled up toward the sky . . . and when he looked back, his wife was already hurrying across the street, moving bravely against the light while buses and taxicabs pressed forward.

He got to his feet to follow her. But an extraordinarily tall man got in   4
front of him, walking quickly, and then a small crowd of women shoppers, everyone hurrying now that the light had turned green. Something held Lawrence back. The tall man was hurrying as if to catch up with Beverly. He was strangely tall, freakishly tall, with silver-gray hair that was bunched around his head in tight little curls, like grapes. He wore a dark coat, and on the back of his neck there was a vivid red birthmark, a stain in the shape of a finger. The shoppers moved forward, in front of Lawrence, and the tall man and Lawrence's wife moved into the distance. All this motion made Lawrence feel slightly dizzy.

The legend about him was his fanaticism about work: Beverly com-   5
plained of this, she worried about it, she was proud of it. He was a doctor and his patients were sacred to him. And so he had better not run after his wife, because she would be alarmed to see him out on the street at this time of day, and because it might be ten or fifteen minutes before he could get away again. She might want him to have lunch with her. She might want him to go into stores with her. Better to stay behind, to stay hidden. So he watched her disappear — his wife hurrying into the midst of the city — and he sat down again, feeling oddly pleased and excited. He felt as if something secret had been revealed to him.

Beside him the young woman was leaning her face to her child, whis-   6
pering. She had a pale, angular face, illuminated by love, or by the child's reflecting face, or by the narrow patch of sunlight that was moving slowly from Lawrence and onto her. Women, seen like this, were gifts to men.

He considered smiling at her. But no, that might be a mistake — this   7
was not a city in which people smiled freely at one another.

Herb Altman came into the office, striding forward with his head slightly 8
lowered. Bald, but only forty-five. He had a portly, arrogant body and his
clothes were always jaunty — today he wore a bright yellow necktie that
jumped in Lawrence's vision.

Shaking hands. 9

"How are you?" 10

"Not well. I can't sleep. I never sleep, you know that," Altman said. 11

He sat and began to talk. His voice was urgent and demanding. As he 12
spoke he shook his head so that his cheeks shivered. Altman's wife Connie
was a friend of Lawrence's wife. It seemed to Lawrence that the women in
their circle were all close friends; in a way they blended into one another.
The husbands, too, seemed to blend into one another. Many of them had
several lives, but the lives were somehow shared. They lived in one dimension but turned up in other dimensions — downtown late in the afternoon,
or in downriver suburbs. Their expensive homes and automobiles and boats
could not quite contain them. Too much energy. Urgent, clicking, demanding words. While Altman talked angrily about his insomnia and switched
onto the complaints of his wife and then onto the complaints of his girl,
Lawrence saw again his own wife in the distance of his imagination, a dream
he had dreamt while awake, moving freely and happily along the sidewalk of
this massive city.

What mystery was in her, this woman he had lived with for so long? 13
They had one child, a daughter. They had known each other for two decades. And yet, seeing her like that, Lawrence had been struck by the mystery of her separateness, her being. . . .

Altman said in a furious whisper, "I'm going to have her followed!" 14

"Your wife?" 15

"Evie. *Evelyn.* Twenty-five years old, a baby, and she tells me the 16
plans she dreams up! She wants me to marry her next year!"

The numerals of Lawrence's watch were greenish-white, glowing up 17
out of a dark face. They were supposed to glow in the dark but they glowed
in the light as well.

"All right," Altman said, seeing Lawrence look at his watch, "so I'm 18
wasting your time with this. So. Check my heart, my blackened lungs, tap
me on the back to see if I have echoes inside, to see what's hollowed
out — I'm a sick man, we both know that. Here I am."

In the end Lawrence did as he always did: refilled Altman's prescrip- 19
tion for barbiturates. It was for six refills, and Altman would be back again in
a few weeks.

At the door Altman paused dramatically. His white shirt front bulged. 20

"Why do they keep after me?" he said. "Larry, what is it? Why are 21
they always after me? I can't sleep at night. I'm planning a trip in my mind
but when I get up I can't remember it — I don't sleep but I don't remember

what I think about. Why are they always after me, those women? What are they doing to me?"

Lawrence and his wife and daughter lived in a brick home that had been 22 painted white, a few blocks from the lake. The house glowed in the air of twilight. It had the ghostly weightless look of something at the bottom of a lake, made perfect. It was a place in which Lawrence might sleep soundly, as he had never slept in his parents' oversized, combative home in Philadelphia. No more of that life! He had blocked out even the memory of that life.

Behind him in the city were his patients and the unhappy memories of 23 his patients. Ten, sometimes twelve hours of ailments — the shame of being sick, of being weak, of uttering words better left unsaid. Office hours were worse than hospital hours. During the day Lawrence's hand turned shaky and reluctant, writing out so many prescriptions, smiling with his prescribed smile, a forty-year-old face that was in danger of wearing out. His patients had too many faces. They were blotched or sullen or impatient or, like Altman's, familiar but eerily distant, demanding something Lawrence could not give and could not understand.

Many of the ailments were imaginary. They existed, yes, but they were 24 imaginary; how to cure them?

The telephone was ringing as he entered his home. He had the idea 25 that it had been ringing for some time. When he went to answer it, in the kitchen, it stopped ringing and he stood with his hand out, a few inches above the receiver, listening to the silence of the house.

His mother is coming to visit, due the next morning on the nine-thirty 26 flight from Philadelphia.

Beverly and Edie are going out again; they get in each other's way by 27 the closet. Edie, fourteen years old and taller than her mother, sticks her arms angrily into her coat. The coat is khaki-colored and lined with fake wool, years old; Edie will not give it up in spite of her mother's pleas. Lawrence stands with the evening newspaper, watching them. It is six-thirty. "Do you have to go out now?" he says.

"I forgot to get new towels. I wanted to get new towels for your 28 mother, I can't let her use those old ones," Beverly says.

"New towels? You're going out now for new towels?" 29

"Everything is sleazy. It isn't good enough for her." 30

Beverly's jaws are hardening. Her eyes are bright, alert, restless. Edie 31 is shiny-faced and almost pretty, but always in a hurry, always bumping into things. It is obvious to Lawrence that his wife and daughter have been arguing about something. Edie knocks against a chair in the foyer and screws up her face. "God!" she winces.

"Did you go shopping downtown today?" Lawrence asks his wife. 32

She is frowning into her purse, looking for something. "No."   33
"I thought I saw you."   34
"Saw me? When?"   35
"A little before noon."   36
She stares at him, closing her purse. There is a cold, bright look   37
around her eyes, a look Lawrence cannot understand. Then she smiles. "Oh,
yes, I was downtown . . . I just drove down and back, looking for some
things I couldn't get out here. . . . I've been running around all day. I had
to pick Edie up at school and take her to the dentist and now . . . now I
have to go out again."
        "You're making too much out of it. My mother doesn't expect you to   38
fuss over her."
        She shakes her head and avoids his eyes. He thinks of the tall, silver-   39
haired man with the birthmark, hurrying along after her as if to catch up
with her.

His mother. The airport. They have met his mother like this many times and   40
each time they say the same things; it seems that the same crowds are at the
airport. His mother begins at once to tell him about the news at home and
she will continue to tell him of funerals and weddings, births, illnesses,
surgery, surprises, all the way home, though she has written him about these
things in her weekly letters.
        "Oh, look at this!" she says in disgust. She holds up her hands for them   41
to see her white gloves, which are soiled and even stained with something
that looks like rust or blood, a very faint red-brown color.
        "I'll wash them out for you, Mother," Beverly says at once.   42
        "Traveling is so dirty. Filthy," Lawrence's mother says.   43
        He recalls her having said that before.   44
        While his mother and his wife talk, Lawrence drives in silence. He's   45
happy that his mother is visiting them. She comes often, several times a
year. Lawrence has the idea that she blames him for having left Philadelphia
and coming to this city of strangers, where he has no relatives. The letters
they write to each other do not seem to express them. Beneath his neat,
typed lines, and beneath her slanted lines in their lavender ink, there seems
to be another dimension, a submerged feeling or memory, that the two of
them can only hint at but cannot express.
        They are approaching Lawrence's home. "I like that house," his   46
mother says flatly, as she always does. This seems to settle something.
Lawrence and Beverly both feel relieved.
        The old family home had been white also. Now Lawrence's mother   47
lives in an apartment favored by other widows, but for decades of her life she
lived in a house the size of a municipal building. In his dreams Lawrence

sometimes climbs the stairway to the third floor, which had been closed off, to look through the stacks of his father's old medical journals, as he did when he was a child. There were bundles of journals. Small towers. He spent many hours looking through them, fascinated.

His mother's presence in his house, his own house, makes Lawrence 48
feel a little displaced. It seems to him that time is confused. His own age is uncertain. But he is a good host to her, helping Beverly out; he is gallant to her. After dinner that night they look through snapshots, another ritual. The snapshots are passed around. Then, leaning toward him, in a sudden stiff motion that makes him realize how his mother is corseted — his wife, also, her body slim and deft but smoothly hard to the touch — she hands him a photograph that had been taken years ago. That photograph again! It is Lawrence, Larry Jr., sitting on a spotted pony at some forgotten fair, a rented pony, Lawrence's dark hair combed down onto his forehead in a way that makes him look like a moron, his stare startled and vacuous, his mouth too timid to smile. Lawrence stares at the photograph. Why does his mother treasure it so much? Why does she always bring it along with the more recent snapshots, as if she doesn't remember she has shown it to him on her last visit?

"Look at that, isn't that darling? A darling boy?" she says stubbornly. 49

Lawrence stares down at his own face, which is blank and stark in the 50 photograph. It was a face that might have become anything. Any personality might have inhabited it. It *was so blank, that face — anything could inhabit it.*

He stands suddenly. His mother and his wife stare at him in alarm. 51
"Larry? What's wrong?" Beverly says. 52
He passes his hand over his eyes. He sits down again. 53
"Nothing." 54
"Did you hear something in the house?" 55
"No. Nothing." 56
Two evenings later he is driving home when a car veers out around 57 him, passing him with its horn blaring. The car is filled with kids — boys and girls — and he thinks he sees Edie in with them. His heart jumps. But he cannot be sure.

When he gets home it is nearly dark. His mother kisses him on the 58 side of the face. She is powdery and yet hard, a precise, stubborn little woman. What do they talk about all day, women? His mother and his wife? They are telling him now about what they have done today. Their chatter is like music, rising in snatches about them, airy and incomplete. It never quite completes itself; it has to continue.

"Is Edie home yet?" he says. 59
"No, not yet," says Beverly. 60
"Where is she?" 61

"She had something after school — choir practice — " 62

"All this time?" 63

"No, not all this time. She's probably at someone's house. She'll be home in a few minuutes." 64

"But you don't know where she is?" 65

"Not exactly. What's wrong? Why are you so angry?" 66

"I'm not angry." 67

When she comes in he will find out nothing from her. Nothing. She will move her body jerkily through the kitchen and to the front closet, she will take off her coat, she will sit slouching at dinner and stare down into her plate or stare dutifully up at him, and he will find out nothing about her, nothing. His heart pounds angrily. Once Beverly said of Edie, "She has all that stuff on her face but you should see her neck — she never washes! I could roll the dirt off her neck with my fingers!" 68

His mother asks him about his day. Did he work hard? Is he tired? 69

He answers her vaguely, listening for Edie to come in. But when she does come in he will find out nothing from her. His mother switches to another topic — complaints about one of his aunts — and he can't follow her. He is thinking of Edie, then he is thinking of his wife. Then he finds himself thinking of one of his patients, Connie Altman. She wept in his office that morning. "I need something to help me sleep at night. I lie awake thinking. Then in the morning I can't remember what I was thinking about. I'm so nervous, my heart pounds, can you give me something stronger to help me sleep? Everything is running out . . ." 70

This puzzled him. "What do you mean, everything is running out?" 71

"There isn't any point. I don't see it. We are all running out, people our age, things are running out of us . . . draining out of us . . . I will have to live out my life in this body . . ." 72

She is a woman of beauty, very small, with childish wrists and ankles. But her face has begun to harden in the past few years. 73

"I need something to help me sleep. Please. I know that in the other room *he* is awake, he can't sleep either, it drives me crazy! I prefer the nights he stays out. At least he isn't in the house, lying awake like me. I don't care who he's with . . . I need something to help me sleep, please. I can't stand my thoughts all night long." 74

His daughter's room. Saturday afternoon. The house is empty for a few hours and he may walk through it, anywhere, because it is his house and all the rooms are his, his property. 75

Edie's room is piled with clothes, school books, shoes, junk. Two of the three dresser drawers are pulled out. The top of the dresser is cluttered. Lawrence's reflection moves into the mirror and he looks at himself in sur- 76 prise — is that really him, Dr. Pryor? He is disappointed. He is even a little angry. His soul is neat, neatly defined as the many cards he carries in his wallet, and as neat as the curve of his haircut against his neck; neat as his files at the office and as his car, which he takes pride in. But his body looks untidy — the shirt rumpled, though he has put it on fresh only that morning — his face sallow, edgy, his hands strangely empty. Is that really Dr. Pryor, that man? How has it happened that he must wake in the morning to this particular face and body, always, this particular human being?

He goes to the dresser, avoiding his own eyes in the mirror, and tugs 77 at the first drawer. A jumble of stockings, black tights, wool socks of various colors, filmy, gauzy things. A spool of white thread rolls harmlessly around. He starts to close the drawer and then remembers that it was partly open. Good. It is good he remembered that. He pulls out the second drawer — underclothes of various colors, pink and yellow and green, things jumbled together, releasing to him an air of fresh, clean laundry. He stares into this drawer. What if it falls out? What if the underclothes fall out and he can't put them back in order again? But they are not in any order, everything is a jumble. He smiles.

He has never come into this room alone in his memory. Never. But 78 being here this afternoon, so close to his daughter and yet safe from her fourteen-year-old's curious, sarcastic eye, he feels oddly pleased. She is very real to him at this moment: She might be standing close behind him, about to break into one of her greetings — "Hiya, buddy!" has been a commonplace remark of hers this past month — or about to hum into his ear one of her slangy, mysterious, banal little tunes.

He finds himself looking through the silky underclothes. Things stick 79 together; there is the crackle of minor electricity. He holds up a half-slip of mint green with tiny white bows on it. Pretty! It is very pretty. He wants to rub it against his face. And now a kind of despair rises in him as he thinks of his and these clothes, his daughter out running around this afternoon at the shopping center with her girlfriends, and these clothes which are now in his possession, here in his room, safe. It is a mystery, his having a daughter. He cannot quite comprehend it. He looks through the drawer farther, this sense of despair rising strongly in him . . . Rolled up in a ball, stuck back in a corner of the drawer, are a pair of white underpants. He picks them up. They have several bloodstains on them, thick and stiff, almost caked. He stares. Why bloodstains? Why here? For a moment he feels nothing, he thinks nothing. He is not even surprised. Then it occurs to him that his daughter was ashamed to put these soiled underpants in the wash, that she had meant to wash them herself but had forgotten, and weeks, maybe months have gone by . . . the blood grown old and hard, the stains impossible to get out . . . she has forgotten about them . . . balled up, rolled up, and stuck in the corner of the drawer, forgotten . . .

His mother is talking with some friends of theirs who have dropped in. An 80 ordinary Sunday afternoon. Beverly is handing drinks around. In the mirror above the fireplace his mother's bluish-white hair bobs weightlessly. Long white candlesticks in holders of silver, on the mantel; the wicks perfectly white, never burnt. What are they talking about so earnestly? Lawrence tries to listen. Beverly is chiding him gently for working so hard — it is a familiar pattern, almost a tune, the words of his mother to his father years ago — and he nods, smiles, he is Dr. Pryor, who works hard. The fact is that he has done nothing all day except sit in his study, at his desk, leafing through medical journals. He has not been able to concentrate on anything.

Ted Albrecht, a friend of many years, is talking in his usual fanciful 81 manner. He is a stockbroker but thinks of himself as a social critic. A short man, with glasses and lively eyebrows; he is considered a friend of Lawrence's, and yet the two men have never talked together, alone together. They always meet at parties, in someone's living room, with groups of other people around.

Ted says, "I guarantee you, a vehement hot time is coming for this na- 82 tion!"

Lawrence has not been able to concentrate on the conversation. He 83 thinks that he may not be able to endure this minute, this very minute.

Voices ring around him. It is a ring of concentric rings, a ring of voices 84 and breaths and bright glances, circling him. Like music, the voices do not come to rest. They pause shrilly; they pause in expectation. Lawrence accepts a drink from his wife, a woman whose face looks oddly brittle. The ice cubes in his glass make him think of the Arctic — pure crystal, pure colorless ice and air, where no germs survive. It is impossible, this minute. Impossible to stand with these people. He does not know what is wrong and yet he understands that it has become impossible, that his body is being pushed to the breaking point, that to contain himself — his physicalness, his being — would take the strength of a wrestler, a man not himself.

The minute expands slowly. Nothing happens. 85

Again, the airport. The reversal of the meeting last week: now she is going 86 home. The airliner will draw up into it a certain number of people, Lawrence's mother among them, and then it will be gone. Now there is a rush of words. Things to be said. His mother complains bitterly of one of his aunts — he nods in agreement, embarrassed that she should say these things in front of Beverly — he nods yes, yes; he will agree to anything. "What could she know? She was never married!" Lawrence's mother says, twisting her mouth. Of Lawrence's father, who died in a boating accident when Lawrence was eighteen, she does not ever speak, exactly; she speaks around him, around that solitary mysterious event, alluding to it with petulant jerks of her stiff little body. Lawrence's father died on the lake, alone. He drowned, alone. The boat must have capsized and he drowned, alone, with no one to witness the death or to explain it.

Lawrence's mother begins to cry. She will back off from them, crying, and then at a certain point she will stop crying, collecting herself, and she will promise to telephone them as soon as she lands in Philadelphia. The visit is concluded. 87

Though it was a weekday evening, they went to Dorothy Clair's art gallery, where a young sculptor was having an opening. Dorothy Clair was a widow some years older than the Pryors, a wealthy woman on the periphery of their social group. It was a champagne opening. Lawrence and his wife were separated, drawn into different groups; Lawrence was not really taking part in the conversation, but he appeared enthusiastic. The champagne went to his head. His mother had stayed with them for nearly a week, the visit had gone well, everything was over. Good. It was a weekday evening but they had gone out as if to reward themselves. 88

Next to Lawrence there was a piece of sculpture — a single column of metal, with sharp edges. It looked dangerous. A woman seemed about to back into it and Lawrence wondered if he should warn her. He could see his own reflection in its surface, blotchy and comic. All the pieces of sculpture were metallic. Some hung from the ceiling, heavily; others hung from the walls. Great massive hulks — not defined enough to be shapes — squatted on the floor. People drifted around the sculpture, sometimes bumping into it. A woman stooped to disentangle her skirt from some wire, a thick ball of wire that had been sprayed with white paint. 89

What were these strange forms? They were oppressive to Lawrence. But no one else seemed to be uneasy. He went to examine the wire — it looked like chicken wire — and he could make no sense of it. Elsewhere in the crowded room there were balls of metal that were distorted, like planets wrenched out of shape. Their shiny surfaces reflected a galaxy of human faces, but the faces were not really human. They were cheerful and blatant and flat, as if there were no private depths to them. . . . How they were all chattering away, those faces! No privacy at all, nothing but the facial mask of flesh: no private depths of anguish or darkness or sweetness, nothing. The faces were all talking earnestly to one another. 90

Lawrence looked for his wife. He saw her across the room, talking to a tall man with silvery hair. It was the man he had seen downtown! Astonished, Lawrence could not move. He stood with his drink in his hand, as metallic and fixed as the pieces of sculpture. These columns punctuated the gallery, each reaching to the ceiling, with flat, shiny surfaces and edges that appeared razor-sharp. They made him think suddenly of the furniture in his 91 parents' house that he had stood up on end, as a child — allowed by his mother to play with the furniture of certain rooms, upending tables and chairs so that he could crawl under them and pretend they were small houses, huts. He had crouched under them, peering out past the legs of tables and chairs. Sometimes his mother had given him a blanket to drape over the piece of furniture.

The man with the silver hair turned and Lawrence saw that it was not the stranger from downtown after all — it was someone he'd known for years. Yet he felt no relief. He was still paralyzed. Beverly, not seeing him, was looking around cautiously, nervously. The man was about to drift into another conversation and leave her. He had a big, heavy handsome head, his silver-gray hair curly and bunched, his face florid and generous and a little too aggressive, too sure of itself. Lawrence felt a sudden dislike for him. And yet he was grateful that he had not become that man — grateful that, in the moment of paralysis and panic, his soul had not flown out of him and into that man, into that other body. It might have happened. Anything might happen!   92

He went out. He walked quickly out of his building and into the midday crowd, in a hurry, and once on the sidewalk he stayed near the curb so that he could walk fast. The day was cold and overcast. He walked several blocks to the end of the street and across the street to the riverfront. There were few people down here, only the most hardy of tourists. No shoppers bothered to come this far. There were no stores here, only concrete and walls and a ferry landing and the water, the grim cold water. He leaned over a railing. He stared down at the lapping water. It was not very clean; there were long streaks of foam in it, as long as six or eight feet, bobbing and curling and twisting like snakes.   93

The discontent of the past two weeks rose in his mind. What was wrong? What had happened? It had begun on that sunlit day when he'd seen his wife from a distance. His wife. His mother arrived the following morning; they picked her up at the airport as always. And his daughter — there had been something about his daughter as well — but he could not remember. In the dirty, bouncy water he saw Edie's face, grinning up at him. But she did not really see him. There was nothing there. He was alone. He thought in a panic of himself and the river: the fact of being alone like this, with the river a few yards beneath him.   94

There was a sensation of deadness around his eyes. His eyes had become hardened, crusted over, like crusts of blood; the wounds where eyes had once been. And now they might fall off. . . ? Another face was pushing its way through. He must scratch at the scabs of his eyes and scratch them off, to make way for the new face, digging the crusts of blood away with his   95 nails. He must tear at himself. He must do it now, this minute . . . for at this minute his body could no longer contain itself, it was like a wrestler with superbly developed muscles bursting through his clothing, tearing his clothing with anger and joy!

The river beneath him was a river of souls: the murky, sour, rebellious   96
souls of all the children he had been meant to father, flowing out of him and helplessly, ferociously downstream. He stared at the water. All of these his children! Sons and daughters of his body! He had been meant to father these thousands, these thousands of millions of souls, and yet he was on the concrete walk, leaning against the guardrail, and the children of his body were flowing by him, bouncing, lapping noisily against the abutment, becoming lost.

For some time he stood in silence. His eyes did ache. He tried to think   97
of what he must do — had he planned something? Why had he come down here? If he were to drown, perhaps scenes of his past life would flash to him. He would see the upended furniture again — the clumsy gold-covered chair with its curved legs and its gauzy bottom, the springs visible through the dark gauze — he would crawl between the legs again, drawing his knees up to his chest, hiding there, sly and safe. He would see the big house, he would see the piles of magazines and he would smell the acrid, lovely odor of loneliness on the third floor of that house; he would pass into that room and live out his life there chastely and silently. But perhaps he would fall into the water screaming. He would thresh his arms and legs — he would sink at once, screaming — and no one could save him. People might come to gawk, but they could not save him. And perhaps he would see nothing at all, no visions, no memories, perhaps it was only a lie about a drowning man living his life again and he would see nothing, nothing, he would drown in agony and be washed downstream, lost.

He glanced at his watch. After one.   98

He hurried back to his office. The receptionist, a pretty Negro woman,   99
chided him for walking in the rain. She took his trench coat from him, shook it, hung it up. In the waiting room — he could see through two partly opened doors — a few people were sitting and had been sitting for a while. He went into his private office. In a few minutes the nurse showed in his first patient of the afternoon: Herb Altman.

"I'm back a little faster this time but everything is the usual. Diagnosis   100
the usual," Altman said flatly. He wore a stylish, wide green tie, mint green. There were tiny white streaks in it that bothered Lawrence's vision.

Shaking of hands.   101

"Maybe somebody should just shoot me. I should croak, eh?" Altman   102
laughed. "Anyway I still can't sleep, Larry. The same damn thing. Give me something strong to help me sleep, eh? And did you hear about that bastard, that investigator, I got to follow Evie? He was a friend of hers! It turned out

he was a friend of hers! He told her everything, he tipped her off. I fired him and I'm dumping her, believe you me, I think even she and my wife are comparing notes on me and laughing and it's no goddam wonder I can't sleep. Maybe I should just croak, eh? Make things easier for everybody? What's your opinion?"

"Let me do just a routine examination," Lawrence said. "You do look a 103 little agitated."

SUBJECT QUESTIONS

1. What seems to be bothering Lawrence Pryor? Does *he* know what is bothering him?
2. Would it be fair to say that this is a story in which nothing happens? Does inaction seem valid subject matter for a short story? How does Oates make it interesting?
3. How many of Lawrence's friends are mentioned in the story? How close is he to them? Is he close to his family?
4. How did Lawrence's father die? Does Oates seem to imply that the death was suicidal? Can you tell from the story whether the father's life was happier than the son's — or very different?
5. At the end, Lawrence seems to be carrying on his work very much as at the beginning. Do you think he has made any adjustment?

STRUCTURE QUESTIONS

1. The incident of the bloodstains is a minor one in the story, one which Lawrence can't even remember at the end. Why do you suppose Oates chose this for the title?
2. The story is composed of half a dozen such minor incidents. How does Oates tie them all together?
3. What does the business about Herb Altman have to do with the story about Lawrence Pryor? Why does Oates bring it up again at the end?
4. Nothing ever comes of Lawrence's suspicions about his wife; what function does the incident play in the story? Does it matter whether or not the reader thinks she is unfaithful?
5. Although Lawrence is alone three times, Oates aranges the story so that most of his thoughts and daydreams occur in the presence of other people — when he ought, perhaps, to be carrying on a conversation. How does this arrangement strengthen the point of the story? (Note particularly Lawrence's detached observations about the people he is with.)

SUGGESTION FOR WRITING

Write a cause and effect analysis of how someone drifted into or was trapped in a situation from which he could not easily extricate himself. Some possible examples: someone who wastes four years of college preparing for a profession not suited to him; someone who cannot pass a required course; a person who becomes engaged to an unsuitable partner.

For L. G.: Unseen for Twenty Years

Adrienne Rich

Adrienne Rich published her first volume of poetry, A Change of World, *in 1951. Since that time she has become a compelling voice in modern poetry. She has published numerous other volumes, winning the National Book Award for Poetry in 1974 for* Diving into the Wreck. *To a greater extent than most writers, she reflects both in subject matter and structure the radical changes in social values which have taken place since 1950. In the "careful" 1950s, Rich wrote what might be called modern-traditional poetry, often employing rhyme and traditional stanza forms. In the revolutionary 1960s, her protests were reflected both in the subject matter and in the stretching and breaking of traditional forms. Since that time, her poetry has been intensely personal, sometimes cryptic but always powerful. Through all the changes, Rich has remained true to a dictum she expressed in an early poem, that "a too-compassionate art is half an art"; that is, effective writing must carefully control and organize the expression of feelings. The following poem was written in 1974.*

A blue-grained line circles a fragment of the mind
drawn in ancient crayon:
out of the blue, your tightstrung smile —

often in the first snow
that even here smells only of itself
even on this Broadway limped by cripples   5
and the self-despising
Still, in that smell, another snow,
another world: we're walking
grey boulevards traced with white   10

in Paris, the early 'fifties
of invincible ignorance:

or, a cold spring:
I clasp your hips on the bike
shearing the empty plain in March   15
teeth gritted in the wind
searching for Chartres:
we doze
in the boat-train

we who were friends and thought   20
women and men should be lovers

Your face: taut as a mask of wires, a fencer's mask
half-turned away, the one night, walking
the City of Love, so cold
we warmed our nerves with wine   25
at every all-night café
to keep on walking, talking
Your words have drifted back for twenty years:

I have to tell you — maybe I'm not a man —
I can't do it with women — but I'd like   30
to hold you, to know what it's like
to sleep and wake together —

the one night in all our weeks of talk
you talked of fear
      I wonder   35

what words of mine drift back to you?
Something like:
     But you're a man, I know it —
the swiftness of your mind is masculine — ?

— some set-piece I'd learned to embroider   40
in my woman's education
while the needle scarred my hand?
Of course, you're a man. I like you. What else could you be?
what else, what else,
what bloody else . . .   45

Given the cruelty of our times and customs,
maybe you hate these memories,
the ignorance, the innocence we shared:

maybe you cruise the SoHo cocktail parties
the Vancouver bar-scene   50
stalking yourself as I can see you still:
young, tense, amorphous, longing —

maybe you live out your double life
in the Berkeley hills, with a wife
who stuns her mind into indifference   55
with Scotch and saunas
while you arrange your own humiliations
downtown

(and, yes, I've played my scenes
of favorite daughter, child-bride, token woman, muse   60
listening now and then
as a drunken poet muttered into my hair:
I can't make it with women I admire —)

maybe you've found or fought
through to a kind of faithfulness   65
in the strange coexistence
of two of any gender

But we were talking in 1952
of the fear of being cripples in a world
of perfect women and men: 70
we were the givens and the stake
and we did badly

and, dear heart, I know, had a lover gestured
you'd have left me
for a man, as I left you,   75
as we left each other, seeking the love of men.

SUBJECT QUESTIONS

1. Would you say that this poem is a commentary on homosexuality or on society? What *does* the poem say?
2. Can you tell why L. G. was unwilling to admit his homosexual tendencies? Why didn't the poet recognize them?
3. If a young man and young woman today are very close friends, does it still seem "natural" that they should become lovers?
4. Does the list of L. G.'s possible courses of action twenty years later

seem a realistic appraisal? (Remember that this poem was written prior to any serious "gay lib" movement.) Is it sympathetic to the man's plight?

5. Does the final stanza say anything about the poet's own success in "seeking the love of men"? Why does she compare herself to L. G.?

STRUCTURE QUESTIONS

1. Does the opening stanza make clear whether the poet has met L. G. again after twenty years or has only recalled him to memory? Is the crayon image effective? What does it imply?
2. Examine the description of the young man on the night he confesses to the poet; does it give sufficient clue to his mental torment?
3. What effect, if any, does the poet's confession of involvement with other homosexuals ("and, yes, I've played my scenes . . .") have on the reader's confidence in her analysis of the homosexual's difficulties?
4. Unlike an essay, a poem tries to suggest far more than it says. Does this poem give sufficient clues to what is left unsaid?
5. From what is given in the poem, try to outline the cause of L. G.'s tension and the effects which his sexual propensities have had. Is it the facts or the full feelings which are left unsaid?

SUGGESTIONS FOR WRITING

1. The words to a great many "bubble-gum" pop songs are of the "they said we were too young" variety, a kind of antisocial "them against us" view of love. Write a paper in which you analyze the causes of this adolescent view.
2. Write a paper analyzing the causes for the widespread preoccupation with love among teen-agers, where one might logically expect other concerns to be more important ('job prospects, what to study in college, and so on). You might consider whether the intensity of this concern varies between males and females, or whether it takes different forms.
3. If you think that social attitudes toward homosexuality have significantly changed since Adrienne Rich wrote this poem, try to explain the reasons for this change in attitude.
4. Some parts of America — Florida, for example — seem much less tolerant of homosexuality than other parts, such as the San Francisco Bay area. Write a paper suggesting some reasons for this difference.

6

VOGUE, VAGUE, OR VERBIAGE? THE WRITTEN WORD

Definition

Most students have been taught — and properly — to go to the dictionary if they cannot tell the meaning of a word from its context. And the development of the modern, carefully compiled dictionary within the last century has been invaluable in furthering communication. Unfortunately, however, the dictionary has its limitations. Consider for a moment how a dictionary goes about defining a word. Normally, it puts the word into a more general classification and then limits its description of that larger class until the definition can refer only to the one word being defined. Thus, "cocker spaniel: any of a breed of small spaniels having short legs, long floppy ears . . ." or "tamale: a native Mexican food having. . . ." This procedure is useful if the general classification is more recognizable than the particular member of it being defined. If readers have a fair idea of what the general class "Mexican food" is like, they are enlightened by the definition of tamale as a "native Mexican food" having certain special characteristics.

But suppose the word to be defined is a very general or abstract concept like "love" or "bravery." The dictionary might classify such a concept as "an emotion" or "an attitude," but its doing so does not tell us much, even if we know what "an attitude" is. Adequate definitions of these broad concepts need much more space than a dictionary can devote to them.

Serious misunderstandings seldom occur from the use of specific or concrete terms like cocker spaniel. Readers who do not know what the word means can use the dictionary to find out. But an abstract term may cause two kinds of difficulty. First, if readers do not know the term, they will get little help from the dictionary. And if they do know the term, their understanding of it may still be quite different from the meaning intended in any particular context. Settlement of the Viet Nam crisis ran into a stalemate partly because of misunderstanding over the meaning of "aggressor." To the United States, the Viet Cong were the aggressors, for they were making war on an established government. But to the NLF and North Viet Nam, "aggressor" was understood to mean "a foreigner who attacks"; when Viet Namese were fighting Viet Namese, there was civil war but not aggression, for no "foreigners" were involved until American forces arrived.

Most abstract terms have only a general *area* of meaning, not a particular meaning on which all can agree. This is because the concept has been abstracted from — drawn out of — a great many particular situations which are considerably varied in their details. Suppose, for instance, a South Pacific tribe witnesses, on three successive days, a tribe member killing a shark to save a friend, another rescuing some children from a burning hut, and a warrior killing seven enemies in one battle. To all of these acts they apply a word meaning "courage." Clearly, they all show courage, though the deeds have little in common except this abstraction, courage. "Courage," then, does not mean "saving children from a burning hut"; the word has a much more general *area* of meaning.

Because no two people have identical sets of experiences, and because the meaning of an abstract concept is derived from experience, both firsthand and vicarious, it follows that an abstract term cannot mean exactly the same to any two people. The meanings of some terms may vary so slightly from person to person that we can use them without fear of serious misunderstanding. Other terms have such an infinite variety of meanings that no one really expects to know quite what someone else means by them. We make a kind of tacit agreement, for instance, that no one will inquire in too much detail what another person means by "love." We simply allow the word so much flexibility that it is possible for a person to express a "love" for mashed potatoes. In between these relatively harmless extremes, however, are a great many terms which are used as though they had a fairly specific and commonly accepted meaning. Not only do serious misunderstandings result from such careless use of abstract words and terms, but important differences in meaning are often obscured. One is likely to hear this type of argument, for example: "The Democratic and Republican parties both believe in the American Way of Life; so there isn't really any significant difference between them." The statement, of course, ignores the fact that "American Way of Life" does not mean the same for both parties — or even for various members of one party. Frequently such statements reflect a deliberate attempt to deceive, as when military leaders cover a disastrous defeat with the phrase "strategic withdrawal."

You should watch for careless use of abstractions in print and try to discover as nearly as possible from the context what writers mean by their terms. Perhaps more important, you should be aware of what *you* mean by terms when you use them, for such careless usage invariably leads to sloppy thinking. You should also make clear in your own writing your meaning of abstract concepts, either by the context in which you use them or, if necessary, by definition. This does not mean that every paper should be prefaced with the awkward and formal "definition of terms" paragraph so common in student themes. For the reader, remember, learns little by "According to Webster, courage means . . ."

But when writers cannot give adequate dictionary definitions, the reader may fairly ask, how do they go about making clear the meanings of their terms? The key is to keep in mind that the meaning of an abstract concept is the sum total of a person's experiences which have that concept in common. The best way, then, for a writer to define a term is to put it back into specific context by giving typical and relevant examples from the writer's own experience. The easiest way to define "book" is to point to one and say, *"This* is a book." The same is true of abstract terms: to define "courage," point out examples of it. Enough instances must be given so that the area of meaning is established.

If one cannot conveniently give sufficient illustrations from one's own experience there are other methods of defining which can be employed. These are the same as the methods of presenting material which have been illustrated thus far in this book: comparison and contrast, classification and division, cause and effect, and process. Suppose, for instance, a writer needed to define "alcoholic." Certainly a description of a typical alcoholic would help — a personal acquaintance would be best. But it would also be helpful to discuss various theories concerning the *cause* of alcoholism, or its social consequences (*effects*). The writer might want to show the *process* by which a person develops into an alcoholic. Or perhaps through *comparison* and *contrast*, the writer would show the difference between a "drinker" and an "alcoholic." Finally, the writer could profitably *classify* alcoholics according to their various mental problems or *divide* them into subgroups. It would be possible for a writer to use all of these methods in a single extended definition. The important consideration is that the reader come to an understanding of the term as nearly as possible like that of the writer. The writer's definition may vary considerably from the reader's, but if the reader sees clearly this difference communication will be effected.

Extended definition is one of the most difficult types of writing; but it can be accomplished if writers will remember to put terms into specific contexts. They need only to watch out for two traps into which students frequently fall. (1) It is not necessary to establish a definition which will be valid for all people in all time. The task of writers is only to convey clearly what *they* mean by their terms. (2) Writers should beware of writing about terms as though they were already defined, that is, of assuming that readers really know from the beginning what writers mean by their terms. Readers cannot possibly know exactly, and the slight differences are significant.

Vogue Words
Are Trific, Right?

William Safire

William Safire (b. 1929) has been a journalist, foreign correspondent, and a speech writer for President Nixon. He is currently a columnist for The New York Times, *where this essay first appeared. Among his books are* Plunging into Politics *(1964) and* The New Language of Politics *(1968; rev. ed., 1972).*

Vogue words are bits of language that slip into American speech, are disseminated far and wide by television talk shows, and make a person appear with-it. Many of the words run a flulike course and disappear, leaving memories of semantic headaches and fevered articulation. Others, like "détente," are formally banished by Presidential fiat. Here is my first annual vogue-word watch, compiled with the help of a few lexicographical colleagues around the country.   1

Vogues from All Over

Is a word merely for the nonce, or worth including in a dictionary? Some stalwart vogues seem to be establishing themselves as permanent features of the language. Among businessmen, "net net" has already faded, but *bottom line* (the "final accounting" or "essence") is spreading. Among youthful linguists, "way to go" has faded, "no way" is borderline, but the familiar *into* — as "he's into slang" — is putting down roots, and lexicographer David Guralnik thinks it may get into non-nonce status.   2

"Getting it together," picked up by lemminglike copywriters for commercials, has been dropped by the coiners who originate these phrases; "mellow," which went the opposite route, is also on the wane, as is "laid back," which might originally have had a sexual connotation but more likely springs from reclining seats on motorcycles. "Heavy," a 40's word for "villain," became a 60's, word for "depressing" but is sinking. *Off the wall,* on the other hand — which comes from the squash court and means "unexpected" or "veering crazily" — shows signs of life.   3

"That bums me out" has already given way to "that cracks me up," and the jazzman's "suss it out" (figure it out) doesn't seem to figure. The   4 disgusted "yecchy," with its comic-strip origins, fades, but the equally disgusted *gross* (ugly, objectionable, and sometimes used admiringly) shows staying power. (To many, a "gross national product" is a derogation of the country's goods.)

Televisionese

The use of the phrase *has learned* to mean "found out" has been growing. "CBS has learned" does three things: (1) removes the need for *sourcing* (a journalism vogue word for identifying the person responsible for a story), (2) gives the impression of being the first to know and to tell the viewer and (3) plugs the network. The report is given as a certainty — much more solid than "reliable sources say" — but conceals, or covers up, the fact that nobody is willing to stand behind the message except the medium.

Private person is the *sine qua non* of soap operas and daytime talk shows. Nobody is an introvert any more; hermits no longer exist; damnable publicity-shunners have drifted from the scene — today, anybody who will not grant an interview is a "very private person."

Bleep has become a usable word-substitute, from the sound made when a word is excised from a tape. Columnist Herb Caen has popularized this as a euphemism, lexicographer Peter Tamony reports — as in: "That's no bullbleep."

Testimony Talk

From the land of "to the best of my knowledge," comes the verb of perjury-avoiding fuzziness; *indicate.* Under cross-examination, nobody ever "said" or "told me" or even "suggested" — rather, they "indicated." *To indicate,* which used to mean "to point to," as "he indicated they went thataway," has now become a cover-up word for "he may have told me this, but if he says no, then maybe I was mistaken." The use of "indicate" indicates guilt.

Cover-up was originally used to describe a specific obstruction of justice. Now this compound word is used to describe a compounded felony. Of the recent vogue words, "cover-up," still too young to lose its hyphen, also stands a good chance of making it into the dictionary, just after the entry for *cover story,* a C.I.A.-ism whose cover appears to have been blown.

Adjectival Jive

Long ago, it was "hep," then it changed to "hip," then, in the 60's, "cool" took hold; now, perhaps from a sanguine view of cool, comes *cold-blooded,* to convey in-group approval.

If a woman is "sexy" she is over 30 and not to be trusted. The replacement is *foxy*, a "counter word" with plenty of connotation but no denotation. (While *lady* has been replaced by "woman" or "person" in liberated discourse, it has taken over the place formerly held by "girl friend." "She's my lady," claims the former "fella," now the *dude*.)

Turning a noun into an adjective is the vogue among fun couples, but the vogue word fades fast: "dynamite" (sometimes pronounced "dyn-o-*mite*," as on the "Good Times" television show), was last year's favorite modifier, as in "Those are dynamite boots," which is being replaced by *killer*, as in "That's a killer whip." 12

Camp Following

"Camp" means "so banal as to be perversely sophisticated." It began as "establishing a camp," which was what the veterans of the Civil War called their reunions, then became a word to define any meeting of an insiders' group, and was taken up by homosexuals to mean the daring use in public of previously private ways. 13

The fashionable-by-being-unfashionable idea has several modern offshoots, not synonymous but related: *kinky, funky,* and *glitzy.* 14

"Kinky," from the Scandinavian "kink," or curl, bend, or twist, became popularized in the United States as "kinky hair," and was applied in the past decade to young fashion, as "offbeat, deliberately bizarre." The word has moved to the sexy, or foxy, world, and now tumbles out of its pornucopia: "Kinky" means perverse or twisted, usually cruel, sex, and the word has held on long enough to merit serious lexicographic-attention. 15

"Funky" has traveled a happier road. Originally a jazz term referring to the smell of cigar smoke, the word bottomed out in meaning as "old cigars, old and decrepit surroundings, just plain old." (Louis Armstrong often referred to "Funky Butt Hall, where I first heard Buddy Bolden play.") Later, as "old" became desirable, "funky" gained its current meaning of "nostalgic," or sweetly memorable, if cornball. (Some of those old cigars were Havanas.) 16

"Glitzy," often used to describe "*kitsch*" (which is unconscious in its tastelessness) comes directly from the German "*glitzen,*" and means "sparkling," or dazzlingly meretricious. 17

In sum, "kinky" has curled away from "funky" in meaning, leaving funkiness next to glitziness, though that may be a glitzening generality. 18

Right?

Where funkiness is next to glitziness, trendiness is surely next to godliness, and nowhere is that better illustrated than in the interrogative reassurance. 19

In the early 70's, the grunted "y'know?" studded the speech of every teen-ager. Put it this way: "I was walking — y'know? — down the street — 20 y'know? — and I ran into this splivvy dude, y'know?" Youth responds quickly to ridicule (adults move slowly, which is why "viable" and "meaningful" linger on) and when others began saying "No, I don't know," "y'know?" began its disappearance.

However, the need for constant verbal reassurance remained. Many 21
people believe they are not being listened to, or believe their listeners do not believe in them as a source of communication. Thus, *right* has emerged, not as something that makes might, but as a word that makes a speaker feel secure, and usually as part of a historical present tense: "Now I'm taking this walk — right? —down the street — right? — minding my own business — right?"

Trific

Finally, the adjective-as-encouragement-to-continue. In some discourses, en- 22
couragement is direct: "keep talking" became "I dig" which became "lay it on me" and now crosses its transcendental *t*'s with *keep it flowing*.

In most current speech, however, a single adjective is preferred. In the 23
30's, this was "fine-'n-dandy." In the 50's, "super" made the grade; in the 60's "fantastic" became a word used not to express amazement, but understanding; and in the early 70's, "beautiful" — usually murmured, head nodding as if in mutual meditation — became the most frequently used word of approval and reassurance. "I found a fish, y'know?" "Beautiful."

Today, the adjective-as-encouragement has become *terrific*, sometimes 24
pronounced with two syllables, "trific." The root meaning — as that which causes one to "wriggle in fear" — changed to "tremble with enthusiasm": after a brief vogue in the early 60's, "terrific" has returned with a rush. "I found a fish — right?" "Trific." Often, the word is repeated, just as "beautiful" used to be: "Now we're sitting around here at The Times — right? and we get this idea — right? for a piece on the way people talk today — right?" "Trific, trific . . ."

SUBJECT QUESTIONS

1. Safire offers an abstract definition of vogue words in his opening sentence. Explain why this is not an adequate definition.
2. Why can't vogue words *stay* in vogue? What happens to them if they become "permanent features of the language"? Can you tell by Safire's essay whether or not there is any way to predict which words will fade and which will become permanent?
3. Using Safire's extended definition, how would you distinguish vogue words from slang words? Are the terms mutually exclusive?

4. Safire explains how vogue words are disseminated (through television talk shows), but not how they "slip into American speech." Could you construct an explanation? In what other important ways are vogue words disseminated besides talk shows?
5. Would you agree that "y'know?" and "right?" reflect "the need for constant verbal reassurance"? What other causes might there be?
6. Judging by the closing section, could you say that Safire's aim is to discourage the use of vogue words?

STRUCTURE QUESTIONS

1. Since the opening abstract definition is not in itself adequate — and Safire does not pretend that it is — what purpose is served by putting it first? (Consider the difference in effect if one moves that sentence to the *end* of the essay.)
2. What purpose is served by the subheadings? (Is Safire going from general to more specific, is he classifying vogue words by subdivisions, or what?) Are they parallel?
3. What is Safire's primary method of definition? Do you find other rhetorical techniques employed?
4. Several times, but not consistently, Safire summarizes the historical development of a vogue word. Are these brief forays integral to his definition? Should there be more of them?
5. Safire's attitude toward at least some words is antagonistic (cf. "has learned" and "indicate"). Does this attitude interfere with the sufficiency of his definition?

SUGGESTION FOR WRITING

Define vogue language as spoken at your college or university. (Your problem may be less in collecting material than in organizing it. You may want to compare and contrast it with the vogue language spoken when you were in high school.)

Noun Overuse Phenomenon Article

Bruce D. Price

A distinguishing characteristic of contemporary English is a very great increase in the percentage of nouns employed in typical writing, not just in scientific writing but even in popular news journals. Here Bruce Price defines the new language, which he calls Nounspeak. The article appeared in Verbatim, *a quarterly journal concerned with modern English usage.*

Have you noticed a new "clunk-clunk" sound in the English language? Phrases such as "patient starter package" for *sample?* "Drug dosage forms" for *pills?* "Health cause" for *sickness?* "Increased labor market participation rates" for *more people working?* This overuse of nouns is a modern trend that has pretty much escaped notice. To put the phenomenon on the intellectual map, I've dubbed it Nounspeak. The allusion is to Newspeak, about which Orwell wrote: "Newspeak was designed not to extend but to diminish the range of thought." 1

The Germanic languages like to pile up nouns. The Romance languages virtually forbid it. The English lexicon, betwixt and between, has traditionally accepted nouns in pairs with no hesitation. Examples are *book store, love affair, deer crossing,* and *state university.* Three nouns in a row used to be the outer limit and is a rare find in English prose before 1950. Now we daily encounter excrescences like "growth trend pattern" and "consumer price inflation" and even, hold your hat, "U.S. Air Force aircraft fuel systems equipment mechanics course" (from a Long Island newspaper). 2

Nounspeak is not grammatically wrong. We're concerned here with good style and with clarity and with avoiding problems for ourselves. *Space ship* is not a problem. *Space ship booster rocket* is the beginning of a problem. Most writers would, I trust, try to find alternate phrasing. But more and more we're having to accept decided problems such as *space ship booster rocket ignition system.* I suggest it's time to back up. 3

Scientists love Nounspeak. Anyone hearing them joust with their mother tongue must lament the change of standards since the Royal Society took as its motto, *Nulla in Verba,* more than 300 years ago. Bureaucrats also 4

Reprinted by permission from © *Verbatim,*® The Language Quarterly, Vol. II, No. 4 (February 1976).

love Nounspeak. Certainly the military loves Nounspeak. Would you ever guess that *target neutralization requirement* means 'the desired dead'? Or that *airplane delivery systems* might mean 'bombs'? Here's the National Academy of Science discussing military research: "Work has included development of empirical and rational formulae for aerosal survival, formulae for predicting human lethal dose, and quantification of disease severity." (They're talking about germs and poisonous gases.) And most of all the "soft sciences," such as psychology, education, sociology and anthropology, love Nounspeak. A prize of some sardonic sort ought to be presented to the behaviorist quoted in *Science Digest* who concocted *place for goods purchase.* It takes a minute to realize he's thinking about 'stores.' The pattern is that people with little to say turn to Nounspeak for pompous packaging, while those with something unsavory to say find friendly camouflage in Nounspeak's abstractions and opacities. Who can forget *body count?*

At a glance Nounspeak might seem a natural development, like the dis-   5
appearance of the distinction between *who* and *whom* or the evolution of a slang word into polite speech, but it is only natural in the sense that foods such as breakfast cereals are a "natural" development in modern society. Normally, a language is shaped by the intellectual writers at the top and the great mass of not-so-intellectual speakers at the bottom. But Nounspeak, like breakfast cereals, is largely an artificial imposition, perpetrated by that growing multitude in the middle with from one to four years of college. Not at all restrained by any sense of educational deficiency, this multitude talks to dazzle its own ears. And to hell with Sir Quiller-Couch.

People aren't *broke* any more. They have a *money problem* or a *bad*   6
money situation. Discontented consumers (real people) have become *consumer discontent* (an abstraction, like so much Nounspeak). Weathermen don't predict *rain* any more: now it's *precipitation activity.*

There may be a metaphysical dimension here. People often have the   7
sensation that they aren't being heard. So they keep lumping noun on noun, as though by saying the same thing two or three times, they'll be understood across the existential void. Can you think of another reason for *Newsweek's* startling duo, *inlet cove?* (One can hardly find two more perfectly synonymous words in English. So why use both?) And *rain postponement dates* recently appeared on a sign in the subway in New York.

Nouns must comfort with their solidity. They seem to pin matters   8
down, to freeze life, to ward off future shock. But it's largely a sham. Life is flux and process. Verbs are truer to this constant change; and expert stylists have always recommended reliance on verbs. Listen to Gertrude Stein railing against nouns in "Lectures in America": "Things once they are named the name does not go on doing anything to them and so why write in nouns. . . . And therefore and I say it again more and more one does not use nouns. . . . Nouns as I say even by definition are completely not interest-

ing." And Gertrude Stein was speaking about nouns in meager doses, not the excesses here labeled Nounspeak.

Poor Gertrude Stein. Alive today, she could not read the front page of [9] any newspaper in the country without finding a surfeit of nouns, many of which can be cut entirely with *no* loss of sense. The favorite free-loaders are *area, situation* and *problem.* One of Nounspeak's major linguistic discoveries is that you can attach any one, or even two of these words to any other English word with no change of meaning. The gain in precision is illusory but the loss of clarity is real.

Nounspeak shares common ground with jargon and bombast and gob- [10] bledygook and prolixity and confusion of whatever sort. But Nounspeak does seem to be the most sharply defined of these phenomena and may be the more interesting in exhibiting its own rudimentary "grammar," the devices by which perfectly fine English is "translated" into Nounspeak.

The first and most obvious of these devices is: never use one noun [11] when two (or three) can be rummaged up. Contemplate these words: *subject; interim; spending; transition; passengers;* and *contract.* Is not each a sturdy soldier of a word, wholly equipped by itself and ready for any mission? But these excellent nouns split in Nounspeak to become: *subject matter; interim period; spending total; transition period; passenger volume;* and *contract agreement.* (All examples are from the press.) Note that nothing is added except the extra syllables. Like germs, one noun splits into two, and then one of those can become two again.

A second technique for subverting English into Nounspeak requires [12] changing strong, aggressive verbs into weak nouns. *We control pests* in English. *We accomplish pest control* in Nounspeak. It's hard to see any good reason for this device. But many variations can be found in the press. The idea is to smash those verbs. Mothers don't *feed* infants, they practice *infant feeding;* teachers don't *educate* any more, they work at *student education;* politicians don't *appeal to voters,* they have *voter appeal;* readers don't *respond,* they show *reader response.*

A third technique diminishes clarity by disdaining the possessive *'s* or [13] *of.* "Nixon had this to say about the Agnew criticism. . . ." Heard on the radio, there is no way of knowing whether Agnew was criticized or criticizing, except by context. Paradigmatically, "B's A" and "A of B" are being changed wholesale into "BA." Thus *rate of change,* which is smooth and flows easily into the brain, becomes *change rate.*

In the years ahead English will depend much more heavily on nouns [14] than Gertrude Stein might like. But it's reasonable to ask that our writers and editors steer us away from Nounspeak's worst excesses. We'll know the tide has turned when the IRS whittles its *Tax Schedule Rate Chart* down to *Tax Rate Chart,* then to the very sensible *Tax Chart,* then — unlikely victory — to *Taxes,* which is what they were trying to say all along.

SUBJECT QUESTIONS

1. If strings of nouns are not grammatically incorrect, what is wrong with using them?
2. Which of the examples cited by Price seem designed to disguise their real meaning rather than to achieve greater accuracy?
3. Does Price give examples of "pompous packaging," the writer's attempt to make a statement sound more important than it is?
4. What was Gertrude Stein's objection to nouns? How does one avoid overusing nouns (or, how is avoidance of noun overuse accomplished)?
5. Near the end of the essay, Price lists three devices or techniques for translating English into Nounspeak. Try using these techniques on a good English sentence to see if you can produce something atrocious.

STRUCTURE QUESTIONS

1. What is the significance of Price's strange title? Is it appropriate?
2. Price defines Nounspeak very simply in the opening paragraph as "this overuse of nouns." What are the inadequacies of this definition?
3. As one might expect, Price's chief method of definition is illustration. What complementary methods does he employ?
4. Would you say that the listing of three techniques toward the end is properly a part of the definition? How does this list clarify the meaning of Nounspeak?
5. In a definition (and condemnation) of Nounspeak, Price ought to be careful to avoid overusing nouns himself. Can you find nouns in the essay which could have been replaced by verbs or adjectives? Is his own style clearly preferable to that of the bad examples he cites? (Note particularly paragraph 8, where Price discusses the advantages of verbs.)
6. In paragraph 10, Price compares Nounspeak to other kinds of bad prose. Should he have tried to make detailed distinctions here?

SUGGESTIONS FOR WRITING

1. Define the jargon or specialized language of one college course you are taking, using the text for your examples.
2. Define the specialized language of an occupation with which you are familiar.

Weasel Words

Carl P. Wrighter

Most of the essays in this section are included to help students improve their writing style. But it is good to be aware of the language aimed at us by others, particularly in advertising, when rhetorical effectiveness may adversely affect our bank balances (especially if we are assured that a loan company which is "the friend of the family" is eager to lend us more spending money when we run out). In the following essay, Carl P. Wrighter defines the "weasel words" used in advertising. An advertising executive himself, Wrighter speaks from experience. Although this essay first appeared in 1972 and many of the examples are outdated, the principles should be clear enough. In fact, recent government attempts to ensure "truth in advertising" have had the ironic effect of encouraging far greater use of weasel words: we no longer hear "actually shrinks," but instead, "in many cases actually helps shrink swollen tissue."

Advertising has power, all right. And advertising works, all right. And what it really boils down to is that advertising works because you believe it. You're the one who believes Josephine the Plumber really knows about stains. You're the one who believes Winston tastes good like a cigarette should. You're the one who believes Plymouth is coming through. The real question is, why do you believe all these things? And the answer is, because you don't yet understand how advertising makes you believe. You don't understand what to believe, or even how to believe advertising. Well, if you're ready to learn how to separate the wheat from the chaff, if you're ready to learn how to make advertising work *for* you, if you're ready to learn how to stop being a sucker, then you're ready to go to work.

Weasel Words: God's Little Helpers

First of all, you know what a weasel is, right? It's a small, slimy animal that eats small birds and other animals, and is especially fond of devouring vermin. Now, consider for a moment the kind of winning personality he must have. I mean, what kind of a guy would get his jollies eating rats and mice?

From *I Can Sell You Anything*, by Carl P. Wrighter. Copyright © 1972 Ballantine Books. Reprinted by permission of Ballantine Books, a Division of Random House, Inc.

Would you invite him to a party? Take him home to meet your mother? This is one of the slyest and most cunning of all creatures; sneaky, slippery, and thoroughly obnoxious. And so it is with great and warm personal regard for these attributes that we humbly award this King of All Devious the honor of bestowing his name upon our golden sword: the weasel word.

A weasel word is "a word used in order to evade or retreat from a direct or forthright statement or position" (Webster). In other words, if we can't say it, we'll weasel it. And, in fact, a weasel word has become more than just an evasion or retreat. We've trained our weasels. They can do anything. They can make you hear things that aren't being said, accept as truths things that have only been implied, and believe things that have only been suggested. Come to think of it, not only do we have our weasels trained, but they, in turn, have got you trained. When *you* hear a weasel word, you automatically hear the implication. Not the real meaning, but the meaning *it* wants *you* to hear. So if you're ready for a little re-education, let's take a good look under a strong light at the two kinds of weasel words.

1. Words That Mean Things They Really Don't Mean

Help

That's it. "Help." It means "aid" or "assist." Nothing more. Yet, "help" is the one single word which, in all the annals of advertising, has done the most to say something that couldn't be said. Because "help" is the great qualifier; once you say it, you can say almost anything after it. In short, "help" has helped help us the most.

> Helps keep you young
> Helps prevent cavities
> Helps keep your house germ-free

"Help" qualifies everything. You've never heard anyone say, "This product will keep you young," or "This toothpaste will positively prevent cavities for all time." Obviously, we can't say anything like that, because there aren't any products like that made. But by adding that one little word, "help," in front, we can use the strongest language possible afterward. And the most fascinating part of it is, you are immune to the word. You literally don't hear the word "help." You only hear what comes after it. And why not? That's strong language, and likely to be much more important to you than the silly little word at the front end.

I would guess that 75 percent of all advertising uses the word "help."

Think, for a minute, about how many times each day you hear these phrases:

> Helps stop . . .
> Helps prevent . . .
> Helps fight . . .
> Helps overcome . . .
> Helps you feel . . .
> Helps you look . . .

I could go on and on, but so could you. Just as a simple exercise, call it homework if you wish, tonight when you plop down in front of the boob tube for your customary three and a half hours of violence and/or situation comedies, take a pad and pencil, and keep score. See if you can count how many times the word "help" comes up during the commercials. Instead of going to the bathroom during the pause before Marcus Welby operates, or raiding the refrigerator prior to witnessing the Mod Squad wipe out a nest of dope pushers, stick with it. Count the "helps," and discover just how dirty a four-letter word can be.

Like

Coming in second, but only losing out by a nose, is the word "like," used   7
in comparison. Watch:

> It's like getting one bar free
> Cleans like a white tornado
> It's like taking a trip to Portugal

Okay. "Like" is a qualifier, and is used in much the same way as   8
"help." But "like" is also a comparative element, with a very specific purpose; we use "like" to get you to stop thinking about the product per se,
and to get you thinking about something that is bigger or better or different
from the product we're selling. In other words, we can make you believe
that the product is more than it is by likening it to something else.

Take a look at that first phrase, straight out of recent Ivory Soap ad-   9
vertising. On the surface of it, they tell you that four bars of Ivory cost
about the same as three bars of most other soaps. So, if you're going to
spend a certain amount of money on soap, you can buy four bars instead of
three. Therefore, it's like getting one bar free. Now, the question you have
to ask yourself is, "Why the weasel? Why do they say 'like'? Why don't
they just come out and say, 'You get one bar free'?" The answer is, of
course, that for one reason or another, you really don't. Here are two possible reasons. One: sure, you get four bars, but in terms of the actual
amount of soap that you get, it may very well be the same as in three bars

of another brand. Remember, Ivory has a lot of air in it — that's what makes it float. And air takes up room. Room that could otherwise be occupied by more soap, So, in terms of pure product, the amount of actual soap in four bars of Ivory may be only as much as the actual amount of soap in three bars of most others. That's why we can't — or won't — come out with a straightforward declaration such as, "You get 25 percent more soap," or "Buy three bars, and get the fourth one free."

Reason number two: the actual cost and value of the product. Did it ever occur to you that Ivory may simply be a cheaper soap to make and, therefore, a cheaper soap to sell? After all, it doesn't have any perfume, or hexachlorophene, or other additives that can raise the cost of manufacturing. It's plain, simple, cheap soap, and so it can be sold for less money while still maintaining a profit margin as great as more expensive soaps. By way of illustrating this, suppose you were trying to decide whether to buy a Mercedes-Benz or a Ford. Let's say the Mercedes cost $7,000, and the Ford $3,500. Now the Ford salesman comes up to you with this deal: as long as you're considering spending $7,000 on a car, buy my Ford for $7,000 and I'll give you a second Ford, free! Well, the same principle can apply to Ivory: as long as you're considering spending 35 cents on soap, buy my cheaper soap, and I'll give you more of it. 10

I'm sure there are other reasons why Ivory uses the weasel "like." Perhaps you've thought of one or two yourself. That's good. You're starting to think. 11

Now, what about that wonderful white tornado? Ajax pulled that one out of the hat some eight years ago and you're still buying it. It's a classic example of the use of the word "like" in which we can force you to think not about the product itself, but about something bigger, more exciting, certainly more powerful than a bottle of fancy ammonia. The word "like" is used here as a transfer word, which gets you away from the obvious — the odious job of getting down on your hands and knees and scrubbing your kitchen floor — and into the world of fantasy, where we can imply that this little bottle of miracles will supply all the elbow grease you need. Isn't that the name of the game? The whirlwind activity of the tornado replacing the whirlwind motion of your arm? Think about the swirling of the tornado, and all the work it will save you. Think about the power of that devastating windstorm; able to lift houses, overturn cars, and now, pick the dirt up off your floor. And we get the license to do it simply by using the word "like." 12

It's a copywriter's dream, because we don't have to substantiate anything. When we compare our product to "another leading brand," we'd better be able to prove what we say. But how can you compare ammonia to a windstorm? It's ludicrous. It can't be done. The whole statement is so ridiculous it couldn't be challenged by the government or the networks. So 13 it went on the air, and it worked. Because the little word "like" let us take you out of the world of reality, and into your own fantasies. . . .

"Like" is a virus that kills. You'd better get immune to it.   14

Other Weasels

"Help" and "like" are the two weasels so powerful that they can stand on   15
their own. There are countless other words, not quite so potent, but equally effective when used in conjunction with our two basic weasels, or with each other. Let me show you a few.

Virtual or *virtually*

How many times have you responded to an ad that said: 16

> Virtually trouble-free . . .
> Virtually foolproof . . .
> Virtually never needs service . . .

Ever remember what "virtual" means? It means "in essence or effect, but not in fact." Important — "but not in fact." Yet today the word "virtually" is interpreted by you as meaning "almost or just about the same as. . . ." Well, gang, it just isn't true. "Not," in fact, means not, in fact. I was scanning, rather longingly I must confess, through the brochure Chevrolet publishes for its Corvette, and I came to this phrase: "The seats in the . . . Corvette are virtually handmade." They had me, for a minute. I almost took the bait of that lovely little weasel. I almost decided that those seats were just about completely handmade. And then I remembered. Those seats were not, *in fact*, handmade. Remember, "virtually" means "not, in fact," or you will, in fact, get sold down the river.

Acts or *works*

These two action words are rarely used alone, and are generally accom-   17
panied by "like." They need help to work, mostly because they are verbs, but their implied meaning is deadly, nonetheless. Here are the key phrases:

> Acts like . . .
> Acts against . . .
> Works like . . .
> Works against . . .
> Works to prevent (or help prevent) . . .

You see what happens? "Acts" or "works" brings an action to the product that might not otherwise be there. When we say that a certain cough syrup "acts on the cough control center," the implication is that the syrup goes to this mysterious organ and immediately makes it better. But the implication here far exceeds what the truthful promise should be. An act is simply a deed. So the claim "acts on" simply means it performs a deed on. What the deed is, we may never know.

The rule of thumb is this: if we can't say "cures" or "fixes" or use any 18 other positive word, we'll nail you with "acts like" or "works against," and get you thinking about something else. Don't. . . .

Can be
This is for comparison, and what we do is to find an announcer who can 19 really make it sound positive. But keep your ears open. "Crest can be of significant value when used in . . . ," etc., is indicative of an ideal situation, and most of us don't live in ideal situations.

Up to
Here's another way of expressing an ideal situation. Remember the 20 cigarette that said it was aged, or "cured for up to eight long, lazy weeks"? Well, that could, and should, be interpreted as meaning that the tobaccos used were cured anywhere from one hour to eight weeks. We like to glamorize the ideal situation; it's up to you to bring it back to reality.

As much as
More of the same. "As much as 20 percent greater mileage" with our 21 gasoline again promises the ideal, but qualifies it. . . .

Feel or *the feel of*
This is the first of our subjective weasels. When we deal with a subjective 22 word, it is simply a matter of opinion. In our opinion, Naugahyde has the feel of real leather. So we can say it. And, indeed, if you were to touch leather, and then touch Naugahyde, you may very well agree with us. But that doesn't mean it is real leather, only that it feels the same. The best way to handle subjective weasels is to complete the thought yourself, by simply saying, "But it isn't." At least that way you can remain grounded in reality.

The look of or *looks like*
"Look" is the same as "feel," our subjective opinion. Did you ever walk 23 into a Woolworth's and see those $29.95 masterpieces hanging in their "Art Gallery"? The look of a real oil painting," it will say. "But it isn't," you will now reply. And probably be $29.95 richer for it.

2. Words That Have No Specific Meaning

If you have kids, then you have all kinds of breakfast cereals in the house.   24
When I was a kid, it was Rice Krispies, the breakfast cereal that went snap,
crackle, and pop. (One hell of a claim for a product that is supposed to offer
nutritional benefits.) Or Wheaties, the breakfast of champions, whatever
that means. Nowadays, we're forced to a confrontation with Quisp, Quake,
Lucky Stars, Cocoa-Puffs, Clunkers, Blooies, Snarkles, and Razzmatazz.
And they all have one thing in common: they're all "fortified." Some are
simply "fortified with vitamins," while others are specifically "fortified with
vitamin D," or some other letter. But what does it all mean?

"Fortified" means "added on to." But "fortified," like so many other   25
weasel words of indefinite meaning, simply doesn't tell us enough. If, for
instance, a cereal were to contain one unit of vitamin D, and the manufacturers added some chemical which would produce two units of vitamin D,
they could then claim that the cereal was "fortified with twice as much
vitamin D." So what? It would still be about as nutritional as sawdust.

The point is, weasel words with no specific meaning don't tell us   26
enough, but we have come to accept them as factual statements closely
associated with something good that has been done to the product. Here's
another example.

Flavor *and* Taste

These are two totally subjective words that allow us to claim marvelous   27
things about products that are edible. Every cigarette in the world has
claimed the best taste. Every supermarket has advertised the most flavorful
meat. And let's not forget "aroma," a subdivision of this category. Wouldn't
you like to have a nickel for every time a room freshener (a weasel in itself)
told you it would make your home "smell fresh as all outdoors"? Well, they
can say it, because smell, like taste and flavor, is a subjective thing. And,
incidentally, there are no less than three weasels in that phrase. "Smell" is
the first. Then, there's "as" (a substitute for the ever-popular "like"), and,
finally, "fresh," which, in context, is a subjective comparison, rather than
the primary definition of "new."

Now we can use an unlimited number of combinations of these   28
weasels for added impact. "Fresher-smelling clothes." "Fresher-tasting tobacco." "Tastes like grandma used to make." Unfortunately, there's no sure
way of bringing these weasels down to size, simply because you can't
define them accurately. Trying to ascertain the meaning of "taste" in any
context is like trying to push a rope up a hill. All you can do is be aware
that these words are subjective, and represent only one opinion — usually
that of the manufacturer.

Style *and* Good Looks

Anyone for buying a new car? Okay, which is the one with the good looks? 29
The smart new styling? What's that you say? All of them? Well, you're
right. Because this is another group of subjective opinions. And it is the
subjective and collective opinion of both Detroit and Madison Avenue that
the following cars have "bold new styling": Buick Riviera, Plymouth Satellite, Dodge Monaco, Mercury Brougham, and you can fill in the spaces for
the rest. Subjectively, you have to decide on which bold new styling is,
indeed, bold new styling. Then, you might spend a minute or two trying to
determine what's going on under that styling. The rest I leave to Ralph
Nader.

Different, Special, *and* Exclusive

To be different, you have to be not the same as. Here, you must rely on 30
your own good judgment and common sense. Exclusive formulas and special combinations of ingredients are coming at you every day, in every way.
You must constantly assure yourself that, basically, all products in any
given category are the same. So when you hear "special," "exclusive," or
"different," you have to establish two things: on what basis are they different, and is that difference an important one? Let me give you a hypothetical example.

All so-called "permanent" antifreeze is basically the same. It is made 31
from a liquid known as ethylene glycol, which has two amazing properties.
It has a lower freezing point than water, and a higher boiling point than
water. It does not break down (lose its properties), nor will it boil away.
And every permanent antifreeze starts with it as a base. Also, just about
every antifreeze has now got antileak ingredients, as well as antirust and
anticorrosion ingredients. Now, let's suppose that, in formulating the
product, one of the companies comes up with a solution that is pink in
color, as opposed to all the others, which are blue. Presto — an exclusivity
claim. "Nothing else looks like it, nothing else performs like it." Or, how
about, "Look at ours, and look at anyone else's. You can see the difference
our exclusive formula makes." Granted, I'm exaggerating. But did I prove a
point?

Summary

A weasel word is a word that's used to imply a meaning that cannot be 32
truthfully stated. Some weasels imply meanings that are not the same as
their actual definition, such as "help," "like," or "fortified." They can act as
qualifiers and/or comparatives. Other weasels, such as "taste" and "flavor,"

have no definite meanings, and are simply subjective opinions offered by the manufacturer. A weasel of omission is one that implies a claim so strongly that it forces you to supply the bogus fact. Adjectives are weasels used to convey feelings and emotions to a greater extent than the product itself can.

In dealing with weasels, you must strip away the innuendos and try to ascertain the facts, if any. To do this, you need to ask questions such as: How? Why? How many? How much? Stick to basic definitions of words. Look them up if you have to. Then, apply the strict definition to the text of the advertisement or commercial. "Like" means similar to, but not the same as. "Virtually" means the same in essence, but not in fact. 33

Above all, never underestimate the devious qualities of a weasel. Weasels twist and turn and hide in dark shadows. You must come to grips with them, or advertising will rule you forever. 34

My advice to you is: Beware of weasels. They are nasty and untrainable, and they attack pocketbooks. 35

SUBJECT QUESTIONS

1. What are the two basic kinds of weasel words? What do they have in common which allows one definition to apply to both types?
2. Presumably an advertising copywriter would prefer telling the truth about a product to misleading the public. Is there anything about the advertising business which encourages use of weasel words even for good products?
3. The government rather effectively prevents false claims in advertising; should it also ban the weasel words which suggest "what couldn't be said"?
4. Wrighter claims that the public ignores such weasel words as "help" and "like" and "virtual" and pays attention only to the stronger statement which follows. Do you think the public is as gullible as he suggests? Is it possible that the public *wants* to believe that products are better than they really are?
5. Consider the advertising of a particular type of product to see how advertisers create demand where none exists. (Commercials for "light" beers would be a good example.) Is the approach different in this kind of commercial from that for a necessary product (such as washing powders)?
6. What is a "weasel of omission"? Think of a current TV commercial employing such a weasel. Is there any "weasel" in the hidden camera comparative taste tests so popular with cola and margarine advertisers?

STRUCTURE QUESTIONS

1. Wrighter's style is deliberately conversational, even though the conversation is necessarily one way. Do you find this style generally effective? Is it ever irritating? Why do you suppose Wrighter chose this style?
2. Identify several of the rhetorical questions employed in this essay. Is the device overworked? Did you ever find your own answers to Wrighter's questions differing from the answers Wrighter provides?
3. Why does Wrighter use a profusion of clichés and slang phrases ("separate the wheat from the chaff," "get his jollies," "take the bait," "come to grips with," etc.)? Do these represent a flaw in the writing, or perhaps a deliberate attempt to sound like a used-car salesman?
4. If the dictionary definition in paragraph 3 is clear, why does Wrighter need the remainder of the essay to define his term? If it is not sufficiently clear, should he have bothered to include it? (Remember, there may be good reason to begin with an inadequate dictionary definition.)
5. In his summary, Wrighter identified three kinds of weasel words, but the essay examines only two kinds at length; should there have been a third section on "weasels of omission"?
6. Identify the rhetorical methods (process, comparison, etc.) which Wrighter has used in his definition. Which would you say is the chief method? Does the essay effectively increase your understanding and awareness of weasel words?

SUGGESTIONS FOR WRITING

1. Write a thirty-second spot radio commercial for a fictitious product. Then identify and analyze the "weasels" you have employed. Select any type of product you wish, such as "an entirely new and different cold remedy which makes you feel like a million dollars in seconds."
2. Either clip a printed advertisement or tape or make notes on a TV or radio commercial. Define the appeal made by the advertisement.

Bombing the Paragraph

Henry Seidel Canby

Henry Seidel Canby (1878–1961) was born in Delaware and received his Ph.D. from Yale, where he became professor of English. He was editor of the Saturday Review of Literature *for many years and published a number of books of criticism as well as* Handbook of English Usage.

Some act of national recovery is needed if the English paragraph is to be saved. Let us recall to the memories of those who were once accustomed to good English what the paragraph was supposed to be before it ran upon the rocks of mass production and was splintered into incoherent sentences. 1

The paragraph was a trim little vessel in the days when journalists still wrote for minds trained to hold more than one thought at a time. Rhetoricians spoke of it as one full step in the development of an idea, and might have compared it with a fan which spreads without losing its unity, increasing its usefulness without changing its control. An idea stated in a single sentence (topic, they used to call it) is self-sufficient only for the very wise or the very simple. Emerson and Thoreau, among Americans, wrote self-sufficient sentences for the wise, and the race of columnists (who call themselves paragraphers) have carried on this tradition of apothegm all the way into wisecrack — a sentence paragraph which is a nut that a sharp mind can bite into. 2

But this is specialists' work. The general utility paragraph led off (in the days of coherence) with a sentence that said simply and definitely what the writer thought. But thought is never so simple as that. It must be qualified, developed, explained, if it is to satisfy the sophisticated. Only the naïve will swallow a generalization without chewing on it. The English paragraph in its prime was raw material made fit for eating by a skillful cook. If the writer began "Democracy depends upon intelligence," he could not leave it at that. Simple minds might be content, but in those days readers were not that simple. They asked why and were prepared to reserve judgment until, item after item, the explanation or argument unrolled to a Q.E.D. at the end of the paragraph. Macaulay, whose diminishing reputation as a historian still leaves him one of the world's great journalists, could fling out a reverbera- 3 ting paragraph as organized and emphatic and lucid as the simplest sentence, which prepared, held, and satisfied the attentive reader by a structure which had all the advantages of a formula without its dangerous simplicity. Frank Cobb of the old *World* could drop his sequent sentences one after another in perfect harmony for a column before the packed theme with which he began had been unpacked and become an organism of thought.

The paragraph, like many other good things, was wrecked by mass 4 production. When newspapers, and then magazines, began to be published for the millions, writers soon found that their readers were short-winded. They would hold their brains together for three or four sentences, not more. News was rewritten for them in short paragraphs, the ramp of the story broken up into little steps; and that was good, especially when the sentences took on the color of contemporary impressionism, for in the reporting of successive incidents, the successive topics are facts which need no logical development. Paragraphs are relatively unimportant in narrative. Not so with editorials and articles. When the writers whose duty it was to exhort or explain discarded the paragraph (the Hearst newspapers began it) and wrote series of short, sharp sentences, each set apart so that it might be easily assimilated by the dumbest readers, they scored at first a great journalistic success. Strong writing, it seemed to be, punches from the shoulder, very persuasive to the man who must have a thought knocked into him, well calculated indeed for a nation of quick readers who seldom read books and lacked the patience (and often the ability) to follow the testing of an idea through a paragraph. And thousands of writers, noting the success with the masses of these disintegrated paragraphs, imitated them, until even when an idea had to be tested, explained, in order to mean anything at all, their paragraphs were still split into groups of pointed sentences, one statement at a time, so that even the feebleminded could read.

That is where we are today in the bulk of English writing outside of 5 books and the better magazines. Unfortunately, however, the immense majority of readers, even among the masses, are not feebleminded. They are, one suspects, beginning to react by not reading at all, or by taking the first punch and dodging all the rest. After all, this method of writing was first devised, not for journalism, but for children's reading-books, where not only paragraphs but long words were split for immature minds. Our journalists have treated their readers like children and they are getting a child's reactions, violent, brief, and oversimplified. They have violated the natural order of thinking and, as a result, give no training and get no response in thought. Like the advertisers and the politicians, they have been playing upon the unformed mass mind for profits, consistently making thought easy in the hope of speedier results. It is a phase of exploitation, and will produce its reactions in both reader and writer, like every other attempt to debase the currency of human intercourse.

SUBJECT QUESTIONS

1. In paragraph 2, Canby gives a one-clause definition of a paragraph. Explain why this is insufficient by itself.
2. Why would topic sentences without supporting paragraphs be sufficient "only for the very wise or the very simple" and not for the rest of us? Does Canby make clear the difference between sufficiency for the wise and for the simple?
3. What exceptions does Canby allow to his generalization that paragraphs should be fully developed? Do these exceptions weaken his position?
4. If the reader's reaction to "childish" writing has been to stop reading at all (paragraph 5), does there seem much hope for a return to proper paragraph writing? Would it be better (or possible) to find a modern substitute instead of returning to the old way of writing paragraphs?
5. Canby's essay was written before the advent of television. Consider the way news and news analysis are presented on television. What effect could the presentation have on problems about which Canby complains?

STRUCTURE QUESTIONS

1. Analogies cannot be used as evidence, but they can help to clarify a point. Identify the analogies Canby uses to clarify his definition and discuss their usefulness.
2. Examine the five paragraphs of Canby's essay. Does each provide the kind of support for a topic idea that he recommends? How is the first paragraph different from the others?
3. Identify the transitional devices Canby uses to lead his reader from one paragraph to the next.
4. In paragraph 3, Canby cites Macaulay and Frank Cobb as examples of writers of first-rate paragraphs. Do the citations, without quoted examples of such paragraphs, strengthen his case? Should Canby have quoted examples?
5. The tone of Canby's essay is somewhat insulting. Is that tone likely to impede his efforts to encourage better paragraph writing? Whom is he insulting?

SUGGESTIONS FOR WRITING

1. Select a mass-audience newspaper or magazine and define the style of its editorial page ("The Playboy Philosophy," for example).

2. Compare the editorial styles of two very different newspapers (such as *The New York Times* and *The Chicago Tribune*) or magazines (such as *Harper's* and *TV Guide*).
3. Analyze the editorial style of your college paper, or compare the editorial page with the sports page.

Connotation

Richard D. Altick

Richard Altick (b. 1915) was born in Pennsylvania and received his Ph.D. at the University of Pennsylvania. He is a professor of English at Ohio State University. His publications are primarily on literary scholarship and include the highly readable The Scholar Adventurers *(1950). The following essay is taken from* Preface to Critical Reading *(rev. ed. 1969).*

Incidents like this are happening every day. A teacher in a college English course has returned a student's theme on the subject of a poem. One sentence in the theme reads, "Like all of Keats's best work, the 'Ode to Autumn' has a sensual quality that makes it especially appealing to me." The instructor's red pencil has underscored the word *sensual,* and in the margin he has written "Accurate?" or whatever his customary comment is in such cases. The student has checked the dictionary and comes back puzzled. "I don't see what you mean," he says. "The dictionary says *sensual* means 'of or pertaining to the senses or physical sensation.' And that's what I wanted to say. Keats's poem is filled with words and images that suggest physical sensation." 1

"Yes," replies the instructor, "that's what the word *means* — according to the dictionary." And then he takes his copy of the *American College Dictionary,* which contains the definition the student quoted, and turns to the word *sensual.* "Look here," he says, pointing to a passage in small type just after the various definitions of the word: 2

SENSUAL, SENSUOUS, VOLUPTUOUS refer to experience through the senses. SENSUAL refers, usually unfavorably, to the enjoyments derived from the senses, generally implying grossness or lewdness: *a sensual delight in eating, sensual excesses.* SENSUOUS refers, favorably or literally, to what is experienced through the senses: *sensuous impressions, sensuous poetry.* VOLUPTUOUS implies the luxurious gratification of sensuous or sensual desires: *voluptuous joys, voluptuous beauty.*[1]

The student reads the passage carefully and begins to see light. The 3

From *Preface to Critical Reading,* Fifth Edition by Richard D. Altick. Copyright 1946, 1951, © 1956, 1960, 1969 by Holt, Rinehart and Winston. Reprinted by permission of Holt, Rinehart and Winston.

[1] Reprinted by permission of Random House, Inc. from *The American College Dictionary.* Copyright 1947 by Random House, Inc.

word *sensual* carries with it a shade of meaning, an unfavorable implication, which he did not intend; the word he wanted was *sensuous*. He has had a useful lesson in the dangers of taking dictionary definitions uncritically, as well as in the vital difference between denotation and connotation.

The difference between the two is succinctly phrased in another of those small-type paragraphs of explanation, taken this time from *Webster's New Collegiate Dictionary:* 4

> *Denote* implies all that strictly belongs to the definition of the word, *connote* all of the ideas that are suggested by the term; thus, "home" *denotes* the place where one lives with one's family, but it usually *connotes* comfort, intimacy, and privacy. The same implications distinguish *denotation* and *connotation.* [2]

The denotation of a word is its dictionary definition, which is what the word "stands for." According to the dictionary, *sensuous* and *sensual* have the same general denotation: they agree in meaning "experience through the senses." Yet they *suggest* different things. And that difference in suggestion constitutes a difference in connotation.

For another elementary example, take the word *tabloid,* the denotation of which refers to small size. For that reason, newspapers with pages that are half as large as regular ones and which specialize in very brief news articles are regularly called tabloids. But because the average tabloid newspaper emphasizes the racy and the bizarre in its attempt to appeal to a certain class of readers, the word's connotation introduces the idea of sensationalism, of "yellow journalism." Thus *tabloid,* not surprisingly, is applied to newspapers in a negative, or pejorative, sense. In such a fashion many words acquire additional meanings which are derived from common experience and usage. (Similarly, the term *prima donna* refers, strictly speaking, to the leading woman in an opera company. By what process has it come to be applied to a certain kind of man or woman, with no reference to opera?) 5

Nothing is more essential to intelligent, profitable reading than sensitivity to connotation. Only when we possess such sensitivity can we understand both what the author *means,* which may be quite plain, and what he wants to *suggest,* which may actually be far more important than the superficial meaning. The difference between reading a book, a story, an essay, or a poem for surface meaning and reading it for implication is the difference between listening to the New York Philharmonic Symphony Orchestra on a battered old transistor radio and listening to it on a high-fidelity stereophonic record player. Only the latter brings out the nuances that are often more significant than the obvious, and therefore easily comprehended, meaning. 6

An unfailing awareness of the connotative power of words is just as 7

---

[2] By permission. From *Webster's New Collegiate Dictionary,* copyright © 1974 by G. & C. Merriam Co., publishers of the Merriam-Webster dictionaries.

vital, of course, to the writer. His ceaseless task is to select the word which will convey exactly what he wants to say. The practiced writer, like the practiced reader, derives his skill from his awareness that though many words may have substantially the same denotation, few are exactly synonymous in connotation. The inexperienced writer, forgetting this, often has recourse to a book like Roget's *Thesaurus*, where he finds, conveniently assembled, whole regiments of synonyms; not knowing which to choose, he either closes his eyes and picks a word at random or else chooses the one that "sounds" best. In either case he is neglecting the delicate shadings in implication and applicability which differentiate each word in a category from its neighbors. Wishing to refer to the familiar terse expressions of wisdom in the Bible, for example, he has a number of roughly synonymous words at his disposal: *maxim, aphorism, apothegm, dictum, adage, proverb, epigram, saw, byword, motto,* among others. But if he chooses *saw* or *epigram* he chooses wrongly; for neither of these words is suitable to designate biblical quotations. (Why?) The way to avoid the all too frequent mistake of picking the wrong word from a list is to refer to those invaluable paragraphs in the dictionary which discriminate among the various words in a closely related group. (If the definition of the word in question is not followed by such a paragraph, there usually is a cross reference to the place where the differentiation is made.) For further help, consult the fuller discussions, illustrated by examples quoted from good writers, in *Webster's Dictionary of Synonyms.* But cheap pocket and desk dictionaries should always be avoided in any work involving word choice. They are frequently misleading because they oversimplify entries which are already reduced to a minimum in the larger, more authoritative dictionaries.

What has been said so far does not mean that the conscientious reader   8
or writer is required to take up every single word and examine it for implications and subsurface meanings. Many words — articles, conjunctions, prepositions, and some adverbs — have no connotative powers, because they do not represent ideas but are used to connect ideas or to show some other relationship between them. Still other words, such as (usually) polysyllabled scientific or technical terms, have few if any connotations; that is, they call forth no vivid pictures, no emotional responses. *Psychomotor* and *cardiovascular* are neutral words in this sense; so are *acetylsalicylic acid* (aspirin) and *crustacean* (shellfish). The single word *eschatology* is colorless compared with the words for its chief concerns: *heaven, hell, death, judgment.* The fact remains, however, that most words which stand for ideas have some connotation, however limited, simply because ideas themselves have connotations. Some technical words, especially when they affect our daily lives, take on more and more connotation as they become familiar: *intravenous, angina pectoris, anxiety neurosis,* for example.

Connotations: Personal and General

There are two types of connotation: personal and general. Personal connota- 9
tions result from our individual experience. The way we react to ideas and
objects, and thus to the words that refer to them (this is why the ideas are
often called "referents"), is determined by the precise nature of our earlier
experience with these referents. Taken all together, the connotations that
surround most of the words in our vocabulary are, though we may not recognize the fact, a complex and intimate record of our life. Our present reaction
to a word may be the cumulative result of all our experiences with the word
and its referent. In the case of another word, our reaction may have been determined once and for all by an early or a particularly memorable experience
with it. A student's reaction to the word *teacher*, for instance, may be determined by all his experience with teachers, which has been subtly synthe-
sized, in the course of time, into a single image or emotional response. In it
are mingled memories of Miss Smith, the first-grade teacher who dried his
tears when he lost a fight in the schoolyard at recess; of Miss Jones, the sixth-
grade teacher who bored her pupils with thrice-told tales of her trip to Mexico ten years earlier; of Mr. Johnson, the high-school gym teacher who
merely laughed when he saw the angry red brush burns a boy sustained
when he inexpertly slid down a rope; of Mr. Miller, the college professor
who somehow packed a tremendous amount of information into lectures that
seemed too entertaining to be instructive. Or, on the other hand, when the
student thinks of *teacher* he may think of a particular teacher who for one
reason or another has made an especially deep impression upon him — such
a person as the chemistry teacher in high school who encouraged him, by example and advice, to make chemistry his life work.

A moment's thought will show the relationship between personal and 10
general connotations as well as the fact that there is no firm line of demarcation between the two types. Since "the mass mind" is the sum total of the individual minds that comprise it, general connotations result when the reaction of the great majority of people to a specific word is substantially the
same. The reasons why one word should possess a certain connotation, while
another word has a quite different connotation, are complex. We shall spend
a little time on the subject later. Here it need only be said that differences in
general connotation derive from at least two major sources. For one thing,
the exact shade of meaning a word possesses in our language is often due to
the use to which it was put by a writer who had especially great influence
over the language because he was, and in some cases, is, so widely read. The
King James version of the Bible, for instance, is responsible for the crystalliz-
ing of many connotations. People came to know a given word from its occurrence in certain passages in the Bible, and thus the word came to connote to

them on *all* occasions what it connoted in those familiar passages; it was permanently colored by particular associations. Such words include *trespass, money changers, manger, Samaritan* (originally the name of a person living in a certain region of Asia Minor), *salvation, vanity, righteous, anoint,* and *charity.* The same is true of many words used in other books which, being widely read and studied, influenced the vocabularies of following generations — Shakespeare's plays, or *Paradise Lost,* or the essays of Addison and Steele.

But general connotation is not always a matter of literary development. It can result also from the experience that men as a social group have had with the ideas which words represent. Before 1938, the word *appease* had an inoffensive connotation. In the edition of *Webster's Collegiate Dictionary* current in that year it was defined simply as "to pacify, often by satisfying; quiet; calm; soothe; allay." But then the word became associated with the ill-fated attempts of Neville Chamberlain to stave off war with Hitler by giving in to his demands, and that association has now strongly colored its meaning. The latest edition of the same dictionary adds to the meaning quoted above this newer one: "to conciliate by political, economic, or other considerations; — now usually signifying a sacrifice of moral principle in order to avert aggression." Laden as the word is with its suggestions of the disaster of Munich, no British or American official ever uses it in referring to a conciliating move in foreign policy for which he wants to win public acceptance. On the other hand, opponents of that move use the word freely to arouse sentiment against it, even though the situation in question may have little or no resemblance to that of Munich. In other words, events have conditioned us to react in a particular way to the verb *appease* and the noun *appeasement.* If our support is desired for a policy of *give and take, live and let live,* or *peaceful coexistence* in international relations, its advocates will use the terms just italicized, as well as *negotiation* and *compromise,* which convey the idea of mutual concessions without sacrifice of principle; or *horse trading,* which has a homely American flavor, suggesting shrewd bargaining with the additional implication that good profit can be made on the deal.

All general connotations thus have their origin in private connotations — in personal, individual, but generally shared reactions to words and the ideas for which they stand. But later, after general connotations have been established, the process works the other way: the individual, who may have had no personal experience with the idea represented by a given word, may acquire a personal attitude toward it by observing how society in general reacts to the word. In the future, men and women who were not yet born when Winston Churchill was delivering his famous Second World War speeches in Britain, or when Adolf Hitler was presiding over mass executions of the Jews, supposedly will continue to react admiringly or with revulsion to their names. In addition, some words pass into and then out of connotative "atmospheres." The word *quisling* probably inspires no feeling whatever in today's student, yet not too long ago it was synonymous with *traitor*. Yet the much older name of Benedict Arnold still serves the same purpose.

Every writer must cultivate his awareness of the distinction between general connotations and personal ones. It is the general ones — those he can be reasonably sure his readers share with him — on which he must rely to convey the accurate spirit of his message. If he uses words for the sake of the additional connotations they have to him alone, he runs the risk of writing in a private shorthand to which he alone holds the key. Since there is no clear dividing line between general and personal connotations, it would, of course, be unrealistic to require that a writer absolutely confine himself to the former. Moreover, some of the subtle richness of poetry, and to some degree of imaginative prose, is derived (assuming that the reader discovers the secret) from the author's use of words in private senses. But in most forms of practical communication, the writer does well to confine himself to words whose connotations, he has reason to assume, are approximately the same to his readers as they are to him.

SUBJECT QUESTIONS

1. Altick cites two passages from college dictionaries in paragraphs 2 and 4. In what way do these passages differ from ordinary dictionary definitions? (See introduction to this section.) Do you see why they are more helpful than the usual definition of a word like "sensual"?
2. Think of some pairs of words having the same denotation but different connotations (carcinoma and cancer, for example, or horse and steed). What accounts for the difference in connotative value?
3. Select a common noun ("dog" or "cat" will do) and construct several very different sentences using that noun. Do the different contexts alter the connotative value of the word?
4. Altick says we should be aware of the difference between personal and general connotations. Can you think of any words which might have a special connotation for you and a different connotation for the class?
5. Altick cites "appease" as a word which has changed connotation as a result of political events. Can you recall any more recent examples of this process?
6. How might cultural differences affect the connotation of words (colors or names of foods, for example)?

STRUCTURE QUESTIONS

1. In "Vogue Words," William Safire began with an abstract definition and then gave illustrative examples. Here Altick begins with an extended example and then presents a dictionary definition. Which procedure seems preferable?
2. Altick might have been tempted to assume that he had defined his term by the end of paragraph 4. What does the remainder of the essay contribute to this definition?
3. If there is "no firm line of demarcation" between personal and general connotations, should Altick have brought up the distinction at all? Does this distinction weaken the reader's grasp of what "connotation" means?
4. Although he cites many examples, Altick does not strive to keep them all on a simple and familiar level. Considering his subject, do you see any justification for his including difficult examples?
5. Paragraph 7 does not seem to be part of Altick's definition at all but advice to writers about word choice. Can its inclusion be justified? How does Altick fit it in? (Consider particularly the transitions between it and paragraphs 6 and 8.)
6. Analogies are used for clarification, not as evidence. Does the analogy in paragraph 6 clarify the distinction Altick is making?

SUGGESTIONS FOR WRITING

1. Write two paragraphs which say the same thing by denotation but which have very different connotations. Try to influence the reader's reaction to each paragraph by the connotative values of the words you use in them.
2. Write a definition of the stereotyped language of some type of television show — western, spy, or hillbilly, for instance. Collect samples, and then analyze them to find distinguishing characteristics. (For instance, a cowboy — cowpoke, that is — almost never says "yes.")

An Ethic of Clarity

Donald Hall

*Donald Hall (b. 1916) is a poet and former English teacher. His poems
have been published in many magazines as well as in separate volumes.
He has also edited and written several successful textbooks on rhetoric
and style.*

Ezra Pound, George Orwell, James Thurber, and Ernest Hemingway don't   1
have much in common: a great poet who became a follower of Mussolini, a
disillusioned left-wing satirist, a comic essayist and cartoonist, and a great
novelist. If anything, they could represent the diversity of modern literature.
Yet one thing unites them. They share a common idea of good style, an idea
of the virtues of clarity and simplicity. This attitude toward style was not unknown to earlier writers, but never before has it been so pervasive and so
exclusive.

Style is the manner of a sentence, not its matter. But the distinction   2
between manner and matter is a slippery one, for manner affects matter.
When *Time* used to tell us that President Truman slouched into one room,
when General Eisenhower strode into another, their manner was trying to
prejudice our feelings. The hotel that invites me to enjoy my favorite beverage at the Crown Room is trying not to sound crass: "Have a drink at the
bar." One linguist, in discussing this problem, took Caesar's "I came; I saw; I
conquered," and revised it as, "I arrived on the scene of the battle; I observed the situation; I won the victory." Here, the matter is the same, but
Caesar's tone of arrogant dignity disappears in the pallid pedantry of the
longer version. It is impossible to say that the matter is unaffected. But, let
us say that this kind of difference, in the two versions of Caesar, is what we
mean by style.

In the expression "good writing" or "good style," the word "good" has   3
usually meant "beautiful" or "proficient" — like a good Rembrandt or a good
kind of soap. In our time it has come to mean honest as opposed to fake. Bad
writing happens when the writer lies to himself, to others, or to both. Probably, it is usually necessary to lie to oneself in order to lie to others; advertising men use the products they praise. Bad writing may be proficient; it may
persuade us to buy a poor car or vote for an imbecile, but it is bad because it

Reprinted with permission of Macmillan Publishing Co., Inc., from *The Modern Stylists* by
Donald Hall. Copyright © 1968 by Donald Hall.

301

is tricky, false in its enthusiasm, and falsely motivated. It appeals to a part of us that wants to deceive itself. I am encouraged to tell myself that I am enjoying my favorite beverage when, really, I am only getting sloshed.

"If a man writes clearly enough any one can see if he fakes," says 4 Hemingway. Orwell reverses the terms: "The great enemy of clear language is insincerity. . . . When there is a gap between one's real and one's declared aims, one turns as it were instinctively to long words and exhausted idioms, like a cuttlefish squirting out ink." Pound talks about the "gap between one's real and one's declared aims" as the distance between expression and meaning. In "The New Vocabularianism," Thurber speaks of the political use of clichés to hide a "menacing Alice in Wonderland meaninglessness."

As Robert Graves says, "The writing of good English is thus a moral 5 matter." And the morality is a morality of truth-telling. Herbert Read declares that "the only thing that is indispensable for the possession of a good style is personal sincerity." We can agree, but we must add that personal sincerity is not always an easy matter, nor is it always available to the will. Real aims, we must understand, are not necessarily conscious ones. The worst liars in the world may consider themselves sincere. Analysis of one's own style, in fact, can be a test of one's own feelings. And certainly, many habits of bad style are bad habits of thinking as well as of feeling.

There are examples of the modern attitude toward style in older 6 writers. Jonathan Swift, maybe the best prose writer of the language, sounds like George Orwell when he writes:

. . . Our English tongue is too little cultivated in this kingdom, yet the faults are nine in ten owing to affectation, not to want of understanding. When a man's thoughts are clear, the properest words will generally offer themselves first, and his own judgment will direct him in what order to place them, so as they may be best understood.

Here Swift appears tautological; clear thoughts only *exist* when they are embodied in clear words. But he goes on: "When men err against this method, it is usually on purpose," purposes, we may add, that we often disguise from ourselves.

Aristotle in his *Rhetoric* makes a case for plainness and truth-telling. 7 "The right thing in speaking really is that we should be satisfied not to annoy our hearers, without trying to delight them: we ought in fairness to fight our cause with no help beyond the bare facts." And he anticipates the modern stylist's avoidance of unusual words: "Clearness is secured by using the words . . . that are current and ordinary." Cicero attacks the Sophists because they are "on the lookout for ideas that are neatly put rather than reasonable. . . ."

Yet, when we quote Cicero, the master rhetorician, on behalf of honest 8 clarity, we must remember that the ancients did not really think of style as we do. Style until recent times has been a division of rhetoric. To learn style, one learned the types of figures of speech, and the appropriateness of each to different levels of discourse — high, middle, and low. The study of style was complex, but it was technical rather than moral. For some writers, Latin was high and the vernacular low, but in the Renaissance the vernacular took in all levels. It is only in modern times that style divorces itself from rhetoric — rhetoric belongs to the enemy, to the advertisers and the propagandists — and becomes a matter of ethics and introspection.

Ezra Pound, like some French writers before him, makes the writer's function social. "Good writers are those who keep the language efficient. That is to say, keep it accurate, keep it clear." We must ask why this idea of the function of good style is so predominantly a modern phenomenon. Pound elsewhere speaks of the "assault," by which he means the attack upon our ears and eyes of words used dishonestly to persuade us, to convince us to buy or to believe. Never before have men been exposed to so many words — written words, from newspapers and billboards and paperbacks and flashing signs and the sides of buses, and spoken words, from radio and television and loudspeakers. Everyone who wishes to keep his mind clear and his feelings his own must make an effort to brush away these words like cobwebs from the face. The assault of the phoney is a result of technology combined with a morality that excuses any technique which is useful for persuasion. The persuasion is for purposes of making money, as in advertising, or winning power, as in war propaganda and the slogans of politicians. Politicians have always had slogans, but they never before had the means to spread their words so widely. The cold war of rhetoric between communism and capitalism has killed no soldiers, but the air is full of the small corpses of words that were once alive: "democracy," "freedom," "liberation." 9

It is because of this assault, primarily, that writers have become increasingly concerned with the honesty of their style to the exclusion of other qualities. Concentration on honesty is the only way to exclude the sounds of the bad style that assault us all. These writers are concerned finally *to be honest about what they see, feel, and know.* For some of them, like William Carlos Williams, we can only trust the evidence of our eyes and ears, our real knowledge of our immediate environment. 10

Our reading of good writers and our attempt to write like them can help to guard against the dulling onslaught. But we can only do this if we are able to look into ourselves with some honesty. An ethic of clarity demands intelligence and self-knowledge. Really, the ethic is not only a defense against the assault (nothing good is ever merely defensive), but is a development of the same inwardness that is reflected in psychoanalysis. One cannot, after all, examine one's motives and feelings carefully if one takes a naïve view that the appearance of a feeling is the reality of that feeling. 11

Sometimes, the assault is merely pompous. Some people say "wealthy" 12

instead of "rich" in order to seem proper, or "home" instead of "house" in
order to seem genteel. George Orwell translates a portion of *Ecclesiastes* into
academic-pompous, for example; Quiller-Couch does something similar with
Hamlet's soliloquy. Years ago, James Russell Lowell ridiculed the newspapers that translated "A great crowd came to see . . ." into "A vast concourse
was assembled to witness. . . ." None of these examples is so funny as a colonel's statement on television that one of our astronauts "has established visual contact" with a piece of his equipment. He meant that the astronaut had
seen it.

Comic as these pomposities are, they are signs that something has gone   13
wrong somewhere. (My father normally spoke a perfectly good plain English,
but, occasionally, when he was unhappy with himself, he would fall off
dreadfully; I remember him once admonishing me at dinner, "It is necessary
to masticate thoroughly.") The colonel must have been worried about the intellectual respectability of the space program when he resorted to phrases
like "visual contact." The lady who speaks of "luncheon" instead of "lunch" is
worried about her social status. She gives herself away. Something has gone
wrong, and it has gone wrong inside her mind and her emotions.

The style is the man. Again and again, the modern stylists repeat this   14
idea. By a man's metaphors you shall know him. When a commencement or-
ator advises students to enrich themselves culturally, chances are that he is
more interested in money than in poetry. When a university president says
that his institution turned out 1,432 B.A.s last year, he tells us that he thinks
he is running General Motors. The style is the man. Remy de Gourmont
used the analogy that the bird's song is conditioned by the shape of the beak.
And Paul Valery said, ". . . what makes the style is not merely the mind
applied to a particular action; it is the whole of a living system extended,
imprinted and recognizable in expression." These statements are fine, but
they sound too deterministic, as if one expresses an unalterable self and can
no more change the style of that self than a bird can change the shape of its
beak. Man is a kind of bird that can change his beak.

A writer of bad prose, to become a writer of good prose, must alter his   15
character. He does not have to become good in terms of conventional morality, but he must become honest in the expression of himself, which means
that he must know himself. There must be no gap between expression and
meaning, between real and declared aims. For some people, some of the
time, this simply means *not* telling deliberate lies. For most people, it means
learning when they are lying and when they are not. It means learning the
real names of their feelings. It means not saying or thinking, "I didn't *mean*
to hurt your feelings," when there really existed a desire to hurt. It means
not saying "luncheon" or "home" for the purpose of appearing upper-class or
well-educated. It means not using the passive mood to attribute to no one in
particular opinions that one is unwilling to call one's own. It means not

disguising banal thinking by polysyllabic writing or the lack of feeling by clichés that purport to display feeling.

The style is the man, and the man can change himself by changing his style. Prose style is the way you think and the way you understand what you feel. Frequently, we feel for one another a mixture of strong love and strong hate; if we call it love and disguise the hate to ourselves by sentimentalizing over love, we are thinking and feeling badly. Style is ethics and psychology; clarity is a psychological sort of ethic, since it involves not general moral laws, but truth to the individual self. The scrutiny of style is a moral and psychological study. By trying to scrutinize our own style, perhaps with the help of people like Orwell and Pound, Hemingway and Thurber, we try to understand ourselves. Editing our own writing, or going over in memory our own spoken words, or even inwardly examining our thought, we can ask *why* we resorted to the passive in this case or to clichés in that. When the smoke of bad prose fills the air, something is always on fire somewhere. If the style is really the man, the style becomes an instrument for discovering and changing the man. Language is expression of self, but language is also the instrument by which to know that self.

SUBJECT QUESTIONS

1. What change does Hall say has taken place in the attitude toward style among contemporary writers? How does he explain this change?
2. In what sense is good style "a moral matter"?
3. Consider the implications of the repeated sentence in paragraph 14, "the style is the man." Do you agree with the thesis? Does a pompous style indicate a pompous person? Does a tangled style imply a mixed-up writer?
4. How, according to Hall, can a poor prose writer become a good one?
5. Do you agree with Hall that a good way to know yourself better is to analyze your prose style? Or do you tend to think that a bad style is simply the result of bad training in composition?

STRUCTURE QUESTIONS

1. At the end of paragraph 2, Hall offers a one-sentence "definition" of style. Is it adequate? Does Hall think it is?
2. Do you find any correspondence between the methods of development Hall employs and logical subdivisions within the essay? What methods does he employ in this problem of definition?
3. Did you find the many quotations from other authors helpful or distracting? Some of the writers Hall cites will not be familiar to freshmen; does it matter that he does not identify them except by name?

4. The last part of the essay is an inducement to writers to improve their own styles. Is it separate from the definition, or is it actually part of the definition?
5. Hall writes much about honesty in style; does his own style seem to you honest? How do you test honesty in style?

SUGGESTIONS FOR WRITING

1. Select two writers whom you admire, and write a comparison and contrast of their styles. Be sure to include enough examples so that the reader can see the difference or similarity.
2. Write a definition of the kind of style you would like to develop for your own writing.

The Apostate

George Milburn

George Milburn (1906–1966) was an American short story writer and novelist. His books include Flannigan's Folly *(1947),* Blackjack Country *(1947), and* No More Trumpets *(1933), from which the following story is taken.*

Harry, you been jacking me up about how I been neglecting Rotary here   1
lately, so I'm just going to break down and tell you something. Now I don't
want you to take this personal, Harry, because it's not meant personal at all.
No, siree! Not *a*-tall! But, just between you and I, Harry, I'm not going to be
coming out to Rotary lunches any more. I mean I'm quitting Rotary! . . .

Now whoa there! Whoa! Whoa just a minute and let me get in a word   2
edgeways. Just let me finish my little say.

Don't you never take it into your head that I haven't been wrestling   3
with this thing plenty. I mean I've argued it all out with myself. Now I'm
going to tell you the whyfor and the whereof and the howcome about this,
Harry, but kindly don't let what I say go no further. Please keep it strictly on
the Q.T. Because I guess the rest of the boys would suspicion that I was
turning highbrow on them. But you've always been a buddy to me, Harry,
you mangy old son of a hoss thief, you, so what I'm telling you is the straight
dope.

II

Harry, like you no doubt remember, up till a few months ago Rotary was   4
about "the most fondest thing I is of," as the nigger says. There wasn't
nothing that stood higher for me than Rotary.

Well, here about a year ago last fall I took a trip down to the university   5
to visit my son and go to a football game. You know Hubert Junior, my boy.
Sure. Well, this is his second year down at the university. Yes, sir, that boy
is getting a college education. I mean, I'm all for youth having a college education.

Of course I think there is such a thing as too much education working a   6
detriment. Take, for instance, some of these longhairs running around

knocking the country right now. But what I mean is, a good, sound, substantial college education. I don't mean a string of letters a yard long for a man to write after his John Henry. I just mean that I want my boy to have his sheepskin, they call it, before he starts out in the world. Like the fellow says, I want him to get his A.B. degree, and then he can go out and get his J.O.B.

Now, Harry, I always felt like a father has got certain responsibilities to   7
his son. That's just good Rotary. That's all that is. You know that that's just good Rotary yourself, Harry. Well, I always wanted Hubert to think about me just like I was a pal to him, or say an older brother, maybe. I don't know that him and I ever was that way in the fullest sense of the word, but God knows I've tried to make things like that between us. I mean I've always wanted to be just a big buddy to Hubert.

I'm not saying that I haven't made a pretty poor job out of it some-   8
times. But anyhow that's the spirit I've tried to get into our relationships ever since he was a little tike. Too many parents never actually get acquainted with their boys, see, Harry? I always encouraged Hubert to come to me and talk things over just like it was man to man. I will admit that since Hubert got older I would sometimes find out about things that he had been keeping from me, especially after he got girl crazy. But however, as I say, Harry, Hubert always knew that all he had to do was come to me, and I would act like a big buddy to him, irregardless.

III

Well, like I was telling you, Harry, I started Hubert in to the university last   9
year, and after he had been there about two months, I thought I would run down and see how he was getting along and go to a football game. So I and Mrs. T. drove over one Friday. We didn't know the town very well, so we stopped at a filling station, and I give Hubert a ring, and he come right on down to where we was to show us the way. Just as soon as he come up, I could see right then that he had something on his mind bothering him.

He called me aside and took me into the filling-station rest-room, and   10
says: "For the love of God, Dad, take that Rotary button out of your coat lapel," he says to me.

Harry, that come as a plenty big surprise to me, and I don't mind   11
telling you that it just about took the wind out of my sails. But I wasn't going to let on to him, so I rared back on my dignity, and says: "Why, what do you mean, take that Rotary button out of my lapel, young man?" I says to him.

"Dad," Hubert says to me, serious, "any frat house has always got a   12
few cynics in it. If you was to wear that Rotary button in your lapel out to the frat house, just as soon as you got out of sight, some of those boys at the house would razz the life out of me," he says.

"Hubert," I says, "there's not a thing that this lapel badge represents   13

that any decent, moral person could afford to make fun of. If that's the kind
of Reds you got out at your fraternity, the kind that would razz a what you
might call sacred thing — yes, sir, a sacred thing — like Rotary, well, I and
your mamma can just go somewheres else and put up. I don't guess the
hotels have quit running," I says to him.

By now I was on my high horse right, see?   14

"Now, Dad," Hubert says, "it's not that. I mean, person'ly I'm awful   15
proud of you. It's just that I haven't been pledged to this fraternity long, see,
and when some of those older members found out you was a Rotarian they
would deal me a lot of misery, and I couldn't say nothing. Person'ly I think
Rotary is all right," he says to me.

"Well, you better, son," I says, "or I'm going to begin to think that   16
you're sick in the head."

The way he explained it, though, Harry, that made it a horse of a dif-   17
ferent tail, as the saying goes, so I give in and took off my Rotary button
right there. Stuck it in my pocket, see? So we went on out and visited at
Hubert's fraternity house, and do you know that those boys just got around
there and treated we folks like we was princes of the blood. I mean you
would of thought that I was an old ex-graduate of that university. And we
saw the big pigskin tussle the next day, fourteen to aught, favor us, and we
had such a scrumptious time all around, I forgot all about what Hubert had
said.

Ever'thing would of been all right, except for what happened later. I   18
guess some of those older boys at the frat house begin using their form of
psychology on Hubert. I mean they finely got his mind set against Rotary,
because when he come home for the summer vacation that was about the
size of things.

IV

I mean all last summer I thought Hubert never would let up. He just kept it 19
up, making sarcastic remarks about Rotary, see? Even when we was on our
vacation trip.

You know we drove out to California and back last summer, Harry.   20
Come back with the same air in the tires we started out with. Well, I
thought it would be kind of nice to drop in and eat with the Hollywood Rotary — you know, just to be able to say I had. So I contacted them and had
ever'thing all fixed. Well, do you know that that boy Hubert made so much
fun of the idea I just had to give it up?

That was the way it was the whole trip. He got his mother around on   21
his side, too. Just to be frank with you, I never got so sick and tired of anything in all my born days.

Well, Harry, I had my dander up there for a while, and all the bicker-   22 ing in the world couldn't of shook me from my stand. But finely Hubert went back to college in September, and I thought I would have a little peace. Then I just got to thinking about it, and it all come over me. "Look here, Mister Man," I says to myself, "your faith and loyalty to Rotary may be a fine thing, and all that, but it's just costing you the fellowship of your own son." Now a man can't practice Rotary in the higher sense, and yet at the same time be letting his own son's fellowship get loose from him. So there it was. Blood's thicker than water, Harry. You'll have to admit that.

Right along in there, Harry, was the first time I begin to attending   23 meetings irregular. I'll tell you — you might not think so — but it was a pretty tough struggle for me. I remember one Monday noon, Rotary meeting day, I happened to walk past the Hotel Beckman just at lunchtime. The windows of the Venetian Room was open, and I could hear you boys singing a Rotary song. You know that one we sing set to the tune of "Last Night on the Back Porch." It goes:

> I love the Lions in the morning,
>   The Exchange Club at night,
> I love the Y's men in the evening,
>   And Kiwanis are all right . . .

Well, I couldn't carry a tune if I had it in a sack, but anyway that's the   24 way it goes. So I just stopped in my tracks and stood there listening to that song coming out of the Hotel Beckman dining-room. And when the boys come to the last verse,

> I love the Optimists in the springtime,
>   The Ad Club in the fall,
> But each day — and in every way —
>   I love Rotary best of all . . .

I tell you, Harry, that just got me. I had a lump in my throat big enough to choke a cow. The tears begin coming up in my eyes, and it might sound ridiculous to hear me tell it now, but I could of broke down and bawled right there on the street. I got a grip on myself and walked on off, but right then I says to myself: "The hell with Hubert and his highbrow college-fraternity ideas; I'm going back to Rotary next week."

V

Well, I did go back the next week, and what happened decided me on taking   25 the step I decided on. Here's what decided me. You know, I never got very well acquainted with Gay Harrison, the new secretary. I mean, of course, I know him all right, but he hasn't been in Rotary only but about a year. Well, on that particular day, I just happened to let my tongue slip and called him

Mister Harrison, instead of by his nickname. Well, of course, the boys slapped a dollar fine on me right then and there. I haven't got no kick to make about that, but the point is, I had a letter from Hubert in my pocket right then, telling me that he had run short of money. So I just couldn't help but be struck by the idea "I wish I was giving Hubert this dollar." So that's what decided me on devoting my time and finances to another kind of fellowship, Harry.

I get down to the university to see Hubert more frequent now, I make it a point to. And the boys come to me, and I been helping them a little on their frat building fund. There's a fine spirit of fellowship in an organization like that. Some boys from the best families of the State are members, too. You might think from what I said that they'd be uppish, but they're not. No, siree. Not a bit of it. I been down there enough for them to know me, now, and they all pound me on the back and call me H.T., just like I was one of them. And I do them, too. And I notice that when they sit down to a meal, they have some songs they sing just as lively and jolly as any we had at Rotary. Of course, like Hubert said, a few of them might have some wild-haired ideas about Rotary, but they're young yet. And as far as I can see there's not a knocker nor a sourbelly among them. Absolutely democratic. 26

It puts me in mind of a little incidence that happened last month when the frat threw a big Dad's Day banquet for us down there. All the fathers of the boys from all over the State was there. Well, to promote the spirit of fellowship between dad and son, the fraternity boys all agreed to call their dads by their first name, just treating the dads like big buddies. So at the table Hubert happened to forget for a minute, and says to me "Dad" something. Well, sir, the president of the frat flashed right out: "All right, Hubie, we heard you call H.T. 'Dad.' So that'll just cost you a dollar for the ice-cream fund." Ever'body had a good laugh at Hubert getting caught like that, but do you know, that boy of mine just forked right over without making a kick. That shows the stuff, don't it, Harry? Nothing wrong with a boy like that. 27

And the whole bunch is like that, ever' one of them. I'll tell you, Harry, the boys at that frat of Hubert's are the builders in the coming generation. Any man of vision can see that. 28

Well, that's that. Now what was you going to say? 29

SUBJECT QUESTIONS

1. What is the father's attitude toward college? What does he expect his son to get out of it?
2. Do you have any clue to the fraternity's objections to Rotary? Do the father's attitudes toward Rotary indicate what those objections might be?

3. Explain the reasoning by which the father finally decides to quit Rotary. Does Milburn make clear why the father fails to see the faults in this reasoning?
4. So far as you can tell from the story, what differences are there between Rotary and the fraternity?
5. What is the significance of the parallel between the fines levied against the father and the son?
6. What hints are there that the father is being "used" by his son's fraternity? Why doesn't he see that he is being used?

STRUCTURE QUESTIONS

1. Do you see any advantage (or disadvantage) to Milburn's making this story a monologue rather than a dialogue between Harry and Hubert, Sr.? Milburn has omitted another ingredient of most short stories — setting. Would anything be gained by describing the setting in which the monologue is delivered?
2. Why does Milburn include many errors in grammar and diction? What do they tell you about the speaker?
3. How would you characterize the father's language? Is it colorful? Original? Does it communicate clearly and effectively?
4. Do you see any relationship between the speaker's thought patterns and the language he uses to express those thoughts? Can language determine thought?
5. Milburn is "defining" or characterizing a type of thinker. How can he do this successfully with only one example? This is a short story, of course. Would you expect an expository essay on this subject to include corroborating evidence?

SUGGESTION FOR WRITING

Write an analysis of the father's language, noticing particularly points at which even his emotional responses seem to be conditioned by the language with which he speaks and thinks.

Sonnet 76, "Why Is My Verse So Barren of New Pride?"

William Shakespeare

William Shakespeare (1564–1616) joined a traveling acting company when he was about 23, and soon began writing plays to help increase the company's receipts. After six years, his reputation was sufficient for him to publish two long poems dedicated to the youthful Earl of South-ampton. Although his sonnets, like his plays, were not intended or prepared for publication, Shakespeare did address most of them to the young earl. They circulated in manuscript form among the earl's friends for many years, until they were finally published in 1609. In Sonnet 76, Shakespeare offers a concise analysis (and illustration) of his own style — a style very different from the flamboyant overstatement of most sonnet writers in his time.

Why is my verse so barren of new pride?
So far from variation or quick change?
Why with the time do I not glance aside
To new-found methods and to compounds strange?
Why write I still all one, ever the same,   5
And keep invention in a noted weed,*
That every word doth almost tell my name,
Showing their birth and where they did proceed?
O know, sweet love, I always write of you,
And you and love are still my argument;   10
So all my best is dressing old words new,
Spending again what is already spent:
For as the sun is daily new and old,
So is my love still telling what is told.

SUBJECT QUESTIONS

1. Does Shakespeare seem to be blaming himself for not following newfangled styles in poetry writing? Does he give any indication that he does not approve of these new styles?
2. What is his defense of his own style?
3. If his subject matter is always the same, does it follow that his style

in a noted weed: in familiar clothing.

must also remain the same? Is there a flaw in Shakespeare's argument here?

STRUCTURE QUESTIONS

1. Considering that the poem is nearly 400 years old, is there any expression other than "noted weed" that would be unfamiliar to a modern reader? Has Shakespeare sufficiently illustrated the simplicity of his own style?
2. Are there any words that might be called "pretentious," bigger than they need be to make the point? What are the four words of more than two syllables?
3. Despite the apparent plainness of the style, Shakespeare has used several implied and direct comparisons (metaphor and simile). Identify several of these; do they seem intended primarily for decoration, or to further the meaning?
4. What is Shakespeare's principal method of defining his style? Do you think comparison and contrast might have worked better?
5. Despite the poem's brevity, Shakespeare repeats himself several times; does this repetition detract from the force of the poem? Does it give any impression about the kind of man who is writing the poem?

SUGGESTION FOR WRITING

Define your own style by writing an analysis of the papers you have written thus far in this class. Try to find identifying characteristics and peculiarities, and be sure to provide adequate illustrations of your observations.

7

FREEDOM AND RESPONSIBILITY

Argument

Argument as an essay form has little in common with the heated discussion which usually terminates a college bull session: it is not a technique for "outshouting" one's opponent in writing. By a devious route through Rome and medieval Europe, its ancestor was the deliberative oration of ancient Athens. The deliberative oration, as taught by Aristotle and others, was a set form for speeches to be delivered before the Athenian Senate on matters of public policy and proposed legislation. Its chief feature was its carefully controlled, logical approach: it was intended to convince the senators of the reasonableness of the speaker's position — not, in our common use of the term "argument," to engage in a verbal free-for-all. Although the speaker might feel strongly about his subject, the aim was to stimulate a spirit of free and serious inquiry, not to overwhelm with rhetoric or to provoke anger.

This same honest, objective, and logical approach characterizes the argument as a literary form today. Although a week or two spent studying argument in a composition course is hardly a substitute for a class in logic, you can learn much by studying the various arguments presented in this section and by writing an argument yourself. You will want to watch for careless logic both in the essays and in your own thinking. You should recognize, for instance, that an opinion, no matter how forcefully presented, is still opinion, not fact. In your own argument you should support your opinions with typical and relevant evidence — facts, observations, and reasons. Rather than slinging mud at possible opponents of your beliefs, you should remember that the purpose of argument is to invite free discussion in the hope of arriving at a workable solution to the problem under consideration. If you as the writer of an argument firmly believe that your solution is "right," you should by all means argue it forcefully; but you can still have the open-minded attitude which allows you to change your position in the light of new evidence. Your job is to search for truth, not obscure it with dogmatism.

Although the original Greek deliberative oration contained some frosting with which we can dispense, a good written argument will contain the four basic ingredients of the old recipe. First, there should be a brief but penetrating introduction to, or analysis of, the problem which needs a solution. This analysis ought to be as objective and honest as the writer can make it; if the writer starts with a slanted interpretation, the aims of argument are defeated at the outset.

The second ingredient is a clear, concise statement of the author's proposed solution. Normally, this immediately follows the analysis of the problem, and it is sometimes repeated in summary at the end of the argument. Or the writer may prefer to save it for the end, as a logical conclusion to the arguments. If possible it should be concentrated into a sentence or two, so that the reader can readily grasp it in its entirety.

The other parts of a good argument are a refutation of an opponent's arguments, if there are any, and a confirmation of the writer's own position. The refutation may be placed before or after the confirmation, or the two may be intermixed. (The writer should remember, however, to save the strongest point for the last, whether it be proof or disproof.) In refuting an opponent's arguments, one ought to recognize that seldom is one side completely right and the other completely wrong; usually, taking sides should be a matter of weighing merits and demerits and then deciding which side has more advantages. A writer who has honestly done this need have no fear of admitting a few merits of the other side or the disadvantages of the position being argued. In no case should the writer resort to mere name-calling instead of disproof. ("Of course we don't want a government-operated medical plan — that's socialism!" or "As any fool can plainly see. . . .")

Because a good argument should be mainly positive, writers will want to concentrate most heavily on their proof. They should be prepared to include as much evidence as their experience and the word limit of their papers will allow. The more specific the evidence, of course, the better. There are two major traps to watch for: insufficient evidence and atypical evidence. One example, no matter how detailed, does not justify a generalization. ("Polio vaccine is worthless. I heard of a child who contracted polio after having three shots.") Although you may wish to concentrate on one piece of evidence, you ought at least to mention others briefly to show that more is available. Second, there is always the danger of selecting from a number of available facts only certain ones which will appear to prove your point. Anyone who has watched political debates on television has probably noticed how both opponents cite numerous statistics to "prove" that they are right. Because the purpose of the argument as an essay form is not to win elections at all costs but to deal honestly with a problem, you will want to avoid either slanting your facts or selecting evidence which does not indicate the general trend of *all* the evidence. This is not always easy to do, but if you strive for integrity you will be much less likely to go wrong. Although you may not solve all the world's problems, you will at least learn something about logical analysis and the objective search for truth.

On Decriminalization

Robert M. Hutchins

Robert M. Hutchins (1899–1977) began his distinguished career as a lecturer at Yale Law School. He was later president, then chancellor, of the University of Chicago (1929–1951), where he fostered many radical educational innovations — guaranteeing that every graduate had a humanistic education in the Great Books, for instance, and granting advanced placement — ideas which have since become standard at most universities. Hutchins was chairman of Encyclopaedia Britannica, *and he was chairman of the Center for the Study of Democratic Institutions in Santa Barbara, California, where he resided. Hutchins was awarded at least a dozen honorary degrees and published many books on experiments in university education and education in a democratic society. The essay which follows first appeared in 1971 in an issue of* Center *magazine devoted to law and order, based on a special conference on that subject held at the Center for the Study of Democratic Institutions.*

At the Center's Conference on Crime Control Legislation James V. Bennett, former director of the United States Bureau of Prisons, estimated the cost of modernizing the penal institutions of the country at eighteen billion dollars. Nobody thought this figure was too high. Many of those present thought it was too low. Whatever the correct figure is, it is a fraction of what it would take to get a modern penal system, for Mr. Bennett was talking only about modernizing buildings. The cost of a well-trained staff in numbers and quality adequate to administer an enlightened program running from conviction through probation and parole would be many billions. More important, it would demand much intelligence, courage, and patience.

The same is true of every department of criminal justice. We need more and better judges, more and better prosecutors, more and better public defenders, more and better police, more and better probation officers and parole boards, and all these groups need more and better facilities. Of course, what they need most of all is more and better ideas.

The demand for more personnel and more facilities would diminish if the President, instead of ranting, would take up the one good idea he has in this field and educate the country to understand and accept it. This is the idea of "decriminalization," which became a sort of central theme of the

Reprinted with permission from *The Center Magazine*, a publication of the Robert Maynard Hutchins Center for the Study of Democratic Institutions, Santa Barbara, California.

conference at the Center and which the President referred to in a speech on March 11. As far as I can recall, it received unanimous support. Even Carl Rauh, of the Department of Justice, endorsed it. The reservations expressed about it had to do with details.

On the main point there was general agreement, and that was that offenses that did not damage the person or property of others, where there was no victim and no complainant, should as far as possible be taken out of the system of criminal justice.

This would remove from the scope of the criminal law people for whom that law can do nothing and who are now the principal burden upon it. Narcotics addicts and alcoholics cannot be helped by terms in the penitentiary. What they need is medical treatment. It was said at the Center's conference that sixty percent at least of all serious crime is drug-related and that alcoholics account for more than fifty percent of the arrests in the country. Although all statistics on crime are unreliable, these figures suggest what would happen if narcotics addicts and alcoholics were regarded as patients rather than criminals.

Some eight to ten million people in this country are said to be using marijuana in open violation of the law. In some states an enormous part of the apparatus of criminal justice is dedicated to detecting and convicting these people and to getting them locked up. If no convincing evidence can be offered that marijuana is more harmful than alcohol or tobacco, the possession and use of marijuana should be legalized. It should follow that the sale of marijuana would be legal as well.

The criminal law cannot stop the traffic in "hard" drugs. As Troy Duster pointed out at the Center's conference, the profits in the business are so large that dealers caught and jailed are immediately replaced. If criminal penalties were removed and the whole business were regulated or owned by government, if something like the British system were introduced, the resources now wasted in tracking down those involved in the drug business could be devoted to the invention of practical solutions to the problem.

Some form of gambling is legal everywhere. Some states have gone so far as to set up state owned gambling institutions. If all restrictions on gambling were removed, the strain it places on the system of criminal justice would be relieved. The hazards to civil liberties would be reduced. The only argument advanced for "no-knock" and wiretapping where "national security" is not involved is that in drug and gambling cases these procedures are necessary to obtain and preserve evidence. If there were no drug or gambling cases nobody would have the face to advocate these procedures.

Drugs turn out to be, too, an important argument for preventive detention: the addict out on bail must engage in crime in order to support his habit. Taking addicts out of the criminal system would minimize the demand to lock up people in order to protect the public from them.

Every reader can make his own list of those acts, now called criminal,   10
which should be considered candidates for "decriminalization." Many readers may differ with some of the examples I have used. This is not material.
The point is that the idea should be accepted and as many acts covered by it
as possible as soon as possible.

Where there is a social problem with which the system of criminal   11
justice is now vainly trying to deal, we do not solve the problem by removing it from the scope of the criminal law. We merely abandon a wasteful and
futile attempt to cope with it. The problem remains. Attempts to take mentally ill persons out of the reach of the criminal law have been a dubious
advantage to them. Most students of the subject agree that a mentally ill
defendant in a criminal case is better off, in those jurisdictions which have
civil commitment, if his illness is not referred to during his trial. If he is sent
to the penitentiary, he has at least some idea when he will get out. If he is
civilly committed he may be detained for years and in the meantime get
little more or better treatment than he would have in prison.

Civil commitment was thought to be a great step forward when it was   12
introduced. The reason that a noble, humanitarian effort has failed to produce better results is the same as that which must be given for the failure of
the system of criminal justice. We as a people do not care to put the necessary intellectual and financial resources into the job. We are therefore an
easy prey for snake-oil salesmen who tell us that if we will only stop "cod-
dling criminals" we shall be secure.

Newsweek quotes Joe Olgiati, who runs a work-training program for   13
probationers in New York, as saying, "If you were to eliminate all cops,
judges, parole officers, and courts, it would have a highly negligible effect on
crime in the streets. In fact, it might even be better. You wouldn't just be
trying to repair what we have now."

The thought does cross one's mind as one listens to the horrors recited   14
in a conference on crime control that it might be better if no criminal were
ever caught. Everybody who is involved with the criminal law seems to be
worse because of his contact with it. For example, the fifty-two percent of
the jail population who are being detained pending trial must be more
dangerous to society as a result of this experience than they were before.

Yet we cannot dispense with the criminal law. Although we know very   15
little about deterrence, it seems probable that the prospect of punishment
does dissuade some people from the commission of some crimes. We should
try to make the system of criminal justice work as swiftly, surely, and fairly
as we can. As Ramsey Clark said at the Center's conference, safety and freedom are not incompatible; the thing to do is to enlarge both. Law and
Order, in the modern interpretation of this slogan, will give us neither.

SUBJECT QUESTIONS

1. When any government agency is not doing the job expected of it, "more money" is the solution normally suggested. Why does Hutchins think that is not a proper solution in this instance?
2. What advantages does Hutchins see in "decriminalization"? Does he give due recognition to the fact that ceasing to call an activity criminal does not eliminate that activity?
3. Does it seem odd that over half the people in jail are not serving sentences but awaiting trial? Can you suggest ways of avoiding the enormous expense this situation necessitates? Are there any major difficulties in your solution?
4. Would you agree that the examples cited are likely areas for decriminalization? Can you suggest others?
5. Do you agree with the statement by Joe Olgiati in paragraph 13? Does Hutchins? Is it possible that the system of law enforcement could cause more crime than it prevents?

STRUCTURE QUESTIONS

1. What exactly is the problem with which Hutchins is concerned? Does he offer a clear statement of a possible solution?
2. Does Hutchins attempt to "open up" discussion with his argument? Does he seem especially concerned that his own solution be the one adopted?
3. Locate Hutchins's admission of the "weakness" in his own solution. How does he turn this weakness to his own advantage?
4. Examine the refutation of the "get tough on lawbreakers" solution to the problem. Does this portion of the argument seem logical, or unfair?
5. Does Hutchins's conclusion in the final paragraph follow logically from his argument? Should he have done more with "swiftness" of criminal justice?

SUGGESTIONS FOR WRITING

1. Write an argument for or against decriminalization in one of the three areas which Hutchins cites as possibilities: marijuana use, hard drug offenses, and gambling. Be sure to base your case on objective reason, not personal feelings or prejudice.
2. Write an argument in which you confront the problem (and expense) of more than half the people in jails not being convicted criminals. (You may of course want to argue that the present system is preferable to other solutions.)

The Truth About the Black Middle Class

Vernon E. Jordan, Jr.

*Vernon Jordan (b. 1935), is a native of Georgia and a foremost civil rights
leader. After graduating from DePauw University he took his law degree
at Howard University and was soon back in Georgia as a civil rights
lawyer. During the integration struggles of the early 1960's, Jordan led
demonstrations, sit-ins, and boycotts and personally led the first black
student through an angry mob of whites onto the campus of the University of Georgia. He became director of the Voter Education Project,
which helped nearly two million black voters to register for the first
time. Jordan was later director of the United Negro College Fund, and in
1972 he became executive director of the National Urban League, one of
the most influential positions in the field of race relations. He has received numerous awards and honorary degrees and has served on a
number of government committees.*

Recent reports of the existence of a vast black middle class remind me of   1
daring explorers emerging from the hidden depths of a strange, newly discovered world bearing tales of an exotic new phenomenon. The media
seem to have discovered, finally, black families that are intact, black men
who are working, black housewives tending backyard gardens and black
youngsters who aren't sniffing coke or mugging old ladies.

And out of this "discovery" a new black stereotype is beginning to   2
emerge. Immaculately dressed, cocktail in hand, the new black stereotype
comes off as a sleek, sophisticated professional light-years away from the
ghetto experience. As I turn the pages of glossy photos of these idealized,
fortunate few, I get the feeling that this new black image is all too comforting to Americans weary of the struggle against poverty and racism.

But this stereotype is no more real than was the old image of the   3
angry, fire-breathing militant. And it may be just as damaging to black
people, for whom equal opportunity is still a theory and for whom a national effort to bring about a more equitable distribution of the fruits of an
affluent society is still a necessity. After all, who can argue the need for
welfare reform, for guaranteed jobs, for integrated schools and better hous-
ing, when the supposed beneficiaries are looking out at us from the pages
of national magazines, smiling at the camera between sips from their Martinis?

The "new" black middle class has been seen recently in prime time [4] on a CBS News documentary; it has adorned the cover of *The New York Times Magazine*, and it has been the subject of a *Time* cover story. But its much ballyhooed emergence is more representative of wishful thinking than of reality. And important as it is for the dedication and hard work of countless black families finally to receive recognition, the image being pushed so hard may be counterproductive in the long run.

The fact is that the black middle class of 1974, like that of earlier [5] years, is a minority within the black community. In 1974, as in 1964, 1954 and in the decades stretching into the distant past, the social and economic reality of the majority of black people has been poverty and marginal status in the wings of our society.

The black middle class traditionally included a handful of profession- [6] als and a far larger number of working people who, had they been white, would be solidly "working class." The inclusion of Pullman porters, post-office clerks and other typical members of the old black middle class was due less to their incomes — which were well below those of whites — than to their relative immunity from the hazards of marginal employment that dogged most blacks. They were "middle class" relative to other black people, not to the society at large.

Despite all the publicity, despite all the photos of yacht-club cocktail [7] parties, that is where the so-called black middle class stands today. The CBS broadcast included a handyman and a postal worker. Had they been white they would be considered working class, but since they were black and defied media-fostered stereotypes, they were given the middle-class label.

Well, is it true that the black community is edging into the middle [8] class? Let's look at income, the handiest guide and certainly the most generally agreed-upon measurement. What income level amounts to middle-class status? Median family income is often used, since that places a family at the exact midpoint in our society. In 1972 the median family income of whites amounted to $11,549, but black median family income was a mere $6,864.

That won't work. Let's use another guide. The Bureau of Labor [9] Statistics says it takes an urban family of four $12,600 to maintain an "intermediate" living standard. Using that measure, the average black family not only is *not* middle class, but earns far less than the "lower, non-poverty" level of $8,200. Four out of five black families earn less than the "intermediate" standard.

What about collar color? Occupational status is often considered a [10] guide to middle-class status, and this is an area in which blacks have made tremendous gains, breaking into occupations unheard of for non-whites only a decade ago. When you look at the official occupation charts, there is a double space to separate higher-status from lower-status jobs such as laborer, operative and service worker. That gap is more than a typographical device. It is an indicator of racial separation as well, for the majority of working whites hold jobs above that line, while the majority of blacks are still confined to the low-pay, low-status jobs below it. At the top of the job pinnacle, in the elite categories of the professions and business, the disparity is most glaring, with one out of four whites in such middle-class jobs in contrast to every tenth black worker.

Yes, there are black doctors, dentists and lawyers, but let no one be fooled into thinking they are typical — these professions include only 2 per cent blacks. Yes, there are black families that are stable, who work, often at more than one job, and who own cars and homes. And yes, they are representative of the masses of black people who work the longest hours at the hardest jobs for the least pay in order to put some meat on the table and clothes on their backs. This should be emphasized in every way possible in order to remind this forgetting nation that there is a dimension of black reality that has never been given its due.   11

But this should not blind us to the realization that even with such superhuman efforts, the vast majority of blacks are still far from middle-class status. Let us not forget that the gains won are tenuous ones, easily shaken from our grasp by an energy crisis, a recession, rampant inflation or nonenforcement of hard-won civil-rights laws.   12

And never let us fall victim to the illusion that the limited gains so bitterly wrenched from an unwilling nation have materially changed the conditions of life for the overwhelming majority of black people — conditions still typified by discrimination, economic insecurity and general living conditions inferior to those enjoyed by the majority of our white fellow citizens.   13

SUBJECT QUESTIONS

1. Is Jordan trying to deny that blacks have made important economic gains? What *is* the main point of his argument?
2. Judging by the examples Jordan gives, do you agree that the news media have created a false impression about black affluence? Might there be a deliberate intention to create a false impression, or do the media simply try to "make news" when there isn't any news?
3. Would you say that newspapers and magazines primarily for blacks, such as *Ebony,* contribute to the notion that blacks are rising into the middle class, or are they more realistic about the plight of minorities?
4. According to Jordan, how have statistics been juggled to include more blacks in the middle class? How does the black middle class differ from the white middle class?

5. What is the danger of believing that blacks are steadily entering the middle class? Would it not encourage acceptance by whites and hope for blacks?
6. What is the "dimension of black reality that has never been given its due"? (See paragraph 11.)

STRUCTURE QUESTIONS

1. Does Jordan begin his argument with a clear statement of the problem? Where does he announce his own position?
2. Because Jordan is arguing against a common assumption, his argument necessarily stresses refutation. Examine the two approaches he uses in the refutation section; do you find the logical reasoning or the statistics the more effective? Could it be said that the statistics are actually part of his confirmation rather than his refutation? (See the introduction to this section.)
3. Does the admission (in paragraph 11) that some gains have been made weaken Jordan's argument? What effect does it have on the reader's "trust" in the writer?
4. The final two paragraphs are somewhat more "rhetorical" than the body of the essay; do they stray from the bounds of argument into persuasion? How does Jordan make these paragraphs effective without resorting to "loaded language"?
5. As a black actively working to improve the plight of blacks, Jordan must feel very strongly about his subject. Does he manage to convey that strong feeling without losing the considered and reasonable tone necessary to good argument?

SUGGESTIONS FOR WRITING

1. Examine several back issues of *Ebony* in your library and decide what impression of blacks is conveyed. Then write an argument for or against the advisability of conveying that impression. Make notes of specific examples and use some in your paper.
2. Write an argument supporting a way you think the disparity of income between whites and minorities could be reduced or eliminated.
3. Suggest and support a way you think the United States could have more mutually beneficial relations with Third World countries.

What I Saw at the Abortion

Richard Selzer

Richard Selzer is a surgeon affiliated with Yale University. He is also a contributing editor to Esquire. *A series of his essays on the human body, which appeared in* Esquire, *was honored in 1975 by the Columbia University Graduate School of Journalism. The following essay also appeared in* Esquire *in 1976.*

I am a surgeon. Particularities of sick flesh is everyday news. Escaping   1
blood, all the outpourings of disease — phlegm, pus, vomitus, even those
occult meaty tumors that terrify — I see as blood, disease, phlegm, and so
on. I touch them to destroy them. But I do not make symbols of them.

What I am saying is that I have seen and I am used to seeing. We are   2
talking about a man who has a trade, who has practiced it long enough to see
no news in any of it. Picture this man, then. A professional. In his forties.
Three children. Lives in a university town — so, necessarily, well —
enlightened? Enough, anyhow. Successful in his work, yes. No overriding
religious posture. Nothing special, then, your routine fellow, trying to do his
work and doing it well enough. Picture him, this professional, a sort of scientist, if you please, in possession of the standard admirable opinions, positions, convictions, and so on — on this and that matter — on *abortion*, for
example.

All right.   3

Now listen.   4

It is the western wing of the fourth floor of a great university hospital. I am   5
present because I asked to be present. I wanted to see what I had never
seen. An abortion.

The patient is Jamaican. She lies on the table in that state of notable   6
submissiveness I have always seen in patients. Now and then she smiles at
one of the nurses as though acknowledging a secret.

A nurse draws down the sheet, lays bare the abdomen. The belly   7
mounds gently in the twenty-fourth week of pregnancy. The chief surgeon
paints it with a sponge soaked in red antiseptic. He does this three times,

each time a fresh sponge. He covers the area with a sterile sheet, an aperture in its center. He is a kindly man who teaches as he works, who pauses to reassure the woman.

He begins. 8

A little pinprick, he says to the woman. 9

He inserts the point of a tiny needle at the midline of the lower portion 10
of her abdomen, on the downslope. He infiltrates local anesthetic into the
skin, where it forms a small white bubble.

The woman grimaces. 11

That is all you will feel the doctor says. Except for a little pressure. But 12
no more pain.

She smiles again. She seems to relax. She settles comfortably on the 13
table. The worst is over.

The doctor selects a three-and-one-half-inch needle bearing a central 14
stylet. He places the point at the site of the previous injection. He aims it
straight up and down, perpendicular. Next he takes hold of her abdomen
with his left hand, palming the womb, steadying it. He thrusts with his right
hand. The needle sinks into the abdominal wall.

Oh, says the woman quietly. 15

But I guess it is not pain that she feels. It is more a recognition that the 16
deed is being done.

Another thrust and he has speared the uterus. 17

We are in, he says. 18

He has felt the muscular wall of the organ gripping the shaft of his 19
needle. A further slight pressure on the needle advances it a bit more. He
takes his left hand from the woman's abdomen. He retracts the filament of
the stylet from the barrel of the needle. A small geyser of pale yellow fluid
erupts.

We are in the right place, says the doctor. Are you feeling any pain? he 20
says.

She smiles, shakes her head. She gazes at the ceiling. 21

In the room we are six: two physicians, two nurses, the patient, and 22
me.

The participants are busy, very attentive. I am not at all busy — but I 23
am no less attentive. I want to see.

I see something! 24

It is unexpected, utterly unexpected, like a disturbance in the earth, a 25
tumultuous jarring. I see something other than what I expected here. I see a
movement — a small one. But I have seen it.

And then I see it again. And now I see that it is the hub of the needle 26
in the woman's belly that has jerked. First to one side. Then to the other

side. Once more it wobbles, is *tugged*, like a fishing line nibbled by a sun-fish.

Again! And I *know!* 27

It is the *fetus* that worries thus. It is the fetus struggling against the 28
needle. Struggling? How can that be? I think: *that cannot be.* I think: the
fetus feels no pain, cannot feel fear, has no *motivation.* It is merely reflex.

I point to the needle. 29

It is a reflex, says the doctor. 30

By the end of the fifth month, the fetus weighs about one pound, is about 31
twelve inches long. Hair is on the head. There are eyebrows, eyelashes. Pale
pink nipples show on the chest. Nails are present, at the fingertips, at the
toes.

At the beginning of the sixth month, the fetus can cry, can suck, can 32
make a fist. He kicks, he punches. The mother can feel this, can *see* this. His
eyelids, until now closed, can open. He may look up, down, sideways. His
grip is very strong. He could support his weight by holding with one hand.

A reflex, the doctor says. 33

I hear him. But I saw something. I saw *something* in that mass of cells 34
understand that it must bob and butt. And I see it again! I have an impulse
to shove to the table — it is just a step — seize that needle, pull it out.

We are not six, I think. I think we are *seven.* 35

Something strangles *there.* An effort, its effort, binds me to it. 36

I do not shove to the table. I take no little step. It would be . . . well, 37
madness. Everyone here wants the needle where it is. Six do. No, *five* do.

I close my eyes. I see the inside of the uterus. It is bathed in ruby gloom. I 38
see the creature curled upon itself. Its knees are flexed. Its head is bent
upon its chest. It is in fluid and gently rocks to the rhythm of the distant
heartbeat.

It resembles . . . a sleeping infant. 39

Its place is entered by something. It is sudden. A point coming. A 40
needle!

A spike of *daylight* pierces the chamber. Now the light is extinguished. 41
The needle comes closer in the pool. The point grazes the thigh, and I stir.
Perhaps I wake from dozing. The light is there again. I twist and straighten.
My arms and legs *push.* My hand finds the shaft — grabs! I *grab.* I bend the
needle this way and that. The point probes, touches on my belly. My mouth
opens. Could I cry out? All is a commotion and a churning. There is a presence in the pool. An activity! The pool colors, reddens, darkens.

I open my eyes to see the doctor feeding a small plastic tube through the 42
barrel of the needle into the uterus. Drops of pink fluid overrun the rim and
spill onto the sheet. He withdraws the needle from around the plastic tubing. Now only the little tube protrudes from the woman's body. A nurse
hands the physician a syringe loaded with a colorless liquid. He attaches it to
the end of the tubing and injects it.

 Prostaglandin, he says. 43

 Ah, well, prostaglandin — a substance found normally in the body. 44
When given in concentrated dosage, it throws the uterus into vigorous contraction. In eight to twelve hours, the woman will expel the fetus.

 The doctor detaches the syringe but does not remove the tubing. 45

 In case we must do it over, he says. 46

 He takes away the sheet. He places gauze pads over the tubing. Over 47
all this he applies adhesive tape.

I know. We cannot feed the great numbers. There is no more room. I know, 48
I know. It is woman's right to refuse the risk, to decline the pain of childbirth. And an unwanted child is a very great burden. An unwanted child is a
burden to himself. I know.

 And yet . . . there is the flick of that needle. I *saw* it. I saw . . . I 49
felt — in that room, a pace away, life prodded, life fending off, I saw life
avulsed — swept by flood, blackening — then *out.*

There, says the doctor. It's all over. It wasn't too bad, was it? he says to the 50
woman.

 She smiles. It is all over. Oh, yes. 51

 And who would care to imagine that from a moist and dark commence- 52
ment six months before there would ripen the cluster and globule, the
sprout and pouch of man?

 And who would care to imagine that trapped within the laked pearl and 53
a dowry of yolk would lie the earliest stuff of dream and memory?

 It is a persona carried here as well as person, I think. I think it is a 54
signed piece, engraved with a hieroglyph of human genes.

 I did not think this until I saw. The flick. The fending off. 55

We leave the room, the three of us, the doctors. 56

 "Routine procedure," the chief surgeon says. 57

 "All right," I say. 58

 "Scrub nurse says first time you've seen one, Dick. First look at a 59
purge," the surgeon says.

"That's right," I say. "First look." 60

"Oh, well," he says, "I guess you've seen everything else." 61

"Pretty much," I say. 62

"I'm not prying, Doctor," he says, "but was there something on your 63
mind? I'd be delighted to field any questions. . ."

"No," I say. "No, thanks. Just simple curiosity." 64

"Okay," he says, and we all shake hands, scrub, change, and go to our 65
calls.

I know, I know. The thing is normally done at sixteen weeks. Well, I've seen 66
it performed at that stage, too. And seen . . . the flick. But I also know that
in the sovereign state of my residence it is hospital policy to warrant the
procedure at twenty-four weeks. And that in the great state that is adjacent,
policy is enlarged to twenty-eight weeks.

Does this sound like argument? I hope not. I am not trying to argue. I 67
am only saying I've *seen*. The flick. Whatever else may be said in abortion's
defense, the vision of that other defense will not vanish from my eyes.

What I saw I saw as that: a *defense*, a motion *from*, an effort *away*. And 68
it has happened that you cannot reason with me now. For what can language
do against the truth of what I saw?

SUBJECT QUESTIONS

1. Do you think Selzer changed his mind as a result of what he saw at
   the abortion? What was the only sight which surprised him?
2. Selzer emphasizes what a fetus is capable of at five or six months.
   Would his argument be invalid if the fetus were in a much earlier
   stage of development?
3. Do you think a report of this sort is likely to cause a reader to change
   his mind about abortions? Would it influence a reader who was un-
   decided?
4. Can you tell from this report anything about the attitude of the doctor performing the operation? Has Selzer painted a sinister picture of
   him? What about the patient?
5. What arguments does Selzer admit in favor of abortions? Does he
   reject them as illogical?

STRUCTURE QUESTIONS

1. What is the point of Selzer's autobiographical sketch at the beginning? Does it influence the reader's attitude toward Selzer's version
   of the abortion? Why does he work in the unpleasant "outpourings
   of disease" in the second sentence?

2. The aim of argument should be to encourage discussion, not to silence it. Is Selzer's essay aimed in the right direction? Does he leave the reader with the impression that he himself is open to reason?
3. Selzer says near the end that he is "not trying to argue." If the essay is in fact an argument, why would Selzer make this disclaimer?
4. Selzer readily summarizes the arguments against his own position. How does he refute them?
5. Criticize the paragraph construction in this essay. Does it seem more appropriate to fiction or expository prose? Why?
6. Discuss Selzer's use of descriptive detail. Does it accomplish its aim?
7. Examine the final paragraph. Is Selzer equating reason with language?

SUGGESTION FOR WRITING

Present your own view on the question of legalized abortion. Try to keep your paper in the realm of argument rather than persuasion. (For suggestions, see the introduction to this section.)

The Case Against All Forms of Government Secrecy

Ramsey Clark

William Ramsey Clark (b. 1927) graduated from the University of Texas and received his law degree from the University of Chicago. He rose through the Department of Justice to become U.S. Attorney General (1967–69). Clark now teaches criminal law at the Brooklyn Law School. As former Attorney General and as author of Crime in America *(1970), Clark is especially well qualified to write about the effectiveness of government secrecy, particularly on crime prevention. This essay was first presented as part of a colloquium on crime in America at the Center for the Study of Democratic Institutions.*

Democratic institutions are founded on assumptions, among them being the belief in the possibility of an informed public. That is why education has always been a major component in democratic theory. So, at the threshold, we see some conflict between secrecy in government and the idea of democracy. Secrecy in government deprives the public of essential information on important governmental matters.

Those who believe in the idea of freedom and in the idea of democracy also believe that the truth will set you free, that to have knowledge is to have the chance to understand, perhaps even to cope. By truth I mean actuality or objective matters capable of discovery. Secrecy in government runs counter to that.

I have come to the conclusion — I came to it some time back — that there should be no acceptance of secrecy in government, that the risks of secrecy in government far exceed any possible benefits. I recently discussed this on a forum at the New School for Social Research with William Colby, Daniel Schorr, and James Wechsler. I found myself a minority of one on the subject. But my experience and my reading tell me that secrecy in government has always been very dangerous. It usually involves the need, or the desire, of authority to deceive the citizens whom it serves.

When you think of things like our bombing in Cambodia, for instance, it must be fairly clear that the Cambodians were aware that they were being bombed by us, and that anyone they could communicate with knew of it if the Cambodians chose to inform them. So, the principal peo-

Reprinted with permission from *The Center Magazine*, a publication of the Robert Maynard Hutchins Center for the Study of Democratic Institutions, Santa Barbara, California.

ple who might not know would be our own people. Take another example, the My Lai massacre. Do we really believe that society is better served by secrecy on such matters? . . .

Many might consider that the ultimate need for secrecy is to be found in the making of the atomic bomb. I think the case can be made, both in principle and in practicality, for those who see it differently, for those who say that had there not been secrecy surrounding the atomic bomb, we would have been much better off. We believed that, somehow or other, we could keep the atomic secret. We killed the Rosenbergs to prove that. Today eight or ten countries have the bomb. Many people believe that, by the year 2000, twenty-five countries will have it.

Bernard Baruch — who is not a favorite of mine — suggested a pooling of atomic knowledge in late 1945. He worked hard for that. While we had the monopoly on atomic knowledge, there was a real potential for what Baruch was proposing. Certainly subsequent history indicates that it would have been far wiser for us to have shared our information. How much of the arms race was necessitated by our policy? What do you do in a world of fear and uncertainty if you think that the people you fear and call your enemy have weapons that can destroy you? You try to find out what they have, and you get the same thing and, if possible, something better for yourself. The arms race follows.

The perils of secrecy are several. Each is serious. Usually the first one we think of is cover-up.

It is appalling to realize that millions in this country are not sure, while millions of others believe, that we, by the deliberate acts of our agents — and since ours is a democratic society, theoretically we share in the responsibility — planned, assisted, or condoned assassinations of foreign leaders. Yet we cannot really find out the truth of the matter. I attended the first press conference that Mrs. Salvador Allende had in this country. She is a shy, private person. She talked for a little while in Spanish. The American reporters paid little attention to the translation. They waited for the questions. The first question was: "Mrs. Allende, did the Central Intelligence Agency murder your husband?" The meaning of that question is, to me, still staggering. First, common sense would tell you that the widow would be the last to know the answer, or be able to judge. Second, here in a free society with our free press, we have to wait until the widow of a political leader comes to our country in order to find out whether our agents killed her husband. . . .

Secrecy becomes a dominant factor in government; it corrupts; it can terribly mislead all who are involved with it; and I think it can destroy the institution that relies on it. So, I have come to the conclusion that the government should have no right to privacy or secrecy.

Of course, some areas require examination. One of the things that

William Colby said in our forum at the New School was, "Well, we have a lot of secrecy in our society. For instance, democracy begins with a secret ballot, and isn't that imperative to democratic government?"

Of course, the obvious answer to that is that the secret is not the 11 government's, it is the individual voter's. What a terrible distortion to turn that around! It is the individual voter who has a right to say how he or she voted. The government has no right to try to discover how he or she voted, or to tell others how he or she voted. People's right to privacy is their right, not the government's. Where a person's life might be endangered by disclosure of certain information about him, if that individual chooses to permit the information to be divulged, it can be divulged. But it is not the government's right to make that decision.

For many, the more difficult exception in favor of non-disclosure, is a 12 criminal investigation during its processing. Obviously, there is such a thing as organized crime. These people have lots of money, and if they could come by and ask the government, at every step of the way, "What are you doing in this case; what is the status of your investigation?," it would be a little difficult to enforce the law. My answer is that if you had principled law, then investigation and information-gathering by agencies that have enforcement or criminal investigative responsibilities would be limited strictly to those situations where there is probable cause to believe that a crime has been committed. But there would be no power or authority in either the Federal Bureau of Investigation or the C.I.A., under this sort of law, to gather general information and to develop dossiers on people.

I was recently with Thomas Emerson, the retired professor of law at 13 Yale University, when he received the dossier the F.B.I. had compiled on him. It weighed ten pounds and ran to 1,500 pages, and it was rather sad. Here is a splendid man, a highly principled man. There was an allegation in his dossier that he had been a student leader in Communist campus activities at the University of Washington. He said he had never been in the Pacific Northwest in his life.

The agents gave the number of the stateroom in which he sailed to 14 England in 1939; he had long since forgotten whether he had even had a stateroom. The amount of money that must have been spent over the years on the surveillance of Tom Emerson is just staggering. He made a speech in Denver once, and the agents, noting that they would not attend a speaking engagement by such a person, said they would have to hire informants, and that this would be costly. There followed a transcript of Emerson's speech. There were several notations in his dossier where it looked like there had been breaking and entering. He had forgotten that he had once lost his address book; he discovered in his dossier that the F.B.I. had his address book. He didn't say the F.B.I. stole it from him. How does he know whether they stole it or whether he dropped it and they picked it up? Apparently they were following him wherever he went.

But the F.B.I. agents spent tens of thousands, probably hundreds of 15 thousands, of dollars over decades, gathering information on an individual who from the standpoint of reason, intelligence, and gentleness, probably represents among the best we have in our country.

I think we need a prohibition of secrecy in government. The Free- 16 dom of Information Act was a very modest beginning. It became law on a happy day, the Fourth of July, 1967. But it has nine major exceptions. The first exception, as you can well guess, is a national-security exception. Another exception is based on the need for confidentiality in decision-making processes. The argument is that unless those processes are secret, people will not be candid, they will not really say what they think.

We are deeply conditioned to secrecy, whether it is in a zoning com- 17 mission meeting or a Supreme Court conference. But if we really want to have democratic institutions, an informed public, and the chance to learn the truth — not to mention survival — we had better start working awfully hard toward the abolition of secrecy in government, and, in Justice Hugo Black's phrase, not be afraid to be free.

SUBJECT QUESTIONS

1. Most of us have been conditioned, with Ramsey Clark, to believe that "the truth will set you free." Will it? Are there some truths (like the My Lai massacre in Viet Nam) that people would rather not know?
2. Does it seem unusual that an Attorney General would argue against government secrecy? For what kinds of secrecy do public prosecutors usually argue?
3. If Clark is correct in his judgment that we encouraged the cold war by keeping secret our knowledge of atomic energy, is this a mistake which cannot now be rectified?
4. Clark believes that secrecy "can destroy the institution that relies on it," but he provides no examples. Can you think of any? Is the CIA a candidate for self-destruction?
5. What is the point of the long story about Professor Thomas Emerson? Was secret surveillance "harmful" in this case?
6. What does Clark think was wrong with the Freedom of Information Act? Why might a zoning commission, for instance, not want to be candid if their discussions were open to the public?

STRUCTURE QUESTIONS

1. One might expect a former Attorney General to write in a style reminiscent of legal documents; do you find in this essay any traces of professional jargon?
2. Clark's position for this argument is stated in paragraph 3; why does he begin with two paragraphs of generalization? Is he arguing from a position presumed to be self-evident?
3. Does Clark spend more time on confirmation of his own view or on refutation of opposing views? Has he made the right decision in this matter? The My Lai massacre is mentioned only briefly, yet it seems more significant than the fully described spying on Professor Emerson. Can the disparity in the amount of attention given to these two occurrences be justified?
4. Are the implications of Clark's concluding statement, that we must "not be afraid to be free," made clear in the course of the essay? Should he have expanded on his meaning here? Is he attempting to stimulate thought, or to end it?
5. Does Clark maintain the objective attitude of proper argument? How can you tell that he cares deeply about his subject?
6. One weakness in this essay may be in the devices for coherence — transitions between ideas. Examine Clark's transitional devices, especially his use of "so" and "of course."

SUGGESTIONS FOR WRITING

1. Write an argument for abolishing (or retaining) the CIA. You may need to do some library research on the functions and activities of the CIA.
2. If there is an area of government activity in which you believe secrecy should (or should not) be maintained, write an argument supporting your position. Remember that your task is to open up discussion, not to close it off.

Politics and the English Language

George Orwell

George Orwell (1903–1950) is best known for his political novels, Animal Farm *(1946) and* 1984 *(1949), both concerned with the effects of political organization on the individual citizen. Orwell was born Eric Blair in India, while his father was in the British civil service. After finishing his schooling at Eton, Orwell himself served five years in Burma with the Imperial Police, finally quitting in disgust at the effects of imperialism on human freedom and dignity. The following essay was written shortly after World War II. While some of the historical references and examples are outdated, the essay has rightly become a classic, and Orwell's argument seems as pertinent today as when he composed it.*

Most people who bother with the matter at all would admit that the English language is in a bad way, but it is generally assumed that we cannot by conscious action do anything about it. Our civilization is decadent and our language — so the argument runs — must inevitably share in the general collapse. It follows that any struggle against the abuse of language is a sentimental archaism, like preferring candles to electric light or hansom cabs to aeroplanes. Underneath this lies the half-conscious belief that language is a natural growth and not an instrument which we shape for our own purposes.

Now, it is clear that the decline of a language must ultimately have political and economic causes: It is not due simply to the bad influence of this or that individual writer. But an effect can become a cause, reinforcing the original cause and producing the same effect in an intensified form, and so on indefinitely. A man may take to drink because he feels himself to be a failure, and then fail all the more completely because he drinks. It is rather the same thing that is happening to the English language. It becomes ugly and inaccurate because our thoughts are foolish, but the slovenliness of our language makes it easier for us to have foolish thoughts. The point is that the process is reversible. Modern English, especially written English, is full of bad habits which spread by imitation and which can be avoided if one is willing to take the necessary trouble. If one gets rid of these habits one can think more clearly, and to think clearly is a necessary first step towards polit-

From *Shooting an Elephant and Other Essays* by George Orwell. Copyright 1945, 1946, 1949, 1950 by Sonia Brownell Orwell; copyright 1973, 1974 by Sonia Orwell. Reprinted by permission of Harcourt Brace Jovanovich, Inc., Mrs. Sonia Brownell Orwell, and Martin Secker & Warburg.

ical regeneration: so that the fight against bad English is not frivolous and is not the exclusive concern of professional writers. I will come back to this presently, and I hope that by that time the meaning of what I have said here will have become clearer. Meanwhile, here are five specimens of the English language as it is now habitually written.

These five passages have not been picked out because they are especially bad — I could have quoted far worse if I had chosen — but because they illustrate various of the mental vices from which we now suffer. They are a little below the average, but are fairly representative samples. I number them so that I can refer back to them when necessary:

(1) I am not, indeed, sure whether it is not true to say that the Milton who once seemed not unlike a seventeenth-century Shelley had not become, out of an experience ever more bitter in each year, more alien [sic] to the founder of that Jesuit sect which nothing could induce him to tolerate.   Professor Harold Laski
(Essay in *Freedom of Expression*)

(2) Above all, we cannot play ducks and drakes with a native battery of idioms which prescribes such egregious collocations of vocables as the Basic *put up with* for *tolerate* or *put at a loss* for *bewilder*.

Professor Lancelot Hogben (*Interglossa*)

(3) On the one side we have the free personality: by definition it is not neurotic, for it has neither conflict nor dream. Its desires, such as they are, are transparent, for they are just what institutional approval keeps in the forefront of consciousness; another institutional pattern would alter their number and intensity; there is little in them that is natural, irreducible, or culturally dangerous. But on the other side, the social bond itself is nothing but the mutual reflection of these self-secure integrities. Recall the definition of love. Is not this the very picture of a small academic? Where is there a place in this hall of mirrors for either personality or fraternity?

Essay on psychology in *Politics* (New York)

(4) All the "best people" from the gentlemen's clubs, and all the frantic fascist captains, united in common hatred of Socialism and bestial horror of the rising tide of the mass revolutionary movement, have turned to acts of provocation, to foul incendiarism, to medieval legends of poisoned wells, to legalize their own destruction of proletarian organizations, and rouse the agitated petty-bourgeoisie to chauvinistic fervor on behalf of the fight against the revolutionary way out of the crisis.

Communist pamphlet

(5) If a new spirit is to be infused into this old country, there is one thorny and contentious reform which must be tackled, and that is the humanization and galvanization of the B.B.C. Timidity here will bespeak canker and atrophy of the soul. The heart of Britain may be sound and of strong beat, for instance, but the British lion's roar at present is like that of Bottom in Shakespeare's Midsummer Night's Dream — as gentle as any sucking dove. A virile new Britain cannot continue indefinitely to be traduced in the eyes, or rather ears, of the world by the effete languors of Langham Place, brazenly masquerading as "standard English." When the Voice of Britain is heard at nine o'clock, better far and infinitely less ludicrous to hear aitches honestly

dropped than the present priggish, inflated, inhibited, school-ma'amish arch braying
of blameless bashful mewing maidens!

Letter in Tribune

Each of these passages has faults of its own, but, quite apart from
avoidable ugliness, two qualities are common to all of them. The first is
staleness of imagery; the other is lack of precision. The writer either has a
meaning and cannot express it, or he inadvertently says something else, or
he is almost indifferent as to whether his words mean anything or not. This
mixture of vagueness and sheer incompetence is the most marked characteristic of modern English prose, and especially of any kind of political writing.
As soon as certain topics are raised, the concrete melts into the abstract and
no one seems able to think of turns of speech that are not hackneyed; prose
consists less and less of *words* chosen for the sake of their meaning, and more
and more of *phrases* tacked together like the sections of a prefabricated hen-
house. I list below, with notes and examples, various of the tricks by means
of which the work of prose-construction is habitually dodged:

Dying metaphors. A newly invented metaphor assists thought by evoking a
visual image, while on the other hand a metaphor which is technically
"dead" (e.g. *iron resolution*) has in effect reverted to being an ordinary word
and can generally be used without loss of vividness. But in between these
two classes there is a huge dump of worn-out metaphors which have lost all
evocative power and are merely used because they save people the trouble
of inventing phrases for themselves. Examples are: *Ring the changes on, take
up the cudgels for, toe the line, ride roughshod over, stand shoulder to
shoulder with, play into the hands of, no axe to grind, grist to the mill, fishing in troubled waters, on the order of the day, Achilles' heel, swan song,
hotbed.* Many of these are used without knowledge of their meaning (what is
a "rift," for instance?), and incompatible metaphors are frequently mixed, a
sure sign that the writer is not interested in what he is saying. Some metaphors now current have been twisted out of their original meaning without
those who use them even being aware of the fact. For example, *toe the line*
is sometimes written *tow the line*. Another example is *the hammer and the
anvil*, now always used with the implication that the anvil gets the worst of
it. In real life it is always the anvil that breaks the hammer, never the other
way about: a writer who stopped to think what he was saying would be aware
of this, and would avoid perverting the original phrase.

Operators or *verbal false limbs.* These save the trouble of picking out appropriate verbs and nouns, and at the same time pad each sentence with extra
syllables which give it an appearance of symmetry. Characteristic phrases are
render inoperative, militate against, make contact with, be subjected to, give

rise to, give grounds for, have the effect of, play a leading part (role) in, make itself felt, take effect, exhibit a tendency to, serve the purpose of, etc., etc. The keynote is the elimination of simple verbs. Instead of being a single word, such as *break, stop, spoil, mend, kill,* a verb becomes a *phrase,* made up of a noun or adjective tacked on to some general-purposes verb such as *prove, serve, form, play, render.* In addition, the passive voice is wherever possible used in preference to the active, and noun constructions are used instead of gerunds (*by examination of* instead of *by examining*). The range of verbs is further cut down by means of the *-ize* and *de-* formations, and the banal statements are given an appearance of profundity by means of the *not un-* formation. Simple conjunctions and prepositions are replaced by such phrases as *with respect to, having regard to, the fact that, by dint of, in view of, in the interests of, on the hypothesis that;* and the ends of sentences are saved from anticlimax by such resounding common-places as *greatly to be desired, cannot be left out of account, a development to be expected in the near future, deserving of serious consideration, brought to a satisfactory conclusion,* and so on and so forth.

Pretentious diction. Words like *phenomenon, element, individual* (as noun), *objective, categorical, effective, virtual, basic, primary, promote, constitute, exhibit, exploit, utilize, eliminate, liquidate,* are used to dress up simple statements and give an air of scientific impartiality to biased judgments. Adjectives like *epoch-making, epic, historic, unforgettable, triumphant, age-old, inevitable, inexorable, veritable,* are used to dignify the sordid processes of international politics, while writing that aims at glorifying war usually takes on an archaic color, its characteristic words being: *realm, throne, chariot, mailed fist, trident, sword, shield, buckler, banner, jackboot, clarion.* Foreign words and expressions such as *cul de sac, ancien régime, deus ex machina, mutatis mutandis, status quo, gleichschaltung, weltanschauung,* are used to give an air of culture and elegance. Except for the useful abbreviations *i.e., e.g.,* and *etc.,* there is no real need for any of the hundreds of foreign phrases now current in English. Bad writers, and especially scientific, political and sociological writers, are nearly always haunted by the notion that Latin or Greek words are grander than Saxon ones, and unnecessary words like *expedite, ameliorate, predict, extraneous, deracinated, clandestine, subaqueous* and hundreds of others constantly gain ground from their Anglo-Saxon opposite numbers.[1] The jargon peculiar to

[1] An interesting illustration of this is the way in which the English flower names which were in use till very recently are being ousted by Greek ones, *snapdragon* becoming *antirrhinum, forget-me-not* becoming *myosotis,* etc. It is hard to see any practical reason for this change of fashion: it is probably due to an instinctive turning-away from the more homely word and a vague feeling that the Greek word is scientific. [AUTHOR'S NOTE.]

Marxist writing (*hyena, hangman, cannibal, petty bourgeois, these gentry, lacquey, flunkey, mad dog, White Guard,* etc.) consists largely of words and phrases translated from Russian, German or French; but the normal way of coining a new word is to use a Latin or Greek root with the appropriate affix and, where necessary, the *-ize* formation. It is often easier to make up words of this kind (*deregionalize, impermissible, extramarital, non-fragmentary* and so forth) than to think up the English words that will cover one's meaning. The result, in general, is an increase in slovenliness and vagueness.

Meaningless words. In certain kinds of writing, particularly in art criticism and literary criticism, it is normal to come across long passages which are almost completely lacking in meaning.[2] Words like *romantic, plastic, values, human, dead, sentimental, natural, vitality,* as used in art criticism, are strictly meaningless, in the sense that they not only do not point to any discoverable object, but are hardly ever expected to do so by the reader. When one critic writes, "The outstanding feature of Mr. X's work is its living quality," while another writes, "The immediately striking thing about Mr. X's work is its peculiar deadness," the reader accepts this as a simple difference of opinion. If words like *black* and *white* were involved, instead of the jargon words *dead* and *living,* he would see at once that language was being used in an improper way. Many political words are similarly abused. The word *Fascism* has now no meaning except in so far as it signifies "something not desirable." The words *democracy, socialism, freedom, patriotic, realistic, justice,* have each of them several different meanings which cannot be reconciled with one another. In the case of a word like *democracy,* not only is there no agreed definition, but the attempt to make one is resisted from all sides. It is almost universally felt that when we call a country democratic we are praising it; consequently the defenders of every kind of regime claim that it is a democracy, and fear that they might have to stop using the word if it were tied down to any one meaning. Words of this kind are often used in a consciously dishonest way. That is, the person who uses them has his own private definition, but allows his hearer to think he means something quite different. Statements like *Marshal Pétain was a true patriot, The Soviet Press is the freest in the world, The Catholic Church is opposed to persecution,* are almost always made with intent to deceive. Other words used in variable meanings, in most cases more or less dishonestly, are: *class, totalitarian, science, progressive, reactionary, bourgeois, equality.*

8

[2] Example: "Comfort's catholicity of perception and image, strangely Whitmanesque in range, almost the exact opposite in aesthetic compulsion, continues to evoke that trembling atmospheric accumulative hinting at a cruel, an inexorably serene timelessness. . . . Wrey Gardiner scores by aiming at simple bull's-eyes with precision. Only they are not so simple, and through this contented sadness runs more than the surface bitter-sweet of resignation" (Poetry Quarterly). [AUTHOR'S NOTE.]

Now that I have made this catalogue of swindles and perversions, let　9
me give another example of the kind of writing that they lead to. This time it
must of its nature be an imaginary one. I am going to translate a passage of
good English into modern English of the worst sort. Here is a well-known
verse from *Ecclesiastes:*

"I returned and saw under the sun, that the race is not to the swift, nor　10
the battle to the strong, neither yet bread to the wise, nor yet riches to men
of understanding, nor yet favour to men of skill; but time and chance hap-
peneth to them all."

Here it is in modern English:　11

"Objective consideration of contemporary phenomena compels the　12
conclusion that success or failure in competitive activities exhibits no tendency to be commensurate with innate capacity, but that a considerable element of the unpredictable must invariably be taken into account."

This is a parody, but not a very gross one. Exhibit (3), above, for in-　13
stance, contains several patches of the same kind of English. It will be seen
that I have not made a full translation. The beginning and ending of the sentence follow the original meaning fairly closely, but in the middle the concrete illustrations — race, battle, bread — dissolve into the vague phrase
"success or failure in competitive activities." This had to be so, because no
modern writer of the kind I am discussing — no one capable of using
phrases like "objective consideration of contemporary phenomena" — would
ever tabulate his thoughts in that precise and detailed way. The whole tendency of modern prose is away from concreteness. Now analyse these two
sentences a little more closely. The first contains forty-nine words but only
sixty syllables, and all its words are those of everyday life. The second contains thirty-eight words of ninety syllables: eighteen of its words are from
Latin roots, and one from Greek. The first sentence contains six vivid
images, and only one phrase ("time and chance") that could be called vague.
The second contains not a single fresh, arresting phrase, and in spite of its
ninety syllables it gives only a shortened version of the meaning contained in
the first. Yet without a doubt it is the second kind of sentence that is gaining
ground in modern English. I do not want to exaggerate. This kind of writing
is not yet universal, and outcrops of simplicity will occur here and there in
the worst-written page. Still, if you or I were told to write a few lines on the
uncertainty of human fortunes, we should probably come much nearer to my
imaginary sentence than to the one from *Ecclesiastes.*

As I have tried to show, modern writing at its worst does not consist in　14
picking out words for the sake of their meaning and inventing images in
order to make the meaning clearer. It consists in gumming together long
strips of words which have already been set in order by someone else, and
making the results presentable by sheer humbug. The attraction of this way
of writing is that it is easy. It is easier — even quicker, once you have the

habit — to say *In my opinion it is not an unjustifiable assumption that* than to say *I think*. If you use ready-made phrases, you not only don't have to hunt about for words; you also don't have to bother with the rhythms of your sentences, since these phrases are generally so arranged as to be more or less euphonious. When you are composing in a hurry — when you are dictating to a stenographer, for instance, or making a public speech — it is natural to fall into a pretentious, Latinized style. Tags like *a consideration which we should do well to bear in mind* or *a conclusion to which all of us would readily assent* will save many a sentence from coming down with a bump. By using stale metaphors, similes and idioms, you save much mental effort, at the cost of leaving your meaning vague, not only for your reader but for yourself. This is the significance of mixed metaphors. The sole aim of a metaphor is to call up a visual image. When these images clash — as in *The Fascist octopus has sung its swan song, the jackboot is thrown into the melting pot* — it can be taken as certain that the writer is not seeing a mental image of the objects he is naming; in other words he is not really thinking. Look again at the examples I gave at the beginning of this essay. Professor Laski (1) uses five negatives in fifty-three words. One of these is superfluous, making nonsense of the whole passage, and in addition there is the slip *alien* for *akin*, making further nonsense, and several avoidable pieces of clumsiness which increase the general vagueness. Professor Hogben (2) plays ducks and drakes with a battery which is able to write prescriptions, and, while disapproving of the everyday phrase *put up with,* is unwilling to look *egregious* up in the dictionary and see what it means; (3), if one takes an uncharitable attitude towards it, is simply meaningless: probably one could work out its intended meaning by reading the whole of the article in which it occurs. In (4), the writer knows more or less what he wants to say, but an accumulation of stale phrases chokes him like tea leaves blocking a sink. In (5), words and meaning have almost parted company. People who write in this manner usually have a general emotional meaning — they dislike one thing and want to express solidarity with another — but they are not interested in the detail of what they are saying. A scrupulous writer, in every sentence that he writes, will ask himself at least four questions, thus: What am I trying to say? What words will express it? What image or idiom will make it clearer? Is this image fresh enough to have an effect? And he will probably ask himself two more: Could I put it more shortly? Have I said anything that is avoidably ugly? But you are not obliged to go to all this trouble. You can shirk it by simply throwing your mind open and letting the ready-made phrases come crowding in. They will construct your sentences for you — even think your thoughts for you, to a certain extent — and at need they will perform the important service of partially concealing your meaning even from yourself. It is at this point that the special connection between politics and the debasement of language becomes clear.

In our time it is broadly true that political writing is bad writing.   15
Where it is not true, it will generally be found that the writer is some kind of
rebel, expressing his private opinions and not a "party line." Orthodoxy, of
whatever color, seems to demand a lifeless, imitative style. The political
dialects to be found in pamphlets, leading articles, manifestos, White Papers
and the speeches of under-secretaries do, of course, vary from party to party,
but they are all alike in that one almost never finds in them a fresh, vivid,
home-made turn of speech. When one watches some tired hack on the platform mechanically repeating the familiar phrases — *bestial atrocities, iron
heel, bloodstained tyranny, free peoples of the world, stand shoulder to
shoulder* — one often has a curious feeling that one is not watching a live
human being but some kind of dummy: a feeling which suddenly becomes
stronger at moments when the light catches the speaker's spectacles and
turns them into blank discs which seem to have no eyes behind them. And
this is not altogether fanciful. A speaker who uses that kind of phraseology
has gone some distance towards turning himself into a machine. The appropriate noises are coming out of his larynx, but his brain is not involved as it
would be if he were choosing his words for himself. If the speech he is making is one that he is accustomed to make over and over again, he may be almost unconscious of what he is saying, as one is when one utters the responses in church. And this reduced state of consciousness, if not
indispensable, is at any rate favorable to political conformity.

In our time, political speech and writing are largely the defence of the   16
indefensible. Things like the continuance of British rule in India, the Russian
purges and deportations, the dropping of the atom bombs on Japan, can
indeed be defended, but only by arguments which are too brutal for most
people to face, and which do not square with the professed aims of political
parties. Thus political language has to consist largely of euphemism, ques-
tion-begging and sheer cloudy vagueness. Defenceless villages are bombarded from the air, the inhabitants driven out into the countryside, the
cattle machine-gunned, the huts set on fire with incendiary bullets: this is
called *pacification*. Millions of peasants are robbed of their farms and sent
trudging along the roads with no more than they can carry: this is called
transfer of population or *rectification of frontiers*. People are imprisoned for
years without trial, or shot in the back of the neck or sent to die of scurvy in
Arctic lumber camps: this is called *elimination of unreliable elements*. Such
phraseology is needed if one wants to name things without calling up mental
pictures of them. Consider for instance some comfortable English professor
defending Russian totalitarianism. He cannot say outright, "I believe in killing off your opponents when you can get good results by doing so." Probably, therefore, he will say something like this:

"While freely conceding that the Soviet régime exhibits certain features   17
which the humanitarian may be inclined to deplore, we must, I think, agree
that a certain curtailment of the right to political opposition is an unavoidable

concomitant of transitional periods, and that the rigors which the Russian people have been called upon to undergo have been amply justified in the sphere of concrete achievement."

The inflated style is itself a kind of euphemism. A mass of Latin words falls upon the facts like soft snow, blurring the outlines and covering up all the details. The great enemy of clear language is insincerity. When there is a gap between one's real and one's declared aims, one turns as it were instinctively to long words and exhausted idioms, like a cuttlefish squirting out ink. In our age there is no such thing as "keeping out of politics." All issues are political issues, and politics itself is a mass of lies, evasions, folly, hatred and schizophrenia. When the general atmosphere is bad, language must suffer. I should expect to find — this is a guess which I have no sufficient knowledge to verify — that the German, Russian and Italian languages have all deteriorated in the last ten or fifteen years, as a result of dictatorship. 18

But if thought corrupts language, language can also corrupt thought. A bad usage can spread by tradition and imitation, even among people who should and do know better. The debased language that I have been discussing is in some ways very convenient. Phrases like *a not unjustifiable assumption, leaves much to be desired, would serve no good purpose, a consideration which we should do well to bear in mind,* are a continuous temptation, a packet of aspirins always at one's elbow. Look back through this essay, and for certain you will find that I have again and again committed the very faults I am protesting against. By this morning's post I have received a pamphlet dealing with conditions in Germany. The author tells me that he "felt impelled" to write it. I open it at random, and here is almost the first sentence that I see: "[The Allies] have an opportunity not only of achieving a radical transformation of Germany's social and political structure in such a way as to avoid a nationalistic reaction in Germany itself, but at the same time of laying the foundations of a co-operative and unified Europe." You see, he "feels impelled" to write — feels, presumably, that he has something new to say — and yet his words, like cavalry horses answering the bugle, group themselves automatically into the familiar dreary pattern. This invasion of one's mind by ready-made phrases *(lay the foundations, achieve a radical transformation)* can only be prevented if one is constantly on guard against them, and every such phrase anaesthetizes a portion of one's brain. 19

I said earlier that the decadence of our language is probably curable. Those who deny this would argue, if they produced an argument at all, that language merely reflects existing social conditions, and that we cannot influence its development by any direct tinkering with words and constructions. So far as the general tone or spirit of a language goes, this may be true, but it is not true in detail. Silly words and expressions have often disappeared, not through any evolutionary process but owing to the conscious action of a minority. Two recent examples were *explore every avenue* and *leave no stone unturned,* which were killed by the jeers of a few journalists. There is a long 20 list of flyblown metaphors which could similarly be got rid of if enough people would interest themselves in the job; and it should also be possible to laugh the *not un-* formation out of existence,[3] to reduce the amount of Latin and Greek in the average sentence, to drive out foreign phrases and strayed scientific words, and, in general to make pretentiousness unfashionable. But all these are minor points. The defence of the English language implies more than this, and perhaps it is best to start by saying what it does *not* imply.

To begin with it has nothing to do with archaism, with the salvaging of obsolete words and turns of speech, or with the setting up of a "standard English" which must never be departed from. On the contrary, it is especially concerned with the scrapping of every word or idiom which has outworn its usefulness. It has nothing to do with correct grammar and syntax, which are of no importance so long as one makes one's meaning clear, or with the avoidance of Americanisms, or with having what is called a "good prose style." On the other hand it is not concerned with fake simplicity and the attempt to make written English colloquial. Nor does it even imply in every case preferring the Saxon word to the Latin one, though it does imply using the fewest and shortest words that will cover one's meaning. What is above all needed is to let the meaning choose the word, and not the other way about. In prose, the worst thing one can do with words is to surrender to them. When you think of a concrete object, you think wordlessly, and then, if you want to describe the thing you have been visualizing you probably hunt about till you find the exact words that seem to fit it. When you think of something abstract you are more inclined to use words from the start, and unless you make a conscious effort to prevent it, the existing dialect will come rushing in and do the job for you, at the expense of blurring or even changing your meaning. Probably it is better to put off using words as long as possible and get one's meaning as clear as one can through pictures or sensations. Afterwards one can choose — not simply *accept* — the phrases that will best cover the meaning, and then switch round and decide what impression one's words are likely to make on another person. This last effort of the mind cuts out all stale or mixed images, all prefabricated phrases, needless repetitions, and humbug and vagueness generally. But one can often be in doubt about the effect of a word or a phrase, and one needs rules that one can rely on when instinct fails. I think the following rules will cover most cases:

(i) Never use a metaphor, simile or other figure of speech which you are used to seeing in print.
(ii) Never use a long word where a short one will do.
(iii) If it is possible to cut a word out, always cut it out.
(iv) Never use the passive where you can use the active.

[3] One can cure oneself of the *not un-* formation by memorizing this sentence: *A not unblack dog was chasing a not unsmall rabbit across a not ungreen field.* [AUTHOR'S NOTE.]

(v) Never use a foreign phrase, a scientific word or a jargon word if you can think of an everyday English equivalent.

(vi) Break any of these rules sooner than say anything outright barbarous.

These rules sound elementary, and so they are, but they demand a deep change of attitude in anyone who has grown used to writing in the style now fashionable. One could keep all of them and still write bad English, but one could not write the kind of stuff that I quoted in those five specimens at the beginning of this article.

I have not here been considering the literary use of language, but merely language as an instrument for expressing and not for concealing or preventing thought. Stuart Chase and others have come near to claiming that all abstract words are meaningless, and have used this as a pretext for advocating a kind of political quietism. Since you don't know what Fascism is, how can you struggle against Fascism? One need not swallow such absurdities as this, but one ought to recognize that the present political chaos is connected with the decay of language, and that one can probably bring about some improvement by starting at the verbal end. If you simplify your English, you are freed from the worst follies of orthodoxy. You cannot speak any of the necessary dialects, and when you make a stupid remark its stupidity will be obvious, even to yourself. Political language — and with variations this is true of all political parties, from Conservatives to Anarchists — is designed to make lies sound truthful and murder respectable, and to give an appearance of solidity to pure wind. One cannot change this all in a moment, but one can at least change one's own habits and from time to time one can even, if one jeers loudly enough, send some worn-out and useless phrase — some *jackboot, Achilles' heel, hotbed, melting pot, acid test, veritable inferno* or other lump of verbal refuse — into the dustbin where it belongs.

SUBJECT QUESTIONS

1. Orwell says the decline of the language "must ultimately have political and economic causes." Does he need to prove that statement or is it self-evident? Can you think of other possible causes?

2. Does Orwell make clear how "an effect can become a cause" in the case of the English language?

3. Orwell does not analyze in depth the five passages he quotes. What is wrong with each? Orwell points out two faults that they all have in common. Do these particular faults relate to his concern with the language of politics?

4. This essay was written just after World II. Has political language become less stale and more precise since then? If possible, examine a paragraph from a recent political speech.

5. Orwell explains in paragraph 16 why political language is intention-

ally vague and misleading. What would happen if it were deliberately clear and honest?

6. How does Orwell propose to cure the problem with which he is concerned? Does he seem overly optimistic about his solution?

STRUCTURE QUESTIONS

1. After the two opening paragraphs, Orwell does not return to the subject of politics until paragraph 15. What has he accomplished in the meantime? Is it an essential part of his argument?
2. Locate the "refutation" portion of Orwell's argument. Why does he place it where it is? He virtually repeats the opponent's objection in paragraph 21. Is there a structural flaw in the essay at this point?
3. Since Orwell is concerned with the mutual interaction of corrupt language and corrupt politics, should his five quotations all have been examples of bad political writing? Or are they? Why does he quote only from a Communist pamphlet instead of liberal or conservative or middle-of-the-road ones? Would such quotes at this point in the essay have altered the writer's relationship with the reader? (You might consider that this essay was written just after World War II.)
4. The six rules Orwell provides near the end might help the individual reader improve his own language. Does Orwell make clear how such improvement would have any effect on politicians' language? Has he let his solution go off in two different directions?
5. Orwell spends much more of his time with the nature of the problem than does the usual argument. Is his decision to do so justified by the nature of the argument?
6. In paragraph 19, Orwell says, "Look back through this essay, and for certain you will find that I have again and again committed the very faults I have been protesting against." Has he done so? If he has, what does the admission accomplish? (One would expect a writer on this subject to be especially careful to avoid the very faults he condemns.) If you do not find many, what might be Orwell's purpose in inviting the reader to look for them?

SUGGESTIONS FOR WRITING

1. Write an argument for (or against) clarity and honesty in political speech-making and writing. You may need to limit yourself to one political issue (nuclear generators, or arms limitation agreements, for instance), and you will probably want to consider the effects of honest pronouncements — on American citizens and on international relations.
2. Write an argument for clearer and simpler terminology in one of the college courses you are taking.

On the Duty of Civil Disobedience

Henry David Thoreau

Henry David Thoreau (1817–1862) was an author and philosopher. Although he published only two books in his lifetime, his edited manuscripts run to twenty volumes. "On the Duty of Civil Disobedience" was published in 1849, just after Mexico had been forced to give up Texas and just before passage of the Second Fugitive Slave Law. Daniel Webster had spoken in favor of the measure, much to Thoreau's disappointment.

I heartily accept the motto — "That government is best which governs least"; and I should like to see it acted up to more rapidly and systematically. Carried out, it finally amounts to this, which also I believe, — "That government is best which governs not at all"; and when men are prepared for it, that will be the kind of government which they will have. Government is at best but an expedient; but most governments are usually, and all governments are sometimes, inexpedient. The objections which have been brought against a standing army, and they are many and weighty, and deserve to prevail, may also at last be brought against a standing government. The standing army is only an arm of the standing government. The government itself, which is only the mode which the people have chosen to execute their will, is equally liable to be abused and perverted before the people can act through it. Witness the present Mexican war, the work of comparatively a few individuals using the standing government as their tool; for, in the outset, the people would not have consented to this measure.

This American government — what is it but a tradition, though a recent one, endeavoring to transmit itself unimpaired to posterity, but each instant losing some of its integrity? It has not the vitality and force of a single living man; for a single man can bend it to his will. It is a sort of wooden gun to the people themselves. But it is not the less necessary for this; for the people must have some complicated machinery or other, and hear its din, to satisfy that idea of government which they have. Governments show us how successfully men can be imposed on, even impose on themselves, for their own advantage. It is excellent, we must all allow. Yet this government never of itself furthered any enterprise, but by the alacrity with which it got out of its way. *It* does not keep the country free. *It* does not settle the West. *It* does not educate. The character inherent in the American people has done all that has been accomplished; and it would have done somewhat more, if the government had not sometimes got in its way. For government is an expedient by which men would fain succeed in letting one another alone; and, as has been said, when it is most expedient, the governed are most let alone by it. Trade and commerce, if they were not made of India-rubber, would never manage to bounce over the obstacles which legislators are continually putting in their way; and, if one were to judge these men wholly by the effects of their actions and not partly by their intentions, they would deserve to be classed and punished with those mischievous persons who put obstructions on the railroads.

But, to speak practically and as a citizen, unlike those who call them-   3
selves no-government men, I ask for, not at once no government, but *at once* a better government. Let every man make known what kind of government would command his respect, and that will be one step toward obtaining it.

After all, the practical reason why, when the power is once in the   4
hands of the people, a majority are permitted, and for a long period continue, to rule is not because they are most likely to be in the right, nor because this seems fairest to the minority, but because they are physically the strongest. But a government in which the majority rule in all cases cannot be based on justice, even as far as men understand it. Can there not be a government in which majorities do not virtually decide right and wrong, but conscience — in which majorities decide only those questions to which the rule of expediency is applicable? Must the citizen ever for a moment, or in the last degree, resign his conscience to the legislator? Why has every man a conscience, then? I think that we should be men first, and subjects afterward. It is not desirable to cultivate a respect for the law, so much as for the right. The only obligation which I have a right to assume is to do at any time what I think right. It is truly enough said, that a corporation has no conscience; but a corporation of conscientious men is a corporation *with* a conscience. Law never made men a whit more just; and, by means of their respect for it, even the well-disposed are daily made the agents of injustice. A common and natural result of an undue respect for law is, that you may see a file of soldiers, colonel, captain, corporal, privates, powder-monkeys, and all, marching in admirable order over hill and dale to the war, against their will, ay, against their common sense and consciences, which makes it very steep marching indeed, and produces a palpitation of the heart. They have no doubt that it is a damnable business in which they are concerned; they are all peaceably inclined. Now, what are they? Men at all? or small movable forts and magazines, at the service of some unscrupulous man in power? Visit the Navy-Yard, and behold a marine, such a man as an American government can make, or such as it can make a man with its black arts — a mere shadow and reminiscence of humanity, a man laid out alive and standing, and already, as one may say, buried under arms with funeral accompaniments, though it may be, —

> Not a drum was heard, not a funeral note,
>> As his corpse to the rampart we hurried;
> Not a soldier discharged his farewell shot
>> O'er the grave where our hero we buried.

The mass of men serve the state thus, not as men mainly, but as 5
machines, with their bodies. They are the standing army, and the militia,
jailors, constables, posse comitatus, etc. In most cases there is no free exercise whatever of the judgment or of the moral sense; but they put themselves on a level with wood and earth and stones; and wooden men can
perhaps be manufactured that will serve the purpose as well. Such command
no more respect than men of straw or a lump of dirt. They have the same
sort of worth only as horses and dogs. Yet such as these even are commonly
esteemed good citizens. Others — as most legislators, politicans, lawyers,
ministers, and office-holders — serve the state chiefly with their heads: and,
as they rarely make any moral distinctions, they are as likely to serve the
Devil, without *intending* it, as God. A very few, as heroes, patriots, martyrs,
reformers in the great sense, and *men,* serve the state with their consciences
also, and so necessarily resist it for the most part; and they are commonly
treated as enemies by it. A wise man will only be useful as a man, and will
not submit to be "clay," and "stop a hole to keep the wind away," but leave
that office to his dust at least: —

> I am too high-born to be propertied,
> To be a secondary at control,
> Or useful serving-man and instrument
> To any sovereign state throughout the world.

He who gives himself entirely to his fellow-men appears to them 6
useless and selfish; but he who gives himself partially to them is pronounced
a benefactor and philanthropist.

How does it become a man to behave toward this American govern- 7
ment to-day? I answer, that he cannot without disgrace be associated with it.
I cannot for an instant recognize that political organization as *my* government
which is the slave's government also.

All men recognize the right of revolution; that is, the right to refuse 8
allegiance to, and to resist, the government, when its tyranny or its inef-
ficiency are great and unendurable. But almost all say that such is not the
case now. But such was the case, they think, in the Revolution of '75. If one
were to tell me that this was a bad government because it taxed certain
foreign commodities brought to its ports, it is most probable that I should
not make an ado about it, for I can do without them. All machines have their
friction; and possibly this does enough good to counterbalance the evil. At
any rate, it is a great evil to make a stir about it. But when the friction comes
to have its machine, and oppression and robbery are organized, I say, let us
not have such a machine any longer. In other words, when a sixth of the

population of a nation which has undertaken to be the refuge of liberty are slaves, and a whole country is unjustly overrun and conquered by a foreign army, and subjected to military law, I think that it is not too soon for honest men to rebel and revolutionize. What makes this duty the more urgent is the fact that the country so overrun is not our own, but ours is the invading army. . . .

> A drab of state, a cloth-o'-silver slut,
> To have her train borne up, and her soul trail in the dirt

Practically speaking, the opponents to a reform in Massachusetts are not a hundred thousand politicians at the South, but a hundred thousand merchants and farmers here, who are more interested in commerce and agriculture than they are in humanity, and are not prepared to do justice to the slave and to Mexico, *cost what it may.* I quarrel not with far-off foes, but with those who, near at home, coöperate with, and do the bidding of, those far away, and without whom the latter would be harmless. We are accustomed to say, that the mass of men are unprepared; but improvement is slow, because the few are not materially wiser or better than the many. It is not so important that many should be as good as you, as that there be some absolute goodness somewhere; for that will leaven the whole lump. There are thousands who are *in opinion* opposed to slavery and to the war, who yet in effect do nothing to put an end to them; who, esteeming themselves children of Washington and Franklin, sit down with their hands in their pockets, and say that they know not what to do, and do nothing; who even postpone the question of freedom to the question of free-trade, and quietly read the prices-current along with the latest advices from Mexico, after dinner, and, it may be, fall asleep over them both. What is the price-current of an honest man and patriot to-day? They hesitate, and they regret, and sometimes they petition; but they do nothing in earnest and with effect. They will wait, well disposed, for others to remedy the evil, that they may no longer have it to regret. At most, they give only a cheap vote, and a feeble countenance and God-speed, to the right, as it goes by them. There are nine hundred and ninety-nine patrons of virtue to one virtuous man. But it is easier to deal with the real possessor of a thing than with the temporary guardian of it.

All voting is a sort of gaming, like checkers or backgammon, with a slight moral tinge to it, a playing with right and wrong, with moral questions; and betting naturally accompanies it. The character of the voters is not staked. I cast my vote, perchance, as I think right; but I am not vitally concerned that that right should prevail. I am willing to leave it to the majority. Its obligation, therefore, never exceeds that of expediency. Even voting *for the right* is *doing* nothing for it. It is only expressing to men feebly your desire that it should prevail. A wise man will not leave the right to the mercy of chance, nor wish it to prevail through the power of the majority. There is but little virtue in the action of masses of men. When the majority shall at length vote for the abolition of slavery, it will be because they are indifferent to slavery, or because there is but little slavery left to be abolished by their vote. *They* will then be the only slaves. Only *his* vote can hasten the abolition of slavery who asserts his own freedom by his vote.

I hear of a convention to be held at Baltimore, or elsewhere, for the   10 selection of a candidate for the Presidency, made up chiefly of editors, and men who are politicians by profession; but I think, what is it to any independent, intelligent, and respectable man what decision they may come to? Shall we not have the advantage of his wisdom and honesty, nevertheless? Can we not count upon some independent votes? Are there not many individuals in the country who do not attend conventions? But no: I find that the respectable man, so called, has immediately drifted from his position, and despairs of his country, when his country has more reason to despair of him. He forthwith adopts one of the candidates thus selected as the only *available* one, thus proving that he is himself *available* for any purposes of the demagogue. His vote is of no more worth than that of any unprincipled foreigner or hireling native, who may have been bought. O for a man who is a *man*, and, as my neighbor says, has a bone in his back which you cannot pass your hand through! Our statistics are at fault: the population has been returned too large. How many *men* are there to a square thousand miles in this country? Hardly one. Does not America offer an inducement for men to settle here? The American has dwindled into an Odd Fellow, — one who may be known by the development of his organ of gregariousness, and a manifest lack of intellect and cheerful self-reliance; whose first and chief concern, on coming into the world, is to see that the Almshouses are in good repair; and, before yet he has lawfully donned the virile garb, to collect a fund for the support of the widows and orphans that may be; who, in short, ventures to live only by the aid of the Mutual Insurance Company, which has promised to bury him decently.

It is not a man's duty, as a matter of course, to devote himself to the   11 eradication of any, even the most enormous wrong; he may still properly have other concerns to engage him; but it is his duty, at least, to wash his hands of it, and, if he gives it no thought longer, not to give it practically his support. If I devote myself to other pursuits and contemplations, I must first see, at least, that I do not pursue them sitting upon another man's shoulders. I must get off him first, that he may pursue his contemplations too. See what gross inconsistency is tolerated. I have heard some of my townsmen say, "I should like to have them order me out to help put down an insurrection of the slaves, or to march to Mexico; — see if I would go"; and yet these very men have each, directly by their allegiance, and so indirectly, at least, by their money, furnished a substitute. The soldier is applauded who refuses to serve in an unjust war by those who do not refuse to sustain the unjust government which makes the war; is applauded by those whose own act and authority he disregards and sets at naught; as if the state were penitent to that degree that it hired one to scourge it while it sinned, but not to that degree that it left off sinning for a moment. Thus, under the name of Order and Civil Government, we are all made at last to pay homage to and support our own meanness. After the first blush of sin comes its indifference; and from immoral it becomes, as it were, *un*moral, and not quite unnecessary to that life which we have made.

The broadest and most prevalent error requires the most disinterested 12 virtue to sustain it. The slight reproach to which the virtue of patriotism is commonly liable, the noble are most likely to incur. Those who, while they disapprove of the character and measures of a government, yield to it their allegiance and support are undoubtedly its most conscientious supporters, and so frequently the most serious obstacles to reform. Some are petitioning the state to dissolve the Union, to disregard the requisitions of the President. Why do they not dissolve it themselves — the union between themselves and the state, — and refuse to pay their quota into its treasury? Do not they stand in the same relation to the state that the state does to the Union? And have not the same reasons prevented the state from resisting the Union which have prevented them from resisting the state?

How can a man be satisfied to entertain an opinion merely, and enjoy 13 *it?* Is there any enjoyment in it, if his opinion is that he is aggrieved? If you are cheated out of a single dollar by your neighbor, you do not rest satisfied with knowing that you are cheated, or with saying that you are cheated, or even with petitioning him to pay you your due; but you take effectual steps at once to obtain the full amount, and see that you are never cheated again. Action from principle, the perception and the performance of right, changes things and relations; it is essentially revolutionary, and does not consist wholly with anything which was. It not only divides states and churches, it divides families; ay, it divides the *individual,* separating the diabolical in him from the divine.

Unjust laws exist: shall we be content to obey them, or shall we en- 14 deavor to amend them, and obey them until we have succeeded, or shall we transgress them at once? Men generally, under such a government as this, think that they ought to wait until they have persuaded the majority to alter them. They think that, if they should resist, the remedy would be worse than the evil. But it is the fault of the government itself that the remedy *is* worse than the evil. *It* makes it worse. Why is it not more apt to anticipate and provide for reform? Why does it not cherish its wise minority? Why does it cry and resist before it is hurt? Why does it not encourage its citizens to be on the alert to point out its faults, and *do* better than it would have them? Why does it always crucify Christ, and excommunicate Copernicus and Luther, and pronounce Washington and Franklin rebels?

One would think, that a deliberate and practical denial of its authority 15
was the only offense never contemplated by government; else, why has it not
assigned its definite, its suitable and proportionate penalty? If a man who has
no property refuses but once to earn nine shillings for the state, he is put in
prison for a period unlimited by any law that I know, and determined only
by the discretion of those who placed him there; but if he should steal ninety
times nine shillings from the state, he is soon permitted to go at large again.

If the justice is part of the necessary friction of the machine of govern- 16
ment, let it go, let it go: perchance it will wear smooth, — certainly the
machine will wear out. If the injustice has a spring, or a pulley, or a rope, or
a crank, exclusively for itself, then perhaps you may consider whether the
remedy will not be worse than the evil; but if it is of such a nature that it
requires you to be the agent of injustice to another, then, I say, break the
law. Let your life be a counter friction to stop the machine. What I have to
do is to see, at any rate, that I do not lend myself to the wrong which I condemn.

As for adopting the ways which the state has provided for remedying 17
the evil, I know not of such ways. They take too much time, and a man's life
will be gone. I have other affairs to attend to. I came into this world, not
chiefly to make this a good place to live in, but to live in it, be it good or
bad. A man has not everything to do, but something; and because he cannot
do *everything*, it is not necessary that he should do *something* wrong. It is
not my business to be petitioning the Governor or the Legislature any more
than it is theirs to petition me; and if they should not hear my petition, what
should I do then? But in this case the state has provided no way: its very
Constitution is the evil. This may seem to be harsh and stubborn and un-
conciliatory; but it is to treat with the utmost kindness and consideration the
only spirit that can appreciate or deserves it. So is all change for the better,
like birth and death, which convulse the body.

I do not hesitate to say, that those who call themselves Abolitionists 18
should at once effectually withdraw their support, both in person and property, from the government of Massachusetts and not wait till they constitute
a majority of one, before they suffer the right to prevail through them. I
think that it is enough if they have God on their side, without waiting for
that other one. Moreover, any man more right than his neighbors constitutes
a majority of one already.

I meet this American government, or its representative, the state gov- 19
ernment, directly, and face to face, once a year — no more — in the person
of its tax-gatherer; this is the only mode in which a man situated as I am necessarily meets it; and it then says distinctly, Recognize me; and the simplest,
most effectual, and, in the present posture of affairs, the indispensablest
mode of treating with it on this head, of expressing your little satisfaction
with and love for it, is to deny it then. My civil neighbor, the tax-gatherer, is
the very man I have to deal with, — for it is, after all, with men and not

with parchment that I quarrel, — and he has voluntarily chosen to be an agent of the government. How shall he ever know well what he is and does as an officer of the government, or as a man, until he is obliged to consider whether he shall treat me, his neighbor, for whom he has respect, as a neighbor and well-disposed man, or as a maniac and disturber of the peace, and see if he can get over this obstruction to his neighborliness without a ruder and more impetuous thought or speech corresponding with his action. I know this well, that if one thousand, if one hundred, if ten men whom I could name, — if ten *honest* men only, — ay, if *one* HONEST man, in this State of Massachusetts, *ceasing to hold slaves,* were actually to withdraw from this copartnership, and be locked up in the county jail therefor, it would be the abolition of slavery in America. For it matters not how small the beginning may seem to be: what is once well done is done forever. But we love better to talk about it: that we say is our mission. Reform keeps many scores of newspapers in its service, but not one man. If my esteemed neighbor, the State's ambassador, who will devote his days to the settlement of the question of human rights in the Council Chamber, instead of being threatened with the prisons of Carolina, were to sit down the prisoner of Massachusetts, that State which is so anxious to foist the sin of slavery upon her sister, — though at present she can discover only an act of inhospitality to be the ground of a quarrel with her, — the Legislature would not wholly waive the subject the following winter.

Under a government which imprisons any unjustly, the true place for a just man is also a prison. The proper place to-day, the only place which Massachusetts has provided for her freer and less desponding spirits, is in her prisons, to be put out and locked out of the State by her own act, as they have already put themelves out by their principles. It is there that the fugitive slave, and the Mexican prisoner on parole, and the Indian come to plead the wrongs of his race should find them; on that separate, but more free and honorable ground, where the State places those who are not *with* her, but *against* her, — the only house in a slave State in which a free man can abide with honor. If any think that their influence would be lost there, and their voices no longer afflict the ear of the State, that they would not be as an enemy within its walls, they do not know by how much truth is stronger than error, nor how much more eloquently and effectively he can combat injustice who has experienced a little in his own person. Cast your whole vote, not a strip of paper merely, but your whole influence. A minority is powerless while it conforms to the majority; it is not even a minority then; but it is irresistible when it clogs by its whole weight. If the alternative is to keep all just men in prison, or give up war and slavery, the State will not hesitate which to choose. If a thousand men were not to pay their tax-bills this year, that would not be a violent and bloody measure, as it would be to pay them, and enable the State to commit violence and shed innocent blood. This is, in fact,

20

the definition of a peaceable revolution, if any such is possible. If the tax-gatherer, or any other public officer, asks me, as one has done, "But what shall I do?" my answer is, "If you really wish to do anything, resign your office." When the subject has refused allegiance, and the officer has resigned his office, then the revolution is accomplished. But even suppose blood should flow. Is there not a sort of blood shed when the conscience is wounded? Through this wound a man's real manhood and immortality flow out, and he bleeds to an everlasting death. I see this blood flowing now.

I have contemplated the imprisonment of the offender, rather than the seizure of his goods, — though both will serve the same purpose, — because they who assert the purest right, and consequently are most dangerous to a corrupt State, commonly have not spent much time in accumulating propery. To such the State renders comparatively small service, and a slight tax is wont to appear exorbitant, particularly if they are obliged to earn it by special labor with their hands. If there were one who lived wholly without the use of money, the State itself would hesitate to demand it of him. But the rich man — not to make any invidious comparison — is always sold to the institution which makes him rich. Absolutely speaking, the more money, the less virtue; for money comes between a man and his objects, and obtains them for him; and it was certainly no great virtue to obtain it. It puts to rest many questions which he would otherwise be taxed to answer; while the only new question which it puts is the hard but superfluous one, how to spend it. Thus his moral ground is taken from under his feet. The opportunities of living are diminished in proportion as what are called the "means" are increased. The best thing a man can do for his culture when he is rich is to endeavor to carry out those schemes which he entertained when he was poor. Christ answered the Herodians according to their condition. "Show me the tribute-money," said he; — and one took a penny out of his pocket; — if you use money which has the image of Caesar on it and which he has made current and valuable, that is, *if you are men of the State,* and gladly enjoy the advantages of Caesar's government, then pay him back some of his own when he demands it. "Render therefore to Caesar that which is Caesar's, and to God those things which are God's," — leaving them no wiser than before as to which was which; for they did not wish to know. . . . 21

I have paid no poll-tax for six years. I was put into a jail once on this account, for one night; and, as I stood considering the walls of solid stone, two or three feet thick, the door of wood and iron, a foot thick, and the iron grating which strained the light, I could not help being struck with the foolishness of that institution which treated me as if I were mere flesh and blood and bones, to be locked up. I wondered that it should have concluded at length that this was the best use it could put me to, and had never thought to avail itself of my services in some way. I saw that, if there was a wall of stone between me and my townsmen, there was a still more difficult one to 22 climb or break through before they could get to be as free as I was. I did not for a moment feel confined, and the walls seemed a great waste of stone and mortar. I felt as if I alone of all my townsmen had paid my tax. They plainly did not know how to treat me, but behaved like persons who are underbred. In every threat and in every compliment there was a blunder; for they thought that my chief desire was to stand the other side of that stone wall. I could not but smile to see how industriously they locked the door on my meditations, which followed them out again without let or hindrance, and *they* were really all that was dangerous. As they could not reach me, they had resolved to punish my body; just as boys, if they cannot come at some person against whom they have a spite, will abuse his dog. I saw that the State was half-witted, that it was timid as a lone woman with her silver spoons, and that it did not know its friends from its foes, and I lost all my remaining respect for it, and pitied it.

Thus the State never intentionally confronts a man's sense, intellectual   23
or moral, but only his body, his senses. It is not armed with superior wit or honesty, but with superior physical strength. I was not born to be forced. I will breathe after my own fashion. Let us see who is the strongest. What force has a multitude? They only can force me who obey a higher law than I. They force me to become like themselves. I do not hear of *men* being *forced* to live this way or that by masses of men. What sort of life were that to live? When I meet a government which says to me, "Your money or your life," why should I be in haste to give it my money? It may be in a great strait, and not know what to do: I cannot help that. It must help itself; do as I do. It is not worth the while to snivel about it. I am not responsible for the successful working of the machinery of society. I am not the son of the engineer. I perceive that, when an acorn and a chestnut fall side by side, the one does not remain inert to make way for the other, but both obey their own laws, and spring and grow and flourish as best they can, till one, perchance, overshadows and destroys the other. If a plant cannot live according to its nature, it dies; and so a man. . . .

When I came out of prison, — for some one interfered, and paid that   24
tax, — I did not perceive that great changes had taken place on the common, such as he observed who went in a youth and emerged a tottering and gray-headed man; and yet a change had to my eyes come over the scene, — the town, and State, and country, — greater than any that mere time could effect. I saw yet more distinctly the State in which I lived. I saw to what extent the people among whom I lived could be trusted as good neighbors and friends; that their friendship was for summer weather only; that they did not greatly propose to do right; that they were a distinct race from me by their prejudices and superstitions, as the Chinamen and Malays are; that in their sacrifices to humanity they ran no risks, not even to their property; that after all they were not so noble but they treated the thief as he had treated them,

and hoped, by a certain outward observance and a few prayers, and by walking in a particular straight though useless path from time to time, to save their souls. This may be to judge my neighbors harshly; for I believe that many of them are not aware that they have such an institution as the jail in their village.

It was formerly the custom in our village, when a poor debtor came out   25
of jail, for his acquaintances to salute him, looking through their fingers, which were crossed to represent the grating of a jail window. "How do ye do?" My neighbors did not thus salute me, but first looked at me, and then at one another, as if I had returned from a long journey. I was put into jail as I was going to the shoemaker's to get a shoe which was mended. When I was let out the next morning, I proceeded to finish my errand, and, having put on my mended shoe, joined a huckleberry party, who were impatient to put themselves under my conduct; and in half an hour, — for the horse was soon tackled, — was in the midst of a huckleberry field, on one of our highest hills, two miles off, and then the State was nowhere to be seen. . . .

I have never declined paying the highway tax, because I am as desirous   26
of being a good neighbor as I am of being a bad subject; and as for supporting schools, I am doing my part to educate my fellow-countrymen now. It is for no particular item in the tax-bill that I refused to pay it. I simply wish to refuse allegiance to the State, to withdraw and stand aloof from it effectually. I do not care to trace the course of my dollar, if I could, till it buys a man or a musket to shoot with, — the dollar is innocent, — but I am concerned to trace the effects of my allegiance. In fact, I quietly declare war with the State, after my fashion, though I will still make what use and get what advantage of her I can, as is usual in such cases.

If others pay the tax which is demanded of me, from a sympathy with   27
the State, they do but what they have already done in their own case, or rather they abet injustice to a greater extent than the State requires. If they pay the tax from a mistaken interest in the individual taxed, to save his property, or prevent his going to jail, it is because they have not considered wisely how far they let their private feelings interfere with the public good.

This, then, is my position at present. But one cannot be too much on   28
his guard in such a case, lest his action be biased by obstinacy or an undue regard for the opinions of men. Let him see that he does only what belongs to himself and to the hour.

I think sometimes, Why, these people mean well, they are only igno-   29
rant; they would do better if they knew how: why give your neighbors this pain to treat you as they are not inclined to? But I think again, This is no reason why I should do as they do, or permit others to suffer much greater pain of a different kind. Again, I sometimes say to myself, When many millions of men, without heat, without ill will, without personal feeling of any kind, demand of you a few shillings only, without the possibility, such is

their constitution, of retracting or altering their present demand, and without the possibility, on your side, of appeal to any other millions, why expose yourself to this overwhelming brute force? You do not resist cold and hunger, the winds and the waves, thus obstinately; you quietly submit to a thousand similar necessities. You do not put your head into the fire. But just in proportion as I regard this as not wholly a brute force, but partly a human force, and consider that I have relations to those millions as to many millions of men, and not of mere brute or inanimate things, I see that appeal is possible, first and instantaneously, from them to the Maker of them and, secondly, from them to themselves. But if I put my head deliberately into the fire, there is no appeal to fire or to the Maker of fire, and I have only myself to blame. If I could convince myself that I have any right to be satisfied with men as they are, and to treat them accordingly, and not according, in some respects, to my requisitions and expectations of what they and I ought to be, then, like a good Mussulman and fatalist, I should endeavor to be satisfied with things as they are, and say it is the will of God. And, above all, there is this difference between resisting this and a purely brute or natural force, that I can resist this with some effect; but I cannot expect, like Orpheus, to change the nature of the rocks and trees and beasts.

I do not wish to quarrel with any man or nation. I do not wish to split   30
hairs, to make fine distinctions, or set myself up as better than my neighbors. I seek rather, I may say, even an excuse for conforming to the laws of the land. I am but too ready to conform to them. Indeed, I have reason to suspect myself on this head; and each year, as the tax-gatherer comes round, I find myself disposed to review the acts and position of the general and State governments, and the spirit of the people, to discover a pretext for conformity.

> We must affect our country as our parents,
> And if at any time we alienate
> Our love or industry from doing it honor,
> We must respect effects and teach the soul
> Matter of conscience and religion,   5
> And not desire of rule or benefit.

I believe that the State will soon be able to take all my work of this sort out of my hands, and then I shall be no better a patriot than my fellow-countrymen. Seen from a lower point of view, the Constitution, with all its faults, is very good; the law and the courts are very respectable; even this State and this American government are, in many respects, very admirable, and rare things, to be thankful for, such as a great many have described them; but seen from a point of view a little higher, they are what I have described them; seen from a higher still, and the highest, who shall say what they are or that they are worth looking at or thinking of at all?

However, the government does not concern me much, and I shall be- 31
stow the fewest possible thoughts on it. It is not many moments that I live
under a government, even in this world. If a man is thought-free, fancy-free,
imagination-free, that which *is not* never for a long time appearing *to be* to
him, unwise rulers or reformers cannot fatally interrupt him.

I know that most men think differently from myself; but those whose 32
lives are by profession devoted to the study of these or kindred subjects content me as little as any. Statesmen and legislators, standing so completely
within the institution, never distinctly and nakedly behold it. They speak of
moving society, but have no resting-place without it. They may be men of a
certain experience and discrimination, and have no doubt invented ingenious
and even useful systems, for which we sincerely thank them; but all their wit
and usefulness lie within certain not very wide limits. They are wont to
forget that the world is not governed by policy and expediency. Webster
never goes behind government, and so cannot speak with authority about it.
His words are wisdom to those legislators who contemplate no essential
reform in the existing government; but for thinkers, and those who legislate
for all time, he never once glances at the subject. I know of those whose
serene and wise speculations on this theme would soon reveal the limits of
his mind's range and hospitality. Yet, compared with the cheap professions of
most reformers, and the still cheaper wisdom and eloquence of politicians in
general, his are almost the only sensible and valuable words, and we thank
Heaven for him. Comparatively, he is always strong, original, and, above all,
practical. Still, his quality is not wisdom, but prudence. The lawyer's truth is
not Truth, but consistency or a consistent expediency. Truth is always in harmony with herself, and is not concerned chiefly to reveal the justice that may
consist with wrong-doing. He well deserves to be called, as he has been
called, the Defender of the Constitution. There are really no blows to be
given by him but defensive ones. He is not a leader, but a follower. His
leaders are the men of '87. "I have never made an effort," he says, "and
never propose to make an effort; I have never countenanced an effort, and
never mean to countenance an effort, to disturb the arrangement as originally made, by which the various States came into the Union." Still thinking
of the sanction which the Constitution gives to slavery, he says, "Because it
was a part of the original compact, — let it stand." Notwithstanding his
special acuteness and ability, he is unable to take a fact out of its merely political relations, and behold it as it lies absolutely to be disposed of by the intellect, — what, for instance, it behooves a man to do here in America today with regard to slavery, — but ventures, or is driven, to make some such
desperate answer as the following while professing to speak absolutely, and
as a private man, — from which what new and singular code of social duties
might be inferred? "The manner," says he, "in which the governments of
those States where slavery exists are to regulate it is for their own consider-

ation, under their responsibility to their constituents, to the general laws of propriety, humanity, and justice, and to God. Associations formed elsewhere, springing from a feeling of humanity, or other cause, have nothing whatever to do with it. They have never received any encouragement from me, and they never will."

They who know of no purer sources of truth, who have traced up its   33
stream no higher, stand, and wisely stand, by the Bible and the Constitution, and drink at it there with reverence and humility; but they who behold where it comes trickling into this lake or that pool, gird up their loins once more, and continue their pilgrimage towards its fountainhead.

No man with a genius for legislation has appeared in America. They are   34
rare in the history of the world. There are orators, politicians, and eloquent men, by the thousand; but the speaker has not yet opened his mouth to speak who is capable of settling the much-vexed questions of the day. We love eloquence for its own sake, and not for any truth which it may utter, or any heroism it may inspire. Our legislators have not yet learned the comparative value of free-trade and of freedom, of union, and of rectitude, to a nation. They have no genius or talent for comparatively humble questions of taxation and finance, commerce and manufactures and agriculture. If we were left solely to the wordy wit of legislators in Congress for our guidance, uncorrected by the seasonable experience and the effectual complaints of the people, America would not long retain her rank among the nations. For eighteen hundred years, though perchance I have no right to say it, the New Testament has been written; yet where is the legislator who has wisdom and practical talent enough to avail himself of the light which it sheds on the science of legislation?

The authority of government, even such as I am willing to submit   35
to, — for I will cheerfully obey those who know and can do better than I, and in many things even those who neither know nor can do so well, — is still an impure one: to be strictly just, it must have the sanction and consent of the governed. It can have no pure right over my person and property but what I concede to it. The progress from an absolute to a limited monarchy, from a limited monarchy to a democracy, is a progress toward a true respect for the individual. Even the Chinese philosopher was wise enough to regard the individual as the basis of the empire. Is a democracy, such as we know it, the last improvement possible in government? Is it not possible to take a step further towards recognizing and organizing the rights of man? There will never be a really free and enlightened State until the State comes to recognize the individual as a higher and independent power, from which all its own power and authority are derived, and treats him accordingly. I please myself with imagining a State at last which can afford to be just to all men, and to treat the individual with respect as a neighbor; which even would not think it inconsistent with its own repose if a few were to live aloof from it,

not meddling with it, nor embraced by it, who fulfilled all the duties of neighbors and fellow-men. A State which bore this kind of fruit, and suffered it to drop off as fast as it ripened, would prepare the way for a still more perfect and glorious State, which also I have imagined, but not yet anywhere seen.

SUBJECT QUESTIONS

1. What two situations prompted Thoreau to write this essay? Is he justified in refusing to cooperate with a government that condones slavery and indulges in armed aggression?
2. If one is confronted with a conflict between the law and his conscience, which should he obey? Would you be willing to disobey your government? A pacifist, even though he does not fight, must pay taxes to support a war; is the government justified in thus forcing him to go against his conscience?
3. Does it logically follow that, if the best governments are those which govern least, the best possible government would govern not at all? Is Thoreau an anarchist?
4. Thoreau does not advocate violent revolution; what does he suggest the citizen should do if he disapproves of his government's activities? Would this solution be effective? How many people would be needed to make it work?
5. Thoreau does not seem to have much faith in the democratic principle of majority rule. Would he have more, or less, faith in an oligarchy? What would happen if every minority acted by Thoreau's principles?
6. Thoreau seems to make one fundamental error: he regards government as an enemy to individualism. But if we had no government at all, how much freedom would we have? Would you conclude that government necessarily requires compromising some freedoms to guarantee more important ones?
7. What would be Thoreau's reaction to modern government? Do you think the increased complexity of life today would force him to modify some of his views? If he were alive today, would he be more likely to vote Democratic or Republican? (The obvious answer to this question may have to be modified in view of what he says about Daniel Webster.)

STRUCTURE QUESTIONS

1. Summarize the position with which Thoreau wants his reader to agree. Does he try to sway the reader into accepting this position, or does he present arguments designed to encourage the reader to do some thinking on his own?

2. Occasionally Thoreau states his opinion without bothering to give supporting evidence. What are some of these assumptions? Why do you suppose Thoreau doesn't support them? Could he have done so?

3. Try outlining the essay. Could Thoreau have made it more effective by organizing it more carefully?

4. What would you say is Thoreau's strongest asset as a writer? What is his most obvious weakness?

5. Does Thoreau succeed in getting the reader to think objectively about the problem of government control? (He may strike some readers as an eccentric, but his purpose was not to be affable. It may be noted that Mahatma Gandhi successfully used Thoreau's idea of passive resistance in his battle for Indian independence.)

SUGGESTIONS FOR WRITING

1. Write an argument on the question of citizens' responsibility to obey their government when it requires them to do something they believe is wrong. (For example, should citizens be forced to pay taxes to support a war, a medical welfare program, or a farm subsidy program of which they don't approve?)

2. Write an argument on the question of a university's right to impose restrictions on its students' private lives (dating hours, dressing for dinner, etc.). If you do not approve of such restrictions, state what action you think the students should take. If you have strong feelings on this subject, take care not to let them interfere with the open search for truth which your paper should stimulate.

The Declaration of Independence

Thomas Jefferson

The Declaration of Independence was written between June 11 and June 28, 1776, mainly by Thomas Jefferson (1743–1826), but with considerable help from Benjamin Franklin and with suggestions from John Adams. After a few minor changes, it was passed by Congress on July 4, and the famous parchment copy of it signed on August 2. The text here is the version authorized by the State Department (1911).

In CONGRESS, July 4, 1776.

THE UNANIMOUS DECLARATION
OF THE THIRTEEN UNITED STATES OF AMERICA.

When in the Course of human events, it becomes necessary for one people 1
to dissolve the political bands which have connected them with another, and to assume among the powers of the earth, the separate and equal station to which the Laws of Nature and of Nature's God entitle them, a decent respect to the opinions of mankind requires that they should declare the causes which impel them to the separation.

We hold these truths to be self-evident, that all men are created equal, 2
that they are endowed by their Creator with certain unalienable Rights, that among these are Life, Liberty, and the pursuit of Happiness.

That to secure these rights, Governments are instituted among Men, 3
deriving their just powers from the consent of the governed.

That whenever any Form of Government becomes destructive of these 4
ends, it is the Right of the People to alter or to abolish it, and to institute new Government, laying its foundation on such principles and organizing its powers in such form, as to them shall seem most likely to effect their Safety and Happiness. Prudence, indeed, will dictate that Governments long established should not be changed for light and transient causes; and accordingly all experience hath shewn, that mankind are more disposed to suffer, while evils are sufferable, than to right themselves by abolishing the forms to which they are accustomed. But when a long train of abuses and usurpations, pursuing invariably the same Object evinces a design to reduce them under absolute Despotism, it is their right, it is their duty, to throw off such Government, and to provide new Guards for their future security.

Such has been the patient sufferance of these Colonies; and such is 5
now the necessity which constrains them to alter their former Systems of

365

Government. The history of the present King of Great Britain is a history of repeated injuries and usurpations, all having in direct object the establishment of an absolute Tyranny over these States. To prove this, let Facts be submitted to a candid world.

He has refused his Assent to Laws, the most wholesome and necessary for the public good. 6

He has forbidden his Governors to pass Laws of immediate and pressing importance, unless suspended in their operation till his Assent should be obtained; and when so suspended, he has utterly neglected to attend to them. 7

He has refused to pass other Laws for the accommodation of large districts of people, unless those people would relinquish the right of Representation in the Legislature, a right inestimable to them and formidable to tyrants only. 8

He has called together legislative bodies at places unusual, uncomfortable, and distant from the depository of their public Records, for the sole purpose of fatiguing them into compliance with his measures. 9

He has dissolved Representative Houses repeatedly, for opposing with manly firmness his invasions on the rights of the people. 10

He has refused for a long time, after such dissolutions, to cause others to be elected; whereby the Legislative powers, incapable of Annihilation, have returned to the People at large for their exercise; the State remaining in the mean time exposed to all the dangers of invasion from without, and convulsions within. 11

He has endeavoured to prevent the population of these States; for that purpose obstructing the Laws for Naturalization of Foreigners; refusing to pass others to encourage their migrations hither, and raising the conditions of new Appropriations of Lands. 12

He has obstructed the Administration of Justice, by refusing his Assent to Laws for establishing Judiciary powers. 13

He has made Judges dependent on his Will alone, for the tenure of their offices, and the amount and payment of their salaries. 14

He has erected a multitude of New Offices, and sent hither swarms of Officers to harass our people, and eat out their substance. 15

He has kept among us, in times of peace, Standing Armies without the Consent of our legislatures. 16

He has affected to render the Military independent of and superior to the Civil power. 17

He has combined with others[1] to subject us to a jurisdiction foreign to our constitution, and unacknowledged by our laws; giving his Assent to their Acts of pretended Legislation: 18

[1] The British Parliament.

For Quartering large bodies of armed troops among us: 19

For protecting them, by a mock Trial, from punishment for any 20
Murders which they should commit on the Inhabitants of these States:

For cutting off our Trade with all parts of the world: 21

For imposing Taxes on us without our Consent: 22

For depriving us in many cases, of the benefits of Trial by Jury: 23

For transporting us beyond Seas to be tried for pretended offenses: 24

For abolishing the free System of English Laws in a neighboring Pro- 25
vince[2] establishing therein an Arbitrary government, and enlarging its Bound-
aries so as to render it at once an example and fit instrument for introducing
the same absolute rule into these Colonies:

For taking away our Charters, abolishing our most valuable Laws, and 26
altering fundamentally the Forms of our Governments:

For suspending our own Legislatures, and declaring themselves in- 27
vested with power to legislate for us in all cases whatsoever.

He has abdicated Government here, by declaring us out of his Protec- 28
tion and waging War against us:

He has plundered our seas, ravaged our Coasts, burnt our towns, and 29
destroyed the lives of our people.

He is at this time transporting large Armies of foreign Mercenaries[3] to 30
compleat the works of death, desolation and tyranny, already begun with circumstances of Cruelty & perfidy scarcely paralleled in the most barbarous
ages, and totally unworthy the Head of a civilized nation.

He has constrained our fellow Citizens taken Captive on the high Seas 31
to bear Arms against their Country, to become the executioners of their
friends and Brethren, or to fall themselves by their Hands.

He has excited domestic insurrections amongst us, and has en- 32
deavoured to bring on the inhabitants of our frontiers, the merciless Indian
Savages, whose known rule of warfare, is an undistinguished destruction of
all ages, sexes and conditions. In every stage of these Oppressions We have
Petitioned for Redress in the most humble terms: Our repeated Petitions
have been answered only by repeated injury. A Prince, whose character is
thus marked by every act which may define a Tyrant, is unfit to be the ruler
of a free people. Nor have We been wanting in attentions to our British
brethren. We have warned them from time to time of attempts by their
legislature to extend an unwarrantable jurisdiction over us. We have reminded them of the circumstances of our emigration and settlement here.
We have appealed to their native justice and magnanimity, and we have conjured them by the ties of our common kindred to disavow these usurpations,

[2] The Quebec Act (1774) promised concessions to the French Catholics, and restored the
French civil law, thus alienating the Province of Quebec from the seaboard colonies in the growing controversy.

[3] German soldiers, principally Hessians, hired by the British for colonial service.

which, would inevitably interrupt our connections and correspondence. They too have been deaf to the voice of justice and of consanguinity. We must, therefore, acquiesce in the necessity, which denounces[4] our Separation, and hold them, as we hold the rest of mankind, Enemies in War, in Peace Friends.

WE, THEREFORE, the Representatives of the UNITED STATES OF   33
AMERICA, in General Congress Assembled, appealing to the Supreme Judge of the world for the rectitude of our intentions, do, in the Name and by Authority of the good People of these Colonies, solemnly publish and declare, That these United Colonies are, and of Right ought to be FREE AND INDEPENDENT STATES; that they are Absolved from all Allegiance to the British Crown, and that all political connection between them and the State of Great Britain, is and ought to be totally dissolved; and that as Free and Independent States, they have full Power to levy War, conclude Peace, contract Alliances, establish Commerce, and to do all other Acts and Things which Independent States may of right do.

And for the support of this Declaration, with a firm reliance on the   34
protection of divine Providence, we mutually pledge to each other our Lives, our Fortunes and our sacred Honor.

SUBJECT QUESTIONS

1. Under what circumstances do the authors claim revolution to be justified? Do you agree? Can you think of other circumstances which might justify rebellion? Can you see any consistency in the attitude of our State Department toward revolution in other countries in the past twenty or thirty years? (Consider, for instance, Red China, Dominican Republic, Cuba, Hungary, Czechoslovakia, and Viet Nam.)
2. Do the authors give the impression that they have exhausted every other recourse before turning to revolution?
3. Consider the long list of reasons given for turning to rebellion; do they strike you as adequate justification? Do you see any that might be interpreted differently?
4. Judging by the one remark about American Indians, do you suppose the new government intended to apply its belief that "all men are created equal" to them?

STRUCTURE QUESTIONS

1. How closely does the Declaration follow the traditional formula for argument? (See introduction.)
2. This is a subject on which the Continental Congress clearly felt

4 Proclaims.

strongly; have the authors maintained objectivity in the presentation of their case? Is it possible for the tone to be objective while the handling of evidence is biased?

3. What reason do they give for making this public declaration? How is the Preamble calculated to affect the reader?

4. Because this argument is a justification for something that has already been decided, rather than an invitation to debate the merits of doing it, one might expect the authors to be less open-minded than in an ideal argument; does this seem to be the case? Can you tell by the wording whether or not there is any deliberate intention to deceive? Does there seem to be any unintentional self-deception?

SUGGESTIONS FOR WRITING

1. Using the criteria for a just rebellion outlined in the Declaration of Independence, write a declaration to fit a hypothetical situation in the present (a commune, for instance, occupies an island off the coast and declares itself an independent nation). Do not merely paraphrase Jefferson; make it your own from start to finish. Be sure to follow the guidelines for argument discussed in the introduction to this section.

2. Write an argument, from a loyalist point of view, that the colonies should *not* declare independence from Britain.

The Bear

William Faulkner

William Faulkner (1897–1962) was born and lived in Mississippi, and most of his fiction deals with southern social problems, from the Reconstruction period to the present. Faulkner received the Nobel Prize for Literature in 1950. The story reprinted here, "The Bear," has Faulkner's usual setting in Mississippi, but the careful reader will find its message to be universal and timeless.

He was ten. But it had already begun, long before that day when at last he wrote his age in two figures and he saw for the first time the camp where his father and Major de Spain and old General Compson and the others spent two weeks each November and two weeks again each June. He had already inherited then, without ever having seen it, the tremendous bear with one trap-ruined foot which, in an area almost a hundred miles deep, had earned itself a name, a definite designation like a living man. 1

He had listened to it for years: the long legend of corncribs rifled, of shotes and grown pigs and even calves carried bodily into the woods and devoured, of traps and deadfalls overthrown and dogs mangled and slain, and shotgun and even rifle charges delivered at point-blank range and with no more effect than so many peas blown through a tube by a boy — a corridor of wreckage and destruction beginning back before he was born, through which sped, not fast but rather with the ruthless and irresistible deliberation of a locomotive, the shaggy tremendous shape. 2

It ran in his knowledge before he ever saw it. It looked and towered in his dreams before he even saw the unaxed woods where it left its crooked print, shaggy, huge, red-eyed, not malevolent but just big — too big for the dogs which tried to bay it, for the horses which tried to ride it down, for the men and the bullets they fired into it, too big for the very country which was its constricting scope. He seemed to see it entire with a child's complete divination before he ever laid eyes on either — the doomed wilderness whose edges were being constantly and punily gnawed at by men with axes and plows who feared it because it was wilderness, men myriad and nameless even to one another in the land where the old bear had earned a name, through which ran not even a mortal animal but an anachronism, indomitable 3

and invincible, out of an old dead time, a phantom, epitome and apotheosis
of the old wild life at which the puny humans swarmed and hacked in a fury
of abhorrence and fear, like pygmies about the ankles of a drowsing elephant:
the old bear solitary, indomitable and alone, widowered, childless, and absolved of mortality — old Priam reft of his old wife and having outlived all
his sons.

Until he was ten, each November he would watch the wagon contain- 4
ing the dogs and the bedding and food and guns and his father and Tennie's
Jim, the Negro, and Sam Fathers, the Indian, son of a slave woman and a
Chickasaw chief, depart on the road to town, to Jefferson, where Major de
Spain and the others would join them. To the boy, at seven, eight, and nine,
they were not going into the Big Bottom to hunt bear and deer, but to keep
yearly rendezvous with the bear which they did not even intend to kill. Two
weeks later they would return, with no trophy, no head and skin. He had
not expected it. He had not even been afraid it would be in the wagon. He
believed that even after he was ten and his father would let him go too, for
those two weeks in November, he would merely make another one, along
with his father and Major de Spain and General Compson and the others,
the dogs which feared to bay at it and the rifles and shotguns which failed
even to bleed it, in the yearly pageant of the old bear's furious immortality.

Then he heard the dogs. It was in the second week of his first time in 5
the camp. He stood with Sam Fathers against a big oak beside the faint
crossing where they had stood each dawn for nine days now, hearing the
dogs. He had heard them once before, one morning last week — a murmur,
sourceless, echoing through the wet woods, swelling presently into separate
voices which he could recognize and call by name. He had raised and cocked
the gun as Sam told him and stood motionless again while the uproar, the invisible course, swept up and past and faded; it seemed to him that he could
actually see the deer, the buck, blond, smoke-colored, elongated with speed,
fleeing, vanishing, the woods, the gray solitude, still ringing even when the
cries of the dogs had died away.

"Now let the hammers down," Sam said. 6

"You knew they were not coming here too," he said. 7

"Yes," Sam said. "I want you to learn how to do when you didn't shoot. 8
It's after the chance for the bear or the deer has done already come and gone
that men and dogs get killed."

"Anyway," he said, "it was just a deer." 9

Then on the tenth morning he heard the dogs again. And he readied 10
the too-long, too-heavy gun as Sam had taught him, before Sam even spoke.
But this time it was no deer, no ringing chorus of dogs running strong on a
free scent, but a moiling yapping an octave too high, with something more
than indecision and even abjectness in it, not even moving very fast, taking a
long time to pass completely out of hearing, leaving then somewhere in the

air that echo, thin, slightly hysterical, abject, almost grieving, with no sense of a fleeting, unseen, smoke-colored, grass-eating shape ahead of it, and Sam, who had taught him first of all to cock the gun and take position where he could see everywhere and then never move again, had himself moved up beside him; he could hear Sam breathing at his shoulder, and he could see the arched curve of the old man's inhaling nostrils.

"Hah," Sam said. "Not even running. Walking." 11

"Old Ben!" the boy said. "But up here!" he cried. "Way up here!" 12

"He do it every year," Sam said. "Once. Maybe to see who in camp 13 this time, if he can shoot or not. Whether we got the dog yet that can bay and hold him. He'll take them to the river, then he'll send them back home. We may as well go back too; see how they look when they come back to camp."

When they reached the camp the hounds were already there, ten of 14 them crouching back under the kitchen, the boy and Sam squatting to peer back into the obscurity where they had huddled, quiet, the eyes luminous, glowing at them and vanishing, and no sound, only that effluvium of something more than dog, stronger than dog and not just animal, just beast, because still there had been nothing in front of that abject and almost painful yapping save the solitude, the wilderness, so that when the eleventh hound came in at noon and with all the others watching — even old Uncle Ash, who called himself first a cook — Sam daubed the tattered ear and the raked shoulder with turpentine and axle grease, to the boy it was still no living creature, but the wilderness which, leaning for the moment down, had patted lightly once the hound's temerity.

"Just like a man," Sam said. "Just like folks. Put off as long as she could 15 having to be brave, knowing all the time that sooner or later she would have to be brave to keep on living with herself, and knowing all the time beforehand what was going to happen to her when she done it."

That afternoon, himself on the one-eyed wagon mule which did not 16 mind the smell of blood nor, as they told him, of bear, and with Sam on the other one, they rode for more than three hours through the rapid, shortening winter day. They followed no path, no trail even that he could see; almost at once they were in a country which he had never seen before. Then he knew why Sam had made him ride the mule which would not spook. The sound one stopped short and tried to whirl and bolt even as Sam got down, blowing its breath, jerking and wrenching at the rein, while Sam held it, coaxing it forward with his voice, since he could not risk tying it, drawing it forward while the boy got down from the marred one.

Then, standing beside Sam in the gloom of the dying afternoon, he 17 looked down at the rotted over-turned log, gutted and scored with claw marks and, in the wet earth beside it, the print of the enormous warped two-toed foot. He knew now what he had smelled when he peered under the kitchen where the dogs huddled. He realized for the first time that the bear which had run in his listening and loomed in his dreams since before he could remember to the contrary, and which, therefore, must have existed in the listening and dreams of his father and Major de Spain and even old General Compson, too, before they began to remember in their turn, was a mortal animal, and that if they had departed for the camp each November without any actual hope of bringing its trophy back, it was not because it could not be slain, but because so far they had had no actual hope to.

"Tomorrow," he said.   18

"We'll try tomorrow," Sam said. "We ain't got the dog yet."   19

"We've got eleven. They ran him this morning."   20

"It won't need but one," Sam said. "He ain't here. Maybe he ain't   21
nowhere. The only other way will be for him to run by accident over somebody that has a gun."

"That wouldn't be me," the boy said. "It will be Walter or Major or —"   22

"It might," Sam said. 'You watch close in the morning. Because he's   23
smart. That's how come he has lived this long. If he gets hemmed up and has to pick out somebody to run over, he will pick out you."

"How?" the boy said. "How will he know —" He ceased. "You mean   24
he already knows me, that I ain't never been here before, ain't had time to find out yet whether I —" He ceased again, looking at Sam, the old man whose face revealed nothing until it smiled. He said humbly, not even amazed, "It was me he was watching. I don't reckon he did need to come but once."

The next morning they left the camp three hours before daylight. They   25
rode this time because it was too far to walk, even the dogs in the wagon; again the first gray light found him in a place which he had never seen before, where Sam had placed him and told him to stay and then departed. With the gun which was too big for him, which did not even belong to him, but to Major de Spain, and which he had fired only once — at a stump on the first day, to learn the recoil and how to reload it — he stood against a gum tree beside a little bayou whose black still water crept without movement out of a canebrake and crossed a small clearing and into cane again, where, invisible, a bird — the big woodpecker called Lord-to-God by Negroes — clattered at a dead limb.

It was a stand like any other, dissimilar only in incidentals to the one   26
where he had stood each morning for ten days: a territory new to him, yet no less familiar than that other one which, after almost two weeks, he had come to believe he knew a little — the same solitude, the same loneliness through which human beings had merely passed without altering it, leaving no mark, no scar, which looked exactly as it must have looked when the first ancestor of Sam Fathers' Chickasaw predecessors crept into it and looked about, club or stone ax or bone arrow drawn and poised; different only because, squatt-

ing at the edge of the kitchen, he smelled the hounds huddled and cringing beneath it and saw the raked ear and shoulder of the one who, Sam said, had had to be brave once in order to live with herself, and saw yesterday in the earth beside the gutted log the print of the living foot.

He heard no dogs at all. He never did hear them. He only heard the 27 drumming of the woodpecker stop short off and knew that the bear was looking at him. He never saw it. He did not know whether it was in front of him or behind him. He did not move, holding the useless gun, which he had not even had warning to cock and which even now he did not cock, tasting in his saliva that taint as of brass which he knew now because he had smelled it when he peered under the kitchen at the huddled dogs.

Then it was gone. As abruptly as it had ceased, the woodpecker's dry, 28 monotonous clatter set up again, and after a while he even believed he could hear the dogs — a murmur, scarce a sound even, which he had probably been hearing for some time before he even remarked it, drifting into hearing and then out again, dying away. They came nowhere near him. If it was a bear they ran, it was another bear. It was Sam himself who came out of the cane and crossed the bayou, followed by the injured bitch of yesterday. She was almost at heel, like a bird dog, making no sound. She came and crouched against his leg, trembling, staring off into the cane.

"I didn't see him," he said. "I didn't, Sam!" 29

"I know it," Sam said. "He done the looking. You didn't hear him nei- 30 ther, did you?"

"No," the boy said. "I—" 31

"He's smart," Sam said. "Too smart." He looked down at the hound, 32 trembling faintly and steadily against the boy's knee. From the raked shoulder a few drops of fresh blood oozed and clung. "Too big. We ain't got the dog yet. But maybe someday. Maybe not next time. But someday."

So I must see him, he thought. *I must look at him.* Otherwise, it 33 seemed to him that it would go on like this forever, as it had gone on with his father and Major de Spain, who was older than his father, and even with old General Compson, who had been old enough to be a brigade commander in 1865. Otherwise, it would go on so forever, next time and next time, after and after and after. It seemed to him that he could never see the two of them, himself and the bear, shadowy in the limbo from which time emerged, becoming time; the old bear absolved of mortality and himself partaking, sharing a little of it, enough of it. And he knew now what he had smelled in the huddled dogs and tasted in his saliva. He recognized fear. *So I will have to see him,* he thought, without dread or even hope. *I will have to look at him.*

It was in June of the next year. He was eleven. They were in camp 34 again, celebrating Major de Spain's and General Compson's birthdays. Although the one had been born in September and the other in the depth of winter and in another decade, they had met for two weeks to fish and shoot squirrels and turkey and run coons and wildcats with the dogs at night. That is, he and Boon Hoggenbeck and the Negroes fished and shot squirrels and ran the coons and cats, because the proved hunters, not only Major de Spain and old General Compson, who spent those two weeks sitting in a rocking chair before a tremendous iron pot of Brunswick stew, stirring and tasting, with old Ash to quarrel with about how he was making it and Tennie's Jim to pour whiskey from the demijohn into the tin dipper from which he drank it, but even the boy's father and Walter Ewell, who were still young enough, scorned such, other than shooting the wild gobblers with pistols for wagers on their marksmanship.

Or, that is, his father and the others believed he was hunting squirrels. 35 Until the third day, he thought that Sam Fathers believed that too. Each morning he would leave the camp right after breakfast. He had his own gun now, a Christmas present. He went back to the tree beside the bayou where he had stood that morning. Using the compass which General Compson had given him, he ranged from that point; he was teaching himself to be a better-than-fair woodsman without knowing he was doing it. On the second day he even found the gutted log where he had first seen the crooked print. It was almost completely crumbled now, healing with unbelievable speed, a passionate and almost visible relinquishment, back into the earth from which the tree had grown.

He ranged the summer woods now, green with gloom; if anything, ac- 36 tually dimmer than in November's gray dissolution, where, even at noon, the sun fell only in intermittent dappling upon the earth, which never completely dried out and which crawled with snakes — moccasins and water snakes and rattlers, themselves the color of the dappling gloom, so that he would not always see them until they moved, returning later and later, first day, second day, passing in the twilight of the third evening the little log pen enclosing the log stable where Sam was putting up the horses for the night.

"You ain't looked right yet," Sam said. 37

He stopped. For a moment he didn't answer. Then he said peacefully, 38 in a peaceful rushing burst as when a boy's miniature dam in a little brook gives way, "All right. But how? I went to the bayou. I even found that log again. I —"

"I reckon that was all right. Likely he's been watching you. You never 39 saw his foot?"

"I," the boy said —"I didn't — I never thought —" 40

"It's the gun," Sam said. He stood beside the fence motionless — the 41 old man, the Indian, in the battered faded overalls and the five-cent straw hat which in the Negro's race had been the badge of his enslavement and was now the regalia of his freedom. The camp — the clearing, the house, the barn and its tiny lot with which Major de Spain in his turn had scratched punily and evanescently at the wilderness — faded in the dusk, back into the immemorial darkness of the woods. *The gun,* the boy thought. *The gun.*

"Be scared," Sam said. "You can't help that. But don't be afraid. Ain't   42 nothing in the woods going to hurt you unless you corner it, or it smells that you are afraid. A bear or a deer, too, has got to be scared of a coward the same as a brave man has got to be."

The gun, the boy thought.   43

"You will have to choose," Sam said.   44

He left the camp before daylight, long before Uncle Ash would wake in   45 his quilts on the kitchen floor and start the fire for breakfast. He had only the compass and a stick for snakes. He could go almost a mile before he would begin to need the compass. He sat on a log, the invisible compass in his invisible hand, while the secret night sounds, fallen still at his movements, scurried again and then ceased for good, and the owls ceased and gave over to the waking of day birds, and he could see the compass. Then he went fast yet still quietly; he was becoming better and better as a woodsman, still without having yet realized it.

He jumped a doe and a fawn at sunrise, walked them out of the bed,   46 close enough to see them — the crash of undergrowth, the white scut, the fawn scudding behind her faster than he had believed it could run. He was hunting right, upwind, as Sam had taught him; not that it mattered now. He had left the gun; of his own will and relinquishment he had accepted not a gambit, not a choice, but a condition in which not only the bear's heretofore inviolable anonymity but all the old rules and balances of hunter and hunted had been abrogated. He would not even be afraid, not even in the moment when the fear would take him completely — blood, skin, bowels, bones, memory from the long time before it became his memory — all save that thin, clear, immortal lucidity which alone differed him from this bear and from all the other bear and deer he would ever kill in the humility and pride of his skill and endurance, to which Sam had spoken when he leaned in the twilight on the lot fence yesterday.

By noon he was far beyond the little bayou, farther into the new and   47 alien country than he had ever been. He was traveling now not only by the old, heavy, biscuit-thick silver watch which had belonged to his grandfather. When he stopped at last, it was for the first time since he had risen from the log at dawn when he could see the compass. It was far enough. He had left the camp nine hours ago; nine hours from now, dark would have already been an hour old. But he didn't think that. He thought, *All right. Yes. But what?* and stood for a moment, alien and small in the green and topless solitude, answering his own question before it had formed and ceased. It was the watch, the compass, the stick — the three lifeless mechanicals with which for nine hours he had fended the wilderness off; he hung the watch and compass carefully on a bush and leaned the stick beside them and relinquished completely to it.

He had not been going very fast for the last two or three hours. He 48 went no faster now, since distance would not matter even if he could have gone fast. And he was trying to keep a bearing on the tree where he had left the compass, trying to complete a circle which would bring him back to it or at least intersect itself, since direction would not matter now either. But the tree was not there, and he did as Sam had schooled him — made the next circle in the opposite direction, so that the two patterns would bisect somewhere, but crossing no print of his own feet, finding the tree at last, but in the wrong place — no bush, no compass, no watch — and the tree not even the tree, because there was a down log beside it and he did what Sam Fathers had told him was the next thing and the last.

As he sat down on the log he saw the crooked print — the warped, 49 tremendous, two-toed indentation which, even as he watched it, filled with water. As he looked up, the wilderness coalesced, solidified — the glade, the tree he sought, the bush, the watch and the compass glinting where a ray of sunshine touched them. Then he saw the bear. It did not emerge, appear; it was just there, immobile, solid, fixed in the hot dappling of the green and windless noon, not as big as he had dreamed it, but as big as he had expected it, bigger, dimensionless, against the dappled obscurity, looking at him where he sat quietly on the log and looked back at it.

Then it moved. It made no sound. It did not hurry. It crossed the 50 glade, walking for an instant into the full glare of the sun; when it reached the other side it stopped again and looked back at him across one shoulder while his quiet breathing inhaled and exhaled three times.

Then it was gone. It didn't walk into the woods, the undergrowth. It 51 faded, sank back into the wilderness as he had watched a fish, a huge old bass, sink and vanish into the dark depths of its pool without even any movement of its fins.

He thought, *It will be next fall.* But it was not next fall, nor the next nor 52 the next. He was fourteen then. He had killed his buck, and Sam Fathers had marked his face with the hot blood, and in the next year he killed a bear. But even before that accolade he had become as competent in the woods as many grown men with the same experience; by his fourteenth year he was a better woodsman than most grown men with more. There was no territory within thirty miles of the camp that he did not know — bayou, ridge, brake, landmark, tree and path. He could have led anyone to any point in it without deviation, and brought them out again. He knew the game trails that even Sam Fathers did not know; in his thirteenth year he found a buck's bedding place, and unbeknown to his father he borrowed Walter Ewell's rifle and lay in wait at dawn and killed the buck when it walked back to the bed, as Sam had told him how the old Chickasaw fathers did.

But not the old bear, although by now he knews its footprints better than he did his own, and not only the crooked one. He could see any one of three sound ones and distinguish it from any other, and not only by its size. There were other bears within these thirty miles which left tracks almost as large, but this was more than that. If Sam Fathers had been his mentor and the back-yard rabbits and squirrels at home his kindergarten, then the wilderness the old bear ran was his college, the old male bear itself, so long unwifed and childless as to have become its own ungendered progenitor, was his alma mater. But he never saw it.   53

He could find the crooked print now almost whenever he liked, fifteen or ten or five miles, or sometimes nearer the camp than that. Twice while on stand during the three years he heard the dogs strike its trail by accident; on the second time they jumped it seemingly, the voices high, abject, almost human in hysteria, as on that first morning two years ago. But not the bear itself. He would remember that noon three years ago, the glade, himself and the bear fixed during that moment in the windless and dappled blaze, and it would seem to him that it had never happened, that he had dreamed that too. But it had happened. They had looked at each other, they had emerged from the wilderness old as earth, synchronized to the instant by something more than the blood that moved the flesh and bones which bore them, and touched, pledged something, affirmed something more lasting than the frail web of bones and flesh which any accident could obliterate.   54

Then he saw it again. Because of the very fact that he thought of nothing else, he had forgotten to look for it. He was still hunting with Walter Ewell's rifle. He saw it cross the end of a long blow-down, a corridor where a tornado had swept, rushing through rather than over the tangle of trunks and branches as a locomotive would have, faster than he had ever believed it could move, almost as fast as a deer even, because a deer would have spent most of that time in the air, faster than he could bring the rifle sights up with it. And now he knew what had been wrong during all the three years. He sat on a log, shaking and trembling as if he had never seen the woods before nor anything that ran them, wondering with incredulous amazement how he could have forgotten the very thing which Sam Fathers had told him and which the bear itself had proved the next day and had now returned after three years to reaffirm.   55

And now he knew what Sam Fathers had meant about the right dog, a dog in which size would mean less than nothing. So when he returned alone in April — school was out then, so that the sons of farmers could help with the land's planting, and at last his father had granted him permission, on his   56 promise to be back in four days — he had the dog. It was his own, a mongrel of the sort called by Negroes a fyce, a ratter, itself not much bigger than a rat and possessing that bravery which had long since stopped being courage and had become foolhardiness.

It did not take four days. Alone again, he found the trail on the first 57 morning. It was not a stalk; it was an ambush. He timed the meeting almost as if it were an appointment with a human being. Himself holding the fyce muffled in a feed sack and Sam Fathers with two of the hounds on a piece of a plowline rope, they lay down wind of the trail at dawn of the second morning. They were so close that the bear turned without even running, as if in surprised amazement at the shrill and frantic uproar of the released fyce, turning at bay against the trunk of a tree, on its hind feet; it seemed to the boy that it would never stop rising, taller and taller, and even the two hounds seemed to take a desperate and despairing courage from the fyce, following it as it went in.

Then he realized that the fyce was actually not going to stop. He flung, 58 threw the gun away, and ran; when he overtook and grasped the frantically pin-wheeling little dog, it seemed to him that he was directly under the bear.

He could smell it, strong and hot and rank. Sprawling, he looked up to 59 where it loomed and towered over him like a cloudburst and colored like a thunderclap, quite familiar, peacefully and even lucidly familiar, until he remembered: This was the way he had used to dream about it. Then it was gone. He didn't see it go. He knelt, holding the frantic fyce with both hands, hearing the abashed wailing of the hounds drawing farther and farther away, until Sam came up. He carried the gun. He laid it down quietly beside the boy and stood looking down at him.

"You've done seed him twice now with a gun in your hands," he said. 60 "This time you couldn't have missed him."

The boy rose. He still held the fyce. Even in his arms and clear of the 61 ground, it yapped frantically, straining and surging after the fading uproar of the two hounds like a tangle of wire springs. He was panting a little, but he was neither shaking nor trembling now.

"Neither could you!" he said. "You had the gun! Neither did you!" 62

"And you didn't shoot," his father said. "How close were you?" 63

"I don't know, sir," he said. "There was a big wood tick inside his right 64 hing leg. I saw that. But I didn't have the gun then."

"But you didn't shoot when you had the gun," his father said. "Why?" 65

But he didn't answer, and his father didn't wait for him to, rising and 66 crossing the room, across the pelt of the bear which the boy had killed two years ago and the larger one which his father had killed before he was born, to the bookcase beneath the mounted head of the boy's first buck. It was the room which his father called the office, from which all the plantation business was transacted; in it for the fourteen years of his life he had heard the best of all talking. Major de Spain would be there and sometimes old General Compson, and Walter Ewell and Boon Hoggenbeck and Sam Fathers and Tennie's Jim, too, were hunters, knew the woods and what ran them.

He would hear it, not talking himself but listening — the wilderness, the big woods, bigger and older than any recorded document of white man fatuous enough to believe he had bought any fragment of it or Indian ruthless enough to pretend that any fragment of it had been his to convey. It was of the men, not white nor black nor red, but men, hunters with the will and hardihood to endure and the humility and skill to survive, and the dogs and the bear and deer juxtaposed and reliefed against it, ordered and compelled by and within the wilderness in the ancient and unremitting contest by the ancient and immitigable rules which voided all regrets and brooked no quarter, the voices quiet and weighty and deliberate for retrospection and recollection and exact remembering, while he squatted in the blazing firelight as Tennie's Jim squatted, who stirred only to put more wood on the fire and to pass the bottle from one glass to another. Because the bottle was always present, so that after a while it seemed to him that those fierce instants of heart and brain and courage and wiliness and speed were concentrated and distilled into that brown liquor which not women, not boys and children, but only hunters drank, drinking not of the blood they had spilled but some condensation of the wild immortal spirit, drinking it moderately, humbly even, not with the pagan's base hope of acquiring the virtues of cunning and strength and speed, but in salute to them.

His father returned with the book and sat down again and opened it. "Listen," he said. He read the five stanzas aloud, his voice quiet and deliberate in the room where there was no fire now because it was already spring. Then he looked up. The boy watched him. "All right," his father said. "Listen." He read again, but only the second stanza this time, to the end of it, the last two lines, and closed the book and put it on the table beside him. "She cannot fade, though thou hast not thy bliss, forever wilt thou love, and she be fair," he said.

"He's talking about a girl," the boy said.

"He had to talk about something," his father said. Then he said, "He was talking about truth. Truth doesn't change. Truth is one thing. It covers all things which touch the heart — honor and pride and pity and justice and courage and love. Do you see now?"

He didn't know. Somehow it was simpler than that. There was an old bear, fierce and ruthless, not merely just to stay alive, but with the fierce pride of liberty and freedom, proud enough of the liberty and freedom to see it threatened without fear or even alarm; nay, who at times even seemed deliberately to put that freedom and liberty in jeopardy in order to savor them, to remind his old strong bones and flesh to keep supple and quick to defend and preserve them. There was an old man, son of a Negro slave and an Indian king, inheritor on the one side of the long chronicle of a people who had learned humility through suffering, and pride through the endurance which survived the suffering and injustice, and on the other side, the chronicle of a people even longer in the land than the first, yet who no longer existed in the land at all save in the solitary brotherhood of an old Negro's alien blood and the wild and invincible spirit of an old bear. There was a boy who wished to learn humility and pride in order to become skillful and worthy in the woods, who suddenly found himself becoming so skillful so rapidly that he feared he would never become worthy because he had not learned humility and pride, although he had tried to, until one day and as suddenly he discovered that an old man who could not have defined either had led him, as though by the hand, to that point where an old bear and a little mongrel of a dog showed him that, by possessing one thing other, he would possess them both.

And a little dog, nameless and mongrel and many-fathered, grown, yet weighing less than six pounds, saying as if to itself, "I can't be dangerous, because there's nothing much smaller than I am; I can't be fierce, because they would call it just a noise; I can't be humble, because I'm already too close to the ground to genuflect; I can't be proud, because I wouldn't be near enough to it for anyone to know who was casting the shadow, and I don't even know that I'm not going to heaven, because they have already decided that I don't possess an immortal soul. So all I can be is brave. But it's all right. I can be that, even if they still call it just noise." [72]

That was all. It was simple, much simpler than somebody talking in a book about youth and a girl he would never need to grieve over, because he could never approach any nearer her and would never have to get any farther away. He had heard about a bear, and finally got big enough to trail it, and he trailed it four years and at last met it with a gun in his hands and he didn't shoot. Because a little dog — But he could have shot long before the little dog covered the twenty yards to where the bear waited, and Sam Fathers could have shot at any time during the interminable minute while Old Ben stood on his hind feet over them. He stopped. His father was watching him gravely across the spring-rife twilight of the room; when he spoke, his words were as quiet as the twilight, too, not loud, because they did not need to be because they would last. "Courage, and honor, and pride," his father said, "and pity, and love of justice and of liberty. They all touch the heart, and what the heart holds to becomes truth, as far as we know the truth. Do you see now?" [73]

Sam, and Old Ben, and Nip, he thought. And himself too. He had been all right too. His father had said so. "Yes, sir," he said. [74]

SUBJECT QUESTIONS

1. Faulkner makes clear from the beginning that Old Ben is more than just a bear; what does he represent?
2. Why do the hunters have no intention of killing Old Ben? If they don't mean to kill him, why do they hunt him every year?
3. Sam Fathers tells the boy that a bear — or a deer or a man — has more to fear from a coward than from a brave man. Do you agree?
4. If the boy must put himself in jeopardy in order to meet the bear, what does the bear mean to the boy? Why does Old Ben sometimes deliberately put *himself* in jeopardy?
5. What three things does the boy need in order to become skillful and worthy?
6. The boy's father explains to him why he didn't kill the bear by reading Keats's "Ode on a Grecian Urn," the point of which is that art, being a distillation of truth, is the only permanent beauty. What connection does that idea have with the boy's action? Does the father's final clarification help?
7. How does the boy explain to himself his refusal to kill Old Ben?

STRUCTURE QUESTIONS

1. This story has been placed in the section on argument, but it obviously does not have the structure of formal argument. In what sense, if any, is it an argument? (You might consider how the story would be changed if Faulkner had let Old Ben hide in a cave instead of exposing himself to danger.)
2. If a short story is to have symbolic meaning, it still ought to function on a literal level — that is, it ought to tell a consistent and comprehensible story. Is this one consistent on both levels?
3. When a writer uses symbols, one of his problems is to make clear what the symbols mean without being blatantly obvious. (The meaning of a symbol may be "felt" or "understood" in context even though it cannot be precisely stated in expository prose.) Did you have any trouble understanding, in the context, what the bear and the fyce stood for? Is the boy also a symbol?
4. Sam Fathers makes a distinction between two words usually considered synonymous, "scared" and "afraid." Should Faulkner have defined the terms to make the difference clear? Why doesn't he?

SUGGESTIONS FOR WRITING

1. Write an argument for (or against) protest and nonconformity in American society.

2. Since things in nature blossom and fade, and since past civilizations have flourished and died, does it follow that our own civilization should die of old age? Write an argument on this subject.
3. Write an argument for or against the idea that freedom needs to expose itself to criticism and danger in order to be true freedom.

First Fight. Then Fiddle. Ply the Slipping String

Gwendolyn Brooks

Gwendolyn Brooks was born in Topeka, Kansas, in 1917 and now lives in Chicago. She has published many volumes of poetry since her first, A Street in Bronzeville (1945). She has won the Pulitzer Prize (1950), two Guggenheim Fellowships, and awards from Poetry and Mademoiselle magazines and the American Academy of Arts and Letters. Brooks is also a book reviewer and has lectured at many colleges and universities. For a full understanding of the following poem, you should know that Gwendolyn Brooks is black, that the poem is addressed to blacks, and that it was written in 1949, long before the civil rights movement had made any serious impact on the white establishment.

First fight. Then fiddle. Ply the slipping string
With feathery sorcery; muzzle the note
With hurting love; the music that they wrote
Bewitch, bewilder. Qualify to sing
Threadwise. Devise no salt, no hempen thing   5
For the dear instrument to bear. Devote
The bow to silks and honey. Be remote
A while from malice and from murdering.
But first to arms, to armor. Carry hate
In front of you and harmony behind.   10
Be deaf to music and to beauty blind.
Win war. Rise bloody, maybe not too late
For having first to civilize a space
Wherein to play your violin with grace.

SUBJECT QUESTIONS

1. Examine the words which describe the music; what kind of music does Brooks advise the black violinist to play?
2. Who are "they" in "the music that they wrote"? Why should the violinist play someone else's music?
3. When the fighting is over, the violin should be encumbered with "no salt, no hempen thing"; what is Brooks getting at here?

4. Does the poet make clear why it is necessary to fight first before playing the violin? Would her audience in 1949 understand without being told?
5. Brooks advises the black to "carry hate" first "and harmony behind." Can beautiful goals be achieved by violent means? Under what circumstances do you think violence is justified? What did the authors of the Declaration of Independence think?

STRUCTURE QUESTIONS

1. If Brooks's advice is to fight first and fiddle later, should the lines about fighting be placed before those on making music? What does Brooks gain in emphasis by reversing the order?
2. Note that the final line returns to violin playing; what effect does this structure have on the total meaning of the poem?
3. Are the phrases which describe beautiful playing themselves beautiful? Is their meaning clear? Do they carry connotations beyond their literal meaning? Would you say that "threadwise" is an unfortunate word choice?
4. Should the lines about fighting be rougher, more "violent"? Does the word choice in these lines fit with the main emphasis of the poem?
5. Can you extract from the poem's meaning a coherent argument? Does your statement of the argument emphasize fighting or making beautiful music? Can you see why Brooks might choose to put this argument in the form of a poem?
6. One might expect advice to fight to be given in an angry tone. Has Brooks maintained the reasoned attitude of good argument?

SUGGESTIONS FOR WRITING

1. Write a prose argument in which you set out the conditions under which one must fight in order to fiddle. (You may, of course, choose to argue that fighting is never justified.)
2. Alfred North Whitehead once argued that history is the study of the ironic difference between people's intentions and the results of their actions. Choose a period of crisis or conflict with which you are familiar (the Civil War, the 1980 Olympic Games, etc.) and write an argument supporting or attacking Whitehead's notion that people never anticipate the results of their intentions.

8

A Matter of Faith

Persuasion

Just as the ancestor of argument was the deliberative oration of the Athenian Senate, so the forefather of persuasion was the forensic oration of Athenian law courts — or judicial assemblies. Its original purpose was to gain acquittal for the defendant. Because lawyers delivering the oration were less interested in arriving at truth than in getting their clients "off the hook," they did not feel obliged to limit their approaches to the logical, objective one of the deliberative oration: an acquittal for illogical or emotional reasons was still an acquittal. Although the rather strict formula for the forensic oration is usually disregarded today, our trial lawyers still use many of the same tactics which Aristotle discussed in his *Rhetoric*. Defense attorneys are likely to distract attention from the specific charge by dragging in character witnesses, or by associating the client's cause with the patriotic or religious feelings of the jury by quoting Abe Lincoln and the Bible.

The ideal persuasion, certainly, would not be deliberately illogical, but it would be much less likely than argument to encourage free and impartial discussion of the problem at hand. The strong feelings about their subjects that writers of argument strive to control can actually be put to use in persuasion to sway the reader to the desired position. Normally, too, writers of persuasion will not be anxious to discuss impartially their opponents' arguments. Although they want to create the impression that their arguments have been presented reasonably and fairly, they are more interested in the reader having a complete emotional conviction that they are right; hence, writers do not want to distract a reader by allowing any implication of serious weakness in their own positions.

The form of a persuasion is basically the same as that of written argument. Normally, it contains the same four parts; analysis of the problem; clear statement of the proposed solution; disproof of the opposition; and positive evidence. In addition persuasion ends with a "peroration," or a final strong emotional appeal. But the difference between persuasion and argument is almost entirely one of attitude: argument seeks to stimulate discussion, persuasion seeks to end it. Writers of persuasion can include anything which does not spoil their cases by the obviousness of the intent — appeals to prejudice and sympathies, appeals to such respected authorities as prophets, movie stars, and baseball heroes, arguments against an opponent's character instead of the opponent's ideas, and so on. They do not have to take pains to ensure that their evidence is typical, relevant, impartial, and sufficient. They can even include brief digressions on related topics that, though they do not constitute proof, will sway the reader by appealing to religious and political convictions, sense of justice and fair play, and so on. When Mark Antony delivered the famous funeral oration in Shakespeare's *Julius Caesar,* for instance, his aim was to convince the mob that Caesar was innocent of the charge of ambition. But Antony did not confine himself to relevant arguments alone. He aroused the people by displaying Caesar's corpse and pointing out the holes made by the daggers of the various assassins; he read Caesar's will; he made much of Brutus's having slain his best friend. In short, he used any argument which would either make the mob believe that his was the "reasonable" side or incense them against the conspirators.

Because the forensic oration was developed to incite the listeners to *do* something — that is, acquit the defendant — persuasion has traditionally been associated with this original aim. Argument can also be used to stimulate the reader to follow a desired course of action, but usually a reader is more likely to be stirred to action when given more motivation than cold logic. Persuasion, then, by combining logic with warmer appeals, is the ideal means of accomplishing such a purpose. (Persuasion can, however, be used simply to sway the reader to believe something without doing anything about it.) If writers wish a reader to take some action, they should be specific about the end they have in mind and should outline clearly the steps (processes) by which the aim can be accomplished. As in any process, the steps should be in proper order and clearly explained. The P.T.A. speaker who convinces an audience that the town needs better schools may achieve nothing without explaining a method of getting better schools. Mark Antony incited the mob to anger, but their anger and energy would gradually have dissipated had not Antony suggested specific action to them — to burn Brutus's house and drive the assassins from Rome. Although audiences or readers may be convinced that "something needs to be done," nothing will be done unless they are told how to do it. Even if writers are not sure that their methods are the best way of achieving their goals, they should still offer them as a tentative plan: they will show that something *can* be done and they may stimulate readers to think of a better plan by giving them something specific to work with.

The greatest danger in writing persuasion is irresponsibility. Students who plan to write persuasion should remember that the aim of writing ought to be honest communication. The freedom to use emotional appeals in persuasion frequently misleads students into thinking that they are free to use dishonest means to gain honest ends. Good persuasion, like good propaganda, does make use of motivations somewhat less respectable intellectually than those used in logical argument; still, writers should believe in the rightness of what they want the reader to do.

Writing persuasion can be an entertaining change of pace from the type of expository prose a student is usually called upon to write. It can also be a useful art: although few students are studying to become politicians or ministers, most of them do have to write home for money occasionally.

The selections illustrating persuasion were chosen from the general area of religion because that is a subject on which logical argument, in the truest sense, is virtually impossible. Many bull sessions on this topic go wrong because the participants fail to realize that it is an area for persuasion rather than argument. Matters of faith are seldom influenced by statistical evidence. You are urged to examine these writings as open-mindedly as possible. You should honestly expose your own ideas to comparison with those presented here, remembering that if a belief is worth having it ought to be able to withstand exposure to differing beliefs.

from The Apology of Socrates

Plato

Socrates was sentenced to death for "corrupting the youth of Athens." His method of teaching was to engage the supposedly wise in cross-examination and thereby prove them not to be wise. The passage which follows is part of his defense of himself at the trial as reported later by his student, Plato (427?–347 B.C.).

Someone will say: And are you not ashamed, Socrates, of a course of life which is likely to bring you to an untimely end? To him I may fairly answer: There you are mistaken: a man who is good for anything ought not to calculate the chance of living or dying; he ought only to consider whether in doing anything he is doing right or wrong — acting the part of a good man or of a bad. . . . 1

Strange, indeed, would be my conduct, O men of Athens, if I, who when I was ordered by the generals whom you chose to command me at Potidaea[1] and Amphipolis and Delium, remained where they placed me, like any other man, facing death — if now, when, as I conceive and imagine, God orders me to fulfill the philosopher's mission of searching into myself and other men, I were to desert my post through fear of death, or any other fear; that would indeed be strange, and I might justly be arraigned in court for denying the existence of the gods, if I disobeyed the oracle because I was afraid of death, fancying that I was wise when I was not wise. For the fear of death is indeed the pretense of wisdom, and not real wisdom, being a pretense of knowing the unknown; and no one knows whether death, which men in their fear apprehend to be the greatest evil, may not be the greatest good. Is not this ignorance of a disgraceful sort, the ignorance which is the conceit that a man knows what he does not know? And in this respect only I believe myself to differ from men in general, and may perhaps claim to be wiser than they are: that whereas I know but little of the world below, I do not suppose that I know: but I do know that injustice and disobedience to a better, whether God or man, is evil and dishonorable, and I will never fear or avoid a possible good rather than a certain evil. And therefore if you let me go now, and are not convinced by Anytus, who said that since I had been prosecuted I must be put to death (or if not, that I ought never to have been 2

[1] Socrates had served in the Athenian infantry during some of the northern campaigns of the Peloponnesian War.

390

prosecuted at all); and that if I escape now, your sons will all be utterly ruined by listening to my words — if you say to me, Socrates, this time we will not mind Anytus, and you shall be let off, but upon one condition, that you are not to inquire and speculate in this way any more, and that if you are caught doing so again you shall die; if this was the condition on which you let me go, I should reply: Men of Athens, I honor and love you; but I shall obey God rather than you, and while I have life and strength I shall never cease from the practice and teaching of philosophy, exhorting anyone whom I meet and saying to him after my manner: "You, my friend — a citizen of the great and mighty and wise city of Athens — are you not ashamed of heaping up the greatest amount of money and honor and reputation, and caring so little about wisdom and truth and the greatest improvement of the soul, which you never regard or heed at all?" And if the person with whom I am arguing, says: "Yes, but I do care"; then I do not leave him or let him go at once; but I proceed to interrogate and examine and cross-examine him, and if I think that he has no virtue in him, but only says that he has, I reproach him with undervaluing the greater and overvaluing the less. And I shall repeat the same words to everyone whom I meet, young and old, citizen and alien, but especially to the citizens, inasmuch as they are my brethren. For know that this is the command of God; and I believe that no greater good has ever happened in the state than my service to the God. For I do nothing but go about persuading you all, old and young alike, not to take thought for your persons or your properties, but first and chiefly to care about the greatest improvement of the soul. I tell you that virtue is not given by money, but that from virtue comes money and every other good of man, public as well as private. This is my teaching, and if this is the doctrine which corrupts the youth, I am a mischievous person. But if anyone says that this is not my teaching, he is speaking an untruth. Wherefore, O men of Athens, I say to you, do as Anytus bids or not as Anytus bids, and either acquit me or not; but whichever you do, understand that I shall never alter my ways, not even if I have to die many times.

Men of Athens, do not interrupt, but hear me; there was an understanding between us that you should hear me to the end; I have something more to say, at which you may be inclined to cry out; but I believe that to hear me will be good for you, and therefore I beg that you will not cry out. I would have you know that if you kill such an one as I am, you will injure yourselves more than you will injure me. Nothing will injure me, not Meletus nor yet Anytus — they cannot, for a bad man is not permitted to injure a better than himself. I do not deny that Anytus may, perhaps, kill him, or drive him into exile, or deprive him of civil rights; and he many imagine, and others may imagine, that he is inflicting a great injury upon him: but there I do not agree. For the evil of doing as he is doing — the evil of unjustly taking away the life of another — is greater far.

And now, Athenians, I am not going to argue for my own sake, as you   4
may think, but for yours, that you may not sin against the God by condemn-
ing me, who am his gift to you. For if you kill me you will not easily find a
successor to me, who, if I may use such a ludicrous figure of speech, am a
sort of gadfly, given to the state by God; and the state is a great and noble
steed who is tardy in his motions owing to his very size, and requires to be
stirred into life. I am that gadfly which God has attached to the state, and all
day long and in all places am always fastening upon you, arousing and persuading and reproaching you. You will not easily find another like me, and
therefore I would advise you to spare me. I dare say that you may feel out of
temper (like a person who is suddenly awakened from sleep), and you think
that you might easily strike me dead as Anytus advises, and then you would
sleep on for the remainder of your lives, unless God in his care of you sent
you another gadfly. When I say that I am given to you by God, the proof of
my mission is this: if I had been like other men, I should not have neglected
all my own concerns or patiently seen the neglect of them during all these
years, and have been doing yours, coming to you individually like a father or
elder brother, exhorting you to regard virtue; such conduct, I say, would be
unlike human nature. If I had gained anything, or if my exhortations had
been paid, there would have been some sense in my doing so; but now, as
you will perceive, not even the impudence of my accusers dares to say that I
have ever exacted or sought pay of anyone; of that they have no witness. And
I have a sufficient witness to the truth of what I say — my poverty.

Someone may wonder why I go about in private giving advice and   5
busying myself with the concerns of others, but do not venture to come
forward in public and advise the state. I will tell you why. You have heard
me speak at sundry times and in diverse places of an oracle or sign which
comes to me, and is the divinity which Meletus ridicules in the indictment.
This sign, which is a kind of voice, first began to come to me when I was a
child; it always forbids but never commands me to do anything which I am
going to do. This is what deters me from being a politician. And rightly, as I
think. For I am certain, O men of Athens, that if I had engaged in politics, I
should have perished long ago, and done no good either to you or to myself.
And do not be offended at my telling you the truth: for the truth is, that no
man who goes to war with you or any other multitude, honestly striving
against the many lawless and unrighteous deeds which are done in a state,
will save his life; he who will fight for the right, if he would live even for a
brief space, must have a private station and not a public one. . . .

SUBJECT QUESTIONS

1. Socrates's defense of himself, although it shows his honesty and apparent innocence, does not seem calculated to win his acquittal.
   Why not?

2. Do you think Socrates might deliberately have put his judges into a position of having to convict him? What might he gain by doing so? What would the world think — or know — of Socrates had he asked for mercy and promised to quit teaching, and thereby been allowed to live?

3. Socrates says that the only way in which he is wiser than other men is that he knows his ignorance and they do not. Of what use, if any, would that sort of wisdom be? Does Socrates show through his speech that he is also wiser than his judges in other ways?

4. What is the rationale behind the concluding statement — "he who will fight for the right, if he would live even for a brief space, must have a private station and not a public one"? How can a reformer accomplish anything unless he secures some position of public power?

5. A reforming politician today, while in some danger of assassination, is in little danger of being put to death by the government. What is more likely to happen to him? Can you think of any politicians in recent years who have had to sacrifice their ideals in order to maintain an influential position in government? Can you think of any who, like Socrates, quit the government in order to maintain their integrity?

6. What is the gist of Socrates's argument that the government should acquit him for their own sakes rather than for his?

7. What parallels do you find between Socrates's trial and that of Jesus?

STRUCTURE QUESTIONS

1. Socrates's defense in its entirety follows the traditional formula for a forensic oration; how much of that formula can you detect in this extract?

2. To what extent, if any, does Socrates rely on emotional rather than rational appeal?

3. If Socrates's approach is primarily rational, what puts this speech in the category of persuasion rather than argument?

4. Examine Socrates's proof that he has been sent to the state by God (paragraph 4); does it constitute valid evidence? Is it "persuasive"?

SUGGESTIONS FOR WRITING

1. Imagine that you are one of Socrates's students and have a chance to speak at his trial. What would you say in defense of Socrates?

2. Write a persuasive essay on the right of the state to censor teachers.

A Free Man's Worship

Bertrand Russell

Bertrand Russell (1872–1970), mathematician and philosopher, also won the Nobel Prize for Literature (1950). Together with Alfred North Whitehead he published the great Principia Mathematica *(1910–13). Thereafter he published three dozen books, mostly on philosophy; his major interest is fairly summarized by the title of one of them:* New Hope *for a* Changing World *(1951). At the time of his death, Lord Russell was perhaps best known as a leader of pacifist movements — he was jailed several times for objecting to government policy and for leading protest demonstrations.* A Free Man's Worship *was written early in his career, when Russell was a young scientist forced to come to grips with the new world which post-Darwinian science had presented to him.*

To Dr. Faustus in his study Mephistopheles told the history of the Creation, saying:

    The endless praises of the choirs of angels had begun to grow wearisome; for, after all, did he not deserve their praise? Had he not given them endless joy? Would it not be more amusing to obtain undeserved praise, to be worshipped by beings whom he tortured? He smiled inwardly, and resolved that the great drama should be performed.

    For countless ages the hot nebula whirled aimlessly through space. At length it began to take shape, the central mass threw off planets, the planets cooled, boiling seas and burning mountains heaved and tossed, from black masses of cloud hot sheets of rain deluged the barely solid crust. And now the first germ of life grew in the depths of the ocean, and developed rapidly in the fructifying warmth into vast forest trees, huge ferns springing from the damp mould, sea monsters breeding, fighting, devouring, and passing away. And from the monsters, as the play unfolded itself, Man was born, with the power of thought, the knowledge of good and evil, and the cruel thirst for worship. And Man saw that all is passing in this mad, monstrous world, that all is struggling to snatch, at any cost, a few brief moments of life before Death's inexorable decree. And Man said: "There is a hidden purpose, could we but fathom it, and the purpose is good; for we must reverence something, and in the visible world there is nothing worthy of reverence." And Man stood aside from the struggle, resolving that God intended harmony to come out of chaos by human efforts. And when he followed the instincts which God had transmitted to him from his ancestry of beasts of prey, he called it Sin, and asked God to forgive him. But he doubted whether he could be justly forgiven, until he invented a divine Plan by which God's wrath was to have been appeased. And seeing the present was bad, he made it yet worse, that thereby the future might be better. And he gave God thanks for the strength that enabled him to forgo even the joys that were possible. And God smiled; and when he saw that Man had become perfect in renunciation and worship, he sent another sun through the sky, which crashed into Man's sun; and all returned again to nebula.

"Yes," he murmured, "it was a good play; I will have it performed again."

Such, in outline, but even more purposeless, more void of meaning, is the world which Science presents for our belief. Amid such a world, if anywhere, our ideas henceforward must find a home. That Man is the product of causes which had no prevision of the end they were achieving; that his origin, his growth, his hopes and fears, his loves and his beliefs, are but the outcome of accidental collocations of atoms; that no fire, no heroism, no intensity of thought and feeling, can preserve an individual life beyond the grave; that all the labours of the ages, all the devotion, all the inspiration, all the noonday brightness of human genius, are destined to extinction in the vast death of the solar system, and that the whole temple of Man's achievement must inevitably be buried beneath the débris of a universe in ruins — all these things, if not quite beyond dispute, are yet so nearly certain, that no philosophy which rejects them can hope to stand. Only within the scaffolding of these truths, only on the firm foundation of unyielding despair, can the soul's habitation henceforth be safely built.

How, in such an alien and inhuman world, can so powerless a creature as Man preserve his aspirations untarnished? A strange mystery it is that Nature, omnipotent but blind, in the revolutions of her secular hurryings through the abysses of space, has brought forth at last a child, subject still to her power, but gifted with sight, with knowledge of good and evil, with the capacity of judging all the works of his unthinking Mother. In spite of Death, the mark and seal of the parental control, Man is yet free, during his brief years, to examine, to criticise, to know, and in imagination to create. To him alone, in the world with which he is acquainted, this freedom belongs; and in this lies his superiority to the resistless forces that control his outward life.

The savage, like ourselves, feels the oppression of his impotence before the powers of Nature; but having in himself nothing that he respects more than Power, he is willing to prostrate himself before his gods, without inquiring whether they are worthy of his worship. Pathetic and very terrible is the long history of cruelty and torture, of degradation and human sacrifices endured in the hope of placating the jealous gods: surely, the trembling believer thinks, when what is most precious has been freely given, their lust for blood must be appeased, and more will not be required. The religion of Moloch — as such creeds may be generically called — is in essence the cringing submission of the slave, who dare not, even in his heart, allow the thought that his master deserves no adulation. Since the independence of

ideals is not yet acknowledged, Power may be freely worshipped, and receive an unlimited respect, despite its wanton infliction of pain.

But gradually, as morality grows bolder, the claim of the ideal world   5
begins to be felt, and worship, if it is not to cease, must be given to gods of
another kind than those created by the savage. Some, though they feel the
demands of the ideal, will still consciously reject them, still urging that
naked Power is worthy of worship. Such is the attitude inculcated in God's
answer to Job out of the whirlwind: the divine power and knowledge are
paraded, but of the divine goodness there is no hint. Such also is the attitude
of those who, in our own day, base their morality upon the struggle for survival, maintaining that the survivors are necessarily the fittest. But others,
not content with an answer so repugnant to the moral sense, will adopt the
position which we have become accustomed to regard as specially religious,
maintaining that, in some hidden manner, the world of fact is really harmoni-
ous with the world of ideals. Thus Man creates God, all-powerful and all-
good, the mystic unity of what is and what should be.

But the world of fact, after all, is not good; and, in submitting our judg-   6
ment to it, there is an element of slavishness from which our thoughts must
be purged. For in all things it is well to exalt the dignity of Man, by freeing
him as far as possible from the tyranny of nonhuman Power. When we have
realised that Power is largely bad, that Man, with his knowledge of good and
evil, is but a helpless atom in a world which has no such knowledge, the
choice is again presented to us: Shall we worship Force, or shall we worship
Goodness? Shall our God exist and be evil, or shall he be recognised as the
creation of our own conscience?

The answer to this question is very momentous, and affects profoundly   7
our whole morality. The worship of Force, to which Carlyle and Nietzche
and the creed of Militarism have accustomed us, is the result of failure to
maintain our own ideals against a hostile universe: it is itself a prostrate submission to evil, a sacrifice of our best to Moloch. If strength indeed is to be
respected, let us respect rather the strength of those who refuse that false
"recognition of facts" which fails to recognise the facts are often bad. Let us
admit that, in the world we know, there are many things that would be better otherwise, and that the ideals to which we do and must adhere are not
realised in the realm of matter. Let us preserve our respect for truth, for
beauty, for the ideal of perfection which life does not permit us to attain,
though none of these things meet with the approval of the unconscious universe. If Power is bad, as it seems to be, let us reject it from our hearts. In
this lies Man's true freedom: in determination to worship only the God
created by our own love of the good, to respect only the heaven which
inspires the insight of our best moments. In action, in desire, we must submit perpetually to the tyranny of outside forces; but in thought, in aspiration,
we are free, free from our fellowmen, free from the petty planet on which

our bodies impotently crawl, free even, while we live, from the tyranny of death. Let us learn, then, that energy of faith which enables us to live constantly in the vision of the good; and let us descend in action, into the world of fact, with that vision always before us.

When first the opposition of fact and ideal grows fully visible, a spirit of   8
fiery revolt, of fierce hatred of the gods, seems necessary to the assertion of freedom. To defy with Promethean constancy a hostile universe, to keep its evil always in view, always actively hated, to refuse no pain that the malice of Power can invent, appears to be the duty of all who will not bow before the inevitable. But indignation is still a bondage, for it compels our thoughts to be occupied with an evil world; and in the fierceness of desire from which rebellion springs there is a kind of self-assertion which it is necessary for the wise to overcome. Indignation is a submission of our thoughts, but not of our desires; the Stoic freedom in which wisdom consists is found in the submission of our desires, but not of our thoughts. From the submission of our desires springs the virtue of resignation; from the freedom of our thoughts springs the whole world of art and philosophy, and the vision of beauty by which, at last, we half reconquer the reluctant world. But the vision of beauty is possible only to unfettered contemplation, to thoughts not weighted by the load of eager wishes; and thus Freedom comes only to those who no longer ask of life that it shall yield them any of those personal goods that are subject to the mutations of Time.

Although the necessity of renunciation is evidence of the existence of   9
evil, yet Christianity, in preaching it, has shown a wisdom exceeding that of the Promethean philosophy of rebellion. It must be admitted that, of the things we desire, some, though they prove impossible, are yet real goods; others, however, as ardently longed for, do not form part of a fully purified ideal. The belief that what must be renounced is bad, though sometimes false, is far less often false than untamed passion supposes; and the creed of religion, by providing a reason for proving that it is never false, has been the means of purifying our hopes by the discovery of many austere truths.

But there is in resignation a further good element: even real goods,   10
when they are unattainable, ought not to be fretfully desired. To every man comes, sooner or later, the great renunciation. For the young, there is nothing unattainable; a good thing desired with the whole force of a passionate will, and yet impossible, is to them not credible. Yet, by death, by illness, by poverty, or by the voice of duty, we must learn, each one of us, that the world was not made for us, and that, however beautiful may be the things we crave, Fate may nevertheless forbid them. It is the part of courage, when misfortune comes, to bear without repining the ruin of our hopes, to turn away our thoughts from vain regrets. This degree of submission to Power is not only just and right; it is the very gate of wisdom.

But passive renunciation is not the whole of wisdom; for not by renun-   11 ciation alone can we build a temple for the worship of our own ideals. Haunting foreshadowings of the temple appear in the realm of imagination, in music, in architecture, in the untroubled kingdom of reason, and in the golden sunset magic of lyrics, where beauty shines and glows, remote from the touch of sorrow, remote from the fear of change, remote from the failures and disenchantments of the world of fact. In the contemplation of these things the vision of heaven will shape itself in our hearts, giving at once a touchstone to judge the world about us, and an inspiration by which to fashion to our needs whatever is not incapable of serving as a stone in the sacred temple.

Except for those rare spirits that are born without sin, there is a cavern   12
of darkness to be traversed before that temple can be entered. The gate of the cavern is despair, and its floor is paved with the gravestones of abandoned hopes. There Self must die; there the eagerness, the greed of untamed desire must be slain, for only so can the soul be freed from the empire of Fate. But out of the cavern the Gate of Renunciation leads again to the daylight of wisdom, by whose radiance a new insight, a new joy, a new tenderness, shine forth to gladden the pilgrim's heart.

When, without the bitterness of impotent rebellion, we have learnt   13
both to resign ourselves to the outward rule of Fate and to recognise that the nonhuman world is unworthy of our worship, it becomes possible at last so to transform and refashion the unconscious universe, so to transmute it in the crucible of the imagination, that a new image of shining gold replaces the old idol of clay. In all the multiform facts of the world — in the visual shapes of trees and mountains and clouds, in the events of the life of Man, even in the very omnipotence of Death — the insight of creative idealism can find the reflection of a beauty which its own thoughts first made. In this way mind asserts its subtle mastery over the thoughtless forces of Nature. The more evil the material with which it deals, the more thwarting to untrained desire, the greater is its achievement in inducing the reluctant rock to yield up its hidden treasures, the prouder its victory in compelling the opposing forces to swell the pageant of its triumph. Of all the arts, Tragedy is the proudest, the most triumphant; for it builds its shining citadel in the very centre of the enemy's country, on the very summit of his highest mountain; from its impregnable watch-towers, his camps and arsenals, his columns and forts, are all revealed; within its walls the free life continues, while the legions of Death and Pain and Despair, and all the servile captains of tyrant Fate, afford the burghers of that dauntless city new spectacles of beauty. Happy those sacred ramparts, thrice happy the dwellers on that all-seeing eminence. Honour to those brave warriors who, through countless ages of warfare, have preserved for us the priceless heritage of liberty, and have kept undefiled by sacrilegious invaders the home of the unsubdued.

But the beauty of Tragedy does but make visible a quality which, in   14
more or less obvious shapes, is present always and everywhere in life. In the

spectacle of Death, in the endurance of intolerable pain, and in the irrevocableness of a vanished past, there is a sacredness, an overpowering awe, a feeling of the vastness, the depth, the inexhaustible mystery of existence, in which, as by some strange marriage of pain, the sufferer is bound to the world by bonds of sorrow. In these moments of insight, we lose all eagerness of temporary desire, all struggling and striving for petty ends, all care for the little trivial things, that, to a superficial view, make up the common life of day by day; we see, surrounding the narrow raft illumined by the flickering light of human comradeship, the dark ocean on whose rolling waves we toss for a brief hour; from the great night without, a chill blast breaks in upon our refuge; all the loneliness of humanity amid hostile forces is concentrated upon the individual soul, which must struggle alone, with what of courage it can command, against the whole weight of a universe that cares nothing for its hopes and fears. Victory, in this struggle with the powers of darkness, is the true baptism into the glorious company of heroes, the true initiation into the overmastering beauty of human existence. From that awful encounter of the soul with the outer world, renunciation, wisdom, and charity are born; and with their birth a new life begins. To take into the inmost shrine of the soul the irresistible forces whose puppets we seem to be — Death and change, the irrevocableness of the past, and the powerlessness of Man before the blind hurry of the universe from vanity to vanity — to feel these things and know them is to conquer them.

This is the reason why the Past has such magical power. The beauty of 15 its motionless and silent pictures is like the enchanted purity of late autumn, when the leaves, though one breath would make them fall, still glow against the sky in golden glory. The Past does not change or strive; like Duncan, after life's fitful fever it sleeps well; what was eager and grasping, what was petty and transitory, has faded away, the things that were beautiful and eternal shine out of it like stars in the night. Its beauty, to a soul not worthy of it, is unendurable; but to a soul which has conquered Fate it is the key of religion.

The life of Man, viewed outwardly, is but a small thing in comparison 16 with the forces of Nature. The slave is doomed to worship Time and Fate and Death, because they are greater than anything he finds in himself, and because all his thoughts are of things which they devour. But, great as they are, to think of them greatly, to feel their passionless splendour, is greater still. And such thought makes us free men; we no longer bow before the inevitable in Oriental subjection, but we absorb it, and make it part of ourselves. To abandon the struggle for private happiness, to expel all eagerness of temporary desire, to burn with passion for eternal things — this is emancipation, and this is the free man's worship. And this liberation is effected by a contemplation of Fate; for Fate itself is subdued by the mind which leaves nothing to be purged by the purifying fire of Time.

United with his fellow-men by the strongest of all ties, the tie of a com- 17 mon doom, the free man finds that a new vision is with him always, shedding over every daily task the light of love. The life of Man is a long march through the night, surrounded by invisible foes, tortured by weariness and pain, towards a goal that few can hope to reach, and where none may tarry long. One by one, as they march, our comrades vanish from our sight, seized by the silent orders of omnipotent Death. Very brief is the time in which we can help them, in which their happiness or misery is decided. Be it ours to shed sunshine on their path, to lighten their sorrows by the balm of sympathy, to give them the pure joy of a never-tiring affection, to strengthen failing courage, to instill faith in hours of despair. Let us not weigh in grudging scales their merits and demerits, but let us think only of their need — of the sorrows, the difficulties, perhaps the blindnesses, that make the misery of their lives; let us remember that they are fellow-sufferers in the same darkness, actors in the same tragedy with ourselves. And so, when their day is over, when their good and their evil have become eternal by the immortality of the past, be it ours to feel that, where they suffered, where they failed, no deed of ours was the cause, but wherever a spark of the divine fire kindled in their hearts, we were ready with encouragement, with sympathy, with brave words in which high courage glowed.

Brief and powerless is Man's life; on him and all his race the slow, sure doom falls pitiless and dark. Blind to good and evil, reckless of destruction, omnipotent matter rolls on its relentless way; for Man, condemned to-day to lose his dearest, to-morrow himself to pass through the gate of darkness, it remains only to cherish, ere yet the blow falls, the lofty thoughts that ennoble his little day; disdaining the coward terrors of the slave of Fate, to worship at the shrine that his own hands have built; undismayed by the empire of chance, to preserve a mind free from the wanton tyranny that rules his outward life; proudly defiant of the irresistible forces that tolerate, for a moment, his knowledge and his condemnation, to sustain alone, a weary but unyielding Atlas, the world that his own ideals have fashioned despite the trampling march of unconscious Power.

18

SUBJECT QUESTIONS

1. Why, when he does not believe in God except as a creation of man's mind, does Russell begin with the fable about God's creation of the world? What is the reader's reaction to it? Is the following a fair analysis of Russell's implication? If there is a god who created man, he must be capricious and arbitrary to have played such a dirty trick on man; hence, even if God exists, he is not worthy of worship.
2. If "Man is the product of causes which had no prevision of the end they were achieving," and if "resistless forces control his outward life," then in what sense can Russell claim that man is free? Is he

overlooking the possibility that even man's thoughts may be determined by natural causes beyond his control? We know, for instance, that body temperature has considerable effect on man's thinking. If his normal body temperature were 105°, like that of birds, his "normal" thinking would resemble what we now call delirium.

3. Russell says that savages still make themselves slaves by worshiping gods which they believe to be omnipotent. Does he mean to imply that anyone who worships an omnipotent god is not quite civilized?

4. Russell assumes without offering proof that "in all things it is well to exalt the dignity of man." Most religions exalt humility and insignificance; some even stress innate depravity. Is Russell being unrealistic in thus placing man on a pedestal, particularly since he recognizes that man is doomed to extinction?

5. Another of Russell's basic assumptions is that "power is largely bad." From this premise he concludes that an all-powerful God would be evil and that "man's true freedom" lies in refusing to worship such a concept. Is there a fallacy in his reasoning here?

6. If man should not worship a god, what is "the free man's worship"?

7. In the last two paragraphs, Russell combines concepts of brotherly love and atheism. But if there is no God-given command to love our fellow men, why should we do it? Surely brotherly love is not natural or instinctive.

STRUCTURE QUESTIONS

1. Examine the language of this essay. Is it objectively denotative, or charged with connotations? Would you say, then, that the language is better suited to the purposes of argument, or of persuasion?

2. Does the essay as a whole invite an open search for truth, or does it assume the truth and try to persuade the reader to accept it?

3. What are some of the premises by which Russell arrives at his conclusions? Does he give evidence to substantiate these premises?

4. Examine the picture of the world which, according to Russell, science shows ours to be. Is it a fair summary? Does it need support?

SUGGESTIONS FOR WRITING

1. Write a persuasive essay on the following question: "If we live in a purposeless, Godless, unfriendly universe and are doomed to extinction, what is the sense in trying to be 'moral' or to improve ourselves?"

2. Write an evaluation of Russell's essay. Refer to the suggestions on secondary evaluation given in the introduction to the section on evaluation (section 9).

The Efficacy of Prayer

C. S. Lewis

C. S. Lewis (1898–1963) was professor of medieval and Renaissance literature at Cambridge. He is most famous for his numerous writings on the
place of Christianity in the modern world, particularly Screwtape Letters.
"The Efficacy of Prayer" originally appeared in The Atlantic Monthly
(January 1959).

Some years ago I got up one morning intending to have my hair cut in prep-   1
aration for a visit to London, and the first letter I opened made it clear I
need not go to London. So I decided to put the haircut off too. But then
there began the most unaccountable little nagging in my mind, almost like a
voice saying, "Get it cut all the same. Go and get it cut." In the end I could
stand it no longer. I went. Now my barber at that time was a fellow Christian
and a man of many troubles whom my brother and I had sometimes been
able to help. The moment I opened his shop door he said, "Oh, I was praying you might come today." And in fact if I had come a day or so later I
should have been of no use to him.

    It awed me; it awes me still. But of course one cannot rigorously prove   2
a causal connection between the barber's prayers and my visit. It might be
telepathy. It might be accident.

    I have stood by the bedside of a woman whose thigh-bone was eaten   3
through with cancer and who had thriving colonies of the disease in many
other bones as well. It took three people to move her in bed. The doctors
predicted a few months of life; the nurses (who often know better), a few
weeks. A good man laid his hands on her and prayed. A year later the patient was walking (uphill, too, through rough woodland) and the man who
took the last X-ray photos was saying, "These bones are as solid as rock. It's
miraculous."

    But once again there is no rigorous proof. Medicine, as all true doctors   4
admit, is not an exact science. We need not invoke the supernatural to
explain the falsification of its prophecies. You need not, unless you choose,
believe in a causal connection between the prayers and the recovery.

    The question then arises, "What sort of evidence *would* prove the ef-   5
ficacy of prayer?" The thing we pray for may happen, but how can you ever

know it was not going to happen anyway? Even if the thing were indisputably miraculous it would not follow that the miracle had occurred because of your prayers. The answer surely is that a compulsive empirical proof such as we have in the sciences can never be attained.

Some things are proved by the unbroken uniformity of our experiences. The law of gravitation is established by the fact that, in our experience, all bodies without exception obey it. Now even if all the things that people prayed for happened, which they do not, this would not prove what Christians mean by the efficacy of prayer. For prayer is request. The essence of request, as distinct from compulsion, is that it may or may not be granted. And if an infinitely wise Being listens to the requests of finite and foolish creatures, of course He will sometimes grant and sometimes refuse them. Invariable "success" in prayer would not prove the Christian doctrine at all. It would prove something much more like magic — a power in certain human beings to control, or compel, the course of nature.

There are, no doubt, passages in the New Testament which may seem at first sight to promise an invariable granting of our prayers. But that cannot be what they really mean. For in the very heart of the story we meet a glaring instance to the contrary. In Gethsemane the holiest of all petitioners prayed three times that a certain cup might pass from Him. It did not. After that the idea that prayer is recommended to us as a sort of infallible gimmick may be dismissed.

Other things are proved not simply by experience but by those artificially contrived experiences which we call experiments. Could this be done about prayer? I will pass over the objection that no Christian could take part in such a project, because he has been forbidden it: "You must not try experiments on God, your Master." Forbidden or not, is the thing even possible?

I have seen it suggested that a team of people — the more the better — should agree to pray as hard as they knew how, over a period of six weeks, for all the patients in Hospital A and none of those in Hospital B. Then you would tot up the results and see if A had more cures and fewer deaths. And I suppose you would repeat the experiment at various times and places so as to eliminate the influence of irrelevant factors.

The trouble is that I do not see how any real prayer could go on under such conditions. "Words without thoughts never to heaven go," says the King in *Hamlet*. Simply to say prayers is not to pray; otherwise a team of properly trained parrots would serve as well as men for our experiment. You cannot pray for the recovery of the sick unless the end you have in view is their recovery. But you can have no motive for desiring the recovery of all the patients in one hospital and none of those in another. You are not doing it in order that suffering should be relieved; you are doing it to find out what happens. The real purpose and the nominal purpose of your prayers are at variance. In other words, whatever your tongue and teeth and knees may do, you are not praying. The experiment demands an impossibility.

Empirical proof and disproof are, then, unobtainable. But this conclu-   11
sion will seem less depressing if we remember that prayer is request and compare it with other specimens of the same thing.

We make requests of our fellow creatures as well as of God: we ask for   12
the salt, we ask for a raise in pay, we ask a friend to feed the cat while we are on our holidays, we ask a woman to marry us. Sometimes we get what we ask for and sometimes not. But when we do, it is not nearly so easy as one might suppose to prove with scientific certainty a causal connection between the asking and the getting.

Your neighbour may be a humane person who would not have let your   13
cat starve even if you had forgotten to make any arrangement. Your employer is never so likely to grant your request for a raise as when he is aware that you could get better money from a rival firm and is quite possibly intending to secure you by a raise in any case. As for the lady who consents to marry you — are you sure she had not decided to do so already? Your proposal, you know, might have been the result, not the cause, of her decision. A certain important conversation might never have taken place unless she had intended that it should.

Thus in some measure the same doubt that hangs about the causal ef-   14
ficacy of our prayers to God hangs also about our prayers to man. Whatever we get we might have been going to get anyway. But only, as I say, in some measure. Our friend, boss, and wife may tell us that they acted because we asked; and we may know them so well as to feel sure, first that they are saying what they believe to be true, and secondly that they understand their own motives well enough to be right. But notice that when this happens our assurance has not been gained by the methods of science. We do not try the control experiment of refusing the raise or breaking off the engagement and then making our request again under fresh conditions. Our assurance is quite different in kind from scientific knowledge. It is born out of our personal relation to the other parties; not from knowing things about them but from knowing *them*.

Our assurance — if we reach an assurance — that God always hears   15
and sometimes grants our prayers, and the apparent grantings are not merely fortuitous, can only come in the same sort of way. There can be no question of tabulating successes and failures and trying to decide whether the successes are too numerous to be accounted for by chance. Those who best know a man best know whether, when he did what they asked, he did it because they asked. I think those who best know God will best know whether He sent me to the barber's shop because the barber prayed.

For up till now we have been tackling the whole question in the wrong   16
way and on the wrong level. The very question "Does prayer work?" puts us

in the wrong frame of mind from the outset. "Work": as if it were magic, or a machine — something that functions automatically. Prayer is either a sheer illusion or a personal contact between embryonic, incomplete persons (ourselves) and the utterly concrete Person. Prayer in the sense of petition, asking for things, is a small part of it; confession and penitence are its threshold, adoration its sanctuary, the presence and vision and enjoyment of God its bread and wine. In it God shows Himself to us. That He answers prayers is a corollary — not necessarily the most important one — from that revelation. What He does is learned from what He is.

Petitionary prayer is, nonetheless, both allowed and commanded to us: 17 "Give us our daily bread." And no doubt it raises a theoretical problem. Can we believe that God ever really modified His action in response to the suggestions of men? For infinite wisdom does not need telling what is best, and infinite goodness needs no urging to do it. But neither does God need any of those things that are done by finite agents, whether living or inanimate. He could, if He chose, repair our bodies miraculously without food; or give us food without the aid of farmers, bakers, and butchers; or knowledge without the aid of learned men; or convert the heathen without missionaries. Instead, He allows soils and weather and animals and the muscles, minds, and wills of men to co-operate in the execution of His will. "God," said Pascal, "instituted prayer in order to lend to His creatures the dignity of causality." But not only prayer; whenever we act at all He lends us that dignity. It is not really stranger, nor less strange, that my prayers should affect the course of events than that my other actions should do so. They have not advised or changed God's mind — that is, His over-all purpose. But that purpose will be realized in different ways according to the actions, including the prayers, of His creatures.

For He seems to do nothing of Himself which He can possibly delegate 18 to His creatures. He commands us to do slowly and blunderingly what He could do perfectly and in the twinkling of an eye. He allows us to neglect what He would have us do, or to fail. Perhaps we do not fully realize the problem, so to call it, of enabling finite free wills to co-exist with Omnipotence. It seems to involve at every moment almost a sort of divine abdication. We are not mere recipients or spectators. We are either privileged to share in the game or compelled to collaborate in the work, "to wield our little tridents." Is this amazing process simply Creation going on before our eyes? This is how (no light matter) God makes something — indeed, makes gods — out of nothing.

So at least it seems to me. But what I have offered can be, at the very 19 best, only a mental model or symbol. All that we say on such subjects must be merely analogical and parabolic. The reality is doubtless not comprehensible by our faculties. But we can at any rate try to expel bad analogies and bad parables. Prayer is not a machine. It is not magic. It is not advice offered to God. Our act, when we pray, must not, any more than all our other acts, be separated from the continuous act of God Himself, in which alone all finite causes operate.

It would be even worse to think of those who get what they pray for as 20 a sort of court favorites, people who have influence with the throne. The refused prayer of Christ in Gethsemane is answer enough to that. And I dare not leave out the hard saying which I once heard from an experienced Christian: "I have seen many striking answers to prayer and more than one that I thought miraculous. But they usually come at the beginning: before conversion, or soon after it. As the Christian life proceeds, they tend to be rarer. The refusals, too, are not only more frequent; they become more unmistakable, more emphatic."

Does God then forsake just those who serve Him best? Well, He who 21 served Him best of all said, near His tortured death, "Why hast thou forsaken me?" When God becomes man, that Man, of all others, is least comforted by God, at His greatest need. There is a mystery here which, even if I had the power, I might not have the courage to explore. Meanwhile, little people like you and me, if our prayers are sometimes granted, beyond all hope and probability, had better not draw hasty conclusions to our own advantage. If we were stronger, we might be less tenderly treated. If we were braver, we might be sent, with far less help, to defend far more desperate posts in the great battle.

SUBJECT QUESTIONS

1. Lewis begins by citing two apparent examples of the efficacy of prayer, then he immediately denies that they constitute valid evidence. Does this denial seem to help or hurt Lewis's thesis? Is it in the nature of a "devastating concession"?
2. Lewis argues that the efficacy of prayer cannot be tested even by "scientific" experiment. Why not? Is his hypothetical controlled experiment merely a poor one, or would any other such experiment also fail?
3. If it cannot be proved that prayers are answered, on what grounds does Lewis believe that they are sometimes answered?
4. Because Lewis does not arrive at his conclusions by scientific induction, his argument must depend on certain undemonstrated assumptions. What are these?
5. If, as Lewis believes, his own answer is at best a "mental model," if "the reality is doubtless not comprehensible by our faculties," why does he try to give an answer at all? Or, to put the same question on a more general level, if religion is extralogical, why do so many people try to write logically about it?

6. Does Lewis mean to imply at the end that the more religious a person is the less likely he is to have his prayers answered?

STRUCTURE QUESTIONS

1. Note that, unlike most writers of persuasion, Lewis tries to avoid an emotional approach and maintain instead an objective, dispassionate tone. Is this tone appropriate to his purpose and subject? Would a different attitude be more effective?
2. What hints do you find that Lewis feels more strongly about his subject than the objective tone implies? Do these seem to be slips on Lewis's part, or deliberate devices? How do they influence the total impact of the essay?
3. At what point in the essay does Lewis abandon strict logic? Is there an accompanying change in language?
4. Examine the analogy between prayer to God and requests to fellow humans. Keeping in mind that an analogy is supposed to clarify but cannot prove a point, would you say that Lewis has used this analogy properly and to good purpose?
5. Does this essay follow the traditional organization of persuasion? Should Lewis have begun with an introductory paragraph instead of plunging immediately into a personal example of his theme?

SUGGESTION FOR WRITING

Write a persuasion essay on some one aspect of religion. (Do not attempt to write a *Summa Theologica* in five hundred words.) The example of Lewis's essay ought to indicate that although persuasion permits emotional appeals, writers should not "wear their hearts on their sleeves." Controlled emotion is much less likely to backfire than uncontrolled emotion. Remember also that dishonest feeling can seldom be disguised. Be sure you either believe what you are arguing or are honest in offering it as a tentative solution. The following list may give you some ideas for a topic of your own:

a. Prayer brings peace of mind
b. Attending church is a waste of time
c. Belief in miracles
d. Literal interpretation of the Bible
e. Religion as a crutch
f. On loving one's enemies

Father Damien

Robert Louis Stevenson

Robert Louis Stevenson (1850–1894) was born in Scotland and died of tuberculosis in Samoa, where he lived his last five years. He was an accomplished novelist, essayist, and poet, and published many books in his short lifetime. His best-known novels are Treasure Island, Kidnapped, *and* Dr. Jekyll and Mr. Hyde. *Despite his prolonged illness, Stevenson was an adventurer and world traveler. He had studied and practiced law before leaving Scotland; thus he was, as both writer and lawyer, especially well equipped to defend Father Damien against the charges of a rival missionary, Dr. Hyde. This "open letter" was first published in Australia, the South Pacific's literary outlet in 1890.*

AN OPEN LETTER TO THE REVEREND DR. HYDE OF HONOLULU

Sydney,
February 25, 1890.

SIR, — It may probably occur to you that we have met, and visited, and [1]
conversed; on my side, with interest. You may remember that you have
done me several courtesies, for which I was prepared to be grateful. But
there are duties which come before gratitude, and offences which justly
divide friends, far more acquaintances. Your letter to the Reverend H. B.
Gage is a document which, in my sight, if you had filled me with bread when
I was starving, if you had sat up to nurse my father when he lay a-dying,
would yet absolve me from the bonds of gratitude. You know enough, doubtless, of the process of canonisation to be aware that, a hundred years after
the death of Damien, there will appear a man charged with the painful office
of the *devil's advocate*. After that noble brother of mine, and of all frail clay,
shall have lain a century at rest, one shall accuse, one defend him. The circumstance is unusual that the devil's advocate should be a volunteer, should
be a member of a sect immediately rival, and should make haste to take
upon himself his ugly office ere the bones are cold; unusual, and of a taste
which I shall leave my readers free to qualify; unusual, and to me inspiring.
If I have at all learned the trade of using words to convey truth and to arouse
emotion, you have at last furnished me with a subject. For it is in the interest of all mankind, and the cause of public decency in every quarter of the
world, not only that Damien should be righted, but that you and your letter
should be displayed at length, in their true colours, to the public eye.

To do this properly, I must begin by quoting you at large: I shall then proceed to criticise your utterance from several points of view, divine and human, in the course of which I shall attempt to draw again, and with more specification, the character of the dead saint whom it has pleased you to vilify: so much being done, I shall say farewell to you for ever. [2]

> *Honolulu,*
> *August 2, 1889.*

Rev. H. B. Gage.

DEAR BROTHER, — In answer to your inquiries about Father Damien, [3] I can only reply that we who knew the man are surprised at the extravagant newspaper laudations, as if he was a most saintly philanthropist. The simple truth is, he was a coarse, dirty man, headstrong and bigoted. He was not sent to Molokai, but went there without orders; did not stay at the leper settlement (before he became one himself), but circulated freely over the whole island (less than half the island is devoted to the lepers), and he came often to Honolulu. He had no hand in the reforms and improvements inaugurated, which were the work of our Board of Health, as occasion required and means were provided. He was not a pure man in his relations with women, and the leprosy of which he died should be attributed to his vices and carelessness. Others have done much for the lepers, our own ministers, the government physicians, and so forth, but never with the Catholic idea of meriting eternal life. — Yours, etc.,

> C. M. Hyde[1]

To deal fitly with a letter so extraordinary, I must draw at the outset on [4] my private knowledge of the signatory and his sect. It may offend others; scarcely you, who have been so busy to collect, so bold to publish, gossip on your rivals. And this is perhaps the moment when I may best explain to you the character of what you are to read: I conceive you as a man quite beyond and below the reticences of civility: with what measure you mete, with that shall it be measured you again; with you, at last, I rejoice to feel the button off the foil and to plunge home. And if in aught that I shall say I should offend others, your colleagues, whom I respect and remember with affection, I can but offer them my regret; I am not free, I am inspired by the consideration of interests far more large; and such pain as can be inflicted by anything from me must be indeed trifling when compared with the pain with which they read your letter. It is not the hangman, but the criminal, that brings dishonour on the house.

---

[1] From the Sydney *Presbyterian*, October 26, 1889.

You belong, sir, to a sect — I believe my sect, and that in which my   5
ancestors laboured — which has enjoyed, and partly failed to utilise, an ex-
ceptional advantage in the islands of Hawaii. The first missionaries came;
they found the land already self-purged of its old and bloody faith; they were
embraced, almost on their arrival, with enthusiasm; what troubles they supported came far more from whites than from Hawaiians; and to these last
they stood (in a rough figure) in the shoes of God. This is not the place to
enter into the degree or causes of their failure, such as it is. One element
alone is pertinent, and must here be plainly dealt with. In the course of their
evangelical calling, they — or too many of them — grew rich. It may be
news to you that the houses of missionaries are a cause of mocking on the
streets of Honolulu. It will at least be news to you, that when I returned
your civil visit, the driver of my cab commented on the size, the taste, and
the comfort of your home. It would have been news certainly to myself, had
any one told me that afternoon that I should live to drag such matter into
print. But you see, sir, how you degrade better men to your own level; and
it is needful that those who are to judge betwixt you and me, betwixt Damien and the devil's advocate, should understand your letter to have been
penned in a house which could raise, and that very justly, the envy and the
comments of the passers-by. I think (to employ a phrase of yours which I admire) it "should be attributed" to you that you have never visited the scene
of Damien's life and death. If you had, and had recalled it, and looked about
your pleasant rooms, even your pen perhaps would have been stayed.

Your sect (and remember, as far as any sect avows me, it is mine) has   6
not done ill in a worldly sense in the Hawaiian Kingdom. When calamity
befell their innocent parishioners, when leprosy descended and took root in
the Eight Islands, a *quid pro quo* was to be looked for. To that prosperous
mission, and to you, as one of its adornments, God had sent at last an opportunity. I know I am touching here upon a nerve acutely sensitive. I know
that others of your colleagues look back on the inertia of your Church, and
the intrusive and decisive heroism of Damien, with something almost to be
called remorse. I am sure it is so with yourself; I am persuaded your letter
was inspired by a certain envy, not essentially ignoble, and the one human
trait to be espied in that performance. You were thinking of the lost chance,
the past day; of that which should have been conceived and was not; of the
service due and not rendered. *Time was,* said the voice in your ear, in your
pleasant room, as you sat raging and writing; and if the words written were
base beyond parallel, the rage, I am happy to repeat — it is the only compliment I shall pay you — the rage was almost virtuous. But, sir, when we
have failed, and another has succeeded; when we have stood by, and another
has stepped in; when we sit and grow bulky in our charming mansions, and a
plain, uncouth peasant steps into the battle, under the eyes of God, and suc-
cours the afflicted, and consoles the dying, and is himself afflicted in his

turn, and dies upon the field of honour — the battle cannot be retrieved as your unhappy irritation has suggested. It is a lost battle, and lost for ever. One thing remained to you in your defeat — some rags of common honour; and these you have made haste to cast away.

Common honour; not the honour of having done anything right, but   7
the honour of not having done aught conspicuously foul; the honour of the inert: that was what remained to you. We are not all expected to be Damiens; a man may conceive his duty more narrowly, he may love his comforts better; and none will cast a stone at him for that. But will a gentleman of your reverend profession allow me an example from the fields of gallantry? When two gentlemen compete for the favour of a lady, and the one succeeds and the other is rejected, and (as will sometimes happen) matter damaging to the successful rival's credit reaches the ear of the defeated, it is held by plain men of no pretensions that his mouth is, in the circumstance, almost necessarily closed. Your Church and Damien's were in Hawaii upon a rivalry to do well: to help, to edify, to set divine examples. You having (in one huge instance) failed, and Damien succeeded, I marvel it should not have occurred to you that you were doomed to silence; that when you had been outstripped in that high rivalry, and sat inglorious in the midst of your wellbeing, in your pleasant room — and Damien, crowned with glories and horrors, toiled and rotted in that pigsty of his under the cliffs of Kalawao —you, the elect who would not, were the last man on earth to collect and propagate gossip on the volunteer who would and did.

I think I see you — for I try to see you in the flesh as I write these sen-   8
tences — I think I see you leap at the word pigsty, a hyperbolical expression at the best. "He had no hand in the reforms," he was "a coarse, dirty man"; these were your own words; and you may think it possible that I am come to support you with fresh evidence. In a sense, it is even so. Damien has been too much depicted with a conventional halo and conventional features; so drawn by men who perhaps had not the eye to remark or the pen to express the individual; or who perhaps were only blinded and silenced by generous admiration, such as I partly envy for myself — such as you, if your soul were enlightened, would envy on your bended knees. It is the least defect of such a method of portraiture that it makes the path easy for the devil's advocate, and leaves for the misuse of the slanderer a considerable field of truth. For the truth that is suppressed by friends is the readiest weapon of the enemy. The world, in your despite, may perhaps owe you something, if your letter be the means of substituting once for all a credible likeness for a wax abstraction. For, if that world at all remember you, on the day when Damien of Molokai shall be named Saint, it will be in virtue of one work: your letter to the Reverend H. B. Gage.

You may ask on what authority I speak. It was my inclement destiny to   9
become acquainted, not with Damien, but with Dr. Hyde. When I visited

the lazaretto, Damien was already in his resting grave. But such information as I have, I gathered on the spot in conversation with those who knew him well and long: some indeed who revered his memory; but others who had sparred and wrangled with him, who beheld him with no halo, who perhaps regarded him with small respect, and through whose unprepared and scarcely partial communications the plain, human features of the man shone on me convincingly. These gave me what knowledge I possess; and I learnt it in that scene where it could be most completely and sensitively understood — Kalawao, which you have never visited, about which you have never so much as endeavoured to inform yourself; for, brief as your letter is, you have found the means to stumble into that confession. *"Less than one-half of the island,"* you say, "is devoted to the lepers." Molokai — *"Molokai ahina,"* the "grey," lofty, and most desolate island — along all its northern side plunges a front of precipice into a sea of unusual profundity. This range of cliff is, from east to west, the true end and frontier of the island. Only in one spot there projects into the ocean a certain triangular and rugged down, grassy, stony, windy, and rising in the midst into a hill with a dead crater: the whole bearing to the cliff that overhangs it somewhat the same relation as a bracket to a wall. With this hint you will now be able to pick out the leper station on a map; you will be able to judge how much of Molokai is thus cut off between the surf and precipice, whether less than a half, or less than a quarter, or a fifth, or a tenth — or, say, a twentieth; and the next time you burst into print you will be in a position to share with us the issue of your calculations.

I imagine you to be one of those persons who talk with cheerfulness of that place which oxen and wainropes could not drag you to behold. You, who do not even know its situation on the map, probably denounce sensational descriptions, stretching your limbs the while in your pleasant parlour on Beretania Street. When I was pulled ashore there one early morning, there sat with me in the boat two sisters, bidding farewell (in humble imitation of Damien) to the lights and joys of human life. One of these wept silently; I could not withhold myself from joining her. Had you been there, it is my belief that nature would have triumphed even in you; and as the boat drew but a little nearer, and you beheld the stairs crowded with abominable deformations of our common manhood, and saw yourself landing in the midst of such a population as only now and then surrounds us in the horror of a nightmare — what a haggard eye you would have rolled over your reluctant shoulder towards the house on Beretania Street. Had you gone on; had you found every fourth face a blot upon the landscape; had you visited the hospital and seen the butt-ends of human beings lying there almost unrecognisable, but still breathing, still thinking, still remembering: you would have understood that life in the lazaretto is an ordeal from which the nerves of a man's spirit shrink, even as his eye quails under the brightness of the sun;

10

you would have felt it was (even to-day) a pitiful place to visit and a hell to dwell in. It is not the fear of possible infection. That seems a little thing when compared with the pain, the pity, and the disgust of the visitor's surroundings, and the atmosphere of affliction, disease, and physical disgrace in which he breathes. I do not think I am a man more than usually timid; but I never recall the days and nights I spent upon that island promontory (eight days and seven nights), without heartfelt thankfulness that I am somewhere else. I find in my diary that I speak of my stay as a "grinding experience": I have once jotted in the margin, "*Harrowing* is the word"; and when the *Mokolii* bore me at last towards the outer world, I kept repeating to myself, with a new conception of their pregnancy, those simple words of the song —

> 'Tis the most distressful country that ever
> yet was seen.

And observe: that which I saw and suffered from was a settlement purged, bettered, beautified; the new village built, the hospital and the Bishop-Home excellently arranged; the sisters, the doctor, and the missionaries, all indefatigable in their noble tasks. It was a different place when Damien came there and made his great renunciation, and slept that first night under a tree amidst his rotting brethren: alone with pestilence; and looking forward (with what courage, with what pitiful sinkings of dread, God only knows) to a lifetime of dressing sores and stumps.

You will say, perhaps, I am too sensitive, that sights as painful abound in cancer hospitals and are confronted daily by doctors and nurses. I have long learned to admire and envy the doctors and the nurses. But there is no cancer hospital so large and populous as Kalawao and Kalaupapa; and in such a matter every fresh case, like every inch of length in the pipe of an organ, deepens the note of the impression; for what daunts the onlooker is that monstrous sum of human suffering by which he stands surrounded. Lastly, no doctor or nurse is called upon to enter once for all the doors of that gehenna; they do not say farewell, they need not abandon hope, on its sad threshold; they but go for a time to their high calling, and can look forward as they go to relief, to recreation, and to rest. But Damien shut-to with his own hand the doors of his own sepulchre.

I shall now extract three passages from my diary at Kalawao.

A. "Damien is dead and already somewhat ungratefully remembered in the field of his labours and sufferings. 'He was a good man, but very officious,' says one. Another tells me he had fallen (as other priests so easily do) into something of the ways and habits of thought of a Kanaka; but he had the wit to recognise the fact, and the good sense to laugh at [over] it. A plain man it seems he was; I cannot find he was a popular."

B. "After Ragsdale's death" [Ragsdale was a famous Luna, or overseer,   14
of the unruly settlement] "there followed a brief term of office by Father
Damien which served only to publish the weakness of that noble man. He
was rough in his ways, and he had no control. Authority was relaxed; Damien's life was threatened, and he was soon eager to resign."

C. "Of Damien I begin to have an idea. He seems to have been a man   15
of the peasant class, certainly of the peasant type: shrewd, ignorant and bigoted, yet with an open mind, and capable of receiving and digesting a re-
proof if it were bluntly administered; superbly generous in the last thing as
well as in the greatest, and as ready to give his last shirt (although not
without human grumbling) as he had been to sacrifice his life; essentially in-
discreet and officious, which made him a troublesome colleague; domineer-
ing in all his ways, which made him incurably unpopular with the Kanakas,
but yet destitute of real authority, so that his boys laughed at him and he
must carry out his wishes by the means of bribes. He learned to have a
mania for doctoring; and set up the Kanakas against the remedies of his regular rivals: perhaps (if anything matter at all in the treatment of such a disease)
the worst thing that he did, and certainly the easiest. The best and worst of
the man appear very plainly in his dealings with Mr. Chapman's money; he
had originally laid it out [intended to lay it out] entirely for the benefit of
Catholics, and even so not wisely; but after a long, plain talk, he admitted his
error fully and revised the list. The sad state of the boys' home is in part the
result of his lack of control; in part, of his own slovenly ways and false ideas
of hygiene. Brother officials used to call it 'Damien's Chinatown.' 'Well,'
they would say, 'your Chinatown keeps growing.' And he would laugh with
perfect good-nature, and adhere to his errors with perfect obstinacy. So
much I have gathered of truth about this plain, noble human brother and father of ours; his imperfections are the traits of his face, by which we know
him for our fellow; his martyrdom and his example nothing can lessen or
annul; and only a person here on the spot can properly appreciate their
greatness."

I have set down these private passages, as you perceive, without cor-   16
rection; thanks to you, the public has them in their bluntness. They are almost a list of the man's faults, for it is rather these that I was seeking: with
his virtues, with the heroic profile of his life, I and the world were already
sufficiently acquainted. I was besides a little suspicious of Catholic testimony;
in no ill sense, but merely because Damien's admirers and disciples were the
least likely to be critical. I know you will be more suspicious still; and the
facts set down above were one and all collected from the lips of Protestants
who had opposed the father in his life. Yet I am strangely deceived, or they
built up the image of a man, with all his weaknesses, essentially heroic, and
alive with rugged honesty, generosity, and mirth.

Take it for what it is, rough private jottings of the worst sides of Da-   17 mien's character, collected from the lips of those who had laboured with and (in your own phrase) "knew the man"; — though I question whether Damien would have said that he knew you. Take it, and observe with wonder how well you were served by your gossips, how ill by your intelligence and sympathy; in how many points of fact we are at one, and how widely our appreciations vary. There is something wrong here; either with you or me. It is possible for instance, that you, who seem to have so many ears in Kalawao, had heard of the affair of Mr. Chapman's money, and were singly struck by Damien's intended wrong-doing. I was struck with that also, and set it fairly down; but I was struck much more by the fact that he had the honesty of mind to be convinced. I may here tell you that it was a long business; that one of his colleagues sat with him late into the night, multiplying arguments and accusations; that the father listened as usual with "perfect good-nature and perfect obstinacy"; but at the last, when he was persuaded — "Yes," said he, "I am very much obliged to you; you have done me a service; it would have been a theft." There are many (not Catholics merely) who require their heroes and saints to be infallible; to these the story will be painful; not to the true lovers, patrons, and servants of mankind.

And I take it, this is a type of our division; that you are one of those 18 who have an eye for faults and failures; that you take a pleasure to find and publish them; and that, having found them, you make haste to forget the overvailing virtues and the real success which had alone introduced them to your knowledge. It is a dangerous frame of mind. That you may understand how dangerous, and into what a situation it has already brought you, we will (if you please) go hand-in-hand through the different phrases of your letter, and candidly examine each from the point of view of its truth, its appositeness, and its charity.

Damien was *coarse*.   19

It is very possible. You make us sorry for the lepers, who had only a   20 coarse old peasant for their friend and father. But you, who were so refined, why were you not there, to cheer them with the lights of culture? Or may I remind you that we have some reason to doubt if John the Baptist were genteel; and in the case of Peter, on whose career you doubtless dwell approvingly in the pulpit, no doubt at all he was a "coarse, headstrong" fisherman! Yet even in our Protestant Bibles Peter is called Saint.

Damien was *dirty*.   21

He was. Think of the poor lepers annoyed with this dirty comrade! But   22 the clean Dr. Hyde was at his food in a fine house.

Damien was *headstrong*.   23

I believe you are right again; and I thank God for his strong head and   24
heart.

Damien was *bigoted*.   25

I am not fond of bigots myself, because they are not fond of me. But   26
what is meant by bigotry, that we should regard it as a blemish in a priest?
Damien believed his own religion with the simplicity of a peasant or a child;
as I would I could suppose that you do. For this, I wonder at him some way
off; and had that been his only character, should have avoided him in life.
But the point of interest in Damien, which has caused him to be so much
talked about and made him at last the subject of your pen and mine, was
that, in him, his bigotry, his intense and narrow faith, wrought potently for
good, and strengthened him to be one of the world's heroes and exemplars.

Damien *was not sent to Molokai, but went there without orders*.   27

Is this a misreading? or do you really mean the words for blame? I have   28
heard Christ, in the pulpits of our Church, held up for imitation on the
ground that His sacrifice was voluntary. Does Dr. Hyde think otherwise?

Damien *did not stay at the settlement, etc.*   29

It is true he was allowed many indulgences. Am I to understand that   30
you blame the father for profiting by these, or the officers for granting them?
In either case, it is a mighty Spartan standard to issue from the house on
Beretania Street; and I am convinced you will find yourself with few supporters.

Damien *had no hand in the reforms, etc.*   31

I think even you will admit that I have already been frank in my   32
description of the man I am defending; but before I take you up upon this
head, I will be franker still, and tell you that perhaps nowhere in the world
can a man taste a more pleasurable sense of contrast than when he passes
from Damien's "Chinatown" at Kalawao to the beautiful Bishop-House at
Kalaupapa. At this point, in my desire to make all fair for you, I will break
my rule and adduce Catholic testimony. Here is a passage from my diary
about my visit to the Chinatown, from which you will see how it is (even
now) regarded by its own officials: "We went round all the dormitories,
refectories, etc. — dark and dingy enough, with a superficial cleanliness,
which he [Mr. Dutton, the lay-brother] did not seek to defend. 'It is almost
decent,' said he; 'the sisters will make that all right when we get them
here.'" And yet I gathered it was already better since Damien was dead,
and far better than when he was there alone and had his own (not always excellent) way. I have now come far enough to meet you on a common ground
of fact; and I tell you that, to a mind not prejudiced by jealousy, all the

reforms of the lazaretto, and even those which he most vigorously opposed, are properly the work of Damien. They are the evidence of his success; they are what his heroism provoked from the reluctant and the careless. Many were before him in the field, Mr. Meyer, for instance, of whose faithful work we hear too little: there have been many since; and some had more worldly wisdom, though none had more devotion, than our saint. Before his day, even you will confess, they had effected little. It was his part, by one striking act of martyrdom, to direct all men's eyes on that distressful country. At a blow, and with the price of his life, he made the place illustrious and public. And that, if you will consider largely, was the one reform needful; pregnant of all that should succeed. It brought money; it brought (best individual addition of them all) the sisters; it brought supervision, for public opinion and public interest landed with the man at Kalawao. If ever any man brought reforms, and died to bring them, it was he. There is not a clean cup or towel in the Bishop-House, but dirty Damien washed it.

Damien *was not a pure man in his relations with women, etc.*   33

How do you know that? Is this the nature of the conversation in that   34
house on Beretania Street which the cabman envied, driving past? — racy details of the misconduct of the poor peasant priest, toiling under the cliffs of Molokai?

Many have visited the station before me; they seem not to have heard   35
the rumour. When I was there I heard many shocking tales, for my informants were men speaking with the plainness of the laity; and I heard plenty of complaints of Damien. Why was this never mentioned? and how came it to you in the retirement of your clerical parlour?

But I must not even seem to deceive you. This scandal, when I read it   36
in your letter, was not new to me. I had heard it once before; and I must tell you how. There came to Samoa a man from Honolulu; he, in a public-house on the beach, volunteered the statement that Damien had "contracted the disease from having connection with the female lepers"; and I find a joy in telling you how the report was welcomed in a public-house. A man sprang to his feet; I am not at liberty to give his name, but from what I heard I doubt if you would care to have him to dinner in Beretania Street. "You miserable little ——" (here is a word I dare not print, it would so shock your ears). "You miserable little ——," he cried, "if the story were a thousand times true, can't you see you are a million times a lower —— for daring to repeat it?" I wish it could be told of you that when the report reached you in your house, perhaps after family worship, you had found in your soul enough holy anger to receive it with the same expressions; ay, even with that one which I dare not print; it would not need to have been blotted away, like Uncle Toby's oath, by the tears of the recording angel; it would have been counted to you for your brightest righteousness. But you have deliberately chosen the

part of the man from Honolulu, and you have played it with improvements of your own. The man from Honolulu — miserable, leering creature — communicated the tale to a rude knot of beach-combing drinkers in a public-house, where (I will so far agree with your temperance opinions) man is not always at his noblest; and the man from Honolulu had himself been drinking — drinking, we may charitably fancy, to excess. It was to your "Dear Brother, the Reverend H. B. Gage," that you chose to communicate the sickening story; and the blue ribbon which adorns your portly bosom forbids me to allow you the extenuating plea that you were drunk when it was done. Your "dear brother" — a brother indeed — made haste to deliver up your letter (as a means of grace, perhaps) to the religious papers; where, after many months, I found and read and wondered at it; and whence I have now reproduced it for the wonder of others. And you and your dear brother have, by this cycle of operations, built up a contrast very edifying to examine in detail. The man whom you would not care to have to dinner, on the one side; on the other, the Reverend Dr. Hyde and the Reverend H. B. Gage: the Apia bar-room, the Honolulu manse.

But I fear you scarce appreciate how you appear to your fellow-men; 37 and to bring it home to you, I will suppose your story to be true. I will suppose — and God forgive me for supposing it — that Damien faltered and stumbled in his narrow path of duty; I will suppose that, in the horror of his isolation, perhaps in the fever of incipient disease, he, who was doing so much more than he had sworn, failed in the letter of his priestly oath — he, who was so much a better man than either you or me, who did what we have never dreamed of daring — he too tasted of our common frailty. "O, Iago, the pity of it!" The least tender should be moved to tears; the incredulous to prayer. And all that you could do was to pen your letter to the Reverend H. B. Gage!

Is it growing at all clear to you what a picture you have drawn of your 38 own heart? I will try yet once again to make it clearer. You had a father: suppose this tale were about him, and some informant brought it to you, proof in hand: I am not making too high an estimate of your emotional nature when I suppose you would regret the circumstance? that you would feel the tale of frailty the more keenly since it shamed the author of your days? and that the last thing you would do would be to publish it in the religious press? Well, the man who tried to do what Damien did, is my father, and the father of the man in the Apia bar, and the father of all who love goodness; and he was your father too, if God had given you grace to see it.

SUBJECT QUESTIONS

1. Presumably Stevenson's original readers in Australia knew much more about Father Damien than does a modern reader. Do you get

enough details in the course of the essay to piece together a clear picture of Damien's self-sacrifice?

2. Stevenson warns at the outset that he intends to "convey truth and to arouse emotion," to take "the button off the foil and to plunge home." Normally such advance notice blunts an essay's persuasive force. Does it do so here? Are there times when the reader enjoys seeing this foil plunged home?

3. If Stevenson's purpose is to vindicate Father Damien, why does he devote so much space to attacks on Dr. Hyde? Does he seem to be more interested in attacking Hyde than in defending Damien? (There are at least two ways in which these attacks are really part of the defense of Damien; do you see what they are?)

4. Why does Stevenson point out that he, like Dr. Hyde, is a Presbyterian? Would the essay's persuasive force be lessened if Stevenson were a Catholic?

5. Can you tell whether or not Stevenson is being fair to the Protestant missionaries in Hawaii? (For a fuller account of these missionaries, see James Michener's novel *Hawaii*.)

6. The quotations from Stevenson's own notebook are hardly flattering to Damien. Why does Stevenson include them?

7. Examine Stevenson's answers to the eight accusations brought by Dr. Hyde. In how many of the answers does he appeal mainly to logic and in how many to emotion?

STRUCTURE QUESTIONS

1. The first task of a writer of persuasion is to make the reader receptive to his position. If the reader is neutral, a few properly connotative words may do the job. If the reader knows little about the subject or is hostile, the writer must devote more time to this part of his persuasion. (Perhaps, like Mark Antony, he will have to pretend to be on the side of his audience: "I come to bury Caesar, not to praise him.") Does Stevenson have any particular problem in swaying the reader to his side? How well chosen is his comparison of Dr. Hyde to the devil's advocate?

2. Does Stevenson successfully refute the charges against Father Damien? (One way of refuting charges is to show that they are not really incriminating.) Does Stevenson attempt to refute all eight charges?

3. Should Stevenson have used more space on "confirmation" — in this instance building up the character of his "client" — and less on refutation?

4. For what reason does Stevenson admit that he has once before heard the rumor of Father Damien's fall from celibacy? Examine the way in which he turns this admission to his own advantage.

5. Examine the last sentence; this is Stevenson's final emotional appeal.

Is its meaning perfectly clear? (Stevenson seems to be equating Father Damien with God.) Could such a sentence be emotionally persuasive even if its logical meaning were vague?

6. Stevenson addresses his "open letter" to Dr. Hyde. Does he intend to persuade Dr. Hyde to change his mind? At whom is the persuasion aimed? Would you judge it to be effective?

SUGGESTIONS FOR WRITING

1. Write a letter to the editor of the local newspaper in which you defend some principle or person recently attacked by the paper.

2. Write a persuasive attack on some university administrator or administrative policy to which you object. (This should probably be for practice, not for publication.)

Packed Dirt, Churchgoing, a Dying Cat, a Traded Car

John Updike

Although John Updike (b. 1932) has written two bestselling novels, Cou-
ples and Rabbit, Run, *he is probably best known as a short story writer.*
His work is found in nearly every collection of contemporary short fic-
tion. The story which follows originally appeared in The New Yorker *and*
was included in Pigeon Feathers *in 1962.*

Different things move us. I, David Kern, am always affected — reassured,   1
nostalgically pleased, even, as a member of my animal species, made
proud — by the sight of bare earth that has been smoothed and packed firm
by the passage of human feet. Such spots abound in small towns: the furtive
break in the playground fence dignified into a thoroughfare, the trough of
dust underneath each swing, the blurred path worn across a wedge of grass,
the anonymous little mound or embankment polished by play and strewn
with pebbles like the confetti aftermath of a wedding. Such unconsciously
humanized intervals of clay, too humble and common even to have a name,
remind me of my childhood, when one communes with dirt down among the
legs, as it were, of presiding fatherly presences. The earth is our playmate,
then, and the call to supper has a piercingly sweet eschatological ring.

The corner where I now live was recently widened so that the cars   2
going back and forth to the summer colony on the Point would not be
troubled to slow down. My neighbor's house was sold to the town and
wrecked and picked clean by salvagers and finally burned in a great bonfire
of old notched beams and splintered clapboards that leaped tree-high
throughout one whole winter day's cold drizzle. Then bulldozers, huge and
yellow and loud, appeared on the street and began to gnaw, it seemed, at
the corner of our house. My third child, a boy not yet two, came running
from the window in tearful panic. After I tried to soothe him with an explanation, he followed me through the house sobbing and wailing " 'Sheen
'Sheen!" while the machines made our rooms shake with the curses of their
labor. They mashed my neighbor's foundation stones into the earth and
trimmed the levelled lot just as my grandmother used to trim the excess
dough from the edge of the pieplate. They brought the curve of the road

right to the corner of my property, and the beaten path that does for a sidewalk in front of my home was sheared diagonally by a foot-high cliff.

Last night I was coming back from across the street, fresh from an   3
impromptu civic lamentation with a neighbor at how unsightly, now that the
snow was melted, the awkward-shaped vacant lot the bulldozers had left
looked, with its high raw enbankment gouged by rivulets and littered with
old chimney bricks. And soon, we concluded, now that spring was here, it
would be bristling with weeds. Crossing from this conversation, I noticed
that where my path had been lopped the cliff no longer existed; feet —
children's feet, mostly, for mostly children walk in our town — had worn
the sharpness away and molded a little ramp by which ascent was easier.

This small modification, this modest work of human erosion, seemed   4
precious to me not only because it recalled, in the slope and set of the dirt, a
part of the path that long ago had led down from my parents' back yard to
the high-school softball field. It seemed precious because it had been
achieved accidentally, and had about it that repose of grace that is beyond
willing. We in America have from the beginning been cleaving and baring
the earth, attacking, reforming the enormity of nature we were given, which
we took to be hostile. We have explored, on behalf of all mankind, this
paradox: the more matter is outwardly mastered, the more it overwhelms us
in our hearts. Evidence — gaping right-of-ways, acres mercilessly scraped,
bleeding mountains of muddy fill — surrounds us of a war that is incapable
of ceasing, and it is good to know that now there are enough of us to exert a
counter-force. If craters were to appear in our landscape tomorrow, the next
day there would be usable paths threading down the blasted sides. As our
sense of God's forested legacy to us dwindles, there grows, in these worn,
rubbed, and patted patches, a sense of human legacy — like those feet of
statues of saints which have lost their toes to centuries of kisses. One thinks
of John Dewey's definition of God as the union of the actual and the ideal.

There was a time when I wondered why more people did not go to church.   5
Taken purely as a human recreation, what could be more delightful, more
unexpected than to enter a venerable and lavishly scaled building kept warm
and clean for use one or two hours a week and to sit and stand in unison and
sing and recite creeds and petitions that are like paths worn smooth in the
raw terrain of our hearts? To listen, or not to listen, as a poorly paid but resplendently robed man strives to console us with scraps of ancient epistles
and halting accounts, hopelessly compromised by words, of those intimations
of divine joy that are like pain in that, their instant gone, the mind cannot
remember or believe them; to witness the windows donated by departed patrons and the altar flowers arranged by withdrawn hands and the whole considered spectacle lustrous beneath its patina of inheritance; to pay, for all

this, no more than we are moved to give — surely in all democracy there is nothing like it. Indeed, it is the most available democratic experience. We vote less than once a year. Only in church and at the polls are we actually given our supposed value, the soul-unit of one, with its noumenal arithmetic of equality: one equals one equals one.

My preaching fouls the words and corrupts me. Belief builds itself unconsciously and in consciousness is spent. Throughout my childhood I felt nothing in church but boredom and an oppressive futility. For reasons my father never explained, he was a dutiful churchman; my mother, who could use her senses, who had read Santayana and Wells, stayed home Sunday mornings, and I was all on her side, on the side of phenomena, in those years, though I went, with the other children, to Sunday school. It was not until we moved from the town and joined a country church that I, an adolescent of fifteen, my head a hotbed of girls and literature, felt a pleasant emotion in church. During Lent — that dull season, those forty suspended days during which Spring is gathering the mineral energy to make the resurrection that the church calendar seizes upon as conveniently emblematic — I ushered with my father at the Wednesday-night services. We would arrive in our old car — I think it was the Chevrolet then — on those raw March nights and it pleasantly surprised me to find the building warm, the stoked furnace already humming its devotions in the basement. The nave was dimly lit, the congregation small, the sermon short, and the wind howled a nihilistic counterpoint beyond the black windows blotted with garbed apostles; the empty pews, making the minister seem remote and small and emblematic, intensified our sensation of huddling. There was a strong sepia flavor of early Christianity: a minority flock furtively gathered within the hostile enormity of a dying, sobbing empire. From the rear, the broad back and baked neck of the occasional dutiful son loomed bullishly above the black straw hats of the mischievous-looking old ladies, gnarled by farmwork, who sat in their rows like withered apples on the shelves of a sweet-smelling cellar. My father would cross and uncross and recross his legs and stare at his thoughts, which seemed distant. It was pleasant to sit beside him in the rear pew. He was not much of a man for sitting still. When my parents and I went to the movies, he insisted on having the aisle seat, supposedly to give his legs room. After about twenty minutes he would leap up and spend the rest of the show walking around in the back of the theatre drinking water and talking to the manager while my mother and I, abandoned, consoled ourselves with the flickering giants of make-believe. He had nothing of the passive in him; a church always became, for him, something he helped run. It was pleasant, and even momentous, when the moment for action came, to walk by his side up the aisle, the thump of our feet the only sound in the church, and to take the wooden, felt-floored plates from a shy blur of white robes and to administer the submission of alms. Coins and envelopes sought to cover the felt. I condescended, stooping gallantly into each pew. The congregation seemed The Others, reaching, with quarters glittering in their crippled fingers, toward mysteries in which I was snugly involved. Even to usher at a church mixes us with the angels, and is a dangerous thing.

The churches of the Village had this Second Century quality. In Manhattan, Christianity is so feeble its future seems before it. One walks to church past clattering cafeterias and ravaged newsies in winter weather that is always a shade of Lent, on pavements spangled with last night's vomit. The expectantly hushed shelter of the church is like one of those spots worn bare by a softball game in a weed-filled vacant lot. The presence of the city beats like wind at the glowing windows. One hastens home afterward, head down, hurrying to assume the disguise — sweaters and suntans — of a non-churchgoer. I tried not to go, but it was not in me not to go. I never attended the same church two Sundays in succession, for fear I would become known, and be expected. To be known by face and name and financial weight robs us of our unitary soul, enrolls us against those Others. Devil's work. We are the others. It is of the essence to be a stranger in church.

On the island the very color of my skin made me strange. This island had been abandoned to the descendants of its slaves. Their church was on a hill; it has since been demolished, I have learned from letters, by a hurricane. To reach it one climbed a steep path made treacherous by the loose rubble of coral rock, jagged gray clinkers that bore no visible relation to the pastel branches that could be plucked, still pliant, from the shallows by Maid's Beach. Dull-colored goats were tethered along the path; their forelegs were tangled in their ropes so tightly that whenever they nodded the bush anchoring them nodded in answer. For windows the church possessed tall arched apertures filled not with stained glass but with air and outward vision; one could see the goats stirring the low foliage and the brightly dressed little girls who had escaped the service playing on the packed dirt around the church. The service was fatiguingly long. There were exhaustive petitionary prayers (for the Queen, the Prime Minister, Parliament) and many eight-versed hymns sung with a penetrating, lingering joy and accompanied by a hand-pumped organ. The organ breathed in and out, loud and soft, and the congregation, largely female, followed its ebb and flow at a brief but noticeable distance; their lips moved behind the singing, so I seemed immersed in an imperfectably synchronized movie. Musical stress, the British accent, and Negro elision worked upon the words a triple harmony of distortion. "Lait eth's waadsa *cull* raio-ind . . ." Vainly seeking my place in the hymn — for without a visual key I was lost — I felt lifted within a sweet, soughing milk, an aspiring chant as patient as the nodding of the goats.

Throughout the service, restless deacons slipped in and out of the windows. Bored myself — for we grow sated even with consolation — I discovered that without moving from my pew I too could escape through those tall portals built to admit the breeze. I rested my eyes on earth's wide circle round. From this height the horizon of the sea was lifted halfway up the sky. The Caribbean seemed a steeply tilted blue plane to which the few fishing boats in the bay below had been attached like magnetized toys. God made the world, Aquinas says, in play.

Matter has its radiance and its darkness; it lifts and it buries. Things com- 10 pete; a life demands a life. On another English island, in Oxford — it is a strange fact about Americans, that we tend to receive our supernatural mail on foreign soil — I helped a cat die. The incident had the signature: decisive but illegible. For six years I did not tell my wife about it, for fear it would frighten her. Some hours before, I had left her at the hospital in the early stages of labor. Wearing a sterilized gown and mask, I had visited her in a white-tiled room along whose walls gleaming gutters stood ready to drain torrents of blood. Her face, scrubbed and polished, was fervent like a child's, and she seemed, lying there swathed in white, ready for nothing so much as a graduation ceremony. She would break off talking, and listen as if to the distant voice of a schoolmistress, and her face would grow rapt, and when the contraction had passed she would sigh and say, "That was a good one," and chatter some more to me of how I would feed myself alone and who I would send the telegrams to.

Shooed from the room, stripped of my mask, I tried to wait, and was 11 told, the comical husband of the American cartoons, to run on home; it would be a time. I went outside and took a bus home. It was the last day of March. I had been born in March, and I had looked forward to welcoming my child to the month; but she was late. We lived on Iffley Road, and around mignight, for some reason — I think to mail a letter, but what letter could have been that important? — I was out walking a few blocks from our flat. The night was cold enough for gloves. The sensations of turning into a father — or, rather, the lack of sensations; the failure of sympathetic pain, the hesitation of dread, the postponement of pride — made the street seem insubstantial. There was not that swishing company of headlights that along an American road throws us into repeated relief. The brick homes, save for an occasional introverted glow in an upstairs window, were dark in the vehement shadows of privacy behind the dry hedges and spiked walls. The streetlamps — wintry, reserved — drained color from everything. Myself a shadow, I noticed another in the center of the road. A puddle of black, as I watched, it curled on itself; its ends lifted from the macadam and seemed to stretch in a yawn. Then it became inert again. I was horrified; the shape was about the size of a baby. When it curled the second time, I went to it, my footsteps the only sound in the street.

It was a cat that had been struck by a car. Struck but not quite killed: a 12 testament to the modest speed and sensible size of English automobiles. By the impersonal witness of the lamps burning in the trees I couldn't be sure what color its fur was — it seemed orange-yellow, tabbied with stripes of dark ginger. The cat was plump and wore a collar. Someone had loved it. Blackness from one ear obscured one side of its head and when I touched it it was like a cup. For the third time, the cat stretched, the tips of its hind feet quivering luxuriously in that way cats have. With a great spastic effort it flipped over onto its other side, but made no cry. The only sound between us was my crooning as I carried it to the side of the street and laid it behind the nearest hedge.

A sallow upstairs light in this home was glowing. I wondered if the cat was theirs. Was it their love invested in my hands? Were they watching as I pushed, crouching, with my burden through their hedge? I wondered if I would be taken for a trespasser, a "poacher"; as an American, I was nervous of English tabus. In my own brutal country it was a not uncommon insult to kill a cat and throw the body into an enemy's yard, and I was afraid that this would be taken that way. I thought of writing a note to explain everything, but I had no paper and pen. I explained to the cat, how I was taking her (I felt it was female) out of the street so no more cars would hit her, how I would put her here in the nice safe dirt behind the hedge, where she could rest and get well. I did not believe she would get well; I think she was dead already. Her weight had felt dead in my hands and when I laid her down she did not stretch or twitch again.

Back in my flat, I discovered that one glove was smeared with blood. Most of the palm and three of the fingers were dyed wine-brown. I hadn't realized there was so much blood. I took off my gloves and carefully wrote a note, explaining that I had found this cat in the middle of the street, still alive, and that I had put it behind this hedge to be safe. If, as I thought, the cat was dead, I hoped that the finders would bury it. After some deliberation, I signed my name and address. I walked back and tucked the note under the cat's body, which seemed at home behind the hedge; it suffered my intrusion a trifle stiffly. It suggested I was making too much fuss, and seemed to say to me, *Run on home.*

Back in my flat once more, I felt abruptly tired, though my heart was pounding hugely. I went to bed and set the alarm for three and read a book. I remember the title, it was Chesterton's *The Everlasting Man.* I turned off the light and prayed for my wife and, though I did not believe myself capable of it, fell asleep. The alarm at three came crashing into some innocent walk of a dream and my frail head felt like a hollow cup. I dressed and went out to the public phone booth a block away and called the hospital. A chirping voice, after some rummaging in the records, told me that several hours ago, in the first hour of April (in the United States it was still March), a perfect female infant had been born. To me.

The next morning, after all the telegrams had been managed, I went back to the hedge, and the cat and my note were gone. Though I had left my address, I never received a letter.

When we returned from England, we bought a car. We had ordered it   17
through my parents from folders they had sent us, and, though its shade of
blue was more naïve, more like a robin's egg, than we had expected, this '55
Ford proved an excellent buy. Whether being shuffled from side to side of
West Eighty-fifth Street every morning or being rammed in second gear up
a washed-out mountain road in Vermont, it never complained. In New York,
hot tar from a roof-patching job rained onto its innocent paint, and in Vermont its muffler was racked and rent on a shelf of rock, and in Massachusetts
it wallowed, its hot clutch stinking, up from repeated graves of snow. Not
only sand and candy wrappers accumulate in a car's interior, but heroisms
and instants of communion. We in America make love in our cars, and listen
to ball games, and plot out wooing of the dollar: small wonder the landscape
is sacrificed to these dreaming vehicles of our ideal and onrushing manhood.

In the beginning, my wife and I would lovingly lave with soap and   18
warm water the unflecked skin of the hood as if it were the thorax of a broad
blue baby, and toward the end we let the gallant old heap rust where it
would. Its eggshell finish grew grizzled with the stains of dropped maple
seeds. Its doors balked at closing; its windows refused to roll down. But I
somehow never believed we would ever trade it in, though the little girl
born across the ocean in the ominous turning of April, now a vocal and
status-conscious democrat of nearly six, applied more and more petulant
pressure. The deal was consummated while my soul had its face turned, and
Detroit the merciless mother contracted to devour her child. But before the
new car arrived, there was a month's grace, and in this grace I enjoyed a
final fling with my car, my first, my only — for all the others will be substitutes. It happened this way:

Dancing at a party with a woman not my wife, it seemed opportune to   19
turn her hand in mine and kiss her palm. For some time her thighs had been
slithering against mine, and, between dances, she developed a nervous
clumsy trick of lurching against me, on tiptoe, and rubbing her breast against
my forearm, which was braced across my chest as I held a cigarette. My first
thought was that I might burn her; my second, that Nature in her gruff ma-
ternal way had arranged one of her opportunities — as my mother, when I
was a child, would unpredictably determine to give me a birthday or Hallow-
e'en party. Obediently I bowed my head and kissed my friend's moist palm.
As it withdrew from the advance, her fingertips caressed my chin in the ab-
sent-minded manner of one fingering the muzzle of an importunate dog. The
exchange transposed us into a higher key; I could hardly hear my own voice,
and our dancing lost all connection with the music, and my hand explored
her spine from a great aerial distance. Her back seemed mysteriously taut
and hard; the body of a strange woman retains more of its mineral content,
not being transmuted, through familiarity, into pure emotion. In a sheltered
corner of the room we stopped dancing altogether and talked, and what I
distinctly remember is how her hands, beneath the steady and opaque ap-

praisal of her eyes, in nervous slurred agitation blindly sought mine and seized and softly gripped, with infantile instinct, my thumbs. Just my thumbs she held, and as we talked she moved them this way and that as if she were steering me. When I closed my eyes, the red darkness inside my lids was trembling, and when I rejoined my wife, and held her to dance, she asked, "Why are you panting?"

After we got home, and surveyed our four children, and in bed read a few pages made unbearably brilliant by their patina of martinis, and turned out the light, she surprised me by not turning her back. Alcohol, with its loosening effect, touches women more deeply than men in this respect; or perhaps, like a matched pair of tuning forks, I had set her vibrating. Irritated by whatever illicit stimulations, we took it out on each other.

To my regret, I survived the natural bliss of satiety — when each muscle is like a petal snugly curved in a corolla of benediction — and was projected onto the wrinkled, azoic territory of insomnia. That feathery anxious embrace of my erect thumbs tormented me in twenty postures. My stomach turned in love of that woman; I feared I would be physically sick and lay on my back gingerly and tried to soothe myself with the caress of headlights as they evolved from bright slits on the wall into parabolically accelerating fans on the ceiling that then vanished: this phenomenon, with its intimations of a life beyond me, had comforted wakeful nights in my earliest childhood. In Sunday school I had been struck by the passage in which Jesus says that to lust after a woman in thought is the same as committing adultery. Now I found myself helplessly containing the conviction that souls, not deeds, are judged. To feel a sin was to commit it; to touch the brink was to be on the floor of the chasm. The universe that so easily permitted me to commit adultery became, by logical steps each one of which went more steeply down than the one above it, a universe that would easily permit me to die. The enormities of cosmic space, the maddening distension of time, history's forgotten slaughters, the child smothered in the dumped icebox, the recent breakdown of the molecular life-spiral, the proven physiological roots of the mind, the presence in our midst of idiots, Eichmanns, animals, and bacteria — all this evidence piled on, and I seemed already eternally forgotten. The dark vibrating air of my bedroom seemed the dust of grave; the dust went up and up and I prayed upward into it, prayed, prayed for a sign, any glimmer at all, any microscopic loophole or chink in the chain of evidence, and saw none. I remembered a movie I had seen as a child in which a young criminal, moaning insanely, is dragged on rubber legs down the long corridor to the electric chair. I became that criminal. My brain in its calcium vault shouted about injustice, thundered accusations into the lustreless and tranquil homogeneity of the air. Each second my agony went unanswered justified it more certainly: the God who permitted me this fear was unworthy of existence. Each instant my horror was extended amplified

God's non-existence, so, as the graph of certain equations fluctuates more and more widely as it moves along the lateral coordinate, or as the magnetic motive-power in atom-smashers accelerates itself, I was caught in a gathering vortex whose unbearably shrill pitch moved me at last to drop my weight on my wife's body and beg, "Wake up, Elaine. I'm so frightened."

I told her of the centuries coming when our names would be forgotten, of the millennia when our nation would be a myth and our continent an ocean, of the aeons when our earth would be vanished and the stars themselves diffused into a uniform and irreversible tepidity. As, an hour before, I had transferred my lust to her, so now I tried to pass my fear into her. It seemed to offend her sense of good taste that I was jealous of future aeons and frantic because I couldn't live through them; she asked me if I had never been so sick I gave up caring whether I lived or died. This contemptible answer — the decrepit Stoic response — required a curious corroboration; eventually, just as I had during the strenuous birth of my fatherhood, I fell asleep, and dreamt of innocent and charming scenes.

The next day, a Saturday, was my birthday. It passed like any day except that underneath the camouflage of furniture and voices and habitual actions I felt death like a wide army invisibly advancing. The newspaper told of nothing but atrocities. My children, wounded and appalled in their competition, came to me to be comforted and I was dismayed to see myself, a gutted shell, appearing to them as the embodiment and pledge of a safe universe. Friends visited, and for the first time in my life I realized that each face is suppressing knowledge of an immense catastrophe; our faces are dams that wrinkle under the strain. Around six the telephone rang. It was my mother calling from Pennsylvania; I assumed she had called because of my birthday, so I chattered humorously about the discomforts of growing old for a minute before she could tell me, her voice growing faint, the news. My father was in the hospital. He had been walking around with chest pains for two weeks and suffered shortness of breath at night. She had finally seduced him into a doctor's office; the doctor had taken a cardiogram and driven him to the hospital. He was a seriously sick man.

Instantly I was relieved. The weight of me rolled away. All day death had been advancing under cover and now it had struck, declared its position. My father had engaged the enemy and it would be defeated.

I was restored to crisp health in the play-world of action. That night we had a few friends in for my birthday party and the next day I took the two older children to Sunday school and went myself to church. The faintly lavender lozenge-panes of the white-mullioned windows glowed and dimmed fitfully. It was a spottily overcast day, spitting a little snow. While I was at church my wife had cooked a lamb dinner and as I drank the coffee it became clear that I must drive to Pennsylvania. My mother and I had agreed I would fly down and visit him in a few days; I would have to see about renting a car at the Philadelphia end. This was potentially awkward because, self-employed, I had no credit card. The awkwardness suddenly seemed easy to surmount. I would drive. The car would be traded in a few days, it had just been greased; I had a vision of escaping our foul New England spring by driving south. In half an hour my bag was packed and in my churchgoing suit I abandoned my family. *Run on home.*

Along Route 128 I picked up a young sailor who rode with me all the way to New York and, for two hours through Connecticut, drove my car. I trusted him. He had the full body, the frank and fleshy blue-eyed face of the docile Titans — guileless, competent, mildly earnest — that we have fattened, an ocean removed from the slimming Latin passions and Nordic anxieties of Europe, on our unprecedented abundance of milk and honey, vitamins and protein. He had that instinctive optimism of the young animal that in America is the only generatrix of hope we have allowed ourselves; until recently, it seemed enough. He was incongruously — and somehow reassuringly — tanned. He had got the tan in Key West, where he had spent twenty-four hours, hitching the rides to and from on Navy jets. He had spent the twenty-four hours sleeping on the beach and selecting souvenirs to send back to his parents and girl friend. His parents lived in Salem, his girl friend in Peabody. He wanted to marry her, but his parents had old-fashioned ideas, they thought he was too young. And a lot of these guys in the service say, Don't get married, don't ever get married. But she was a nice girl, not so pretty or anything, but really nice: he really wanted to marry her.

I asked him how old he was. He was twenty-two, and was being trained as an airplane mechanic. He wanted at the end of his hitch to come back to Salem and live. He figured an airplane mechanic could find some sort of job. I told him, with a paternal firmness that amazed my ears, to marry her; absolutely; his parents would get used to it. The thing about parents, I told him, was that secretly, no matter what you did, they liked you anyway. I told him I had married at the age of twenty-one and had never for a minute been sorry.

He asked me, "What do you do? Teach?"

This impressed me. My grandfather had been a teacher, and my father was a teacher, and from my childhood up it had been assumed by the people of our neighborhood that I in turn would become a teacher.

"No," I said. "I'm a writer."

He seemed less offended than puzzled. "What do you write?"

"Oh — whatever comes into my head."

"What's the point?"

"I don't know," I told him. "I wish I did."

We talked less freely after that. At his request I left him off in wet twilight at a Texaco station near the entrance of the New Jersey Turnpike. He hoped to get a ride from there all the way to Washington. Other sailors

26

27

28

29

30

31

32

33

34

35

were clustered out of the rain in the doorways of the station. They hailed him as if they had been waiting for him, and as he went to them he became, from the back, just one more sailor, anonymous at sea. He did not turn and wave goodbye. I felt I had frightened him, which I regretted, because he had driven for me very well and I wanted him to marry his girl. In the dark I drove down the pike alone. In the first years of my car, when we lived in Manhattan, it would ease up to seventy-five on this wide black stretch without our noticing; now the needle found its natural level at sixty. The windshield wipers beat, and the wonderland lights of the Newark refineries were swollen and broken like bubbles by the raindrops on the side windows. For a dozen seconds a solemn cross of colored stars was suspended stiffly in the upper part of the windshield: an airplane above me was coming in to land.

I did not eat until I was on Pennsylvania soil. The Howard Johnsons in Pennsylvania are cleaner, less crowded, more homelike in their furnishings. The decorative plants seem to be honestly growing, and the waitresses have just a day ago removed the Mennonite cap from their hair, which is still pulled into a smooth bun flattering to their pallid, sly faces. They served me with that swift grace that comes in a country where food is still one of the pleasures. The familiar and subtle irony of their smiles awakened in me that old sense, of Pennsylvania knowingness — of knowing, that is, that the truth is good. They were the innkeeper's daughters, God had given us crops, and my wagon was hitched outside.

When I returned to the car, the music on the radio had changed color. The ersatz hiccup and gravel of Atlantic Seaboard hillbilly had turned, inland, backwards into something younger. As I passed the Valley Forge intersection the radio relived a Benny Goodman quintet that used to make my scalp freeze in high school. The speedometer went up to seventy without effort.

I left the toll road for our local highway and, turning into our dirt road, I was nearly rammed from behind by a pair of headlights that had been pushing, Pennsylvania style, six feet behind me. I parked beside my father's car in front of the barn. My mother came unseen into the yard, and, two voices calling in the opaque drizzle, while the dogs yapped deliriously in their pen, we debated whether I should move my car further off the road. "Out of harm's way," my grandfather would have said. Complaining, I obeyed her. My mother turned as I carried my suitcase down the path of sandstone steppingstones, and led me to the back door as if I would not know the way. So it was not until we were inside the house that I could kiss her in greeting. She poured us two glasses of wine. Wine had a ceremonial significance in our family; we drank it seldom. My mother seemed cheerful, even silly, and it took an hour for the willed impetus of gaiety to ebb away. She turned her head and looked delicately at the rug and the side of her neck blushed as she told me, "Daddy says he's lost all his faith."

Since I had also lost mine, I could find nothing to say. I remembered, in the silence, a conversation I had had with my father during a vacation from college. With the habitual simplicity of his eagerness to know, he had asked me, "Have you ever had any doubts of the existence of a Divine Being?"

"Sure," I had answered.   40

"I never have," he said. "It's beyond my ability to imagine it. The   41
divinity of Jesus, yes; but the existence of a Divine Being, never." He stated this not as an attempt to influence me, but as a moderately curious fact he had that moment discovered about himself.

"He never was much one for faith," my mother added, hurt by my fail-   42
ure to speak. "He was strictly a works man."

I slept badly; I missed my wife's body, that weight of pure emotion,   43
beside me. I was enough of a father to feel lost out of my nest of little rustling souls. I kept looking out of the windows. The three red lights of the chimneys of the plant that had been built some miles away, to mine low-grade iron ore, seemed to be advancing over our neighbor's ridged field toward our farm. My mother had mistaken me for a stoic like my father and had not put enough blankets on the bed. I found an old overcoat of his and arranged it over me; its collar scratched my chin. I tipped into sleep and awoke. The morning was sharply sunny; sheep hustled, heads toppling, through the gauzy blue sky. It was authentic spring in Pennsylvania. Some of the grass in the lawn had already grown shiny and lank. A yellow crocus had popped up beside the BEWARE OF THE DOG sign my father had had a child at school make for him.

I insisted we drive to Alton in my car, and then was sorry, for it   44
seemed to insult their own. Just a few months ago my father had traded in on yet one more second-hand car: now he owned a '53 Plymouth. But while growing up I had been ambushed by so many mishaps in my father's cars that I insisted we take the car I could trust. Or perhaps it was that I did not wish to take my father's place behind the wheel of his car. My father's place was between me and Heaven; I was afraid of being placed adjacent to that far sky. First we visited his doctor. Our old doctor, a man who believed that people simply "wore out" and nothing could be done about it, had several years ago himself worn out and died. The new doctor's office, in the center of the city, was furnished with a certain raw sophistication. Rippling music leaked from the walls, which were hung with semi-professional oils. He him-self was a wiry and firm-tongued young man not much older than myself but venerable with competence and witnessed pain. Such are the brisk shep-herds who hop us over the final stile. He brought down from the top of a fil-ing cabinet a plaster model of the human heart. "Your own heart," he told me, "is nice and thin like this; but your dad's heart is enlarged. We believe the obstruction is here, in one of these vessels on the outside, luckily for your dad."

Outside, in the streets of Alton, my own heart felt enlarged. A white   45
sun warmed the neat façades of painted brick; chimneys like peony shoots
thrust through budding treetops. Having grown accustomed to the cramped,
improvised cities of New England, I was patriotically thrilled by Alton's
straight broad streets and superb equipment of institutions. While my
mother went off to buy my daughter a birthday present, I returned a book
she had borrowed to the Alton Public Library. I had forgotten the deep
aroma of that place, mixed of fust and cleaning fluid and binder's glue and
sweet pastry baking in the shop next door. I revisited the shelf of P. G.
Wodehouse that in one summer I had read straight through. I took down
Mulliner Nights and looked in the back for the stamped date, in '47 or '48,
that would be me. I never thought to look for the section of the shelves
where my own few books would be placed. They were not me. They were
my children, mysterious and self-willed.

In driving to the hospital on Alton's outskirts, we passed the museum   46
grounds, where every tree and flower-bed wore a name-tag and black swans
drifted through flotillas of crumbled bread. As a child I had believed literally
that bread cast upon the waters came back doubled. I remembered that
within the museum there were mummies with astonished shattered faces; a
tiny gilt chair for a baby Pharaoh; an elephant tusk carved into thousands of
tiny Chinamen and pagodas and squat leafy trees; miniature Eskimo villages
that you lit up with a switch and peeped into like an Easter egg; cases of arrowheads; rooms of stuffed birds; and, upstairs, wooden chests decorated
with hearts and pelicans and tulips by the pious "plain people" and iridescent glassware from the kilns of Baron von Steigel and slashing paintings of
Pennsylvania woodland by the Shearers and bronze statuettes of wrestling
Indians that stirred my first erotic dreams and, in the round skylit room at
the head of the marble stairs, a black-rimmed pool in whose center a naked
green lady held to her pursed lips a shell whose lucent contents forever
spilled from the other side, filling this whole vast upstairs — from whose
Palladian windows the swans in their bready pond could be seen trailing fan-
shaped wakes — with the music and chill romance of falling water. The world
then seemed an intricate wonder displayed for my delight with no price
asked. Above the trees across the pond one saw rose glints of the hospital, an
orderly multitude of tall brick rectangles set among levelled and lovingly
tended grounds, an ideal city of the ill.

I had forgotten how grand the Alton hospital was. I had not seen its   47
stately entrance, approached down a grassy mall bright with the first flush of
green, since, at the age of seven, I had left the hospital unburdened of my
tonsils. Then, too, it had been spring, and my mother was with me. I
recalled it to her, and she said, "I felt so guilty. You were so sick."

"Really? I remember it as so pleasant." They had put a cup of pink rub-   48
ber over my nose and there had been a thunderous flood of the smell of cot-

ton candy and I opened my eyes and my mother was reading a magazine beside my bed.

"You were such a hopeful boy," my mother said, and I did not look at her face for fear of seeing her crying.   49

I wondered aloud if a certain girl in my high school class were still a nurse here.   50

"Oh, dear," my mother said. "Here I thought you came all this way to see your poor old father and all you care about is seeing — " And she used the girl's maiden name, though the girl had been married as long as I had.   51

Within the hospital, she surprised me by knowing the way. Usually, wherever we went, it was my father or I who knew the way. As I followed her through the linoleum maze, my mother's shoulders seemed already to have received the responsible shawl of widowhood. Like the halls of a palace, the hospital corridors were lined with patient petitioners. Negro girls electrically dramatic in their starched white uniforms folded bales of cotton sheets; gray men pushed wrung mops. We went through an Exit sign, down a stairway, into a realm where gaunt convalescents in bathrobes shuffled in and out of doorways. I saw my father diagonally through a doorway before we entered his room. He was sitting up in bed, supported sultanlike by a wealth of pillows and clad in red-striped pajamas.   52

I had never seen him in pajamas before; a great man for the shortest distance between two points, he slept in his underclothes. But, having been at last captured in pajamas, like a big-hearted lion he did not try to miminize his humiliation, but lay fully exposed, without a sheet covering even his feet. Bare, they looked pale, gentle, and oddly unused.   53

Except for a sullen lymphatic glow under his cheeks, his face was totally familiar. I had been afraid that his loss of faith would show, like the altered shape of his mouth after he had had all his teeth pulled. With grins we exchanged the shy handshake that my going off to college had forced upon us. I sat on the window sill by his bed, my mother took the chair at the foot of the bed, and my father's roommate, a tanned and fortyish man flat on his back with a crushed vertebra, sighed and blew smoke toward the ceiling and tried, I suppose, not to hear us. Our conversation, though things were radically changed, followed old patterns. Quite quickly the talk shifted from him to me. "I don't know how you do it, David," he said. "I couldn't do what you're doing if you paid me a million dollars a day." Embarrassed and flattered, as usual, I tried to shush him, and he disobediently turned to his roommate and called loudly, "I don't know where the kid gets his ideas. Not from his old man, I know that. I never gave that poor kid an idea in my life."   54

"Sure you did," I said softly, trying to take pressure off the man with the painful back. "You taught me two things. Always butter bread toward the edges because enough gets in the middle anyway, and No matter what happens to you, it'll be a new experience."   55

To my dismay, this seemed to make him melancholy. "That's right, 56
David," he said. "No matter what happens to you, it'll be a new experience.
The only thing that worries me is that *she*" — he pointed at my mother —
"will crack up the car. I don't want anything to happen to your mother."

"The car, you mean," my mother said, and to me she added, "It's a sin, 57
the way he worships that car."

My father didn't deny it. "Jesus I love that car," he said. "It's the first 58
car I've ever owned that didn't go bad on me. Remember all those heaps we
used to ride back and forth in?"

The old Chevy was always getting dirt in the fuel pump and refusing to 59
start at awkward hours. Once, going down Fire Hill, the left front wheel had
broken off the axle; my father wrestled with the steering wheel while the
tires screamed and the white posts of the guard fence floated calmly toward
my eyes. When the car slid sideways to a stop just short of the embankment
my father's face was stunned and the corners of his mouth dribbled saliva. I
was surprised; it had not occurred to me to be frightened. The '36 Buick had
drunk oil, a quart every fifty miles, and loved to have flat tires after midnight, when I would be gliding home with a scrubbed brain and the smell of
lipstick in my nose. Once, when we had both gone into town and I had
dropped him off and taken the car, I had absent-mindedly driven home
alone. I came in the door and my mother said, "Why, where's your father?"

My stomach sank. "My Lord," I said, "I forgot I had him!" 60

As, smiling, I took in breath and prepared to dip with him into remini- 61
scence of these adventures, my father, staring stonily into the air above his
pale and motionless toes, said, "I love this place. There are a lot of wonderful
gentlemen in here. The only thing that worries me is that mother will crack
up the car."

To my horror I saw that my mother, leaning forward red-faced in the 62
chair at the foot of the bed, was silently crying. He glanced at her and said to
me, "It's a funny feeling. The night before we went to see the doctor I woke
up and couldn't get my breath and realized I wasn't ready to die. I had
always thought I would be. It's a funny feeling."

"Luckily for your dad," "all his faith," "wonderful gentlemen": these 63
phrases were borne in on me with a dreadful weight and my tongue seemed
pressed flat on the floor of its grave. The pajama stripes under my eyes
stirred and streamed, real blood. I wanted to speak, to say how I needed
him and to beg him not to leave me, but there were no words, no form of
words available in our tradition. A pillar of smoke poured upward from the
sighing man in the other bed.

Into this pit hesitantly walked a plain, painfully clean girl with a pad 64
and pencil. She had yellow hair, thick lips, and, behind pink-rimmed glasses,
large eyes that looked as if they had been corrected from being crossed.
They flicked across our faces and focussed straight ahead in that tunnel-

vision gaze of those who know perfectly well they are figures of fun. The
Jehovah's Witnesses who come to the door wear that funnelled expression.
She approached the bed where my father lay barefoot and, suppressing a
stammer, explained that she was from Lutheran Home Missions and that
they kept accounts of all hospitalized Lutherans and notified the appropriate
pastors to make visitations. Clearly she had measured my father for a rebuff;
perhaps her eyes, more practiced in this respect than mine, spotted the ex-
ternal sign of loss of faith that I had missed. At any rate my father was a Lutheran by adoption; he had been born and raised a Presbyterian and still
looked like one.

"That's *aw*fully nice of you," he told the girl. "I don't see how you peo- 65
ple do it on the little money we give you."

Puzzled, she dimpled and moved ahead with her routine. "Your 66
church is — ?"

He told her, pronouncing every syllable meticulously and consulting 67
my mother and me as to whether the word "Evangelical" figured in the official title.

"That would make your pastor Reverend — " 68

"Yeah. He'll be in, don't worry about it. Wild horses couldn't keep 69
him away. Nothing he likes better than to get out of the sticks and drive into
Alton. I didn't mean to confuse you a minute ago; what I meant was, just last
week in church council we were talking about you people. We couldn't figure out how you do anything on the little money we give you. After we've
got done feeding the furnace and converting the benighted Hindoo there
isn't anything left over for you people that are trying to help the poor devils
in our own back yard."

The grinning girl was lost in this onslaught of praise and clung to the 70
shreds of her routine. "In the meantime," she recited, "here is a pamphlet
you might like to read."

My father took it from her with a swooping gesture so expansive I got 71
down from the window sill to restrain him physically, if necessary. That he
must lie still was my one lever, my one certainty about his situation. "That's
awfully nice of you," he told the girl. "I don't know where the hell you get
the money to print these things."

"We hope your stay in the hospital is pleasant and would like to wish 72
you a speedy recovery to full health."

"Thank you; I know you're sincere when you say it. As I was telling my 73
son David here, if I can do what the doctors tell me I'll be all right. First
time in my life I've ever tried to do what anybody ever told me to do. The
kid was just telling me, 'No matter what happens to you, Pop, it'll be a new
experience.'"

"Now if you will excuse me I have other calls to pay." 74

"Of course. You go right ahead, sick Lutherans are a dime a dozen.   75
You're a wonderful woman to be doing what you're doing."

And she left the room transformed into just that. As a star shines in our   76
heaven though it has vanished from the universe, so my father continued to
shed faith upon others. For the remainder of my visit with him his simple
presence so reassured me, filled me with such a buoyant humor, that my
mother surprised me, when we had left the hospital, by remarking that we
had tired him.

"I hadn't noticed," I said.   77

"And it worries me," she went on, "the way he talks about the movies   78
all the time. You know he never liked them." When I had offered to stay
another night so I could visit him again, he had said, "No, instead of that
why don't you take your mother to the movies?" Rather than do that, I said,
I would drive home. It took him a moment, it seemed, to realize that by my
home I meant a far place, where I had a wife and children; though at the
time I was impatient to have his consent, it has since occurred to me and
grieved me that during that instant his face was blank he was swallowing the
realization that he was no longer the center of even his son's universe. Having swallowed, he told me how good I had been to come all this way to see
him. He told me I was a good son and a good father; he clasped my hand. I
felt I would ascend straight north from his touch.

I drove my mother back to her farm and got my bag and said goodbye   79
on the lawn. The little sandstone house was pink in the declining sunlight;
the lawn was a tinkling clutter of shy rivulets. Standing beside the BEWARE OF
THE DOG sign with its companion of a crocus, she smiled and said, "This is
like when you were born. Your father drove through a snowstorm all the way
from Wheeling in our old Ford." He had been working with the telephone
company then; the story of his all-night ride was the first myth in which I
was a character.

Darkness did not fall until New Jersey. The hour of countryside I saw   80
from the Pennsylvania Turnpike looked enchanted — the branches of the
trees underpainted with budding russet, the meadows nubbled like new car-
pets, the bronze sun slanting on Valley Forge and Levittown alike. I do not
know what it is that is so welcome to me in the Pennsylvania landscape, but
it is the same quality — perhaps of reposing in the certainty that the truth is
good — that is in Pennsylvania faces. It seemed to me for this sunset hour
that the world is our bride, given to us to love, and the terror and joy of the
marriage is that we bring to it a nature not our bride's.

There was no sailor to help me drive the nine hours back. New Jersey   81
began in twilight and ended in darkness, and Manhattan made its gossamer
splash at its favorite hour, eight o'clock. The rest of the trip was more and
more steeply uphill. The Merritt Turnpike seemed meaninglessly coquet-

tish, the light-controlled stretch below Hartford maddeningly obstinate, and the hour above that frighteningly empty. Distance grew thicker and thicker; the intricate and effortful mechanics of the engine, the stellar infinity of explosive sparks needed to drive it, passed into my body, and wearied me. Repeatedly I stopped for coffee and the hallucinatory comfort of human faces, and after every stop, my waiting car, companion and warm home and willing steed, responded to my pressure. It began to seem a miracle that the car could gather speed from my numb foot; the very music on the radio seemed a drag on our effort, and I turned it off, obliterating time. We climbed through a space fretted by scattered brilliance and bathed in a monotonous wind. I had been driving forever; furniture, earth, churches, women, were all things I had innocently dreamed. And through those aeons my car, beginning as a mechanical spiral of molecules, evolved into something soft and organic and consciously brave. I lost, first, heart, then head, and finally any sense of my body. In the last hour of the trip I ceased to care or feel or in any real sense see, but the car, though its soul the driver had died, maintained steady forward motion, and completed the endless journey safely. Above my back yard the stars were frozen in place, and the shapes of my neighbors' houses wore the wonder that children induced by whirling.

Any day now we will trade it in; we are just waiting for the phone to ring. I know how it will be. My father traded in many cars. It happens so cleanly, before you expect it. He would drive off in the old car up the dirt road exactly as usual and when he returned the car would be new, and the old was gone, gone, utterly dissolved back into the mineral world from which it was conjured, dismissed without a blessing, a kiss, a testament, or any ceremony of farewell. We in America need ceremonies, is I suppose, sailor, the point of what I have written.

82

SUBJECT QUESTIONS

1. The story concludes with the statement, "We in America need ceremonies, is I suppose, sailor, the point of what I have written." Who is the "sailor" to whom the statement is addressed? Why to him?
2. Can you see this concluding statement as the point of the four episodes? What does the story of the dead cat have to do with ceremonies?
3. The narrator, David, several times refers to his loss of faith. Why, then, does he feel the need for ceremonies? Why does he bother to go to church?
4. What connection does Updike make between "packed dirt" and a religious impulse? What does John Dewey's definition of God have to do with this? (See paragraph 4.)
5. Twice in the dying cat episode occurs the direction, "Run on home," which is repeated in the traded car episode; and at the end David

leaves his dying father to "run on home." What special significance do you think Updike attaches to this command?

6. After a night of torment over his own insignificance in a dying universe, David is "relieved" to hear that his father is dying: "I was restored to crisp health in the play-world of action." Does the author intend for us to take David as a crass, uncaring son? What does he mean by the "play-world of action"? If action is the play-world, what is the real world?

7. Explain David's statement that churchgoing is "our most available democratic experience." Do you agree?

STRUCTURE QUESTIONS

1. Even the lengthy title implies that this story is about four separate episodes. What organizing principle, if any, justifies Updike's putting them together in one story?

2. Narrative poets frequently tie their poems, particularly ballads, together with refrains. Consider the effectiveness of Updike's use of this technique in fiction.

3. Until the fourth episode, we have only one indication that the narrator is "David" rather than the author, and the reader may feel that he is reading autobiography instead of fiction. What devices does Updike employ to give this impression? Why would he want to create such an impression?

4. Modern fiction writers seldom stop their narrative to comment on and interpret what happens (as in paragraph 4, for instance); are these commentaries necessary to understand the story? Do they interfere with emotional impact?

5. Because this is fiction, Updike does not use the traditional organization of persuasion. Does he manage to convey his beliefs effectively through fiction? Is Updike trying to "persuade" the reader, or only explain to him his own views? What advantages might fiction have as an instrument of persuasion?

SUGGESTION FOR WRITING

In an account of a personal experience, or a related series of experiences, show how you arrived at some conviction. Try to tell the story in such a way as to persuade the reader to your point of view.

Dover Beach

Matthew Arnold

Matthew Arnold (1822–1888), son of a headmaster at Rugby, was a social critic. The best-known of his many books is Culture and Anarchy, *a criticism of the tastes and values of the middle class. "Dover Beach" is perhaps the best example of his meditative poetry, reflecting the nineteenth century's deep doubts about the purpose of the universe and man's place in it aroused by new scientific discoveries and particularly by the publication of Darwin's* Origin of Species.

The sea is calm to-night,
The tide is full, the moon lies fair
Upon the Straits; — on the French coast, the light
Gleams, and is gone; the cliffs of England stand,
Glimmering and vast, out in the tranquil bay.   5
Come to the window, sweet is the night air!
Only, from the long line of spray
Where the sea meets the moon-blanched land,
Listen! you hear the grating roar
Of pebbles which the waves draw back, and fling,   10
At their return, up the high strand,
Begin, and cease, and then again begin,
With tremulous cadence slow, and bring
The eternal note of sadness in.

Sophocles long ago   15
Heard it on the Ægean, and it brought
Into his mind the turbid ebb and flow
Of human misery; we
Find also in the sound a thought,
Hearing it by this distant northern sea.   20

The sea of faith
Was once, too, at the full, and round earth's shore
Lay like the folds of a bright girdle furled;
But now I only hear
Its melancholy, long, withdrawing roar,   25
Retreating to the breath

440

Of the night-wind, down the vast edges drear
And naked shingles of the world.

Ah, love, let us be true
To one another! for the world, which seems   30
To lie before us like a land of dreams,
So various, so beautiful, so new,
Hath really neither joy, nor love, nor light,
Nor certitude, nor peace, nor help for pain;
And we are here as on a darkling plain   35
Swept with confused alarms of struggle and flight,
Where ignorant armies clash by night.

SUBJECT QUESTIONS

1. What is it about the sea which reminds Arnold of human misery? Isn't the opening picture one of calm beauty rather than of misery?
2. What is the reasoning behind Arnold's conclusion that love is all he can have faith in? Is his "evidence" primarily logical, or emotional?
3. Arnold assumes that the universe is unconcerned with him. Does he reciprocate with unconcern for the universe in his decision to trust only love? What is his attitude toward nature?
4. To what is Arnold referring in the concluding figure about ignorant armies in conflict?
5. Why does Arnold bring Sophocles into the poem? Does he represent something?

STRUCTURE QUESTIONS

1. The poem is divided into four stanzas; are these logical divisions or melodic divisions?
2. Analyze the rhyme schemes of the four stanzas. Do you find any correlation between the tightness of the rhyme and the idea expressed in each stanza?
3. Which lines seem to you to imitate most successfully the sound and rhythm of the sea? Do these imitations have any effect on the meaning of the poem, or are they exercises in poetic ingenuity?
4. Consider the way in which Arnold indicates transitions in thought with metrical variations. (Two good examples of this technique occur in the second stanza.)
5. The normal meter of this poem is iambic; why does Arnold vary this slightly in the last line? Consider other variations from iambic; do they serve any purpose? Are they weaknesses in the poem? Should Arnold have made the lines all the same length?
6. Evaluate the strengths and weaknesses of this poem as persuasion.

Does poetry seem to have any particular advantage over prose as a medium of persuasion?

7. What is the effect of the repetitious structure in lines 33 and 34? Explain how these lines help tie the last stanza to the rest of the poem.

SUGGESTIONS FOR WRITING

1. Write a persuasive essay defending or attacking the proposition "All you need is love."
2. Write a persuasive essay defending or attacking the proposition "An active faith is beneficial even when it does not have the support of scientific evidence."

Choy's Religion

Ann Steiner

In its December, 1976, issue, Esquire ran a special section on new religious movements and mind-expanding substitutes for conventional religion. This poem by Ann Steiner concluded the section.

Crandall Ming Choy started a new religion.
Called it Eat Your Baloney Before You
                 Get Your Chocolate Pudding.
Everybody came to worship.
They came from India.   5
They came from Paterson, New Jersey.
They came from Cuernavaca.
Everybody kept coming and coming
Till nobody nowhere was staying away.

And all the stores closed.   10
And spider webs grew in the Palace Theater.

Thanksgiving was taken off the calendar.
So was April.
                 And May.

Because Ming Choy proclaimed April and May   15
Unnecessary.

And so proclaimed they were in fact.

Along with Thanksgiving,
                 the Palace Theater,

And stores.   20

And that, my friends, was that.

Until Ralph K. Green came along with another religion.

He called his Read Your Books
                    Before You Watch TV.
Which lasted about two weeks.   25
A hell of a lot longer than

Pearlie Livingston's religion, Try My Gefilte Fish
Or You Don't Get Any Kugel.

Which lasted six minutes on the *Tonight* show.

So if you want to start a religion,   30
Stick with Crandall Ming Choy.

SUBJECT QUESTIONS

1. What element is shared by the three religions Steiner discusses? Is that element characteristic of most religions?
2. On what basis does Steiner prefer Choy's religion over the other two?
3. If Choy were going to proclaim any two months "unnecessary," why would he choose April and May?
4. Is it clear why Choy also banishes Thanksgiving, movie theaters, and stores?
5. What do you think Steiner's purpose was in writing this poem?

STRUCTURE QUESTIONS

1. Would the persuasive force of this poem have been altered had Steiner used real sects as examples instead of fictitious ones?
2. Examine Steiner's poem for characteristic poetic devices such as rhyme, metrical norm, vivid imagery, accumulated connotations. Is the style suited to her subject and purpose? Suppose she had made the poem more "beautiful"?
3. The eighteenth-century satirists believed that the best way to attack an idea was through ridicule rather than violence or intellectual argument. Why would that method be especially appropriate in the case of religious cults? Has Steiner made the right choice in her method of attack?
4. One difficulty with satire is that any positive incitement may be lost in the negative persuasion. Can you tell if Steiner wants to persuade her readers to any positive position?

SUGGESTION FOR WRITING

Write an essay in which you attempt to persuade the reader toward a particular religious view or philosophical position. (Or you may attempt to dissuade the reader from some view.)

9

LOOKING AHEAD

Evaluation

The ability to evaluate, to judge, to decide that one way is better than another is one of the great distinguishing characteristics of the human mind. It is what enables us to make use of our abilities to see likenesses and differences, to form generalizations from particulars, and to accumulate knowledge purposefully, instead of indiscriminately like a pack rat saving objects. The discovery of scientific information, for instance, is not nearly so valuable to us as the ability to assess its importance — to see the significance of new facts in relation to known facts.

Evaluation is a practice in which learned minds are constantly indulging and of which everyone is more or less capable. Every time we make a decision we first evaluate the advantages and disadvantages of each possible course of action. We may not do this very carefully or logically, but we do it. Take a familiar example: A student whose alarm clock rings at 7:30 is faced with a decision. "Should I get up and go to my 8 o'clock class? Should I stay in bed and get some much-needed rest? Should I wander over to the student union for a leisurely and nourishing breakfast of black coffee and cigarette smoke?" The student may be handicapped by an inability to think clearly at this time of day but will still evaluate various factors: "I need sleep more than I need food. If I went to class, the professor would put me to sleep. But I sleep better in a prone position than sitting at a desk." A good evaluation, certainly, would be done much more carefully than that, but the basic process would be similar. Con-

447

sider all the pertinent facts and implications and pass judgment in the light of each possibility's relative merits.

Evaluation, whether it is simple or complex, always presupposes the existence of some standard of judgment. Standards may vary greatly with different people and may not be very explicitly formulated, but for any judgment there must be a standard. A teacher who evaluates a student theme compares it to certain standards of excellence: "The organization is fair, sentence structure good, clarity excellent, spelling and punctuation atrocious." Then the teacher decides what its overall grade should be. A student does the same thing in deciding "That was a good movie" or "She is a poor teacher." What makes a good movie? — photography, acting, directing, significance of plot, continuity, and so on. The evaluator may not have such explicit standards, however, and perhaps judges from a vague notion, accumulated by watching many movies, that a movie ought to evoke certain emotional responses. But almost no one is totally uncritical — that is, without any standards of judgment.

It will easily be seen from the preceding examples that the amount and diversity of one's experience have much to do with one's ability to evaluate. Young children who have seen few movies will be tempted to boo the villain and shout warnings to the good guy; they will admire the good guy and detest the bad guy even if the latter is a much better actor. Similarly, second graders are not nearly as capable of judging teaching effectiveness as are college students. And beginning teachers, lacking the experience which comes from reading thousands of papers of varying quality, may also lack that ability to know automatically what grade a paper should receive. They must make up in eagerness and carefulness what they lack in experience. Of the two aspects of experience, variety is probably more important for good evaluation than mere quantity of experience. Persons who have read much poetry but all of it comparatively easy (Service, Whitman, and Sandburg, for example) will still have trouble evaluating the more difficult poetry of Wallace Stevens or Dylan Thomas. Their standards of judgment are simply too limited. A story is told of an African tribal chief who was taken to hear his first symphonic concert in an experiment to determine whether or not good music is naturally appealing to someone without prior training. The chief was quite pleased when the orchestra members were tuning their instruments, but the symphony itself left him coldly unappreciative.

In discussing standards of evaluation it is important to keep in mind that standards can be — and usually are — relative instead of absolute. We hold most standards tentatively, with an awareness that there may be specific instances to which a generally valid standard does not apply. Most people who endorse the principle "Thou shalt not kill" do not hold it absolutely but mean "In *most cases* thou shalt not kill." If one person kills another and we are called upon to evaluate the criminality of the act, we make an exception to the principle if the person was fighting in a war, acting in self-defense, or executing a convict. Our courts even distinguish "degrees" of murder: premeditated, unpremeditated, accidental, and justifiable. This same relativity of principles applies in most other areas as well. English teachers may normally mark off heavily for errors in punctuation or sentence structure, but they are likely to be much more forgiving in these matters with papers that show considerable insight and imagination. We say that the hero of a tragedy ought to have a recognizable "tragic flaw," but we readily admit that *Hamlet* is great even though its hero has no such flaw.

Evaluation as an essay form can be of three different types. One of these is *primary* evaluation: evaluation of a state of affairs or past action, such as a judgment of the accomplishments of Theodore Roosevelt's administration or of UNESCO's success in fostering mutual understanding among nations. Another type is *secondary*, an evaluation of *someone else's* judgment. This includes book reviews and judgments of paintings, poems, movies — works which express the values of the artist. The process for this kind of evaluation is the same as for primary evaluation except that two sets of standards must be considered: those of the original author or artist and those of the reviewer or critic. Normally, such an evaluation is organized in three parts, answering the following questions: (1) What was the author trying to do? (2) How well did the author accomplish his aims? (3) To what extent was the work worth doing? The answers to the first two questions should be in terms of the standards implied by the original author. If an artist was trying to produce an abstract painting it would hardly be fair to condemn the work for being insufficiently representational — that is, not "looking like" the scene which inspired it. The answer to the third question depends on the standards of the reviewer or critic. If the critic believes that abstract painting is foolish experimentation and that this particular painting cannot be great because it is abstract, such a judgment should come in the third rather than the second part. Thus a critic might conclude that the artist succeeded very well in what the artist was trying to do but that the attempt was not worth the effort.

You should remember that any evaluation, no matter how carefully worked out, is still opinion rather than fact. A viewer may be convinced that a certain movie was the "worst" of the year, and perhaps it was that bad if judged by a standard such as acting or plot.

But perhaps its producer, whose standard of judgment is monetary, might judge it to be "great" if a few suggestive scenes cause it to bring in considerable amounts of money. This is not to say, however, that all evaluations are equally valuable. Enlightened opinion can tell us much; snap judgments tell us little except something about the intellectual nature of the person making the judgment. Students who write evaluations should take pains to judge carefully and fairly, to consider as much relevant information as possible, to know and make clear what their standards of judgment are, and to recognize that they may not be the only applicable standards. Pursued properly, evaluation can be a rewarding experience and a valuable contribution to civilization. Done improperly, it can be a mere excuse for perpetrating one's prejudices.

Although *self-evaluation*, the third type, is on a subject obviously familiar to the writer, it is a very difficult kind of writing to handle competently. And it is the one type of writing which is generally more useful to the writer than to his reader. The great Dr. Samuel Johnson always kept a journal, and he urged his friend Boswell to do the same on the grounds that any person, no matter how successful or important he was, could profit by occasionally making a self-evaluation. He found that people, too easily losing sight of their personal values and goals, can drift through life discovering too late that they have not accomplished what they set out to do or anything else worthwhile.

Self-evaluation is especially valuable to students for they are in the process of committing themselves to sets of standards and aims which will in large measure determine what the rest of their lives will be like. Students who come to school with exalted and narrow-minded notions of their chosen careers, whether they be in medicine, engineering, or creative writing, are likely to be making tragic mistakes if they stagger through programs for which they are not suited and refuse to consider other possible major fields. Again, unless they evaluate themselves periodically students may go through college thinking that a C-average and a house presidency are adequate recommendations for a job, and then suddenly discover too late that they want to go on to graduate school.

In spite of the obvious benefit from occasional self-evaluation, students are likely to encounter considerable difficulty in doing it. People don't like to admit that they are making mistakes or that their values are wrong; consequently, it is easier to avoid the possibility of having to make such an admission by dismissing self-evaluation as a "waste of time" or by substituting for honest analysis a few hasty rationalizations. Someone has said, however, that students' greatest advantage is their right to be wrong: students who are afraid of making mistakes never learn as much as the ones who expose their ideas to the criticism of teachers and fellow students. Although a ten-year veteran of a specialized occupation can hardly afford to admit having chosen the wrong career, students can admit it — and change — without too much inconvenience. If they can forget their fear of being wrong and make honest efforts to evaluate themselves justly, they can learn a great deal about themselves and at the same time gain clearer vision of where they are going and where they want to go.

A complete self-evaluation contains the answers to two questions: (1) Am I accomplishing my aims and living up to my standards? (2) Are my standards, basic assumptions, and goals the right ones for me? For most students, the first question is probably much easier to answer than the second, for the latter calls into question values which the student has been accumulating for years and may have had no doubts about before coming to college. Evaluating these values involves the same kind of difficulty faced by a person who takes a college biology course after having been taught at home or at church that the whole notion of evolution is atheistic nonsense. But because anyone's set of values is likely to include contradictions and unwarranted assumptions, it is particularly worthwhile to examine them before committing one's whole life to them. Most of our "cherished" goals are either handed to us or accumulated unconsciously, so that we have no real reason for being fiercely loyal to them. It would profit any student to make a complete self-evaluation at least as often as once every school year. The difficulty of the attempt ought to be compensated for by the knowledge that it is the student's own life which is at stake. It is because self-evaluation can be of such vital importance — and because backing off and examining one's self objectively is such a difficult task — that this subject has been reserved for the last part of the text.

I Can Write

Theodore Roethke

Theodore Roethke (1908–1963) raised himself by sheer will and energy from unpromising beginnings in a tough neighborhood of Saginaw, Michigan, to become one of the most sensitive and respected of modern American poets. At the time of his death, he was professor of English and artist-in-residence at the University of Washington and had won almost every important award given to poets, including a Pulitzer Prize, a National Book Award, the Bollingen Prize, and the Poetry Society of America Prize. The price he paid for tremendous mental output was recurrent mental exhaustion. Despite a series of nervous breakdowns, Roethke was a devoted, demanding, and first-rate teacher who trained a number of the best contemporary American poets. At the time he wrote the following essay, Roethke was a student at Michigan State University, struggling to make the transition from beer-drinking jock to serious student. After the undistinguished beginnings he refers to in the essay, he went on to graduate magna cum laude and to be accepted both at Michigan State, for law school, and at Harvard University, for graduate work in English. Much of Roethke's success as a writer was due to his careful observation of his surroundings: throughout his career he kept voluminous notebooks, and his pockets were usually stuffed with notes of observations and ideas for poems.

I expect this course to open my eyes to story material, to unleash my too dormant imagination, to develop that quality utterly lacking in my nature — a sense of form. I do not expect to acquire much technique. I expect to be able to seize upon the significant, reject the trivial. I hope to acquire a greater love for humanity in all its forms.

I have long wondered just what my strength was as a writer. I am often filled with tremendous enthusiasm for a subject, yet my writing about it will seem a sorry attempt. Above all, I possess a driving sincerity, — that prime virtue of any creative worker. I write only what I believe to be the absolute truth, — even if I must ruin the theme in so doing. In this respect I feel far superior to those glib people in my classes who often garner better grades than I do. They are so often pitiful frauds, — artificial — insincere. They have a line that works. They do not write from

1

2

From *On the Poet and His Craft: Selected Prose of Theodore Roethke* by Theodore Roethke. Reprinted by permission of University of Washington Press.

the depths of their hearts. Nothing of theirs was ever born of pain. Many an incoherent yet sincere piece of writing has outlived the polished product.

I write only about people and things that I know thoroughly. Perhaps I have become a mere reporter, not a writer. Yet I feel that this is all my present abilities permit. I will open my eyes in my youth and store this raw, living material. Age may bring the fire that molds experience into artistry.

I have a genuine love of nature. It is not the least bit affected, but an integral and powerful part of my life. I know that Cooper is a fraud — that he doesn't give a true sense of the sublimity of American scenery. I know that Muir and Thoreau and Burroughs speak the truth.

I can sense the moods of nature almost instinctively. Ever since I could walk, I have spent as much time as I could in the open. A perception of nature — no matter how delicate, how subtle, how evanescent, — remains with me forever.

I am influenced too much, perhaps, by natural objects. I seem bound by the very room I'm in. I've associated so long with prosaic people that I've dwarfed myself spiritually. When I get alone under an open sky where man isn't too evident — then I'm tremendously exalted and a thousand vivid ideas and sweet visions flood my consciousness.

I think that I possess story material in abundance. I have had an unusual upbringing. I was let alone, thank God! My mother insisted upon two things, — that I strive for perfection in whatever I did and that I always try to be a gentleman. I played with Italians, with Russians, Poles, and the "sissies" on Michigan Avenue. I was carefully watched, yet allowed to follow my own inclinations. I have seen a good deal of life that would never have been revealed to an older person. Up to the time I came to college then I had seen humanity in diverse forms. Now I'm cramped and unhappy. I don't feel that these idiotic adolescents are worth writing about. In the summer, I turn animal and work for a few weeks in a factory. Then I'm happy.

My literary achievements have been insignificant. At fourteen, I made a speech which was translated into twenty-six languages and used as Red Cross propaganda. When I was younger, it seemed that everything I wrote was eminently successful. I always won a prize when I entered an essay contest. In college, I've been able to get only one "A" in four rhetoric courses. I feel this keenly. If I can't write, what can I do? I wonder.

When I was a freshman, I told Carleton Wells that I knew I could write whether he thought so or not. On my next theme he wrote "You can Write!" How I have cherished that praise!

It is bad form to talk about grades, I know. If I don't get an "A" in this course, it wouldn't be because I haven't tried. I've made a slow start.

I'm going to spend Christmas vacation writing. A "B" symbolizes defeat to me. I've been beaten too often.

I do wish that we were allowed to keep our stories until we felt that   11
we had worked them into the best possible form.

I do not have the divine urge to write. There seems to be something   12
surging within, — a profound undercurrent of emotion. Yet there is none
of that fertility of creation which distinguishes the real writer.

Nevertheless, I have faith in myself. I'm either going to be a good   13
writer or a poor fool.

SUBJECT QUESTIONS

1. What does Roethke expect to gain from his writing course? Judging from your own writing course, are these realistic expectations? Is Roethke aware that the course will not "give" him anything which he does not work to gain?
2. What does Roethke think are his chief weaknesses as a writer? Are they weaknesses which can be overcome through training and practice?
3. Would you agree that insincere but polished writing is more likely to receive a top grade than sincere but unpolished writing? Is good writing necessarily "born of pain"? Do you think it true that sincere thoughts are harder to polish than insincere ones?
4. If Roethke is such a lover of nature, why do you suppose he keeps trying to write about people? Would he do better to start with nature writing?
5. Does Roethke make clear whether he thinks "driving sincerity" or "fertility of creation" more important to a good writer? Which would you say is more important? Can these qualities be learned?
6. In what ways does Roethke see himself as different from the other students? Do you think he is being fair, or resentful?

STRUCTURE QUESTIONS

1. As this self-evaluation was not intended for publication, one might expect it to be more random than coherent. Does it have unity if not coherence?
2. By what standards does Roethke judge himself as a writer? Does he make these standards clear?
3. Can you judge from this writing whether or not Roethke is being honest with himself? What clues have you? Does he at any point seem a victim of self-deception?
4. Roethke admits that grades should not be a standard for judging his

writing potential; does he in fact use grades as one standard of judgment?
5. If Roethke were preparing this essay as a written assignment, how might he have organized his material to better effect?

SUGGESTIONS FOR WRITING

1. Write an evaluation of this essay, in terms not of sincerity but of writing quality. You may put it in the form of an essay from instructor to student, pointing out, with specific examples, both the strengths and weaknesses of the writing.
2. Write a self-evaluation of your writing abilities. Be sure to make clear your standards of judgment.

The Summit of the Years
John Burroughs

John Burroughs (1837–1921) was an American naturalist, a close friend of Walt Whitman. He began his career as a schoolteacher, but soon went to the woods and built a secluded cabin (called Slabsides), where he lived alone for twenty-two years. His first published book was Notes on Walt Whitman as Poet and Person *(1867). He subsequently wrote many nature books, including* Locusts and Wild Honey *(1879),* Ways of Nature *(1905),* Bird and Bough *(1906),* The Summit of the Years *(1914), and* The Breath of Life *(1915). He was considered in his time America's finest nature writer and has been admired by many later writers, including Theodore Roethke in the essay above. The self-evaluation which follows was written when Burroughs was seventy-five and almost at the end of his long career.*

The longer I live the more my mind dwells upon the beauty and the wonder of the world. I hardly know which feeling leads, wonderment or admiration. After a man has passed the psalmist's deadline of seventy years, as Dr. Holmes called it, if he is of a certain temperament, he becomes more and more detached from the noise and turmoil of the times in which he lives. The passing hubbub in the street attracts him less and less; more and more he turns to the permanent, the fundamental, the everlasting. More and more is he impressed with life and nature in themselves, and the beauty and the grandeur of the voyage we are making on this planet. The burning questions and issues of the hour are for the new generations, in whom life burns intensely also. 1

My life has always been more or less detached from the life about me. 2 I have not been a hermit, but my temperament and love of solitude, and a certain constitutional timidity and shrinking from all kinds of strife, have kept me in the by-paths rather than on the great highways of life. My talent, such as it is, is distinctly a by-path talent, or at most, a talent for green lanes and sequestered roadsides; but that which has most interested me in life, Nature, can be seen from lanes and by-paths better even than from the turnpike, where the dust and noise and the fast driving obscure the view or distract the attention. I have loved the feel of the grass under my feet, and the sound of the running streams by my side. The hum of the wind in the tree-tops has always been good music to me, and the face of the fields has often comforted me more than the faces of men.

In my tranquil seclusion I am often on the point of upbraiding myself 3 because I keep so aloof from the struggles and contentions and acrimonious debates of the political, the social, and the industrial world about me. I do not join any of the noisy processions, I do not howl with the reformers, or cry Fire! with the alarmists. I say to myself, What is all this noisy civilization and all this rattling machinery of government for, but that men may all have just the sane and contented life that I am living, and on the same terms that I do. They can find it in the next field, beyond the next hill, in the town or in the country — a land of peace and plenty, if one has peace in his heart and the spirit of fair play in his blood.

Business, politics, government, are but the scaffoldings of our house 4 of life; they are there that I may have a good roof over my head, and a warm and safe outlook into the beauty and glory of the universe, and let them not absorb more time and energy than the home itself. They have absorbed very little of mine, and I fancy that my house of life would have just as staunch walls, and just as many windows and doors, had they not absorbed so much of other men's. Let those who love turmoil arm for turmoil: their very arming will bring it; and let those who love peace disarm for peace: the disarming will hasten it. Those also serve who mind their own business and let others mind theirs.

I know that all this clamor and competition, all this heat and friction 5 and turmoil of the world, are only the result of the fury with which we play the game of our civilization. It is like our college football, which is brutal and killing, and more like war than like sport. Why should I be more than an amused or pained spectator?

I was never a fighter; I fear that at times I may have been a shirker, 6 but I have shirked one thing or one duty that I might the more heartily give myself to another. He also serves who sometimes runs away.

From the summit of the years I look back over my life, and see what I 7 have escaped and what I have missed, as a traveler might look back over his course from a mountain-top, and see where he had escaped a jungle or a wilderness or a desert, and where he had missed a fair field or a fountain, or pleasant habitations. I have escaped the soul-killing and body-wrecking occupations that are the fate of so many men in my time. I have escaped the greed of wealth, the "mania of owning things," as Whitman called it. I have escaped the disappointment of political ambition, of business ambition, of social ambition; I have never been a cog in anybody's wheel, or an attachment to the tail of anybody's kite. I have never lost myself in the procession of parties, or trained with any sect or clique. I have been fortunate in being allowed to go my own way in the world.

It is a question whether in escaping a college education I made a hit 8 or a miss. I am inclined to the opinion that a little systematic training, especially in science, would have been a gain, though the systematic grind in literature which the college puts its students through, I am glad to have escaped. I thank heaven that in literature I have never had to dissect Shakespeare or Milton, or any other great poet, in the class-room, and that I have never had to dissect any animal in the laboratory. I have had the poets in their beautiful and stimulating unity and wholeness, and I have had the animals in the fields and woods in the joy of their natural activities. In my literary career I have escaped trying to write for the public or for editors; I have written for myself. I have not asked, "What does the public want?" I have only asked, "What do I want to say? What have I lived or felt or thought that is my own, and has its root in my inmost being?"

I have few of the aptitudes of the scholar, and fewer yet of the   9
methodical habits and industry of the man of business. I live in books a certain part of each day, but less as a student of books than as a student of life. I go to books and to nature as a bee goes to the flower, for a nectar that I can make into my own honey. My memory for the facts and the arguments of books is poor, but my absorptive power is great.

There is no one, I suppose, who does not miss some good fortune in   10
his life. We all miss congenial people, people who are going our way, and whose companionship would make life sweeter for us. Often we are a day too early, or a day too late, at the point where our paths cross. How many such congenial souls we miss we know not, but for my part, considering the number I have met, I think it may be many.

I have missed certain domestic good fortunes, such as a family of   11
many children (I have only one), which might have made the struggle of life harder, but which would surely have brought its compensations. Those lives are, indeed, narrow and confined which are not blessed with several children. Every branch the tree puts out lays it open more to the storms and tempests of life; it lays it open also to the light and the sunshine, and to the singing and the mating birds. A childless life is a tree without branches, a house without windows.

I missed being a soldier in the armies of the Union during the Civil   12
War, which was probably the greatest miss of my life. I think I had in me many of the qualities that go to the making of a good soldier — love of adventure, keenness of eye and ear, love of camp-life, ability to shift for myself, skill with the gun, and a sound constitution. But the rigidity of the military system, the iron rules, the mechanical unity and precision, the loss of the one in the many — all would have galled me terribly, though better men than I willingly, joyously, made themselves a part of the great military machine.

I got near enough to the firing line during our Civil War, — when   13
Early made his demonstration against the Capital in 1864, and I was a clerk

in the Treasury Department, — to know that I much prefer the singing of the birds to the singing of hostile bullets.

War is a terrible business.   14

II

From youth to age I have lived with nature more than with men. In youth   15
I saw nature as a standing invitation to come forth and give play to myself;
the streams were for fishing and swimming, the woods were for hunting
and exploring, and for all kinds of sylvan adventure; the fields were for
berries and birds' nests, and color, and the delight of the world of grasses;
the mountains were for climbing and the prospects and the triumphs of
their summits.

The world was good; it tasted good, it delighted all my senses. The   16
seasons came and went, each with its own charms and enticements. I was
ready for each and contented with each. The spring was for the delights of
sugar-making, and the returning birds — the naked maple woods flooded
with the warm creative sunshine, the brown fields slipping off their covering of snow, the loosened rills, the first robin, the first phoebe, the first
song sparrow — how all these things thrilled one! The summer was for
bare feet, light clothes, freedom from school, strawberries, trout, hay-
making, and the Fourth of July. Autumn was for apples, nuts, wild
pigeons, gray squirrels, and the great dreamy tranquil days; winter for the
fireside, school, games, coasting, and the tonic of frost and snow. How the
stars twinkled in winter! how the ice sang, and whooped on the ponds! how
the snow sculpturing decked all the farm fences! how the sheeted winds
stalked across the hills!

Oh, the eagerness and freshness of youth! How the boy enjoys his   17
food, his sleep, his sports, his companions, his truant days! His life is an
adventure, he is widening his outlook, he is extending his dominion, he is
conquering his kingdom. How cheap are his pleasures, how ready his en-
thusiasms! In boyhood I have had more delight on a haymow with two
companions and a big dog — delight that came nearer intoxication — than
I have ever had in all the subsequent holidays of my life. When youth goes,
much goes with it. When manhood comes, much comes with it. We exchange a world of delightful sensations and impressions for a world of
duties and studies and meditations. The youth enjoys what the man tries to
understand. Lucky is he who can get his grapes to market and keep the
bloom upon them, who can carry some of the freshness and eagerness and
simplicity of youth into his later years, who can have a boy's heart below a
man's head.

The birds have always meant much to me; as a farm-boy they were   18
like a golden thread that knit the seasons together. In early manhood I

turned to them with the fondness of youth, reinforced with an impetus obtained from literature. Books, especially the poets, may do this for a man; they may consecrate a subject, give it the atmosphere of the ideal, and lift it up in the field of universal interest. They seem to have done something like that for me in relation to birds. I did not go to books for my knowledge of the birds, except for some technical knowledge, but I think literature helped to endow them with a human interest to me, and relate them to the deeper and purer currents of my life. What joy they have brought me! How they have given me wings to escape the tedious and the deadening! I have not studied them so much as I have played with them, camped with them, gone berrying with them, summered and wintered with them, and my knowledge of them has filtered into my mind almost unconsciously.

The bird as a piece of living nature is what interests me, having vital   19
relations to all out-of-doors, and capable of linking my mind to itself and its surroundings with threads of delightful associations. The live bird is a fellow passenger; we are making the voyage together, and there is a sympathy between us that quickly leads to knowledge. If I looked upon it as something to be measured and weighed and tabulated, or as a subject for laboratory experimentation, my ornithology would turn to ashes in my hands.

The whole of nature, directly or indirectly, goes with him who gives   20
his mind to objects in the open air. The observer of bird-life in the open has heaven and earth thrown in. Well, I need not harp on this string. All lovers of life in the open know what I would say. The book of living nature is unlike other books in this respect: one can read it over and over, and always find new passages and new meanings. It is a book that goes to press new every night, and comes forth fresh every morning.

III

I began by saying how much the beauty and wonder of the world occupies   21
me these later years. How these things come home to me as life draws near the end. I am like a man who makes a voyage and falls so much in love with the ship and the sea that he thinks of little else and is not curious about the new lands before him. I suppose if my mind had dwelt much upon the other world toward which we are headed, and which is the main concern with so many passengers, I should have found less to absorb and instruct me in this. In fact, the hypothetical other world has scarcely occupied me at all, and when it has, I have thought of it as a projection from this, a kind of Brocken shadow cast by our love of life upon futurity. My whole being is so well, so exquisitely attuned to this world, that I have instinctively felt that it was for this world that I was made.

I have never been able to see how I could be adjusted to two worlds 22 unless they were much alike. A better world I have never wanted. I could not begin to exhaust the knowledge and the delights of this one. I have found in it deep beneath deep, worlds within a world — an endless series of beautiful and wonderful forms forever flowing out of itself. From the highest heavens of the telescope, to the minutest organisms of the microscope, all is beautiful and wonderful, and passeth understanding.

SUBJECT QUESTIONS

1. Unlike Roethke's self-evaluation, written at the beginning of his career, Burroughs's was written near the end of his career. What pitfalls might there be in a self-evaluation by a writer at the top of his profession? Does Burroughs avoid them? Does he make good use of his advantage of "perspective"?
2. Burroughs says that at times he is "on the point" of blaming himself for keeping aloof from the world's troubles; how does he justify not having become more involved?
3. Except for the reference to the Civil War, what clues are there that this essay was written three-quarters of a century ago? Do the world's troubles seem very much different now?
4. What things has Burroughs's life as a recluse enabled him to "escape"? Do these seem to be things one ought to avoid? Do most people want to avoid them?
5. What experiences does Burroughs regret having missed? Do the pleasures outweigh the regrets? Why would he have wanted more children? Does he regret not going to college? (Note that he had learned to write well without going to college.)
6. As a general rule, elderly people tend to dwell on the present and on their childhood; the years between twenty and sixty are of little concern to them. Is this true of Burroughs? What do old age and youth have in common which makes them blend so well in the minds of the elderly?

STRUCTURE QUESTIONS

1. What is the logic of the division into three numbered sections?
2. A prerequisite for good evaluation is a willingness to be just and honest in self-judgment. Does Burroughs maintain this attitude? Point out passages which tell the reader that Burroughs at least intends to be honest.
3. What are the chief standards by which Burroughs evaluates his life? When these standards are not the "usual" ones, does he make clear that they are personal and not necessarily ideal for everyone?

4. To what extent would you say that Burroughs's standards mesh with his understanding of his own personality? At which points did his chosen way of life fail to fulfill aspects of his personality? Does he keep the standards constant?

5. Burroughs's writing style is more vivid and less "conversational" than most modern prose; were you comfortable with it, or did it seem "artificial"? Examine a passage closely (paragraph 17 is a good example), noting particularly the parallel structure and the use of active verbs and concrete nouns to keep the philosophical passages from becoming abstract.

SUGGESTIONS FOR WRITING

1. Undertake an honest analysis of your own personality in the way that Burroughs has done with his in paragraph 2. Then evaluate the degree to which your goals and standards mesh with your personality. (It is not expected that everything will be in harmony: you may be very hot-tempered and still think gentleness ideal.)

2. Write a "stock-taking" evaluation, in which you judge your progress against your expectations and standards. It may be convenient to limit this exercise to one aspect of your life, such as academic work. Remember to make your standards clear and to be honest with yourself.

We'll Never Conquer Space

Arthur C. Clarke

Arthur C. Clarke (b. 1917), noted British scientist and writer, is probably best known to Americans for his novel and screenplay, 2001: A Space Odyssey (1968). But he has written dozens of books, both fiction and nonfiction, on the space program and space travel, including First on the Moon (1970) with the astronauts who made the trip. Clarke was an RAF pilot in World War II, and he has won numerous awards for science writing. It may seem surprising, considering his involvement in the space program, to find him writing an article entitled "We'll Never Conquer Space." Written in 1960, it is characteristic of Clarke's thought on the subject throughout his career.

Man will never conquer space. Such a statement may sound ludicrous, now   1
that our rockets are already 100 million miles beyond the moon and the first
human travelers are preparing to leave the atmosphere. Yet it expresses a
truth which our forefathers knew, one we have forgotten — and our descendants must learn again, in heartbreak and loneliness.

Our age is in many ways unique, full of events and phenomena which   2
never occurred before and can never happen again. They distort our thinking, making us believe that what is true now will be true forever, though
perhaps on a larger scale. Because we have annihilated distance on this
planet, we imagine that we can do it once again. The facts are far otherwise,
and we will see them more clearly if we forget the present and turn our
minds toward the past.

To our ancestors, the vastness of the earth was a dominant fact control-   3
ling their thoughts and lives. In all earlier ages than ours, the world was
wide indeed, and no man could ever see more than a tiny fraction of its immensity. A few hundred miles — a thousand, at the most — was infinity.
Only a lifetime ago, parents waved farewell to their emigrating children in
the virtual certainty that they would never meet again.

And now, within one incredible generation, all this has changed. Over   4
the seas where Odysseus wandered for a decade, the Rome-Beirut Comet
whispers its way within the hour. And above that, the closer satellites span
the distance between Troy and Ithaca in less than a minute.

Psychologically as well as physically, there are no longer any remote 5
places on earth. When a friend leaves for what was once a far country, even
if he has no intention of returning, we cannot feel that same sense of irrevocable separation that saddened our forefathers. We know that he is only
hours away by jet liner, and that we have merely to reach for the telephone
to hear his voice.

In a very few years, when the satellite communication network is es- 6
tablished, we will be able to see friends on the far side of the earth as easily
as we talk to them on the other side of the town. Then the world will shrink
no more, for it will have become a dimensionless point.

But the new stage that is opening up for the human drama will never 7
shrink as the old one has done. We have abolished space here on the little
earth; we can never abolish the space that yawns between the stars. Once
again we are face to face with immensity and must accept its grandeur and
terror, its inspiring possibilities and its dreadful restraints. From a world that
has become too small, we are moving out into one that will forever be too
large, whose frontiers will recede from us always more swiftly than we can
reach out towards them.

Consider first the fairly modest solar, or planetary, distances which we 8
are now preparing to assault. The very first Lunik made a substantial impression upon them, traveling more than 200 million miles from the earth — six
times the distance to Mars. When we have harnessed nuclear energy for
spaceflight, the solar system will contract until it is little larger than the earth
today. The remotest of the planets will be perhaps no more than a week's
travel from the earth, while Mars and Venus will be only a few hours away.

This achievement, which will be witnessed within a century, might ap- 9
pear to make even the solar system a comfortable, homely place, with such
giant planets as Saturn and Jupiter playing much the same role in our
thoughts as do Africa or Asia today. (Their qualitative differences of climate,
atmosphere and gravity, fundamental though they are, do not concern us at
the moment.) To some extent this may be true, yet as soon as we pass
beyond the orbit of the moon, a mere quarter-million miles away, we will
meet the first of the barriers that will separate the earth from her scattered
children.

The marvelous telephone and television network that will soon enmesh 10
the whole world, making all men neighbors, cannot be extended into space.
It will never be possible to converse with anyone on another planet.

Do not misunderstand this statement. Even with today's radio equip- 11
ment, the problem of sending speech to the other planets is almost trivial.
But the messages will take minutes — sometimes hours — on their journey,
because radio and light waves travel at the same limited speed of 186,000
miles a second.

Twenty years from now you will be able to listen to a friend on Mars, 12 but the words you hear will have left his mouth at least three minutes earlier, and your reply will take a corresponding time to reach him. In such circumstances, an exchange of verbal messages is possible — but not a conversation.

Even in the case of the nearby moon, the 2½-second time lag will be [13] annoying. At distances of more than a million miles, it will be intolerable.

To a culture which has come to take instantaneous communication for [14] granted, as part of the very structure of civilized life, this "time barrier" may have a profound psychological impact. It will be a perpetual reminder of universal laws and limitations against which not all our technology can ever prevail. For it seems as certain as anything can be that no signal — still less any material object — can ever travel faster than light.

The velocity of light is the ultimate speed limit, being part of the very [15] structure of space and time. Within the narrow confines of the solar system, it will not handicap us too severely, once we have accepted the delays in communication which it involves. At the worst, these will amount to twenty hours — the time it takes a radio signal to span the orbit of Pluto, the outermost planet.

Between the three inner worlds, the earth, Mars, and Venus, it will [16] never be more than twenty minutes — not enough to interfere seriously with commerce or administration, but more than sufficient to shatter those personal links of sound or vision that can give us a sense of direct contact with friends on earth, wherever they may be.

It is when we move out beyond the confines of the solar system that we [17] come face to face with an altogether new order of cosmic reality. Even today, many otherwise educated men — like those savages who can count to three but lump together all numbers beyond four — cannot grasp the profound distinction between solar and stellar space. The first is the space enclosing our neighboring worlds, the planets; the second is that which embraces those distant suns, the stars, and it is literally millions of times greater.

There is no such abrupt change of scale in terrestrial affairs. To obtain a [18] mental picture of the distance to the nearest star, as compared with the distance to the nearest planet, you must imagine a world in which the closest object to you is only five feet away — and then there is nothing else to see until you have travelled a thousand miles.

Many conservative scientists, appalled by these cosmic gulfs, have de- [19] nied that they can ever be crossed. Some people never learn; those who sixty years ago scoffed at the possibility of flight, and ten (even five!) years ago laughed at the idea of travel to the planets, are now quite sure that the stars will always be beyond our reach. And again they are wrong, for they have failed to grasp the great lesson of our age — that if something is possible in theory, and no fundamental scientific laws oppose its realization, then sooner or later it will be achieved.

One day, it may be in this century, or it may be a thousand years from   20
now, we shall discover a really efficient means of propelling our space vehicles. Every technical device is always developed to its limit (unless it is
superseded by something better) and the ultimate speed for spaceships is the
velocity of light. They will never reach that goal, but they will get very close
to it. And then the nearest star will be less than five years' voyaging from the
earth.

Our exploring ships will spread outwards from their home over an   21
ever-expanding sphere of space. It is a sphere which will grow at almost —
but never quite — the speed of light. Five years to the triple system of
Alpha Centauri, ten to the strangely-matched doublet Sirius A and B, eleven
to the tantalizing enigma of 61 Cygni, the first star suspected to possess a
planet. These journeys are long, but they are not impossible. Man has always
accepted whatever price was necessary for his explorations and discoveries,
and the price of Space is Time.

Even voyages which may last for centuries or millennia will one day be   22
attempted. Suspended animation has already been achieved in the laboratory, and may be the key to interstellar travel. Self-contained cosmic arks
which will be tiny traveling worlds in their own right may be another solution, for they would make possible journeys of unlimited extent, lasting generation after generation.

The famous Time Dilation effect predicted by the Theory of Relativity,   23
whereby time appears to pass more slowly for a traveler moving at almost
the speed of light, may be yet a third. And there are others.

Looking far into the future, therefore, we must picture a slow (little   24
more than half a billion miles an hour!) expansion of human activities outwards from the solar system, among the suns scattered across the region of
the galaxy in which we now find ourselves. These suns are on the average
five light-years apart; in other words, we can never get from one to the next
in less than five years.

To bring home what this means, let us use a down-to-earth analogy.   25
Imagine a vast ocean, sprinkled with islands — some desert, others perhaps
inhabited. On one of these islands an energetic race has just discovered the
art of building ships. It is preparing to explore the ocean, but must face the
fact that the very nearest island is five years' voyaging away, and that no possible improvement in the technique of shipbuilding will ever reduce this
time.

In these circumstances (which are those in which we will soon find our-   26
selves) what could the islanders achieve? After a few centuries, they might
have established colonies on many of the nearby islands and have briefly
explored many others. The daughter colonies might themselves have sent
out further pioneers, and so a kind of chain reaction would spread the original culture over a steadily expanding area of the ocean.

But now consider the effects of the inevitable, unavoidable time lag. 27
There could be only the most tenuous contact between the home island and
its offspring. Returning messengers could report what had happened on the
nearest colony — five years ago. They could never bring information more
up to date than that, and dispatches from the more distant parts of the ocean
would be from still further in the past — perhaps centuries behind the
times. There would never be news from the other islands, but only history.

All the star-borne colonies of the future will be independent, whether 28
they wish it or not. Their liberty will be inviolably protected by Time as well
as Space. They must go their own way and achieve their own destiny, with
no help or hindrance from Mother Earth.

At this point, we will move the discussion on to a new level and deal 29
with an obvious objection. Can we be sure that the velocity of light is indeed
a limiting factor? So many "impassible" barriers have been shattered in the
past; perhaps this one may go the way of all the others.

We will not argue the point, or give the reasons why scientists believe 30
that light can never be outraced by any form of radiation or any material object. Instead, let us assume the contrary and see just where it gets us. We
will even take the most optimistic possible case and imagine that the speed
of transportation may eventually become infinite.

Picture a time when, by the development of techniques as far beyond 31
our present engineering as a transistor is beyond a stone axe, we can reach
anywhere we please instantaneously, with no more effort than by dialing a
number. This would indeed cut the universe down to size and reduce its
physical immensity to nothingness. What would be left?

Everything that really matters. For the universe has two aspects — its 32
scale, and its overwhelming, mind-numbing complexity. Having abolished
the first, we are now face-to-face with the second.

What we must now try to visualize is not size, but quantity. Most peo- 33
ple today are familiar with the simple notation which scientists use to describe large numbers; it consists merely of counting zeroes, so that a
hundred becomes 10^2, a million, 10^6, a billion, 10^9 and so on. This useful
trick enables us to work with quantities of any magnitude, and even defense-
budget totals look modest when expressed as $\$5.76 \times 10^9$ instead of
$\$5,760,000,000$.

The number of other suns in our own galaxy (that is, the whirlpool of 34
stars and cosmic dust of which our sun is an out-of-town member, lying in
one of the remoter spiral arms) is estimated at about 10^{11} — or written in
full, 100,000,000,000. Our present telescopes can observe something like 10^9
other galaxies, and they show no sign of thinning out even at the extreme
limit of vision.

There are probably at least as many galaxies in the whole of creation as 35
there are stars in our own galaxy, but let us confine ourselves to those we

can see. They must contain a total of about 10^{11} times 10^9 stars, or 10^{20} stars altogether. One followed by twenty other digits is, of course, a number beyond all understanding.

Before such numbers, even spirits brave enough to face the challenge of the light-years must quail. The detailed examination of all the grains of sand on all the beaches of the world is a far smaller task than the exploration of the universe.   36

And so we return to our opening statement. Space can be mapped and crossed and occupied without definable limit; but it can never be conquered. When our race has reached its ultimate achievements, and the stars themselves are scattered no more widely than the seed of Adam, even then we shall still be like ants crawling on the face of the earth. The ants have covered the world, but have they conquered it — for what do their countless colonies know of it, or of each other?   37

So it will be with us as we spread outwards from Mother Earth, loosening the bonds of kinship and understanding, hearing faint and belated rumors at second — or third — or thousandth-hand of an ever-dwindling fraction of the entire human race.   38

Though Earth will try to keep in touch with her children, in the end all the efforts of her archivists and historians will be defeated by time and distance, and the sheer bulk of material. For the number of distinct societies or nations, when our race is twice its present age, may be far greater than the total number of all the men who have ever lived up to the present time.   39

We have left the realm of human comprehension in our vain effort to grasp the scale of the universe; so it must always be, sooner rather than later.   40

When you are next outdoors on a summer night, turn your head toward the zenith. Almost vertically above you will be shining the brightest star of the northern skies — Vega of the Lyre, twenty-six years away at the speed of light, near enough the point of no return for us short-lived creatures. Past this blue-white beacon, fifty times as brilliant as our sun, we may send our minds and bodies, but never our hearts.   41

For no man will ever turn homewards from beyond Vega, to greet again those he knew and loved on the earth.   42

SUBJECT QUESTIONS

1. Why does Clarke think a few minutes' time lag in communication between planets will be "unbearable"? Does he weaken his point by admitting later that this time lag would not be enough to hinder commerce or administration?
2. Would the time lag of ten years for a two-way communication between Earth and the nearest star be enough to hinder commerce or administration? (Try thinking of some communication sent by a pres-

ident ten years ago and the response that might come back today.) What communication difficulties would exist on Vega, twenty-six light years away? (For instance, the problem an American astronaut might have if he wanted to change the beneficiary of his life insurance policy.)

3. Is Clarke being shortsighted in his estimation of what the space program can achieve? Or do you think he has been too willing to admit possibilities — such as traveling faster than the speed of light? Would you agree with his precept that if something is theoretically possible, sooner or later it will be achieved?

4. If, as Clarke conjectures, we could eventually "dial" ourselves to any part of the universe, then what would prevent us from mastering space? How much would the present world population need to increase before we could send one person to each solar system just in the observable universe (10^{20} people)? If the population doubles every forty years, how long would it take to attain the available manpower?

5. Why do you think Clarke backs off, in his eloquent conclusion, from the possibility that we might someday be able to dial ourselves anywhere instantly?

STRUCTURE QUESTIONS

1. In paragraph 2, Clarke says we can see the problem more clearly "if we forget the present and turn our minds toward the past." Does his comparison with past views help to enlighten the present?

2. In paragraph 18, Clarke tries to give a notion of distance by comparison with objects five feet and a thousand miles distant. Does this reduction in scale help the reader grasp the vast difference in distances? Is the later analogy with island shipbuilders helpful?

3. Considering the complexity of his subject, has Clarke made it intelligible to a college-level reader? Has he distorted the subject by oversimplifying? (This is a danger in some areas of science.)

4. In this essay, Clarke changes his standards temporarily from what is now known to be theoretically possible to what might eventually be possible. Why does he do this? Can the reader follow with him when he changes his standards? (Note that he returns to the original standards at the end.)

5. Do you have the feeling that Clarke is trying to force an opinion on the reader or that he presented his evaluation objectively and justly? If the reader knows that Clarke is a science fiction writer, is he more or less likely to accept Clarke's final judgment?

SUGGESTIONS FOR WRITING

1. If you are familiar with the world of outer space, write your own evaluation of the feasibility of travel there.
2. Clarke has omitted the arguments against spaceships exceeding the speed of light. Explain and evaluate these arguments if you know them.
3. Evaluate some other physical project under consideration with which you are familiar — irrigating Arabia with icebergs towed from the Arctic, for instance, or large-scale water desalination projects.

The Cosmic Prison

Loren C. Eiseley

Loren Eiseley (1907–1977) was born in Lincoln, Nebraska. After dropping out of college during the depression of the 1930s and riding the rails for a few years, he finished his education and later became chairman of anthropology, provost, and Benjamin Franklin Professor of Anthropology and the History of Science at the University of Pennsylvania. He was a member of the National Parks Advisory Board and published many books on humans and the environment, including The Immense Journey *(1957),* The Unexpected Universe *(1969),* The Night Country *(1971), and his autobiography (1976). The following passage, from* The Invisible Pyramid *(1970), follows a discussion similar to Arthur Clarke's above, about the vastness of the universe and humans being trapped by sheer distances.*

There are other confinements, however, than that imposed by the enormous distances of the cosmos. One could almost list them. There is, for example, the prison of smells. I happen to know a big black hunting poodle named Beau. Beau loves to go for walks in the woods, and at such times as I visit his owners the task of seeing Beau safely through his morning adventures is happily turned over to me.

Beau has eyes, of course, and I do not doubt that he uses them when he greets his human friends by proffering a little gift such as his food dish. After this formality, which dates from his puppyhood, has been completed, Beau reverts to the world of snuffles. As a long-time and trusted friend, I have frequently tried to get Beau to thrust his head out of the world of smells and actually to see the universe. I have led him before the mirror in my bedroom and tried to persuade him to see himself, his own visible identity. The results, it turns out, are totally unsatisfactory, if not ludicrous. Beau peers out from his black ringlets as suspiciously as an ape hiding in a bush. He immediately drops his head and pretends to examine the floor. It is evident he detests this apparition and has no intention of being cajoled into some dangerous, undoggy wisdom by my voice.

He promptly brings his collar and makes appropriate throaty conversation. To appease his wounded feelings, I set out for a walk in the woods. It is necessary to do this with a long chain, and a very tight grasp upon it. Beau is

471

a big, powerful animal, and ringlets or no, he has come from an active and carnivorous past. Once in the woods all this past suddenly emerges. One is dragged willy-nilly through leaf, thorn, and thicket on intangible trails that Beau's swinging muzzle senses upon the wind.

His deep, wet nose has entered a world denied to me — a mad world whose contours and direction change with every gust of air. I leap and bound with a chafed wrist through a smell universe I cannot even sense. Occasionally something squawks or bounds from under our feet and I am flung against trees or wrapped around by a flying chain.

On one memorable occasion, after a rain, Beau paused, sniffing suspiciously between two rocks on a hillside. Another rabbit, I groaned mentally, taking a tighter hold on the chain. Beau then began some careful digging, curving and patting the soil aside in a way I had never before witnessed. A small basin shaped by Beau's forepaws presently appeared, and up from the bottom of it welled a spring-fed pool in which Beau promptly buried his snout and lapped long and lustily of water that I am sure carried the living tastes and delicate nuances of information disseminated from an unseen watershed.

Beau had had a proper drink of tap water before we started from home, but this drink was different. I could tell from the varied, eager slurping sounds that emanated from Beau. He was intoxicated by living water that dim primordial memories had instructed him how to secure. I looked on, interested and sympathetic, but aware that the big black animal lived in a smell prison as I, in my way, lived in a sight prison. Our universes intersected sufficiently for us to be aware, in a friendly fashion, of each other, but Beau would never admit the mirror image of himself into his mind, and try as I would, the passing breeze would never inform me of the shadowy creatures that passed unglimpsed in the forest.

There are, of course, still other prisons in the universe than those dominated by the senses of smell or sight or temperature. Some involve the length of a creature's lifetime, as in the case of five-year-old Beau, who gambols happily about his master, knowing him to be one of the everlasting immortals of his universe.

The dream that there are men elsewhere in the universe, alleviating the final prison of human loneliness, dies hard. Nevertheless, a wise remark Santayana made many years ago should discourage facile and optimistic thinking upon this very point. "An infinite number of solar systems," the philosopher meditated, "must have begun as ours began, but each of them must have deviated at one point from ours in its evolution, all the previous incidents being followed in each case by a different sequel." In voicing this view, Santayana betrays a clearer concept of the chance-filled course of genetics and its unreturning pathways than that of some astronomers. The Mendelian pathways are prisons of no return. Advances are made, but always a door swings shut behind the evolving organism. It can no longer mate with its one-time progenitors. It can only press forward along roads that increasingly will fix its irrevocable destiny.

Ours is a man-centered age. Not many months ago I was perusing a work on space when I came across this statement by a professional astronomer: "Other stars, other planets, other life, and other races of men are evolving all along, so that the net effect is changeless." Implied in this remark was an utter confidence that the evolutionary process was everywhere the same, ran through the same succession of forms, and emerged always with men at the helm of life, men presumably so close to ourselves that they might interbreed — a supposition fostered by our comic strips.

In the light of this naive concept — for such it is — let us consider just two worlds we know about, not worlds in space, but continents on our own planet. These continents exist under the same sun and are surrounded by the same waters as our own; their life bears a distant relationship to ours but has long been isolated. Man never arose in the remote regions of South America and Australia. He only reached them by migration from outside. They are laboratories of age-long evolution that tell us much about the unique quality of the human experience.

The southern continents of our earth do not maintain the intimacy of faunal exchange that marks the Holarctic land masses encircling the basin of the polar sea. Instead, they are lost in the southern latitudes of the oceans, and for long intervals their faunas have evolved in isolation. These lands have been, in truth, "other worlds."

The most isolated of these worlds is Australia. With the insignificant exception of a few late drifters from outside, this marsupial world is not merely an ancient world. It is a world in which ground life, originally represented by a few marsupial forms, has, since the Mesozoic era, evolved untroubled by invading placental mammals from without. Every possible ecological niche from forest tree to that of underground burrower has been occupied by the evolutionary radiation of a slower-brained mammal whose young are born in a far more embryonic condition than that of the true Placentalia.

This world remained unknown to Western science until the great exploratory voyages began. Somewhere in the past, life had taken another turn. Chance mutation, "total contingency" in the words of the American paleontologist William King Gregory, had led to another universe. The "world" of Australia contained no primates at all, nor any hint of their emergence. Upon that "planet" lost in the great waters they were one of an infinite number of random potentialities that had remained as unrealized as the whole group of placental mammals of which the Primate order is a minor part.

If we now turn to South America, we encounter still another isolated evolutionary center — but one not totally unrelated to that of Eurasia. Here, so the biogeographers inform us, an attenuated land bridge, at intervals completely severed, has both stimulated local evolutionary development and at times interrupted it by migrations from North America. Our concern is with just one group of animals, the South American monkeys. They are anatomically distinct from the catarrhine forms of the Old World, and constitute an apparent parallel emergence from the prosimians of the early Tertiary.

Once more, however, despite the fact that the same basic primate stock is involved, things have gone differently. There are no great apes in the New World, no evidence of ground-dwelling experiments of any kind. Though fewer carnivores are to be found on the South American grasslands than in Africa, the rain-forest monkeys, effectively equipped with prehensile tails, still cling to their archaic pathways. One can only observe that South America's vast rivers flow through frequently flooded lowlands, and that by contrast much of Africa is high, with open savanna and parkland. The South American primates appear to be confined to areas where descent to the ground proved less inviting. Here ended another experiment that did not lead to man, though it began within the same order from which he sprang. Another world had gone astray from the human direction. **15**

If, some occasionally extrapolate, man was so ubiquitous, so easy to produce, why did two great continental laboratories, Australia and South America — "worlds," indeed — fail to reproduce him? They failed, we may assume, simply because the great movements of life are irreversible, the same mutations do not occur, circumstances differ in infinite particulars, opportunities fail to be grasped, and so, what once happened is no more. The random element is always present, but it is selected on the basis of what has preceded it. **16**

There appears to be nothing foreordained about the human emergence, nor any trend demanding man's constant reappearance, either on what we have seen to be the separate "worlds" of this world or elsewhere. There can no more be a random duplication of man than there is a random duplication of such a complex genetic phenomenon as fingerprints. The situation is not one that is comparable to a single identical cast of dice, but rather it is an endless addition of new genes building on what has previously been incorporated into a living creature through long ages. Nature gambles, but she gambles with constantly new and altering dice. It is this well-established fact that enables us to call long-range evolution irreversible. **17**

Finally, there are even meteorological prisons. The constant circulation of moisture in our atmosphere actually played an important role in creating the first vertebrates and, indirectly, man. If early rivers had not poured from the continents into the sea, the first sea vertebrates to penetrate streams above sea level would not have evolved a rigid muscular support, the spine, to enable them to wriggle against down-rushing currents. And if man, in his **18** early history, had not become a tree climber in tropical rain-forests, he would never have further tilted that same spine upright or replaced the smell prison of the horizontal mammal with the stereoscopic, far-ranging "eye-brain" of the higher primates. If space permitted, such final dice throws, in which leaf and grass, wave and water, are inextricably commingled with the chemistry of the body, could be multiplied. The cosmic prison is subdivided into an infinite number of unduplicable smaller prisons, the prisons of form.

We are now in a position to grasp, after an examination of the many   19
prisons that encompass life, that the cosmic prison many men, in the excitement of the first moon landing, believed we had escaped, still extends immeasurably beyond us. The lack of any conceivable means of travel and the shortness of our individual lives both prevent the crossing of such distances. Even if we confined ourselves to unmanned space probes of far greater sophistication than those we now possess, their homing messages through the void could be expected to descend upon the ruined radio scanners of a civilization long vanished, or upon one whose aging scholars would have long since forgotten what naive dreams had been programmed into such instruments. We have detected that we exist in a prison of numbers, otherwise known as light-years. We are also locked in a body that responds to biological rather than sidereal time. That body, in turn, receives the universe through its own senses and through no others.

At every single turn of thought a lock snaps shut upon us. As societal   20
men we bow to a given frame of culture — a world view we have received from the past. Biologically each of us is unique, and the tight spiral of the DNA molecules conspires to doom us to mediocrity or grandeur. We dream vast dreams of utopias and live to learn the meaning of a Greek philosopher's judgment: "The flaw is in the vessel itself" — the flaw that defeats all governments.

By what means, then, can we seek escape from groveling in mean   21
corners of despair? Not, certainly, by the rush to depart upon the night's black pathways, nor by attention to the swerving wind vane of the senses. We are men, and despite all our follies there have been great ones among us who have counseled us in wisdom, men who have also sought keys to our prison. Strangely, these men have never spoken of space: they have spoken, instead, as though the farthest spaces lay within the mind itself—as though we still carried a memory of some light of long ago and the way we had come. Perhaps for this reason alone we have scanned the skies and the waters with what Henry Vaughan so well labeled the "Ecclips'd Eye," the eye incapable of quite assembling the true meaning of the universe but striving to do so "with Hyeroglyphicks quite dismembered."

These are the words of a seventeenth-century mystic who has mentally   22
dispatched inward vision through all the creatures until coming to man, who

"shines a little" and whose depths he finds it impossible to plumb. Thomas Traherne, another man of that century of the Ecclips'd Eye, when religion was groping amid the revelations of science, stated well the matter of the keys to the prison.

"Infinite love," he ventured, "cannot be expressed in finite room. Yet it must be infinitely expressed in the smallest moment . . . Only so is it in both ways infinite." 23

Can this insight be seen to justify itself in modern evolutionary terms? I think it can. 24

Close to a hundred years ago the great French medical scientist Claude Bernard observed that the stability of the inside environment of complex organisms must be maintained before an outer freedom can be achieved from their immediate surroundings. What Bernard meant was profound but is simple to illustrate. 25

He meant that for life to obtain relative security from its fickle and dangerous outside surroundings the animal must be able to sustain stable, unchanging conditions within the body. Warm-blooded mammals and birds can continue to move about in winter; insects cannot. Warm-blooded animals such as man, with his stable body temperature, can continue to think and reason in outside temperatures that would put a frog to sleep in a muddy pond or roll a snake into a ball in a crevice. In winter latitudes many of the lower creatures are forced to sleep part of their lives away. 26

It took many millions of years of evolutionary effort before life was successful in defending its internal world from the intrusion of the heat or cold of the outside world of nature. Yet only so can life avoid running down like a clock in winter or perishing from exposure to the midday sun. Even the desert rattlesnake is forced to coil in the shade of a bush at midday. Of course our tolerance is limited to a few degrees of temperature when measured against the great thermometer of the stars, but this hard-won victory is what creates the ever active brain of the mammal against the retarded sluggishness of the reptile. 27

A steady metabolism has enabled the birds and mammals to experience life more fully and rapidly than cold-blooded creatures. One of the great feats of evolution, perhaps the greatest, has been this triumph of the interior environment over exterior nature. Inside, we might say, has fought invading outside, and inside, since the beginning of life, has by slow degrees won the battle of life. If it had not, man, frail man with his even more fragile brain, would not exist. 28

Unless fever or some other disorder disrupts this internal island of safety, we rarely think of it. Body controls are normally automatic, but let them once go wrong and outside destroys inside. This is the simplest expres- 29 sion of the war of nature — the endless conflict between the microcosm and macrocosm.

Since the first cell created a film about itself and elected to carry on the   30 carefully insulated processes known as life, the creative spark has not been generalized. Whatever its principle may be, it hides magically within individual skins. To the day of our deaths we exist in an inner solitude that is linked to the nature of life itself. Even as we project love and affection upon others, we endure a loneliness that is the price of all individual consciousness: the price of living.

It is, though overlooked, the discontinuity beyond all others: the sepa-   31 ration both of the living creature from the inanimate and of the individual from his kind. These are star distances. In man, moreover, consciousness looks out isolated from its own body. The body is the true cosmic prison, yet it contains, in the creative individual, a magnificent if sometimes helpless giant.

John Donne spoke for that giant in each of us. He said: "Our creatures   32 are our thoughts, creatures that are borne Gyants . . . My thoughts reach all, comprehend all. Inexplicable mystery; I their Creator am in a close prison, in a sick bed, anywhere, and any one of my Creatures, my thoughts is with the Sunne and beyond the Sunne, overtakes the Sunne, and overgoes the Sunne in one pace, one steppe, everywhere."

This thought, expressed so poignantly by Donne, represents the final   33 triumph of Claude Bernard's interior microcosm in its war with the macrocosm. Inside has conquered outside. The giant confined in the body's prison roams at will among the stars. More rarely and more beautifully, perhaps, the profound mind in the close prison projects infinite love in a finite room. This is a crossing beside which light years are meaningless. It is the solitary key to the prison that is man.

SUBJECT QUESTIONS

1. If the dog Beau can see and hear, in what sense is he a "prisoner" of the world of smell? Doesn't he experience the same world people do? Does the fact that dogs are color blind make any difference?
2. What is the basis for Eiseley's judgment that belief in humans on other planets is "naive"?
3. Is the fact that humans never evolved in South America and Australia any reason to argue that they could not evolve on other planets? What makes the argument more cogent than, say, an argument that humans did not evolve on Mars or the moon and therefore cannot be on distant planets?
4. How could Eiseley answer the usual argument that with an almost

infinite number of stars, human life must have been duplicated somewhere? If it had been duplicated, what would be the chances of its existing now, or of our being able to contact it?
5. What is so important about the "triumph of the interior environment over exterior nature"?
6. What, according to Eiseley, is the only way we can escape the prison of our own bodies? Is it surprising to find a modern scientist arriving at such an ancient conclusion?

STRUCTURE QUESTIONS

1. This complex essay touches on many subjects, from space exploration to a black poodle. How does Eiseley unify all this material?
2. Are the transitions from one subject to the next clearly marked? Did you have any trouble following Eiseley's turns of thought?
3. To evaluate man's place in time and space is a large order. Has Eiseley based his judgments mainly on verifiable evidence or on conjecture? Are they consistently reasonable?
4. One check on evaluators' "honesty" is to see whether they arrive at any conclusions which they would prefer not to have to make. Does this happen in Eiseley's essay?
5. The story of the dog Beau seems a long one to use simply to explain the prison of smells, when other prisons are dealt with much more quickly. Can the length be justified? Should the other points have been explained just as fully?
6. Do you find the vocabulary of this essay appropriate for college students, challenging, or too difficult? Could Eiseley have said the same things in simpler language? Are there any places where the diction seems pretentious or pompous, or is the diction necessitated by the subject matter?

SUGGESTIONS FOR WRITING

1. Evaluate the human imaginative capacity to "roam at will among the stars." Using Eiseley's hints at the end of his essay, consider the value of an imaginative mind in a "prison" of body, time, and space.
2. Select one of the "prisons" discussed by Eiseley (climate or sight, for example) and try to evaluate its effect on humankind's development. It may of course be seen as an opportunity for advance as well as a limitation.
3. Toward the end of his essay, Eiseley mentions people's capacity to love; evaluate the past or possible future effects of this capacity on human development.

The Long Childhood

J. Bronowski

Jacob Bronowski (1908–1974), Polish-born British scientist and author, became famous in England as the narrator of a television series on atomic energy and other scientific subjects. Trained at Cambridge in mathematics, he began his research in physics and ended it in biology at the Salk Institute in California after he became convinced that physics was making possible instruments of destruction which politicians could not manage responsibly. A scholar of wide-ranging interests, Bronowski was head of the projects division of UNESCO, director of research for the British Coal Board, and author of several volumes on English litera-ture, particularly on the poet William Blake. The essay which follows is a shortened version of the final chapter from his last book, The Ascent of Man *(1974).*

I begin this last essay in Iceland because it is the seat of the oldest democ-   1
racy in Northern Europe. In the natural amphitheatre of Thingvellir, where
there were never any buildings, the Allthing of Iceland (the whole community of the Norsemen of Iceland) met each year to make laws and to receive
them. And this began about AD 900, before Christianity arrived, at a time
when China was a great empire, and Europe was the spoil of princelings and
robber barons. That is a remarkable beginning to democracy.

But there is something more remarkable about this misty, inclement   2
site. It was chosen because the farmer who had owned it had killed, not
another farmer but a slave, and had been outlawed. Justice was seldom so
even-handed in slave-owning cultures. Yet justice is a universal of all cultures. It is a tightrope that man walks, between his desire to fulfil his wishes,
and his acknowledgement of social responsibility. No animal is faced with
this dilemma: an animal is either social or solitary. Man alone aspires to be
both in one, a social solitary. And to me that is a unique biological feature.
That is the kind of problem that engaged me in my work on human specificity, and that I want to discuss.

It is something of a shock to think that justice is part of the biological equip-   3
ment of man. And yet it is exactly that thought which took me out of physics

479

into biology, and that has taught me since that a man's life, a man's home, is a proper place in which to study his biological uniqueness.

It is natural that by tradition biology is thought of in a different way: that the likeness between man and the animals is what dominates it. Back before the year AD 200 the great classic author of antiquity in medicine, Claudius Galen, studied, for example, the forearm in man. How did he study it? By dissecting the forearm in a Barbary ape. That is how you have to begin, necessarily using the evidence of the animals, long before the theory of evolution comes to justify the analogy. And to this day the wonderful work on animal behaviour by Konrad Lorenz naturally makes us seek for likeness between the duck and the tiger and man; or B. F. Skinner's psychological work on pigeons and rats. They tell us something about man. But they cannot tell us everything. There must be something unique about man because otherwise, evidently, the ducks would be lecturing about Konrad Lorenz, and the rats would be writing papers about B. F. Skinner.

Let us not beat about the bush. The horse and the rider have many anatomical features in common. But it is the human creature that rides the horse, and not the other way about. And the rider is a very good example, because man was not created to ride the horse. There is no wiring inside the brain that makes us horse riders. Riding a horse is a comparatively recent invention, less than five thousand years old. And yet it has had an immense influence, for instance on our social structure.

The plasticity of human behaviour makes that possible. That is what characterises us; in our social institutions, of course, but for me, naturally, above all in books, because they are the permanent product of the total interests of the human mind. They come to me like the memory of my parents: Isaac Newton, the great man dominating the Royal Society at the beginning of the eighteenth century, and William Blake, writing the *Songs of Innocence* late in the eighteenth century. They are two aspects of the one mind, and both are what behavioural biologists call 'species-specific.'

How can I put this most simply? I wrote a book recently called *The Identity of Man.* I never saw the cover of the English edition until the book reached me in print. And yet the artist had understood exactly what was in my mind, by putting on the cover a drawing of the brain and the *Mona Lisa,* one on top of the other. In his action he demonstrated what the book said. Man is unique not because he does science, and he is unique not because he does art, but because science and art equally are expressions of his marvellous plasticity of mind. And the *Mona Lisa* is a very good example, because after all what did Leonardo do for much of his life? He drew anatomical pictures, such as the baby in the womb in the Royal Collection at Windsor. And the brain and the baby is exactly where the plasticity of human behaviour begins.

I have an object which I treasure: a cast of the skull of a child that is two   8
million years old, the Taung baby. Of course, it is not strictly a human child.
And yet if she — I always think of her as a girl — if she had lived long
enough, she might have been my ancestor. What distinguishes her little
brain from mine? In a simple sense, the size. That brain, if she had grown
up, would have weighed perhaps a little over a pound. And my brain, the
average brain today, weighs three pounds.

    I am not going to talk about the neural structures, about one-way con-   9
duction in nervous tissues, or even about the old brain and the new, because
that apparatus is what we share with many animals. I am going to talk about
the brain as it is specific to the human creature.

    The first question we ask is, Is the human brain a better computer — a   10
more complex computer? Of course, artists in particular tend to think of the
brain as a computer. So in his *Portrait of Dr Bronowski* Terry Durham has
symbols of the spectrum and the computer, because that is how an artist
imagines a scientist's brain. But of course that cannot be right. If the brain
were a computer, then it would be carrying out a pre-wired set of actions in
an inflexible sequence.

    By way of example, think of a very beautiful piece of animal behaviour   11
described in my friend Dan Lehrman's work on the mating of the ring-dove.
If the male coos in the right way, if he bows in the right way, then the
females explodes in excitement, all her hormones squirt, and she goes
through a sequence as part of which she builds a perfect nest. Her actions
are exact in detail and order, yet they are untaught, and therefore invariable;
the ring-dove never changes them. Nobody ever gave her any set of bricks to
learn to build a nest. But you could not get a human being to build anything
unless the child had put together a set of bricks. That is the beginning of the
Parthenon and the Taj Mahal, of the dome at Sultaniyeh and the Watts
Towers, of Machu Picchu and the Pentagon.

    We are not a computer that follows routines laid down at birth. If we   12
are any kind of machine, then we are a learning machine, and we do our important learning in specific areas of the brain. Thus you see that the brain has
not just blown up to two or three times its size during its evolution. It has
grown in quite special areas: where it controls the hand, for instance, where
speech is controlled, where foresight and planning are controlled. I shall ask
you to look at them one by one.

Consider the hand first. The recent evolution of man certainly begins with   13
the advancing development of the hand, and the selection for a brain which
is particularly adept at manipulating the hand. We feel the pleasure of that in
our actions, so that for the artist the hand remains a major symbol: the hand
of Buddha, for instance, giving man the gift of humanity in a gesture of calm,

the gift of fearlessness. But also for the scientist the hand has a special gesture: we can oppose the thumb to the fingers. Well, the apes can do that. But we can oppose the thumb precisely to the forefinger, and that is a special human gesture. And it can be done because there is an area in the brain so large that I can best describe its size to you in the following way: we spend more grey matter in the brain manipulating the thumb than in the total control of the chest and the abdomen.

I remember as a young father tiptoeing to the cradle of my first daugh-   14
ter when she was four or five days old, and thinking, 'These marvellous fingers, every joint so perfect, down to the finger nails. I could not have designed that detail in a million years.' But of course it is exactly a million years that it took me, a million years that it took mankind, for the hand to drive the brain and for the brain to feed back and drive the hand to reach its present stage of evolution. And that takes place in a quite specific place in the brain. The whole of the hand is essentially monitored by a part of the brain that can be marked out, near the top of the head.

Take next an even more specifically human part of the brain which does not   15
exist in animals at all: for speech. That is localised in two connected areas of the human brain; one area is close to the hearing centre, and the other lies forward and higher, in the frontal lobes. Is that pre-wired? Yes, in one sense, because if we do not have the speech centres intact we cannot speak at all. And yet, does it have to be learned? Of course it does. I speak English, which I only learned at the age of thirteen; but I could not speak English if I had not before learned language. You see, if you leave a child speaking no language until the age of thirteen, then it is almost impossible for it to learn at all. I speak English because I learned Polish at the age of two. I have forgotten every word of Polish, but I learned *language*. Here as in other human gifts the brain is wired to learn.

The speech areas are very peculiar in another way that is human. You   16
know that the human brain is not symmetrical in its two halves. The evidence is familiar to you in the observation that, unlike other animals, men are markedly right-handed or left-handed. Speech also is controlled on one side of the brain, but the side does not vary. Whether you are right-handed or left-handed, speech is almost certainly on the left. There are exceptions, in the same way that there are people who have their heart on the right, but the exceptions are rare: by and large speech is in areas in the left half of the brain. And what is in the matching areas on the right? We do not exactly know, so far. We do not exactly know what the right-hand side of the brain does in those areas which are devoted to speech on the left. But it looks as if they take the input that comes by way of the eye — the map of a two-dimensional world on the retina — and turn it or organise it into a three-dimen-

sional picture. If that is right, then in my view it is clear that speech is also a way of organising the world into its parts and putting them together again like movable images.

The organisation of experience is very far-sighted in man, and is lodged in a third area of human specificity. The main organisation of the brain is in the frontal lobes and the prefrontal lobes. I am, every man is, a highbrow, an egghead, because that is how his brain goes. By contrast, we know that the Taung skull is not just that of a child that died recently and that we have mistaken for a fossil, because she still has a rather sloping forehead. [17]

Exactly what do these large frontal lobes do? They may well have several functions, certainly, and yet do one very specific and important thing. They enable you to think of actions in the future, and wait for a reward then. Some beautiful experiments on this delayed response were first done by Walter Hunter round about 1910, and then refined by Jacobsen in the 1930s. The kind of thing that Hunter did was this: he would take some reward, and he would show it to an animal and then hide it. The results found in the darling of the laboratory, the rat, are typical. If you take a rat and, having shown it the reward, you let it go at once, the rat of course goes to the hidden reward immediately. But if you keep the rat waiting for some minutes, then it is no longer able to identify where it ought to go for its reward. [18]

Of course, children are quite different. Hunter did the same experiments with children, and you can keep children of five or six waiting for half an hour, perhaps an hour. Hunter had a little girl whom he was trying to keep amused while keeping her waiting, and he talked to her. Finally she said to him, 'You know, I think you're just trying to make me forget.' [19]

The ability to plan actions for which the reward is a long way off is an elaboration of the delayed response, and sociologists call it 'the postponement of gratification.' It is a central gift that the human brain has to which there is no rudimentary match in animal brains until they become quite sophisticated, well up in the evolutionary scale, like our cousins the monkeys and the apes. That human development means that we are concerned in our early education actually with the postponement of decisions. Here I am saying something different from the sociologists. We *have* to put off the decision-making process, in order to accumulate enough knowledge as a preparation for the future. That seems an extraordinary thing to say. But that is what childhood is about, that is what puberty is about, that is what youth is about. . . . [20]

In man, before the brain is an instrument for action, it has to be an instrument of preparation. For that, quite specific areas are involved; for ex- [21]

ample, the frontal lobes have to be undamaged. But, far more deeply, it depends on the long preparation of human childhood.

In scientific terms we are neotenous; that is, we come from the womb   22 still as embryos. And perhaps that is why our civilisation, our scientific civilisation, adores above all else the symbol of the child, ever since the Renaissance: the Christ child painted by Raphael and re-enacted by Blaise Pascal; the young Mozart and Gauss; the children in Jean Jacques Rousseau and Charles Dickens. It never struck me that other civilisations are different until I sailed south from here out of California, four thousand miles away to Easter Island. There I was struck by the historical difference.

Every so often some visionary invents a new Utopia: Plato, Sir Thomas   23 More, H. G. Wells. And always the idea is that the heroic image shall last, as Hitler said, for a thousand years. But the heroic images always look like the crude, dead, ancestral faces of the statues on Easter Island — why, they even look like Mussolini! That is not the essence of the human personality, even in terms of biology. Biologically, a human being is changeable, sensitive, mutable, fitted to many environments, and not static. The real vision of the human being is the child wonder, the Virgin and Child, the Holy Family.

When I was a boy in my teens, I used to walk on Saturday afternoons   24 from the East End of London to the British Museum, in order to look at the single statue from the Easter Islands which somehow they had not got inside the Museum. So I am fond of these ancient ancestral faces. But in the end, all of them are not worth one child's dimpled face.

If I was a little carried away in saying that at Easter Island, it was with   25 reason. Think of the investment that evolution has made in the child's brain. My brain weighs three pounds, my body weighs fifty times as much as that. But when I was born, my body was a mere appendage to the head; it weighed only five or six times as much as my brain. For most of history, civilisations have crudely ignored that enormous potential. In fact the longest childhood has been that of civilisation, learning to understand that.

For most of history, children have been asked simply to conform to the   26 image of the adult. We travelled with the Bakhtiari of Persia on their spring migration. They are as near as any surviving, vanishing people can be to the nomad ways of ten thousand years ago. You see it everywhere in such ancient modes of life: the image of the adult shines in the children's eyes. The girls are little mothers in the making. The boys are little herdsmen. They even carry themselves like their parents.

History, of course, did not stand still between the nomad and the Renais-   27 sance. The ascent of man has never come to a stop. But the ascent of the young, the ascent of the talented, the ascent of the imaginative: that became very halting many times in between.

Of course there were great civilisations. Who am I to belittle the 28
civilisations of Egypt, of China, of India, even of Europe in the Middle
Ages? And yet by one test they all fail: they limit the freedom of the imagination of the young. They are static, and they are minority cultures. Static,
because the son does what the father did, and the father what the grandfather did. And minority, because only a tiny fraction of all that talent that
mankind produces is actually used; learns to read, learns to write, learns
another language, and climbs the terribly slow ladder of promotion.

In the Middle Ages the ladder of promotion was through the Church; 29
there was no other way for a clever, poor boy to go up. And at the end of the
ladder there is always the image, the icon of the godhead that says, 'Now you
have reached the last commandment: Thou shalt not question.'

For instance, when Erasmus was left an orphan in 1480, he had to 30
prepare for a career in the Church. The services were as beautiful then as
now. Erasmus may himself have taken part in the moving Mass *Cum Giubi-
late* of the fourteenth century, which I have heard in a church that is even
older, San Pietro in Gropina. But the monk's life was for Erasmus an iron
door closed against knowledge. Only when Erasmus read the classics for
himself, in defiance of orders, did the world open for him. 'A heathen wrote
this to a heathen,' he said, 'yet it has justice, sanctity, truth. I can hardly
refrain from saying "Saint Socrates, pray for me!" '

Erasmus made two lifelong friends, Sir Thomas More in England and 31
Johann Frobenius in Switzerland. From More he got what I got when I first
came to England, the sense of pleasure in the companionship of civilised
minds. From Frobenius he got a sense of the power of the printed book.
Frobenius and his family were the great printers of the classics in the 1500s,
including the classics of medicine. Their edition of the works of Hippocrates
is, I think, one of the most beautiful books ever printed, in which the happy
passion of the printer sits on the page as powerful as the knowledge.

What did those three men and their books mean — the works of Hip- 32
pocrates, More's *Utopia, The Praise of Folly* by Erasmus? To me, this is the
democracy of the intellect; and that is why Erasmus and Frobenius and Sir
Thomas More stand in my mind as gigantic landmarks of their time. The democracy of the intellect comes from the printed book, and the problems that
it set from the year 1500 have lasted right down to the student riots of today.
What did Sir Thomas More die of? He died because his king thought of him
as a wielder of power. And what More wanted to be, what Erasmus wanted
to be, what every strong intellect wants to be, is a guardian of integrity.

There is an age-old conflict between intellectual leadership and civil author- 33
ity. How old, how bitter, came home to me when I came up from Jericho on
the road that Jesus took, and saw the first glimpse of Jerusalem on the
skyline as he saw it going to his certain death. Death, because Jesus was then

the intellectual and moral leader of his people, but he was facing an establishment in which religion was simply an arm of government. And that is a crisis of choice that leaders have faced over and over again: Socrates in Athens; Jonathan Swift in Ireland, torn between pity and ambition; Mahatma Gandhi in India; and Albert Einstein, when he refused the presidency of Israel.

I bring in the name of Einstein deliberately because he was a scientist, 34 and the intellectual leadership of the twentieth century rests with scientists. And that poses a grave problem, because science is also a source of power that walks close to government and that the state wants to harness. But if science allows itself to go that way, the beliefs of the twentieth century will fall to pieces in cynicism. We shall be left without belief, because no beliefs can be built up in this century that are not based on science as the recognition of the uniqueness of man, and a pride in his gifts and works. It is not the business of science to inherit the earth, but to inherit the moral imagination; because without that man and beliefs and science will perish together. . . .

. . . If we are anything, we must be a democracy of the intellect. We must 35 not perish by the distance between people and government, between people and power, by which Babylon and Egypt and Rome failed. And that distance can only be conflated, can only be closed, if knowledge sits in the homes and heads of people with no ambition to control others, and not up in the isolated seats of power.

That seems a hard lesson. After all, this is a world run by specialists: is not 36 that what we mean by a scientific society? No, it is not. A scientific society is one in which specialists can indeed do the things like making the electric light work. But it is you, it is I, who have to know how *nature* works, and how (for example) electricity is one of her expressions in the light *and* in my brain.

. . . Will it be possible to find happy foundations for the forms of 37 behaviour that we prize in a full man and a fulfilled society? We have seen that human behaviour is characterised by a high internal delay in preparation for deferred action. The biological groundwork for this inaction stretches through the long childhood and slow maturation of man. But deferment of action in man goes far beyond that. Our actions as adults, as decision makers, as human beings, are mediated by values, which I interpret as general strategies in which we balance opposing impulses. It is not true that we run our lives by any computer scheme of problem solving. The problems of life are insoluble in this sense. Instead, we shape our conduct by finding principles to guide it. We devise ethical strategies or systems of values to ensure that what is attractive in the short term is weighed in the balance of the ultimate, long-term satisfactions.

And we are really here on a wonderful threshold of knowledge. The ascent of man is always teetering in the balance. There is always a sense of uncertainty, whether when man lifts his foot for the next step it is really going to come down pointing ahead. And what is ahead for us? At last the bringing together of all that we have learned, in physics and in biology, towards an understanding of where we have come: what man is.

Knowledge is not a loose-leaf notebook of facts. Above all, it is a responsibility for the integrity of what we are, primarily of what we are as ethical creatures. You cannot possibly maintain that informed integrity if you let other people run the world for you while you yourself continue to live out of a ragbag of morals that come from past beliefs. That is really crucial today. You can see it is pointless to advise people to learn differential equations, or to do a course in electronics or in computer programming. And yet, fifty years from now, if an understanding of man's origins, his evolution, his history, his progress is not the commonplace of the schoolbooks, we shall not exist. The commonplace of the schoolbooks of tomorrow is the adventure of today, and that is what we are engaged in.

And I am infinitely saddened to find myself suddenly surrounded in the west by a sense of terrible loss of nerve, a retreat from knowledge into — into what? Into Zen Buddhism; into falsely profound questions about, Are we not really just animals at bottom; into extra-sensory perception and mystery. They do not lie along the line of what we are now able to know if we devote ourselves to it: an understanding of man himself. We are nature's unique experiment to make the rational intelligence prove itself sounder than the reflex. Knowledge is our destiny. Self-knowledge, at last bringing together the experience of the arts and the explanations of science, waits ahead of us.

It sounds very pessimistic to talk about western civilisation with a sense of retreat. I have been so optimistic about the ascent of man; am I going to give up at this moment? Of course not. The ascent of man will go on. But do not assume that it will go on carried by western civilisation as we know it. We are being weighed in the balance at this moment. If we give up, the next step will be taken — but not by us. We have not been given any guarantee that Assyria and Egypt and Rome were not given. We are waiting to be somebody's past too, and not necessarily that of our future. . . .

SUBJECT QUESTIONS

1. Why, in an essay on the uniqueness of man's evolution, does Bronowski begin by writing about democracy and justice?
2. How does the human brain differ from a complex computer?
3. In what three areas is the human brain conspicuously more developed than the brains of other animals?

4. What difference does it make that the human brain is not fully developed at birth?
5. What does Bronowski see as the chief failing of the civilizations of Egypt, Greece, China, India, and medieval Europe? Has our present civilization corrected that failing?
6. What does Bronowski mean by "democracy of the intellect"? Does he want all intellects to be equal or to think alike?
7. What "terrible loss of nerve" in modern society bothers Bronowski? Why does he think we should not be concerned with mysticism and the occult?

STRUCTURE QUESTIONS

1. Even in this shortened version, Bronowski's essay is somewhat sprawling; does it have a unifying principle? Is the title appropriate?
2. By what standards does Bronowski judge the human brain to be special? Does he make clear that these are standards important only to man?
3. By what standards does he judge previous civilizations to have been inadequate? Are these the same standards by which the future should be judged?
4. Although his writing is largely abstract, Bronowski does cite many examples of past civilizations and of individual thinkers. Do these examples aid in understanding his thoughts?
5. Toward the end of his essay, Bronowski says that our actions as humans must be guided by "ethical strategies or systems of values." Should he have specified what these strategies ought to be? Should he explain what is wrong with the "ragbag of morals that come from past beliefs"? Does he at least make clear the direction in which mankind should be moving?

SUGGESTIONS FOR WRITING

1. Bronowski considers that the best chance for the continued "ascent of man" is utilizing what he calls the "long childhood." Offer your own assessment of man's chances for improvement. Be sure to make clear your standards of judgment.
2. If you have changed — or are thinking of changing — your academic or occupational goals, write a self-evaluation centered on those goals.

Will Our World Survive?

John J. McKetta

Dr. McKetta is professor of chemical engineering at the University of Texas, Austin. He is chairman of the Texas Atomic Energy Commission and of the National Air Quality Management Committee. He has also served on the boards of industrial companies and has been an officer in several professional societies.

There is an entire spectrum from zero to infinity, of views and actions on almost any problem.   1

Let's take the pollution problem, for example. We all know there are   2
still some companies and cities who put toxic gases and liquids into our air and streams. It's almost unbelievable that many of our large cities still discharge raw sewage, or only partially treated sewage into our streams. Both industry and the cities should be stopped immediately from these flagrant violations.

On the other extreme, we have those people who wish to have distilled   3
water in the streams and zero particulates in the atmosphere. These are impossible concentrations and could not be attained even if we had no people on this earth. The answer, obviously, is somewhere between these two extremes.

We're all deeply concerned about reports of the destruction of our en-   4
vironment as a result of technological recklessness, overpopulation, and the lack of consideration to the preservation of nature. As chairman of the National Air Quality Management Committee, I have to read great amounts of technical literature in this area. I've turned up a lot of information that I'd like to share with you.

Is Our Oxygen Really Disappearing?

My first surprise concerns the air we breathe. You have been reading that   5
we are seriously depleting the oxygen in the atmosphere and replacing it with toxic substances such as carbon monoxide.

We've always been taught that oxygen in our atmosphere is supplied   6
by green plants using the process of photosynthesis. We know that plants

take in carbon dioxide and through activation by sunlight, combine CO_2 with water to make starches and cellulose, and give off oxygen. In this way the whole chain of plant and animal life is sustained by energy from the sun. When the vegetable or animal materials thus produced are eaten, burned, or allowed to decay they combine with oxygen and return to the carbon dioxide and water from whence they came. We all know this. Then, what is the surprise?

Surprise number one is that most of the oxygen in the atmosphere   7 doesn't come from photosynthesis. The evidence is now overwhelming that photosynthesis is just inadequate to have produced the amount of oxygen that is present in our atmosphere. The amount of oxygen produced by photosynthesis is just exactly enough to convert the plant tissue back to the carbon dioxide and water from which it came. The net gain in oxygen due to photosynthesis is extremely small. The oxygen in the atmosphere had to come from another source. The most likely possibility involves the photodissociation of water vapor in the upper atmosphere by high energy rays from the sun and by cosmic rays.

This means that the supply of oxygen in the atmosphere is virtually un-   8 limited. It is not threatened by man's activities in any significant way. If all the organic material on earth were oxidized, it would reduce the atmospheric concentration of oxygen by less than 1 per cent. We can forget the depletion of oxygen in the atmosphere and get on with the solution of more serious problems.

Will Carbon Monoxide Kill Us All?

As you know, the most toxic component of automobile exhaust is carbon   9 monoxide. Each year man adds 270 million tons of carbon monoxide to the atmosphere. Most of this comes from automobiles.

People are concerned about the accumulation of this toxic material   10 because they know that it has a life in dry air of about three years. Monitoring stations on land and sea have been measuring the carbon monoxide content of the atmosphere.

Since there are nine times more automobiles in the northern hemi-   11 sphere than in the southern hemisphere it is expected that the northern hemisphere will have a much higher concentration of atmospheric carbon monoxide. The true measurements show, however, that there is no difference in CO amounts between the hemispheres and that the overall concentration in the air is not increasing at all. In fact they've found higher concentrations of CO over the Atlantic and Pacific oceans than over land.

Early in 1971 scientists at the Stanford Research Institute in Palo Alto   12 disclosed that they had done some experiments in smog chambers containing soil. They reported that carbon monoxide rapidly disappeared from the chamber. After sterilizing the soil they found that the carbon monoxide did not disappear. They quickly identified that organisms were responsible for CO disappearance. These organisms, on a world wide basis, are using all of the 270 million tons of the CO made by man for their own metabolism, thus enriching the soils of the forest and the fields.

This does not say carbon monoxide is any less toxic. It does say that, in 13 spite of man's activities, carbon monoxide will never build up in the atmosphere to a dangerous level except on a localized basis. To put things in perspective, let me point out that the average concentration of CO in Austin, Texas, is about 1.5 parts per million. In downtown Houston, in heavy traffic, it sometimes builds up to 15 or 20 p.p.m. In Los Angeles it gets to be as high as 35 p.p.m. In parking garages and tunnels it is sometimes 50 p.p.m.

Here lies surprise number two for you — do you know that the CO 14 content of cigarette smoke is as high as 42,000 p.p.m.? The CO concentration in practically any smoke-filled room grossly exceeds the safety standards we allow in our laboratories. Of course 35 to 50 p.p.m. CO should not be ignored but there are so many of us who subject ourselves to CO concentrations voluntarily (and involuntarily) that are greater than those of our worse polluted cities, including those in the Holland Tunnel in New York, without any catastrophic effects. It is not at all unusual for CO concentrations to reach 100-200 p.p.m. range in poorly ventilated, smoke-filled rooms. Incidentally, if a heavy smoker spends several hours without smoking in highly polluted city air containing 35 p.p.m. of CO concentration, the concentration of CO in his blood will actually decrease. In the broad expanse of our natural air, CO levels are totally safe for human beings. We all know that we should not start our automobiles in closed unventilated garages.

Will Oxides of Nitrogen Choke Us to Death?

One cannot help but be extremely impressed by the various research efforts 15 on the part of petroleum, automotive, and chemical companies to remove oxides of nitrogen from the products of combustion in the tail pipe gas of our automobiles. You've read about the brilliant work of Dr. Haagen-Smit that showed that the oxides of nitrogen play a critical role in the chain reaction of photochemical smog formation in Los Angeles. Oxides of nitrogen are definately problems in places where temperature inversions trap the air.

But we've all known for many years that nature also produces oxides of 16 nitrogen.

The number three surprise (and shock) is that most of the oxides of ni- 17 trogen come from nature. If we consider only nitric oxide and nitrogen dioxide the best estimates are 97 per cent is natural and only 3 per cent is man made. If we also consider nitrous oxide and amines, then it turns out that 99 plus per cent is natural and less than 1 per cent is man made.

The significance of this is that even if we are 100 per cent successful in our removal of the oxides of nitrogen from combustion bases, we will still have more than 99 per cent left in the atmosphere which is produced by nature. [18]

Did Lake Erie Really Succumb?

We've all read for some time that Lake Erie is dead. It's true that the beaches are no longer safe in the Cleveland area and the oxygen content at the bottom of the lake is decreasing. This is called eutrophication. The blame has been placed on phosphates as the cause of this situation. Housewives were urged to curb the use of phosphate detergents. In fact, for several years phosphate detergents were taken off the market. There's been a change in law since scientific evidence proved that the phosphate detergents were not the only culprits and never should have been removed from the market in the first place. [19]

Some studies show clearly that the cause of the eutrophication of Lake Erie has not been properly defined. This evidence suggests that if we totally stopped using phosphate detergents it would have no effect whatever on the eutrophication of Lake Erie. Many experiments have now been carried out that bring surprise number four — that it is the organic carbon content from sewage that is using up the oxygen in the lake and not the phosphates in the detergents. One must be extremely careful in these studies since the most recent report by Dr. D. W. Shindler states that phosphorus is the culprit rather than the organic carbon. But the reason that the Cleveland area beaches are not swimmable is that the coliform bacterial count is too high, not that there is too much detergent in the water. [20]

Enlarged and improved sewage treatment facilities by Detroit, Toledo, Sandusky, and Cleveland will be required to correct this situation. Our garbage disposal units do far more to pollute Lake Erie than do the phosphate detergents. If we put in the proper sewage treatment facilities, the lake will sparkle blue again in a very few years. [21]

Incidentally, we've all heard that Lake Superior is so much larger, cleaner, and nicer than Lake Erie. It's kind of strange then to learn that in 1972 and 1973 more tons of commercial fish were taken from Lake Erie than were taken from Lake Superior. [22]

Is DDT Really Our Deadly Foe?

DDT and other chlorinated compounds are supposedly endangering the lives of mankind and eliminating some bird species by the thinning of the egg shells of birds. There is a big question mark as to whether or not this is true. Even if it is true, it's quite possible that the desirable properties of [23]

DDT so greatly outnumber the undesirable ones that it might prove to be a serious mistake to ban entirely this remarkable chemical.

Many of you heard of Dr. Norman E. Borlaug, the Nobel Peace Prize 24 winner. He is opposed to the banning of DDT. Obviously he is a competent scientist. He won the Nobel prize because he was able to develop a new strain of wheat that can double the food production per acre anywhere in the world that it is grown.

Dr. Borlaug said "If DDT is banned in the United States, I have 25 wasted my life's work. I have dedicated myself to finding better methods of feeding the world's starving population. Without DDT and other important agricultural chemicals, our goals are simply unattainable."

DDT has had a miraculous impact on arresting insect borne diseases 26 and increasing grain production from fields once ravaged by insects. According to the World Health Organization, malaria fatalities alone dropped from 4 million a year in the 1930s to less than 1 million per year in 1968. Other insect borne diseases, such as encephalitis, yellow fever, and typhus fever showed similar declines.

Surprise number five is that it has been estimated that 100 million 27 human beings who would have died of these afflictions are alive today because of DDT. Incidentally, recent tests indicate that the thinning of bird egg shells may have been caused by mercury compounds rather than DDT. . . .

Many people feel that mankind is the one responsible for the disap- 28 pearance of animal species. The abundance of evidence indicates that he has very little to do with it. About 50 species are expected to disappear during this century. It is also true that 50 species became extinct last century and 50 species the century before that and so on.

Dr. T. H. Jukes of the University of California points out that about 29 100 million species of plant and animal life have become extinct since life began on this planet, about 3 billion years ago. Animals come and animals disappear. This is the essence of evolution as Mr. Darwin pointed out many years ago. Mankind is a relatively recent visitor here.

Surprise number six is that one of man's failures is that he has not been 30 successful in eliminating a single insect species — in spite of his all-out war on certain undesirable ones in recent years.

Is Mankind the Real Polluter?

Here's the seventh surprise! The late Dr. William Pecora reported that all of 31 man's air pollution during his thousands of years of life on earth does not equal the amount of particulate and noxious gases from just three volcanoes (Krakatoa, near Java — 1883; Mt. Katmai, Alaska — 1912; Hekla, Iceland — 1947).

Dr. Pecora pointed out that nature's pure water is not so pure after all.   32
Here are a few examples:

1. The natural springs feeding the Arkansas and Red Rivers carry approximately 17 tons of salt per minute.
2. The Lemonade Springs in New Mexico carry approximately 900 pounds H_2SO_4 per million pounds of water. (This is more than ten times the acid concentration in coal mine discharges.)
3. The Mississippi River carries over 2 million tons of natural sediment into the Gulf of Mexico each day.
4. The Paria River of Arizona and Utah carries as much as 500 times more natural sediment per unit volume than the Mississippi River. The Mississippi sediment concentration ranges from 100 to 1,000 mg. per liter. The Paria River concentration has been measured as high as 780,000 mg. per liter during 1973.

Should We Go Back to the Good Old Days?

Dr. Isaac Asimov admonishes us not to believe the trash about the happy   33
lives that people once had before all this nasty industrialization came along.
There was no such thing. One of his neighbors once asked him "What has all
these 2,000 years of development of industry and civilization done for us?
Wouldn't we have been happier in 100 B.C.?" Dr. Asimov said "No, chances
are 97 out of 100 that, if you were not a poor slave, you'd be a poor farmer,
living at bare subsistence level."

When people think of ancient times, they think of themselves as   34
members of aristocracy. They are never slaves, never peasants, but that's
what most of them would be.

My wife once said to me "If we lived a hundred years ago we'd have no   35
trouble getting servants." I said, "If we'd lived 150 years ago, we'd be the
servants."

Let's consider what life was really like in America just 150 years ago.   36
For one thing, we didn't have to worry about pollution very long — because
life was very brief. Life expectancy of males was about 38 years. The work
week was 72 hours. The women's lot was even worse. They worked 98 hours
a week scrubbing floors, making clothes by hand, bringing in fire wood,
cooking in heavy iron pots, fighting off insects without pesticides. Most of
the clothes were rags by present day standards. There were no fresh vegetables in winter. Vitamin deficiency diseases were prevalent. Homes were cold
in winter and sweltering in the summer.

Epidemics were expected yearly and chances were high that they   37
would carry off some members of the immediate family. If you think the
water pollution is bad now, it was deadly then. In 1793 one person in every

five in the city of Philadelphia died in a single epidemic of typhoid as a result
of polluted water. Many people of that time never heard a symphony orchestra or traveled more than 20 miles from their birthplace during their entire
lifetime. Many informed people do not want to return to the "paradise" of
150 years ago. Perhaps the simple life was not so simple.

Are Nuclear Plants Latter Day Witches?

Dr. A. Letcher Jones points out that in every age we have people practicing   38
witchcraft in one form or another. We all think the people of New England
were irrational in accusing certain women of being witches without evidence
to prove it.

Suppose someone accused you of being a witch? How could you prove   39
you were not? It is impossible to prove unless you can give evidence. It is
precisely this same witchcraft practice that is being used to deter the construction of nuclear power plants. The opponents are saying these plants are
witches and it is up to the builders and owners to prove they are not. The
scientific evidence is that nuclear power plants constructed to date are the
cleanest and least polluting devices for generating electricity so far developed
by man. We need electricity to maintain the standard of living we have
reached, but to the extreme environmentalists we are witches. We should be
burned at the stake.

We hear the same accusations about lead compounds from the gasoline   40
engine. Our Environmental Protection Agency has no evidence that there
has ever been a single case of death, or even illness, from lead in the air
coming from burning of gasoline, but they still insist we remove the lead
from gasoline.

To the EPA we are witches. They have no evidence — no proof — we   41
are pronounced guilty! And yet you know gasoline needs some additives to
prevent engine knocks. If we don't use tetraethyl-lead we'll have to use aro-
matic compounds. Some aromatics are carcinogenic. We know that! The use
of unleaded gasoline also can use up to 12 per cent more crude oil. (Incidentally, the real reason for removing lead from gasoline was because it was suspected that lead poisoned the catalyst in the emission control unit. Now we
have some evidence that it isn't the lead but ethylene bromide which is the
poisoner.)

Is There Real Hope for Our Survival?

From what we read and hear it would seem we are on the edge of impend-   42
ing doom. A scientific evaluation of the evidence does not support this conclusion. Of course we have many undesirable problems attributed to technological activities. The solution of these problems will require a technical

understanding of their nature, not through emotion. They cannot be solved unless properly identified, which will require more technically trained people — not less.

Thomas Jefferson said if the public is properly informed, the people   43
will make wise decisions. The public has not been getting all of the facts on matters relating to ecology. This is the reason some of us are speaking out on this subject today — as technical people and as citizens.

In summary, let me state we are not on the brink of ecological disaster.   44
Our O_2 is not disappearing. There will be no build up of poisonous CO. The waters can be made pure again by adequate sewage treatment plants. The disappearance of species is natural. A large percentage of pollution is natural pollution and would be here whether or not man was on this earth. We cannot solve our real problems unless we attack them on the basis of what we know rather than what we don't know. Let us use our knowledge and not our fears to solve the real problems of our environment.

SUBJECT QUESTIONS

1. Why, according to Dr. McKetta, do we not need to worry about depleting the supply of oxygen by burning fossil fuels?
2. What happens to the millions of tons of carbon monoxide that automobiles and industry discharge into the air? Is McKetta suggesting that smog is not so bad because smoky rooms are worse?
3. McKetta says that 97 percent of the nitrogen oxides are natural. Does he consider than the 3 percent added by man might upset a natural balance?
4. McKetta points out the many benefits of DDT. Should he have admitted the role of DDT in the world population explosion? Is the population explosion a good argument against the use of DDT?
5. Granted that the dodo would have disappeared without man's intervention, does McKetta ignore the man-caused danger to the existence of such species as eagles and whales? Name some creatures that man has tried and failed to eradicate.
6. Do you think McKetta has given a fair account of life before industrial pollution, one hundred fifty years ago? Is he suggesting that pollution is the price for lowering the seventy-two-hour work week and other improvements?

STRUCTURE QUESTIONS

1. In our ecology-conscious society, most of McKetta's readers are probably predisposed to feel differently than he does about pollution. What opening strategies does he use to get a fair hearing?
2. Does McKetta seem to be unconcerned about human welfare? Can

you tell what his chief values are? Should he have stated them more clearly?
3. Evaluate McKetta's strategy in using the analogy between witch-hunts and criticism of nuclear power plants. What element does he find common to both situations?
4. McKetta has to discuss some complicated chemical processes and employ some formidable statistics. Does he make this difficult subject understandable to the layman without grossly oversimplifying? Has he avoided the technical jargon of his trade?
5. Do the last three paragraphs form a suitable conclusion to this essay? What is the strongest part of that conclusion? Does McKetta need the summary of his points in the last paragraph?
6. In an essay of this sort, it is important that the reader not feel that the writer represents special interest groups. Do you feel that McKetta has given an objective — if optimistic — evaluation of the pollution problem?

SUGGESTIONS FOR WRITING

1. Write an evaluation of the concern for time schedules in modern society — or in school.
2. Write an evaluation of some other current concern which you think might create problems — the passion for keeping records, for instance, which affects even college football.
3. As a library research project, evaluate the seriousness of some pollution problem of local or national importance (the pollution of Lake Erie, for instance).

To Err Is Human

Lewis Thomas

Dr. Lewis Thomas (b. 1913) is one of America's most distinguished pathologists and pediatricians. He has held important posts at leading medical colleges and served as dean of the school of medicine at Yale University and as president of the Sloan-Kettering Cancer Center in New York City. He has won numerous awards and holds nearly a dozen honorary degrees from Princeton, Duke, Columbia, Johns Hopkins, and other universities. Although he had written hundreds of specialized articles for medical journals, his first book was for the layman: The Lives of a Cell: Notes of a Biology Watcher *(1974), which won the National Book Award. Thomas's constant theme in that book is symbiosis — the mutual interdependence of living organisms. In one essay he wrote, "The whole dear notion of one's own self — marvelous old free-willed, free-enterprising, autonomous, independent, isolated island of a Self — is a myth." The essay which follows is from his most recent book,* The Medusa and the Snail: And More Notes of a Biology Watcher *(1979).*

Everyone must have had at least one personal experience with a computer error by this time. Bank balances are suddenly reported to have jumped from $379 into the millions, appeals for charitable contributions are mailed over and over to people with crazy-sounding names at your address, department stores send the wrong bills, utility companies write that they're turning everything off, that sort of thing. If you manage to get in touch with someone and complain, you then get instantaneously typed, guilty letters from the same computer, saying, "Our computer was in error, and an adjustment is being made in your account."

These are supposed to be the sheerest, blindest accidents. Mistakes are not believed to be part of the normal behavior of a good machine. If things go wrong, it must be a personal, human error, the result of fingering, tampering, a button getting stuck, someone hitting the wrong key. The computer, at its normal best, is infallible.

I wonder whether this can be true. After all, the whole point of computers is that they represent an extension of the human brain, vastly improved upon but nonetheless human, superhuman maybe. A good computer can think clearly and quickly enough to beat you at chess, and some of them have even been programmed to write obscure verse. They can do anything we can do, and more besides.

It is not yet known whether a computer has its own consciousness, 4 and it would be hard to find out about this. When you walk into one of those great halls now built for the huge machines, and stand listening, it is easy to imagine that the faint, distant noises are the sound of thinking, and the turning of the spools gives them the look of wild creatures rolling their eyes in the effort to concentrate, choking with information. But real thinking, and dreaming, are other matters.

On the other hand, the evidences of something like an *unconscious,* 5 equivalent to ours, are all around, in every mail. As extensions of the human brain, they have been constructed with the same property of error, spontaneous, uncontrolled, and rich in possibilities.

Mistakes are at the very base of human thought, embedded there, 6 feeding the structure like root nodules. If we were not provided with the knack of being wrong, we could never get anything useful done. We think our way along by choosing between right and wrong alternatives, and the wrong choices have to be made as frequently as the right ones. We get along in life this way. We are built to make mistakes, coded for error.

We learn, as we say, by "trial and error." Why do we always say that? 7 Why not "trial and rightness" or "trial and triumph"? The old phrase puts it that way because that is, in real life, the way it is done.

A good laboratory, like a good bank or a corporation or government, 8 has to run like a computer. Almost everything is done flawlessly, by the book, and all the numbers add up to the predicted sums. The days go by. And then, if it is a lucky day, and a lucky laboratory, somebody makes a mistake: the wrong buffer, something in one of the blanks, a decimal misplaced in reading counts, the warm room off by a degree and a half, a mouse out of his box, or just a misreading of the day's protocol. Whatever, when the results come in, something is obviously screwed up, and then the action can begin.

The misreading is not the important error; it opens the way. The next 9 step is the crucial one. If the investigator can bring himself to say, "But even so, look at that!" then the new finding, whatever it is, is ready for snatching. What is needed, for progress to be made, is the move based on the error.

Whenever new kinds of thinking are about to be accomplished, or 10 new varieties of music, there has to be an argument beforehand. With two sides debating in the same mind, haranguing, there is an amiable understanding that one is right and the other wrong. Sooner or later the thing is settled, but there can be no action at all if there are not the two sides, and the argument. The hope is in the faculty of wrongness, the tendency toward error. The capacity to leap across mountains of information to land lightly on the wrong side represents the highest of human endowments.

It may be that this is a uniquely human gift, perhaps even stipulated   11 in our genetic instructions. Other creatures do not seem to have DNA sequences for making mistakes as a routine part of daily living, certainly not for programmed error as a guide for action.

We are at our human finest, dancing with our minds, when there are   12 more choices than two. Sometimes there are ten, even twenty different ways to go, all but one bound to be wrong, and the richness of selection in such situations can lift us onto totally new ground. This process is called exploration and is based on human fallibility. If we had only a single center in our brains, capable of responding only when a correct decision was to be made, instead of the jumble of different, credulous, easily conned clusters of neurones that provide for being flung off into blind alleys, up trees, down dead ends, out into blue sky, along wrong turnings, around bends, we could only stay the way we are today, stuck fast.

The lower animals do not have this splendid freedom. They are   13 limited, most of them, to absolute infallibility. Cats, for all their good side, never make mistakes. I have never seen a maladroit, clumsy, or blundering cat. Dogs are sometimes fallible, occasionally able to make charming minor mistakes, but they get this way by trying to mimic their masters. Fish are flawless in everything they do. Individual cells in a tissue are mindless machines, perfect in their performance, as absolutely inhuman as bees.

We should have this in mind as we become dependent on more com-   14 plex computers for the arrangement of our affairs. Give the computers their heads, I say; let them go their way. If we can learn to do this, turning our heads to one side and wincing while the work proceeds, the possibilities for the future of mankind, and computerkind, are limitless. Your average good computer can make calculations in an instant which would take a lifetime of slide rules for any of us. Think of what we could gain from the near infinity of precise, machine-made miscomputation which is now so easily within our grasp. We could begin the solving of some of our hardest problems. How, for instance, should we go about organizing ourselves for social living on a planetary scale, now that we have become, as a plain fact of life, a single community? We can assume, as a working hypothesis, that all the right ways of doing this are unworkable. What we need, then, for moving ahead, is a set of wrong alternatives much longer and more interesting than the short list of mistaken courses that any of us can think up right now. We need, in fact, an infinite list, and when it is printed out we need the computer to turn on itself and select, at random, the next way to go. If it is a big enough mistake, we could find ourselves on a new level, stunned, out in the clear, ready to move again.

SUBJECT QUESTIONS

1. On what basis does Thomas suggest that computers can make "human errors"?
2. Thomas thinks that "mistakes are at the very base of human thought," "perhaps even stipulated in our genetic instructions." Is it just as likely that errors result from *failures* in the thought process?
3. Why do we learn more from "trial and error" than from "trial and triumph"? If you can succeed at a task the first time you try, why bother to learn from trial and error?
4. Would you agree that new thoughts arise only from disagreement? What would a college bull session be like if everyone agreed about everything?
5. What does Thomas say would happen if our minds were not capable of making errors? What are the implications of this effect? Wouldn't we return to a kind of Garden of Eden? Would it be fair to reply to Thomas that we have not done very well in a world where error is common?
6. Is it possible to program computers to make the sorts of profitable errors Thomas envisages in the final paragraph? Is it likely that the new computers will make such errors without being programmed to do so?

STRUCTURE QUESTIONS

1. The subject of Thomas's evaluation is the human capacity to err. Should he begin and end his essay with discussion of computers rather than human brains?
2. Thomas has based his evaluation on a single value or standard; what is it? Should he have explained more fully why he thinks it *is* a value?
3. To explain how mistakes lead to discovery, Thomas gives a generalized example of a hypothetical laboratory. Does he make his point clearly? Would a real and specific example have been better?
4. It is always difficult to write "popular" science, to explain in layman's terms without distorting with imprecise language and simplified generalizations. Has Thomas succeeded in conveying his position clearly? Do you think he has badly distorted his scientific evidence?
5. Paragraph 12 is a good example of Thomas's tactic of expressing the generalization abstractly and then bringing it to everyday level, if not with clichés, at least with familiar "dead metaphors." Examine that paragraph and judge whether or not the strategy succeeds.

SUGGESTIONS FOR WRITING

1. Envision a world in which everyone agrees and no one makes mistakes; evaluate that world, making clear by what standards you are judging it.

2. Select a specific area of human endeavor (chemistry, soccer — something with which you are familiar) and apply to it the principle which Thomas expresses in paragraph 7. Use factual examples rather than hypothetical ones where possible.

Harrison Bergeron

Kurt Vonnegut, Jr.

Kurt Vonnegut, Jr. (b. 1922) is probably the most influential novelist among college students since J. R. R. Tolkien. Vonnegut was a biochemistry student at Cornell and Carnegie Institute, and he later studied anthropology at the University of Chicago. During World War II, he was captured during the Battle of the Bulge and later as a POW witnessed the holocaust of the fire-bombing of Dresden, which had a tremendous impact on him. His novel Slaughterhouse-Five, *about the Dresden bombing, was made into a very successful movie in 1972. Among his best novels are* Cat's Cradle *(1963) and* God Bless You, Mr. Rosewater *(1965). Vonnegut is also a successful playwright; his* Happy Birthday, Wanda June *(1970) was a Broadway hit. As a renegade scientist, Vonnegut often offends critics with irreverent attacks on their cherished beliefs. Although he has many followers, many people regard him simply as a good science fiction writer. But while Vonnegut can be iconoclastic and often wildly funny, he is a serious writer with a rare gift of prophecy. "Harrison Bergeron" illustrates on a simpler level the qualities which makes his novels major works of fiction.*

The year was 2081, and everybody was finally equal. They weren't only equal before God and the law. They were equal every which way. Nobody was smarter than anybody else. Nobody was better looking than anybody else. Nobody was stronger or quicker than anybody else. All this equality was due to the 211th, 212th, and 213th Amendments to the Constitution, and to the unceasing vigilance of agents of the United States Handicapper General.

Some things about living still weren't quite right, though. April, for instance, still drove people crazy by not being springtime. And it was in that clammy month that the H-G men took George and Hazel Bergeron's fourteen-year-old son, Harrison, away.

It was tragic, all right, but George and Hazel couldn't think about it very hard. Hazel had a perfectly average intelligence, which meant she couldn't think about anything except in short bursts. And George, while his intelligence was way above normal, had a little mental handicap radio in his ear. He was required by law to wear it at all times. It was tuned to a government transmitter. Every twenty seconds or so, the transmitter would send out some sharp noise to keep people like George from taking unfair advantage of their brains.

George and Hazel were watching television. There were tears on Hazel's cheeks, but she'd forgotten for the moment what they were about. 4

On the television screen were ballerinas. 5

A buzzer sounded in George's head. His thoughts fled in panic, like bandits from a burglar alarm. 6

"That was a real pretty dance, that dance they just did," said Hazel. 7

"Huh?" said George. 8

"That dance — it was nice," said Hazel. 9

"Yup," said George. He tried to think a little about the ballerinas. 10
They weren't really very good — no better than anybody else would have been, anyway. They were burdened with sashweights and bags of birdshot, and their faces were masked, so that no one, seeing a free and graceful gesture or a pretty face, would feel like something the cat drug in. George was toying with the vague notion that maybe dancers shouldn't be handicapped. But he didn't get very far with it before another noise in his ear radio scattered his thoughts.

George winced. So did two out of the eight ballerinas. 11

Hazel saw him wince. Having no mental handicap herself, she had to ask George what the latest sound had been. 12

"Sounded like somebody hitting a milk bottle with a ball peen hammer," said George. 13

"I'd think it would be real interesting, hearing all the different sounds," said Hazel, a little envious. "All the things they think up." 14

"Um," said George. 15

"Only, if I was Handicapper General, you know what I would do?" said Hazel. Hazel, as a matter of fact, bore a strong resemblance to the Handicapper General, a woman named Diana Moon Glampers. "If I was Diana Moon Glampers," said Hazel, "I'd have chimes on Sunday — just chimes. Kind of in honor of religion." 16

"I could think, if it was just chimes," said George. 17

"Well — maybe make 'em real loud," said Hazel. "I think I'd make a good Handicapper General." 18

"Good as anybody else," said George. 19

"Who knows better'n I do what normal is?" said Hazel. 20

"Right," said George. He began to think glimmeringly about his abnormal son who was now in jail, about Harrison, but a twenty-one-gun salute in his head stopped that. 21

"Boy!" said Hazel, "that was a doozy, wasn't it?" 22

It was such a doozy that George was white and trembling, and tears stood on the rims of his red eyes. Two of the eight ballerinas had collapsed to the studio floor, were holding their temples. 23

"All of a sudden you look so tired," said Hazel. "Why don't you stretch out on the sofa, so's you can rest your handicap bag on the pillows, honeybunch." She was referring to the forty-seven pounds of birdshot in a canvas bag, which was padlocked around George's neck. "Go on and rest the bag for a little while," she said. "I don't care if you're not equal to me for a while." ²⁴

George weighed the bag with his hands. "I don't mind it," he said. "I don't notice it any more. It's just a part of me." ²⁵

"You been so tired lately — kind of wore out," said Hazel. "If there was just some way we could make a little hole in the bottom of the bag, and just take out a few of them lead balls. Just a few." ²⁶

"Two years in prison and two thousand dollars fine for every ball I took out," said George. "I don't call that a bargain." ²⁷

"If you could just take a few out when you came home from work," said Hazel. "I mean — you don't compete with anybody around here. You just set around." ²⁸

"If I tried to get away with it," said George, "then other people'd get away with it — and pretty soon we'd be right back to the dark ages again, with everybody competing against everybody else. You wouldn't like that, would you?" ²⁹

"I'd hate it," said Hazel. ³⁰

"There you are," said George. "The minute people start cheating on laws, what do you think happens to society?" ³¹

If Hazel hadn't been able to come up with an answer to this question, George couldn't have supplied one. A siren was going off in his head. ³²

"Reckon it'd fall all apart," said Hazel. ³³

"What would?" said George blankly. ³⁴

"Society," said Hazel uncertainly. "Wasn't that what you just said?" ³⁵

"Who knows?" said George. ³⁶

The television program was suddenly interrupted for a news bulletin. It wasn't clear at first as to what the bulletin was about, since the announcer, like all announcers, had a serious speech impediment. For about half a minute, and in a state of high excitement, the announcer tried to say, "Ladies and gentlemen —" ³⁷

He finally gave up, handed the bulletin to a ballerina to read. ³⁸

"That's all right —" Hazel said of the announcer," he tried. "That's the big thing. He tried to do the best he could with what God gave him. He should get a nice raise for trying so hard." ³⁹

"Ladies and gentlemen —" said the ballerina, reading the bulletin. She must have been extraordinarily beautiful, because the mask she wore was hideous. And it was easy to see that she was the strongest and most graceful of all the dancers, for her handicap bags were as big as those worn by two-hundred-pound men. ⁴⁰

And she had to apologize at once for her voice, which was a very ⁴¹ unfair voice for a woman to use. Her voice was a warm, luminous, timeless melody. "Excuse me —" she said, and she began again, making her voice absolutely uncompetitive.

"Harrison Bergeron, age fourteen," she said in a grackle squawk, "has just escaped from jail, where he was held on suspicion of plotting to over-throw the government. He is a genius and an athlete, is under-handicapped, and should be regarded as extremely dangerous." 42

A police photograph of Harrison Bergeron was flashed on the screen upside down, then sideways, upside down again, then right side up. The picture showed the full length of Harrison against a background calibrated in feet and inches. He was exactly seven feet tall. 43

The rest of Harrison's appearance was Halloween and hardware. No-body had ever borne heavier handicaps. He had outgrown hindrances fas-ter than the H-G men could think them up. Instead of a little ear radio for a mental handicap, he wore a tremendous pair of earphones, and spectacles with thick wavy lenses. The spectacles were intended to make him not only half blind, but to give him whanging headaches besides. 44

Scrap metal was hung all over him. Ordinarily, there was a certain symmetry, a military neatness to the handicaps issued to strong people, but Harrison looked like a walking junkyard. In the race of life, Harrison car-ried three hundred pounds. 45

And to offset his good looks, the H-G men required that he wear at all times a red rubber ball for a nose, keep his eyebrows shaved off, and cover his even white teeth with black caps at snaggle-tooth random. 46

"If you see this boy," said the ballerina, "do not — I repeat, do not — try to reason with him." 47

There was the shriek of a door being torn from its hinges. 48

Screams and barking cries of consternation came from the television set. The photograph of Harrison Bergeron on the screen jumped again and again, as though dancing to the tune of an earthquake. 49

George Bergeron correctly identified the earthquake, and well he might have — for many was the time his own home had danced to the same crashing tune. "My God —" said George, "that must be Harrison!" 50

The realization was blasted from his mind instantly by the sound of an automobile collision in his head. 51

When George could open his eyes again, the photograph of Harrison was gone. A living, breathing Harrison filled the screen. 52

Clanking, clownish, and huge, Harrison stood in the center of the studio. The knob of the uprooted studio door was still in his hand. Bal-lerinas, technicians, musicians, and announcers cowered on their knees be-fore him, expecting to die. 53

"I am the Emperor!" cried Harrison. "Do you hear? I am the Em-peror! Everybody must do what I say at once!" He stamped his foot and the studio shook. 54

"Even as I stand here —" he bellowed, "crippled, hobbled, sick- 55
ened — I am a greater ruler than any man who ever lived! Now watch me
become what I *can* become!"

Harrison tore the straps of his handicap harness like wet tissue paper, 56
tore straps guaranteed to support five thousand pounds.

Harrison's scrap-iron handicaps crashed to the floor. 57

Harrison thrust his thumbs under the bar of the padlock that secured 58
his head harness. The bar snapped like celery. Harrison smashed his head-
phones and spectacles against the wall.

He flung away his rubber-ball nose, revealed a man that would have 59
awed Thor, the god of thunder.

"I shall now select my Empress!" he said, looking down on the cower- 60
ing people. "Let the first woman who dares rise to her feet claim her mate
and her throne!"

A moment passed, and then a ballerina arose, swaying like a willow. 61

Harrison plucked the mental handicap from her ear, snapped off her 62
physical handicaps with marvelous delicacy. Last of all, he removed her
mask.

She was blindingly beautiful. 63

"Now —" said Harrison, taking her hand, "shall we show the people 64
the meaning of the word dance? Music!" he commanded.

The musicians scrambled back into their chairs, and Harrison 65
stripped them of their handicaps, too. "Play your best," he told them, and
I'll make you barons and dukes and earls."

The music began. It was normal at first — cheap, silly, false. But 66
Harrison snatched two musicians from their chairs, waved them like batons
as he sang the music as he wanted it played. He slammed them back into
their chairs.

The music began again and was much improved. 67

Harrison and his Empress merely listened to the music for a while 68
— listened gravely, as though synchronizing their heartbeats with it.

They shifted their weights to their toes. 69

Harrison placed his big hands on the girl's tiny waist, letting her 70
sense the weightlessness that would soon be hers.

And then, in an explosion of joy and grace, into the air they sprang! 71

Not only were the laws of the land abandoned, but the law of gravity 72
and the laws of motion as well.

They reeled, whirled, swiveled, flounced, capered, gamboled, and 73
spun.

They leaped like deer on the moon. 74

The studio ceiling was thirty feet high, but each leap brought the 75
dancers nearer to it.

It became their obvious intention to kiss the ceiling. 76

They kissed it. 77

And then, neutralizing gravity with love and pure will, they remained 78
suspended in air inches below the ceiling, and they kissed each other for a
long, long time.

It was then that Diana Moon Glampers, the Handicapper General, 79
came into the studio with a double-barreled ten-gauge shotgun. She fired
twice, and the Emperor and the Empress were dead before they hit the
floor.

Diana Moon Glampers loaded the gun again. She aimed it at the 80
musicians and told them they had ten seconds to get their handicaps back
on.

It was then that the Bergerons' television tube burned out. 81

Hazel turned to comment about the blackout to George. But George 82
had gone out into the kitchen for a can of beer.

George came back in with the beer, paused while a handicap signal 83
shook him up. And then he sat down again, "You been crying?" he said to
Hazel.

"Yup," she said. 84
"What about?" he said. 85
"I forget," she said. "Something real sad on television." 86
"What was it?" he said. 87
"It's all kind of mixed up in my mind," said Hazel. 88
"Forget sad things," said George. 89
"I always do," said Hazel. 90
"That's my girl," said George. He winced. There was the sound of a 91
rivetting gun in his head.

"Gee — I could tell that one was a doozy," said Hazel. 92
"You can say that again," said George. 93
"Gee — " said Hazel, "I could tell that one was a doozy." 94

SUBJECT QUESTIONS

1. Vonnegut has cast his evaluation of a trend in modern society in the form of a science fiction story about the future. Do you see any signs that we are heading toward the situation he predicts?
2. Why, in this theoretical culture of 2081, are handicaps given to the physically and mentally advantaged? To achieve equality, is it necessary to reduce everyone to the lowest common denominator?
3. Do the people in this future society seem to approve of the efforts of the Handicapper General? What does George think about having to wear handicaps? How does Hazel feel about them? What quality of medical care do you suppose they receive?
4. Twenty-five years ago, there were many programs in American education for gifted students; today "special education" money goes

primarily to programs for the mentally, physically, and culturally handicapped. Do you see in this changed emphasis a tendency toward Vonnegut's prophecy?

5. What are some of the problems caused by court insistence on equality in college athletics programs for men and women? Do the advantages outweigh the difficulties? What about the tendency toward economic equality between blue-collar and white-collar workers? (Truck drivers, for instance, now earn higher average salaries than college professors.) What are the good, and the bad, long-term results of such a situation?

6. Certainly physically and mentally gifted people have a distinct advantage in life; should something be done to level out this advantage? (Should a genius and a mentally retarded person have equal right to attend medical school, for instance?)

STRUCTURE QUESTIONS

1. In order to make his point forcefully, Vonnegut has created a kind of *reductio ad absurdum*. Should he have kept it on a more realistic level?

2. Does Vonnegut weaken his case against total equality by having superboy Harrison Bergeron want to become emperor? Does he mean to suggest that the alternative to equality is dictatorship?

3. What point, if any, is made by giving Harrison the ability to leap to the ceiling and neutralize gravity? Should Vonnegut have made the boy more "normal"?

4. The story ends with the old "you can say that again" joke. Is it appropriate here, or has Vonnegut made a tactical error? Is it fitting that the television set burns out?

5. As this text has stressed from the beginning, specific details are among a writer's most effective tools. Point out some of the apparently gratuitous details which contribute to the force of this story (the ballerina's apology when reading the news bulletin, for instance).

SUGGESTIONS FOR WRITING

1. Select one area in which attempts are being made to provide equality and evaluate the success of those attempts (college athletic programs, medical school admissions policies, corporation hiring policies, and so on).

2. Suppose, through cloning or another genetics program, people could be made equal without having to be handicapped as in Vonnegut's story. Write your own ideas of what such a society would be like.

The Second Coming
William Butler Yeats

William Butler Yeats (1865–1939) was an Irish poet and dramatist, a
leader of the "Irish literary revival." He wrote many volumes of poetry
and prose and verse plays, and he helped to establish the Abbey
Theatre, still Dublin's most famous theater. Yeats was awarded the
Nobel Prize for Literature in 1923 and was chosen one of the first
senators when Ireland achieved its independence from Great Britain. He
has been one of the most admired and influential poets of the twentieth
century. Yeats outlived his gloomy prediction in the following poem by
twenty years, but it might not have been much different had he written
it just before his death at the beginning of World War II.

Turning and turning in the widening gyre
The falcon cannot hear the falconer;
Things fall apart; the center cannot hold;
Mere anarchy is loosed upon the world,
The blood-dimmed tide is loosed, and everywhere   5
The ceremony of innocence is drowned;
The best lack all conviction, while the worst
Are full of passionate intensity.

Surely some revelation is at hand;
Surely the Second Coming is at hand;   10
The Second Coming! Hardly are those words out
When a vast image out of *Spiritus Mundi*
Troubles my sight: somewhere in sands of the desert
A shape with lion body and the head of a man,
A gaze blank and pitiless as the sun,   15
Is moving its slow thighs, while all about it
Reel shadows of the indignant desert birds.
The darkness drops again; but now I know
That twenty centuries of stony sleep
Were vexed to nightmare by a rocking cradle,   20
And what rough beast, its hour come round at last,
Slouches towards Bethlehem to be born?

SUBJECT QUESTIONS

1. Yeats wrote this peom in 1919, when his native Ireland was in the midst of revolution and the world had just experienced its first world war. Would you expect his assessment of the current world situation to be considerably different?
2. Do you think it is generally true that the "best lack all conviction, while the worst / Are full of passionate intensity"? Was there ever a time when the worst were the ones who lacked conviction? Does the twentieth century particularly encourage good people to lack conviction?
3. What is the reference to the creature in the desert? Is the image consonant with Yeats's view that history repeats itself in two thousand-year cycles?
4. The "Second Coming" usually refers to a belief in the second coming of Christ; is this what Yeats has in mind?
5. In the line "Were vexed to nightmare by a rocking cradle," is Yeats suggesting that Christianity caused the world's present troubles? What else might the line mean?

STRUCTURE QUESTIONS

1. The poem is divided into two stanzas of unequal length; why did Yeats make this division where he did?
2. Does the poem have a regular meter or rhyme scheme? Why would Yeats not want to cast his poem into a traditional form such as a sonnet? (Consider the relation of subject to structure.)
3. Can this poem be understood without knowing Yeats's private mythology? Is it necessary to know at least some history?
4. By what standard or standards does Yeats judge his contemporary world? Is his judgment easier to understand than his prophecy for the future? Might there be a reason for leaving the prophecy somewhat vague?
5. Examine the images which Yeats uses; are the most "impressive" ones those which also convey their meaning best? Is there a difference in the way images are employed in the two stanzas?

SUGGESTIONS FOR WRITING

1. Using Yeats's standard of judgment, evaluate the present prospects for world peace and harmony. Does the "center" seem likely to "hold" now?
2. Take some source of conflict with which you are familiar, and evaluate its prospects of peaceful settlement. (You may choose a global conflict if you wish, but you may feel more at ease with a local campus issue.)

To the student:

If we are to make *Subject and Structure* a better book next time, we need to know what students think of what we've already done. Would you help us by filling out this questionnaire and returning it to: Little, Brown and Company, College English, 34 Beacon Street, Boston, Massachusetts 02106.

School_____ Course title_____

School address: City_____ State _____

Instructor's name _____

What did you think of the selections?	Definitely keep	Keep	Drop	Didn't read
1. Turning Points				
Malcolm X, "The First Major Turning Point"				
Hughes, "Salvation"				
Allen, "A Whole Society of Loners and Dreamers"				
Dell, "My Sixth Christmas"				
Didion, "On Self-Respect"				
Anderson, "Death in the Woods"				
Frost, "Acquainted with the Night"				
Sexton, Anne, "The Abortion"				
2. The World about Us				
Dillard, "Seeing"				
Dillard, "The Death of a Moth"				
Steinbeck, "The Turtle"				
Sexton, Patricia Cayo, "East Harlem"				
Hoagland, "City Walking"				
Twain, "Uncle John's Farm"				
Hemingway, "The Big Two-Hearted River, Part I"				
Stafford, "Traveling through the Dark"				
3. Playschools and Colleges				
White, "Education"				
Norman, "Pedestrian Students and High-Flying Squirrels"				
Neill, "Summerhill Education vs. Standard Education"				
Wolynski, "Confessions of a Misspent Youth"				
Whitehead, "Universities and Their Function"				
Trilling, "Of This Time, of That Place"				
Wallace, "In a Spring Still Not Written Of"				
4. The Programmed Citizen				
Thomas, "Choosing the Class of '83"				
Hull, "The Peter Principle"				
Clerk, "The Art of the Memorandum"				
Ashmore, "Jesse Jackson's Revolutionary Message"				
Mitford, "To Bid the World Farewell"				
Donleavy, "The Gentleman's Guide to Suicide"				
Dickson, "Computers Don't Argue"				
Auden, "The Unknown Citizen"				
5. The Family under Stress				
Goodman, "The Wrong Side of the Generation Gap"				
Tiger, "Omnigamy: The New Kinship System"				
Bettelheim, "Untying the Family"				
Laucks, "Do We Need the Family"				
Shorris, "The Cowards of Christmas Eve"				

	Definitely keep	Keep	Drop	Didn't read
Joyce, "Counterparts"				
Oates, "Bloodstains"				
Rich, "For L. G.: Unseen for Twenty Years"				

6. Vogue, Vague, or Verbiage? The Written Word

	Definitely keep	Keep	Drop	Didn't read
Safire, "Vogue Words Are Trific, Right?"				
Wrighter, "Weasel Words"				
Price, "Noun Overuse Phenomenon Article"				
Canby, "Bombing the Paragraph"				
Altick, "Connotation"				
Hall, "An Ethic of Clarity"				
Milburn, "The Apostate"				
Shakespeare, "Sonnet 76, " 'Why Is My Verse So Barren of New Pride?' "				

7. Freedom and Responsibility

	Definitely keep	Keep	Drop	Didn't read
Hutchins, "On Decriminalization"				
Jordan, "The Truth about the Black Middle Class"				
Selzer, "What I Saw at the Abortion"				
Clark, "The Case against All Forms of Government Secrecy"				
Orwell, "Politics and the English Language"				
Thoreau, "On the Duty of Civil Disobedience"				
Jefferson, "The Declaration of Independence"				
Faulkner, "The Bear"				
Brooks, "First Fight. Then Fiddle."				

8. A Matter of Faith

	Definitely keep	Keep	Drop	Didn't read
Plato, from "The Apology of Socrates"				
Russell, "A Free Man's Worship"				
Lewis, "The Efficacy of Prayer"				
Stevenson, "Father Damien"				
Updike, "Packed Dirt, Churchgoing, a Dying Cat, a Traded Car"				
Arnold, "Dover Beach"				
Steiner, "Choy's Religion"				

9. Looking Ahead

	Definitely keep	Keep	Drop	Didn't read
Roethke, "I Can Write"				
Burroughs, "The Summit of the Years"				
Clarke, "We'll Never Conquer Space"				
Eiseley, "The Cosmic Prison"				
Bronowski, "The Long Childhood"				
McKetta, "Will Our World Survive?"				
Thomas, "To Err Is Human"				
Vonnegut, "Harrison Bergeron"				
Yeats, "The Second Coming"				

Please add any comments or suggestions _____

_____

_____

May we quote you in our promotional efforts for this book?___yes___no

Date_____ Signature _____

Mailing address_____